T4-ABM-406

CultureGrams™

World Edition 2006

volume 3

Africa

This volume contains 47 country reports featuring 25 categories:

Land and Climate
History
Population
Language
Religion
General Attitudes
Personal Appearance
Greetings
Gestures
Visiting
Eating
Family
Dating and Marriage
Diet
Recreation
The Arts
Holidays
Commerce
Government
Economy
Transportation and Communications
Education
Health
Events and Trends
Contact Information

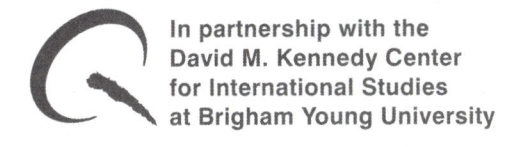

In partnership with the
David M. Kennedy Center
for International Studies
at Brigham Young University

WITHDRAWN
MILAN PUBLIC LIBRARY

This book (Volume III) includes CultureGrams™ 2006 World Edition cultural reports for Africa.

Related CultureGrams™ 2006 World Edition volumes (Volumes I, II, and IV) include cultural reports for The Americas, Europe, and Asia and Oceania, respectively.

This book was printed using the following fonts: Helvetica Neue, Swiss 721, Times New Roman.

The CultureGrams™ series is published in Provo, Utah, U.S.A.

ISBN-13: 978-1-931694-95-7 (v.3)
ISBN-10: 1-931694-95-8 (v.3)

ISBN-13: 978-1-931694-97-1 (4 vol. set)
ISBN-10: 1-931694-97-4 (4 vol. set)

© 2005 ProQuest Information and Learning Company and Brigham Young University. It is against the law to copy, reprint, store, or transmit any part of this publication in any form by any means without written permission from ProQuest.

Contents

VOLUME III

Introduction v
Africa. vii
CultureGrams™
    Algeria 1
    Angola. 5
    Benin. 9
    Botswana 13
    Burkina Faso 17
    Cameroon 21
    Cape Verde 25
    Central African Republic 29
    Chad 33
    Comoros 37
    Congo 41
    Egypt. 45
    Equatorial Guinea 49
    Eritrea. 53
    Ethiopia 57
    Gabon. 61
    The Gambia 65
    Ghana. 69
    Guinea 73
    Guinea-Bissau 77
    Ivory Coast 81
    Kenya 85
    Lesotho 89
    Libya. 93
    Madagascar 97
    Malawi 101
    Mali. 105
    Mauritania 109
    Mauritius. 113
    Morocco 117
    Mozambique 121
    Namibia. 125
    Niger 129
    Nigeria 133
    Rwanda. 137
    Senegal 141
    Sierra Leone 145
    Somalia. 149
    South Africa 153
    Sudan 157
    Swaziland 161
    Tanzania 165
    Togo. 169
    Tunisia. 173
    Uganda 177
    Zambia 181
    Zimbabwe 185
Country Data Tables
    Capitals. A-2
    Population and Area A-4
    Development Data A-6
Concepts and Terminology A-11
Glossary of Cultural Terms A-15

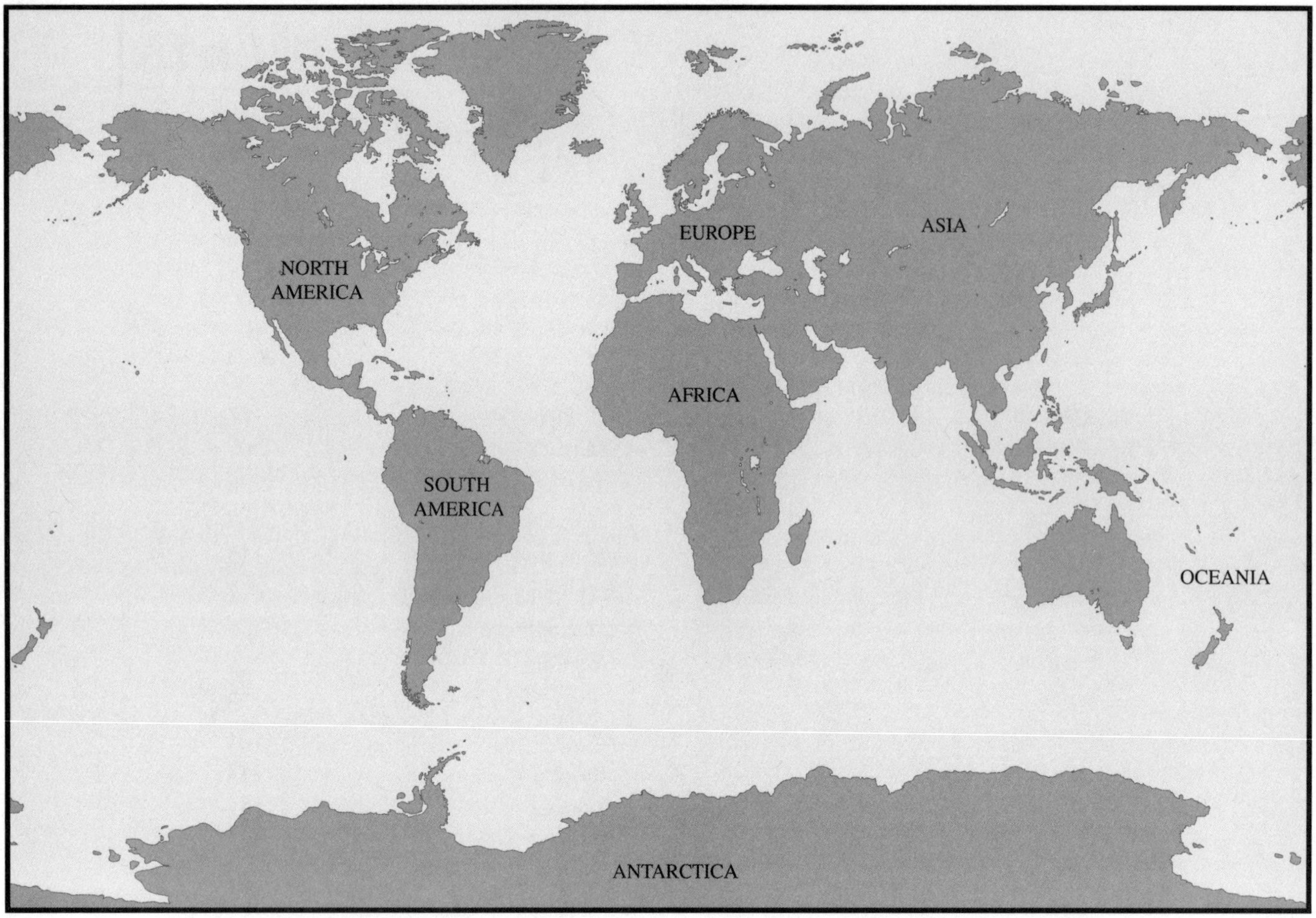
NORTH
AMERICA
EUROPE
ASIA
AFRICA
SOUTH
AMERICA
OCEANIA
ANTARCTICA

Introduction

Because learning about other countries and cultures makes a difference—to you, your community, and the world at large—we have created CultureGrams. Our reports give you a framework for understanding and appreciating how other people live and think. In a small way, they let you stand in someone else's shoes, an experience which becomes the basis for tolerance, respect, mutual understanding, and communication. CultureGrams helps you take each culture on its own terms and appreciate it for the gifts it brings to the world table: its religions and worldviews, arts and traditions, peoples and languages.

What Is a Culture?

Broadly, a culture can be said to be those beliefs, traditions, and institutions that create and mediate individual, community, and national identity. History and geography are defining elements, but they are not the only elements. Ethnicity, economics, religion, and other factors all shape, and are shaped by, a culture. This is why each CultureGram has 25 different categories: we want you to see each culture's many facets and draw connections between them.

Why Are CultureGrams Unique?

The CultureGrams World Edition is a concise reference tool created by natives and long-time residents to give you an insider's perspective. Its information ranges from mile-high views of a nation, its society, and institutions to close-up views of communities, families, and individuals. Each report seeks a balance between generality and breadth, on one hand, and detail and depth on the other. This tension lets us create multidimensional and realistic portraits of a place and its peoples. Moreover, CultureGrams are updated annually and reviewed by natives and experts periodically to ensure that the reports reflect changes in the culture.

For the Teacher

If you teach history, geography, a foreign language, ESL, or current events—among other subjects—you can use CultureGrams as the basis for in-class discussions, debates, presentations, research papers, reports, and reading and writing exercises. Use CultureGrams to help students make connections and form hypotheses about how various aspects of a culture are related. Compare and contrast the cultures of countries as diverse as Niue and Ghana. For example, you could compare family structure, look at the correlation between economy and religion, or see how the language of instruction affects education. Make your own UN or national parliament and debate social, political, and economic issues. Or have a culture fair and ask students to act as a citizen of the country they have been assigned. No matter how you use CultureGrams, you will find that your students learn more about themselves and the world than you ever thought possible.

CultureGrams
People. The World. You.

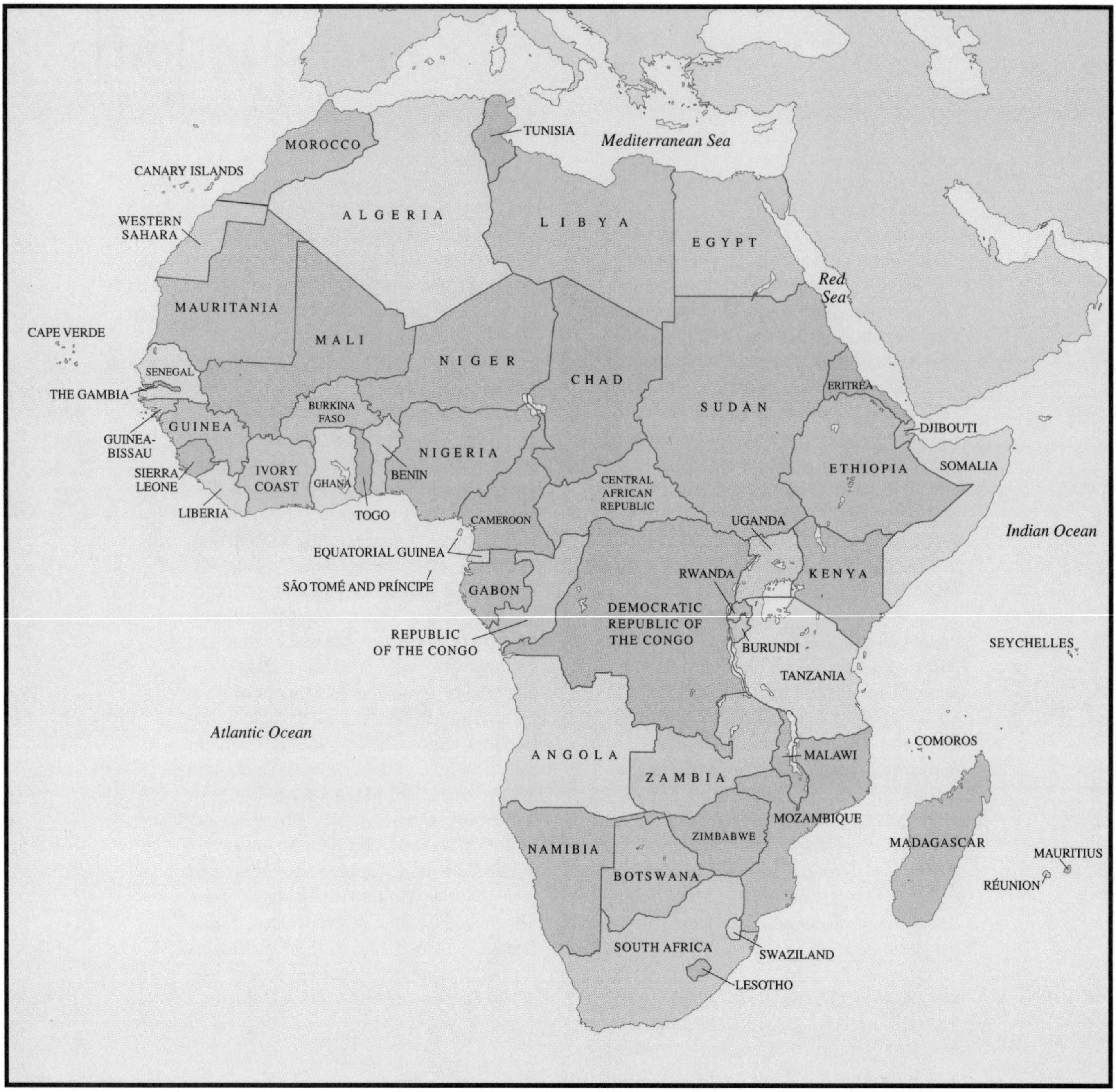

TUNISIA
Mediterranean Sea
MOROCCO
CANARY ISLANDS
ALGERIA
LIBYA
EGYPT
WESTERN SAHARA
Red Sea
MAURITANIA
CAPE VERDE
MALI
NIGER
CHAD
SENEGAL
THE GAMBIA
ERITREA
SUDAN
BURKINA FASO
GUINEA
DJIBOUTI
GUINEA-BISSAU
NIGERIA
ETHIOPIA
SOMALIA
SIERRA LEONE
IVORY COAST
GHANA
BENIN
CENTRAL AFRICAN REPUBLIC
LIBERIA
TOGO
CAMEROON
UGANDA
Indian Ocean
EQUATORIAL GUINEA
RWANDA
KENYA
SÃO TOMÉ AND PRÍNCIPE
GABON
DEMOCRATIC REPUBLIC OF THE CONGO
REPUBLIC OF THE CONGO
BURUNDI
SEYCHELLES
TANZANIA
Atlantic Ocean
COMOROS
MALAWI
ANGOLA
ZAMBIA
MOZAMBIQUE
MADAGASCAR
ZIMBABWE
NAMIBIA
MAURITIUS
BOTSWANA
RÉUNION
SOUTH AFRICA
SWAZILAND
LESOTHO

Africa

AN OVERVIEW

Africa is a vast continent of some 11,700,000 square miles (30,300,000 square kilometers), divided into 53 independent nations, and ranks second only to Asia in size. The African continent represents about 20 percent of the earth's total landmass, yet its population hovers around 10 percent of the world's total population. Though the growth rate continues to be high—despite the widespread AIDS epidemic—Africa ranks only third in the world, behind Asia and Europe (including western Russia), in continental population.

Most of the African landmass is high in elevation with comparatively few mountain ranges. The highest point, Mount Kilimanjaro, rises to an elevation of 19,340 feet (5,895 meters) above the East African plains in Tanzania. The Nile is the longest river in the world and flows more than 4,000 miles (6,400 kilometers) from its origin at Lake Victoria to the Mediterranean Sea. Other major rivers include the Congo, the Niger, and the Zambezi. There are a number of islands off the coast of Africa, the largest of which is Madagascar, the world's fourth largest island (229,000 square miles, or 593,000 square kilometers). Divided into almost equal halves by the equator, Africa has warm temperatures most of the year, though these are moderated somewhat in high elevations and by ocean currents along the coast.

Africa divides geographically and culturally in two. The Sahara Desert, nearly the size of the United States, dominates the landscape of northern Africa. Culturally and historically, North Africa is predominantly Mediterranean, Arabic, and Muslim. South of the Sahara is Black Africa. Though many West African countries are Muslim, and there are Swahili pockets (of Arab influence) in East Africa, Africa south of the Sahara has an incredible diversity of peoples, cultures, and languages. More than one thousand languages and dialects are spoken, and economies vary from mostly developed (South Africa) to pastoral, horticultural/agricultural to hunting and gathering. Most of the current political boundaries of African countries were drawn up by European colonial powers in the mid- to late 19th century; thus, many peoples found themselves divided into two or three different geographical sections, each belonging to a different colony. Since independence from Europe, beginning in the 1960s and finally ending with Namibian independence in 1990, African nations have had to struggle with a colonial legacy as well as increasing populations, heavy urbanization, low economic growth, civil war, ethnic violence, educational franchise, limited health care delivery, and disease. They have done so with widely varying degrees of success and failure. While the continent as a whole is rich in natural and human resources, and while there is great social and economic potential for Africans, the future of Africa is simply impossible to predict.

David Crandall, Ph.D.
Department of Anthropology
Brigham Young University

CultureGrams World Edition 2006
People's Democratic Republic of Algeria

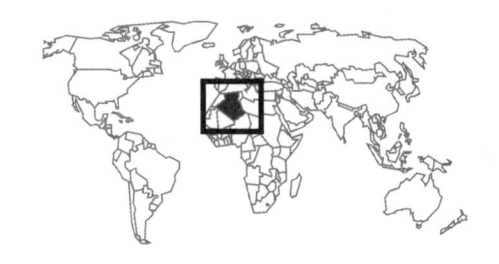

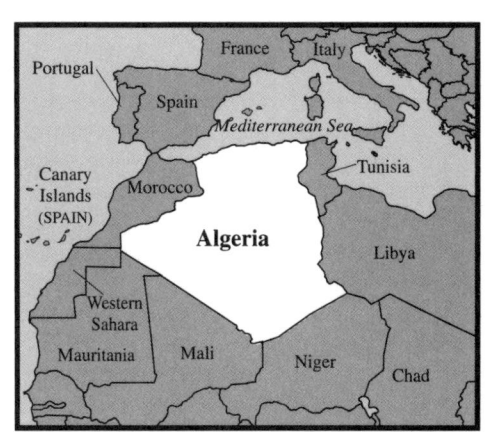

BACKGROUND

Land and Climate. Algeria, with an area of 919,590 square miles (2,381,740 square kilometers), is the world's tenth largest and Africa's second largest country; it is about three and a half times the size of Texas. About 90 percent of the population inhabits the northern coastal region, called the Tell. Central and southern Algeria form part of the vast Sahara Desert, where only an occasional oasis is capable of supporting life. The Tell is separated from the Sahara by the Atlas mountain range and the highlands of the Hauts Plateaux. The Hoggar Mountains, located near the southern border, are a water source for nearby communities. Only 3 percent of Algeria's land is arable.

The Tell enjoys a mild Mediterranean climate and moderate rainfall, with a winter rainy season that extends from December to March. In Algiers, the capital, the average daily high temperature in January is 61°F (16°C); in August it is about 86°F (30°C). Temperatures in the interior of Algeria can be much hotter. Humidity on the coast runs about 60 percent; it is less than 20 percent in the interior. A hot, sandy wind called the *sirocco* is common during summer, when all regions of the country are hot and dry.

History. Algeria's earliest inhabitants were not a homogenous people, but collectively they were called Berbers (from the Greek word *barbaros*, or *barbarian*) by Greeks and Romans. The term was adopted by successive invaders and is still used by non-Berbers today. A movement among indigenous Berbers has developed to collectively call themselves Imazighen (Amazigh, singular), meaning "free men." Algeria was conquered by the Phoenicians, whose Carthaginian Empire flourished (ca. 800–146 B.C.) until its destruction by the Romans. The Romans and then the Vandals held the coastal region until the Umayyad (Arab) invasion in the seventh century A.D. The cities of Algiers, Oran, Constantine, and Annaba owe their development to this period. The Umayyads introduced Islam to the Imazighen, who in the eighth century regained control of the region and established their own Islamic empire. Several indigenous empires followed until the 13th century, when immigrating Bedouins introduced the nomadic lifestyle.

From the early 1500s, the area was part of the Ottoman Empire. During this time, Barbary Coast pirates consistently attacked European ships and disrupted trade. This piracy was one reason France invaded in 1830. Fighting between French forces and local resistance groups lasted for several years, but Algeria eventually became a French-controlled territory and, ultimately, a department of the French Republic. Present-day borders were set in 1902.

A smoldering independence movement erupted into open warfare in 1954. After years of bitter fighting and more than a million deaths, Algeria was granted independence in 1962. After a challenging period of adjustment, Algeria emerged as a socialist republic. Ahmed Ben Bella was the first Algerian president.

The National Liberation Front (FLN) was the only political party until 1989, when the FLN set forth a new constitution for a multiparty system. Local and regional elections in 1990 were to be followed by full national elections in 1991. The Islamic Salvation Front (FIS) gained surprising victories in the 1990 elections and appeared to be heading for victory in 1991. To prevent the FIS from taking power, the military took control, canceled election results, and banned the FIS. Algeria soon slid into economic and political chaos. In 1994, a governing council appointed General Liamine Zeroual as president.

Algeria

Meanwhile, the FIS developed an armed resistance and a substantial guerrilla army. More radical militants of the Armed Islamic Group (GIA) began killing anyone deemed a supporter of the military regime. Human-rights abuses by government forces, as well as factional fighting on both sides of the conflict, contributed to the crisis.

In multiparty elections in 1995, Zeroual was elected president by a wide margin. By a 1996 referendum, the constitution was amended to ban political parties based on religion, create an upper house of parliament, and grant broader authority to the president. The GIA and other fundamentalist terrorists intensified a series of civilian massacres and terrorist bombings that have continued to the present and killed more than 100,000 people. In 1998, government forces began killing rebels but did not effectively stop their activities.

The upper house of parliament was seated through indirect elections in 1997 and gave Zeroual's party, the National Democratic Rally (RND), a majority of seats. In April 1999 elections, six of the seven presidential candidates pulled out of the contest to protest government favoritism. Thus unopposed, army-backed former foreign minister Abdelaziz Bouteflika became Algeria's first civilian president.

Promising an end to the violence and a restoration of national unity, Bouteflika called for a referendum supporting reconciliation with the militants. The referendum passed, and many militants took advantage of the government's offer of amnesty by laying down their weapons. Thousands of militants were released from prison. Although a state of emergency continues, the violence has largely subsided. In April 2004, Bouteflika defeated five opposition candidates to win reelection to a second five-year term.

THE PEOPLE

Population. Algeria's population of 32.1 million is growing annually at 1.3 percent. Nearly one-third of all residents are younger than age 15. About half of the population lives in urban areas. The capital, Algiers, has about 2.5 million residents; Oran has roughly 1 million.

About 83 percent of Algerians are of Arabic descent or mixed heritage (Amazigh/Arab), while 16 percent are of Amazigh lineage. The Imazighen and Arabs are well integrated, although some Imazighen (especially the Mozabit of the Sahara) do not intermarry with other groups. The Imazighen call themselves by different names (Kabyle, Shawya, Mozabit, Tuareg, etc.). They inhabit primarily the Aures and Djurdjura Mountains or desert regions due to a historical tendency to seek refuge from invading armies.

Language. Arabic is the official language. Tamazight, spoken by Imazighen, is also a national language; it has many regional variants. French, the primary language of business before 1992, is less prominent but remains important. Algerian Arabic incorporates many French and Amazigh words into daily speech. Standard Arabic is used for school instruction, government administration, and media reports. The Algerian dialect is used in casual conversation. Its vocabulary is primarily Arabic, but Amazigh influences its grammar and pronunciation. The Algerian dialect can be understood by speakers of other North African Arabic dialects but not by Middle East Arabic speakers. Imazighen speak many variations of Tamazight (Kabyle, Shawya, etc.) and Arabic.

Religion. Although Islam is the state religion, Algeria is not an Islamic republic. Still, since 99 percent of the people are Sunni Muslim, Islamic philosophy is deeply rooted in their minds, hearts, and behavior. Islamic scripture, the *Qur'an* (Koran), is considered the complete word of God. Muslims revere major Judeo-Christian prophets, but they accept Muhammad as the last and greatest emissary of *Allah* (God). Friday is the day of worship, when men go to mosque for a sermon and prayer. As in other Islamic countries, women pray in a different area of the mosque. Islam is practiced every day through dress, dietary codes, five daily prayers, and constant references to *Allah*. About 1 percent of the people are Christian or Jewish.

General Attitudes. Algerians are formal and courteous with strangers but warm and expressive among friends. They may be frank and even personal in expressing opinions, although it is impolite to publicly offend another person. Urban Algerians are becoming more individualistic, a character trait at odds with the traditional habit of placing group needs over personal ones. Algerians value family solidarity, intelligence, honesty, loyalty, courage, social status, and simplicity. Manliness is admired, as are traditional feminine qualities. Most Algerians want to buy a home, own a car, be healthy, and provide their children with a good education.

Outside observers may see Algerian politics as a battle between secular society and a fundamentalist religion. However, many Algerians believe the tension is more accurately described as a social revolution. Widening socio-economic gaps in 1991 between the rich and poor—as well as rising crime, corruption, and materialism—were the primary complaints of some educated conservatives. When they appealed to the structure, safety, and equality of Islam, the religion became a powerful and unifying symbol for all disenchanted people. The ensuing conflict was between supporters and opponents of the 1992 military takeover. Most supporters were secularists opposed to democracy. Opponents were secularists who favored democracy as well as Islamists, who continue to be divided between those who insist on an Islamic, nondemocratic state and those who support a democracy influenced by Islamic principles. Terrorists seek to establish a strict, non-democratic Islamic state.

Personal Appearance. Most urban men and about half of all urban women wear Western-style attire, but some urban dwellers and most rural people wear traditional North African styles. For women, this includes a blouse and skirt covered in public by a long, full dress whose color varies from region to region. In the east it is mainly dark, and in the west and central areas it is mainly white, but red, brown, and green dresses can be found all over. Some women wear veils in public; few Imazighen do. Most cover their hair with a scarf in public. Women wear a considerable amount of jewelry, an important part of their dowry and financial security. Although secular urban women may have Western hairstyles, most Algerian women have long, braided hair.

Traditional attire for men may include long, flowing robes or a long shirt, vest, and loose fitting pants. Head coverings are common. Most men have a mustache, the traditional symbol of manhood. In fact, to curse someone's mustache is one of the worst possible insults. Men who wear beards do so mostly as an expression of religious orientation.

CUSTOMS AND COURTESIES

Greetings. Greetings are genuinely cordial and open. They are usually accompanied by a handshake and frequently an embrace (between members of the same sex). Anything less friendly is considered impolite. Men shake hands with women unless one or both of them avoids contact with the opposite sex on religious grounds. Some Algerians follow the French custom of kissing each other on both cheeks when embracing. Others may hold and kiss the other person's right hand. Although different situations call for different greetings, a few phrases are appropriate in most cases. *Ahlan wa sahlan* (May your way be easy) is an Arabic welcome. *Marhaban bikoum* (Hello to you) is also common.

People address strangers and acquaintances by title and family name. Informally, the title may be combined with one's given name. Elders, always greeted first, are often called "uncle" or "aunt," even if not related. Friends and relatives use given names, whereas people within the same social or religious circles address one another as "brother" or "sister," often combined with the first or last name, depending on the degree of familiarity. Imazighen show respect to their elders, including siblings, by addressing them using the terms *dada* (for males) or *nana* (for females).

Gestures. Algerians commonly use hand gestures during or instead of conversation. Two clasped hands is a greeting at a distance. Men often slap the palm of a friend's hand to express something like "brilliant," "good joke," or "touché." Pressing a flat right hand to the heart shows appreciation or thanks. To ask for patience, one joins the right hand's fingertips, palm up, and moves it up and down slightly. The index finger may be extended to indicate a warning, but it is impolite to point directly at someone or something. Algerians avoid using the left hand for gestures. One passes items with the right hand or both hands. Facial gestures, such as expressing doubt by tightening the lips and raising the eyebrows, are also common. Algerians take care not to let the bottom of the foot point at others, and they do not place feet on furniture.

Visiting. Visiting is a social occasion in Algeria. Guests usually are offered refreshments, and it is impolite to refuse them. Hosts typically serve mint tea or coffee and pastries. Algerians visit parents and siblings weekly whenever possible. Close friends also visit one another frequently and without prior arrangement. Others are expected to make plans in advance. Fridays and holidays are popular times for visiting.

Men and women tend to socialize separately. In traditional homes or on formal occasions, they occupy different rooms. Even in Westernized families, they congregate in separate corners of the living room after eating a meal together.

Visitors, especially invited guests, often take gifts to their hosts. In urban areas, guests might give flowers, but food (pastries, fruit, etc.) is the most common gift throughout Algeria. During nonsocial visits, people like to spend considerable time on small talk before shifting the conversation to the intended subject.

Eating. Urban families usually eat main meals together, but rural or traditional men and women eat separately. In many urban homes, the father serves the meat, and each person takes portions of other foods from serving dishes. The eldest is served first. Rural families are more likely to eat from a common bowl, females after males. Some foods (meat, desserts) are eaten with the right hand, but most are eaten with utensils. Bread is sometimes used as a scoop. Throughout Algeria, people wash their hands and say *Bismi Allah* (In the name of God) before eating. After the meal, they say *Elhamduli Allah* (Praise be to God) and wash their hands. Meals are followed by tea.

LIFESTYLE

Family. The Algerian family is an important, private, and male-dominated entity, often including three or more generations (parents, married sons and their families, and unmarried children) in a single home. However, multigenerational families in a single home are becoming less common. Families have an average of four or five children. Smaller, nuclear families are found in cities. Although some Algerians live in apartments, most prefer large, concrete homes with four or five rooms. High walls surround the home and its vegetable garden.

Mothers care for the children and household, while fathers are responsible for income and discipline. Children are expected to obey parents and take care of them in their old age. An employed man provides not only for his family but also for the families of any unemployed brothers.

Dating and Marriage. Algerians do not date in the Western sense of dating. Marriage represents the linking of families, not just individuals. Consequently, matchmaking is often a family affair, with parents playing a major role. Romantic love is seen as something that grows with time after marriage.

Not all Algerians have traditional weddings, nor are all weddings similar. However, festivities may last as long as three days. Men and women usually have separate parties prior to getting married. At one, henna (a red dye made from the henna plant) is applied to the bride's hands and feet and to the groom's hands to signify the approaching change in life. Each betrothed person saves a portion of the henna and sends it to the other; doing so has nearly the same significance as exchanging rings. Before all of this, it is customary for the families to hold an engagement ceremony at a mosque and in each home. Both families agree on the dowry and prepare for wedding festivities, including the henna ritual. On the wedding day, the groom's family calls for the bride at her home. After they are served food and drink, they take the bride to the groom's home (traditionally riding on a horse, camel, or mule, but now in a nice car), where he is waiting or will appear later in the evening for the ceremony and wedding night.

Diet. *Couscous*, a pasta-like semolina (made from wheat particles) often cooked with lamb or chicken and vegetables, is perhaps Algeria's most popular dish—particularly for special occasions. *Tajine* is a meat-and-vegetable stew named for the type of pot in which it is cooked. Rich sauces are a common feature. *Chorba* is a soup made with small pieces of meat and vermicelli. Staple grains are wheat, rice, maize, and barley. Local produce includes oranges, grapes, watermelon, tomatoes, potatoes, onions, green beans, and cauliflower. Although pastries like *makrout* (a semolina pastry with date filling) are popular, fruit is nearly always served for dessert. Devout Muslims do not eat pork or drink alcohol.

Recreation. Soccer is the most popular sport in Algeria. Only men attend matches at stadiums; schoolgirls might attend boys' school matches. Algerians also play basketball, volleyball, and handball. Women participate in sports, especially track, but far less often than men. Families go to the beach or on picnics. Individuals like to take walks, although rural women are always accompanied by relatives. For winter recreation, women watch television and socialize at home, while men play cards or dominoes in cafés. Algerians play the guitar, flute, and *gaspa* (a long bamboo flute).

The Arts. Algerian jewelry and textiles are traditional arts that continue to thrive. Intricate metalworking and inlaid stone is characteristic of traditional jewelry. Swords, daggers, and other metalwork are often highly stylized. Knotted wool Algerian rugs are popular for their bold colors and geometric form. Artisans hand-tool leather items, especially boots and saddles. *Raï* music, a popular, danceable Algerian musical style sung

Algeria

by both men and women, has gained some international renown and blends U.S., European, and North African musical elements. A week-long *Raï* festival is held annually.

Holidays. National holidays include New Year's Day, Labor Day (1 May), Independence Day (5 July), and Revolution Day (1 Nov.). Muslim holy days are set according to the lunar calendar. *Aid al Fitr*, a two-day feast at the end of *Ramadan*, is a time for visiting, feasting, and worshiping. *Ramadan* is the month in which the *Qur'an* was revealed to Muhammad, so each day Muslims do not eat, drink, or smoke from sunrise to sunset. After an evening prayer (*tarawih*), they eat and visit with family and friends. *Aid al Adha* is a two-day event held in conjunction with the summer pilgrimage to Makkah, Saudi Arabia. It also commemorates Abraham's willingness to sacrifice his son. *Mouharem* (the lunar calendar's New Year), *Achoura* (celebrated one month after *Aid al Adha*), and *Al Mawlid* (Muhammad's birthday) are also religious holidays.

Commerce. Normal business hours are Saturday through Wednesday, from 8 a.m. to noon and from 2 to 6 p.m. The Western (Gregorian) calendar is used for business. Urban Algerians buy staple foods from state-owned (and in some cases privately owned) supermarkets. Small shops are more common in rural areas. Many people buy perishables such as bread, meat, and vegetables every day. In remote areas, meat and vegetables are only available on weekly market days.

SOCIETY

Government. Algeria has a strong executive president (currently Abdelaziz Bouteflika) elected to a five-year term and a prime minister (currently Ahmed Ouyahia) appointed by the president. Parliament's lower house is the 389-seat National Assembly, whose members are directly elected to five-year terms. The upper house is the National Council. Of its 144 members, one-third are appointed by the president and two-thirds are chosen by local councils. Members of the National Council serve six-year terms. Legislation passed by the National Assembly must be approved by the National Council. The country is divided into 48 *wilayaat* (prefectures). The voting age is 18.

Economy. Algeria's main exports include crude oil, other petroleum products, and natural gas. With four major natural gas deposits, Algeria holds about 3 percent of the world's total reserves. Agriculture employs about one-quarter of the labor force, but the country is not self-sufficient in food production. Nomadic herding is the primary economic activity in the sparsely populated desert regions. Light industry, food processing, and the mining of iron, phosphates, lead, and zinc are also important sectors of the economy.

The gross domestic product per capita is relatively high due to oil revenues. Most Algerians have a low income, and many have been impacted by inflation, high unemployment, political strife, and the withdrawal of foreign companies.

The state controls most industries. The public sector is large: the government employs more than one-quarter of the labor force. Such a large bureaucracy has led to low productivity. The currency is the Algerian *dinar* (DZD).

Transportation and Communications. Most highways are paved, but desert roads are less reliable. Some people have cars

DEVELOPMENT DATA
Human Dev. Index* rank . . . . 108 of 177 countries
   Adjusted for women. . . . . 89 of 144 countries
Real GDP per capita $5,760
Adult literacy rate . . . . 78 percent (male); 60 (female)
Infant mortality rate . . . . 32 per 1,000 births
Life expectancy . . . . 68 (male); 71 (female)

but more rely on buses, especially in major cities. Travel by train is possible but not popular. Seven international airports link Algeria's major cities with other countries. As with transportation, communications systems are good in the north but less reliable in the south. Telephones are concentrated in cities. The state controls local radio and television, but urban Algerians can access international television via satellite. Internet access is extremely limited. Newspapers print only authorized material or risk being suspended.

Education. Schooling is free and compulsory to age 15. Instruction is mainly in Arabic. Beginning at age six, students attend nine years at a "fundamental" school that stresses basic skills, science, and technology. More than three-fourths of all pupils go on to secondary school. Boys are more likely than girls to complete those three years. Algeria has a few large and several small universities. Other students can obtain training at vocational schools and technological institutes.

Health. Algerians receive free or low-cost care in hospitals, clinics, and mobile health facilities. Lines are long, so many prefer the expensive care of private facilities. Disease, poverty, and malnutrition are still serious, but the health of Algerians is better than a decade ago. These improvements are partly the result of improved prenatal education and a massive immunization campaign.

AT A GLANCE

Events and Trends.
- President Bouteflika won more than 80 percent of the vote in the April 2004 election. His nearest opponent won just 8 percent. Although opposition groups argued the election was fraudulent, international observers declared it to be transparent and fair.
- President Jacques Chirac of France visited Algeria in March 2003 to meet with President Bouteflika and to sign a cooperation agreement between the two nations. Although Chirac also went to Algeria in 2001, the 2003 trip was the first official state visit by a French president since France granted Algeria independence in 1962.
- A government report released in 2003 showed that Algerians are marrying much later than in the past. Half of all Algerians over the age of 15 are single. The average age at which men marry is 33; for women, the average age is 30. The report blamed a housing shortage and unemployment for the increase in the number of unmarried Algerians.

Contact Information. Embassy of Algeria, 2137 Wyoming Avenue NW, Washington, DC 20008; phone (202) 265-2800; web site www.algeria-us.org.

CultureGrams
People. The World. You.

ProQuest Information and Learning Company
300 North Zeeb Road, P.O. Box 1346
Ann Arbor, Michigan 48106 USA
Toll Free: 1.800.528.6279
Fax: 1.800.864.0019
www.culturegrams.com

© 2005 ProQuest Information and Learning Company and Brigham Young University. It is against the law to copy, reprint, store, or transmit any part of this publication in any form by any means without written permission from ProQuest. This document contains native commentary and original analysis, as well as estimated statistics. The content should not be considered strictly factual, and it may not apply to all groups in a nation. *UN Development Programme, Human Development Report 2004 (New York: Oxford University Press, 2004).

CultureGrams World Edition 2006

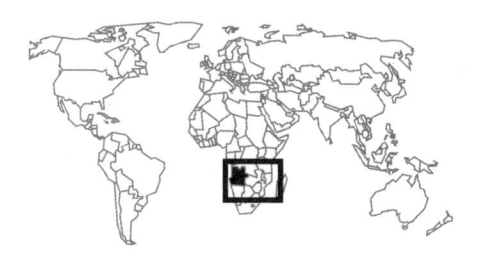

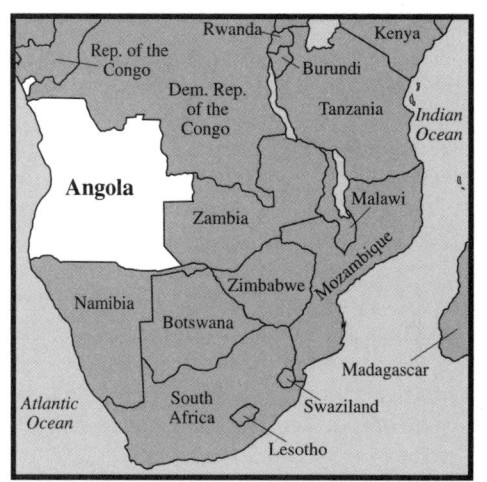

Republic of Angola

BACKGROUND

Land and Climate. Nearly three times the size of California, Angola covers 481,350 square miles (1,246,700 square kilometers) of southwestern Africa. Angolan territory includes oil-rich Cabinda Province, which is separated from the rest of Angola by territory belonging to the Democratic Republic of the Congo. A narrow plain on Angola's Atlantic coast rises sharply to a large central plateau, where elevations range between 2,000 and 8,000 feet (approximately 600 to 2,400 meters). Tropical forests are found in northern Angola, while open savannas cover the south and east. Years of war and hunting devastated Angola's populations of elephant, giraffe, rhinoceros, and other wildlife, as animals fled to neighboring countries or were killed. Efforts are underway to repopulate some species.

Angola's central plateau has a mild but wet climate. Nearly all of the region's annual precipitation (40 to 60 inches, or 100 to 150 centimeters) falls during the wet (or hot) season from October to April. During this period, the daily high temperature is usually at least 79°F (26°C). Temperatures are lower during the dry (or cool) season, from May to September. The southern coastal plain is generally cooler and more arid than the interior because of the Benguela Current, a cold Atlantic current that flows northward along the coast.

History. Beginning in the 6th century A.D., Bantu groups migrated south across the Congo River, displacing and integrating with the existing populations. Portuguese explorers arrived at the end of the 15th century and encountered powerful societies such as the Kingdom of Congo and the Kingdom of Ndongo. The king of the Ndongo was called the *ngola*, from which Angola derives its name. The Portuguese established a colony and a slave trade, sending captives to colonies in the Americas. By the time slavery was abolished in the 19th century, huge sections of Angola had been depopulated.

Portugal's attempts to exert greater control over the colony's interior in the 20th century were met with stiff local resistance. A nationalist movement grew during the 1950s, leading to a guerrilla war for independence in 1961. After a coup in Portugal, the new government there was eager to end the costly war. On 11 November 1975, it granted Angola independence.

The transition to nationhood did not go smoothly, largely because of a power struggle between the three nationalist groups: the National Front for the Liberation of Angola (FNLA), the National Union for the Total Independence of Angola (UNITA), and the Popular Movement for the Liberation of Angola (MPLA). The resulting civil war became a proxy conflict for the Cold War rivalry between the Soviet Union and the United States. The left-wing MPLA fought with the help of Soviet weapons and Cuban soldiers. U.S. weapons and South African soldiers supported UNITA and the FNLA.

By 1976, the MPLA, which was based in the capital Luanda, had received broad international recognition as the nation's legitimate government, and MPLA leader Agostinho Neto was named president. When Neto died in 1979, he was succeeded by José Eduardo dos Santos. The FNLA surrendered in 1984, but UNITA leader Jonas Savimbi continued the campaign against the MPLA. As Cold War tensions eased in the late 1980s, South Africa and Cuba agreed to withdraw their forces. The war appeared to be over when treaties in 1989 and 1991 led to national multiparty elections in 1992. However, Savimbi resumed fighting after placing second to Dos Santos in the first round of the presidential election. A 1994 treaty and the deployment of UN peacekeepers ushered in a period of relative

Angola

peace, but in 1998 disagreements between Dos Santos and Savimbi again led to war.

The MPLA gained key victories in the years that followed. In February 2002, Savimbi was killed in battle. Two months later, after 27 years of civil conflict and the loss of 1.5 million lives, the MPLA and UNITA signed a peace accord that finally ended the war. Although a decades-old separatist conflict continues in Cabinda Province, the peace has endured in the rest of the country, where Angolans now work to resettle refugees, reunite families, clear landmines, and reconstruct the infrastructure.

THE PEOPLE

Population. Estimates of Angola's population range between 11 and 15 million. An accurate count is impossible because of the ongoing movement of displaced people. Approximately 40 percent of the population lives in urban areas. Luanda, the capital and largest city, has about 3.5 million inhabitants. Angola has a young population, with 44 percent under age 15.

Angola's largest ethnic group is the Ovimbundu (37 percent of the population), followed by the Kimbundu (25 percent) and Bakongo (13 percent). Smaller groups are the Lunda-Quioco, Nhaneca-Humbe, Ganguela, Ovambos, and Herero. The San, or Bosquimanes, (also known as "Bushmen") are nomads and gatherers comprising a very small and diminishing portion of the population in the south. Ethnic groups tend to be concentrated in particular regions. For example, the Ovimbundu live primarily in central and western Angola, the Kimbundu around Luanda, and the Bakongo in the northwest. About 2 percent of Angolans are of mixed Portuguese and African origin (*mestiços*). Europeans (mostly of Portuguese origin) comprise 1 percent.

Language. Portuguese, the official national language, is used in government, schools, and commerce. Most urban Angolans but very few rural Angolans speak Portuguese. This is due in part to a lack of formal education in rural areas and the isolation of some groups during the civil war. Local languages spoken in Angola include Umbundo (by the Ovimbundu), Kimbundu (by the Kimbundu), and Kikongo (by the Bakongo). People displaced in urban centers often discontinue speaking their native language, and urban children usually favor Portuguese over their parents' native language. Since the war's end, native language learning has become part of the school curriculum, and there is a growing feeling among educated Angolans that the nation's linguistic heritage should be preserved.

Religion. The vast majority of Angolans are Christians. Due to Portuguese influence, Catholics comprise the largest denomination, followed by various Protestant faiths. Traditional animist beliefs remain strong, especially in rural areas. People often combine animist practices with their Christian beliefs. Many Angolans rely on traditional healers (*curandeiros*, or *kimbondeiros*) and believe that witches (*feiticeiros*, or *macumbeiros*) can free them from a problem or help them obtain wealth. Gains from witchcraft are believed to come at the expense of others, and many deaths and accidents are attributed to witchcraft.

General Attitudes. Angolans generally have a friendly, joyful, and generous nature. They like to feast, celebrate, dance, and sing. People in cities tend to be more outspoken and boisterous than those in rural areas. Rural Angolans generally are more attached to traditions than are their urban compatriots. Although Angolans have experienced the traumas of war, they are not a cynical or combative people. There is a strong belief among generations under age 40 that the war was not theirs. During the war years, people lived in fear and deprivation. Many rural Angolans fled their homes in the country, leaving possessions behind, to arrive in cities. There they struggled in a different and sometimes hostile environment. Because of these hardships, Angolans tend to live in the present: tomorrow might not bring the simple joys of today's moments, and if the day brings sadness, it will be forgotten tomorrow.

Personal Appearance. Urban Angolans generally wear Western clothing. They like to dress well when going out, even if only for everyday tasks such as shopping. Older urban men may wear a two-piece suit on formal occasions. Among younger businessmen, a three-piece suit and tie is the norm. It is still common for women, especially in rural areas, to wear a blouse, an African-style wraparound dress, and a colorful shawl tied around the neck or head. A shawl may also be wrapped around the back to carry a child. Young urban women often prefer jeans or other casual Western clothing. In rural communities, if people have nice clothes, they prefer to reserve them for the most important events, such as a wedding or church service. Traditional clothing still exists among some ethnic groups. For example, Mumuilas women in southern Angola wear elaborate beadwork and bracelets on their neck, arms, and legs.

CUSTOMS AND COURTESIES

Greetings. Female friends and friends of the opposite sex greet by kissing one another once on each cheek. Good male friends may greet with a brief hug and several slaps on the back. Otherwise, people shake hands. Portuguese greetings include *Bom dia, como está?* (Good day, how are you?) and the informal *Oi* or *Olá* (both meaning "Hi"). A young man might say to another *Meu camba, fixe?* (Friend, are you okay?). A common Umbundo greeting is *Walale* (meaning "Good morning," but literally translated as "How did you pass the night?"). The reply is generally *Ndalale* (I passed the night well, and you?).

One addresses an elderly man with a respectful term such as *Kota* (Elder) or *Tio* (Uncle), even when no family relationship exists. An elderly woman is called *Mãe* or *Mamá* (Mother) or *Tia* (Aunt). In formal situations, the Portuguese titles *Senhor* (Mr.) or *Senhora* (Mrs.) precede the person's last name.

When people part, they might say *Boa continuação* (Have a nice day), *Feliz noite* (Good night), or the informal *Tcháu* (Good-bye).

Gestures. Holding the hand flat and pointing the index finger of the other hand into the palm means "I want to speak to you." Pointing an index finger at someone can be interpreted as aggression. Giving the "thumbs up" is a common way to say "Everything is okay!" If a person is busy talking with someone but wishes to greet another person, the greeter lifts the palm of the hand. The other person will reply with the same gesture. Public displays of affection between people of the opposite sex are discouraged, especially in rural areas. As a sign of friendship, friends of the same sex may hold hands. It is not uncommon, or considered rude, for people to spit, pick their nose, or scratch their body in public.

Visiting. In rural areas, friends and family members usually visit unannounced. Urban people may telephone ahead. If the home does not have a doorbell, visitors attract attention by clapping their hands three or four times. Even if very poor, the host will do everything possible to make guests feel comfortable. Guests are offered a beer or another alcoholic drink (even in the morning) or a soft drink. For a special celebratory meal called a *contribuição*, guests are asked in advance to bring food or drinks (or money to pay for them), in part to avoid gate-crashers.

Eating. Breakfast is called *mata-bicho*, literally meaning "kill the beast" (the one growling in an empty stomach). For most families, especially in rural areas, breakfast consists primarily of *tchisangua* (a drink made of water, ground cornmeal, and sugar). At lunch and dinner, the staple is *funge* (a paste of ground cornmeal, similar to thick porridge) or *pirão* (a paste of ground cassava). In rural areas, people eat with their hands. In cities, people use utensils. When guests fill the dining table, children eat in the kitchen or outside. Guests are served first and are expected to eat the best portions. Although cities have restaurants, they are unaffordable for most Angolans. Instead, people usually eat out by buying a hamburger or *churrasco* (a piece of grilled chicken) cooked on a charcoal stove at a roadside food stand.

LIFESTYLE

Family. Three decades of war have severely disrupted the traditional family structure. Ninety percent of families lost someone in the conflict. Widows head many families. When both parents are lost, children live with aunts or uncles if possible, but older children must often care for younger siblings themselves. Orphaned street kids, usually from rural areas, have swelled city centers looking for means of subsistence. Rural families have returned to home regions they fled during the war. The government, aided by non-governmental organizations, has established a nationwide television program to help reunify family members.

In Angola, the traditional family is an extended one, with three generations often living together. The head of the family is the eldest man (*o mais velho*, meaning "the elder"). Housing in cities is scarce, so adult children usually remain with their parents until they can afford to build or buy their own house. The entire family usually lives in one room; the kitchen is a separate structure. Women are responsible for household tasks, though all family members, even young children, are expected to contribute to the upkeep of the home. In many households, children cook meals, herd livestock, and carry water and firewood. Older children take care of younger siblings and cousins.

Dating and Marriage. In urban areas, young people begin casual dating during teenage years. Rural communities are more traditional and close-knit, and young people who date usually intend to marry.

A traditional *alambamento* usually takes place before a Christian wedding can be considered. In this ceremony, the prospective groom offers a bride-price (drinks, clothing, poultry, goats, or other goods) to the bride's family, and conditions of the marriage are discussed. Lengthy negotiations often precede an agreement. Prices and practices differ from one ethnic group to another. For example, a Bakongo *alambamento* is an elaborate ritual with an expensive bride-price, so Bakongo men are sometimes said to prefer wives from other ethnic groups because the bride-price is cheaper. In some cases, the *alambamento* is considered a wedding, after which the husband and wife start their life together; they later marry in a registry office and/or the church. Sometimes the *alambamento* serves as an engagement, and the bride stays in her parents' home until the wedding.

Urban marriages are expensive celebrations, usually taking place at the end of the week. The bride and groom wear formal Western wedding clothing (a suit for men and a white bridal dress for women). The couple has wedding photos taken at public fountains or other scenic locations, and the wedding party drives in a long procession of cars through the city, honking their horns. Although these processions often paralyze traffic, other drivers usually honk back to show their approval to the passing couple. The celebrations continue in a restaurant or at home, where guests enjoy food and dancing until late in the night.

Diet. Staples are *funge* (in central and southern Angola) and *pirão* (in the north). These are served with dried and salted fish, fresh fish, or (on special occasions) meat. Accompanying the meal may be green-leaf dishes, such as *quisaca* (dried and ground cassava leaves cooked in water) or *jimbôa* (a cooked leafy vegetable similar to spinach). Beans and *jindungo* (small hot peppers) are frequently added. Another popular dish is *calulú*, made of fish, vegetables, and palm oil. Urban residents may eat steak, rice, or pasta. Seasonal fruits include mangos, avocadoes, and papaya. A favorite with children is the white-and-pink edible interior of *múcua* (the fruit of the baobab tree), which is also made into ice cream.

Recreation. Soccer is the most popular sport in Angola, followed by basketball and handball. Children play soccer and other games using a ball made of tightly-bound rags. Boys make toy cars using tin cans and other scrap metal, pushing them along the street with long sticks. In rural areas, adults play a strategy game called *wela* (in Umbundo) or *kwela* (in Kimbundu); the game is played with beads or seeds placed in holes on a wooden board or in the ground. The most popular urban recreational activity is watching *novelas*, television soap operas mostly made in Brazil. In wartime, the shows were an escapist diversion that provided some measure of continuity in people's lives. Young people go to bars to socialize and play pool or chess. House parties are common. During the hot season, Angolans living in coastal regions may go to the beach. Angolans can rarely afford to travel for leisure.

The Arts. The nation enjoys a rich musical tradition, which has been influenced by music from Brazil, Cuba, and Cape Verde. *Semba* and *kizomba* are the most established local styles, but new styles have recently emerged, including *kuduro*, which is heavily influenced by rap and rhythm and blues.

Provincial museums feature masks and other indigenous arts. Some of the Quioco (Tchokwé) people's masks are internationally renowned pieces of artwork. Masks are carved in ebony, while ivory is frequently used for small statues and bracelets. Soapstone is used for carvings in southern Angola.

Holidays. Public holidays are New Year's Day, Martyrs of the Colonial Repression Day (4 January, marking a 1961 uprising in Baixa de Cassange), Beginning of the Armed Struggle Day (4 February, marking a 1961 uprising in Luanda), Carnival (the day before Ash Wednesday), International Women's Day (8 Mar.), Peace and National Reconciliation Day (4 Apr.), Easter (including Good Friday), International Workers' Day (1 May), International Children's Day (1 June), Birthday of Agostinho Neto (17 Sept.), All Soul's Day (2 Nov.), Independence Day (11 Nov.), and Christmas (25 Dec.).

Commerce. Most offices and shops observe a midday break. They are open Monday to Friday from 8 a.m. to 12:30 p.m. and from 2 to 5:30 p.m. Urban shops sometimes stay open as late as 7:30 p.m. On Saturday, shop hours are generally 8 a.m. until at least 12.30 p.m. In Luanda and some other cities, people now have access to supermarkets, which may stay open until 10:00 p.m. Open-air markets operate throughout the week in

Angola

both urban and rural areas; prices increase on weekends. Street trading by peddlers is common. In Luanda, groups of youths sell their wares to drivers at traffic lights or in traffic jams. Women known as *zungueiras*, or *kitandeiras*, sell fruit and other goods on street corners or by walking through the city carrying their products on their heads.

SOCIETY

Government. Angola's president (currently José Eduardo dos Santos) is both chief of state and head of government. The prime minister (currently Fernando da Piedade Dias dos Santos Nando) is appointed by the president. The unicameral National Assembly (*Assembleia Nacional*) has 220 members. Presidential and parliamentary elections were last held in 1992; the next elections are scheduled to take place no later than 2006. The voting age is 18. Angola's 18 provinces are administered by presidentially appointed governors. Local officials govern rural areas, although the village chief (*soba*) has some powers, including the distribution of land to new arrivals and returning refugees (*regressados*). Villagers select the chiefs on the basis of age and experience.

Economy. Angola is rich in resources, including oil, diamonds, gold, iron, timber, and fish. The economy relies most heavily on the oil industry, which is responsible for about half of Angola's GDP and 90 percent of its exports. Angola is the second-largest crude oil producer in sub-Saharan Africa, after Nigeria. Still, the economy has yet to recover from the effects of war, and Angolans remain some of the world's poorest people. Most do not share in the benefits of the oil wealth. Rural Angolans practice subsistence agriculture, with corn, beans, peanuts, cassava, potatoes, and sweet potatoes the principal crops. Many urban people earn a living by trading imported food or goods on the informal market. Angola's currency is the *kwanza* (AOA).

Transportation and Communications. Paved roads, many requiring extensive repairs, connect provincial capitals. Other roads are unpaved and, during the wet season, often become flooded and impassable. Traveling off the main roads can be extremely dangerous, as Angola remains one of the world's most heavily mined countries. Land-mine accidents increase during the wet season, when people drive on the road shoulders to avoid mud. Most rural people travel locally on foot or by bicycle. Privately owned minibuses transport passengers in urban areas. Vehicle ownership has dramatically increased in cities in recent years; traffic congestion in Luanda is severe. Traffic moves on the right. One government-owned airline and several private ones fly to provincial capitals. The reconstruction of the rail system is underway.

The government owns most media outlets, including two television channels, the majority of radio stations, and the nation's only daily newspaper. The government produces a daily television news program in each of the main local languages. Private radio stations broadcast in major cities. Because most Angolans do not have a regular electricity supply, transistor radios are the main source of information. Most private weekly newspapers are published in Luanda. Mobile phones outnumber telephone land lines. Computer and internet use is limited, though internet cafés can be found in cities.

DEVELOPMENT DATA
Human Dev. Index* rank . . . . 166 of 177 countries
    Adjusted for women. . . . . NA
Real GDP per capita $2,130
Adult literacy rate . . . . 56 percent (male); 28 (female)
Infant mortality rate . . . . 193 per 1,000 births
Life expectancy. . . . . 39 (male); 42 (female)

Education. Officially, schooling in Angola is mandatory through the sixth grade. In practice, there are not enough schools or teachers for this law to be enforced. The government and non-governmental organizations are working to reconstruct schools damaged or abandoned during the war. In rural areas, school may be held under a shade tree or in a shop, church, or home. Classes are crowded due to a lack of trained teachers. Former teachers are being re-recruited. University education is offered only in major urban centers. Parents of the small wealthy minority send their children abroad for secondary and tertiary education, mainly to Portugal, South Africa, Namibia, the United Kingdom, and the United States.

Health. No health insurance system exists, so individuals must pay for all medical costs. Medical facilities lack equipment and trained staff, particularly in rural areas. Malaria is the primary contributor to a high mortality rate for children under age 5 (260 deaths per 1,000 live births). Waterborne diseases such as cholera and diarrhea are common because of the lack of access to clean water. Angola's official HIV/AIDS infection rate is 6 percent (the lowest rate in southern Africa), though many believe the real rate is much higher. The spread of HIV/AIDS was slowed by a lack of population movement during the war years. Now that the war is over and there is a much freer circulation of people, Angola is at risk of having the disease become a major health problem.

AT A GLANCE
Events and Trends.
- Between March and May 2005, an outbreak of the highly contagious Marburg virus killed nearly 300 people in northern Angola. The Marburg virus is a form of haemorrhagic fever similar to Ebola. Ninety percent of those infected died within days. The cause of the outbreak is unknown, though it may have been started by human consumption of contaminated wild animal meat.
- In February 2005, thousands of people demonstrated in Cabinda to demand autonomy for the province. Government troops are deployed in Cabinda Province to combat the Front for the Liberation of the Enclave of Cabinda (FLEC), which has sought independence for the province since 1974. Oil is a major issue in the war, as Cabinda produces more than half of Angola's oil revenue.

Contact Information. Embassy of Angola, 2100–2108 16th Street NW, Washington, DC 20009; phone (202) 785-1156; web site www.angola.org.

© 2005 ProQuest Information and Learning Company and Brigham Young University. It is against the law to copy, reprint, store, or transmit any part of this publication in any form by any means without written permission from ProQuest. This document contains native commentary and original analysis, as well as estimated statistics. The content should not be considered strictly factual, and it may not apply to all groups in a nation. *UN Development Programme, Human Development Report 2004 (New York: Oxford University Press, 2004).

CultureGrams™
People. The World. You.

ProQuest Information and Learning Company
300 North Zeeb Road, P.O. Box 1346
Ann Arbor, Michigan 48106 USA
Toll Free: 1.800.528.6279
Fax: 1.800.864.0019
www.culturegrams.com

CultureGrams 2006 World Edition

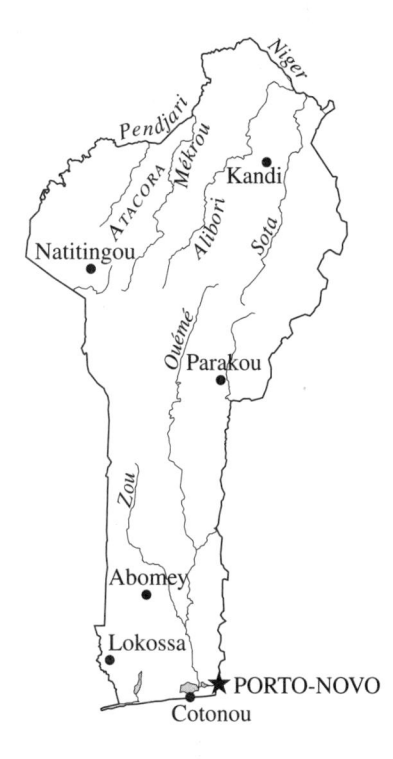

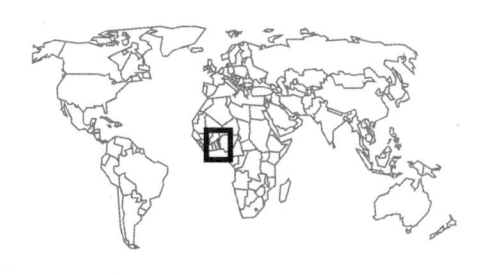

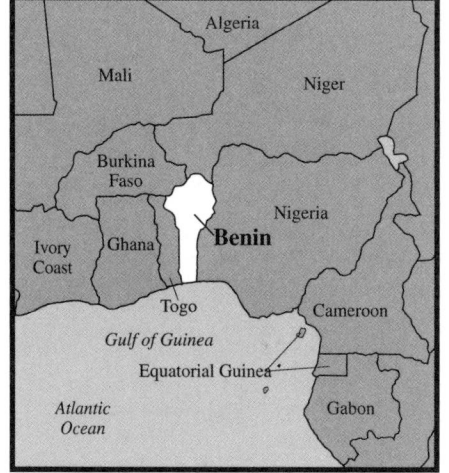

Republic of Benin

BACKGROUND

Land and Climate. Benin is a small western African nation located between Togo and Nigeria. Covering 43,482 square miles (112,620 square kilometers), it is just smaller than Pennsylvania. From its coast on the Atlantic Ocean, Benin runs only 420 miles (680 kilometers) to the northern border. Rolling hills and plains dominate the landscape, but the Atacora Mountains provide variety in the north. Major rivers include the Ouémé, Zou, Pendjari, Mékrou, Alibori, Sota, and Niger. The capital is Porto-Novo.

Benin's north is generally higher in elevation, is covered by savannah, and has a drier climate. Most rain falls between June and September. Between November and February, the dry harmattan winds blow from north to south to moderate the hot temperatures. Harmattan winds also carry fine red dust that coats all surfaces and hangs in the air. Without the wind, daytime temperatures find their peak in March and April at above 100°F (37°C). The lower-lying south has tropical forests and experiences four seasons: a long rainy season between March and July, followed by a short hot season until September; and a short rainy season to November, followed by a long hot season until March. Southern temperatures are slightly cooler (95°F, or 35°C) than in the north, but the climate is more humid.

Deforestation has destroyed many southern forests, but ceiba, ebony, mahogany, and palm trees are still found. Elephants, lions, antelopes, monkeys, boars, crocodiles, wildebeests, and snakes all inhabit Benin. Many snakes are poisonous, and the python is considered sacred.

History. The history of Benin (called Dahomey until 1975) cannot be separated from the history of the powerful Fon kingdom of Danhomê. The kingdom was known for its slave trade and production of palm oil and for having an army of women (the Amazons). Other kingdoms were prominent at the same time as Danhomê, such as the Kingdom of Porto-Novo in the south and the northern kingdoms of Borgu, Nikki, Djougou, and Kouande. Danhomê expanded its northern frontier in the early 1800s to acquire more slaves from neighboring tribes. It also fiercely resisted French incursions beginning in 1857. In 1893, the French finally defeated King Gbehanzin, the hero of the resistance, and gradually spread their administrative control throughout the region. By 1904, Dahomey was fully integrated into French West Africa.

Independence came in 1960, but the first 12 years were marked by regional strife, trade union and student strikes, and six military coups. No one could unite the nation until Major Matthieu Kérékou seized power. He eventually (1974) adopted Marxism-Leninism as the official ideology, renamed the country the People's Republic of Benin, and governed with a strong hand until 1989.

When communism disintegrated in Europe, Kérékou sponsored a national conference in which it was decided that Benin would become a multiparty democracy with regularly scheduled elections. Although the transition period was unstable due to strikes and opposition activities, national elections were held on schedule in 1991. Nicéphore Soglo defeated Kérékou to become president of the newly declared Republic of Benin. The peaceful transfer of power was followed by another relatively peaceful election in 1996 in which Kérékou was elected president. Despite this stability, Benin remains mired in poverty, and the current government is working to stimulate economic growth by implementing reforms, privatizing state enterprises, and encouraging foreign investment.

Benin

THE PEOPLE

Population. The population of 7.25 million grows annually at 2.9 percent. Benin's diversity of ethnic groups is the result of migrations, conquests, and the mixing of groups over time. The Fon is the largest single group, with 47 percent of the population. Other peoples include the Adja (12 percent) and Bariba (10), as well as the Yoruba and Aizo peoples. In the north, a number of smaller groups form 5 percent of the population; these include the Dendi, Betamari, Berba, Kountemba, Ouama, Peuhl, and others. More recent immigrants include Togolese, Ghanaians, and Nigerians. Southern and northern Beninese do not always have good relations. Southerners sometimes consider the northerners primitive, while northerners may characterize southerners as untrustworthy. Despite these views, the vast diversity of people in Benin are able to work together in a democracy. Two-thirds of all people live in the south, particularly between Abomey and Cotonou, the main commercial city. Cotonou claims 12 percent of the total population, but most people (70 percent) live in rural areas.

Language. French, the official language, is used in government and education. No one of the more than 60 indigenous languages has been accepted as a national language, so French remains the unifying tongue. And while many rural adults have trouble speaking French, their children in school speak it with greater fluency. The Adja-Fon language group (Fon, Adja, Houéda, Popo, Mahi, Mina, Goun, etc.) dominates in the south and central regions. Yoruba is also widely spoken in these areas. Bariba and many other languages are spoken in the north. People usually speak at least three local languages. From 1975 to 1990, the government encouraged the use of major national languages in radio and television broadcasts. In the 1990s, local languages were added to help educate and inform more people. English, Spanish, German, and Russian are offered in secondary schools, and some Beninese can understand Nigerian Pidgin English.

Religion. Although Christianity has had a presence in Benin since the 17th century, indigenous belief systems such as animism and voodoo permeate the country's culture. Most Beninese believe in a supreme God (*Mahu* among the Fon and *Olorun* or *Olodumare* among the Yoruba) and in a life after death. They attach great importance to worshiping ancestors who protect them against misfortune. Accordingly, death is regarded as an important family event, and in some cases, funeral rites are elaborate. Divination is a central feature of local faith; people regularly consult an oracle about significant events or decisions they wish to undertake. People worship the supreme God through traditional divinities (*Voodoos* among the Fon and *Orisha* among the Yoruba). Most families have a fetish to which they pray and offer sacrifices to get help from these local gods.

Even Beninese who have adopted Christianity or Islam continue to practice fetish worship and other indigenous rites. They do not see the rules of organized religion as particularly binding or exclusive. Indeed, forms of Christianity that integrate African practices are developing quickly, and there is little religious conflict between groups. Fifteen percent of Benin's population is Christian, mostly Catholic. Islam (also 15 percent) is practiced mostly in the north.

General Attitudes. Although attitudes and values differ between ethnic groups, some common traits are characteristic. For instance, the concept of privacy does not exist for Beninese the way it does for North Americans. Most Beninese wonder why anyone would actually want to be alone. They take life at a fairly casual pace and have a good sense of humor that allows them to laugh at life's trivial problems. Humor does not extend to sarcasm, however, which is viewed as insulting. The Beninese are proud of their heritage. Most value hard work and material success, but these come second to family priorities and friendship bonds. Beninese are hospitable and generous; they will help relatives in need even when they are themselves poor. Trust is a primary component of a strong friendship. Misconceptions between the north and south are partly due to the fact that northerners are more traditional and reserved than southerners, who have greater exposure to Western ideas and education.

Personal Appearance. Cleanliness and neatness are very important. People take great care to maintain and iron their clothing, shower daily, and dress as well as possible. Urban residents wear anything from Western shirts, trousers, and suits to traditional fashions. Men's casual clothing often consists of a pair of loose trousers and a long-sleeved shirt that can reach to the knees. Formal outfits consist of three embroidered pieces: trousers, a long shirt, and a top usually called a *boubou* or *agbada*. Tailors produce these with both imported fabrics and local material. Around the house, rural men might wear a cloth about the waist and a small *dashiti* top or short-sleeved shirt, or they might wrap the waist cloth up to cover the chest and one shoulder.

Rural and urban women often wear a *pagne* (wraparound skirt). This can be long or short depending on one's age and marital status. A loose *boumba* (blouse) completes the outfit. Women wear a long *boubou* on formal occasions. A *boubou* is often ornately embroidered and quite colorful. Many women wear a head wrap and dress modestly.

CUSTOMS AND COURTESIES

Greetings. A proper greeting always precedes conversation. When joining or leaving a small group, one greets each individual. Men usually shake right hands. The oldest person initiates the handshake. Women only shake hands with men if the man initiates. To show special respect, particularly to an older person, one bows slightly and grasps one's right elbow with the left hand during a handshake. Men may snap fingers when they shake hands. Many urban relatives and friends tend to kiss three or four times alternately on the cheeks. Some people might add a kiss on the mouth for special occasions.

The Fon ask *A fon dagbe a?* (Did you wake up well?), while the Yoruba say *E karo* (Good morning). Similar expressions are used in other languages. People of the same age and status address each other by first name or nickname. Titles are reserved for official functions. It is disrespectful to call older people by their first names. Instead, one uses familial terms such as "brother" or "sister" (*fofo* or *dada* among the Fon). If an eldest child is named Dossa, parents may be called "Dossa's mother" (*Dossanon*) or "Dossa's father" (*Dossato*).

Gestures. Everyday conversation is accompanied by many gestures and sounds. To express exasperation, people might alternate slapping the back of one hand with the palm of the other, or women might hit the side of their thighs. A clicking sound made in the back of the throat expresses agreement. It is considered offensive to beckon someone with the index finger; instead, one waves all fingers of the right hand with the palm facing down. Public displays of affection are unacceptable, but friends of the same gender often hold hands or touch when talking or walking. Using the left hand for gestures is unclean and considered bad luck.

Showing respect for elders is vital. One does not interrupt an older person in conversation, nor does one talk to an elder with hands in the pockets or while chewing gum or wearing a hat. Avoiding eye contact shows deference to elders. Among equals, eye contact can indicate frankness.

Visiting. Visiting friends and relatives is regarded as considerate, and it is not necessary to notify them in advance. Visitors are welcomed warmly and offered water, both to drink and to wash off the dust from the roads. The host may take a sip before offering it to guests, and in rural areas, guests often spill a bit on the earth to show respect for the dead.

If visitors arrive during a meal, hosts feel obligated to offer some food. Visitors should accept at least a bite, as it is rude not to taste the food, but they can politely decline to eat the entire meal. Visitors ask for permission to leave; when the host agrees, the host walks the visitors at least to the door and sometimes further. Reciprocity is an important part of relationships, so today's guest is expected to be tomorrow's host.

While most visiting takes place in the home, the marketplace is also a popular point of social contact. Every town has a market day once a week or so, where people enjoy meeting.

Eating. Eating habits depend on one's activities. Rural workers may eat breakfast and lunch in the fields. They return home for dinner at night. Non-agricultural wage earners may have three substantial meals, or just one meal and snacks, depending on their financial means. Urban dwellers often have breakfast sometime between 7 and 10 a.m., lunch between 1 and 3 p.m., and dinner between 7 and 10 p.m. Spoons and other utensils may be used for some foods, but the right hand is generally preferred, especially for *eba* (see Diet), or pounded yam. At home, people eat from a common bowl (children share one and parents share another). Families eat together, and the father usually is served first. In northern areas, however, when male guests are present, the wife does not eat with them. Guests receive the best portions of food. Sniffing food is impolite.

LIFESTYLE

Family. The traditional family structure consists of an extended family living in a compound of separate houses. The compound is surrounded by a wall or fence and has a common courtyard with a well, space for animals, and a cooking area. Such a family expects to work hard together to meet basic needs, and all members expect to share the fruits of labor. Tolerance and support are key elements to family interaction, and it is considered a curse to have bad relations within the family unit. While this structure is preferred and remains mostly intact in rural areas, it is undergoing profound change in cities, where nuclear families are more common and where the idea of working together has taken different forms. Because the desire is still strong to share in what others have accomplished, some conflicts have arisen and society is struggling to keep the traditional family system working.

Polygamy is legal and practiced by half (or more) of the population. It is common among all ethnic groups and religions. Northern men are more likely than southern men to have two wives. Women do much of the work in the family, but the father is its head. Women are responsible for raising children, caring for the home, buying and selling, and helping their husband plant and harvest the crops. Men have the primary responsibility for agriculture. Children take on chores at an early age. Most families have more than two children and prefer to have at least one son to perpetuate the family name.

Dating and Marriage. While urban dating is becoming more casual, traditional dating is geared toward marriage. Depending on the area's customs, young people might socialize at local ceremonies, dance parties, dinners, or family functions such as marriages or funerals. Rural and northern marriages are more likely to be arranged than southern ones.

Wedding traditions vary widely. Most Beninese attach a great deal of importance to customary and religious marriages. Christians and Muslims mix their respective customs with local ways. A common practice is negotiating the bride-price. Women elders from the bride's family preside over a ceremony where they accept the groom's gifts and officially agree to the marriage, which is considered an alliance between two families. This bride-price, which legislation has sought to discourage, and the cost of a proper wedding can be so high that the wedding might be postponed for months or years until sufficient finances are available. In such cases, couples may live together and have children as if married.

Diet. Beninese prefer hot and spicy foods. The basic daily meal is a spicy stew eaten with a doughy porridge made from corn flour (called *wo* or *amiwo* in local languages and *pâte* in French) in the south, yam flour (*amala* or *loubo*) in Yoruba areas, or millet and sorghum flour in the north. Side dishes are pounded yam, fried or boiled yam and cassava, sweet potatoes, and fried bananas and *gari*, a kind of grits made from cassava. Beninese also eat *gari* with any kind of stew or soup, or they thin it and drink it like a porridge with sugar or milk. Boiled in water, *gari* is served as *eba*, a side dish eaten with stew. Beans are popular. Rice, which is mostly imported, is increasingly consumed. Stews have many ingredients: vegetables and leaves, okra, peanuts, palm nut pulp, and so on.

People eat a variety of tropical fruits (bananas, mangoes, oranges, avocados, tangerines, pineapples, and papaya) and snacks in the morning or late afternoon. They save meat for special occasions because it is so expensive; favorite types include chicken, goat, beef, and a special delicacy, *agouti* (sugarcane rat). The entire animal is eaten with no part being wasted. French cuisine is found in urban areas. Fresh seafood is plentiful in the south.

Recreation. Beninese enjoy getting together. Many social activities are closely related to family events, agriculture (planting or harvesting), and religious ceremonies. People also love soccer and other games such as lawn bowling, handball, wrestling, boxing, and basketball. Televisions are scarce, but people have access to one somewhere in the village, and large groups often get together to watch favorite programs or soccer matches. Only a few people can afford to go to a restaurant or on beach outings. The Beninese enjoy playing cards, checkers, or *adji* (a mathematical and probability game) outdoors.

The Arts. Performances of music and dance are common, and traditional musical rhythms such as *massegohoun* and *gogo* have been adapted to modern styles. Beninese sculptors create works in stone, wood, and iron. Some pieces, such as ceremonial masks, have religious purposes. Statues of human figures are created for their artistic value while drawing on religious themes. Many forms of art serve domestic functions, such as ornately carved tables and chairs. Colorful appliqué wall tapestries depict symbolic animals and historical events.

Holidays. The biggest holidays are New Year's Day and Easter, which are celebrated with days of eating and dancing. Other important holidays include National Voodoo Day (10 Jan.), International Workers' Day (1 May), Independence Day (1 Aug.), Christmas Day, *Odun Idi* (feast at the end of the Muslim holy month of *Ramadan*), and *Odun Lea* (Muslim Feast of

Benin

the Sacrifice). Rural people hold local celebrations. In the north, April often is reserved for festive funeral parties in honor of certain death anniversaries.

Commerce. Government offices are open weekdays from 8 a.m. to noon and 3 to 6:30 p.m. Banks usually close by 5 p.m. Private businesses operate on their own schedules. Business should be initiated only after a greeting and social conversation. Shop prices usually are fixed, but bargaining is essential at open markets. Merchants respect a good bargainer and see the exchange as a game as well as a transaction. The most famous market, called *Tokpa* or *Dantokpa* (meaning "near the river"), is held in Cotonou. Street hawkers informally sell their goods at crossroads. A vendor's first customer each day is said to determine the seller's luck: if the customer makes a purchase, the vendor will have many sales; if not, the vendor will not expect a good day. Therefore, the vendor often gives his first customer a very good price to encourage a sale.

SOCIETY

Government. Benin is a multiparty democracy. The president (currently Matthieu Kérékou) acts as chief of state and head of government and is directly elected to a five-year term. The National Assembly has 83 members, elected to four-year terms. The voting age is 18. More than 50 political parties are active within Benin's six provinces, but only a handful have legislative representation. While the government works to unite the country, regional politics remain important.

Economy. Benin is one of the poorest countries in the world. Although it profits from oil revenue, this wealth is concentrated in the hands of a few. Most people rely on subsistence farming and sometimes fishing for their livelihood. In fact, 90 percent of all agricultural output comes from small farms. Agriculture accounts for 35 percent of export earnings. Major crops include corn, cassava and other tubers, groundnuts, sorghum, soy, and millet. Cotton is the chief export crop, but cash crops such as coffee, cocoa, palm oil, and tobacco are also produced in small quantities. Industry employs only 2 percent of the workforce. Crude oil is the country's most important export. Remittances from Beninese working abroad are also vital to the economy. Benin imports far more than it exports, and a great deal of illegal trade is conducted across Benin's borders, particularly with Nigeria. The currency is the *CFA franc* (XOF).

Transportation and Communications. Benin's few roads are mostly unpaved. Urban public transport hardly exists, although inexpensive taxis do operate in cities and between towns. Taxi-motorcycles called *zemidjans* have become a substitute for taxis in cities and large towns. Many people also have their own motorcycles and some have cars. Minimal traffic laws make driving hazardous.

Private telephones are rare, but the number of public phones is increasing. Benin has one government-operated television station, and broadcasts from neighboring countries can sometimes be received. Abundant newspapers enjoy a wide urban readership. Rural people receive news from private radio stations and through village meetings, but they primarily exchange messages and news at the market.

Education. The government tried to replace its French-based educational system in the 1970s, but it failed for a number of reasons. While it allowed people to learn written local languages (most languages are oral) instead of French, facilities and materials were lacking. In recent years, more private and Catholic schools have opened, and the curriculum is reverting to the French model. Nevertheless, the challenges remain the same: to create a school system flexible enough to take into account changing national realities, to help reduce unemployment, and to absorb the vast majority of children younger than 15, who represent 47 percent of the total population. The dropout rate is high. Reasons often involve finances. Children are important members of the family labor pool and cannot be spared for many years of schooling, which begin at age six. Only about one in ten children gains a secondary education. Most students at all levels are boys. Abomey has a university with a medical school. Other professional schools (for nursing, administration, and teaching) are also available.

Health. Benin lacks a national healthcare system, but government social centers are working to educate people about immunizations and infant nutrition. These efforts are slowly helping Beninese to overcome a distrust of preventive care and to understand that some traditional food taboos cause malnutrition. Doctors are few, as most go abroad to practice. Many diseases afflict Benin (yellow fever, malaria, cholera, typhoid fever). While some diseases, such as river blindness and guinea worm, have become less common, others such as HIV/AIDS continue to affect more of the population. Indigenous (mostly herbal) medicines are still highly trusted, and the government is trying to integrate them with modern treatments. Medical training and modern equipment are badly needed.

DEVELOPMENT DATA
Human Dev. Index* rank . . . . 161 of 177 countries
  Adjusted for women. . . . . 130 of 144 countries
Real GDP per capita $1,070
Adult literacy rate . . . . 55 percent (male); 26 (female)
Infant mortality rate . . . . 86 per 1,000 births
Life expectancy. . . . . 49 (male); 53 (female)

AT A GLANCE

Events and Trends.
- In March 2005, a U.S. telecommunications company, Titan corporation, admitted that it had paid more than US$2 million in bribes to improve its business prospects in Benin. The company agreed to pay US$13 million in criminal penalties and $15.5 nillion to settle a civil lawsuit brought by the Securities and Exchange Commission (SEC).
- In July 2004, authorities intercepted traffickers smuggling 27 Beninese and Nigerian children into other West African countries to work as laborers. This type of child trafficking occurs when families allow their children to be taken to more prosperous nations and work in labor camps, in the hope that the children may send home small remittances.

Contact Information. Embassy of Benin, 2124 Kalorama Road NW, Washington, DC 20008; phone (202) 232-6656.

CultureGrams
People. The World. You.

ProQuest Information and Learning Company
300 North Zeeb Road, P.O. Box 1346
Ann Arbor, Michigan 48106 USA
Toll Free: 1.800.528.6279
Fax: 1.800.864.0019
www.culturegrams.com

CultureGrams World Edition 2006

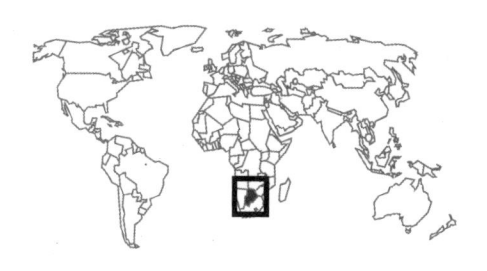

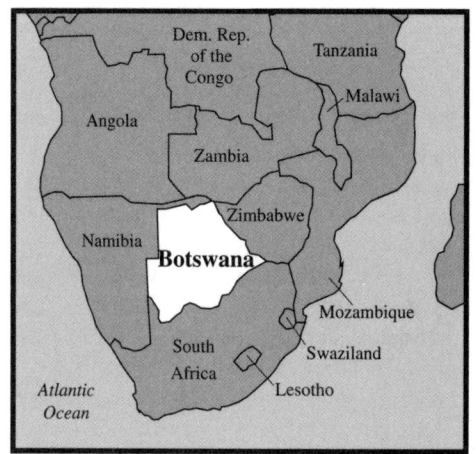

Republic of Botswana

BACKGROUND

Land and Climate. Botswana, a landlocked country in southern Africa, covers 231,800 square miles (600,370 square kilometers). It is about the same size as France. Eighty percent of its territory (west of most cities) is covered by the Kgalagadi (Kalahari) Desert, which consists of savanna grasses and shrubs but virtually no water. Gently rolling hills form the eastern border. The Okavango Delta, the world's largest inland delta, is found in the north. Its wetlands, as well as the country's many national parks, harbor a wide variety of animal and plant life.

Reservoirs provide water for major urban areas, but most water comes from wells. Small dams catch rain runoff for cattle, which far outnumber the human population. Drought cycles are common. Summer is from October to April, with temperatures often above 100°F (37°C). During winter, which lasts from May to August, days are typically windy and sunny. Temperatures may go below freezing at night in some parts of the country.

History. Tswana ethnic groups began moving into Botswana from the southeast in the early 1500s. They displaced and absorbed other peoples as they spread out to claim all land that had surface water or was suitable for grazing and agriculture. Various chiefdoms developed over the next several decades.

Ethnic disputes beginning in the mid-1700s left Tswana chiefdoms vulnerable to invasions by refugee armies from Zulu wars in Natal (now in South Africa). These wars began in the early 1800s and caused great upheaval in southern Africa. *Boer* (white settler) encroachment from 1852 onward led major Tswana chiefs, under the direction of Khama III, to seek protection through the British government. The British, eager to secure a labor supply for their South African mines and a route to newly discovered gold in Matabeleland (Zimbabwe), established the Bechuanaland Protectorate in 1885.

In the 20th century, unrest in the Rhodesias (now Zambia and Zimbabwe) and apartheid in South Africa led various groups to form political parties and demand independence from Britain. The Bechuanaland Democratic Party (BDP) led the way to independence in 1966. The founders of the BDP, Sir Seretse Khama and Sir Ketumile Masire, were declared president and vice president, respectively, of the new Republic of Botswana.

Their BDP (now the Botswana Democratic Party) is credited with maintaining one of the most stable democracies in Africa. Khama won three consecutive elections. When he died in 1980, Masire succeeded him as president. Masire went on to win reelection three times before retiring in 1998. The BDP's Festus Mogae, who served as Masire's vice president, took over from Masire and was confirmed as president in 1999 elections. He secured a second term in November 2004 elections as the BDP continued its longstanding majority in the National Assembly.

THE PEOPLE

Population. Botswana's population is about 1.56 million. The population is shrinking at a rate of 0.89 percent, due in large part to a high rate of HIV/AIDS infection. Forty percent of the population is younger than age 15.

Descendants of the original Tswana peoples (Kwena, Ngwato, Ngwaketse, Kgatla, Tawana, Lete, Tlokwa, and Rolong) constitute about half of the total population. These groups essentially consider themselves to be one people because they descend from a common ancestor, but they tend

Botswana

to concentrate in different areas. The other half of the population is composed of the Kalanga, Kgalagadi, Birwa, Tswapong, Yei, Mbukushu, Subiya, Herero, and Khoesan groups. Whites, Indians, and other Asians compose small minorities.

While a majority of the population lives in rural areas, many people are moving to cities for work and education. Gaborone, the capital, is a rapidly growing city; about one-third of Gaborone's population (currently 170,000) lives in Old Naledi, Botswana's largest shantytown. Most people live in the eastern part of the country, where the railroad is located, soil supports agriculture, and rain falls sufficiently to sustain life.

Language. Although English is the official language of government and secondary education, most people speak the national language, Setswana. Primary schooling is conducted in Setswana. For many, Setswana is a second language because each minority group speaks its own language. For instance, the Tjikalanga language (also called Ikalanga) is predominant in the northeast. Like Setswana, these other languages are Bantu tongues and are related.

In Bantu languages, the noun prefix is the key to grammatical connections. For example, the *mo-* prefix can refer to a person. Thus, a *Motswana* is a Tswana person. The plural of *mo* is *ba*. So *Batswana* means "Tswana people" (and citizens of Botswana, regardless of ethnicity). There are seven other two-letter noun classes. Non-Bantu tongues are known collectively as Khoesan (or Sarwa).

The only languages in print are English and Setswana, but Bible publishers are trying to codify every language in Africa. Ikalanga is a written language in Zimbabwe.

Religion. Religious freedom is protected under the constitution, but Christianity is accepted as an official religion in the sense that the school day and official functions begin with prayer. Schoolchildren sing Christian hymns before classes begin, but religious instruction is not compulsory.

Christianity was introduced in the early 1800s by missionaries (David Livingstone and others) traveling from South Africa. This opened the interior of Africa to exploitation by European hunters and slave traders. Because Christianity was often viewed as a means to Western technology, education, and health care, many chiefs allowed missions on their lands. During his reign (1835–1923), Chief Khama III, who converted to Christianity in 1862, tried to abolish many traditional practices (polygamy, initiation ceremonies, passing widows to a deceased man's brother, rainmaking ceremonies, and other rites) that conflicted with Christian teachings. But some outlawed traditions remain part of village life.

It is estimated that as many as half of all Batswana continue to exclusively follow aspects of their indigenous beliefs. The other half are Christian; Catholics and Protestants together comprise approximately one-fourth of the population. Many local churches combine traditional beliefs with those of Western Christianity. The largest of these churches is the Zion Christian Church; another major congregation is the Spiritual Healing Church.

General Attitudes. Society is founded on traditional law, with the community as the core of Tswana life and the chief as the symbol of unity. Traditionally, schools, roads, and health clinics were built through local organization. This practice of self-help, evident in such Setswana words as *ipelegeng* (carry yourselves), continues today, even though the government is now more responsible for infrastructure. Each individual is expected to benefit the community. The more a person does, the greater that person's status within the group. Anything that can benefit the group is valued, such as one's educational level, integrity, and generosity. People are expected to house traveling relatives for as long as necessary, and working family members are expected to support those without jobs. Batswana generally try to avoid conflict. Public criticism is inappropriate, as is raising one's voice in anger.

Personal Appearance. Western dress is common in most areas. Urban men wear business suits and ties, and women wear fashionable dresses or a skirt and blouse. Some young urban women wear pants. Rural women often wear a wrap over their dresses to protect them from dirt. Mothers carry their babies on their backs in fabric slings. Older men wear overalls to protect their clothing. Many men wear hats, except in the *kgotla* (meeting place), and rural women cover their heads with a kerchief. Both sexes typically have short hair.

Cleanliness and neatness are important. Smooth hands and longer fingernails are a status symbol for men, indicating they can pay someone else to do their farming or manual labor. For a rural woman, rough hands are considered honorable because they indicate that she works hard.

Many Batswana attend church services wearing uniforms that distinguish their denominations. People also display their political party's colors through clothing. Women of the Herero ethnic group, which migrated from Namibia in 1904, wear a long bouffant-skirted costume introduced in Namibia by German missionary wives. The heavy, colorful dress may require as much as 10 yards of fabric. A woman arranges a matching headdress to indicate her marital status.

CUSTOMS AND COURTESIES

Greetings. Greetings are important; failing to greet someone is rude. To show respect when greeting, particularly to an elder or superior, one shakes with the right hand while supporting one's elbow with the left hand. The handshake is less of a grasp and more a matter of palms and fingertips touching. A slight head bow may also be added to lower one's eye level below that of an elder. A younger person will wait for an elder to initiate the greeting. Likewise, someone approaching a person or group will greet first.

A common adult greeting is *Dumela, Rra/Mma, O tsogile jang?* (Greetings, sir/madam, how did you wake?). The response is *Ke tsogile sentle* (I awoke well). At social gatherings, people greet those they know and are introduced to others. Children and peers use informal greetings. For instance, the Setswana reply to *O kae?* (How are you?) is *Ke teng* (literally, "I am here," meaning "fine"). *Tsamaya sentle* (Go well) is said to one departing and *Sala sentle* (Stay well) is said to one staying.

Greeting customs vary for other ethnic groups. For example, among the Kalanga the younger person always greets first. Young children greet elders by extending both hands or clapping; the elder responds by kissing both hands and saying *Wa muka?* (Are you well?).

Children may be named for some circumstance related to their birth and also given a pet name by which they are known at home. Students often give themselves nicknames for use at school. Traditionally, the father's first name became the child's surname. Now, however, the child takes the father's surname. Upon the birth of her first child, a woman is thereafter referred to as the mother of that child (e.g., *Mma Jamey* in Setswana or *Bakajamey* in Tjikalanga).

Gestures. One may press the hands (palms and fingers)

together in front of the chest before accepting a gift with both hands. Gifts are given with both hands or with the right hand supported by the left at the elbow. Batswana use a variety of gestures to suggest "no," "no thanks," or that something is all gone. One way is to rotate the wrist with fingers outstretched or pointing down. Hitchhikers rapidly wave their right hand with arm extended to hail a vehicle.

It is impolite to walk between two people in conversation. If passing through cannot be avoided, one bows below the level of the conversation and says *Intshwarele* (Excuse me). One can best show respect for elders during conversation by looking down toward the ground rather than into their eyes. Public displays of affection are inappropriate.

Visiting. Relatives visit one another as often as they can. Because Batswana value personal relationships, they welcome unannounced visitors. Most visits cannot be arranged in advance due to a lack of telephones. Hosts offer guests water or tea to drink. They will invite anyone who arrives at mealtime to eat with the family. Guests who are not hungry at least try the food and take some home. Urban relatives often bring staples and household goods as gifts, while people from rural areas bring in-season crops. Acquaintances are not expected to bring gifts. Hosts accompany departing guests to the gate or even part of the way home (if traveling on foot) to show they were welcome.

Socializing takes place at the standpipe (where people get water), general stores, and church activities. Men socialize at local *chibuku* depots (bars selling sorghum beer).

Eating. Eating habits vary between urban and rural settings, but sharing is the common denominator. For most, family meals involve eating from common bowls or plates. Visitors receive separate plates. Children share a bowl among them. Drinks are never shared; each person has a cup. Batswana use utensils but eat some foods with their hands. They frequently eat outside in the shade of a nearby tree. Everyone usually leaves a little food behind to indicate the meal has been filling. Guests often say *Ke itumetse* (I am pleased) to thank the hosts. Smelling food before eating it implies something is wrong with it. Leftovers are kept for later or are given to departing guests.

LIFESTYLE

Family. Batswana historically lived in large villages with their agricultural and grazing lands at a distance. With women at the lands and men at cattle posts, families were separated much of the time. In colonial times, many men worked in South African mines. Later, the youth moved to cities in search of work. Families remained tied through an extended family network. Today, schooling and employment keep families apart. Women are primarily responsible for the family, agriculture, and entrepreneurial pursuits. They head most rural families with support from nearby relatives. Children take on chores at an early age.

A fenced family compound contains several *rondavels* (round, thatched dwellings), a cooking area, and an outhouse. Animals are penned within the compound, which women keep clear of grass and debris. More modern homes are made of cinder blocks with cement floors.

Dating and Marriage. The migration of young Batswana from their home villages to urban areas dramatically impacts the way they socialize. Interaction in villages is rather restricted, but urban youth meet at discos and other sites. School competitions and youth clubs also provide contact.

Because of the expense and obligations involved in formal marriage, more than half of all couples live together rather than marry. Those who do marry may choose rites under either civil or customary law. Customary celebrations involve two or more days of eating, drinking, dancing, and speeches. The family of the groom pays a negotiated *bogadi* (bride-price) to the family of the bride. The bride-price shows respect for the bride's parents, thanks them for raising the woman, and helps compensate them for the loss of a productive member of the family.

Diet. *Bogobe* (porridge) made from *mabele* (sorghum), maize, or millet (in the northeast) is a staple food. *Bogobe* is served soft and often soured for breakfast but served thick for the midday and evening meals. *Paleche* (white maize), although vulnerable to drought, is replacing sorghum as the primary grain. Many people have tea or *mageu* (a thick sorghum drink) instead of porridge for breakfast. Some enjoy *fat cakes* (deep-fried dough) with tea for breakfast or lunch. *Bogobe* is accompanied by a relish, such as a popular relish made of onions, chicken stock, and tomato sauce. Batswana eat seasonal fruits and vegetables and raise goats and chicken for meat. *Phane* worms, a delicacy gathered from the *mophane* trees in the northeast, are dried in hot ashes and eaten. Men slaughter cattle for special occasions. Rice replaces *bogobe* at weddings.

Recreation. Batswana enjoy visiting, dancing, singing, and playing sports. Young men play *football* (soccer), often competing on village teams. Schools offer track-and-field and ball sports (soccer, softball, volleyball, and netball) to all students. Track-and-field competitions at local, regional, and national levels bring great prestige to a winning student and his or her school.

The Arts. Schools sponsor choirs and traditional dance groups, which perform at public events. Traditional dancing is popular in villages, where women play drums to provide the dancers with rhythm. Young urban professionals like ballroom dancing, and most Batswana enjoy African disco and *kwasa kwasa*, a Congolese style of dance music.

Batswana folk artists produce basketry and pottery using natural dyes and materials. Stylized animals commonly adorn these crafts. Jewelry is worked in silver, although animal hair and glass beads are also used. Many domestic textile items (blankets, tablecloths, and floormats) are woven from wool and decorated with geometric patterns. Khoesan men sew and tan leather items, which the women beautify with beads made from ostrich eggshells. These folk arts are cultivated for tourism and international sale.

Holidays. Batswana celebrate the New Year (1–2 Jan.), Easter (Friday–Monday), Ascension, President's Day (third weekend in July), Botswana Day (30 Sept.–1 Oct.), Christmas, and Boxing Day (26 Dec.). For Christmas, people return to their home villages to celebrate with relatives. Family members do not exchange gifts, but they usually receive new clothes. Boxing Day comes from the British tradition of giving small boxed gifts to service workers or the poor on the day after Christmas. It is now a day to visit and relax. Batswana also go home for a four-day weekend on President's Day. During this weekend, government-sponsored programs begin with prayer and include traditional dancing, singing, speeches, and praise poems. Easter is a time for church and family.

Commerce. It is customary for Batswana to exchange formal greetings before conducting business. Business hours generally extend from 8 or 9 a.m. until about 5 p.m. Many offices and shops close for an hour at about 1 p.m. Botswana has few

Botswana

factories, so most of the goods available at the nation's wholesale and retail businesses are imported.

SOCIETY

Government. Botswana is a parliamentary republic. The president (currently Festus Mogae) is head of state and head of government. The 57-seat National Assembly elects the president to a five-year term. Members of the National Assembly are directly elected to five-year terms. Major political parties include the BDP, the Botswana National Front (BNF), and the Botswana Congress Party (BCP) The voting age is 18. Botswana has never experienced a coup or been ruled by a dictator. Factors contributing to this include Tswana cohesion and tolerance, a pastoralist heritage, traditional local democracy, a sound economy based on diamond mining, and well-educated and strong leaders.

A 15-member House of Chiefs, representing major ethnic groups, advises the National Assembly on legislation pertaining to custom and tradition. Judiciary cases involving customary law are heard in the *kgotla* by local chiefs and *headmen*, while statutory cases are heard in the Magistrates' Courts or the High Court. There is also an appeals court.

Villages are divided into *wards* (neighborhoods), each with a *headman* (an elder appointed by the village chief) and a *kgotla* (meeting place). Decisions at the *ward* and village levels are made in the *kgotla* by all adult males through a consensus process. Women may express opinions but remain in the back of the *kgotla*. The chief's *kgotla* is used to consider matters that cannot be settled at the *ward* level. Local councils govern schools and health clinics.

Economy. Botswana has enjoyed a stable economy since independence. Diamonds account for more than three-fourths of export revenue. The government is trying to diversify to guard against world price fluctuations. Other exports include copper, nickel, and beef. The currency is the *pula* (BWP). The word *pula* (meaning "rain") is also used as a greeting or at the end of speeches to mean "Good wishes."

Despite relative stability, problems exist. High unemployment has a significant impact on the younger Batswana. A shortage of skilled labor keeps industrial growth low, and land deterioration hampers agriculture. Despite a relatively high gross domestic product per capita, more than 60 percent of the nation's cattle, a traditional measure of wealth, are owned by less than 10 percent of the population. Hence, economic prosperity is enjoyed by a small percentage of people.

Transportation and Communications. A paved highway and a rail line parallel the eastern border, linking the major towns. The train is used for longer distances. Rural people often walk long distances or hitchhike. If given a ride, they pay bus fare to the driver. Some families use bicycles locally. A minority own cars, but more urban residents are buying them. Buses or *combies* (minibuses) run between towns and major villages. The Trans-Kgalagadi Highway crosses the desert into Namibia.

Few people, even in towns, have telephones, but pay phones are located in post offices. Radio Botswana, a government-run station, broadcasts in Setswana and English. Private radio stations also operate. Television stations include a government-run station and two private stations. Independent newspapers enjoy freedom of the press and wide circulation; the government sends free copies of the *Daily News* to schools.

DEVELOPMENT DATA

Human Dev. Index* rank . . . . 128 of 177 countries
    Adjusted for women . . . . 102 of 144 countries
Real GDP per capita $8,170
Adult literacy rate . . . . 76 percent (male); 82 (female)
Infant mortality rate . . . . 70 per 1,000 births
Life expectancy . . . . 40 (male); 42 (female)

Education. Botswana has a very high elementary completion rate. The abolition of school fees in 1987 marked the first step in offering primary and secondary schooling to all children. Increased school construction was the next step, and helping young children learn English before junior secondary school is now a priority. Lack of English skills and lack of rural senior schools prevent two-thirds of Junior Certificate (JC) holders from advancing. The Brigades (units providing technical training) and other vocational programs accept some JC students.

Senior secondary graduates qualify for higher education by earning the Cambridge Overseas School Certificate and performing one year of community service. Botswana houses a number of institutions of higher education: the University of Botswana, a National Health Institute, six teacher-training colleges, a polytechnic institute, and an agricultural college.

Health. Botswana has many commonly diagnosed illnesses that are related to poverty and malnutrition. Still, nurse-staffed primary-care clinics are within reach of most people. Doctors practice in cities and larger towns. For many Batswana, traditional healers' herbal medicine and charms provide a popular alternative to Western medicine. Malaria, schistosomiasis, and sleeping sickness are found in the north. Botswana currently faces a devastating HIV/AIDS epidemic; an estimated 37 percent of the nation's adult population is infected with the virus.

AT A GLANCE

Events and Trends.

- The BDP won 44 of the 57 seats in the National Assembly in November 2004 elections. The opposition Botswana National Front won 12 seats, and the Botswana Congress Party won just 1 seat. Although opposition parties complained about their limited access to the media, especially the government-run television station, election observers declared the vote to be free and fair.

- By the end of 2004, more than 35,000 citizens of Botswana were receiving antiretroviral drugs to combat the effects of HIV/AIDS. Much of the funding for the drugs comes from overseas donors. Because Botswana is seen as a test case for the effectiveness of antiretroviral drug campaigns, it currently is home to 10 percent of the patients who receive them worldwide.

Contact Information. Embassy of Botswana, 1531–1533 New Hampshire Avenue NW, Washington, DC 20036; phone (202) 244-4990.

© 2005 ProQuest Information and Learning Company and Brigham Young University. It is against the law to copy, reprint, store, or transmit any part of this publication in any form by any means without written permission from ProQuest. This document contains native commentary and original analysis, as well as estimated statistics. The content should not be considered strictly factual, and it may not apply to all groups in a nation. *UN Development Programme, Human Development Report 2004 (New York: Oxford University Press, 2004).

CultureGrams
People. The World. You.

ProQuest Information and Learning Company
300 North Zeeb Road, P.O. Box 1346
Ann Arbor, Michigan 48106 USA
Toll Free: 1.800.528.6279
Fax: 1.800.864.0019
www.culturegrams.com

CultureGrams World Edition 2006 — Burkina Faso

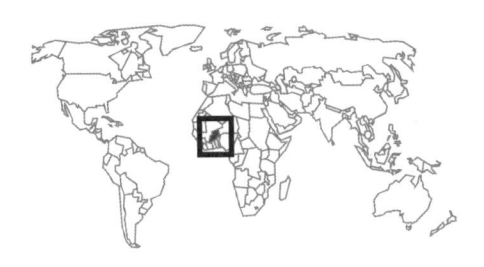

BACKGROUND

Land and Climate. Burkina Faso's name means "the land of upright and courageous people." This landlocked nation covers an area of 105,869 square miles (274,200 square kilometers), making it somewhat larger than Colorado. The mostly flat northern quarter, called the Sahel, is characterized by sand dunes and a dry climate. Half the nation is covered by the central plateau, and forests are most common in the fertile south. Burkina Faso's highest elevations include Mount Tenakourou (2,300 feet, or 750 meters) and Mount Naouri (1,372 feet, or 447 meters). The country's main rivers are the Mouhoun, Nakambe, and Nazinon. Most precipitation falls during the rainy season (June–October). The dry season (November–February) is generally warm, though cooled by a consistent harmattan (a dry, dusty) wind. Daytime temperatures average 85°F (30°C) year-round, but soar to 110°F (43°C) during the hot season (March–May).

History. Before the colonial period, the region was dominated by several powerful kingdoms, the most important of which were the Mosse, Gurma, Emirat of Liptako, and Guriko. These kingdoms reached their pinnacle by the turn of the 11th century. Although Portuguese explorers named the three major rivers, it was the French who conquered and colonized the land in the late 19th century. In 1904, the Burkinabè (Bur-keen-ah-BAY) territories became attached to the High Senegal–Niger French Colony until it dissolved in 1919. The territories then became a colony called Upper Volta.

The French dissolved Upper Volta in 1932 and distributed its territory among Côte d'Ivoire (Ivory Coast), French Sudan (now Mali), and Niger. However, the French reestablished Upper Volta in 1947 and a peaceful struggle for independence was waged throughout the 1950s. Two rival leaders emerged from that movement. One of them, Daniel Ouezzin Coulibaly, died in 1958 and his opponent, Maurice Yameogo, then reconciled with the African Democratic Rally (RDA), of which Coulibaly had been a prominent member. Yameogo was subsequently chosen as the country's first president upon independence on 5 August 1960.

Yameogo's regime was viewed as corrupt and undemocratic, and he was overthrown after a trade union uprising in a 3 January 1966 military coup. Lieutenant Sangoulé Lamizana took power as president. During the 1970s, Upper Volta's four trade unions, among the most powerful in Africa, were able to force political reform. For example, after a nationwide strike in 1980, Lamizana was overthrown in a coup. The coup leader was, in turn, ousted in 1982 by Commandant Jean-Baptiste Ouédraogo, but division among his supporting officers led to a 1983 coup by Captain Thomas Sankara.

For many, the charismatic Sankara soon became (and remains) a hero. He changed the country's name to Burkina Faso in 1984, made peace with Mali over a territorial dispute, and espoused a socialist ideology. Sankara believed the people should be self-sufficient and not rely on Western aid, and he developed policies toward that goal. Yet in 1987, Sankara's closest associate, Captain Blaise Compaoré, staged a bloody coup in which Sankara and 12 other leaders were killed.

Despite Sankara's popularity, few Burkinabè protested the coup because of Compaoré's strength. Some dissenters were punished, but an armistice with opponents soon followed and a new constitution was issued in 1990. Presidential elections in 1991 were followed by multiparty legislative elections in 1992. Compaoré was elected president. Democratization then proceeded slowly but in a stable atmosphere. Compaoré was

Burkina Faso

constitutionally prohibited from seeking a second term; however, parliament amended the constitution in 1997 to make Compaoré eligible for the November 1998 presidential race. Despite an opposition boycott, Compaoré was reelected president. In December 1998, the suspected assassination of newspaper owner Norbert Zongo set off riots and protests. His death remains a divisive issue.

Following the outbreak of civil war in Ivory Coast in 2002, Ivory Coast's government accused Burkina Faso of backing northern rebels. Although the government of Burkina Faso denied involvement in the war, Burkinabè immigrants living in Ivory Coast became targets of violence by government supporters. With many citizens of Burkina Faso dependant on remittances from relatives in Ivory Coast, the conflict continues to have severe economic and social costs for Burkina Faso.

THE PEOPLE

Population. Burkina Faso's population of 13.6 million is growing annually at 2.6 percent. Eighty percent of all Burkinabè live in rural areas. The nation's two largest cities are the capital, Ouagadougou (often abbreviated as Ouaga), and Bobo Dioulasso. The Mossi (roughly 50 percent of the population) inhabit the central plateau. A number of smaller groups comprise the remaining 50 percent of the population, including the Fulani (15 percent) in the north; the Gurmantche or Gurma (10 percent) in the east; the Bissa and Gourounsi in the southeast; the Lobi and Dagari in the southwest; and the Bobo, Bwaba, Samo, and Senoufo in the west. Most Burkinabè are tolerant of other ethnic groups and religions, and rivalries tend to be good-natured.

Language. More than 60 languages are used in Burkina Faso, but the most widely spoken are Mooré (by the Mossi), Dioula (a trade language used by many groups, including the Bwaba, Bobo, and Senoufo), Fulfuldé (by the Fulani), and Gurmantchéma (by the Gurma). French is the official language of government and education but is only spoken by 15 to 20 percent of the population. Burkinabè use Dioula and Fulfuldé to communicate with ethnic groups in neighboring countries. These languages and Mooré are used in some television and radio broadcasts and are taught at the university level for literature and language students.

Religion. Both Muslims and Christians inhabit Burkina Faso, interacting on each other's holidays and respecting the others' traditions and beliefs. Burkinabè from all ethnic groups belong to each religion, although Fulani are less likely to be Christians. Estimates differ as to how many people belong to each group, but Muslims comprise at least 40 percent of the population. Christians (10–15 percent) are most often Roman Catholic, but Protestant groups are also active. Christians tend to have Christian first names and Muslims use Islamic names.

Traditional animist beliefs are practiced exclusively by as many as half of all people; practitioners retain their Burkinabè names. Animist traditions act as unifying factors in Burkina Faso's tolerant religious climate, since many Muslims and Christians combine animist practices with their religion. It is not uncommon for them to consult a diviner or to participate in ritual dances. Masks play an important part in animist rituals. For example, dancers wear them to ward off bad luck or to perform agricultural rites. The shape and color of a mask depend on the ethnic group and purpose of the wearer. Fetishes, *gris-gris* (an amulet or incantation), and totems are used by animists for various purposes, such as protection or luck.

General Attitudes. Burkinabè admire those who are warm, friendly, and generous. Honesty, wisdom, and loyalty are valued, as well as an ability to control one's tongue. They have strong family values centered on sharing and on respect for customs and tradition. A financially successful individual is responsible for the rest of the extended family. The elderly are highly respected. Young people are expected to do whatever older relatives, teachers, or neighbors ask. Humility and generosity are the most desired personal traits, while individualism and bragging are least tolerated. Although family ties are strong, individuals actually are quite independent. Moving into one's own home, even if it lacks running water or electricity, is an important goal; renting is considered a temporary situation.

Personal Appearance. Burkinabè wear both African and Western clothing. In rural settings, men wear a Muslim robe (*boubou*) while women wear a wraparound skirt (*pagne*) with a blouse or T-shirt. In cities, women wear elaborate, colorful African outfits made of locally designed or imported fabrics. Men often wear the *tenue de fonctionnaire* (civil servant suit, with shirt and pants made of the same cloth). Men also wear slacks or jeans with shirts made of colorful *pagnes*. Both rural and urban dwellers buy used clothing imported from Europe, Asia, and the United States. However, as civic leaders call for consumption of local products, embroidered traditional outfits have become more popular attire for social events. Women often have elaborate hairstyles and change them every few months. Braided extensions, wigs, and "spikes" of hair (made by wrapping hair with black thread) are common. Although on the decline, traditional face scarring is still sometimes practiced in rural areas by some (among the Mossi and Bwaba, for example) to distinguish between ethnic groups.

CUSTOMS AND COURTESIES

Greetings. Before engaging in any social activity, Burkinabè take time to greet each other and shake hands. Greetings include inquiries about family, health, and work. Urban people who have not seen each other for some time may kiss each cheek. One may show respect by bowing one's head. Or when shaking hands, one might touch the other person's right hand or arm at the elbow level with one's left hand. Male friends may touch their right fists to their hearts after shaking hands. Urban and educated men may also touch foreheads as they shake hands, particularly if they are greeting a friend after a long separation. In the countryside, women may kneel to express respect. In Muslim settings, men often will not shake hands with women, as Islamic principles dictate minimal contact between unrelated men and women. Not greeting all those in a room or at a table is considered rude.

Acquaintances are addressed by first name, while the names of elders are preceded by *Monsieur* (Mr.) or *Madame* (Mrs.). French greetings range from the informal *Salut, comment ça va?* (Hi, how are you?) to the more formal *Bonjour* (Good day) and *Bonsoir* (Good evening). In Mooré, as in many of the national languages, greetings depend on the time of day or the activities performed by the person being greeted. Common salutations include *Ne y yibeogo* (Good morning), *Ne y zaabre* (Good afternoon), or simply *Kibare* (Hi). In Dioula, one says *A ni sogoma* (Good morning) or *Somogo do?* (How is your family?); in Fulfuldé, one says *Jam waali* (Good morning) or *Jam sukaabe?* (How are the kids?). Answers to greetings are always positive, even if circumstances are not.

Gestures. Burkinabè use the right hand to greet people, pass items, and eat. Using the left hand, especially for greeting or eating, is offensive. Men and women hold hands in public with friends of the same gender, but displays of affection between men and women are inappropriate. To motion to someone using the index finger is considered disrespectful; instead, one motions with the palm of the hand down. It is rude to call someone's name unless the person is nearby. If the person is farther away, it is polite to whistle or make a loud *psst* noise in order to get his or her attention. Burkinabè express disgust at events or actions by rounding the lips and making a noise by sucking air through the front teeth.

Visiting. Visiting friends and relatives is an important part of Burkinabè culture. Visits generally occur during the evening, sometimes during *siesta* (a nap or rest time from around noon to 3 p.m.), and at any time on the weekend. Most visits are spontaneous and visitors are allowed to stay as long as they wish. People announce their arrival by clapping their hands (instead of knocking) or saying *ko ko ko*; they wait to be invited in. In areas influenced by Islam, people announce themselves by saying *Salaam ale kum* (Peace be upon you), to which the host responds *Ale kum Salaam* (And peace to you) as a way of inviting the visitors in.

Guests are always offered a place to sit and water to drink; refusing to drink is socially inappropriate, even if one is not thirsty. After a *siesta*, Burkinabè often make tea or coffee to share with friends and family. Tea-making is an important social ritual among men. It can take half an hour to prepare each of the three rounds on a bed of charcoal; the third round is the weakest brew. Burkinabè also enjoy having guests over for a meal or evening socializing. If guests are just dropping by, they are not expected to bring a gift. However, rural people visiting from another village for several days commonly give their hosts chickens, eggs, cola nuts, salt, or sugar.

Eating. Food is not treated casually and meals are eaten in general silence. Rural men usually eat together in a circle on the floor, sharing a common platter and using the fingers of the right hand. Using the left hand is forbidden. Women and children eat together in a different section of the compound. If offered food, guests must take a few bites or risk offending the host.

Urban families tend to eat together, and they use a dining table and utensils more often than their rural counterparts. Most single urban men eat their meals at street-side stands or in the numerous open-air bars where tasty meat kabobs (*brochettes*) and roasted chicken are sold; some hire young men or women to cook meals for them at home. Cities and villages usually have *dolo cabarets* (local beer stands), tended by women, where both men and women gather for a drink, food, discussion of local events, and gossip.

LIFESTYLE

Family. Large families are the norm in Burkina Faso, especially in rural areas, where a family might have 10 or more children. Children live with their parents until they get married. When elderly parents need care, they usually live with their eldest son. Burkina Faso's traditional social network is based on the extended family and guarantees that family members will help a relative in need.

Rural families often live in a compound, with separate sleeping quarters for men and women. A mother generally cares for her children until they are weaned at around age three. At this time, boys move from sleeping in the mother's house to sleeping in the father's house. Both boys and girls are cared for by their parents until they reach adulthood, but boys generally receive more support than girls. Once girls marry, they are perceived as having changed families.

In polygamous families, wives share chores, including cleaning the courtyard and preparing family meals. Rural women have few property rights and can be sent back to their families if their husbands are unsatisfied with them. In matriarchal families within such ethnic groups as the Dagari, women have more rights. In urban settings, women are more often educated and able to find jobs. This gives them greater autonomy and decision-making power.

Dating and Marriage. Although casual dating is becoming the norm in urban areas, marriages in the countryside are usually still arranged. Often for women the only way out of an arranged marriage is to run away. Marriage expenses are shared by the groom, his parents, and the extended family. In many cases, however, couples do not formalize their relationship and simply begin living together, after which they are referred to as husband and wife. The average marriage age is 22 for men and between 18 and 20 for women. Islamic laws allow a man to have as many as four wives if he can care equally for each. Polygamy is decreasing in urban centers due to the cost of raising and educating a family, but it is still practiced in rural areas.

Diet. Burkina Faso's main staple is sorghum, millet, or corn flour cooked into a hard porridge known as *tô*. Rural people usually eat *tô* twice a day with a variety of sauces made from peanuts and indigenous plants and vegetables, such as sorrel and okra. A rural breakfast usually consists of leftovers from the previous night. Urban families with more financial means often prefer to eat their meals with rice rather than *tô*. People eat *couscous* and pasta cooked with meat on special occasions. Due to recent dam, fishery, and gardening projects, fresh fish and fruits are more plentiful in major cities.

Recreation. Burkinabè enjoy visiting each other and meeting at *dolo cabarets*. Men play cards and board games such as checkers. Women often meet to do each other's hair. On Saturdays, urban dwellers pack popular bars to dance to the rhythm of African, *Zouk* (Haitian), and reggae music. These bars are also known for their kabobs and broiled, spicy fish. Soccer is the most popular sport in Burkina Faso, followed by cycling, boxing, volleyball, basketball, and handball. On many Sundays in Ouagadougou, local businesses sponsor cycling races. During the harvest (October–November) and on holidays, villagers enjoy wrestling matches and traditional dances.

The Arts. Burkinabè arts are varied. The Fulani make colorful cotton blankets used as wedding gifts or decorations. Artisans carve sacred ancestral masks and figures of deity. Oral history is performed by *djeli* (praise singers, or *griot*) at civic ceremonies, and storytelling is common at festivals. Traditional music and instruments are heard at religious and secular activities. Dance troupes are often invited to perform at funerals and other events. The *balafon* (a wooden xylophone) and calabash gourds beaten with metal rings are common instruments.

Burkina Faso annually hosts a major festival. On even years, a large international arts festival (everything from theater to weaving) is held. On odd years, the biggest film festival in Africa is held in the capital. FESPACO (Pan African Film and Television Festival of Ouagadougou) promotes African films and filmmakers.

Holidays. Burkina Faso's national public holidays include New Year's Day, *Fête du 3 janvier* (commemoration of the 3 January 1966 uprising), Labor Day (1 May), Revolution Day

Burkina Faso

(4 August, for the 1983 revolution), and Independence Day (5 Aug.). Political holidays are marked by speeches and parades. Other holidays include International Women's Day (8 Mar.) and various religious celebrations. Important Muslim dates include a feast at the end of the holy fasting month of *Ramadan*; *Tabaski*, the feast that honors Abraham for his willingness to sacrifice his son; and *Mouloud*, the birth of Muhammad. Christian Burkinabè celebrate Easter, Ascension, Assumption (15 Aug.), and Christmas. End-of-the-year festivities remain the most important, and Burkinabè of all creeds join together to celebrate the New Year.

Commerce. A cash economy dominates rural and urban areas, although occasionally some people barter or use payment-in-kind. Still, most rural Burkinabè provide for their own needs and have little cash. Each town has an open-air market where most business is conducted. Market days are held every day in big cities and every three days in small towns and villages. In the west, market days are held once a week. Due to the lack of refrigeration, most families shop for food every day, either in the market or at small neighborhood stores operated out of people's homes. Busy, informal roadside stands located near markets and taxi or train stations offer clothing, used books, and buckets and suitcases made of recycled material. The largest cities have a few department stores, which are open from 7:30 a.m. to noon and from 3 to 5 p.m.

SOCIETY

Government. Burkina Faso is a parliamentary democracy. Its president (currently Blaise Compaoré) is head of state. The prime minister (currently Ernest Paramanga Yonli) is appointed by the president and acts as head of government. The Assembly of Peoples' Deputies has 111 seats; its delegates are elected to five-year terms. Local traditional chiefs exercise considerable influence and power.

Economy. The economy depends largely on subsistence agriculture and raising cattle. Most Burkinabè are subsistence farmers; production is difficult to maintain because of drought and poor soil. Mining opportunities remain under-exploited, but manganese and limestone are found in the north, gold in the west, and copper in the east. Principal exports are crafts, cotton, shea nuts, cattle, and gold. Imports include manufactured and chemical products, cereals, petroleum, vehicles, and machinery. France is the main trading partner. Burkina Faso uses the currency common to francophone African countries, the *CFA franc* (XOF). The economy is not yet diversified enough to respond to weather irregularities, global market events, or population growth.

Transportation and Communications. Due to the lack of a developed public transportation system, the average person walks. Many Burkinabè own *mobylettes* (mopeds) or bicycles. Some observers have described Ouagadougou as the moped capital of Africa. A railway links Ouaga to Abidjan (capital of Ivory Coast). A few paved roads, covering about 2,500 miles (4,023 kilometers), exist inside the country; the best is between Ouaga and Bobo Dioulasso, both of which also have taxis, "bush-taxis" (trucks or minibuses), and buses for intra- and intercity travel. Unpaved roads (about 7,500 miles, or 12,070 kilometers) may not be passable in the rainy season.

DEVELOPMENT DATA
Human Dev. Index* rank . . . . 175 of 177 countries
   Adjusted for women . . . . 143 of 144 countries
Real GDP per capita $1,100
Adult literacy rate . . . . 19 percent (male); 8 (female)
Infant mortality rate . . . . 99 per 1,000 births
Life expectancy . . . . 45 (male); 46 (female)

Phone service is available in urban areas and in villages located on roads between larger towns. Mobile phone use is increasing. Mail service exists where there is a post office, but word of mouth and passing letters via bus and truck drivers are some of the quickest and most reliable ways to relay information. One national and two private television stations and four FM radio stations broadcast daily. Few rural people have access to television, but shortwave radios are common. There are several independent newspapers. A number of internet cafés operate in Ouaga and Bobo Dioulasso.

Education. The educational system is based on the French model. Mastery of French largely determines one's success because all instruction is in French. Since young children starting school have no French background, they do not understand or learn well. Elementary school lasts six years; secondary has seven years. Classes can be extremely large. Primary enrollment is estimated at 36 percent; about one-fourth of these students go on to the secondary level. Many students drop out because they can no longer afford school fees. All rates are lower for girls and rural students. Few adult women can read or write. Rural schools often lack teachers, so students might miss certain subjects for months or longer. Entrance to one of the country's three universities is available to those who pass difficult exams; usually only a small percentage pass.

Health. Burkinabè face numerous health problems, including dysentery, hepatitis, diarrhea, malaria, and HIV/AIDS. The infant mortality rate remains high due to malnutrition and malaria. The government is trying to improve health conditions, and primary-care clinics have recently been built in all cities. All provinces have regional hospitals, but these are overburdened and underequipped. Most patients or families must pay for hospital stays and medicines; civil servants have some health benefits.

AT A GLANCE

Events and Trends.
- In November 2004, a summit of 36 French-speaking nations was held in Burkina Faso to discuss the conflict in neighboring Ivory Coast. The summit renounced the decision by Ivory Coast's government to launch attacks on rebel forces, ending an 18-month cease-fire.
- In April 2004, army captain Luther Ouali was jailed for 10 years after being found guilty of leading an October 2003 plot to overthrow President Compaoré. Six other defendants were also found guilty.

Contact Information. Embassy of Burkina Faso, 2340 Massachusetts Avenue NW, Washington, DC 20008; phone (202) 332-5577.

CultureGrams
People. The World. You.

ProQuest Information and Learning Company
300 North Zeeb Road, P.O. Box 1346
Ann Arbor, Michigan 48106 USA
Toll Free: 1.800.528.6279
Fax: 1.800.864.0019
www.culturegrams.com

CultureGrams 2006 World Edition

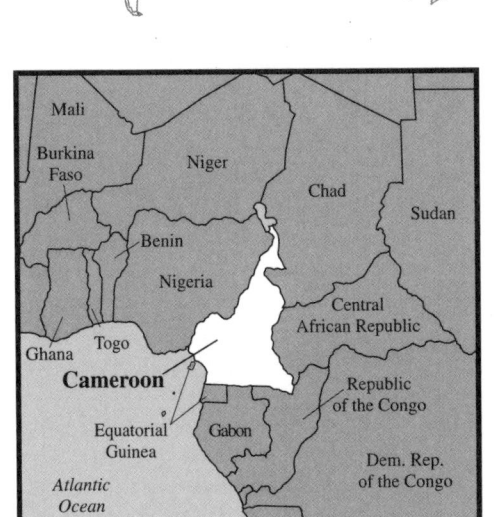

Republic of Cameroon

BACKGROUND

Land and Climate. Located slightly north of the equator, Cameroon (183,567 square miles, or 475,440 square kilometers) is not much larger than California. The north, from Lake Chad to Garoua, is dominated by a dry plain where Sahara winds and hot temperatures are standard from October to May. Cooler winds and rain between June and September allow for farming and grazing. A plateau of 2,000 to 4,000 feet (600–1,200 meters) covers much of central, southern, and eastern Cameroon. Here, dry-season daily heat is relieved at night and by occasional showers. Rains from May to October bring abundant water to the plateau's cities and farms. In wetter grasslands above 4,000 feet (1,200 meters), the November to April dry season is cooler; rains are heavy for several weeks after midyear. Rich volcanic soils provide for agriculture in this area. Mount Cameroon (Mount Po) is an active volcano. The narrow Atlantic coastal lowland is hot and humid all year. Douala's average high is 90°F (32°C). The lowlands support large areas of rubber, banana, cocoa, oil palms, and timber. Logging is depleting forests in the south and east.

History. Bantu tribes inhabited Cameroon's highlands more than 1,500 years ago and began spreading south into Pygmy lands as they cleared forests for new farms. Fulani migrated to the north from western Africa in the 13th century A.D., bringing Islam with them and encountering Hausa already there.

Cameroon's colonial name comes from the prawns (*cameros* in Portuguese) that 15th-century explorers found in the Wouri River. During the colonial era, southern Cameroon supplied the Atlantic slave and commodity trades, while northern peoples participated in the Muslim culture and economy of the Fulani and Hausa south of the Sahara. Germany united the south and north into a colony between 1884 and 1916. Germany's defeat in World War I led to Cameroon's partitioning between France and Britain. The French tightly ruled the east from the capital, Yaoundé. The smaller British area to the west was ruled more loosely from Nigeria.

Anticolonialism grew after 1945, and independence was achieved in French Cameroon in 1960. In 1961, voters in the southern portion of British Cameroon chose to join in a federation with the new republic; those in the north chose to unite with Nigeria. Cameroon's former French and British areas kept separate educational, legal, civil service, and legislative structures until a 1972 referendum adopted a national, one-party system along French lines.

Ahmadou Ahidjo, a northern Muslim, was president from 1960 until his resignation in 1982. The presidency was then filled by his prime minister, Paul Biya, a southern Christian. After resisting a 1984 rebellion designed to reinstate Ahidjo, Biya dismantled the opposition. He submitted to public pressure and allowed the introduction of multiparty politics in 1992, but subsequent elections have been marred by boycotts and allegations of fraud. Biya maintains a firm hold on power. His party, the Cameroon People's Democratic Movement (RDPC), dominates the National Assembly.

THE PEOPLE

Population. Cameroon's population of 16.1 million is growing at 1.97 percent annually. More than half the people live in rural areas, but cities are growing rapidly. Douala, the center of commerce and industry, is home to more than two million residents. The capital, Yaoundé, hosts more than one million.

Cameroon is often known as "Africa's crossroads" because of its many ethnic groups. The largest groups are the Bamileke

Cameroon

(in the west), Fulani (north), and Beti (south). The Beti are also known as the Pahouin. No single group comprises more than 20 percent of the population, and most comprise less than 1 percent. Cameroon's more than two hundred ethnic groups have widely different backgrounds—from Fulani kingdoms to small bands of Pygmies that live and hunt in southern forests. More typical are the farming and trading central and western peoples (half the population) with independent chiefdoms and rich cultural traditions. On the whole, the ethnic groups respect and tolerate each other; disputes are generally localized.

Language. Cameroon has some 240 languages; nearly 100 have written forms. Cameroonians commonly speak several local languages. French and English are the nation's official languages, and most urban residents can speak and read one of them. University graduates often speak both to some degree. Rural people generally are not fluent in either. French is used primarily in the eight francophone provinces colonized by France. English is common in the two anglophone provinces once governed by Britain.

No local language is used widely enough to have official status. Some languages have regional dominance, such as Fulfulde in the north, Ewondo near the capital, and Douala on the coast. Pidgin English, an ever-evolving tongue with roots in English and other European languages, emerged during colonization to facilitate trade and communication between ethnic groups who could not communicate otherwise. Today it continues to perform this function in Yaoundé (alongside French), as well as in the anglophone provinces and neighboring areas.

Religion. More than half the population is Christian, with about twice as many Catholics as Protestants. About one-fourth is Muslim (mostly Sunni). Most of the rest follow indigenous beliefs. Christians and Muslims often respect and continue to practice some local beliefs. The merging of religions does not create contradictions for believers; they adopt the elements they feel enhance their faith's overall value. Indigenous beliefs are especially evident in death rites, traditional medicine, and family relationships. Fortune-tellers (*ngambe*) are popular and witchcraft (*muyongo*) is still feared.

General Attitudes. Complicated leadership patterns basically center on those with title and rank, either inherited or earned through education or wealth. Leaders often maintain a support base by providing favors to family members, villagers, and those of the same ethnic group or social class. Cameroon is a group-oriented society; everyone has a place in the group and each group has a clear leader. Individualism is not encouraged. When one person benefits from something (such as a high wage), the group expects a share.

Family and friendship ties are strong and obligations run deep. For example, even distant relatives or "junior" siblings (a half sibling or someone from the village) can expect a family to house and feed them, regardless of the hardship it might cause. Guests cannot be asked to leave except in rare cases. The practice is accepted because the host family assumes it will someday benefit from the same network. Deep, complex bonds also exist between fellow students or local residents of the same sex and age. These bonds mean that service, respect, and cooperation usually come before personal interest. Social change is disrupting this system, but it remains important.

Personal Appearance. Cameroonians consider a clean, well-groomed appearance and fashionable dress the marks of good character. All but the very poor have formal clothing for special occasions. Muslim men in the north usually wear the *boubou*, an embroidered flowing robe. In western grasslands, men wear vibrant multicolored robes and matching headwear for ceremonies; beads, certain designs, shells, feathers, porcupine quills, and ivory often indicate particular royal or social status. These men otherwise wear modest Western clothing, especially in urban areas.

Women wear a colorful *pagne* (a wraparound dress; *rapa* in Pidgin) around their waist with a matching blouse. A woman might wear more than one *pagne*, either as a head covering or as an overskirt to cover work clothes while in public. Muslim women cover their heads outside of home, often wear a lot of jewelry, and color their hands and feet with patterns using henna (a plant dye). More intricate designs are drawn on their legs and arms for special occasions, such as weddings. Women might apply rich oils to their skin for a glossy appearance. People strive to keep feet clean; men prefer shoes to sandals.

CUSTOMS AND COURTESIES

Greetings. Men take handshakes seriously and use them to greet friends or even coworkers they see every day. In francophone areas, a brief handshake is preferred. Family or close friends may also brush alternate cheeks while they "kiss the air." In anglophone provinces, a slightly firmer handshake is most common. If one's hand is dirty, one offers the wrist. Hugs are reserved for family and close friends. Close male friends, as well as young people of the same age and gender, snap the middle finger and thumb while pulling the hands away from a handshake. Most Cameroonians recognize seniority (defined by gender, age, or prestige) by bowing the head or touching the right arm with the left hand during a handshake. To show special respect, a man might bow from the waist, while a woman might curtsy; in the north, women may kneel. One avoids eye contact with respected individuals but does not turn one's back to them. People do not touch or approach traditional royalty until they are told how to act.

Formal greetings include *Good morning* (*Bonjour* in francophone areas) and *Good afternoon* (*Bonsoir*). Local phrases vary widely but are followed by inquiries about family welfare. A person responds to the informal greeting of *Ha na?* (Pidgin for "How are you?") with *Normal* (Fine) or *Fine* (Great). In Fulfulde, people ask *Jam na?* (How are you?) and respond *Jam* (fine). In Mungaka (spoken near the city of Bamenda), the morning question is *Oo la ndi?* (Will you still sleep?) and the answer is *Oo sat ni?* (Have you arisen?).

Since one's place in society is more important than one's name, Cameroonians address others of seniority by title. Even younger siblings use titles for older siblings. Peers might use nicknames that reflect a person's role in a group. Professionals and officials are always called by their formal titles.

Gestures. Cameroonians use the right hand for passing an object, greeting, or eating. A person who uses the left accidentally or out of necessity apologizes. One points with head gestures or by puckering the lips. Legs may be crossed at the ankles but not the knees and not in front of those with higher authority. In some areas, women do not cross their legs in front of men. For all, it is important to keep the soles of the feet from pointing at others. A quick head nod indicates agreement. Nodding up quickly and audibly taking in breath means "yes" and shrugging means "no." Cameroonians make clicking sounds with the tongue to indicate agreement or astonishment. People often display pleasure by dancing. Grief may be shown by placing the hand on one's opposite shoulder and bowing the head, or by resting hands on top of the head (one hand on top of the other). People beckon by waving all fingers with the palm down. A hand extended and cupped upward is a request that something be shared. Public displays of affection are not acceptable, but peers of the same gender may hold hands or arms while talking.

Visiting. Cameroonians enjoy visiting family and friends, especially on Fridays after mosque or Sundays after church. Social visits are casual and relaxed, except in more conservative homes where rank and gender distinctions are important. In such homes, women and children rarely appear; if they do, they are not introduced. Unannounced visits are common, although strangers are expected to arrange visits in advance. One greets each individual at a small gathering and offers a general greeting to larger groups. Hosts need not stay the entire time with guests, who are content to sit long periods without conversation.

Hosts offer guests something to eat and drink, even if they have to send a child out to buy something. Visitors who drop by during a meal are asked to join in. Invited friends might bring food or drink as a gift. Food is not acceptable from visitors without a close relationship to the hosts because the food may be interpreted as questioning the host's means or hospitality; these visitors can present other gifts. Guests offer gifts for children through the parents. Good hosts will accompany their guests a distance from the home or send a companion along if it is after dark. One removes street shoes before entering a Muslim home. Business matters are not discussed during social visits. Northern Muslims show deference to a chief by removing their shoes about 100 yards away before visiting. Foreigners and government officials, considered on the same level as chiefs, do not remove their shoes.

Eating. Cameroonians eat the main meal in the evening. Food is not taken for granted, so formal meals are often blessed, and elders are served first. Rural women eat by the cooking fire with younger children, not with the men or older boys; women also serve the meal.

Diners wash their hands in a common bowl before and after eating. Most people eat with the right hand and Muslims do so from communal bowls. Bottles are opened in the drinker's view; the host leaves the cap loose and the guest pours. A guest must taste offered food; smelling it first is an insult. Satiated guests eat at least a small portion and then say they have eaten recently. In many areas, not being hungry is considered being sick, so guests generally are expected to eat plenty. Cameroonians would rather share a meal and eat less than eat alone. On entering small restaurants, diners wish others *Bon appétit* (Good appetite). They leave money on the table after eating.

LIFESTYLE

Family. Rural families often have as many as 10 children. Urban families are smaller. Young children are cared for by their mothers until weaned. At that point, older female siblings and relatives share in raising them. Fathers become more involved with their sons regarding career choices, marriage, and property issues. Often, a child is raised by rural grandparents, especially if the parents work in the city. By age 10, children are farming, herding, or doing domestic work. Cousins may be as close as siblings but birth order and degree of relatedness are not forgotten. The elderly receive basic needs and affection within the family compound. Cameroonians remember ancestors by drinking in their honor after pouring some of their drink on the ground.

Men raise cash crops and may hunt or work for wages; women farm food crops. Men are expected to provide for their families what their wives cannot produce on the farm. Women are expected to be fertile, keep a clean house, cook well, and raise respectful children. A woman can be sent back to her family by an unsatisfied husband. Urban women are more likely to get an education and enter the job market.

Dating and Marriage. Marriage is a highly regarded status to which nearly all Cameroonians aspire, but it is often viewed more as a social contract than an affectionate relationship. Arranged marriages may involve months or years of negotiations that create obligations after marriage for relatives on both sides, but couples can also meet on their own. Women marry on average by age 20, men by 27, though the average is younger in rural areas and older in cities.

Couples might engage in one or more weddings (civil, traditional, and religious), depending on their social situation. A civil union may come first, followed some years later by religious and/or traditional ceremonies. These are delayed most often by the high bride-price a groom must pay his bride's family for raising her; he can pay in cash or in kind (cattle, food).

Men may have many girlfriends in addition to one or more wives. Civil law allows as many as four wives, but some ethnic groups allow for many more (especially among royalty). Urban men are less likely to have multiple wives. Women are raised to be mothers more than wives. Their extended family will help provide for their children if they are not married.

Diet. Staple foods vary by region but include corn, millet, cassava, groundnuts (peanuts), yams, rice, potatoes, and plantains. *Fufu*, a common dish, is a stiff paste made by boiling flour (corn, millet, cassava, or rice). *Garri* is grated cassava that is dried over a fire until light and flaky. Meat is a luxury for villagers. Northern people sometimes eat beef, lamb, goat, and chicken. *Bush meat* (snake, monkey, porcupine, etc.) is a delicacy in the south. Sauces made from fish, meat, or vegetables are often cooked in palm, cottonseed, or peanut oil and seasoned with hot peppers. An urban breakfast might include tea or coffee, fruit, and bread. Rural breakfasts consist mostly of leftovers from the previous evening. Energy snacks and street foods include raw sugarcane, boiled eggs, roasted corn, fresh fruit, and nuts. Beer is popular on social occasions, but water is the main drink in the home. Muslims usually prefer tea to coffee.

Recreation. Team sports and individual athletics are sponsored by companies and urban social clubs. Soccer is the most popular sport. Inter-village soccer tournaments are organized during the months when school is out (June, July, August). Men and women in schools and cities play team handball, volleyball, and basketball. A marathon traditionally is run up and down Mount Cameroon (elevation 13,450 feet, or 4,100 meters) each year. Traditional board games played with seeds or pebbles are popular. Savings societies sponsor monthly feasts that provide recreation for many adults. Urban workers and students use any vacation time to return to their native villages. Movies, videos, and television are popular in cities. In rural areas, people pay a small admission fee to watch videos at a local "video-club" consisting of a television and VCR in an outdoor courtyard. Live music, dances, radios, and portable cassette players are popular throughout the country.

The Arts. Modern Cameroonian music is a fusion of world influences and indigenous styles such as *makossa* and *bikutsi*. Many Cameroonian musicians have gained international popularity. Traditional musical instruments include drums and lutes made from hollowed gourds and wood. Statues and relief carvings portray scenes from local oral literature. Ritual masks

Cameroon

are still produced, with styles varying by region. Cameroon hosts several cultural and arts organizations.

Holidays. Cameroon's national holidays include New Year's Day, Youth Day (11 Feb.), Labor Day (1 May), and Unification Day (20 May). Unification Day marks the 1972 union of the French and British zones. Some religious holidays have national recognition, including Easter, Assumption (15 Aug.), and Christmas. For Muslims, the most important holidays include *Fête du Ramadan* (*Ramadan* feast) at the end of the holy month of fasting, and the *Fête de Mouton* (lamb feast) held 40 days later in honor of Abraham's willingness to sacrifice his son. At the *Fête du Ramadan*, children get new clothing and sweets. Many villages also have annual festivals or dances.

Commerce. The cash economy dominates in urban areas, but bartering and payment-in-kind still exist in rural areas. Most retailing is done curbside, from market stands, in small shops, or out of converted cargo containers. Douala and Yaoundé have the largest department stores. Multinational banks dominate trade and finance, but credit unions handle local savings and investments. People often form or join *tontines* (*njangis* in anglophone provinces)—savings societies with as many as 20 members (men and/or women). Members pool their capital, provide loans to each other, and sponsor social activities. Doing business is considered a delicate matter, and taking one's time is essential. Stores are usually open from 7:30 or 8 a.m. to 4 or 5 p.m. In francophone areas, businesses close for lunch at noon or 12:30 and reopen at 2 p.m. Street vendors do business late into the evening. Urban stores commonly close on Saturday afternoon and Sunday, except in the north.

SOCIETY

Government. Cameroon is a unitary republic. The president (currently Paul Biya) is chief of state and appoints a prime minister (currently Peter Mafany Musonge) as head of government. Several parties are represented in the 180-seat National Assembly; members are elected to five-year terms. The voting age is 20. Local courts for domestic and land law are maintained by hereditary kings in the north and west and appointed chiefs elsewhere. These rulers enjoy strong loyalty among many ethnic groups and are consulted about national politics. Each of the nation's 10 provinces is led by a governor, and each province is divided into several divisions and sub-divisions led by prefects and mayors. Many rural people prefer to consult a village chief rather than take matters to a government official.

Economy. Economic prosperity depends largely on oil, coffee, and cocoa prices. Because oil reserves may run out in the future, Cameroon is trying to diversify its economy. Agriculture employs a majority of the labor force in either growing or processing food. Cash crops include coffee, cocoa, cotton, rubber, and timber. Major crops specific to Cameroon's north include corn and onions; in the south, manioc and pineapples are key products. The south has a better-developed infrastructure than the north and has greater access to products and services. Economic growth has been inhibited by poor management and corruption. Cameroon uses the currency common to francophone African countries, the *CFA franc* (XAF).

Transportation and Communications. Paved roads connect

DEVELOPMENT DATA
Human Dev. Index* rank . . . . 141 of 177 countries
  Adjusted for women . . . . 111 of 144 countries
Real GDP per capita $2,000
Adult literacy rate . . . . 77 percent (male); 60 (female)
Infant mortality rate . . . . 69 per 1,000 births
Life expectancy . . . . 46 (male); 48 (female)

major cities, but many areas are isolated. Unpaved roads are often impassable in the rainy season. Vans or sedans provide local public transportation. Taxis are available in cities. Many people travel by foot, bicycle, or motorcycle taxi. The domestic airline connects five cities. Telephones are concentrated in large urban areas. Mail service is unreliable, but "hand mail" passes via taxi drivers to shops where mail can be retrieved. Families can announce funerals and celebrations on the radio. Even more effective is *radio trottoir* (pavement radio), a system of verbal relays that passes news and information with great speed.

Education. The education system remains divided between French and English models, though it is governed by one government ministry. Rural children enter school knowing neither French nor English, while urban children know at least one of them. Primary school enrollment is higher in the south than the north. More boys than girls actually finish school. Secondary school enrollment is low due to fees, exam failures, space shortages, and parental choice. Muslim children memorize *Qur'an* (Koran) passages at evening *Qur'anic* schools. There is a full university in Yaoundé and smaller universities in four other cities. Informal education and apprenticeships provide vital vocational skills.

Health. Hospitals, while able to provide emergency services, often cannot provide basic (especially long-term) care. Patients' families must supply food, medicine, and some care. Villages often have local clinics staffed by nurses. Although government vaccination campaigns have targeted polio and measles, Cameroonians face a full range of diseases, including malaria, cholera, and AIDS.

AT A GLANCE

Events and Trends.

- President Biya secured reelection to another seven-year term in October 2004, winning more than 70 percent of the vote. According to a 1996 constitutional amendment, which limits the president to two terms, Biya will be required to step down at the end of his current term in 2011.
- A longtime border dispute between Cameroon and Nigeria remains unresolved. A 2002 ruling by the International Court of Justice (ICJ) granted the oil-rich Bakassi Peninsula to Cameroon, but Nigeria failed to transfer the disputed region to Cameroon by the ICJ-mandated deadline in September 2004.

Contact Information. Embassy of Cameroon, 2349 Massachusetts Avenue NW, Washington, DC 20008; phone (202) 265-8790.

CultureGrams™
People. The World. You.

ProQuest Information and Learning Company
300 North Zeeb Road, P.O. Box 1346
Ann Arbor, Michigan 48106 USA
Toll Free: 1.800.528.6279
Fax: 1.800.864.0019
www.culturegrams.com

CultureGrams World Edition 2006

Republic of Cape Verde

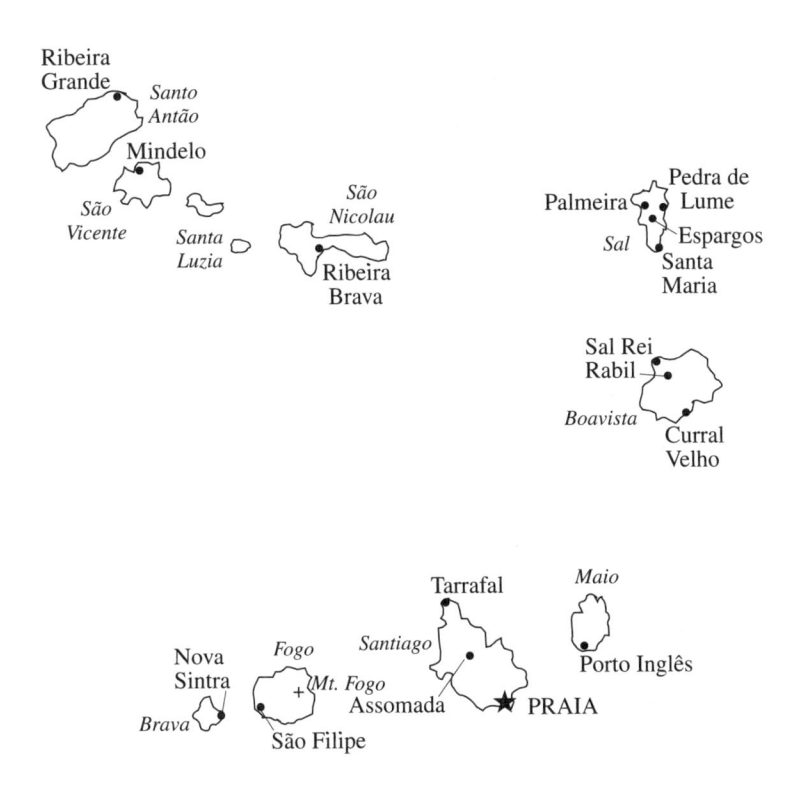

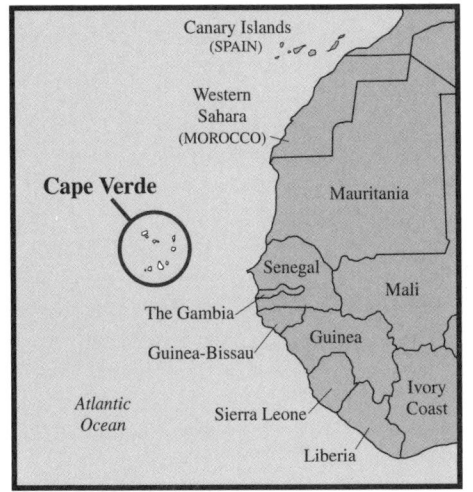

BACKGROUND

Land and Climate. Cape Verde (natively called Cabo Verde) is an archipelago located some 278 miles (445 kilometers) off the West African coast. There are two island groups, consisting of a total of ten principal islands, of which one (Santa Luzia) is uninhabited. Cape Verde's land area is 1,557 square miles (4,033 square kilometers), which is a bit larger than Rhode Island. The capital is Praia, located on Santiago.

The islands are arid and of volcanic origin. Fogo's 9,281-foot (2,829-meter) volcano last erupted in 1995. Sahelian vegetation is prevalent in many areas, although the high rate of soil erosion does not favor plant life. Vegetation is most prevalent in Brava, Santo Antão, and parts of Fogo, Santiago, and Maio. Many of the islands are mountainous.

The average temperature in Cape Verde is 75°F (25°C). The dry season spans November to July, while the rainy season begins in August and ends in October. Rains fall irregularly and sometimes not at all for years. Harmattan winds from Africa's deserts blow dust and dry air to Cape Verde between January and March.

History. Portuguese navigators arrived in the Cape Verde archipelago in the 15th century. Prior to this, West African groups such as the Wolof, Serere, and Lebou may have inhabited some of the islands. Within 10 years, the Portuguese brought slaves to Cape Verde from the Guinea Coast in order to develop sugar plantations. The plantations proved unproductive given the inhospitable climate. Cape Verde came to be used by Portugal as a crossroads for trading slaves, gold, and other valuables.

The islands' more recent history began jointly with Guinea-Bissau. In 1955, the African Party for the Independence of Guinea and Cape Verde (PAIGC) was organized by Amilcar Cabral, Luís Cabral, Aristides Pereira, Pedro Pires, and others. After some 20 years of guerrilla warfare against Portugal, both Cape Verde and Guinea-Bissau gained independence. Cape Verde became independent in 1975, and the PAIGC eventually became the PAICV (African Party for the Independence of Cape Verde). Amilcar Cabral, the movement's leader, was assassinated in 1973 in Conakry, Guinea. Pereira was then elected president, and Pires became prime minister. They led the government under a single-party system until 1990.

In the nation's first multiparty elections in 1991, António Mascarenhas Monteiro was elected president and Carlos Veiga became prime minister. Their Movement for Democracy Party (MPD) won by a landslide over the PAICV. Mascarenhas ran unopposed and was reelected in 1996. However, the PAICV returned to power in legislative and presidential elections held in 2001.

THE PEOPLE

Population. Cape Verde's population of about 415,000 is growing at an annual rate of 0.7 percent. The most populated islands include Santiago (48 percent of the nation's total population), São Vicente (13), Santo Antão (13), and Fogo (10). The largest cities are Praia (150,000 inhabitants) and Mindelo (60,000). About 55 percent of the population lives in urban areas. Cape Verde has a young population, with 40 percent under age 15 and only around 7 percent over age 64.

People call themselves *Caboverdianos* or *Crioulos*. Most Caboverdians (71 percent) are descendants of a mixture of Black Africans and Portuguese, while 28 percent are Black African and 1 percent are European. Because of high emigration rates, there are more Caboverdians living abroad (mainly

Cape Verde

in the United States, Portugal, Netherlands, and France) than in Cape Verde itself.

Language. Cape Verde's official language is Portuguese. However, most people use the national language, Crioulo, on a daily basis. Crioulo is a mixture of Portuguese, African, and other languages. A project to publish a Crioulo dictionary is currently underway, but the language remains an oral one. This is due in part to linguistic variations among the islands. Since the majority of people do not speak or write Portuguese well, many have difficulty understanding all the information in newspapers, on television, or on the radio. Use of Portuguese is a sign of education and social status; many in rural areas cannot understand it. Because of this, television and radio stations broadcast a small amount of news programming in Crioulo. Some educated people speak English and French, which are subjects offered in secondary school.

Religion. Freedom of worship is allowed and religious differences are accepted. Nearly all Caboverdians are Christian. More than 80 percent of them belong to the Roman Catholic Church. About 12 percent are Protestant, and the rest belong to other groups. People are very religious in Cape Verde, as shown by the large attendance at Mass and by the many sayings of a religious nature used in everyday conversation. Every town and county has a patron saint, whom the residents honor with an annual three-day festival around the saint's name day. On Sunday, churches are crowded, and one must come early to get a seat. The Catholic Church has a great deal of political and social influence in Cape Verde. In fact, some people credit it for the MDP's electoral win in 1991.

General Attitudes. Compared to those in the industrialized world, people in Cape Verde do things at a relaxed pace. For example, while going to work people stop to greet friends even though doing so may make them a few minutes late. A person who does not stop to greet his or her acquaintances often is considered *ingrato* (ungrateful).

To avoid confrontation, Caboverdians do not state opinions directly, and they are uncomfortable with direct apologies. Except in political discussions, they almost never reject an idea or invitation. People are hospitable, generous, and friendly. They are also open to the outside world, as twice as many Caboverdians live away from the islands as on them. In general, individualism is not promoted among Caboverdians. All deem it their responsibility to take care of neighbors. Privacy is not highly valued; people do not like to be alone. Traditionally, one's wealth is to be used to help the less fortunate in the family and not simply to be enjoyed alone. For example, expatriate Caboverdians feel obliged to send money and gifts to relatives in Cape Verde. Aid from abroad can amount to more than twice the average income on the islands and is a significant source of support for nearly every family. Many Caboverdians who leave the country for work elsewhere eventually return to vacation, start a business, or retire.

Personal Appearance. Caboverdians value cleanliness. They may bathe and change clothes several times a day. In urban areas, Western-style clothing dominates. Most people dress neatly but informally. Even high-ranking public officials wear short-sleeved shirts to work. Older people dress more conservatively than the younger generation, wearing longer dresses or darker colors, for example. Older women often cover their head with a scarf. Caboverdians dress up in their finest clothing when going to the city or to church. Teenagers also dress up when they go to the *praça* (town plaza). For young Caboverdian men, shirts with English inscriptions, such as the names of U.S. sports teams and cities, are especially popular.

In rural areas, Caboverdians might mix Western clothing with more traditional styles, but their appearance is always neat and clean. Rural women favor dresses (or blouses with wraparound skirts) and a headscarf. They may also wear a *pano* (apron). Rural men wear lightweight shirts and pants and sometimes a wide-brimmed or other kind of hat. Young women and adults usually do not wear shorts.

CUSTOMS AND COURTESIES

Greetings. People generally exchange a handshake and a long greeting when they meet. Greetings are an important precursor to conversation. Especially in informal introductions or after a long separation, women give and receive kisses from both sexes. Parents or elders also may be greeted with kisses. Most of the time, greetings are in Crioulo. Dialects vary between islands, but the most standard phrase is *Modi ki bu sta?* (How are you?). The response is *N'sta bom* (I am fine). After initial greetings, it is polite to inquire after the welfare of the person's family. When conducting business, especially with strangers, one uses the Portuguese *Como está?* (How are you?). In response, a person answers *Estou bem* (I am fine).

One respectfully addresses older people with a title before their name: *Senhor* (Mr.), *Senhora* (Mrs.), *Dona* (Lady), *Tio* (Uncle), or *Tia* (Aunt). It is also a sign of respect to address parents and relatives by familial titles: *Papá* or *Pai* (Father), *Mamá* or *Mãe* (Mother), *Tio*, or *Tia*. Friends address each other by first name or nickname. Nearly everyone has a nickname—either a shortened version of a given name or something that describes appearance or personality. For example, José would be called *Zé* (ZAY), or Maria de Luz would be *Milu* (MEE-loo). Someone with a lighter skin tone might be called *Zé Branco* (White José). It is also common to combine a nickname with the person's mother's name: *Zé de Maria* (José of Maria).

Gestures. In Cape Verde, one beckons by turning the palm toward a person and curling the fingers down, as if waving. It is not proper to beckon the elderly. To indicate "no," people commonly shake their finger back and forth, sometimes while clicking the tongue.

People stand in close proximity and often touch each other while conversing. This is an important part of communication. Members of the same sex hold hands while talking or walking as a gesture of friendship. A person should ask permission before passing between two people who are conversing. Eye contact during conversation is important among peers. However, it is a sign of respect to look down when talking to older persons or to teachers. Caboverdians, who generally are music-oriented people, tend to whistle their favorite tunes in public.

Visiting. Caboverdians regularly visit friends and relatives. Neglecting this important social custom is considered rude. It is not necessary to call ahead, and most informal visits are unannounced. Hosts are hospitable and treat their guests well. In most cases, guests are offered a drink and some sweets. Guests arriving at mealtime are invited to eat. Declining a drink or a meal is not considered impolite, but doing it consistently would probably be offensive. When invited to dinner, guests are not expected to contribute to the meal. Nevertheless, it is common practice to reciprocate a dinner invitation. Sometimes, a guest may bring a small gift to the host.

When invited to an event, guests say they will try to attend, even if they know it will not be possible. Saying "no" directly to an invitation may offend the inviting party, since it is interpreted as not valuing the invitation.

Caboverdians are not so conscious of time as people in industrialized nations. They often are late, even by an hour or more. This is especially true at dances. If a dance is scheduled to start at 9 p.m., guests might not begin to arrive until 10:30 and the dance may not begin before midnight. Arriving late at a home does not insult a host. The host simply assumes the guest had something to do prior to arriving.

People frequently socialize outside of their homes in Cape Verde. In fact, people in cities or villages gather daily at the *praça* between 6 and 8 p.m. to discuss their day, make plans for the weekend, or talk about issues affecting the country.

Eating. Caboverdians usually eat breakfast between 7 and 9 a.m. and lunch between noon and 2 p.m. After eating lunch, many people finish off their two-hour break with a short nap. Around 5 p.m., Caboverdians have coffee or tea with bread, cookies, or cakes. They eat supper around 8 or 9 p.m. Rural residents often have just two meals, lunch between 11 a.m. and 1 p.m. and dinner between 7 and 9 p.m.

In formal settings, Caboverdians eat with forks, knives, and spoons. More frequently, however, they use only spoons. The family typically eats together. Dinner guests might eat alone or with the family's male members, while the women and younger children eat later or separately in the kitchen. Guests receive the best pieces of food on the best plates the family owns. When people gather at a restaurant or café, it is not uncommon for the wealthiest person to pay for the entire meal. In any case, a person who invites someone for dinner, a drink, or something else pays for the food and drink of the guest. Tips are not required in restaurants or taxis, but they are welcomed.

LIFESTYLE

Family. In Cape Verde, the average family has five or six children. Nuclear families are rare, and many children are cared for by siblings and members of the extended family, such as aunts or grandparents. The extended family unit is important to each person; group (family) success takes precedence over individual success. Some elderly parents live with their children. Adult children often live in their parents' house until they marry, even if they have a job. Adult children who do live away from home are expected to give their mother money on a regular basis. Many women work outside the home; they comprise 29 percent of the labor force. Regardless of their responsibilities outside the home, women generally are expected to do all household cleaning and cooking and to care for the children. Although men are culturally recognized as the head of the family, women's responsibilities often make them the effectual leaders. More than one-third of households are headed by single mothers.

Most homes are modest. Only about half of rural houses have access to electricity. Rural homes are made of concrete or stone, stone being plentiful in the islands. Urban homes are more commonly made of cement. Smoothed concrete, paint, glass windows, and tile floors are characteristics of affluent homes.

Dating and Marriage. Dating customs in Cape Verde are similar to those in Western countries; young people meet at school, community events, work, or the *praça*. Couples enjoy going to movies, dancing, going to the beach, and having parties. Young people are free to choose their mates, but families often have input or play an integral role in planning a couple's wedding and other celebrations.

Many couples live together instead of marrying or until they can afford the expensive wedding celebrations. A church ceremony typically is preceded by a party the night before during which invited guests visit both the bride's and groom's houses to light fireworks. After the ceremony, all the guests participate in a car parade, honking and cheering the bride and groom, who are seated in the final car. The parade ends at the bride's house, where the celebration continues with dancing, visiting, and gifts of money for the new couple. At some point during the party, the groom claims his bride and takes her to his home. Fidelity is important in marriage, but male infidelity is generally tolerated. Men often have children by several women.

Diet. The most commonly eaten foods in Cape Verde are rice, beans, and corn. Rice, although imported, is relatively inexpensive; beans and corn are grown locally. Rice is often served with fish and beans (black or pinto). Corn is often served with beans, pork, manioc, and sweet potatoes. *Cachupa* is the national dish. It is a stew made of corn and meat or fish with manioc (cassava) that is cooked slowly in water. Fish and fish products are important to the diet.

People eat locally grown produce such as bananas, papayas, mangoes, tomatoes, potatoes, cabbage, carrots, onions, and green peppers. Most Caboverdians enjoy sweets at any time of day, cakes and marmalades being among the favorites. Two popular sweets include *doce de leite* (made of milk, sugar, and lemon) and *doce de coco* (made of coconut and sugar). *Grogue*, a strong rum made from sugarcane, is the national drink.

Recreation. In their leisure time, Caboverdians visit friends and family, go to the beach, and play *futebol* (soccer). *Futebol* is the most popular sport, and people watch or listen to game broadcasts with undivided attention. Portuguese teams are favored. In recent years, basketball and some other sports have increased in popularity. People watch television soap operas and dramas in the evening. Singing and dancing are favorite activities among all ages.

The Arts. The culture of Cape Verde reflects its dual Portuguese and African heritage. Stories, proverbs, and improvised poetry and singing are highly valued. Crioulo is the language of poetry, while Portuguese is used for prose. Distinctive Cape Verdian literature began to appear in 1936 with the journal *Claridade* (*Clarity*), an anti-dictatorial publication that opposed European-dominated arts. Baltasar Lopes da Silva's novel *Chiquinho* is widely considered the country's best piece of literature. Folk arts include cane and cloth weaving, tapestry work, and unglazed red clay pottery.

Music and dancing are a fundamental part of Caboverdian culture. Cape Verde's unique music and dance styles include the *morna*, *coladeira*, and *funáná*. *Morna* has a slow rhythm and melancholy lyrics, while *coladeira* is more upbeat and joyful. *Funáná* is even livelier and has a strong beat; it was forbidden before independence but survived in the countryside. *Funáná* is now the nation's most popular dance music. String instruments such as the *guitarra* (a cittern-like instrument), the *viola* (a kind of guitar), the *cavaquinho* (ukulele), and the violin are widely used. *Gaitas* (accordions) and percussion instruments are also important to Caboverdian music.

Holidays. Cape Verde's official holidays are New Year's Day, National Hero's Day (20 Jan.), Women's Day (8 Mar.), Ash Wednesday, Easter, Labor Day (1 May), Children's Day (1 June), Independence Day (5 July), All Saints' Day (1 Nov.), and Christmas. In February, *Carnaval* is celebrated all over the

Cape Verde

country. National Hero's Day commemorates the death of Amilcar Cabral, who led the fight for independence. Other national heroes also are honored on this day. While every fifth of July is a holiday, an official celebration takes place only every five years to minimize the financial costs of celebrating Independence Day. Workers usually receive two or three days off from work for their local patron saint's festival.

Commerce. Businesses are open from 8 a.m. to noon and from 3:00 to 6 p.m., Monday through Friday. Some offices use an 8 a.m. to 4 p.m. schedule, with a shorter (30-minute) lunch break. Banks and post offices may use either of these schedules. Summer hours often extend from 7:30 a.m. to 1:30 p.m. with no break for lunch. Although the price of goods may be negotiable in some open-air markets, it is generally fixed. The main open-air market, *Sukupira*, is in Praia. Staple goods, sold mostly in stores, are purchased less frequently, while fresh foods may be purchased several times a week.

SOCIETY

Government. Having established a multiparty democratic system within 16 years of independence, Cape Verde considers itself an example of a genuine African democracy. The country is a republic divided into 17 districts and administered through a parliamentary democracy. The president (currently Pedro Pires) is head of state, and the prime minister (currently José Maria Pereira Neves) is head of government. Both leaders serve five-year terms. The National People's Assembly deliberates on, amends, and adopts national laws, plans, and budgets. The assembly has 72 directly elected members. According to the 1992 constitution, six of the legislators are elected by and represent citizens living abroad. The voting age is 18.

Economy. Relatively speaking, Cape Verde is a poor country. About two-thirds of the people are considered wage earners, but many do not earn enough to meet basic needs. Unemployment is chronically high. Industries such as fishing and lobster harvesting suffer from limited or underdeveloped resources. Clothing, fish, bananas, hides, and salt are the main exports, while much of the country's food and consumer items are imported. Most rural people work in construction or live from fishing or subsistence farming. Urban residents are mainly government employees, small retail-business owners, or fishermen. Without aid from the international community, as well as remittances from Caboverdians living abroad, the country's standard of living would be considerably lower. The currency is the Cape Verdean *escudo* (CVE).

Transportation and Communications. Most areas in Cape Verde are accessible by road, and private cars or taxis and vans provide most transportation on the main islands. Buses are used in Praia and Mindelo. On small islands, people walk or get rides from passing motorists. Interisland transportation by sea is available for both passengers and freight. Air travel is available between some of the islands, although atmospheric dust from the harmattans sometimes makes it impossible.

The country has several television and radio stations, and it also receives some foreign television broadcasts. Most Caboverdians have access to telephone service. The postal system, now privatized like the phone system, is reliable and reasonably fast.

DEVELOPMENT DATA
Human Dev. Index* rank . . . . 105 of 177 countries
  Adjusted for women . . . . 83 of 144 countries
Real GDP per capita $5,000
Adult literacy rate . . . . 85 percent (male); 68 (female)
Infant mortality rate . . . . 49 per 1,000 births
Life expectancy . . . . 67 (male); 73 (female)

Education. Enrollment in primary schools (for seven- to twelve-year-old students) is compulsory, and 85 percent of children within this age group attend. About 48 percent of the school-age population attends secondary schools, while less than 1 percent of Caboverdians hold a college degree. Cape Verde has no university, so the country relies on overseas fellowships to provide its people with higher education. The government pays all educational costs.

Cape Verde's dropout rates in primary and secondary schools are high for many reasons. First, classes are taught in Portuguese, creating a learning barrier for the majority of children, who speak Crioulo at home. Also, it is difficult for rural people to appreciate the value of education. It is not seen as necessary for earning a living. Economic constraints further compound the situation. For instance, the relatively high cost of transportation in rural areas, coupled with the need for children to help with work at home, can lead even eager students to drop out.

Health. The government pays for healthcare costs. However, the waiting lines at the hospital are costly in terms of time, and the quality of care is not always adequate. This is due to the lack of equipment and to understaffing. All serious procedures require a trip abroad. Most people in urban areas, but only half of all rural residents, have access to safe drinking water. Cholera epidemics are difficult to control because of poor sanitation conditions. Outbreaks of malaria, typhoid, hepatitis A, and polio are not uncommon. Still, conditions are improving slowly and people are living longer.

AT A GLANCE

Events and Trends.
- In January 2005, U.S. State Department officials and the ambassador of Cape Verde to the United States signed a joint declaration on science and technology cooperation between the two nations. The agreement allows Cape Verde to receive assistance in several fields, including oceanography, fisheries sciences, water resource management, and natural resource conservation.
- Pedro Pires of the PAICV defeated Carlos Veiga of the MPD by just 17 votes to secure the presidency in 2001 elections. Both men previously held the position of prime minister. The next presidential elections are set for 2006.

Contact Information. Embassy of Cape Verde, 3415 Massachusetts Avenue NW, Washington, DC 20007; phone (202) 965-6820.

© 2005 ProQuest Information and Learning Company and Brigham Young University. It is against the law to copy, reprint, store, or transmit any part of this publication in any form by any means without written permission from ProQuest. This document contains native commentary and original analysis, as well as estimated statistics. The content should not be considered strictly factual, and it may not apply to all groups in a nation. *UN Development Programme, Human Development Report 2004 (New York: Oxford University Press, 2004).

CultureGrams™
People. The World. You.

ProQuest Information and Learning Company
300 North Zeeb Road, P.O. Box 1346
Ann Arbor, Michigan 48106 USA
Toll Free: 1.800.528.6279
Fax: 1.800.864.0019
www.culturegrams.com

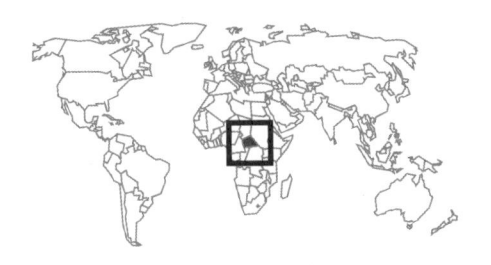

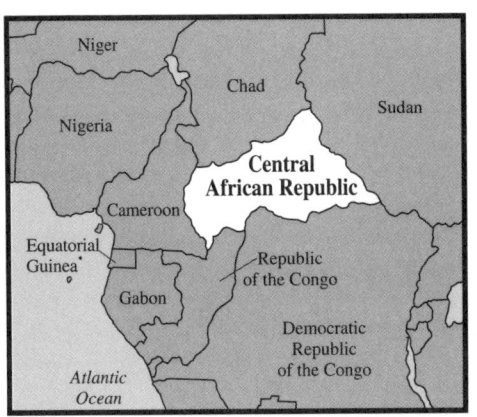

CultureGrams World Edition 2006
Central African Republic

BACKGROUND

Land and Climate. The Central African Republic covers 240,533 square miles (622,980 square kilometers) and is a little smaller than Texas. Dense rain forests grow in the south, which forms part of the Congo River Basin. Farther north, the land becomes drier and rises in elevation, but most of the country is covered by savanna. The Central African Republic is landlocked. Only the Oubangui River can be used by large boats during the rainy season.

The weather is almost always humid. Generally, daytime temperatures are hot, but nights cool off to 55°F (13°C) during November and December, when cold winds blow off the northern desert. The rainy season (May–November) is shorter in the north than in the south. A second rainy season in late February or early March is called the "mango rains" because it allows growing mangoes to fatten before the harvest. Rain and strong winds during this time knock many ripening mangoes from the trees.

The Central African Republic has implemented a variety of conservation projects. Northern and southwestern reserves protect wildlife and rain forests. Although elephant hunting is banned, poaching is still a problem.

History. Central Africa has an ancient heritage, but little of it is recorded. Just prior to French control of the region in 1887, it was inhabited by the Aka (Pygmy) and peoples migrating inland to escape the coastal slave trade. The French established the area as the Ubangi-Shari territory in 1894 and united it with Chad in 1906 as the Ubangi-Shari-Chad colony. In 1910, the colony was united with the Congo and Gabon as the Federation of French Equatorial Africa. Ubangi-Shari became autonomous in 1958 and independent in 1960. At independence, the name was changed to Central African Republic.

David Dacko served as the country's first postindependence president but was overthrown in a 1966 coup led by his uncle, Colonel Jean-Bedel Bokassa. In 1976, the brutal and capricious Bokassa created a monarchy and crowned himself Emperor Bokassa I. Dacko staged a coup in 1979 while Bokassa was out of the country and restored the republic. In 1987, Bokassa returned and was convicted of murder and jailed. He was released in 1993 and died in 1996.

General André Kolingba overthrew Dacko in 1981. The military ran the government until 1985, and Kolingba created the Rassemblement Démocratique Centrafricain (RDC) as the only legal party in 1986. Elections in 1987 were used to approve a new constitution and a six-year term in office for Kolingba. By the 1990s, however, in a climate of bleak economic conditions, other parties became active and posted candidates in 1993 elections. Ange-Félix Patassé was elected. Despite his efforts to improve economic conditions, government payrolls were often not met. In protest, the army mutinied three times in 1996. Patassé asked French troops to restore order to the capital city of Bangui, sections of which were devastated by heavy fighting. A hopeful January 1997 truce ended in March with renewed fighting. UN-sponsored African peacekeeping forces battled mutinous soldiers until a June 1997 truce was reached.

By mid-1998, the UN peacekeeping mission remained, but most French troops had withdrawn and fighting had subsided. Elections in late 1998 were fair but did not lead to national reconciliation. No party gained a majority of parliamentary seats. When violence and instability persisted, the United Nations extended the peacekeeping mission. President Patassé recommended holding elections to bring stability to the nation; he

Central African Republic

retained the presidency in a contested election held in September 1999.

UN soldiers left the country in February 2001, but political and social volatility increased in their wake. In March 2003, rebel troops under former army general Francois Bozize seized Bangui when Patassé was out of the country. Bozize took over the presidency, dissolved parliament, and established a transitional government to prepare the nation for new elections. Voters approved a new constitution in a December 2004 referendum. When parliamentary and presidential elections were held in March 2005, Bozize defeated 10 other candidates to remain in office.

THE PEOPLE

Population. The population of 3.7 million is growing annually at 1.6 percent. More than 500,000 people live in and around Bangui. Roughly half of the nation's population lives in small towns and villages, but urban areas are growing rapidly. About 43 percent of the population is younger than 15 years old.

More than 80 ethnic groups inhabit the Central African Republic, but two form a majority: the Gbaya (34 percent) and Banda (27 percent). Smaller groups include the Mandjia (21), Sara (10), Mboum, M'Baka, Sango, and others. A significant Aka population lives along the southwest border. The Mbororo, descendants of the Fulbé (or Fulani), are migratory herders who do not consider themselves Central Africans. Others also recognize the Mbororo (*Peul* in French) as distinctly different, even though they are active in society and government. A number of Portuguese, Greek, and Arab merchants live in urban areas. Tens of thousands of refugees from Sudan, Chad, and the Democratic Republic of the Congo also live in the country.

Language. Sango and French are the two main languages, but each ethnic group also has its own language. Sango (a Bantu tongue) is the national language. It was spread years ago as a trade language. French is the official language but is used mostly in government. Generally, people are fluent in their own tongue and Sango. French is spoken only by the more educated (about 10 percent).

The government promotes Sango because the language reinforces national identity. It recently introduced Sango as the language of instruction in primary school. Many official speeches are made in Sango rather than French, especially if the audience is primarily Central African. The national radio, Radio Centrafrique, broadcasts in both Sango and French.

Religion. Several religions are practiced in the Central African Republic. About half of the population is Christian, mainly Catholic and Baptist. About 15 percent of the population is Muslim. Other Central Africans practice local religions. Even Christians and Muslims maintain traditional beliefs or combine local practices with Christianity or Islam. For example, funerals may be less Catholic and more African. A belief in magic is widespread. People also seek the services of local charmers for guidance.

General Attitudes. Central Africans are friendly, gentle, and generous. Strangers are greeted with smiles. There is a strong sense of community among the people, including a deep commitment to the family and loyalty to one's ethnic group. Young people attending school away from home can expect to live with relatives, no matter how distant the relationship.

Central Africans tend to live in the present. With many immediate daily concerns and limited resources, they spend money when they get it. Those with money left over are expected to share it with family members who need it. Saving money is considered a sign of greed and is not common. Although the future seems uncertain, Central Africans feel they have no control over it and so do not dwell on it. Instead, they genuinely appreciate and enjoy the present.

Ethnic groups and clans have strong internal bonds and often have identifying characteristics such as specific trades, customs, or facial features (which include tattoos, scars, and henna leaf designs).

Personal Appearance. Central Africans take pride in being clean and well dressed. Wealthier urban men may wear a shirt and slacks or a Western-style suit. A *complet*, also popular, consists of pants and a matching shirt jacket that buttons to the collar. A common traditional outfit consists of pants and a matching *boubou* made from bright, locally produced fabric. A *boubou* may be cut as a pullover-style shirt, but a *grand boubou* is more like a robe that reaches the man's knees or feet. Embroidery on the front is popular.

Urban women commonly wear traditional styles. One outfit is a tight-fitting, short-sleeved blouse with a matching *pagne* (long wraparound skirt). Wealthier women might wear a short and a long *pagne* at the same time. The way a woman ties her *pagne* and allows the cloth to drape over her body conveys a number of unspoken messages, such as marital status. Women usually wear some sort of head wrap; they must wear a scarf to enter a church. Gold jewelry is a status symbol. Hairstyles can be elaborate. Girls learn at an early age to braid and weave hair.

Rural people and the urban poor dress modestly. They often wear secondhand Western clothing or a combination of local styles with Western T-shirts. Villagers often go barefoot to save their shoes for special occasions.

CUSTOMS AND COURTESIES

Greetings. A handshake is used in formal and social settings, along with verbal greetings. If close friends meet informally, they might begin a greeting by slapping right hands together. Then, each would grasp the other person's middle finger with the thumb and middle finger and "snap." Women sometimes kiss each other on alternating cheeks.

After these physical gestures, inquiries about one's health, family, and crops usually follow. This is true even when people meet by chance; just a passing "Hello" to a friend or coworker is not polite. A common Sango greeting is *Bara ala!* or *Bala mo!* (Greetings to you!), followed by *Tonga na nyen?* (How is it going?) or *Ala yeke senge?* or *Mo yeke?* (Are you okay?). French greetings include *Bonjour* (Good day) or *Salut!* (Greetings!), followed by *Ça va?* (Everything okay?). French is not used in villages.

How one addresses a person depends on the situation. Formally, one uses a title alone or with the last name. Respected older men may be addressed as *baba* (Sango for "father") and women as *mama* (mother). Informally, one may use first or last names, nicknames, or family affiliation (brother, sister, cousin). A very close friend may be called *ita* ("brother" or "sister") or *cousin* (cousin). Each person in a small group is greeted individually. To greet a larger group, one might raise both hands, palms facing the group, and say *Bara ala kwé* (Sango for "Greetings, everyone").

Gestures. Central Africans beckon by extending the hand, fingers out and palm down, and waving the fingers inward. During conversation, one can indicate "yes" by raising the eyebrows. This gesture is sometimes accompanied by a quick inhalation or a glottal clicking sound. One might ask "What?" or even "How are you?" by holding the hand out next to the body, palm open and down with the fingers relaxed, and flipping the hand over. Surprise or shock may be expressed by slapping the forehead with an open hand, sometimes saying *Aye!* or *Mama!* A hissing sound may be used to attract attention. Children often cross their arms over their stomachs as a sign of respect when speaking to a person of authority. Pointing with one finger is impolite. Forming a circle with the thumb and index finger means "zero." One may show respect when shaking hands by supporting the right wrist with the left hand and bowing slightly. Young friends of the same age and sex often hold hands while walking and talking.

Visiting. Visiting is a popular way to spend free time; it is common for a person to "drop in" uninvited at a friend's home. After greeting those present, the visitor is offered a chair or stool (*barambo*) and something to drink. Hosts may ask visitors to sit inside the home, but it is more common to sit outside on the porch or in the shade of a nearby tree. The visitor usually is given the nicest place to sit. During the visit, everyone might talk or listen to the radio. Sometimes very little is said and everyone just relaxes. Visitors arriving at mealtime are asked to share the meal. It is impolite to refuse offers of food, drink, or a seat.

Invited guests are not necessarily expected to be prompt. Hosts are patient with late guests and accommodating of those who arrive early. The host will often accompany a departing guest for a short distance.

Eating. At mealtime, people (especially children) may sit on the ground or on low stools around the food, which may be on a mat or a low table. Townspeople often have Western-style tables and chairs. While people might use plates and utensils, they generally use their hands to eat food from a common bowl. The right hand is used unless the type of food requires both hands. Before and after the meal, soap and water are passed around to wash the hands. In villages, men and boys eat together. Girls and young boys eat near their mother by the cooking fire. The mother eats last because she usually is still preparing food while others are eating. If guests are present, they receive the best meat. It is impolite for children to eat a large portion of meat or to talk during the meal.

Central Africans generally snack throughout the day. Popular snack foods include peanuts, small pieces of grilled meat, *makala* (fried dough), fried sweet potatoes, hard-boiled eggs, *kanda* (meat, fish, fruit, or termites wrapped in a leaf and steamed), and *mangbele* (cassava dough wrapped and boiled in leaves). The average person rarely eats at a restaurant. Among those who do eat out, hosts pay for anyone they invite. Friends who decide together to eat out pay for their own meals.

LIFESTYLE

Family. The extended family is the basic social unit; it includes the mother, father, children, grandparents, aunts, uncles, and cousins. They may live together in one home, and great emphasis is placed on taking care of elderly relatives. Adults often consider nieces and nephews as daughters and sons. Families are relatively large and can seem larger because men may have more than one wife (or girlfriend). Each wife or girlfriend lives apart from the others. Women are responsible for raising their children and providing the family with food. The man provides money for school, clothing, and the home.

Special pride is taken in introducing someone as, for example, *mon frère, même mère, même père* (my brother, same mother, same father). *Un frère* (a brother) might be a half brother or other relation. *Un cousin* (a cousin) could be a very distant relative. *Ita ti mbi* (in Sango) can mean "brother," "sister," "half brother," "cousin," or even "close friend."

Central Africans will travel great distances to attend the funeral of a relative or close friend. The family of the deceased must lodge, feed, and pay the return trip for all such visitors. Funeral events can last from a customary three days to a month depending on the importance of the deceased. Newborns who die are buried as soon as possible to encourage their quick "return" in the form of another baby.

Homes may be made of mud or cement bricks, a dirt or cement floor, and a thatched or tin roof. The kitchen may be a thatched hut away from the home where women cook over an open fire; outhouses are also located away from the home. The wealthy might have a kitchen and bathroom attached to their homes. People spend little time in the home because they are busy with daily activities.

Dating and Marriage. Rural inhabitants follow traditional courtship customs. Parents sometimes arrange a marriage, and older men sometimes take young women as wives. In larger urban areas, men and women usually choose their own spouse. Although illegal, the practice of paying a bride-price to the bride's family is common. Depending on the groom's financial status and reputation, the bride-price can be quite high. It consists of money, clothing, animals, jewelry, household items, food for the wedding party, and other items. A wedding party can last for days. Men are allowed, by custom, to have relationships outside of marriage, but women are not. Polygamy is common but less so than in the past. The poorest can afford only one wife.

Diet. Lunch is the main meal of the day; dinner consists of leftovers or fruit. A traditional meal is *ngunza* with *gozo*. *Ngunza* is a thick sauce made from ground cassava leaves, tomato paste, and peanut butter. A *kpu* (similar to a giant mortar and pestle) is used to grind the leaves and prepare many other foods. *Gozo* is a thick paste made by soaking cassava root in water, drying it in the sun, grinding it into flour, and boiling it. *Gozo* is then formed into concave balls to scoop up *ngunza*. Meals may also include sauces with fish or meat (beef, chicken, goat, sheep, gazelle, monkey, snake, and even elephant). The country produces a variety of fruits and vegetables, including sweet potatoes, tomatoes, avocados, bananas, oranges, grapefruit, guavas, papaya, pineapples, and mangoes. Imports include powdered milk, flour, rice, and noodles. Banana and palm wine are common drinks.

Recreation. Because girls and women do household work, tend the fields, and do the shopping, recreation mostly applies to men and boys. They enjoy playing and watching soccer and basketball. Amateur teams compete in the capital and in each large town. Some towns sponsor scout troops.

Schools provide all students with some recreation. Basketball, soccer, handball, and track-and-field are popular. Children also like to sing and play games at recess. Some schools have other extracurricular activities, such as theater. Church groups provide social activities, too.

The Arts. Music is important to Central Africans. Popular music such as *zokela* blends traditional and Western music. Congolese music is most popular for entertainment, but folk music accompanies ceremonies and festivals. Traditional instruments include banana tree xylophones and *sanza*, a thumb piano. Each ethnic group has a distinct style and ensemble of skin drums and log drums. Specific drumming rhythms

Central African Republic

are used for certain events. Music is integral to most religious events. Oral histories are performed by older villagers through a call-and-response progression of songs and chants.

Fine artists often incorporate traditional themes, materials, and images into modern compositions. Contemporary folk arts include pottery, basket and mat weaving, and wood carving. Artists carve stools, figurines, masks, and musical instruments. Folk arts and historical artifacts are preserved in the Boganda Museum in Bangui.

Holidays. Central Africans observe New Year's Day, *Fête du Travail* (Labor Day, 1 May), *Fête des Mères* (Mother's Day, end of May), Independence Day (13 Aug.), and last, the Declaration of Independence from France (1 Dec.). The latter is the biggest holiday, celebrated countrywide with parades and festivities. Schoolchildren practice for months to perform on this day. For Mother's Day, men stay home to cook and women get together to socialize, play sports, and dance.

Christians celebrate Easter and Christmas. Muslims have a great feast at the end of *Ramadan* (the month during which Muslims fast from sunup to sundown) and for *Tabaski* (Feast of the Sacrifice, which honors Abraham's willingness to sacrifice his son).

Commerce. Offices are generally open Monday through Friday until early afternoon. Shops are open Monday through Saturday from early to late, with a long break in the afternoon. Some outdoor markets are open only in the morning or afternoon. Many open on Sunday, a popular day for shopping and socializing. Prices in open markets are negotiable, but some staple foods are sold at fixed prices. Post offices sell stamps in the morning; those with public telephones stay open later so people can make calls. Socializing precedes most business meetings.

SOCIETY

Government. The president (currently Francois Bozize) is chief of state and has most executive powers. The prime minister (currently Celestin Gaombalet) is head of government. Members of the 105-seat National Assembly are elected to five-year terms. There is a separate judicial branch, although constitutional court judges are appointed by the president. The country's 16 prefectures are divided into sub-prefectures. Each town has an elected mayor. In addition, a *makunji* (village chief) is elected in each village. The responsibilities of the *makunji* depend on the strength of the mayor. All citizens may vote at age 21.

Economy. The economy is based on agriculture, and most people are subsistence farmers. Coffee, cotton, tobacco, peanut and palm oils, and wood are exported and used locally; food crops and livestock are raised for domestic consumption. Diamonds and timber account for most export earnings. Industry usually centers on food processing and textiles. France is an important trade partner. It also provides loans and grants to the country. The currency is the *CFA franc* (XAF).

The country's real gross domestic product per capita reflects the wealth of a small number of people rather than the great poverty among the vast majority of people (e.g., subsistence farmers) who do not earn an income or do not earn enough to meet basic needs.

DEVELOPMENT DATA
Human Dev. Index* rank .... 169 of 177 countries
Adjusted for women.......... 138 of 144 countries
Real GDP per capita $1,170
Adult literacy rate .... 65 percent (male); 34 (female)
Infant mortality rate .... 92 per 1,000 births
Life expectancy .... 39 (male); 41 (female)

Transportation and Communications. The main form of intercity transportation is the *taxi brousse* (bush-taxi); this can be a small pickup or a van. They are affordable but crowded and overloaded with luggage. People also hitchhike, while some have mopeds or bicycles. Short trips (up to 30 miles, or 48 kilometers) are sometimes made on foot. Very few roads are paved. Post offices handle mail and telephone services. People often "send" letters with travelers going in the appropriate direction, or they transmit messages via national radio.

Education. Children begin primary school at age seven. Attendance is mandatory, but fewer than half of the eligible students are enrolled. Some cannot afford registration fees or do not have enough clothing or food to stay in school. Books are scarce, so teachers write lessons on the board and students copy them in their notebooks. About 10 percent go on to secondary school. Successful graduates may go to the university in Bangui or to a technical school. Some study abroad.

Health. The Central African Republic lacks adequate health care. Healthcare professionals are often dedicated but underpaid. Public clinics exist in cities, but equipment is usually outdated and patients are required to provide their own anesthetics and medicine (available at pharmacies). Public facilities are virtually nonexistent in villages. Private clinics operate in the capital. Missionaries run rural clinics. Traditional healers in rural areas treat illness with organic medicine and rituals. If children survive to age six, they have a good chance of living to adulthood. Women often have children in their late teens, and many die in childbirth. Malaria, hepatitis, AIDS, polio, intestinal parasites, and river blindness are common.

AT A GLANCE

Events and Trends.
- Most election observers declared the March 2005 parliamentary and presidential poll to be fair, though several losing presidential candidates accused President Bozize of fraud. Among them was General André Kolingba, who ruled the Central African Republic from 1981 to 1993.
- In June 2003, three months after Bozize took power in a coup, the countries neighboring the Central African Republic officially recognized him as the nation's legitimate leader. However, the Central African Republic was not invited to attend a summit of the African Union (AU) in July 2003 due to an AU policy of not inviting leaders who seize power by force.

Contact Information. Embassy of the Central African Republic, 1618 22d Street NW, Washington, DC 20008; phone (202) 483-7800.

CultureGrams™
People. The World. You.

ProQuest Information and Learning Company
300 North Zeeb Road, P.O. Box 1346
Ann Arbor, Michigan 48106 USA
Toll Free: 1.800.528.6279
Fax: 1.800.864.0019
www.culturegrams.com

© 2005 ProQuest Information and Learning Company and Brigham Young University. It is against the law to copy, reprint, store, or transmit any part of this publication in any form by any means without written permission from ProQuest. This document contains native commentary and original analysis, as well as estimated statistics. The content should not be considered strictly factual, and it may not apply to all groups in a nation. *UN Development Programme, Human Development Report 2004 (New York: Oxford University Press, 2004).

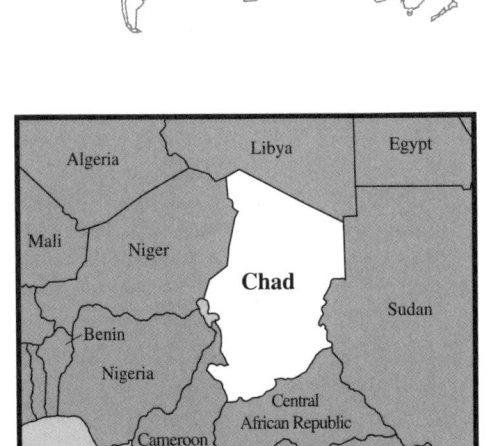

CultureGrams World Edition 2006
Republic of Chad

BACKGROUND

Land and Climate. Chad covers 495,755 square miles (1,284,000 square kilometers) of central Africa. This landlocked country is a giant basin surrounded by mountains on all sides but the west, including the spectacular Tibesti Mountains in the north. The nation's highest peak is the Tibesti's Emi Koussi (11,204 feet, or 3,415 meters). Chad's three climatic regions are the hot, dry Sahara in the north; a flat, arid center; and a fertile savanna in the south. The Chari and Logone rivers, abundant in fish, feed Lake Chad, which is shrinking dramatically from drought.

From June to October, the subtropical southwest receives abundant rain. In the hot season (March–May), temperatures average 104 to 113°F (40–45°C). Temperatures from December to February average 80°F (27°C) and can drop to 55°F (18°C) at night. Hot-season harmattan winds blowing off the desert turn the sky yellow with dust in many parts of the country. The desert receives only a few inches of rain, if any, each year. Small underground streams and oases support Chad's sparse Saharan population. The desert is hotter by day and often colder by night than elsewhere in the country. Drought, the expanding Sahara, civil war, and deforestation have decimated wildlife. Recovery is beginning at the Zakouma Game Reserve.

History. Chad was home to many ancient civilizations. Arab traders introduced Islam in the late seventh century A.D. Various kingdoms followed, including the legendary 10th-century Sao civilization and the competing 13th-century kingdoms of the Kanem, Ouaddai, Baguirmi, and Bornu.

Chad was largely ignored by the West until the French and Italians divided their Saharan territories in the late 19th century. The area now called Chad went to the French, who were unable to solidify colonial rule until 1920. The new borders united disparate and sometimes hostile groups in a poorly governed country called Tchad. Hence, its modern history speaks more of war than of peace.

Upon independence in 1960, Chadians elected François Tombalbaye as president. His policies angered Muslims and other groups; the army assassinated him in 1975. The presidency then changed hands a few times before the country erupted into civil war in 1979. Libya, France, and the United States all backed various factions. One rebel leader, Hissène Habré, eventually seized the presidency in 1982. With French and U.S. assistance, Chad then fought Libya—partially for ownership of the Aozou Strip, a reportedly oil- and uranium-rich band of desert on the Chad-Libya border. Libya withdrew in 1988, and the international court of justice recognized Chad's territorial claim in 1994.

Army colonel Idriss Déby deposed Habré in 1990. In 1993, a National Sovereign Conference was called to organize democratic elections. Voters approved a new constitution in March 1996 and national elections were held in July 1996. Déby was elected president and Chad seemed ready for a more peaceful future. However, insurgencies stemming from ethnic or political rivalries have hindered stability and continued the nation's social upheaval.

THE PEOPLE

Population. Chad has a population of 9.5 million, growing at a rate of 3 percent annually. About 75 of the population lives in rural areas. N'Djamena, located on the western border with Cameroon, is the capital and largest city. About half of all Chadians live in the fertile south, one-third in the center, and

Chad

the rest in or north of the Sahara. The advancing desert is driving many northern Muslim nomads south, where most people are Christians or animists.

No ethnic group can be said to dominate Chad. The Sara family includes the N'Gambaye in the southwest and the Goulaye, Sara Maj Ngai, and Sara-Kibba in the south. Smaller southern groups include the Moundang, Mboum, Moussai, and Massa. Muslims include Arabs, Toubou, Hadjerai, Kotoko, Kanembou, Baguirmi, Maba, Zakawa, and Gorane. The latter two groups are Saharan nomads. Nonindigenous nomads (Fulani, Mbororo) also traverse Chad. The country is home to Libyan, Cameroonian, Nigerian, and Yemeni merchants, as well as European missionaries and development workers. Tens of thousands of Sudanese and Central Africans live in border refugee camps.

Language. Chad's official languages are French and classical Arabic; few people speak either of them. Chadian Arabic—an oral language that combines Arabic, French, Fulani, and local dialects—is used for cross-ethnic communication (e.g., at the market). Muslim children learn some Arabic in *Qur'anic* (Koranic) schools, but most Chadian Arabic speakers do not read or speak classical Arabic. More than one hundred languages are spoken in Chad, including Central African Sara and its linguistic cousin, N'Gambaye. Chad's nomads primarily speak one of 30 dialects of Chadian Arabic. Nonindigenous nomads usually speak Fulani. Secondary students prefer English to French as a course of study, but French is the language of instruction. Children are adept at learning languages and often speak several local tongues by age seven.

Religion. Religion is important to daily life and is more likely to create divisions in the population than ethnicity is. Chad's population is roughly half Muslim, 25 percent Christian, and 25 percent animist. Islam was not a unifying religion until the late 19th century, and Christianity was not widely accepted until the 1920s. Even today, Muslims and Christians blend animist traditions with formal religion. Muslims might buy *gris-gris* (charms) or drink ink used to print verses from the *Qur'an* (Koran) in order to ward off evil or disease. Animists strive to maintain harmony with their natural environment by placating spirits, especially those of ancestors. Many southern youth undergo the *yondo*, a secret adult initiation ritual. Belief in magic and witchcraft is widespread, and most Chadians consult diviners.

General Attitudes. Individually, Chadians are friendly and generous. They avoid personal conflicts and strive to be pleasant in public. However, years of war, strikes, and poverty have taken their toll. Tensions among Chadians arise from lifestyle differences between ethnic and religious groups, as well as historical conflicts (e.g., northern Muslims raided and enslaved the Sara until the 20th century).

Chadians treasure their sense of humor, which joins with ingenuity to help them get by with few resources. Many believe their future is in the hands of Deity and that an individual's main task is to not disrupt social order. Most people would rather endure hardships than be accused of selfishness or arrogance. Chadians are community oriented. People are expected to share their incomes with less-fortunate relatives. Social status is gained by wealth and by how much of it a person shares.

Personal Appearance. Cleanliness is very important and Chadians keep their clothing clean, ironed, and mended. Mothers keep their children clean and will scold them when they get dirty. Women wear a *pagne* (ankle-length wraparound cloth tucked at the side). Married women add a second *pagne* as an apron. Short-sleeved shirts with wide, patterned necklines and a matching head wrap complete the outfit. In the south, women often wear their hair in elaborate braids. Muslim women conceal their clothing with a head-to-toe covering and a veil. Some northern women use tree thorns to insert dye in patterns on their chin and lips.

Southern men wear secondhand Western clothing or more traditional attire, such as a *complet* (long-sleeved tunic over baggy, but tapered, pants). Muslim men wear a *boubou* (ankle-length, long-sleeved robe over baggy pants). Elaborate embroidery on these outfits indicates wealth. Muslim men travel with an ornate dagger tucked into one sleeve and the head protected by a carefully wrapped turban. The average Chadian wears foam or plastic sandals; shoes are for the rich. Many southerners are ritually scarred with patterns reflecting their ethnic group. It is a high compliment to tell a person he or she has put on weight; corpulence is a sign of wealth and leisure.

CUSTOMS AND COURTESIES

Greetings. Proper greetings are essential to Chadians. When joining a group or visiting a home, one shakes hands with all, beginning with elders, and then men before women. In a large group, raising both palms and saying *Lalé* is sufficient. Friends often hold hands during an entire greeting. The left hand is not used in any exchange of greetings or items; it is reserved for personal hygiene.

When shaking an elder's hand, one kneels or bows, sometimes supporting the right elbow with the left hand to signify the weight of one's respect for the other person. In the north, one also might touch one's heart to indicate the honor felt in greeting the person. If greeting in Sara, one might say *Lafia ngai* (Much peace) and/or *I baii?* (How are you?). The response to the latter is *M'to kari* (I'm fine). Arabic greetings usually begin with an exchange of *Salaam alek(i)* (Peace be upon you) and *Wa alek asalaam* (And peace be upon you). *Lalé* is derived from this greeting. Inquiries about health, home, family, and crops usually follow. *Kaif al hal?* (How is your health?) is answered with *Afé, al hamdulilah* (Fine, praise be to *Allah*). At parting one says *Aw lafia* (in Sara) or *Amshee afé* (in Arabic), meaning "Go in peace." Parents are addressed as the mother or father of their eldest child (*Am-djoua*, meaning "mother of Djoua"). Elders are addressed as "mother" or "father" in the local language. Many men call each other *Chef* (chief) at work or use the title to show respect to another man.

Gestures. People knock by clapping outside someone's gate or front door. Children ask questions in school by raising a hand and snapping the fingers. To agree, a person clicks the tongue against the palate and thrusts the chin upward. To beckon, one motions with all fingers of the right hand with the palm facing down. Flipping a palm from facedown to faceup is a way of asking "Where are you going?" or "What are you doing?" One gets a subordinate's attention by hissing. A man may kneel to greet his wife's parents or important elders. Chadians help older people of the same gender (e.g., a young woman might carry a bundle from market for an older woman).

Visiting. Chadians visit friends and relatives regularly. Unannounced visits occur daily, especially evenings and Sundays. People socialize outside in the shade; they rarely go in the house. Visitors are given the best chair or cleanest mat to sit on. Guests, even unwelcome guests, are served water on arrival; favored guests then receive tea or hot, sweetened milk, and sometimes *Hadjilidj* nuts. Muslim women may greet male guests and serve tea, but they do not stay. Female friends visit each other in the women's separate cooking/eating area. Children may not touch guests without permission, but they often roll out mats or take a visitor's packages for them. Hosts accompany departing guests a short distance and may give honored visitors a live chicken.

Visitors are welcome at any meal, but it is impolite to arrive purposefully at mealtime. When invited to a funeral or family celebration, guests are expected to contribute money to help offset costs. On holidays, entire families visit neighbors and are treated to food and drink at each stop; children may receive candy or small coins.

Eating. Breakfast is optional and light (usually leftovers from the day before or tea and bread). Lunch is the main meal; dinner is at sundown. Women cook on a three-rock fire (the rocks support a pot) or a charcoal basket (*ganoon*). People wash their hands before a meal. Men and guests eat first, separate from the rest of the family; children eat from the leftovers and then women eat after all have been served. Eating is not a time for conversation. Some people have tables, but diners usually sit on mats around a common platter; feet may not point at food. Chadians use the right hand to scoop food from the portion directly in front of them. Meat is reserved for men, and the best parts (e.g., heart, head, neck, and intestines) are served to guests. Leftovers will include some meat. People begin eating only after a prayer or signal from the host or parent. It is rude for guests to refuse food. It is rude to eat or snack in public, except at the market. During the holy month of *Ramadan*, devout Muslims fast from sunrise to sundown. Meals are eaten at night. Chadians abide by certain food taboos across religious and ethnic lines. These include not giving eggs to children for fear they will become thieves or will not learn to speak, and limiting how much a pregnant woman eats so that her baby will not grow too large to deliver.

LIFESTYLE

Family. Family is the cornerstone of Chadian society. A man has as many wives and children as his income, religion, and tastes allow. Islam permits four wives. Christianity discourages more than one. The man has a hut or tent in the family compound; wives and children live in separate structures nearby. Adult children may live in or near the compound. Aging parents generally live with or near a son. Men make family decisions but women run the household, often with their own money. Rural southern women usually have more autonomy than do Muslim women, who often cannot leave the family compound without their husband's permission.

The children of co-wives are considered brothers and sisters, although siblings of the same mother maintain the closest bonds. Children have many chores at home, and girls tend younger siblings until they are old enough to help cook, shop, or do laundry. Children are expected to obey their parents without question; they can be disciplined by any adult. Funerals bring relatives and friends from all over to mourn for at least four days; women cry with each other, but men do not cry.

Dating and Marriage. Many marriages are arranged by families, but youth also meet at the market or dances. Southern youth might date discreetly. Rural Muslim girls do not date. Young women marry in their teens; men are usually in their twenties. A suitor gets to know a girl's father and brothers before he is allowed to spend time with her. Men find it difficult to pay the bride-price ($50 to $500, depending on the bride's status or beauty) and often wait to marry. New wives may be resented by first wives or may be welcomed as household helpers.

Muslim weddings are lavish events that can last up to four days. Southern weddings are brief and involve only payment of the bride-price. Often, a couple is considered married if the woman becomes pregnant. Divorce is uncommon; marital problems usually are resolved before a local chief.

Diet. Chad's national food is *boule*, a heavy porridge formed into a ball and dipped in sauce. Northerners prefer corn *boule*; southerners use millet. Sorghum, cassava, and groundnut (peanut) *boule* are also common. Another staple food is *bouillie*, a millet-and-peanut porridge flavored with lemon and sometimes sugar. *Tan kul* (long sauce) is mixed with fish, meat, or beans for special occasions in the south. Northern sauces tend to be spicier and meatier. *Nashif* is made of chopped beef with a spicy tomato sauce. It traditionally is eaten with *kissar*, a light sourdough crêpe. Okra, garlic, *piment* (a powdery, red pepper), bouillon, and dried tomato flour flavor nearly every sauce. Peanut paste and dried fish are common protein sources, since meat and fresh fish are expensive. Goat is a common meat. Guavas and mangoes are seasonally plentiful in the south, as are dates in the north. Rice and pasta are reserved for special occasions or eaten by the wealthy. Arabs typically eat *esh* (boiled millet flour) with *moulah* (sauce). For herders, dairy products comprise a large part of the diet. Milk is heated with sugar and cardamom or made into a sour yogurt or clarified butter. Women earn extra income by brewing and selling millet beer (*bili-bili*). Market snacks may include cookies, bread, or crickets and termites toasted in oil.

Recreation. Women visit each other to talk, drink, and braid hair. Men have more time to tell stories, drink tea, and play cards and strategy games. Young men play soccer; urban boys also like basketball. Children enjoy rhyming, hand-clapping, and dancing games, as well as rope skipping. Sundays and market days in southern villages are festive times for people to enjoy *bili-bili* and dancing. Women often organize a *parivente*, a fund-raising party with free food but expensive beer. Urban dwellers enjoy dancing in open-air bars. Chad's few movie theaters and video clubs often show martial arts or other action films. People rarely travel for pleasure, only for family or special business.

The Arts. Chad's art traditions are varied. France's influence can be seen in architecture and the fine arts. Contemporary art is exhibited by the National Museum, founded in 1962. Indigenous arts thrive as well. Artisans work metal and make musical instruments, papyrus boats, and woven baskets. The influence of the Arab population on the arts has been primarily in the area of music. Traditional music may consist of a vocal soloist accompanying himself with a lute. Lutes are hand made from wood, gourds, or metal. Strings may be added or removed depending on the requirements of the performance.

Holidays. Chad's national holidays include New Year's Day, International Women's Day (8 Mar.), Labor Day (1 May), Independence Day (11 Aug.), Proclamation of Independence Day (28 Nov.), and President Déby Day (1 Dec.). Government holidays are celebrated with military parades, decorated streets, marching bands, traditional dancing, Arab horsemen, and speeches. On Women's Day, women parade, play soccer, race bikes, dress as men, and are served meals by men dressed as women.

Muslims celebrate *Aid al Fitr*, a feast at the end of *Ramadan*. They also celebrate *Tabaski* (Feast of the Sacrifice) to honor

Chad

Abraham's willingness to sacrifice his son, and *Maoloeud*, the prophet Muhammad's birthday. These are times to share wealth, dress up, visit, and enjoy special foods. Christian holidays are Easter and Christmas.

Commerce. Muslim men dominate trade in Chad. Cities and large towns have a permanent *souq* (open-air market) with stands, street tables, and small boutiques. Towns and villages have smaller weekly markets, which serve an important social and political, as well as commercial, purpose. Small neighborhood stands sell spices, peanuts, batteries, matches, and cigarettes. Bargaining and bartering are expected. Urban markets are open all day beginning at 7 a.m. Weekly markets close for an afternoon break. Business hours are from 7 a.m. to 6 p.m. with a two-hour break at 2 p.m.

Women often pool their money to buy fresh produce (like tomatoes) to dry, process, and later sell in the off-season. Many sell spices and prepared foods, especially at truck stops. Nomad women sell milk and yogurt at markets. A woman's income is vital to her family's welfare. Agricultural cooperatives pool money to fund village projects or provide credit to members.

SOCIETY

Government. The president (currently Idriss Déby) is head of state and elected to a five-year term. The prime minister (currently Pascal Yoadimnadji) is head of government and appointed by the president. Members of the 155-seat National Assembly are elected to four-year terms. The voting age is 18. Chad's 14 prefectures are led by presidential appointees. Villages grouped into a *canton* (county) usually are led by local traditional chiefs. Serious criminal cases are heard in civil courts. Local disputes are heard by traditional chiefs, some of whom consult diviners to assess a person's guilt. Public shamings or beatings are traditional local punishments.

Economy. Chad is one of the world's poorest countries. Drought, distance to markets, and political instability have all contributed to a troubled economy. Subsistence farmers and fishers comprise 85 percent of the labor force. Only 4 percent is employed in industry: cotton ginning; grain milling; agricultural processing; and manufacturing beer, textiles, sugar cubes, and cigarettes. Cotton is the most important export, followed by beef, gum arabic, and fish. Strikes are common due to lack of wages. Many people hope petroleum deposits will help alleviate poverty, but the corruption that hinders other economic growth will likely keep oil profits in powerful hands. The currency is the *CFA franc* (XAF).

Transportation and Communications. Travel is difficult in Chad, which has only 200 miles (322 kilometers) of paved roads and no railways. Dirt roads connecting major cities are frequently flooded. Local "bush-taxis" (*taxi brousse*) are small pickup trucks that carry goods and passengers between towns. Two buses offer sporadic service between southern cities. Taxi service is good in the capital and in Moundou. Otherwise, people walk, bicycle, or travel by donkey. Only skilled guides and drivers can cross the Sahara. In the wet season, the postal service relies on market trucks and missionaries to distribute mail to villages. The largest city in each prefecture has some public telephones. Villagers can send Morse code messages from a post office. Radio is the primary source of information. Radio Chad broadcasts primarily in French, Arabic, and Sara. N'Djamena's French-literate residents enjoy a relatively free press.

Education. Chad's education system, based on the French model, begins with first grade at age six and can continue to the equivalent of the second year of college. Many students drop out after sixth grade, and few are educated beyond junior high (*collège*). Fees, lack of resources, frequent strikes, the need for girls to help at home, and other factors hinder many Chadians from getting an education. Many parents dislike Western-style education; they want a curriculum that prepares children to farm and develop their communities.

Classes meet in the morning or the afternoon, six days a week. French is the language of instruction. There are few books and the average teacher has 64 or more students. Since teachers lack regular government paychecks, parent associations often must pay their salaries. Church missions sponsor private schools. Chad's small university has a three- or four-year waiting list.

Health. Chadians are subject to malaria, diarrhea, measles, meningitis, and AIDS. These ailments, as well as hunger, work to shorten life. Many women die in childbirth. Only about one-fourth of the population has access to clean water. People prefer herbs and traditional healers to the poorly staffed and understocked medical clinics. Funding comes primarily from private donations and grants, but these can do little more than provide some medicines, first-aid training, and a few doctors. Mission clinics provide care to those who can afford it. A preventive health program (vaccinations, prenatal consultations, health and hygiene education) is in place, but people generally expect shots from doctors, not advice.

DEVELOPMENT DATA

Human Dev. Index* rank . . . . 167 of 177 countries
 Adjusted for women. . . . . 135 of 144 countries
Real GDP per capita $1,020
Adult literacy rate . . . . 55 percent (male); 38 (female)
Infant mortality rate . . . . 95 per 1,000 births
Life expectancy . . . . 44 (male); 46 (female)

AT A GLANCE

Events and Trends.
- Since 2003, huge numbers of Sudanese refugees have fled to Chad to escape fighting in Sudan's Darfur region. Camps in eastern Chad hosted an estimated 200,000 Sudanese refugees by 2005.
- The National Resistance Army, a rebel group in eastern Chad, signed a peace deal with the government in 2003, ending years of fighting in the region. However, hostilities continue between the government and another rebel group, the Democratic Movement for Justice, in northern Chad.

Contact Information. Embassy of Chad, 2002 R Street NW, Washington, DC 20009; phone (202) 462-4009.

© 2005 ProQuest Information and Learning Company and Brigham Young University. It is against the law to copy, reprint, store, or transmit any part of this publication in any form by any means without written permission from ProQuest. This document contains native commentary and original analysis, as well as estimated statistics. The content should not be considered strictly factual, and it may not apply to all groups in a nation. *UN Development Programme, Human Development Report 2004 (New York: Oxford University Press, 2004).

CultureGrams™
People. The World. You.

ProQuest Information and Learning Company
300 North Zeeb Road, P.O. Box 1346
Ann Arbor, Michigan 48106 USA
Toll Free: 1.800.528.6279
Fax: 1.800.864.0019
www.culturegrams.com

Union of the Comoros

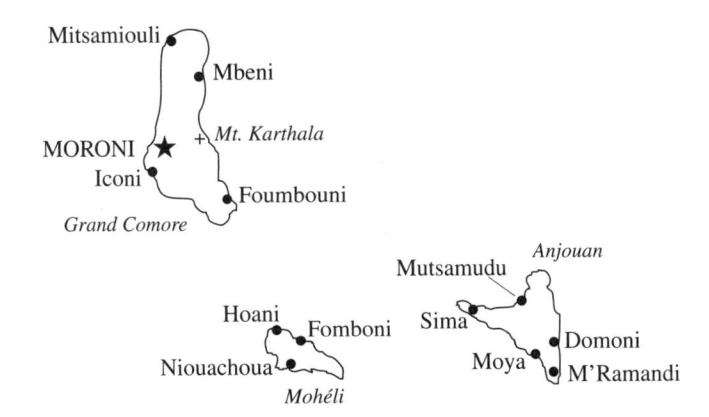

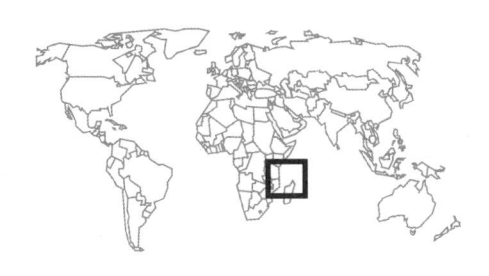

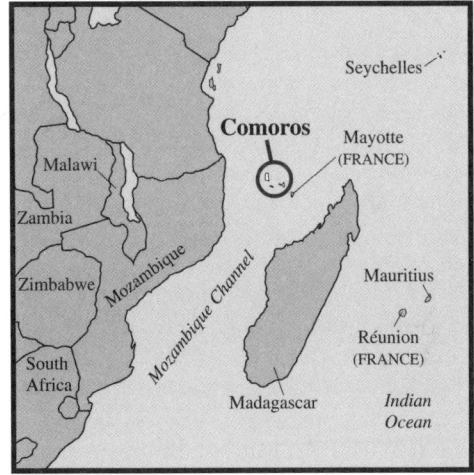

BACKGROUND

Land and Climate. Comoros is located to the northwest of Madagascar in the Mozambique Channel of the Indian Ocean. The nation is comprised of three islands: Anjouan (Nzduani), Mohéli (Mwali), and Grand Comore (Ngazidja). Together, the islands are about the same size as Delaware, covering 838 square miles (2,171 square kilometers).

These volcanic islands were formed in succession from east to west, Grand Comore being the youngest. It has less-evolved soil than the other islands and so lacks their ability to support agriculture. All the islands are mountainous; Grand Comore is dominated by Mount Karthala (7,800 feet, or 2,400 meters), which has a large active volcanic crater. Mayotte Island to the southeast is geologically the oldest member of the Comoros Archipelago, but it is a French territory and not part of the nation of Comoros.

The hot, humid rainy season (*Kashkazi*) generally runs from November to March, but it varies annually. The pleasant season of *Kusi* (April–September) has warm, clear, breezy days and cool nights. Comorian waters are home to the ancient coelacanth fish, thought to be long extinct before one was seen in South African waters in 1938.

History. Africans arriving in the 13th century were thought to be the first inhabitants, but discoveries in 1990 led to theories that Persians may have actually settled the islands in the 800s. Malagasy people from Madagascar came in the 16th century, but the population remained small until the islands were used by Arab slave traders as holding areas.

Arab slave traders set up towns, and mainland Africans formed their own communities. Over time, the islands were divided into various opposing sultanates. Except for pirates and a few other sailors, Europeans paid the islands little attention until the 19th-century "scramble for Africa." The French, having occupied Madagascar, became interested in Comoros to counter a British presence in East Africa and the Seychelles. A sultan on Grand Comore allied with the French in the 1870s, and by 1886 the entire four-island archipelago was proclaimed a French protectorate.

In 1958, Comorians voted to remain a French overseas territory while assuming responsibility for internal affairs. Saïd Mohammed Cheik became president of the Council of Government. Though he served mostly as a figurehead, he gave Comorians their first sense of self-determination. In 1962, Cheik moved the capital from Mayotte to Moroni on Grand Comore. In a 1974 referendum on independence, 94 percent of the total population voted for autonomy, but 64 percent of Mayotte's residents voted to remain under French control. Hence, when the Federal Islamic Republic of the Comoros became independent in 1975, France maintained possession of Mayotte. Comoros still claims the island, on which France supports a large naval base, because of the overall popular vote for independence.

After only a few months in office, Ahmed Abdallah, elected as the first postindependence president, was overthrown by a socialist visionary named Ali Soilihi. Soilihi was assisted by European mercenaries led by Frenchman Bob Denard. Soilihi's austere policies managed to boost agricultural production and increase the number of schools. However, his strict approach alienated Comorians, his economic policies were not appreciated by Western donors, and his criticism of many Islamic traditions offended Muslim nations. Having little foreign or domestic support, Soilihi was overthrown in 1978 by Abdallah (with Denard's help).

Comoros

Abdallah led the country away from the socialist economy, but he could not maintain order without Denard's assistance. Comorian resentment of the mercenaries grew, and by 1989, Abdallah had planned to oust Denard with help from France and South Africa. In November 1989, Abdallah was murdered at home and Denard took control for several weeks until France forced his departure.

Supreme Court judge Saïd Mohammed Djohar was elected president in 1990. Economic crisis and political unrest soon gripped the country, and Bob Denard returned in 1995 to lead a coup against the unpopular Djohar. France invaded and arrested Denard, sending him to jail in France. Elections in 1996 brought Mohamed Taki to office as president.

In October 1997, residents of Anjouan and Mohéli voted to secede from the Republic. An invasion of Anjouan from Grand Comore was repulsed by the breakaway islands. Mohéli later renounced its secession. Yet another coup in April 1999 brought Colonel Assoumani Azzali to power. In February 2001, Grand Comore and Anjouan agreed to reunite under a new constitution that granted each of the three islands greater autonomy. To reflect this looser association, the nation adopted a new name: the Union of the Comoros. Azzali was declared the winner of April 2002 presidential elections marred by violence, low voter turnout, and a boycott by the two opposition candidates. Legislative elections were held in April 2004. Despite tensions between Azzali and his opponents, the new union remains tentatively in place.

THE PEOPLE

Population. The nation's population of about 652,000 is growing at a rate of 2.9 percent annually. Roughly 43 percent of the population is younger than age 15, and about 65 percent lives in rural areas. Moroni and Mutsamudu are the largest cities. Grand Comore has the most residents, followed by Anjouan and Mohéli. Comoros has no true ethnic divisions, but the population is divided by language and other factors. Most Comorians are descendants of both Arab slave traders and the African mainlanders brought as slaves to be shipped north to the Arabian Peninsula and Nile Basin. Those with more Arab ancestry tend to enjoy higher social status than others. A few families have Malagasy or Asian ethnicity.

Language. French and Arabic are official languages. French is used for official business and government. Indigenous languages are Bantu tongues derived from Swahili. Shingazidja is spoken on Grand Comore. Shinzduani is Anjouan's language, and Shimwali is spoken on Mohéli. People understand each other's languages, as well as the Shimaore spoken on Mayotte. Comorians traditionally use the Arabic script, but the Roman alphabet is being promoted.

Four- and five-year-olds attending *Qur'anic* schools learn Arabic, and while few adults speak it, most read the alphabet. Many Comorians know some French. Since French is the language of school instruction, anyone with a secondary education will be fairly fluent. English is offered in school, but usually only workers connected to travel can speak it.

Religion. Nearly all Comorians are Sunni Muslims, and Islamic traditions play a key role in daily life. Muslims accept the *Qur'an* (Koran) to be the final word of *Allah* (God) as revealed to the prophet Muhammad, revered as the last and greatest prophet. Devout Muslims pray five times daily. In even the smallest villages, mosques issue the call to prayer regularly. On Friday, all men (even less devout ones) go to their town's largest mosque for the noon prayer.

Non-Islamic (mostly indigenous African) beliefs are present, but they have largely been incorporated into Islamic practices. Many Comorians maintain a belief in good and evil spirits; they use *gris-gris* (charms) to ward off the evil ones. Some attend special ceremonies to bring out spirits. Other religions are tolerated. Most foreigners are Christians; large towns have both Catholic and Protestant churches.

General Attitudes. As Muslims, Comorians believe all events occur according to *Allah's* will. This faith is expressed as fatalism, a belief that events are set in advance and that people are powerless to change them. Thus, Comorians often feel there is little they do to control their conditions. However, Comorians have a wonderful sense of humor. They enjoy a good joke and often exchange humorous light insults with friends.

Individual needs are subordinate to the family's needs. People expect to share in both the successes and failures of family members. Within the larger community, sharing one's wealth is a way to increase social standing and influence, both of which are highly desired. Comorians also desire material possessions, the acquisition of which is seen as the will of *Allah*. Gifts from relatives working in France are particularly prized.

Personal Appearance. Quite conscious of their appearance, Comorians dress well in public. The traditional Islamic emphasis on cleanliness is not taken lightly. Urban men usually wear Western-style shirts and slacks. They have a nice suit for formal occasions. Elders, rural men, and urban men going to a mosque more often wear the traditional white robe (*kandu*). Regardless of their outfit, men usually wear an embroidered cap (*kofia*). Shorts and a sloppy appearance are frowned upon. Most adults wear plastic flip-flops on their feet, although professionals wear shoes to work.

Women typically wear Western-style dresses with colorful patterns and nearly always carry a printed shawl (*leso*) that often serves as a head covering. They rarely wear pants except in cities. Anjouan women often wear a *shiromani* (traditional cloth) over their dresses (or skirt and blouse) and pulled up over their heads. Women on all Comorian islands occasionally wear a face mask made of ground sandalwood that is considered a cosmetic and a skin lightener.

CUSTOMS AND COURTESIES

Greetings. Comorian men shake hands at every opportunity. They offer a verbal greeting to women, as touching women in public is considered improper. In private, among relatives, men and women may kiss on the cheek. Women might also greet female friends with a kiss.

Comorians exchange several greetings, depending on the level of formality. The Shingazidja version of an exchange between social equals is *Edje* (an informal "Hello") followed by *Ye yapvo?* (What's up?). More formal terms are required for greeting elders, professionals, or strangers. *Bariza husha* (Good morning), *Bariza hazi?* (How is work?), and *Bariza masihu* (Good evening) are all common Shingazidja phrases. In fact, *Bariza* can precede anything to form a greeting.

On Anjouan, *Djedje?* (How how?) is the most common informal greeting, followed by *Habari?* (News?). Mohéli has similar greetings. Comorians also use traditional Muslim Arabic terms such as *Asalaam alaikum* (Peace be unto you). A positive response is often followed by the Arabic expression *Insha'Allah* (God willing) or *Alhamdul'illah* (Thanks be to God).

When calling out to someone, Grand Comorians precede the addressee's name with *Bo* (e.g., *Bo Mbaraka!*). Comorians often address people by titles such as *mwana hangu* (my child/brother) for good friends, *coco* for a grandmother, *fundi* for a teacher or craftsman, and *mzé* for an elder man.

Gestures. Comorians beckon by opening and closing a hand, palm facing down or out. They indicate direction with the index finger. Members of the same sex often hold hands while walking, but members of the opposite sex do not touch in public. After a shared joke, it is common to slap each other's hands and laugh. One expresses polite refusal by placing a hand on the chest while verbally thanking the offerer. Various other hand gestures are used in the course of conversation.

A child respectfully greets an elder with both hands cupped and extended while saying *Kwezi*. In response, the elder clasps the child's hands and says *Mbona*. The exchange is like asking for and receiving a blessing. On Anjouan, the elder raises the cupped hands to the child's forehead before saying *Mbona*.

Visiting. Comorians make informal daily visits to close friends; it is impolite to lose contact with any friend or family member for more than a few days. Extended families are large, so social obligations are numerous. People enjoy having guests in their homes. It is a special honor to host a foreigner.

Within a village, Comorians visit freely without prior arrangement. Time for visiting is usually set aside from 4 to 6 p.m. When one visits someone in another town, it is polite to give advance notice (*oulaha*) and thereby allow the hosts time to prepare. Hosts offer guests food and drink; refusing these refreshments is impolite. Weekday visits are short (an hour or less) but weekend visits can take the entire afternoon and include at least one meal. Visitors usually bring gifts only when returning from foreign travel.

Eating. Comorians eat cold leftovers, if anything, for breakfast, along with hot, sweet tea. The afternoon meal includes a sauce-covered starchy food, like cassava or green bananas, and meat. *Putu*, a hot pepper sauce, seasons all types of food. Dinner, the main meal, features a rice dish.

Affluent urban families eat at a table with Western utensils. Otherwise, families eat on a mat on the floor, everyone sitting cross-legged around several shared plates of food. Rural women usually eat apart from men, especially if guests are present. If a guest eats with the entire family, he or she is considered a very close friend. Comorians wash hands in a dish of water before and after eating. Utensils (generally spoons) are not uncommon, but people eat most often with the hand (right only). At large gatherings, food is served buffet-style and guests stand and eat from many plates. They take a handful of rice from a large common bowl and compress it with sauce before putting it in their mouths. No one eats until a short blessing has been offered.

Some urban men eat at restaurants when they cannot go home for lunch, but most Comorians (especially in rural areas) consider eating out embarrassing; it implies a person is poorly fed at home, has no family, or has marital problems.

LIFESTYLE

Family. Most Comorians live with or near their extended family. These families are especially large in villages where polygamy is common. Men are in charge of family finances and property, while women control the household. Men do little domestic work; they farm or fish for the family's subsistence. Women seldom leave home except to do chores or for holidays, although some urban women do have outside jobs. In general, women are not submissive and are proud of their traditional role.

Children use their father's given name as their own surname. At about age 18, sons might build themselves a *paillotte* (thatched hut) near the family home. They still eat at home and take part in family activities, but they sleep and entertain guests in their own dwelling. Daughters live at home and care for younger siblings until they marry. Elders live with the adult children when they can no longer live alone.

Dating and Marriage. Comorians do not date in the Western sense. A couple seen together is assumed to be romantically involved. Wealthy urban youth might go to dance clubs, but most socializing is discreet.

The most conspicuous social "statement" in Comoros is the Grand Marriage. Any man who wishes to be a full-fledged member of the community's group of elders, or *Notables*, must marry off at least his eldest daughter in a Grand Marriage. Maternal uncles can also give a Grand Marriage for nieces. This highly expensive, multiceremony event lasts more than a week. Families save for it for years and can expend their life's savings hosting the entire village for dances and meals. Guests offer expensive gifts, which are recorded so the recipients can properly reciprocate in the future. A Grand Marriage that involves much local purchasing benefits the community and so brings greater status to the host. The groom and both families also gain greater status for their roles in the wedding. The bride's father builds the newlyweds a house. If any problems occur, the husband must leave and the woman keeps the house.

The Grand Marriage began simply as a celebratory event, but it has taken on great social importance. On Grand Comore, rising competition between families to host better ceremonies has serious implications. Families save so much for the event that they spend less on basic needs. Some go into debt, which is passed on to future generations. Couples can marry without a Grand Marriage, and many do, but the respective families will not join the highest social class until a Grand Marriage is held.

Diet. Comorians mostly eat imported rice, usually topped by a fish or meat sauce. Plentiful local fish (tuna, barracuda, wahoo, and red snapper) are the main source of protein. Cassava (manioc root) is eaten fried, boiled, or grilled. Taro, green bananas, breadfruit, and potatoes (both white and sweet) are served often. Chicken, goat, and imported beef are popular meats. Islam forbids eating pork. Comorians love to spice their foods with *putu*. Most people have access to bread, and fruit is plentiful. Oranges, bananas, pineapple, papaya, mangoes, passion fruit, litchis, and others are eaten seasonally. Coconut is used in some sauces. Urban markets sell tomatoes, onions, cucumbers, and green beans. Cloves, cinnamon, saffron, and cardamom are indigenous spices. People drink water, tea, and fruit juice with meals.

Recreation. Soccer is the most popular sport and each town has a team that competes at the national level. Young men enjoy basketball and volleyball. There are no real movie theaters, but most villages have a video hut that plays videos for a small admission price. Television is available in towns with electricity, but only a French overseas broadcast is receivable. Comorian youth like to organize village dances. Musical tastes range from Western pop to reggae to traditional wedding dance music. Men spend free time walking, visiting, and playing games such as cards, dominoes, or *mdraha* (a pebble-and-board game). On weekends, families and friends might take a picnic to the beach.

The Arts. Islamic influences are quite visible in Comoros's cultural arts. Mosques are among the most ornate buildings on

Comoros

the islands and serve as the center of religious life. Most national holidays are Islamic holy days and are celebrated with folk music and dance. Gongs, tambourines, and five-stringed lutes are common traditional instruments. Recently, folk music has been mixed with reggae and other modern musical forms to create a style unique to the islands. Wood carving is perhaps the most prominent folk art. Artists carve decorative domestic items such as shutters, boxes, and candleholders.

Holidays. National holidays include New Year's Day (1 Jan.), the Lunar New Year, Labor Day (1 May), and Independence Day (6 July). Islamic holidays are based on the lunar calendar and so vary every year. During *Ramadan*, the holy month of fasting, people do not eat or drink from dawn to dusk, but nights are filled with activity and eating. At the end of the month is the most celebrated holy day, *Id-al-Fitr*. Comorians visit, share gifts, and feast all day long. Forty days later, *Id-al-Adha* honors Abraham for his willingness to sacrifice his son. Comorians celebrate Muhammad's birth for a month, and *Maulid*, his actual birthday, is a national holiday.

Commerce. Business hours are 8 a.m. to 6 p.m., but most offices close for at least two hours for lunch. Stores are closed Friday afternoon and Sunday. Pakistani and Indian merchants operate on a large commercial scale and have considerable economic influence. Open markets offer produce and meat, and stores have basic supplies; specialty items are only available in larger cities. Store prices are set, but market prices are negotiable. Comorians conduct business in their homes only if they are well acquainted.

SOCIETY

Government. The nation's president (currently Assoumani Azzali) is head of state and head of government. According to the 2001 constitution, Anjouan, Mohéli, and Grand Comore each elect an island president every four years. The national presidency must rotate among the island presidents, allowing each island to control the national presidency for one out of every three terms. Elections for the 33-seat Assembly of the Union are held every five years. The voting age is 18.

Economy. Comoros is called the Perfume Islands because it is the world's leading exporter of ylang-ylang, the oil base of many French perfumes. Comoros also exports vanilla, cinnamon, and cloves. With the once-valuable world market in these commodities rapidly shrinking, the country finds itself in a difficult situation. Other agricultural products include coconuts, bananas, and cassava (tapioca). Half of all food, and especially rice, a Comorian staple, is imported.

Some 80 percent of the labor force works in agriculture, which generates only 40 percent of the economy. There are no factories or other productive industries and few small businesses. The economy relies on foreign aid and remittances from Comorians who work abroad. Most people are subsistence farmers and do not earn a wage. Isolation and political instability have made severe economic conditions even worse. The currency is the Comorian *franc* (KMF).

Transportation and Communications. Comoros has few roads, but most are paved. Private, unregulated "bush-taxis" (usually small pickups or minibuses) connect all villages on each island. Moroni and Mutsamudu have city taxis. Boats ferry passengers and cargo between islands. The islands are connected by flights from Air Comoros airlines, which also flies to Madagascar. Grand Comore's international airport receives traffic from neighboring countries and Europe. Mutsamudu boasts a deepwater port for large ships.

A few private radio stations broadcast in addition to the main government station. The national weekly newspaper, *Al-Watwan*, is found in cities. Private homes rarely have telephones, but each island has public pay phones. Limited internet access is available. All international mail must go through Paris.

Education. The educational system is based on the French model, but it does not function effectively. Schooling is free and every village has an elementary school (*école primaire*), but teachers are poorly trained and often not paid. Only about 30 percent of all students finish elementary school, and even fewer go on to junior high (*collège*). A small number continue to high school (*lycée*) and take the graduation exam. There is a teacher-training college but no university. Formal education is geared toward academics. Because there are no state-funded technical training schools, many youths take apprenticeships with craftsmen instead of going to school.

Health. Malaria is the greatest health problem in Comoros, but diarrhea and intestinal parasites also are common. Although cities and towns have hospitals, basic supplies and equipment are lacking. Patients provide their own medications and food. A new public hospital in Mitsudjé (south of Moroni) offers the nation's best care.

DEVELOPMENT DATA
Human Dev. Index* rank . . . . 136 of 177 countries
  Adjusted for women. . . . . 108 of 144 countries
Real GDP per capita $1,690
Adult literacy rate . . . . 64 percent (male); 49 (female)
Infant mortality rate . . . . 77 per 1,000 births
Life expectancy. . . . . 59 (male); 62 (female)

AT A GLANCE

Events and Trends.
- The Assembly of the Union held its opening session in June 2004, two months after elections were held. The session marked the first time a national legislature had convened since the dissolution of the former legislature, the Federal Assembly, in 1999.
- Fifteen people were injured when security forces fired on a political march in Moroni in November 2003. The troops later claimed they thought the marchers intended to overthrow President Azzali. The marchers declared the event to be a peaceful protest against the Azzali government.

Contact Information. Permanent Mission of Comoros to the United Nations, 866 United Nations Plaza, Suite 418, New York, NY 10017; phone (212) 750-1637.

CultureGrams World Edition 2006

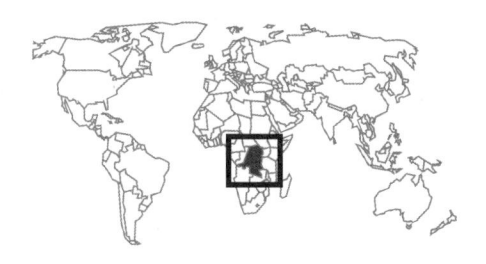

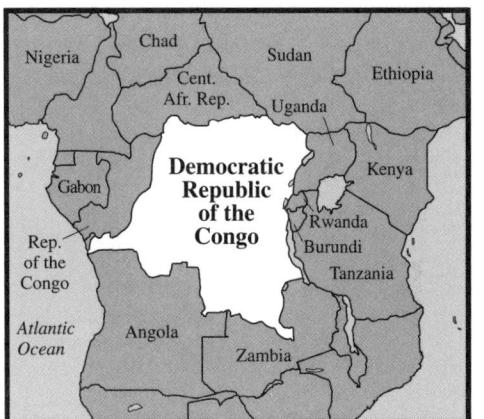

Democratic Republic of the Congo

BACKGROUND

Land and Climate. The Democratic Republic of the Congo covers 905,563 square miles (2,345,410 square kilometers), an area roughly the size of the United States east of the Mississippi River. Most of Congo lies within the vast lowland basin of the Congo River, the world's fifth largest river and one of Africa's most renowned waterways. The country features tropical rain forests in the central and western regions, grasslands in the north and south, and mountains in the east. The Mitumba Mountains, on Congo's eastern border, are part of Africa's Great Rift system. Other major mountain ranges include the Ruwenzori and Virunga, both in the northeast. The Garamba National Park, on Congo's northeastern border, shelters rare species such as the okapi and white rhino.

Congo is situated almost entirely within the equatorial zone. Temperatures in the eastern mountains and the southeastern savanna are cool from May to September, and they occasionally drop below freezing. The rain forests experience high humidity and warm temperatures throughout the year. Annual rainfall varies from 40 inches (100 centimeters) in the south to 80 inches (200 centimeters) in the central Congo River Basin. The dry season is from June to August, when southern temperatures cool. Otherwise, temperatures average between 70 and 85°F (20–30°C) all year.

History. Bantu peoples from western Africa migrated into the Congo Basin thousands of years ago. Several kingdoms existed in the centuries before Europeans arrived. The Kongo Kingdom controlled the southwest when the Portuguese arrived in the late 1400s. Little European intervention took place until the late 1800s, when Leopold II of Belgium formed an international trading company to exploit the Congo region's rich resources. The so-called Congo Free State, recognized by the Conference of Berlin in 1884, became, in effect, a feudal estate. Leopold enslaved the people and plundered the land. His harsh treatment of the region inspired Joseph Conrad's novella *Heart of Darkness*, Mark Twain's *King Leopold's Soliloquy*, and other publications. These eventually aroused an international outcry, and the Belgian Parliament was moved to seize the domain from King Leopold in 1908. The area then became known as the Belgian Congo.

After World War II, and following the trend in much of Africa, the Congolese negotiated with Belgium for their independence. In 1960, the new country was named the Democratic Republic of the Congo. The first prime minister, Patrice Lumumba, was a champion of the independence movement and is still revered as a hero today.

Soon after the first elections, the Katanga province in the southeast seceded, Lumumba was murdered by political rivals, and unrest spread throughout the region. UN troops could not restore peace. Mobutu Sese Seko eventually seized power in 1965 with help from Western nations. In 1971, he began an "Africanization" campaign and renamed the country the Republic of Zaire, after the Portuguese name for the Congo River. Zairians were told to reject foreign influences, and cities and individuals were required to replace their Christian or other foreign names with African names. Western-style clothing was banned.

Mobutu ruled a one-party dictatorship through the Popular Movement of the Revolution (MPR). He robbed the national treasury, living in luxury while ignoring the needs of his people. Under pressure from the political opposition in 1990, he lifted the ban on political parties and allowed a 1991 national political conference to draft a framework for a transitional

Congo

government and free elections. Unfortunately, Mobutu refused to accept most of the conference's decisions as binding. He did agree initially to the appointment of his chief rival, Étienne Tshisekedi, as prime minister. But when Tshisekedi began challenging Mobutu's authority, the two became locked in a power struggle. Much of the nation's infrastructure stopped working. Rampaging underpaid soldiers, corruption, and a collapsed economy plunged the country into chaos.

Total collapse was averted with minor political reform in 1994, but the war in Rwanda began to spill over into Zaire. One million Hutu refugees from Rwanda swelled makeshift camps in eastern Zaire. When armed Hutus from among these refugees began killing ethnic Tutsis in Zaire in 1996, the Rwandan government organized a Tutsi militia that quickly defeated Zairian troops helping the Hutus. The Tutsi militia soon allied with the forces of longtime Congo rebel Laurent Kabila. Most Hutu refugees were later sent back to Rwanda. Kabila's forces marched rapidly on major cities, often being joined by Zairian troops as they surrendered. In May 1997, Kabila entered Kinshasa to the relief of its war-weary citizens. Kabila declared himself president and changed Zaire's name back to the Democratic Republic of the Congo. Mobutu died in exile in September 1997.

Promises of democracy were tainted by Kabila's refusal to include Tshisekedi in his government. Kabila also banned political parties and suppressed political demonstrations. He justified his actions as necessary for stability, but people wondered whether they had exchanged one dictator for another. In August 1998, many of Kabila's allies accused him of corruption, nepotism, and an anti-Tutsi bias. They joined with ethnic Tutsi rebels in the east to spark a new round of civil war. Angola, Zimbabwe, and Namibia fought on Kabila's behalf, citing their own national interests in Congo. Rwanda and Uganda allied with the rebel movement, which soon controlled most of eastern Congo. The rebels split into two factions in 1999; Uganda backed one (the Movement for the Liberation of Congo, or MLC) and Rwanda the other (the Rally for Congolese Democracy, or RCD). All six nations and the two rebel groups involved in the war signed the 1999 Lusaka Accord, but its cease-fire was promptly violated.

In January 2001, Kabila was assassinated by one of his bodyguards, and Kabila's son Joseph took over as president. Though politically inexperienced, Joseph Kabila initiated peace measures that led to a treaty in December 2002. The war, which had cost a staggering three million lives, was declared over. Foreign troops left the country, and the leaders of the MLC and the RCD were granted positions in a transitional government in June 2003.

The 2002 peace agreement has held, but the government in Kinshasa has been unable to assert control over large sections of the country. Fighting between rival militias in eastern Congo has continued, with civilians often the targets of violence. Despite the efforts of UN peacekeepers to bring stability to the region, lawlessness and violence remain widespread.

THE PEOPLE

Population. Congo's population of 58.3 million is growing at 3.0 percent annually. More than 48 percent of the population is younger than age 15. Urban populations are growing rapidly. Kinshasa, the nation's capital and largest city, is home to at least seven million people.

There are more than two hundred distinct African ethnic groups in Congo; Bantu peoples account for the majority (80 percent). The three largest Bantu groups are the Mongo, Luba, and Kongo. The Mangbetu-Azande ethnic group is the fourth largest. These four comprise about 45 percent of the total population. Smaller groups include the Hutu, Tutsi, Pygmy, Nilo-Saharan, and various Afro-Asiatic peoples. The few foreigners who remain in Congo live mostly in Kinshasa's Gombe neighborhood. West Africans (known as Ndingari), Lebanese, and Indians form an important merchant class. Congo is also home to large populations of refugees who have fled conflicts in neighboring countries.

Most Congolese ethnic groups coexist in peace on a daily basis. They intermarry, live in mixed communities, and handle their differences without violence. Tensions rise when one group believes another has an advantage or level of control over something, but this rarely leads to fighting. Political foes have exploited such tensions in civil conflicts, especially in the east where opposing groups from other countries reside. This has been the prime contributor to the nation's ethnic violence.

Language. Broadcasting, local business, daily communication, and primary school instruction occur in one of the four national Bantu languages: Lingala (in Kinshasa and the west), Kikongo (in the west and southwest), Tshiluba (in central and southern Congo), and Swahili (in the east). Most people speak their own ethnic language as well as one or more of the four national languages.

Urban residents might speak a mixture of local languages and French. Under Mobutu, French was the country's official language. Used for international commerce, education, and government administration, it was spoken by only about 10 percent of the population. Lingala was used in the military and bureaucracy.

Religion. Eighty percent of the population is Christian: 50 percent is Roman Catholic and 20 percent belongs to various Protestant organizations. Another 10 percent participates in the indigenous Christian sect known as Kimbanguism, a Protestant offshoot established in the early 20th century by Simon Kimbangu. Many Christians also mix traditional animist beliefs with Christianity. About 10 percent of the people are Muslim, residing mainly in the east but also in Kinshasa. The remaining 10 percent follow traditional beliefs exclusively. Regardless of one's faith, religion plays an important role in daily life. People regularly attend worship services and participate in public prayers.

General Attitudes. Most Bantu peoples share a common cultural heritage, distinguished by their genuine concern for the welfare of others. They will nearly always share their food with others in need, no matter how little they may have themselves. Congolese are courteous and friendly. They laugh easily and enjoy living. Congolese are careful not to offend.

In many groups, speech is often abrupt. Congolese may make requests without a "Please" and accept help without a "Thank you." Indeed, Lingala was specifically promoted by Belgian colonialists for use in official institutions (such as the police force) because of its directness. Even if a person does not say "Please" (*Bolimbisi* in Lingala or *Tafadhali* in Swahili) or "Thank you" (*Botondi* in Lingala or *Aksanti* in Swahili), he or she will show gratitude or politeness through actions.

The desires of family, friends, and colleagues are expected to override personal concerns. Individualism at the expense of the family is frowned upon. Time is elastic; Lingala uses the same word, *lobi*, for both "yesterday" and "tomorrow." People are considered more important than schedules, and appointments or events may begin as much as an hour late.

Because there are so few wealthy people in Congolese society, they are accorded great respect. Education is highly valued and people work hard to find a way to pay for their children's schooling. The poor express education as a priority goal if their circumstances improve. Even children who live and beg in the streets of Kinshasa express a desire to go to school.

Personal Appearance. A neat and clean appearance is important to Congolese, even for those who live in poverty. They keep clothing clean and ironed. Western-style clothing is common in most urban areas. Congolese women wear a long, tailored dress, called a *pagne* or (in Lingala) *liputa*, made of a 5-yard length of fabric. Adults rarely wear shorts or immodest attire. However, children wear shorts. Some rural Congolese continue to wear traditional clothing or traditional items mixed with Western clothing.

CUSTOMS AND COURTESIES

Greetings. In urban areas, men and women generally shake hands, smile, and greet each other verbally. Upon entering a room for the first time, a person shakes hands with each individual. Close friends greet first with a handshake, followed by a hug and three alternating kisses to the cheek (men might simply touch alternating temples). The urban elite greet with the French term *Bonjour* (Good day). But *Mbote* (Hello) is more common. It is followed by *Sango nini?* (What's new?) among Lingala speakers. Outside urban areas, men usually do not shake hands with women but will shake hands with men. Some rural women greet men by clapping their hands a few times and bowing slightly. In the eastern and southeastern parts of the country, the Swahili greeting *Jambo* (Hello) is common.

Gestures. Pointing directly at a person with the index finger is impolite. One beckons by waving all fingers. Objects are passed with the right hand or both hands, never the left alone, as the left is traditionally reserved for personal hygiene. When shaking hands, if one's right hand is soiled, one offers the wrist instead. Hand gestures often accompany or replace verbal communication. For example, to indicate a bus or place is completely full, one taps the fist two or three times with an open palm.

Visiting. Visiting is important to the Congolese and hospitality is customary. Most visiting occurs in the home. Family and close friends often drop by unannounced, but strangers are expected to make arrangements in advance. When a person first visits a Congolese home, a gift is not appropriate. Visitors may give small gifts, such as food or an item for the house, after a relationship has been established. A visitor must be invited in before entering a home and he or she must be invited to sit before being seated. Good friends and extended family members have greater liberty to make themselves at home. Children are expected to greet each adult with a handshake and perhaps a kiss on the cheek. They usually are then dismissed while the adults socialize.

If a Congolese offers to share a meal, the guest is expected first to show reluctance to join the host's table. But the guest should ultimately accept the offer. Not doing so is impolite. Even if guests are not hungry, they should try some of the food as a gesture of goodwill. The Congolese often judge guests' sincerity by the way they eat. If hosts do not offer a meal, they usually serve refreshments. At the end of the visit, it is common for the host family to offer money to guests to pay for the taxi or bus ride home.

Eating. Congolese eat a light breakfast (perhaps tea and bread or leftovers from the day before) and a larger meal in the late afternoon or early evening. Meals usually are eaten with the fingers of the right hand only. When Congolese use utensils, they observe the continental style of eating; the fork is in the left hand and the knife remains in the right. Men and women eat from separate communal bowls. When sharing a bowl, people eat only from the space directly in front of them. Only the eldest is permitted to distribute meat with both hands to those eating the meal. Diners wash their hands before and after each meal.

LIFESTYLE

Family. Although family structure varies greatly between ethnic groups, they all place emphasis on group goals and family welfare. Large extended families usually live under the same roof or in a group of closely joined homes. In western Congo, families are mostly matriarchal; the mother's brother, rather than her husband, is the male with the greatest authority in the family. In other areas, patriarchal and polygamous families are common. Urban families, particularly among the more affluent, tend to be more patriarchal and include fewer relatives in the extended family. Women care for the children and household. Because many women sell produce and goods at the market, they are often the primary force in the informal economy. Children are expected to be polite and obedient to adults. They take on chores early in life, and older girls help their mothers with most daily tasks.

Dating and Marriage. Casual dating occurs only among the wealthy in large urban areas. Dating in rural areas usually leads to marriage. Traditionally, marriage is a family affair and is at least partly arranged by parents. A complete wedding usually includes three ceremonies: civil, church, and traditional. The process can take months and is very expensive. Prospective grooms must present the bride's family with gifts and money. This custom prevents many young people from marrying, at least in the traditional way.

Diet. Staple foods include cassava, rice, potatoes, bananas, yams, beans, corn, fish, peanuts, and various fruits and vegetables. Common fruits include mangoes, oranges, *pawpaws*, and coconuts. Sugarcane is also grown in Congo. People must purchase some perishable foods on a daily basis. Adequate supplies of food are hard to find in some areas, and malnutrition and starvation affect as much as 10 percent of the nation's children.

Recreation. Soccer is the most popular sport. Even urban girls are beginning to play. Rural Congolese enjoy gatherings that consist of dancing and drum music. Many urban people spend their leisure time socializing, dancing, or listening to music.

The Arts. Musical styles that originated in Congo are popular not only locally but also in many other parts of Africa and around the world. Among the most celebrated is *soukous*, which combines guitars, percussion, and horns in an upbeat, Latin-influenced dance rhythm. *Soukous* is also referred to as *rumba* or *lingala* and has generated related forms such as *kwasa kwasa* and *ndombolo*. Congolese musicians who have achieved international success include singers Papa Wemba and Koffi Olomide and bands Wenge Musica and Zaiko Langa Langa. Traditional music is still important, so instruments such as the *likembe* (a board with thin metal strips plucked with the thumbs) are common. Folk art has a strong presence throughout the country; popular forms include baskets, wood carvings, and jewelry. Painting and sculpture are concentrated in urban areas.

Holidays. Congo's holidays include New Year's Day, the

Congo

Commemoration of the Martyrs of Independence (4 Jan.), Easter, Labor Day (1 May), Independence Day (30 June), Parents' Day (1 Aug.), Veterans' Day (17 Nov.), and Christmas.

Commerce. Most people live in small villages and farm small plots of land or catch fish. In the cities, business hours vary. Businesses may open anytime from 7 to 9 a.m. and close between 4 and 5 p.m. Government offices close by 4 p.m. People purchase daily goods from open-air markets and small shops. In Kinshasa, most residents live by trading or working in the informal street economy.

SOCIETY

Government. President Joseph Kabila is Congo's chief of state and head of government. He has broad powers over all three branches of government. Under the terms of the 2002 peace agreement, leaders of the country's two main rebel groups, the MLC and the RCD, were installed as vice presidents in June 2003. Each group also received seven leadership positions in government ministries. An interim parliament will be in place until elections are held.

Economy. Political chaos and neglect have left Congo's economy in ruin, and most of the population lives in dire poverty. Although only about 3 percent of the nation's total area is under cultivation, the bulk of the labor force is involved in agriculture. Subsistence farmers produce staples such as cassava and corn. Other agricultural products include coffee (the nation's most important cash crop), sugar, palm oil, rubber, tea, bananas, and timber. The national currency is the Congolese *franc* (CDF), although the U.S. dollar is used for most major transactions.

Vast mineral deposits and other natural resources make Congo potentially one of the richest nations in Africa, but this potential remains largely untapped and even lost. Congo is one of the world's largest producers of diamonds, a resource that rebel groups and foreign armies used to fund their campaigns during the civil war. Congo could be a principal cobalt and copper supplier, but many of these mines are not functioning. Other abundant natural resources include oil, gold, silver, zinc, tin, uranium, bauxite, iron ore, coal, and timber. Even if goods are produced, they are difficult to transport. If peace can be established in all parts of the country, it may be possible for the government to use mineral wealth to build roads, refurbish and expand the railway, and support other development projects.

Inland waterways give Congo great potential for hydroelectric energy. It has one of the largest dams in Africa, the Inga Dam near the mouth of the Congo River. Power is transmitted more than 1,000 miles (1,600 kilometers) from the Inga to the southern copper-mining region—one of the world's longest direct-current hydroelectric transmission lines.

Transportation and Communications. The Congo River is the nation's major route for both commercial and passenger transportation. Congo's few paved roads are in disrepair and are difficult to travel. Many dirt roads are impassable in the rainy season. Public transportation in cities is all but nonexistent. Private trucks provide transportation, along with taxis in larger cities, but fuel is expensive and scarce. Hence, most people walk distances up to about 6 miles (10 kilometers).

DEVELOPMENT DATA
Human Dev. Index* rank . . . . 168 of 177 countries
    Adjusted for women . . . . 136 of 144 countries
Real GDP per capita $650
Adult literacy rate . . . . 74 percent (male); 52 (female)
Infant mortality rate . . . . 95 per 1,000 births
Life expectancy . . . . 40 (male); 42 (female)

Only wealthy Congolese have private phones, and there are no public phones. Telephone service shops offer access for a fee per minute. Radio messages are broadcast to areas where conventional telephone service does not exist. Mobile phone use is also beginning to be established in some of these areas. Shops offering internet access are becoming popular in Kinshasa. The press is free but faces some restrictions. As many as 15 newspapers are regularly published in Kinshasa. A number of television and radio stations also operate.

Education. Like the economy, the education system has faltered. Facilities and staff are lacking, and enrollment levels are very low. Few viable institutions exist in interior rural areas. A severe "brain drain" of the skilled and educated is undermining the country's ability to provide adequate teaching. However, the country's three public universities (in Kinshasa, Lubumbashi, and Kisangani) still operate alongside several private institutions.

Health. Congo has few physicians. Medical help is available in Kinshasa, but adequate health care is a serious problem in rural areas. Medical supplies are lacking throughout the country. International relief organizations or traditional healers are often the only sources of care. Malaria, yellow fever, AIDS, and cholera are widespread. Preventive medicine and mosquito nets are available but too expensive for the average person. Disease epidemics are common. Outbreaks of the deadly Ebola virus have occurred in rural areas where people come into contact with infected animals. Other diseases afflicting people include measles, hepatitis, tuberculosis, and sleeping sickness.

AT A GLANCE

Events and Trends.
- In March 2005, the International Criminal Court (ICC) in The Hague, Netherlands, held its first hearing on war crimes allegedly committed during the Congolese civil war. The ICC was established in 2002 to try cases of genocide, war crimes, and crimes against humanity.
- After nine Bangladeshi soldiers in the UN peacekeeping force were killed in Congo's northeast in February 2005, a peacekeeper offensive resulted in more than 50 deaths among the militia believed to be responsible. More than 13,000 UN troops are stationed in Congo.

Contact Information. Embassy of the Democratic Republic of the Congo, 1726 M Street NW, Suite 601, Washington, DC 20036; phone (202) 234-7690.

© 2005 ProQuest Information and Learning Company and Brigham Young University. It is against the law to copy, reprint, store, or transmit any part of this publication in any form by any means without written permission from ProQuest. This document contains native commentary and original analysis, as well as estimated statistics. The content should not be considered strictly factual, and it may not apply to all groups in a nation. *UN Development Programme, Human Development Report 2004 (New York: Oxford University Press, 2004).

CultureGrams
People. The World. You.

ProQuest Information and Learning Company
300 North Zeeb Road, P.O. Box 1346
Ann Arbor, Michigan 48106 USA
Toll Free: 1.800.528.6279
Fax: 1.800.864.0019
www.culturegrams.com

Arab Republic of Egypt

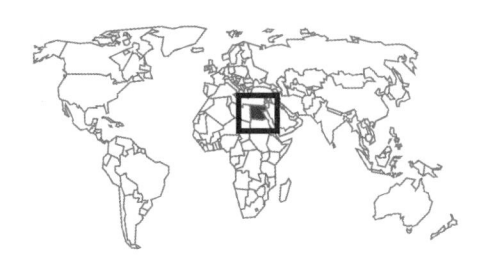

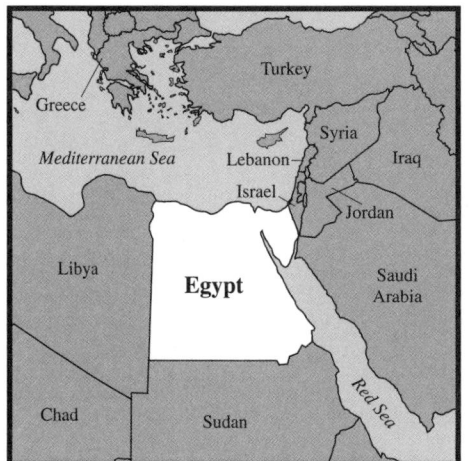

BACKGROUND

Land and Climate. Covering an area of 386,662 square miles (1,001,449 square kilometers), Egypt is just larger than the states of Texas and New Mexico combined. Most of Egypt is dry and arid desert, spotted with small, inhabited oases. Part of the Sahara Desert is in southwestern Egypt. The Nile River, the longest river in Africa, runs north through Egypt into the Mediterranean Sea, providing a fertile delta area and the lifeblood for the country. Before the Aswan Dam was built in southeastern Egypt, the Nile Delta was subject to seasonal flooding. Now the dam regulates water flow and allows for more predictable crop planting, although it has also caused some environmental problems.

Summers are hot and humid with daily high temperatures reaching 108°F (42°C) in some areas. Winters have a moderate climate, with lows near 40°F (4°C). Annual rainfall ranges from virtually nothing in the desert to about 8 inches in the Nile Delta. In the spring, the *Khamasiin* (a hot, driving, dusty wind) blows.

History. The earliest recorded Egyptian dynasty united the kingdoms of Upper and Lower Egypt around 3110 B.C. Today's Egyptians are proud of the Pharaonic heritage that followed. In 525 B.C., Egypt came under Persian control. Alexander the Great's conquest in 332 B.C. brought Greek rule and culture to Egypt. As one of the first nations visited by Christian missionaries (the apostle Mark), Egypt was Christianized within three centuries and followed a Coptic patriarch. Because of Byzantine religious persecution, Egyptians welcomed the Muslim invasion that began in A.D. 642. By the eighth century, Egypt had become largely Muslim. For centuries, Egypt was ruled by successive Islamic dynasties, including the Ottoman Turks in the 16th century. France's Napoleon invaded in 1798, but Egypt was still associated with the Ottoman Empire until World War I.

France and Britain vied for influence over Egypt throughout the 19th century, during which time Viceroy Muhammad Ali successfully governed and reformed Egypt (1805–48). France and Britain exerted increasing control over Egyptian affairs after the completion of the Suez Canal in 1869, and Britain made Egypt a protectorate in 1914. Although given official independence in 1922, the Egyptians regard 1952 as the beginning of their real independence. In that year, a revolution overthrew the British-supported monarchy. Gamal Abdel Nasser ousted the first president of Egypt in 1954 and became an influential leader and statesman. Nasser was responsible for a number of reforms, including universal education, land reform, nationalization of major industries and banks, and Egyptian leadership of the Arab world. He governed until his death in 1970.

During Nasser's tenure, Egypt fought two wars that involved Israel (1956 and 1967) and lost the Sinai Peninsula in 1967. Upon Nasser's death, Anwar el-Sadat became president. His government orchestrated a war (1973) in which Egypt regained a foothold in the Sinai. Sadat liberalized economic policy and signed a peace treaty with Israel (1979) that returned the Sinai to Egypt. In 1981, Sadat was assassinated by Muslim fundamentalists who disagreed with his policies. He was succeeded by Vice President Hosni Mubarak.

Fundamentalists, led by the Islamic Brotherhood, began pressing in 1991 for an Islamic state that would shun Western art, music, literature, and values. Their quest to overthrow Egypt's secular state has included pressing the government to restrict freedom of expression, liberal education, and secular

Egypt

law; committing violent acts against Coptic Christians, Western tourists, and government installations; and making assassination attempts. Although crackdowns have been harsh, Islamic extremists remain the greatest threat to the government.

Egypt is recognized as a leader among Arab nations, both politically, culturally, and economically. Egypt was the first Arab nation to sign a peace treaty with Israel (1979). President Mubarak has taken an active role in the peace process with Israel. He also has reached out to former enemies, such as Sudan and Iran, to improve relations and regional stability. Domestically, his government has reduced inflation, liberalized trade restrictions, moved to privatize state companies, deregulated some industries, and implemented other reforms that have led to economic growth. Mubarak was reelected to a fourth presidential term in June 1999. His government continues to steer a middle road that maintains Egypt's traditions while adapting to modernity.

THE PEOPLE

Population. Egypt's population of 76.1 million is growing annually at 1.8 percent. The majority (90 percent) descends from both native Egyptians and Arabs who conquered Egypt in the seventh century. The rest of the population is composed of Nubians (who live in southern Egypt), Bedouin nomads, Greeks, Italians, and Syro-Lebanese.

Nearly all Egyptians live on the arable land along the Nile River because the rest of the country is mostly desert. Cairo, the capital, has between 14 and 16 million inhabitants. An exact count is impossible due to migrants, informal residents (as many as 5 million), and other factors. Alexandria claims more than 3 million residents. About one-third of Egyptians are younger than 15 years old.

Language. Arabic is the official language of Egypt. Written Arabic differs from the standard Egyptian dialect (Cairene) spoken in daily life. Egyptians are enormously proud of Cairene Arabic and its rich expressions. Wordplays, jokes, clichés, and riddles in Cairene Arabic are an integral part of Egyptian culture. Arabic is the language of instruction in schools. English is also a part of the national curriculum.

Religion. More than 90 percent of all Egyptians are Sunni Muslims. Islamic theology is rooted deeply in the minds, hearts, and behavior of the people. Islamic scripture, the *Qur'an* (Koran), is considered the final, complete word of *Allah* (God). Muslims accept and revere all major Judeo-Christian prophets from Adam to Jesus, but they proclaim Muhammad to be the last and greatest prophet. Although Egypt is officially a secular state, Islamic principles guide the nation's laws, business relations, and social customs.

Islam also permeates daily life through dress and dietary codes, frequent prayers, and constant references to *Allah's* will or blessings. Muslims are obliged to pray five times daily, always facing Makkah, Saudi Arabia. On Friday, the Islamic day of worship, men gather in the mosque to offer *Jum'a* (the Friday midday prayer) and to hear a sermon; women pray at home or in a separate part of the mosque. During the rest of the week, prayers may be performed elsewhere (at home, work, or even in public places).

Coptic Christians, whose religion dates back to the first century A.D., are Egypt's largest religious minority. Their population is estimated to be more than seven million.

General Attitudes. Egyptians generally prefer a relaxed and patient life, characterized by the phrase *Ma'alesh*, meaning roughly "Don't worry" or "Never mind." This term is used to dismiss concerns or conflicts that are inevitable or not serious. Both business and leisure activities are governed by the concept of *Insha'allah* (If *Allah* wills), which dominates all aspects of Muslim life. Patience also influences life, as the people view events in an expanded time frame.

Egyptians are expressive and emotional. They are known for their sense of humor, which has helped them endure difficult living conditions with great composure. Part of Egyptian humor is a love for riddles (which are especially common during the Muslim holy month of *Ramadan*), jokes, sarcasm, and wordplay. Egyptians often identify with community groups to the point that personal needs become secondary to those of the group. Generosity is an integral part of this sense of community, and homelessness is fairly rare, even in crowded Cairo.

Society is engaged in a serious debate over its future course; that is, both secularists and Islamists are battling for the hearts of Egyptians. Secularists desire Egypt to remain a secular state in which multiculturalism, a free press, and diversity can flourish. The Islamists see greater devotion to Islamic principles in schools, government, and the arts as the answer to Egypt's problems with poverty, government corruption, and other social ills. Both sides of the debate have strong followings throughout the country.

Personal Appearance. Both modest Western-style clothing and traditional attire are common in urban areas. Business representatives usually wear business suits. Trends toward fundamental Islamic practices have led many women to return to stricter observance of Islamic dress codes. Most rural women cover the hair and body (except the face and hands) completely when in public. Rural men often wear the *gallebeyya* (a long, dress-like robe). Many men also wear a head covering, particularly if they are from the south. A beard coupled with the traditional *gallebeyya* can be a sign of religious faith. Visitors to a mosque remove shoes before entering and wear clothing that covers the entire body.

CUSTOMS AND COURTESIES

Greetings. Warmth in personal relations is important to Egyptians, and greetings are often elaborate. Because social classes play a key role in society, phrases used for greetings depend largely on the differences between the individuals' social classes. Generally, however, friends of the same sex shake hands and kiss on the right and left cheeks. If the greeting comes after a long absence, the kisses may be repeated more than once and even end with a kiss on the forehead. Close relatives may greet members of the opposite sex with a hug and a kiss on the cheek, particularly if they have not seen each other for a long time or if they are not close in age.

A man greets a woman with a handshake only if the woman extends her hand first. Otherwise, the greeting is verbal. One does not use first names unless invited to do so. Good friends exchange first names in informal settings, but they may add a title to the first name in formal settings. To thank someone for a compliment, one responds with an equally respectful compliment on the same subject or wishes *Allah's* blessings.

Gestures. Physical distance between members of the same sex is closer than in the United States and much farther apart between members of the opposite sex. In fact, good friends of the same sex may walk hand in hand in public. Yet, except for married or engaged couples that walk arm in arm, a man does not touch a woman in public. It is impolite for the bottom of one's foot to point at another person, and therefore one does not prop the feet on a table or chair in the presence of others. Walking in front of a praying person is also considered impolite.

Visiting. Because personal relationships with friends and relatives are so vital, visiting is one of the most important pastimes in Egypt. Not visiting for a long period is a sign of the relationship's insignificance. Married children often visit parents on Fridays and holidays.

It is common for guests to take a gift to the host. Gifts usually reflect the guest's social and financial position in relation to the host as well as the closeness of the relationship. Guests typically are modest about the gift's significance and try to leave it behind without saying a word. However, the host may choose to open the gift, especially if it is food (sweets or fruit), and express his or her gratitude. One passes and receives gifts with either both hands or only the right hand, not the left. Alcohol, prohibited by Islam, is not given as a gift to Muslims. Business visits usually begin with light conversation over coffee or tea to establish trust and confidence.

Eating. Egyptians prepare elaborate and expensive meals when they have guests. Sometimes a person will not eat everything on the plate because leftover food is a symbol of abundance and a compliment to the host for providing so well. Or, in restaurants, food is left as a sign of wealth (indicating one can afford to leave food behind). Egyptians eat finger food with the right hand. When they use Western utensils (mostly in large urban areas), they eat in the continental style, with the fork in the left hand and the knife in the right.

LIFESTYLE

Family. Families are extremely important in Egypt. In most homes, a young woman is protected by her brothers and may even be accompanied by them in public. Traditionally, a man's honor is based on how well he protects the women in his care. In rural areas, a young woman may discontinue her schooling when she comes of age. It is customary for extended families, including families of brothers and sisters, to live under the same roof. However, increased urbanization is changing this tradition toward a home with only a nuclear family. Still, families maintain close ties, and cousins are often as close as siblings. The thought of putting the elderly in a rest home is repulsive to most Egyptians; children expect to support their parents in old age. Parents often play a key role in planning the future of their children; their influence ranges from the choice of profession to the selection of a mate. Egyptians value this support as a source of emotional security.

Dating and Marriage. Although attitudes are changing in Westernized circles, dating is not widespread. Public displays of affection are frowned upon. Moral purity is highly valued in a woman and is usually a key requirement in the marriage contract. Traditionally, marriages were arranged between heads of families, often with little input from the couple involved. Now, individuals have more say as to whom they wish to marry. Because marriages join not just two people but two families, both families are heavily involved in wedding preparations. Housing is expensive and hard to acquire in the cities; engagements may last until the couple saves enough money for their own apartment and furnishings.

A family-reform law enacted in 2000 allows women to initiate divorce on grounds of incompatibility; previously, it was nearly impossible for women to get a divorce on any grounds. Under the law, women are not entitled to alimony and must return any money given at the time of marriage.

Diet. Egyptians eat rice, bread, fish, lamb, chicken, turkey, and stuffed vegetables. *Tahina* (sesame-seed paste), tomatoes, yogurt, and cucumbers are also eaten with meals. The *Qur'an* prohibits the consumption of pork and alcohol. Traditional foods include flat Egyptian bread (*aish*) and fava beans prepared as *foul* or *ta'miyya*. Meat is expensive and eaten only occasionally. Bread is inexpensive and eaten with every meal. The word for "bread" is the same as the word for "life" (*aish*).

Recreation. Soccer is the national sport. Sport clubs offer urban residents tennis, swimming, and horseback riding. Many urban Egyptians enjoy going to the movies; a wide variety of Egyptian and foreign films are shown. In the Middle East, Egypt is well-known for its dedication to cultural arts—evident in its cinema and television programming. Many enjoy watching television, even in rural areas. While wealthy men socialize in private clubs, men of all other classes go to coffee shops to play table games such as backgammon and dominoes, have refreshments, and relax with friends. Many coffee shops cater to specific groups or professions (barbers, plumbers, etc.). Women socialize in the home.

The Arts. Egypt continues to be the hub of culture and art for the Arab world and an important influence abroad. Music, dance, literature (oral and written), film, and traditional crafts are highly developed and draw on eclectic influences. Revered singers such as Umm Kalthum and Abd al-Halim Hafiz blend a poetry of longing and emotion in a traditional style; such songs may extend for hours. Copts, Nubians, Sufis, and others have their own styles and instruments. Young people enjoy pop, *shaabi*, and *al-jil*—blends of Western, folk, and Arabic music. Belly dancing and its music are deeply rooted in Egyptian culture and are performed at weddings and other events.

Egyptians have always loved poetry. Genres such as the short story and novel emerged following a literary renaissance at the turn of the century. Contemporary writers, such as 1988 Nobel Prize–winning novelist Naguib Mahfouz, continue a rich literary tradition. Egypt is the main producer of Arabic-language films and television shows. Artisans practice carpet weaving, calligraphy, metalwork, glasswork, and woodwork.

Holidays. The Western (Gregorian) calendar is used for all business and government purposes, but the lunar calendar is used to calculate the dates of Muslim holidays. The lunar year is about 11 days shorter than the Western calendar year, so the Gregorian dates for holidays differ from year to year. During the month of *Ramadan*, Muslims go without food or drink from sunrise to sundown and eat only in the evening. '*Aid al Fitr* is a three-day feast held at the end of *Ramadan*. Another major religious holiday is '*Aid al Adha* (Feast of the Sacrifice), which commemorates Abraham's willingness to sacrifice his son. Muslims also celebrate the prophet Muhammad's birthday (*al-Mawlid*). National holidays include Labor Day (1 May), Anniversary of the Revolution (23 July), Armed Forces Day (6 Oct.), and the lunar New Year. *Sham el-Nasseem* is celebrated at the beginning of spring.

Commerce. Business hours are generally from 8:30 a.m. to 1:30 p.m. and from 4:30 to 7 p.m., Saturday through Thursday. Government offices are open from 8 a.m. to 3 p.m. In the summer, many workers take a longer lunch break because of the heat and then work later in the cool evening. Shops are generally closed on Friday afternoon, but work is not prohibited. Street vendors are common, and people in high-rise apartments will often lower a basket from balconies to purchase something from a passing salesman. Also common are outdoor *souks* (markets), where businesses sell their products and

Egypt

prices are negotiable. During the month of *Ramadan*, business hours are often cut back by an hour, and work slows down in many areas. However, many shops open again in the evening.

SOCIETY

Government. The Arab Republic of Egypt is divided into 26 governorates. The president (currently Hosni Mubarak) is chief of state. The prime minister (currently Ahmed Nazif) is head of government. The president serves terms of six years and appoints the prime minister. The legislative branch consists of a 454-seat People's Assembly and a 264-seat *Shura* Council. Because the *Shura* Council acts as a consultative body, the People's Assembly is the primary legislature. Ten representatives in the People's Assembly are appointed by the president; the remaining 444 are elected to five-year terms. In the *Shura* Council, 176 members are elected to six-year terms and 88 are appointed by the president. Citizens are required to vote at age 18. Mubarak's party (the National Democratic Party) dominates the People's Assembly, but some opposition parties and independents also hold seats. Religious-based political parties are banned.

Economy. More than one-third of Egyptians are employed in agricultural pursuits, such as growing corn, wheat, cotton, rice, barley, and fruit. Egypt also produces cheese and dairy products. Chief industries include food processing, textiles, chemicals, cement, petroleum, and metals. Egypt exports cotton, petroleum, yarn, and textiles. Important natural resources are oil, natural gas, lead, and other minerals. The Suez Canal is a vital source of income. Tourism is the country's most important industry. Threats and acts of violence have occasionally shaken tourist confidence, but the government has renewed an emergency powers law that gives security forces expanded powers. With economic reform Egypt has lowered inflation and improved the climate for international investment. Still, large sections of the population remain impoverished. Women earn only one-fourth of the nation's income. The currency is the Egyptian pound (EGP).

Transportation and Communications. The River Bus (water taxi) is a common means of public transportation along the Nile River. In urban areas, people travel by car, bus, and taxi. Cairo has a modern, efficient subway, the first in the Middle East; unfortunately, with such a large population, Cairo's transportation system is still overburdened. The Nile River is used for transporting goods and people as well as for recreational tours. Egyptians often travel between cities by train, bus, and even taxi. There is also a domestic airline. In rural areas, some still travel by donkey or camel.

Applying for and getting a phone are expensive and take a long time; people without phones make calls from a central phone office. Mobile phone access is widely available; internet access is growing. There are five main television stations and seven radio networks.

Education. The government subsidizes free education through the university level, although not everyone is able to take advantage of these subsidies. In 1962, Nasser abolished fees for state-run institutions and guaranteed employment to all university graduates. These policies have significantly increased the number of students and college graduates. But

DEVELOPMENT DATA
Human Dev. Index* rank . . . . 120 of 177 countries
  Adjusted for women. . . . . 99 of 144 countries
Real GDP per capita $3,810
Adult literacy rate . . . . 67 percent (male); 44 (female)
Infant mortality rate . . . . 34 per 1,000 births
Life expectancy . . . . 67 (male); 71 (female)

they have also strained resources (physical facilities, textbooks, equipment, and teachers) already in short supply. Many college graduates are unable to find work outside the government, which is currently the nation's largest employer. Many men (even those working in government) have to learn a trade to supplement their family's income.

Most children who begin primary schooling now also complete it. A significant number go on to secondary school. The building of more schools in rural areas has opened some educational opportunities to the poor. Universities are located in most urban centers, and nearly half of all students are women.

Health. Egypt has many excellent doctors, but medical facilities are limited, especially in rural areas. Typhoid, bilharzia, and other diseases are endemic in Egypt. A UN program sends doctors and volunteers into villages for one-week clinics (medical caravans) to provide hygiene education (such as how to brush teeth), examine children, dispense medicine, give shots, administer first aid, and teach family planning. The government has expanded this program by establishing a hospital in every small city. In addition, a daily four-hour satellite television broadcast covers health topics from fertility to newborn care. Private hospitals for the wealthy are equipped with the latest medical technology.

AT A GLANCE

Events and Trends.
- In December 2004, Egypt released a convicted Israeli spy in exchange for six Egyptian students accused of plotting to kill Israeli soldiers. The prisoner swap was viewed as a sign of improving ties between Egypt and Israel. Relations had deteriorated since 2000 as a result of the escalation of the Palestinian-Israeli conflict.
- The military funeral of longtime Palestinian leader Yasser Arafat was held in Cairo in November 2004. The funeral, which was not open to the public, was attended by foreign dignitaries. Arafat died while undergoing medical treatment in France. He was buried in the West Bank town of Ramallah, where thousands of mourners gathered.
- More than 30 people died in series of simultaneous bomb attacks targeting Israeli tourists on Egypt's Sinai Peninsula in October 2004.

Contact Information. Embassy of Egypt, 3521 International Court NW, Washington, DC 20008; phone (202) 895-5400. Egyptian Tourist Authority, 630 Fifth Avenue, Suite 2305, New York, NY 10111; phone (212) 332-2570; web site www.egypttourism.org.

© 2005 ProQuest Information and Learning Company and Brigham Young University. It is against the law to copy, reprint, store, or transmit any part of this publication in any form by any means without written permission from ProQuest. This document contains native commentary and original analysis, as well as estimated statistics. The content should not be considered strictly factual, and it may not apply to all groups in a nation. *UN Development Programme, Human Development Report 2004 (New York: Oxford University Press, 2004).

CultureGrams
People. The World. You.

ProQuest Information and Learning Company
300 North Zeeb Road, P.O. Box 1346
Ann Arbor, Michigan 48106 USA
Toll Free: 1.800.528.6279
Fax: 1.800.864.0019
www.culturegrams.com

Republic of Equatorial Guinea

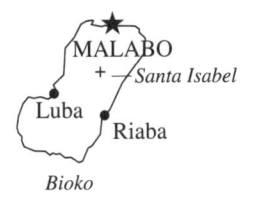

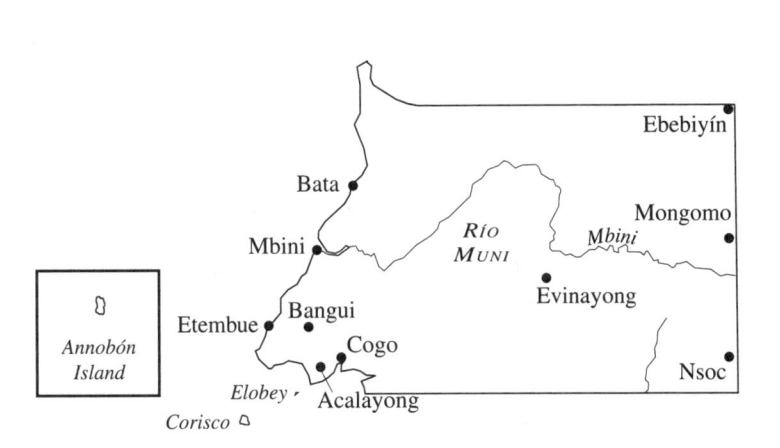

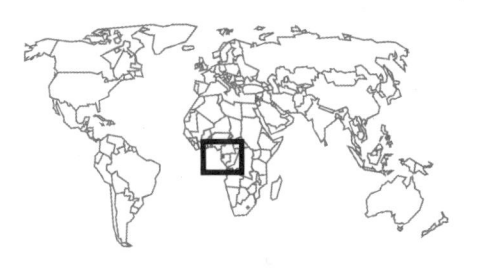

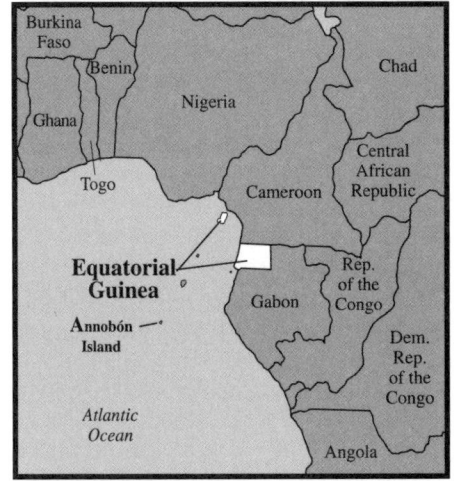

BACKGROUND

Land and Climate. About the size of Maryland, Equatorial Guinea consists of a small continental portion and several small islands. It covers 10,830 square miles (28,050 square kilometers). Río Muni, the continental portion, lies between Gabon and Cameroon on Africa's west coast just north of the equator. Equatorial Guinea's largest river, Río Mbini, divides this section of the country roughly in half.

Bioko is Equatorial Guinea's largest island and the site of the nation's capital city, Malabo. The island is about 19 miles (30 kilometers) from the Cameroon coast, far enough north of Río Muni (about 95 miles, or 150 kilometers) to make transportation and communication difficult. Bioko has fertile volcanic soil and a 9,865-foot (3,007-meter) peak, Santa Isabel. The nation's considerable oil reserves are also at Bioko. Annobón Island lies 370 miles (590 kilometers) southwest of Bioko. Corisco Island is just off the southwest corner of Río Muni.

The entire country is covered by dense rain forest and has a humid climate. The average temperature is 80°F (27°C). Bioko is generally hotter and wetter than Río Muni.

History. The histories of Bioko and Río Muni are strikingly different. Río Muni remained isolated from contact with the West until the 20th century. However, the people of the Bubi ethnic group on Bioko retreated upland as the natural harbor of Malabo changed from Portuguese to Spanish to British and then back to Spanish hands between the late 1400s and early 1900s. During this time, Malabo was primarily a slave-trading center, except during the British occupation of 1827 to 1843. During the first half of the 1900s, Spain developed the infrastructure to support cocoa plantations on the island. Because of that system, Bioko has a higher income and literacy rate and has better health care than the mainland.

Conflicting claims to the mainland were settled in the Treaty of Paris (1900), which set the borders for Río Muni and gave it to the Spanish. The lives of the indigenous people (mostly Fang) of Río Muni were not really affected until the 1920s when Europeans established coffee production there. Río Muni and Bioko were joined artificially by the Spanish as Spanish Guinea.

In 1959, Spanish Guinea was made part of Spain, and all indigenous peoples gained full citizenship. Representatives were sent to the parliament in Madrid. In 1963, a measure of autonomy was granted and a joint legislative body was set up. On 12 October 1968, full independence for Equatorial Guinea was granted peacefully, and Francisco Macías Nguema became the first president in a multiparty election.

An attempted coup and attacks on Spanish citizens in Malabo were among events that led to tighter political controls. In 1972, Macías assumed complete control over the government and declared himself president for life. He deteriorated into a brutal ruler, and all government functions completely eroded except for internal security. The economy existed only due to Spanish, Cuban, Soviet, and Chinese assistance. Under Macías, about one-third of the population was either exiled or executed. Twenty thousand Nigerians left, which greatly disrupted Bioko's cocoa production, the nation's primary source of income. Churches, banks, and schools ceased to operate.

On 3 August 1979, Teodoro Obiang Nguema Mbasogo, the commander of the national guard and a nephew of Macías, staged a successful coup, and Macías was executed after a trial attended by international observers. Obiang Nguema assumed the presidency but also ruled with tight control. Equatorial Guinea struggled to overcome the darkest years of trouble. In

Equatorial Guinea

a single-candidate election in 1989, Obiang Nguema was elected to a seven-year term as president. The country legalized a multiparty system in a new 1992 constitution, but elections were not held until 1996. Opposition parties had posted presidential candidates but withdrew in protest over polling irregularities. Obiang Nguema was therefore reelected to another seven-year term in an unopposed victory.

In 1998, after the discovery of oil on Bioko, calls for Bioko's independence grew louder, rebel factions attacked military bases, and tensions between the Bubi and Fang became rather serious. The government cracked down on militants and their sympathizers. Dozens of Bubi were arrested. Meanwhile, legislative elections in March 1999 gave the ruling Democratic Party of Equatorial Guinea (PDGE) 75 of parliament's 80 seats. The opposition accused the PDGE of rigging the election and demanded that the results be annulled. When the government refused, the five opposition members refused to sit in parliament.

Prior to December 2002 presidential elections, the government jailed nearly 70 opposition party members for conspiracy to overthrow the president, though they argued that Obiang Nguema had fabricated the charges to eliminate his political rivals and assure his victory in the elections. When opposition leaders withdrew from the elections, citing fraud, Obiang Nguema won the contest with nearly 100 percent of the vote.

Equatorial Guinea's oil production has increased more than ten times since the 1990s, and it continues to rise. The sudden influx of oil revenue has given Equatorial Guinea one of the fastest-growing economies in the world. However, critics of the government argue that corruption has prevented most people from seeing the benefits of the economic boom.

THE PEOPLE

Population. The population of about 523,000 is growing at 2.4 percent annually. Roughly half of Equatoguineans live in rural areas. The country's two largest cities, Malabo (on Bioko) and Bata (on the coast of Río Muni), each have between 50,000 and 100,000 residents. The population is young, with 42 percent younger than age 15.

Equatorial Guinea's predominant ethnic group is the Fang (80 percent of the population), whose traditional territory is Río Muni. The Fang, a Bantu people, migrated from what is now southern Sudan over a 250-year period and have inhabited Río Muni and surrounding areas for about 150 years. The traditional territory of the Bubi (15 percent) is the island of Bioko. The Bubi came to Bioko from the shores of Cameroon and Río Muni. Annobón Island is inhabited by Angolan people, brought there by the Portuguese.

Language. Because Equatorial Guinea was colonized by Spain, Spanish is the official language and the primary language of business, government, public schools, and urban life. However, it usually is not spoken in the home. French, spoken in surrounding countries, is increasingly influential, and Pidgin English is common in the markets. Local languages, none of which are written, prevail in villages. If a transaction requires writing, Spanish is used. However, most traditional transactions do not require writing, and people have good mental skills for keeping track of such dealings. Fang is spoken in Río Muni, and Bubi is spoken in rural areas of Bioko. Annobónese is spoken on Annobón and Coriscan on the island of Corisco. Ndoe and Kombe are spoken by their respective groups.

Religion. Due to colonization, the population is 83 percent Roman Catholic. While people actively honor the Catholic calendar (celebrating holidays and saints' days), they commonly mix traditional African practices with Western rites. An example is the Fang *defunción*, a three-day celebration to honor the passing of the dead, which occurs four to six months after the death. Clan members may come from all over the country to take part in traditional dancing and feasting and to hear the *nvet* (a traditional stringed rhythm instrument) player create a bridge to ancestors through his song, which assists the soul's passage to the beyond. Traditional healers continue to play a religious role, and polygamy is accepted among many who profess Catholicism. Other Christian denominations do exist, and some Muslims and Baha'is live in the country.

General Attitudes. Equatoguineans are warm, friendly, and generous. Mainlanders generally are known as being more gregarious than islanders. However, all ethnic groups love a celebration. Village life, in particular, revolves around the celebration of life's passages (birth, marriage, death) and the Catholic calendar.

Generosity is both in people's nature and part of clan obligation, which requires a person to share gains with members of the extended family and support those in difficult circumstances. This generosity provides for a type of social security for the elderly and disabled, but it also makes the improvement of an individual's economic situation difficult.

Traditional religious beliefs, mixed with Catholicism, focus heavily on the unexplainable and the mysterious. Fate is accepted without question. Equatoguineans highly respect elders, village officials, and political figures. They take pride in the clan, village, and nation.

Personal Appearance. The average person commonly wears secondhand Western clothing, sold at low cost by Christian missionaries or in the market. Dress in urban areas is more formal than in villages. Traditional clothing is highly valued but too expensive for most people. Rural Equatoguineans reserve their best colors and fashions for celebrations and church. Women generally prefer to wear dresses rather than pants or shorts, even when working their fields in the rain forest.

CUSTOMS AND COURTESIES

Greetings. Greetings are accompanied by enthusiastic handshaking and sometimes a small bow. Equatoguineans greet each person in a small group. If the hand is dirty, one extends a wrist or forearm. In cities, Spanish greetings such as *¡Buenos días!* (Good day) and *¡Buenas noches!* (Good evening) are common. Acquaintances may greet women with a light kiss on each cheek.

In villages, handshakes with local greetings are more common. For example, *Mbolo* (Hello) is common on the continent. Rural Fang women often greet each other by pressing both forearms together (palm to elbow), bowing slightly at the hips and knees, and issuing a long, low, guttural *Sah* (Hello). The Fang, who consider their ethnic group a family, also ask each other where they are going or have been. This custom of keeping track of family members is such a habit that the Fang often ask the question of non-Fang people.

In cities, the use of titles and proper honorifics is important when addressing someone. People commonly use *Señor* (Mr.), *Señora* ("Ms." or "Mrs."), or an official title with a person's last name. Respected older people may be addressed as *Don* or *Doña* with their first name. Rural people use first names, which often have a Spanish origin, or African nicknames when addressing one another.

Equatorial Guinea

Gestures. Equatoguineans use hand gestures during conversation and for many of life's situations. For example, the hands pressed together in prayer position and opened up as if empty can mean anything from "nothing left" to "such is life." Drawing the fingers closed with the palm facing down indicates "come here." In Fang, *ka* means "no" and is often accompanied by a finger wagging back and forth close to the face.

People stand close to one another, often touching while they talk. Holding hands or locking arms while talking or walking is common for men and children. Such physical contact is not appropriate for members of the opposite sex. Even husbands and wives do not display affection in public.

Visiting. Equatoguineans are very social, and visiting is an important way to establish and maintain social contacts. A visit is considered a gift in itself, but people also might take fruit or bread to their hosts. Visits usually are returned. People drop by unannounced in villages but might make prior arrangements in the cities. Arranged visits rarely begin on time, as the concept of time is more flexible than in Western countries.

Hosts may offer visitors water, beer (in the city), *tope* (palm wine), *malamba* (cane alcohol), or a meal. Although one may refuse refreshments, it is polite to at least taste some of the food offered. However, since Equatoguineans often have personal taboos concerning a particular food, hosts are not offended by a refusal to eat a certain item.

When one enters a village, it is polite to visit the *abaa*, a hut made of bamboo and palm leaves, and greet the elderly men who socialize there and work on crafts.

Eating. Urban residents tend to follow Spanish eating customs, with a light breakfast of coffee or tea and bread, a main meal at midday, and a light dinner between 8 and 10 p.m. In rural areas, people often eat only a light midmorning meal and supper just before dusk. When invited for dinner among the Fang, guests might eat alone in a reception room reserved for the male head of household, or senior male family members may eat with the guests. Women serve the meal and then eat in the kitchen with the children.

People use Western utensils for most meals. Only in very informal settings do they eat food with their hands. Then, even peanut pastes and sauces, bundled in banana leaves tied with melango fiber, become finger foods. It is improper to drink from a common container; therefore, when glasses are not available, individuals pick an appropriate type of leaf and form a leaf cup.

LIFESTYLE

Family. As in many parts of Africa, polygamous extended family structures still dominate Equatorial Guinea's rural life, while nuclear families are more common in cities. "The family" actually refers to the entire clan, which once also implied a village. The power structure revolves around gender, age, and clan status. This system leaves women with limited power, although they do control the production of food. The kitchen is the center of family life. Each wife in an extended family has her own kitchen (used for both sleeping and cooking) or her own cooking-fire area, where she is the authority figure. The husband has his own building, and wives take turns spending time with him there. Wives also share responsibility for child care and household chores.

Cousins are considered siblings; aunts and uncles are considered mothers and fathers. Children must obey their elders, even older siblings, but especially their various mothers and fathers. It is not uncommon for children to be sent to live with other family members. Large families are prized as a sign of wealth, health, and virility; having six or more children is common. Women grow the food, cook, clean, serve, haul water and firewood, and raise the children. Men are responsible for hunting, building and maintaining houses, making tools and baskets, and clearing the *fincas* (agricultural plots in the forest) twice a year.

Dating and Marriage. Young urban Equatoguineans like to date by going to late-night discos. Young people in rural areas more commonly meet at large celebrations that involve other clans, but discos are becoming popular for them as well.

Many marriages are still arranged. When two people marry, a three-day wedding celebration of dancing and feasting marks the woman's acceptance into her husband's clan. This celebration is preceded by negotiations between the two families on the bride-price (paid to the bride's family), which can be extremely high.

Because of the expense, young people often enter into a common-law relationship and begin having children before they are actually married. Any children born before the wedding technically belong to the woman's father, but the groom can take the children when he pays the bride-price and formally marries. In the rare case of divorce, the bride-price must be returned to the husband, who retains the children, while the woman returns to her family.

Diet. Cassava and other starchy roots, which adapt well to rainforest agriculture, are the main staple foods. Fermented cassava (*yuca* in Spanish, *mbo* in Fang) sticks are eaten with nearly every meal. Meat is the preferred source of protein when available and may include anything from goats and chickens to rodents, monkeys, and snakes. Fish is also a traditional favorite. Peanuts, another staple, are prepared in many different ways, such as peppery leaf-roasted rolls, peanut brittle, or sauce. A favorite dish is ground squash seeds made into a curd similar to tofu. Papaya, pineapples, bananas, plantains, and other fruits are abundant. Cities are more influenced by Spanish cuisine and have access to seafood, bread, and pasta.

Recreation. Social visiting is the primary leisure activity in Equatorial Guinea. The expression *Voy a pasear* (I am going visiting) describes a common weekend pastime. Drumming, dancing, and singing are also popular activities during holidays and family events. Soccer is the only group sport, but it is very popular and every village has a soccer field. A traditional strategy board game is played with rocks and seeds.

The Arts. Dances frequently accompany festivals and holidays. Community members perform dances that represent a theme related to daily life, such as courtship. A small ensemble of musicians accompanies dancers by playing drums, wooden xylophones, thumb pianos, and the *nvet* (see Religion). Popular music in Malabo and Bata consists of imported styles, such as *soukous* from the Democratic Republic of the Congo and *makossa* from Cameroon. Decorative masks are an important part of festival traditions. The nation's painters and sculptors create a blend of traditional and modern styles. Bata and Malabo have cultural centers that hold art exhibits and music and theater performances.

Holidays. National holidays include New Year's Day, Easter (including Good Friday), Labor Day (1 May), Corpus Christi, the President's Birthday (5 June), Armed Forces Day (3 Aug.), Constitution Day (15 Aug.), Independence Day (12 Oct.), Immaculate Conception Day (8 Dec.), and Christmas. Easter is the most important holiday, with a week of celebrations from

▼ **AFRICA**

Equatorial Guinea

Palm Sunday to Easter Sunday. Independence Day is marked by large gatherings, singing, and food.

Commerce. Generally, hours for businesses, banks, and government offices are 7:30 a.m. to 2:30 p.m. Stores operate from 8 a.m. to 1 p.m. and from 4 to 7 p.m. Bargaining is uncommon, even at open-air markets. In rural areas, traditional patterns such as clan obligations have a substantial impact on business negotiations.

SOCIETY

Government. Equatorial Guinea is a unitary republic. The constitution provides the president (currently Teodoro Obiang Nguema Mbasogo) with extensive powers; he is commander-in-chief of the military and minister of defense. The president is elected to a seven-year term and appoints all cabinet members and the prime minister (currently Miguel Abia Biteo Borico), who has only limited powers. The unicameral House of Representatives of the People has 80 members elected to five-year terms. Parties in opposition to the ruling PDGE include the Convergence for Social Democracy Party and the Popular Union. Each of the nation's seven provinces has a governor appointed by the president. When not in conflict with constitutional law, tribal laws and customs are usually honored by the judicial system.

Economy. About 90 percent of Equatoguineans are engaged in subsistence agriculture. The main agricultural exports are cocoa beans and coffee. Cocoa production, which dropped in the Macías years, has revived. Equatorial Guinea's conversion in 1985 to West Africa's regional currency, the *CFA franc* (XAF), provided a much needed stepping-stone out of economic isolation.

Timber harvesting is relied upon to attract foreign capital. However, most timber is shipped out as raw logs; very little manufacturing takes place in Equatorial Guinea. More significant growth has been achieved in the petroleum industry. Major international firms began offshore drilling in the 1990s, and oil now accounts for 90 percent of export revenue. The potential for increased trade with neighboring countries exists for local food crops such as cassava, taro, pineapples, and coconuts. Spain is Equatorial Guinea's main trading partner. Other major partners include China, Japan, the United States, and France.

Gross national product per capita figures are artificially high, reflecting the country's oil revenue. Most farmers do not earn a wage. The wealthy hold most assets, and corruption keeps new oil wealth from benefiting local people.

Transportation and Communications. For common people, the accepted mode of transportation is walking. Few Equatoguineans can afford bicycles. "Bush-taxis," which are privately owned cars for hire, are the only transportation to rural areas. They collect passengers at the market and leave when full; there are no schedules. For many people, a ride in a "bush-taxi" is a special event for which they save. There are two or three weekly flights between Bata and Malabo, as well as to other countries in the region. There is also a weekly flight to Spain.

A radio-phone system connects district capitals, but people otherwise do not have access to telephones. Television and radio broadcasts are controlled by the government-owned media company. Communication is often hindered by problems with the power system. Electricity in Malabo is sporadic, and local power stations can supply the city with only one-third of its electricity needs. There are no national or private newspapers or magazines.

Education. While the majority of all children attend primary school, only about 10 percent are enrolled in secondary school. Malabo offers an academically oriented agricultural vocational school. Bata has a post-secondary vocational program that offers courses in agriculture, metalworking, and carpentry, but placement is limited. The Catholic Church has made important contributions to primary and secondary education, as well as to health.

Health. The population's primary health problems are malaria, diarrhea (among young children), and intestinal parasites. Availability of Western health resources is generally poor, with very few doctors and clinics. In most parts of the country, people still rely on traditional tribal medicine to provide effective care for many health problems.

DEVELOPMENT DATA
Human Dev. Index* rank . . . . 109 of 177 countries
Adjusted for women. . . . . 86 of 144 countries
Real GDP per capita $29,780
Adult literacy rate . . . . 93 percent (male); 76 (female)
Infant mortality rate . . . . 87 per 1,000 births
Life expectancy. . . . . 48 (male); 51 (female)

AT A GLANCE

Events and Trends.
- In March 2004, police in Zimbabwe impounded an airplane that had flown more than 60 alleged mercenaries from South Africa. Shortly after, Equatorial Guinean authorities arrested another 15 men and charged them with collaborating with the group in Zimbabwe on a plot to overthrow President Obiang Nguema. Trials for the two groups were held between August and November 2004. In Equatorial Guinea, fourteen men were found guilty of charges linked to the coup plot; one man died in custody amid allegations of torture. At the Zimbabwe trial, only the group's leader and two pilots were found guilty of coup-related charges. The others were sentenced for violating immigration and aviation laws.
- Equatorial Guinea is now the third largest oil producer in sub-Saharan Africa, behind only Nigeria and Angola. The nation produced roughly 350,000 barrels of crude oil per day in 2004.

Contact Information. Embassy of Equatorial Guinea, 2020 16th Street NW, Washington, DC 20009; phone (202) 518-5700.

© 2005 ProQuest Information and Learning Company and Brigham Young University. It is against the law to copy, reprint, store, or transmit any part of this publication in any form by any means without written permission from ProQuest. This document contains native commentary and original analysis, as well as estimated statistics. The content should not be considered strictly factual, and it may not apply to all groups in a nation. *UN Development Programme, Human Development Report 2004 (New York: Oxford University Press, 2004).

CultureGrams
People. The World. You.

ProQuest Information and Learning Company
300 North Zeeb Road, P.O. Box 1346
Ann Arbor, Michigan 48106 USA
Toll Free: 1.800.528.6279
Fax: 1.800.864.0019
www.culturegrams.com

CultureGrams 2006 World Edition

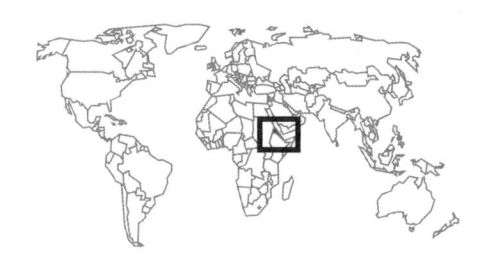

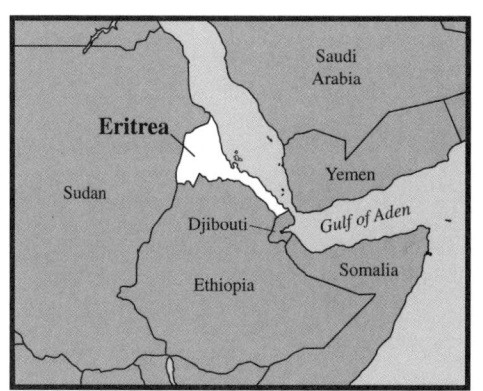

State of Eritrea

BACKGROUND

Land and Climate. Eritrea sits on the Horn of Africa, bordering the Red Sea. It consists of the mainland and the Dahlak Archipelago. Covering 46,842 square miles (121,320 square kilometers), Eritrea is a bit larger than Pennsylvania. Central highlands rise to an elevation of more than 8,000 feet (2,500 meters) near the east coast, forming an escarpment of the Great Rift Valley. Western elevations are lower. In the southeast, the Danakil Depression lies below sea level; it has been the location of some of the world's hottest recorded temperatures.

The semiarid highland climate is mild and dry; temperatures rarely fall to freezing. Precipitation in the rainy season (June–September) varies by elevation and is not always dependable. Rain also falls between October and February on foothills and lowlands east of the northern escarpment, creating an extra growing season. In recent years, dry conditions have cut crop production. Given a history of recurring drought in some areas, officials expect sustainable agriculture to be possible only with improved irrigation.

History. Eritrea's original inhabitants were joined successively by people from the Nile River area and by Egyptians, Cushites, and Semites. The region later was influenced by Greeks, Turks, Egyptians, and Persians. The name *Eritrea* comes from the Greek *erythrea* (red).

After 1885, Italy colonized the region, establishing some industries and confiscating land suitable for farming. Asmara, the capital, still displays a distinct Italian influence. Italian forces eventually conquered Ethiopia as well in 1935. Ethiopia's emperor Haile Selassie I requested intervention from the League of Nations. In response, the Allied powers of World War II eventually halted Italy's advances and forced its surrender at Asmara in 1941.

Britain governed Eritrea as a protectorate until 1952, when the United Nations recommended a federation with Ethiopia. Ethiopia moved to annex Eritrea as a province in 1962. The Eritrean Liberation Front organized initial resistance against the annexation, and the Eritrean People's Liberation Front (EPLF) later led the movement. After Marxists deposed Haile Selassie I in 1974, the liberation movement gained popularity. Over the next two decades, the EPLF steadily captured territory and arms. It also set up schools, industries, and a hospital. By 1990, it occupied the strategic port city of Massawa.

Ethiopia's dictator Mengistu Haile-Mariam was eventually forced from power by groups trying to overthrow him. The EPLF took advantage of the ensuing chaos to capture Asmara in May 1991 and force the Ethiopian army to abandon Eritrea. Independence from Ethiopia was declared on 24 May 1993, after 98 percent of Eritreans voted for it. Eritrea joined the United Nations and other organizations and established diplomatic ties with many countries. In 1993, Ethiopia (under new leadership) and Eritrea signed an Agreement of Friendship and Cooperation to establish good relations and trade links, and to grant Ethiopia sea access through Massawa.

Eritreans were soon working to repair their war-damaged nation. In 1996, Eritrea was billed as an African phenomenon because of enormous strides in revitalizing the economy, cleaning up cities, cracking down on crime, and establishing a democratic society—without Western aid. In 1997, Eritrea began drafting a new constitution, introduced its own currency (the *nakfa*), and held regional elections in preparation for future national elections.

Relations with Ethiopia soured over Eritrea's adoption of a new currency (Eritrea stopped using Ethiopia's currency) and

Eritrea

then over a border dispute in May 1998. Eritrea crossed into Ethiopian territory and touched off a border war that killed hundreds of people in a few weeks. The fighting spread as animosity and nationalism grew to a feverish pitch. Trench warfare raged along the border, claiming thousands of lives. All diplomatic efforts failed to end the bloodshed and economic upheaval.

By June 2000, some 100,000 people had been killed in heavy fighting on both sides. Finally, the two nations signed a peace treaty brokered by the Organization for African Unity (OAU). Although an international court of arbitration in The Hague, Netherlands, ruled on the placement of the nations' boundaries, Eritrea and Ethiopia have failed to reach consensus on the issue. A matter of national pride for both countries, the border dispute continues to cloud their relations.

THE PEOPLE

Population. Eritrea has a population of 4.4 million, growing at 2.6 percent annually. About 85 percent of Eritreans live in rural areas. The largest ethnic groups are the highland Tigrinya (50 percent) and the Tigre (33 percent) of both highland and lowland areas. The remaining population is composed of Saho, Bilen, Afar, Hadareb, Kunama, Nara, and Rashaida minorities.

Language. Eritrea has no official language. Tigrinya, Arabic, and English are all used in government. Tigrinya is spoken by highlanders and is related to Tigre, spoken in the western and eastern lowlands. Tigrinya and Tigre, like Arabic, are Semitic tongues. Arabic, native to the Rashaida, is widely used in commerce. Minority groups speak their native languages but are familiar with Tigrinya or Arabic. Except for the Rashaida and Hadareb (whose language is called To Bedawi), the language names are the same as their respective ethnic group name.

Religion. Most Eritreans follow Islam or Christianity (roughly 40 percent each), but indigenous religious beliefs are still widespread. Although Roman Catholics and Protestants are found among the more affluent and Westernized Eritreans, most Christians are Orthodox. The Eritrean Orthodox Church has its own bishop but maintains ties to the Ethiopian Orthodox Church. The church is conservative, uses the Ge'ez language (an ancient Sabian language) in prayers and worship, and incorporates both monks and married priests in its clergy.

Whereas most Christians reside in the highlands, Sunni Muslims tend to inhabit the lowlands. They include nearly all of the Saho, Nara, and Rashaida, as well as many Tigre and Kunama. Muslims adhere to Islam's Five Pillars, which include professing *Allah* as God and Muhammad as his prophet; praying towards Makkah, Saudi Arabia, five times daily; making a pilgrimage at least once to Makkah; giving alms; and fasting from sunup to sundown during the month of *Ramadan*.

During the war for independence, fighters (30 percent were women) of different religions often married. These intermarriages and the unity of religious leaders during war are factors in the country's religious freedom and tolerance. By law, neither religion nor ethnicity can be the basis of a political party.

General Attitudes. Eritreans are optimistic, hardworking, committed people who love their country and their independence. National pride was at stake in the recent war with Ethiopia and is one reason why resolution was difficult to reach. Eritreans generally respected the EPLF, whose leaders worked to promote cooperative effort, equality among ethnic groups, and equal participation by women. While crime is often a major problem for societies in transition, it is less common in Eritrea. Although Eritreans believe in community cooperation and friendliness, they also value self-sufficiency. Eritreans are willing to face war, poverty, and other hardships as they build their nation. Indeed, the war with Ethiopia increased Eritreans' willingness to sacrifice; people accepted the economic and personal setbacks as a matter of patriotism. At the same time, many Eritreans are disappointed that in the years since independence, presidential elections have been postponed and the People's Front for Democracy and Justice (PFDJ), which evolved from the EPLF, remains the only party in government.

Personal Appearance. Western-style clothing is popular in urban areas. Rural dress is more traditional. Many highland Christian women wear white cotton dresses with a woven border at the hem, or embroidery on the bodice and skirt, and a shawl with a matching border. Their hair customarily is braided in tight, narrow rows up front but is left free and fluffy behind. Highland men wear a long-sleeved, knee-length white shirt over white trousers. They also wear white cotton shawls with colored borders. Work clothing or "daily dress" is less decorated and is made of heavy off-white cotton.

Muslim men wear *jalabiyas* (long gowns) and embroidered caps with turbans. Women usually cover their dresses with black or colorful cloth called *luiet*. The cloth can be loosely draped or tailored. Some Muslim women wear veils that cover all of the face but the eyes. Throughout Eritrea, women use henna as a skin conditioner, hair tint, or dye to decorate their hands and feet.

CUSTOMS AND COURTESIES

Greetings. Greeting styles vary by region and ethnic group. Highlanders greet with a handshake. Nudging right shoulders during a handshake is common between male villagers and former fighters. Urban dwellers of the opposite or same sex who are relatives or acquaintances shake hands and "kiss the air" while brushing alternate cheeks three times. Verbal greetings depend on the time of day but nearly always involve an inquiry about one's well-being. *Salaam* (Peace) is a general greeting or parting phrase. Muslims grasp and kiss each other's right hands, ask *Kefelhal?* (How are you?), and answer *Hamdellah* or *Marhaba* (both roughly mean "Fine").

Friends call one another by nickname. Eritreans address older people by title (equivalents of "Mr.," "Mrs.," "Miss," "Aunt," "Uncle") and name. They use professional titles in formal situations. The use of second-person plural shows respect. A person's given name is followed by the father's name, so that Mhret, the daughter of Tesfai, is called *Mhret Tesfai*.

Gestures. Eritreans use the right hand for eating and making gestures. They also use it alone or together with the left hand to pass or receive items. A hand held high is a greeting, whereas a hand waved back and forth indicates a negative response. Snapping fingers shows agreement. To beckon, one waves all fingers with the palm facing out. Pointing with a finger to indicate location is fine, but pointing at people is impolite. In discussion, old men often gesture with their fly whisks to emphasize a point or indicate direction. Seated girls keep their legs uncrossed—knees touching and covered—with elbows on their knees as a sign of respect.

Visiting. In Eritrea, relatives and good friends visit each other often and without invitation. Guests may be offered food or asked to join the family for an upcoming meal, which they may accept or politely decline. They are always served tea or coffee. The latter involves a prescribed sequence of roasting and pounding the coffee beans. The coffee is then boiled, heavily sweetened, and served in small cups. Three customary rounds might be accompanied by fresh popcorn or *himbasha* (a bread made with cumin and raisins). People enjoy the prolonged conversation encouraged by this coffee ceremony.

When visiting on special occasions, townspeople often take villagers gifts of coffee or sugar; villagers take urban dwellers local produce, a chicken, food (such as bread), or firewood (which is precious due to soil erosion and deforestation).

Special events require an invitation and involve women and men socializing separately. Wedding guests take *ingera* (sour bread) for the feast or they contribute to its cost. *Ga'at*, a thick barley porridge, is served at gatherings to welcome new babies. When someone dies, friends and relatives gather for the burial. For at least 12 days, they attend the bereaved family, cook their meals, divert their attention with games and entertainment, help receive many visitors, and collect money for the family.

Eating. Among highlanders, adults and children eat separately. Among other Eritreans, families eat together, although children eat separately when guests are present. If the guests are close friends or relatives, the hostess usually eats with them. However, if she does not know the guests well or they are more distant relatives, she serves the guests during the meal and must either eat before the guests arrive or after they leave.

To begin each meal, the oldest man takes a piece of bread, blesses it, and offers some to each person. Diners eat with the right hand from a large communal tray set on a low table. Each person eats only the portion directly in front of him or her. In Christian homes, mealtime etiquette is stressed because it is said that heaven is watching. Restaurants offer traditional and Italian foods. Tipping is common only in hotel restaurants.

LIFESTYLE

Family. For Eritreans, the family as a group is more important than any of its individual members. Each member will sacrifice as necessary for the good of the group or for future generations. A family unit typically consists of parents, four or more children, and frequently grandparents. Respected for their wisdom, the elderly are always cared for by adult children. After marriage, a son and his wife usually live with his parents for at least two years before establishing their own home.

Village men are farmers. Women work on the farm and do all household work. Chores, especially food preparation, can be lengthy. Some urban women work outside the home and employ house servants.

Village homes, usually made of stone, have thatched or metal roofs and concrete or dirt floors. City dwellings, made of stone or brick, have metal roofs, tiled floors, and water and electricity. Nomadic and seminomadic peoples (Afar, Hadareb, Rashaida, and Tigre) have different lifestyles than the settled population. Accordingly, their homes are portable or built with whatever materials they find when they settle temporarily. Regardless of the style, homes are kept clean and neat.

Dating and Marriage. Families arrange nearly all marriages in Eritrea. Among the monogamous Tigrinya, parents suggest marriage partners to establish family alliances. The couple involved usually makes the final decision to marry, although some rural couples may not be acquainted before they wed. The bride is often some 10 years younger than the groom; in cities, she will have completed secondary school before getting married.

The wedding celebration involves at least a week's food preparation and requires a month to brew *suwa* (a beer) and *miyess* (a fermented drink made of honey). Following the morning church ceremony, the bride's family sponsors a banquet. After a display of gifts from both families, the couple enters the banquet to share a meal with their guests. Some urban couples also cut a tiered wedding cake. For two or three weeks, the couple stays at home while relatives provide their meals.

Among Muslims, wedding festivities include the bride's arrival on a camel and a feast where guests sit on floor mats to eat from bowls. Muslim men may have as many as four wives if they can provide for all equally. Due to the economic burden, this practice is diminishing.

Diet. Eritreans traditionally enjoy a wide variety of foods, but culinary skills and food levels are not yet what they were before the war. The preferred meal is meat (chicken, beef, or goat or sheep mutton) cooked with onion, garlic, red pepper, spices, and clarified butter. *Shuro*, a typical meal of garbanzo bean flour and spices, is similarly cooked. Lentils or other vegetables are served. Spicy main dishes, eaten for lunch or dinner, are complemented by *ingera* (also called *taitah*), a sour pancake bread made of *teff* (a local grain), millet, or corn flour fermented in water. Breakfast may be tea served with honey and unleavened *k'itcha* bread, bits of bread (*fit fit*) and yogurt, *ga'at* and yogurt, *himbasha* bread, or leftovers.

Orthodox Christians eat no animal products on Wednesdays and Fridays and during Lent (the 40 weekdays from Ash Wednesday to Easter). Muslims abstain from pork and alcohol.

Recreation. Frequently, entire families participate in annual church festivals, make social visits, and help relatives prepare food for weddings or babies' baptisms. Urban dwellers often return to their home villages for such celebrations.

In Asmara, espresso coffee bars are popular meeting spots, especially for men. Villages have tea shops. Women visit mostly in each other's homes. They also get together to weave baskets used to store and serve food.

Eritrean boys enjoy soccer, bicycle racing, a game similar to field hockey, and a game that is similar to horseshoes but uses stones. Both boys and girls play *gebetta*, a strategy game played with pebbles on a playing surface they create by making depressions in the ground. Girls enjoy drumming and dancing.

The Arts. As one of Africa's oldest inhabited nations, Eritrea has a rich tradition of oral literature. Storytelling and oral poetry have been an integral part of Eritrean culture for centuries, and poets and storytellers are revered. Illuminated manuscripts and other religious art survive from the Early Christian period. Artisans produce leather and woodworking, jewelry, and pottery. Early Christian, Arab, Turkish, Italian, and other influences have added to traditional architectural styles. Music, singing, and dance play an important role in daily life and at festivals or during holidays.

Holidays. Eritrea's holidays include New Year's Day (1 Jan.), International Women's Day (8 Mar.), Independence Day (24 May), Martyr's Day (20 June, a day for remembering war dead), and the Anniversary of the Start of the Armed Struggle (1 Sept.). Christian holidays include Christmas (7 Jan.); *Timket*, the baptism of Jesus, also in January; *Fasika* (Easter); and *Meskel*, the finding of the True Cross by St. Helena, in late September.

Muslims celebrate *Eid el Fitr* at the end of *Ramadan*, the holy month of fasting in which they go without food and drink

Eritrea

each day from dawn to dusk. Forty days later, they observe *Eid el Adha* to mark the completion of the pilgrimage to Makkah and to honor Abraham for his willingness to sacrifice his son. *Eid Milad el-Nabi* honors the prophet Muhammad.

Commerce. Government offices and businesses are open weekdays, 8 a.m. to 5 p.m., with a two-hour closing for lunch. Most are also open Saturday mornings. Shops and markets are open mornings and late afternoons. Before people conduct office business, they converse socially for several minutes. Bargaining is officially discouraged in favor of posted prices. Although this rule is observed in urban shops, bargaining occurs frequently at open-air markets.

SOCIETY

Government. After independence, the EPLF installed the Provisional Government of Eritrea (PGE). In 1994, the EPLF separated from the PGE and became a political party, the People's Front for Democracy and Justice (PFDJ). A Transitional National Assembly consists of the PFDJ's 75-member Central Committee, 15 representatives of Eritrean nationals living abroad, and 60 members from the Constituent Assembly drafting the constitution. The latter group comes from the regional assemblies elected in January 1997. The Transitional Assembly is mandated to govern until national elections. Elections scheduled for 1998 were delayed by the war; a date for new elections has not been set. President Isaias Afewerki continues to be the transitional head of government. The voting age is 18.

Economy. Although Eritrea has a potentially strong economy, it remains one of the world's poorest nations. War crippled its economy and severely damaged its workforce. About 80 percent of all people depend on subsistence agriculture for their living. Rural food levels are often inadequate. Drought and landmines affect agricultural production. The country relies heavily on remittances from Eritreans living abroad. Current exports include sesame seeds, gum arabic, leather shoes, beer, and refined petroleum. A steel plant makes steel with melted down tanks.

Potentially productive economic sectors include tourism, marine resources (fishing and petroleum), trade (Eritrea is situated on the world's busiest shipping lane), and mining for gold, copper, silver, marble, potash, and iron ore. A liberal investment code allows foreign capital to supplement local efforts. Solar and other technology is being explored as an alternative to wood and charcoal. Eritrea's currency is the *nakfa* (ERN).

Transportation and Communications. Major roads crossing the country are under repair; most city streets are paved, while country roads are not. Public buses serve even remote villages and are the most common transport within cities. Taxis are available in urban areas.

Telephones are used mostly by government and business offices. Public phones are found at central urban locations. The government administers the postal system and provides radio and television broadcasts. It also prints weekly English and semiweekly Arabic and Tigrinya newspapers.

Education. Eritrea's education system is not yet extensive, and few children are able to attend school. Of those who do attend, less than one-quarter finish grade six. Few graduate from sec-

DEVELOPMENT DATA
Human Dev. Index* rank . . . . 156 of 177 countries
   Adjusted for women . . . . 127 of 144 countries
Real GDP per capita $890
Adult literacy rate . . . . 68 percent (male); 46 (female)
Infant mortality rate . . . . 76 per 1,000 births
Life expectancy . . . . 51 (male); 54 (female)

ondary school. Nevertheless, education is highly valued. The national goal is to have mandatory free education up to seventh grade that will emphasize skills needed to develop rural areas. To that end, schools are under repair or construction, teachers are in training, and instructional materials are in development. For the first several years, students are taught in their native tongue but can study English and Arabic or Tigrinya. From the sixth grade on, instruction is in English. Adult literacy and education classes are available for adults who wish to finish elementary and secondary school.

Health. Maternity and child care are high priorities of the Primary Health Care Programme (PHCP) because the population is young and growing rapidly. Common health problems include malnutrition, malaria, parasitic and upper respiratory infections, diarrhea, and other diseases.

Comprehensive medical services are centralized in a few hospitals. The plan is to have a hospital in each of the eight provinces, with healthcare centers at the subprovincial, district, and village levels. Doctors and nurses are in short supply, but the PHCP has posted more than 1,500 healthcare workers to various communities. The University of Asmara runs the College of Health Sciences to train nurses.

AT A GLANCE
Events and Trends.

- Ethiopia's Prime Minister Meles Zenawi announced in November 2004 that his government had reconsidered its position on its border dispute with Eritrea and that it would be willing to accept a 2003 ruling by an international court of arbitration. Ethiopia had opposed the ruling because it gave Eritrea control of the town of Badme, the flashpoint for the nations' war. Though not strategically or economically significant, Badme became a symbol of victory in the war. Meles stated that Ethiopia would seek further dialogue with Eritrea to implement the ruling.

- More than three thousand UN peacekeepers are stationed in Eritrea and Ethiopia. Although the troops were initially deployed for a short-term mission to separate the two sides and oversee the marking of the border, the inability of Eritrea and Ethiopia to agree on the border's position extended the peacekeeping operation.

Contact Information. Embassy of Eritrea, 1708 New Hampshire Avenue NW, Washington, DC 20009; phone (202) 319-1991.

Federal Democratic Republic of Ethiopia

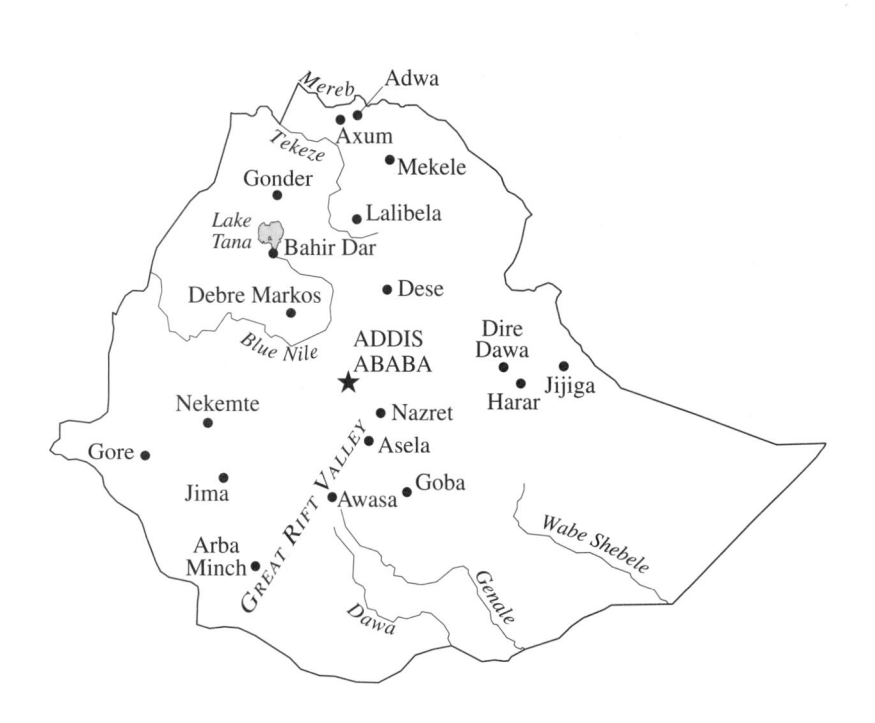

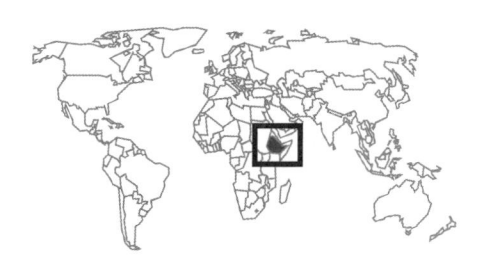

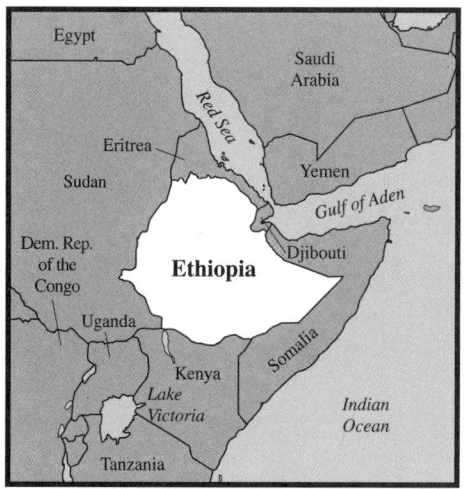

CultureGrams World Edition 2006

BACKGROUND

Land and Climate. Ethiopia, a landlocked and mountainous country on the Horn of Africa, covers 435,184 square miles (1,127,127 square kilometers); this is about the size of California and Texas combined. It has access to the Red Sea through a port in Djibouti. Ethiopia has a variety of climates and terrains. The Great Rift Valley, which is subject to earthquakes, separates the northwestern highlands from the southeastern mountains. Located at an elevation of 8,000 feet (2,400 meters) in the center of the country, the capital city of Addis Ababa has a moderate climate. Most of Ethiopia's lakes are situated along the Great Rift Valley. The largest, Lake Tana, is the source of the Blue Nile. Many rivers originating in Ethiopia flow to neighboring countries.

In the western lowlands, the hottest days average 95°F (35°C) but can rise to 120°F (49°C). Temperatures in the highlands average between 60°F (16°C) and 74°F (23°C). The rainy season is from mid-June to mid-September in the highlands, and the period from October to February is extremely dry. Rainfall varies widely from year to year, a factor that causes extreme problems for agriculture and animal husbandry, the two main sources of sustenance for Ethiopians. Despite its rocky and arid landscapes, however, Ethiopia is home to a great variety of plant and animal species.

History. Ethiopia is the oldest independent country in Africa, known anciently as Abyssinia. Legend has it that Ethiopian monarchs are descendants of Solomon and the Queen of Sheba. Ethiopians converted to Christianity during the Axumite period, primarily under the reign of King Ezana in the fourth century A.D. The Solomonic dynasty lasted until 960, when it was replaced by the Zague dynasty. The Solomonic dynasty returned to power from 1267 to 1974, though it was often divided by warfare between opposing factions. Christian Ethiopia began warring with neighboring Islamic states in the 13th century and was nearly defeated in the 16th century by Ottoman Turks. Islam first gained influence in Ethiopia in the 17th century.

Around 1885, Italy colonized the coast and tried to move inland. Italian forces were defeated at Adwa in 1896 by the Ethiopian army under Emperor Menilek II. That victory spared Ethiopia further aggression until the 1930s. Mussolini's Italian army invaded and occupied Ethiopia in 1935. In 1941, the British helped exiled Emperor Haile Selassie I regain control. He had been Ras Taferi Makonen, regent to the Empress Zauditu (daughter of Menilek II) during the 1920s. He took the throne from the empress and declared himself Emperor Haile Selassie I. His autocratic rule after 1941 created the economic and political turmoil that led to his fall in 1974. After his death a year later, the country was declared a socialist state called the People's Democratic Republic of Ethiopia.

Mengistu Haile-Mariam came to power in 1977 as leader of the provisional government. A 1987 constitution established a national assembly, which elected Mengistu president. He ruled as a dictator. Mengistu faced several problems, including an ongoing civil war (that began in 1961) between government forces and the Eritrean People's Liberation Front (EPLF). Other ethnic groups were also working to topple the government. The fighting, the Marxist economy, and poor harvests brought severe famine to millions of Ethiopians in the 1980s.

An attempted 1989 coup prompted Mengistu to announce economic reforms in 1990, but fighting intensified in 1991 and Mengistu left the country. When rebels surrounded Addis Ababa, the government collapsed. The Ethiopian People's

Ethiopia

Revolutionary Democratic Front (EPRDF) assumed central power. At the same time, the EPLF took control of Eritrea, which gained full independence in 1993. Eritrea granted Ethiopia access to the sea through the port city of Massawa, and the two nations established close ties.

The new Ethiopian leader, Meles Zenawi of the EPRDF, set up a provisional government to sponsor multiethnic elections under a new constitution. Multiparty elections were held in May 1995, but some parties boycotted the polling to protest the EPRDF's domination of the electoral process. The EPRDF swept most seats in a landslide victory. Meles became prime minister. Ethiopia was renamed the Federal Democratic Republic of Ethiopia. The country began to repatriate thousands of refugees stranded in Sudan and started developing a viable economy. However, political tensions continued to divide people, making it difficult for the nation to establish democratic institutions.

Relations with Eritrea were strained in 1997 when Eritrea stopped using the Ethiopian currency, and relations broke down completely in 1998 over a border dispute. Fighting escalated into full-scale war, killing some 100,000 people. A peace treaty ended the war in June 2000. However, despite a border demarcation ruling by an international court of arbitration, the two countries have still failed to resolve the border issue.

THE PEOPLE

Population. Ethiopia's population of 67.9 million is growing by about 1.89 percent per year. The Amhara ethnic group of northwestern Ethiopia accounts for about 30 percent of the population. The Tigreans in the north comprise almost 12 percent. The Oromo (35 percent) live in central Ethiopia, while the Somali (6 percent) live in the southeast. Other groups include the Beni-Shangul, Afar, Sidamo, Guraghe, and Walayta. At least another 65 very small ethnic groups live in Ethiopia. Addis Ababa is the nation's largest city, with more than three million residents.

Historical tensions between various regions remain a problem, and small guerrilla movements still fight for separation. Some groups oppose the government's demarcation of state boundaries based on ethnic majorities. These factors have helped intensify ethnic tensions, and critics allege the EPRDF is encouraging ethnic conflict by organizing the government along ethnic lines rather than stressing shared identities.

Language. Amharic, a Semitic language related to Hebrew and Arabic, is the official national language and is used in commerce and administration. It and Tigrinya are written in a Sabian script. Oromifaa is written in a Latin script. Somali, Guaraginga, Arabic, and more than 80 other languages (of which there are more than 200 dialects) are spoken in Ethiopia. Rural people often speak only their own particular dialect. Residents of towns and cities usually speak Amharic or Oromifaa in addition to their native language. Ge'ez is the ancient Sabian language of the Ethiopian Orthodox Church used in prayers and worship. English is taught in secondary schools, but only the educated urban elite can speak it.

Religion. About 45 percent of the population belongs to the Ethiopian Orthodox Church, a leading influence in the culture since the fourth century. Indeed, Ethiopian Christians stress that while Christianity was introduced by European colonizers in other African countries, it was adopted by Ethiopian rulers in A.D. 332—before many Western nations were exposed to it. Ethiopian Orthodox doctrine is most similar to Roman Catholicism in its emphasis on celebrating Mass and reverencing icons and patron saints. Some people living around Axum claim that the biblical Lost Ark of the Covenant is in their hands, but they have not permitted anyone to see it. The average Ethiopian has little knowledge of this lost ark, but there are many arks of covenant (called *tabots*) in the country's various churches. During religious holidays, arks in the region are gathered together for a celebration. On feast days in each month, certain saints, angels, and religious fathers are remembered by those Christians who have chosen them as patrons. Christianity's legacy can be seen in many ancient structures, including stone churches in Lalibela.

Muslims account for 35 percent of the population, generally among the Oromo. Other Ethiopians follow traditional animist beliefs that stress a reverence for all living things.

General Attitudes. Although attitudes vary widely among Ethiopia's many ethnic groups, one common trait is friendliness. Ethiopians generally appreciate others who are humble, honorable, and pleasant. Aggressive, loud, or demanding behavior demonstrates poor character. Ethiopians are often reluctant to show emotion, a characteristic attributed to the nation's years of hardship. Courtesy and concern for others also pervade the Ethiopian personality. Most Ethiopians are concerned about finding or maintaining a source of income and will do whatever is necessary to provide for their families.

Despite many years of conflict, most individuals favor peaceful solutions to problems and look forward to greater prosperity and harmony. However, the war with Eritrea strengthened nationalist feelings in Ethiopia, and many considered victory a matter of national pride; this is one factor that has kept a resolution at bay.

Personal Appearance. For the most part, Ethiopian men and women working as professionals or in offices wear Western-style clothing. Most other women wear traditional dresses. For holidays and other important occasions, Ethiopians of the northern and central regions wear traditional white cotton clothing decorated with various designs. Some items are embroidered in bright colors; others are bordered in hand woven silk. A matching cloth covers women's heads. This cloth is also used as a shawl by both men and women.

CUSTOMS AND COURTESIES

Greetings. Greetings are courteous and warm in Ethiopia. Relatives and friends often kiss on each cheek. New acquaintances shake hands gently with one or both hands. Phrases vary among ethnic groups, but some form of "How are you?" is typical. In Amharic, friends and peers say *Endemin neh?* to a male or *Endemin nesch?* to a female. A more formal Amharic greeting is *Tena Yistilin* (God give you health). In Oromifaa, one greets members of either sex with *Akam jirta?* The Tigrinya form is *Kamelaha?* for a man, or *Kamelehee?* for a woman.

In all areas of Ethiopia, one greets an elderly person by lowering or bowing the head to show deference. The elderly greet grandchildren by kissing them on the forehead; in return, they receive kisses on their knees. People are addressed by their titles (Mr., Mrs., Miss, Doctor, etc.) and given names. There are no surnames. One's given name is followed by one's father's given name, which is not used to address that person. Parents can be greeted by the name of their first child (e.g., "How are you, Mary's father?" or "Hello, Solomon's mother").

Gestures. Ethiopians keep a reasonable distance during conversation and avoid prolonged eye contact. Pointing with the finger or foot is not appropriate; one uses the entire hand. People avoid passing items or food with the left hand. Keeping one's hands at the side (not in pockets) during conversation is considered polite. Trilling the tongue is an expression of excitement or happiness. Slowly nodding the head indicates reflection or sorrow; quicker nods indicate agreement. Walking between two or more conversing people is considered rude. It is customary for people to treat the elderly with respect and deference.

Visiting. In Ethiopia, visiting is an important social function. Rural dwellers visit friends and family frequently and without advance notice. They are always warmly welcomed. Hosts nearly always serve guests something to drink. In most cases, men and women converse freely and enjoy a relaxed visit. In some Muslim homes, men and women do not socialize together. Many people in the east meet to chew *chat*, a leafy plant that produces a mildly stimulating effect when chewed. One removes the shoes when chewing *chat* or when in a Muslim home.

Urban visits may also occur unannounced between family and friends, but advance invitation or notice generally is required of others. Ethiopians enjoy inviting friends over for an evening of socializing, although the Amhara consider the home to be highly private.

Eating. Ethiopians eat two or three daily meals, depending on their income. Children eat separate from or before their parents, except on holidays or on special occasions. People wash their hands before the meal is served; the father, the oldest person, or any guest washes first. Diners eat from a common platter, taking food with the fingers of the right hand from the space on the platter directly in front of them. In most areas, hosts expect guests to eat and drink without reservation. Hosts may occasionally say "Please eat," until the food is finished. After the meal, people enjoy coffee, which often is served with elaborate ceremony. Urban Ethiopians often go to cafés and restaurants, although doing so was traditionally frowned upon as lazy or a sign of a poor home life.

LIFESTYLE

Family. The extended family is strongly patriarchal throughout Ethiopia. Sons usually bring their brides to live with or near their father's family, and three or more generations in the male line frequently live under one roof or in one family compound. Polygamy, once common among Muslims, is becoming less widely practiced. Age is highly respected in Ethiopia, and adult children care for their elderly parents. Only 3 percent of the population is older than age 65.

In rural areas, a father builds a separate house in the compound for each son before a wedding. He also gives each son a plot of land to farm. In the absence of the father, the eldest adult son leads the family. Women are responsible for household and compound upkeep and for child care. Their duties and privileges are well-defined and they often lead sheltered lives. While women may have certain legal rights, such as property inheritance, cultural practice often overrides these rights. Many men died during the years of fighting. The resulting female-headed households tend to be the poorest and most marginalized in the country.

Dating and Marriage. Western-style dating is becoming common in large cities, where young people more often choose their spouses. In more traditional settings, marriage represents the union of two families, and individual choice of spouse is limited. Weddings can be costly, elaborate family events lasting two or three days.

Diet. Porridge made from corn, barley, oats, or sorghum flour boiled with milk is the most common food in nearly all regions of the country. The porridge is flavored with butter and eaten with a wooden spoon. The Guraghe enjoy *kitfo*, a finely chopped, raw red meat mixed with butter, cheese, and vegetables. *Kitfo* is served with *koocho*, a bread prepared from the stem of a plant called *inset*. *Injera* and *wat* are popular highland dishes. *Injera*, used as bread, is made from a native grain known as *teff*, while *wat* is a stew made with chicken, beef, or vegetables. *Berbere*, a red hot pepper, is often used to spice *wat* or is served separately with raw meat. Available fruits include oranges, bananas, mangoes, papaya, avocados, grapes, tomatoes, and lemons. The most common vegetables are potatoes, carrots, cabbage, and onions.

Strict religious dietary and fasting customs affect what Ethiopians eat. For example, Orthodox Christians do not eat pork or meat from closed-hoofed animals; they also abstain from dairy products and meat on Wednesdays, Fridays, and during Lent (the 40 weekdays from Ash Wednesday to Easter). Muslims do not eat pork. During the holy month of *Ramadan*, they fast from sunrise to sundown each day.

Recreation. Urban Ethiopians watch television, go to sporting events, eat at restaurants, go to movies, take their children out for sweets, and so forth. Rural residents rarely have access to electricity. They go to community meetings, attend their local burial society meetings (*idir*) or savings club (*equib*), and play with their children. All Ethiopians enjoy visiting friends and relatives. Chess, checkers, and cards are popular games. Soccer is the most popular sport for men and boys, along with track-and-field. Rural sports include *gena* (like field hockey) and *guugs* (horse racing). Rural women usually do not play sports but socialize at home.

The Arts. Early Ethiopian Christians built many ancient structures, including 11 churches in Lalibela carved from stone in the 12th and 13th centuries. The walls of these churches are often covered with paintings. Mosques reflect broader Islamic architecture. Most art was religious until the 1930s, when European influences brought new styles. Painters have since explored various subjects and styles.

Music is used in religious ceremonies and for entertainment. Following the Mengistu dictatorship, when censorship and other government control of music performance and production were rife, popular and traditional music flourished again. Special instruments include the *begena* (lyre), the *kebero* (drum), and the *tsenatsil* (a kind of rattle). *Azmaris* (traveling singers) are important to the musical tradition. Despite Western influences, Ethiopian music remains popular. Other traditional arts include basket weaving, embroidery, carpet weaving, wood carving, and jewelry making.

Holidays. Major holidays include the Victory of Adwa (2 Mar.), Victory Day (5 May), Downfall of the Communist Regime (28 May), Ethiopian New Year (in September), and *Meskel* (a festival that celebrates the finding of the True Cross on which Christ was crucified; end of September).

In addition to the various holidays for saints and angels, Christians celebrate Christmas (7 Jan.), Epiphany (20 Jan.), and Easter (Friday–Sunday). Muslims mark *Id al-Fatar* (three-day feast at the end of *Ramadan*), *Id al-Adha* (Feast of the Sacrifice, also called *Arefa*), and *Moulid* (birth of the prophet Muhammad).

Meskel was celebrated before the advent of Christianity and Islam and has been adapted by all faiths. It comes at the end of winter. Each religion or culture celebrates it in different

Ethiopia

ways, but some customs are similar. Urban people visit friends and relatives in the countryside. On the eve of *Meskel*, each person places a tree branch vertically into a pile. There is a dance around the pile, and a community elder then lights the branches on fire. In the morning, most families slaughter a sheep or goat for a feast; some people pool their money to buy a bull. Families and neighbors gather to eat, sing, and dance.

Ethiopia follows the Coptic calendar. Each of 12 months has 30 days, and a 13th month has 5 or 6 days. There is a seven-year difference between the Coptic and Gregorian calendars. Therefore, 2004 in Western societies is 1997 in Ethiopia. Also, the 24-hour day begins at sunrise, not midnight, so 7 a.m. is locally called "one o'clock."

Commerce. Business is conducted using Western time and calendar standards. In large cities, offices are open from 8:30 a.m. to 1 p.m. and from 3 to 8 p.m., Monday through Friday. Saturday hours are 9 a.m. to 1 p.m. Government offices close at 6 p.m. on weekdays. Rural Ethiopians generally produce their own food and rely on open-air markets for products such as soap, sugar, clothing, and so on. Urban residents purchase most items from markets.

SOCIETY

Government. Ethiopia's prime minister (currently Meles Zenawi) is head of government and has strong executive authority. A ceremonial president (currently Girma Woldegiorgis) is head of state. Parliament's upper chamber, the Federal Council (108 members), is elected by state assemblies. The lower chamber, the Council of People's Representatives (548 members), is elected by popular vote. Representatives in both bodies serve five-year terms. The voting age is 18. Ethiopia is divided into nine ethnically-based states and two self-governing city administrations (Addis Ababa and Dire Dawa). Each has its own parliament and council of ministers, but leaders are ultimately responsible to the federal government.

Economy. Nearly all Ethiopians are subsistence farmers with little or no access to the resources necessary to pursue goals beyond feeding and clothing a family. Only about 12 percent of the land is arable. Rural wealth is often measured by the size of a person's herds. Coffee is the main cash crop, accounting for more than half of all export earnings. Other important crops include *teff*, wheat, millet, pulse, barley, and *chat*. Ethiopia also exports animal hides. Drought, soil erosion, and war have all contributed to the poor economy and periodic famines. Despite its poverty, Ethiopia has the potential to achieve economic self-sufficiency. Areas of focus include mining and gold exploration. The currency is the *birr* (ETB).

Transportation and Communications. In cities, transportation is relatively easy to find and is affordable for the majority of Ethiopians. Taxis, buses, and a train that travels between Addis Ababa and the country of Djibouti are available. Ethiopian Airlines flies to most major cities. In rural communities, people travel on foot, horseback, camels, donkeys, or mules.

The telephone network in major cities and towns is fairly good, although public phones are in short supply and direct-dial services are not always available. Rural residents rely on the mail and word of mouth for communication. One television station and four radio stations broadcast in Ethiopia.

DEVELOPMENT DATA
Human Dev. Index* rank . . . . 170 of 177 countries
  Adjusted for women . . . . 137 of 144 countries
Real GDP per capita $780
Adult literacy rate . . . . 49 percent (male); 34 (female)
Infant mortality rate . . . . 102 per 1,000 births
Life expectancy . . . . 45 (male); 46 (female)

Education. Education is not yet compulsory in Ethiopia, and less than half of all school-aged children are enrolled. About one-third of all students finish primary schooling, which begins at age seven, and go on for secondary school at age thirteen. Girls attend less often than boys; only one-fourth of adult women are literate. Until 1991, many children (who have now reached adulthood) fought in the civil war and were unable to get an education. Primary school instruction is in the chief language of each region.

Health. Addis Ababa and other major cities have some medical facilities, but most Ethiopians do not have access to proper medical care. The nation has few physicians, life expectancy remains very low, and infant mortality is extremely high. Malnutrition and diseases such as malaria, meningitis, cholera, and yellow fever are common, and outbreaks wreak havoc because few citizens are vaccinated. Only about one-fourth of the population has access to safe water.

AT A GLANCE
Events and Trends.
- Prime Minister Meles announced in November 2004 that his government had reconsidered its position on its border dispute with Eritrea and that it would be willing to accept a 2003 demarcation ruling by an international court of arbitration. Ethiopia had opposed the ruling because it gave Eritrea control of the town of Badme, the flashpoint for the nations' war. Though not strategically or economically significant, Badme became a symbol of victory in the war. Meles stated that Ethiopia would seek further dialogue with Eritrea to implement the ruling.
- Many of Ethiopia's farmers have replaced their coffee bean crops with *chat* crops in recent years due to sharp decreases in coffee prices. Coffee production has fallen dramatically since the late 1990s in the Harar province, a region renowned worldwide for the quality of its coffee beans.

Contact Information. Embassy of Ethiopia, 3506 International Drive NW, Washington, DC 20008; phone (202) 364-1200; web site www.ethiopianembassy.org. Permanent Mission of Ethiopia to the United Nations, 866 Second Avenue, Third Floor, New York, NY 10017; phone (212) 421-1830.

© 2005 ProQuest Information and Learning Company and Brigham Young University. It is against the law to copy, reprint, store, or transmit any part of this publication in any form by any means without written permission from ProQuest. This document contains native commentary and original analysis, as well as estimated statistics. The content should not be considered strictly factual, and it may not apply to all groups in a nation. *UN Development Programme, Human Development Report 2004 (New York: Oxford University Press, 2004).

CultureGrams
People. The World. You.

ProQuest Information and Learning Company
300 North Zeeb Road, P.O. Box 1346
Ann Arbor, Michigan 48106 USA
Toll Free: 1.800.528.6279
Fax: 1.800.864.0019
www.culturegrams.com

CultureGrams 2006 World Edition

Gabon
(Gabonese Republic)

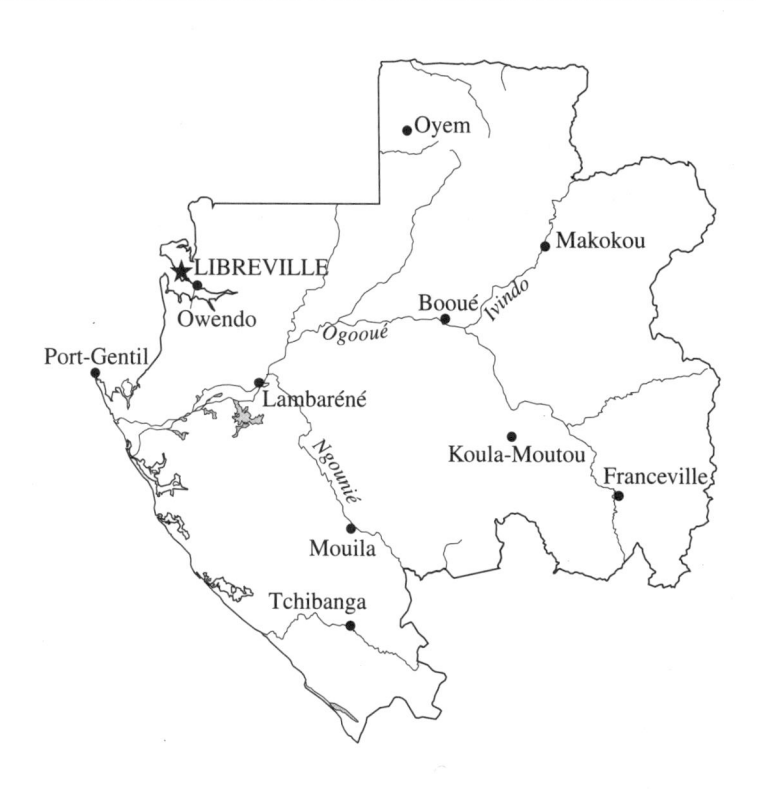

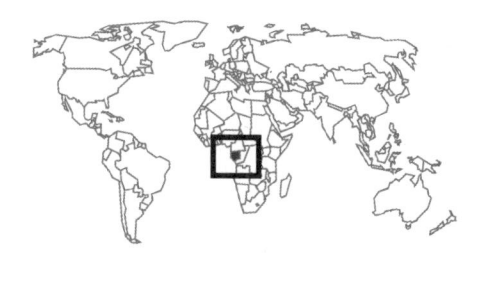

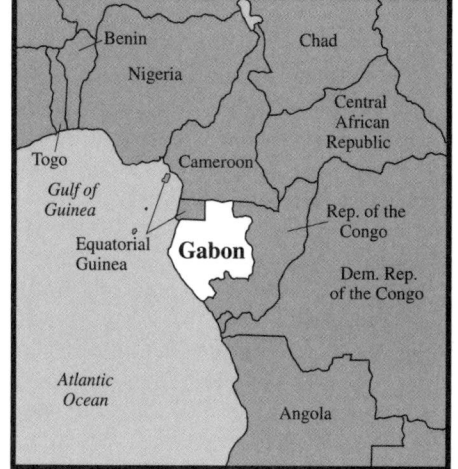

BACKGROUND

Land and Climate. Gabon straddles the equator on Africa's west coast. It is about the same size as Colorado, covering 103,347 square miles (267,670 square kilometers), and is situated in the drainage basin of the Ogooué River. About three-fourths of the country is low-lying equatorial rain forest, which is harvested for timber. The southeast is mostly savanna. Gabon's climate is hot in the rainy seasons (September–December, February–May) and moderate in the dry seasons (May–September, December–February). The capital city of Libreville has an average temperature in January of 80°F (27°C) and in July of 75°F (24°C). It receives about 99 inches (252 centimeters) of rain each year.

Gabon's tropical and coastal forests are dotted with small towns and villages. Although the Gabonese practice a sort of slash-and-burn agriculture, their small population has thus far left the forests mostly intact. However, larger-scale logging threatens the virgin forests, which harbor countless species of plants and wildlife (many endangered and some yet unknown). Four-fifths of Africa's gorillas and chimpanzees live in Gabon. By opening the forests, the mostly French and Lebanese logging firms may also be uncovering dangerous diseases (such as that caused by the Ebola virus found in Gabon).

History. The earliest inhabitants of Gabon were groups collectively known as Pygmies. Migrations of Bantu peoples (A.D. 1000) resulted in Bantu domination of the area. The southernmost part of Gabon was ruled by the powerful Bantu Bakongo Empire, centered at the mouth of the Congo River. When the Portuguese arrived in the 1400s, the rest of Gabon was comprised of small migratory villages of hunting and farming Bantus. Soon, the export of slaves and ivory to Europe began. These exports were replaced with timber and rubber by the early 1800s. Coastal traders eventually allied themselves with France. Interior people first resisted French colonization, but Western explorers, traders, and missionaries opened the area in the 1800s to eventual incorporation into French Equatorial Africa (present-day Gabon, Cameroon, Chad, Republic of the Congo, and Central African Republic).

Gabon experienced little development during the colonial era because of its small population and dense forests. Independence was granted in 1960, but the borders were based on French Equatorial Africa's artificial internal boundaries rather than natural ethnic groupings. The first president of Gabon was Leon M'ba. He died in 1967 and was succeeded by Albert-Bernard Bongo.

Bongo instituted a relatively tolerant one-party rule. In the 1970s, Gabon joined the Organization of Petroleum Exporting Countries (OPEC), and Bongo adopted Islam, changing his first name to El Hadj Omar. Protests and strikes in 1990 and 1991 forced Bongo to loosen political restrictions and legalize opposition parties. In 1991 elections, more than 40 parties ran for seats in the National Assembly. Bongo's party, the Gabonese Democratic Party (known by its French acronym, PDG), won a majority, and Bongo was reelected in 1993. Bongo was reelected again in December 1998 with a large majority. Now more than a decade since the introduction of a multiparty system, Bongo and the PDG still dominate Gabonese politics.

THE PEOPLE

Population. The population of Gabon is estimated to be about 1.4 million, but official data are not considered accurate. Annual population growth is roughly 2.5 percent. Gabon is

Gabon

home to more than 40 ethnic groups (most of them Bantu-speaking). The largest group is the Fang, comprising 30 percent of the population. Others include Eshira, Bapuna, Adouma, Mbeda, Bakota, Omyene, Okande, and Bateke. The 40,000 Pygmies who live in the rain forest have little or no contact with outside groups. Gabon is also home to many immigrants, especially from other French-speaking African nations, who work as teachers, shopkeepers, tailors, dressmakers, cabdrivers, and laborers. A large number of Western workers manage many of Gabon's export industries. Libreville, the nation's largest city, is home to about one-third of the total population. Other major cities are Port-Gentil, Franceville, and Lambaréné. More than half of the people live in rural towns and villages.

Language. French is Gabon's official language. Nearly all publishing and broadcasting occurs in French, and it is the most commonly heard language in cities. Taught in schools, it is the only language the Gabonese have in common and is basically the only written language. Local languages are primarily oral, although Christian missionaries have helped put some into written form. Most Gabonese speak both French and their ethnic group's native tongue. People usually are not fluent in another ethnic group's language, even though many different groups live close to one another. In the north, Fang is more common than French.

Religion. About 60 percent of the population is Roman Catholic, 20 percent is Protestant, and the remaining people practice local animist beliefs or are Muslim. Most Muslims are immigrants from other countries. Going to church is a popular social occasion, especially for women and girls. Most Christian clergy are from the West, but meetings are influenced by African music and are conducted in the local language by village elders. In their daily lives, people mix local beliefs with Christianity, often turning in times of emergency to tradition rather than to Western religion.

General Attitudes. The Gabonese are generally polite and kind. Although they may get loud and angry in disputes, they prefer to quickly resolve problems and rarely harbor hard feelings. The Gabonese are considered outspoken and even argumentative among some West African neighbors. Certain ethnic groups do not often say "please" and "thank you" because there is no tradition for these words in their languages. Regardless of whether a person uses the words, he or she acknowledges kindness and consideration from others and usually will repay favors.

The Gabonese tend to accept life as it is. They see themselves first as members of a family (including the extended family, and the village in rural areas), then as part of an ethnic group, and finally as Gabonese and Africans. People who live in the interior (rural areas away from major cities) do not enjoy many benefits from Gabon's oil wealth and are often frustrated with the lack of jobs, medicines, and educational opportunities. City residents have shared that frustration when oil prices have been low. Riots and other problems have strained the nation's ability to achieve its democratic and economic goals.

Personal Appearance. The Gabonese wear both Western and African clothing. People like to be neatly groomed and dressed as well as possible. Modesty and cleanliness are important. The Gabonese borrow their African fashions from neighboring countries; skilled tailors are found in every town. Women like elaborate, braided hairstyles—some sticking straight out, others in intricate loops, and others tied in bunches—and they change them often. Women might wear loose-fitting dresses made of colorful, embroidered fabric or a colorful *pagne* (wraparound skirt) with a blouse. Urban men might wear Western suits or, more often, just shirts and pants. Muslims also might wear a *boubou*, a loose-fitting, long-sleeved, embroidered cotton shirt extending to midcalf that is worn over loose-fitting pants. Fabrics are colorful and designs are often bold. The youth wear shorts or other casual attire.

CUSTOMS AND COURTESIES

Greetings. The Gabonese shake hands and smile each time they meet, even if several times a day. If the hand is dirty, one extends a closed fist (palm down) so the greeter can "shake" the wrist or forearm. Urban friends might hug and brush alternating cheeks while "kissing the air." In small groups, one greets each individual. In larger gatherings, one can raise both hands to the group and say *Bonjour tout le monde* (Hello, everyone). People of the same sex, especially men, often hold hands while talking or walking. It is improper, especially in rural areas, for members of the opposite sex to do this. Rural women might clasp each other's forearms when greeting. Shaking another person's hand with both hands is a sign of respect.

Urban greetings include the French *Bonjour* (Good day) and *Bonsoir* (Good evening). The Fang *Mbolo* (Hello) is common throughout Gabon. Greetings include asking about one's family and health. Older people may be addressed as *mama* or *papa*. People of about the same age may address each other by first name or as *mon frère* (my brother) or *ma soeur* (my sister). At work, *Monsieur* (Mr.), *Madame* ("Ms." or "Mrs."), or a title is used with the last name.

Gestures. A closed fist with the thumb extended up means "good." Hitting a raised, closed left fist with the right palm open means *beaucoup* (many, much). Hooking one's right thumbnail behind a front tooth and snapping it to make a loud clicking sound indicates a statement is true. To point, one quickly extends puckered lips. The Gabonese show enthusiasm by shaking the wrist rapidly to make the fingers slap together. A person expresses frustration or "nothing" by clapping the hands together once and then opening the arms wide to the side. One indicates "come here" by holding the hand vertical, palm facing out, and waving the fingers in unison so they touch the palm several times. To hail a taxi, one waves an extended arm, palm down, from shoulder to waist. Muslims object to contact with one's left hand. It is impolite to touch someone's head.

Visiting. Visiting is common after work or on weekends in urban areas and anytime one is home in villages. Most rural socializing takes place Sunday after morning church services. Hospitality is important, and hosts frequently offer food to guests, especially if a meal is in progress. Hosts always offer a drink and quickly refill an empty glass. A guest who is not hungry should at least taste offered food. Guests usually are not expected to bring gifts, but friends might bring food or drink. In urban areas, a new acquaintance might make a vague appointment ("I'll drop by next week") before visiting, but most visits are unplanned. Rural Gabonese might invite passing friends in for a drink; it is impolite to refuse, even if one has something else to do. Rural women socialize in the *cuisine* (kitchen), where much of daily life usually takes place. Kitchens generally are separate from the living quarters (*salon*), as open cooking fires are often used. The *salon* consists of a living room and bedrooms. Rural men often socialize and work together in open-air structures called *corps de gars*.

Invited guests are not expected to arrive on time. Guests customarily return the favor of an invitation at a later date. It is polite to knock before entering a home. If the door is open, the visitor imitates the knocking sound by saying *Kokoko*. One does not enter without announcing one's presence.

Eating. An urban breakfast, eaten around 7 a.m., may include bread, croissants, butter, marmalade, eggs, yogurt, and coffee. Lunch might be around noon; dinner is after dark, even as late as 9 p.m. Most urban Gabonese use utensils but eat certain foods with the hand.

In villages, breakfast may consist of leftovers from the day before, but adults also might have bread and coffee or hot chocolate. *Beignets* (deep-fried doughnutlike food eaten plain or with sugar) are widely available from vendors. Adults usually are working around lunchtime, so children returning from school eat a light meal or leftovers. Adults also eat light; while working, they might harvest fruit for a quick snack. The main meal is eaten in the evening (usually after 7 p.m.) when work is done. Rural Gabonese often eat with the right hand or a spoon from a common bowl. Men and older boys usually eat in the *salon*. Women and young children eat in the *cuisine*. The father often has his own bowl. Small families might eat together in the *cuisine*. In this case, adults share one bowl and children share another. Guests are given a separate bowl.

LIFESTYLE

Family. The Gabonese feel great loyalty toward family members. Family obligations require the Gabonese to extend hospitality (food, lodging, and expenses) to any member of the extended family who asks for it, even for a prolonged period of time. Traditionally, an extended family lives in a large compound of several buildings, usually sharing cooking, child care, and other chores. A man, his wife (or wives), their children, and often cousins or other relatives live in the compound. A man with more than one wife provides each with a separate home and kitchen whenever possible. Since this is expensive, the trend is to have only one wife. Still, an unmarried man may have children by more than one woman, and married men often have mistresses. A child's aunts and uncles frequently have equal status to parents.

A village functions as an extension of the family. Villagers who move to urban areas have a spirit of unity with fellow villagers they meet there. They make regular visits back home; students might return on weekends or holidays to work and visit with family and friends.

Dating and Marriage. Western-style dating occurs mostly among the urban educated. Rural courtship involves the boy visiting the girl at her parents' home. An engaged couple may date outside the home. The family often has great influence in the choice of a marriage partner. Girls are sometimes promised to a future husband at a very young age, although the wedding does not take place (if at all) until after puberty. A groom often must give gifts (*dot*) to the bride's family when they get engaged and when they marry. Young men find it difficult to afford *dot*, so many do not formally wed. The Gabonese generally marry within their ethnic group but outside of their village to avoid marrying relatives. Women are often encouraged to have a child or two before marriage to prove fertility. These children frequently are raised by the woman's mother and are not taken into marriage. If a marriage fails, the *dot* must be repaid and children born in wedlock remain with the father.

Diet. The most widely grown food is cassava (*manioc*). A typical meal consists of either plantains (boiled and mashed) or *bâton de manioc*, a dough-like paste made from cassava. It is served with meat or fish in urban areas and with fresh meat among villagers who have had a successful hunt. Rural Gabonese dry or smoke meat to preserve it. People might eat imported sardines or locally caught fish when meat is unavailable. The main course is often a stew in peanut butter or palm oil sauce. Hot peppers (*piment*) are frequently used as a spice. Water is the most common drink, but palm wine and canned soda are also popular.

Yams, taro, peanuts, and corn are major crops grown in Gabon. Coffee, cocoa, sugarcane, and palm oil are produced for commercial purposes. There are many tropical fruits: papaya, bananas, pineapples, mangoes, avocados, and *atangas* (a violet, bitter fruit about the size of a golf ball). *Atangas* are often boiled until soft enough to eat. Some non-Gabonese call this fruit "bush butter" and use it as a spread. *Odika*, a substance made from the pits of wild mangoes, is used to make a gravy-like sauce referred to as *chocalat* (chocolate) because of its dark color.

In remote areas, people hunt wild animals (gazelles, pangolins, snakes, crocodiles, boars, monkeys, etc.) and grow food for themselves. Insects, such as termites or palm grubs, are not an uncommon part of the rural diet.

Recreation. Visiting is the most common leisure activity in Gabon. Women socialize while braiding each other's hair. Soccer is Gabon's most popular sport, followed by basketball. Television is available in many parts of the country. Dancing to drums and local music is usually a part of weddings, religious ceremonies, and other occasions. A popular, traditional strategy game called *songo* (in Fang) is played with pebbles or seeds on a wooden board. Young people like tag, jump rope, and tug-of-war. Children are very creative in making their own toys (cars, dolls, airplanes, games) from scraps and forest materials.

The Arts. Folklore and other forms of oral literature maintain a strong influence in Gabonese life. Stories are often sung, accompanied by instruments such as the harp. These performances, as well as various dances, are prominent features of Gabonese celebrations. Though regarded more as an art form today, wooden masks traditionally played a large role in religious rituals and rites of passage. These masks vary in style according to region and tribal affiliation. Gabonese sculpture uses traditional motifs in modern formats. Popular folk arts include domestic items such as baskets made from palm, bamboo, and other vegetation.

Holidays. Official public holidays include such Christian holy days as *Pâques* (Easter), *Pentecôte* (Pentecost), *Toussaint* (1 November, All Saints' Day), and *Noël* (Christmas). The Islamic holy days of *Fin du Ramadan* (a feast at the end of *Ramadan*, a month of fasting) and *Fête de Mouton* (a feast to honor Abraham's willingness to sacrifice his son) are observed according to their dates on the lunar calendar. The Gabonese celebrate *Jour de l'An* (New Year's Day) and *Fête du Travail* (May Day, 1 May). *Fête National* commemorates independence on 17 August.

Commerce. A few minutes of greetings and small talk precede discussions of business. Businesses generally open between 7 and 9 a.m. and close for lunch at noon. Most heavy work is done in the morning; light work is reserved for the hot afternoon. When the long lunch break is over at around 3 p.m., business and work resume until early evening. Small food shops are open through lunch, late in the evening, and on weekends. In these shops and in open-air markets, prices are negotiable.

Gabon

The largest outdoor market is *Mont Bouet* in Libreville. Most private shops are owned by non-Gabonese (usually from other West African countries).

SOCIETY

Government. Gabon is governed by a president (currently Omar Bongo) and a prime minister (currently Jean-François Ntoutoume-Émane). The president appoints the prime minister and is elected to a seven-year term. Although the president has the most authority, an effort has been made to balance that by increasing the prime minister's duties. The 120-seat National Assembly (*Assemblée Nationale*) was joined in 1997 by a 91-seat Senate. Members of the National Assembly serve five-year terms; members of the Senate serve six-year terms. Everyone 21 and older must vote. Political parties include the PDG, the National Rally of Woodcutters, and a number of smaller parties.

Economy. Historically, Gabon's major exports were *okoumé* (a hardwood) and soft woods used to make plywood. Timber exports continue, but they have been exceeded by oil exports since the 1970s. Oil constitutes one-third of Gabon's gross domestic product (GDP) and 80 percent of the country's exports. Manganese and uranium are also exported. Export industries are owned mostly by French and Lebanese companies. Most food and other commodities are imported, making Libreville one of the most expensive cities in the world.

Because of the value of Gabon's exports, its real GDP per capita is relatively high for Africa. However, most wealth is in the hands of a small minority, and the average person does not earn a decent income. The majority of people (65 percent) are engaged in subsistence agriculture. Gabon has the potential to give its people economic opportunities, but corruption, oil price fluctuations, and lower global demand for uranium have all hindered development. Unemployment is high. Gabon is trying to diversify its economy to reduce dependence on oil and to create jobs. The currency is the *CFA franc* (XAF).

Transportation and Communications. Only the wealthy and government officials have access to private cars. Animals are not often used for transportation, and bicycles and motorcycles are rare, so people mostly walk. They travel long distances by way of an *occasion*, a "bush-taxi," which is often crowded. *Occasion* passengers pay a commonly understood fare and take their luggage, food, and animals with them. Roads between major cities are not paved and are difficult to travel during the rainy seasons. Air Gabon airlines provides service to many areas, but flights are too expensive for the average Gabonese. The Trans-Gabonais railway provides daily service between Libreville and Franceville. Goods are transported by rail from Libreville to Franceville and then by truck or air to other interior destinations, making imports more expensive in the interior than in the capital. The post office provides reliable mail and phone service between many locations. Mail moves slowly because it is all sorted at the capital, regardless of its origin or destination.

Education. Gabon follows the French system of education, in which students attend school for as many as 13 years and end with a *bac* (baccalaureate) exam. Free education is guaranteed to all, even though the government reduces spending when oil revenues fall. In the past, many schools were run by churches. But the government, which sets curriculum and appoints teachers, is replacing cleric administrators with government officials.

Nearly all children are enrolled in and finish primary school, which lasts six years. Only one-fifth continue on for seven years of secondary school. Rural schools lack books and other critical supplies. Girls are less likely to finish school. Students who pass the *bac* may attend one of Gabon's two universities at no cost. Living expenses are paid for university students who maintain passing grades. College graduates often work for the government.

Health. In Gabon's national healthcare system, doctors' services are free but medicine is not. Serious medical problems can be treated only in Libreville. Village clinics are not well equipped. Hospital patients are responsible for their own bedding and food. Villagers must travel to the nearest town or city for medical care. Villagers might visit a local "healer" as well as, or instead of, a town doctor. Albert Schweitzer's famous hospital in Lambaréné is now run by the government. HIV/AIDS is a growing problem. Outbreaks of the deadly Ebola virus periodically strike rural areas where people come into contact with infected animals.

DEVELOPMENT DATA
Human Dev. Index* rank . . . . 122 of 177 countries
    Adjusted for women . . . . NA
Real GDP per capita $6,590
Adult literacy rate . . . . 74 percent (male); 53 (female)
Infant mortality rate . . . . 54 per 1,000 births
Life expectancy . . . . 56 (male); 58 (female)

AT A GLANCE
Events and Trends.
- Chinese president Hu Jintao visited Gabon in February 2004 for discussions with President Bongo. The visit followed an agreement allowing a French oil company to export Gabonese oil to China.
- In July 2003, Gabon's parliament amended the nation's constitution to eliminate restrictions on the number of terms the president can hold office. Opposition leaders condemned the amendment, as it will allow President Bongo to hold power for life.
- In 2002, President Bongo announced plans to create an extensive national park system covering approximately 10,000 square miles (26,000 square kilometers), or 10 percent of Gabon's total area. Conservationists praised the nation's effort to preserve its forests.

Contact Information. Embassy of Gabon, 2034 20th Street NW, Washington, DC 20009; phone (202) 797-1000.

CultureGrams 2006 World Edition

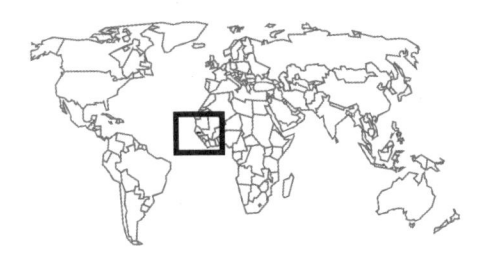

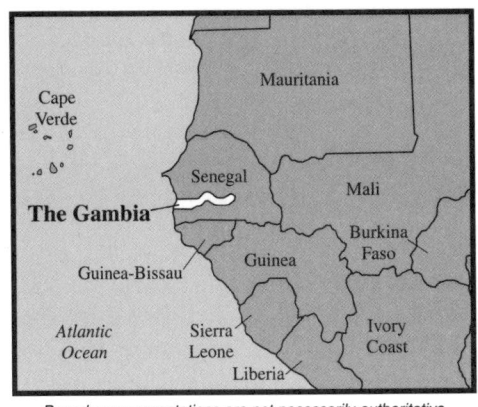

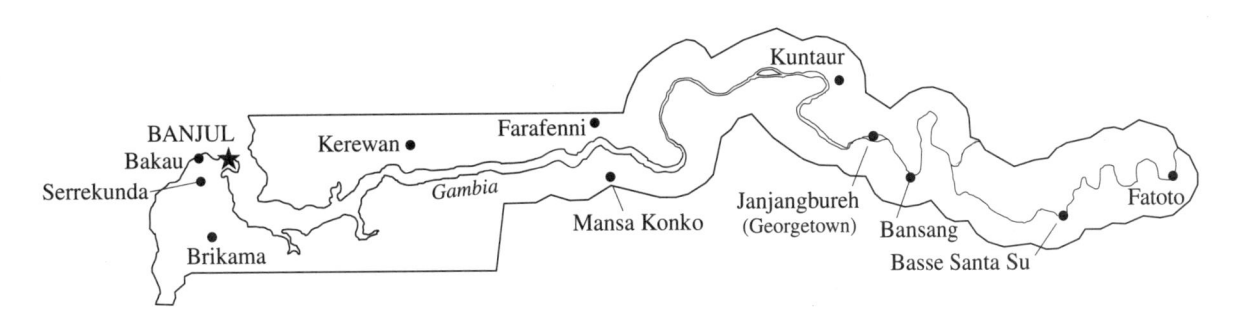

Republic of The Gambia

BACKGROUND

Land and Climate. The Gambia is located on the coast of West Africa, about 10 degrees latitude north of the equator. It is one of Africa's smallest countries, occupying a narrow strip of land on both sides of the River Gambia, about 250 miles (400 kilometers) in length. Covering 4,363 square miles (11,300 square kilometers), The Gambia is slightly larger than Maryland and is surrounded on three sides by Senegal. The River Gambia allows some transport from the Atlantic coast to points inland. The capital, Banjul, is an island that is connected to the mainland by a bridge. Surrounding Banjul are various urban areas that collectively are called the Kombos. Savannas cover much of the country; marshes are found along the River Gambia.

The Gambia experiences a humid, rainy season from June to September. The dry season lasts from May to October, with slightly cooler temperatures from November to February. However, the "cold" season's overnight temperatures are still above 70°F (21°C). Days heat up in advance of the rainy season, during which the average high temperature is 88°F (31°C); temperatures are even higher upriver.

History. The Gambia was once part of various large African empires, including the Serrahule and Mandinka empires of the fifth and sixth centuries. The country's modern history is closely linked to the River Gambia. The Portuguese are believed to have been the first Europeans to navigate the river in 1455, but it was not recognized as a European possession until 1783 when the British claimed the river and its surrounding territory. The British remained in the area until 1965 when The Gambia became an independent state and a member of the British Commonwealth. In 1970, the country became a republic and enjoyed relative peace and multiparty democracy under the leadership of President Dawda K. Jawara.

In July 1981, political turmoil led to an attempted coup while Jawara was in England for the wedding between Prince Charles and Princess Diana. The coup ended when Senegalese troops intervened at Jawara's request. As a result, the two countries joined together in closer union, establishing a Senegambia confederation in September 1981. Close diplomatic relations and the loose confederation continued until 1989, when Senegal withdrew. Jawara, who had been reelected several times and was considered personally popular, faced strong opposition in the 1992 elections but still won with a majority.

In July 1994, Lieutenant Yahya Jammeh seized power in a bloodless coup, forcing Jawara to flee to Senegal. Jammeh suspended the constitution, banned political activity, and detained top military and government officials. He promised a swift return to civilian rule, but his timetable of four years seemed too long for the international community. Western donor nations withdrew aid and pressed Jammeh to move up scheduled elections. Balloting occurred in 1996, but opposition groups had very little opportunity to campaign, and Jammeh won a sizeable victory. Another election in 2001 had similar results. Jammeh has continued to espouse the virtues of a one-party state.

THE PEOPLE

Population. The population of 1.5 million is growing at 2.98 percent annually. The Gambia has five major ethnic groups: the Mandinka (42 percent); Fulani, or Fula (18); Wolof (16); Jola (10); and the Serrahule (9). About 5 percent of the population is comprised of a community of Europeans, U.S. citizens, Mauritanians, Lebanese, Syrians, and people from neighboring countries.

The Gambia

Descendants of the Mali Empire, the Mandinkas make up most of the ruling class and hold most civil-service positions. Most Mandinka settlements are upriver, east of the capital, but a few are found in the Banjul area. The Fulanis migrated from the Guinea highlands. Wolofs are from the Senegambia area; it is believed that they and the Jolas have always lived in the region. The Serrahules, who are primarily traders in the Basse and Banjul areas, migrated from Mali and Mauritania. About 80 percent of Gambians live in rural areas. Most urban residents live in the various cities of the Kombos on the South Bank, which is much more developed than the North Bank.

Language. Although English is the official language, most Gambians speak Wolof, Mandinka, and/or Fula on a daily basis. Official business and school instruction has traditionally been conducted in English, although some schools now teach local languages. Most Gambians who have attended school speak some English, and Gambians with contacts in Senegal also speak French. French is encouraged in the high school curriculum. Wolof is the commercial language. Other languages spoken by smaller groups include Creole, Jola, Serere, and Serrehule. Gambian languages are not usually written, but Latin or Arabic characters are sometimes used to write them.

Religion. About 85 percent of Gambians are Muslim, 13 percent are Christian, and 2 percent are animist. Religious differences are not divisive and people tolerate each other's beliefs. They may not often intermarry, but they respect one another. Religious freedom is guaranteed. Most Christians live in the cities of Banjul, Bakau, and Serrekunda, whereas Muslims reside throughout the country.

Muslims basically believe in *Allah* as God and Muhammad as his prophet. Muslims pray five times daily, give alms to the poor, and try to make a pilgrimage to Makkah (Mecca), Saudi Arabia, at least once in their lifetime. Devout Muslims also fast each year during the month of *Ramadan*, going without food or drink from sunrise to sunset each day. Most entertainment is suspended temporarily during *Ramadan* because of the fast, which commemorates *Allah's* revelation of the *Qur'an* to Muhammad.

General Attitudes. Gambians are generally self-confident, outgoing, and positive about life. They are usually open and hospitable toward strangers because sharing and openness are valued over secrecy and individualism. People eat and spend what they have today, hoping *Allah* will provide for tomorrow. Most lead lives of great simplicity.

Gambians are proud of their heritage, but many are also curious about Western civilization. Most Gambians are pleased to host international guests; this is known as *tarranga*. Gambians believe in strong family bonds, honesty, friendliness, sharing, respect, and communal effort. These values are changing as Gambia becomes more modern. For example, elders (especially those with gray hair) traditionally are considered wise and irreproachable—one should not speak boldly to elders but rather listen carefully to their advice. Yet the Western concept of children standing up to their parents has led some Gambians to do the same, and now it is not uncommon to see a child talk back to a parent.

Gambians prefer to take their time with activities. Appointment times are given in general terms (e.g., before or after one of the five Muslim prayers). Further, if something cannot be done today, it will be done tomorrow or the next day. This attitude is not as prevalent in farming communities, since work must be done according to the seasons.

Personal Appearance. Most Gambians value neatness and modesty. Professional men usually wear dress pants, shirts, and ties in offices. Many mix Western and African clothing (e.g., Western pants with an African shirt). Wolof and Fula traditional attire for men includes *chaya* (baggy drawstring pants with many extra folds between the legs that provide ventilation in the heat). Older men wear *kaftans* (long tailored robes) or *warambas* (shorter, more flowing robes). Schoolchildren wear uniforms. Only children wear shorts.

Older women wear traditional shirts called *grandmbuba* or *dendiko ba* and skirts called *faano*. Younger women often wear a *dagit* (skirt-and-blouse outfit). Most women braid their hair. For holidays, many women buy hair extensions to weave into their hair for added length.

CUSTOMS AND COURTESIES

Greetings. Proper greetings come before a conversation or formal business. The younger person usually initiates a handshake and a greeting such as the Arabic *Salaam Malekum* (May peace be upon you); the older person responds with *Malekum Salaam* (May it be upon you, too). When greeting an elder, one may start by saying the elder person's first name once and his last name several times. Inquiries then are made about an individual's health and that of his or her family. Greetings may last a minute or two. If a girl greets an elder, she might shake hands, but she may also dip her knees toward the ground to show respect. Traditionally, the girl would actually kneel, but the gesture is more of a curtsy today. Boys do not kneel or curtsy when they greet elders. Persons in a group are greeted individually. If one's hand is dirty from work or eating, one offers the wrist for shaking instead of the hand.

One addresses a person of the same age group as one's parents as *mother, aunt, father,* or *uncle*, regardless of their relation to the greeter; these titles are combined with the first names (*Auntie Marie*). This greeting is especially common around Banjul, Serrekunda, and other cities. In other towns, the Mandinka greeting *Summo lay?* (How are your people?) is common. The customary response is *Ibbi jay* (They are fine). The Wolof also use *Na ka nga def?* (How are you?) and respond *Ma ngi fi rek* (I am all right; I am here).

Gestures. To beckon, Gambians wave all fingers inward with the palm facing down. They avoid using the left hand for most activities (shaking hands, passing items, eating), but it is used to shake hands with someone departing on a long trip as a sign of wishing a safe journey. Direct eye contact with older people is disrespectful. The index finger is a sign of good luck and safety. For instance, some Gambians dip the finger in food to taste before eating; it is believed this can prevent food poisoning. Dipping the index finger is also a substitute for praying before a meal; another way to bless the food is by saying *Bissimilai* (which is also to be expressed before riding a bus or taxi or welcoming a new resident to a village). When one yawns, one must cover the mouth and then touch the forehead. Burping after a meal is considered a positive comment on the food and is often followed by a word of thanks to the cook or *Allah* for providing the meal.

Visiting. Visiting friends and relatives is a common way to maintain strong relationships. Gambians normally visit without prior notice. Guests are always welcome and rarely turned away. Even if the host is about to leave, he or she will stay a while to talk with the guest. People chat about local developments: who is marrying whom, who has died, when the next naming ceremony will be, harvests, and so on. Visits are most common in the late afternoon or evening when the sun is mild and there is enough shade to be outside. The normal greeting takes place first with both parties standing. The host then offers a drink such as *attaya* (green tea with sugar) or the more expensive *lay* (condensed milk with sugar). It is common for people to visit during mealtime, in which case the guest is expected to share the meal. If preparations have not begun, the hosts might cook a chicken for their guests; chicken is expensive so this is a way to honor guests.

Visitors with a mango or other fruit tree at home often bring some fruit to their hosts. Guests from other towns normally bring gifts ranging from vegetables to chickens. When returning to the family home after a long absence, a Gambian is expected to bring gifts. When a guest leaves, a host may offer a gift in the form of taxi fare. Although most visiting is done at home, some is done at work or in public places.

Eating. Most Gambians eat three meals a day. Breakfast is usually sometime between 7 and 9 a.m., lunch between 1 and 3 p.m., and dinner between 7 and 9 p.m. However, many wage earners do not have lunch until after 4 p.m., when government offices close. During busy farming seasons, mothers send prepared lunches with children to their fathers in the fields. Gambian men usually squat on a floor mat to eat; women may sit on a low stool or bench. Although some urban Gambians eat with utensils, most people eat with their hands from communal bowls. The youngest person uses the left thumb and index finger to steady the bowl while the rest eat with right hands. Food does not have to be finished. It is impolite for children to reach for meat; they must wait to be given a portion. Children also look down while eating and do not talk. Leftovers are divided equally among them. Eating and drinking at the same time is not acceptable, so drinks are served after a meal. If soft drinks are served, water will be served first. In large families, women and young children eat separately from men and older boys. Elders may receive their own bowl.

Gambians eat at market stalls or small restaurants when away from home for the day. While eating on the streets is uncommon for adults, people might eat peanuts or oranges sold at street stands. Children might eat on the street and elders may chew kola nuts or bitter kola. Kola nuts are round and contain a mild stimulant; bitter kola is elongated and bitter but is not a stimulant.

LIFESTYLE

Family. The Gambian family structure is based on the extended family. Three generations may live together in one household. Gambians usually address each other by name but refer in conversation to one another by their family title (*brother, sister, aunt, grandfather,* etc.). It is common to call more than one person *father* or *mother*, and there are various kinds of "relatives." If not related by blood, people may become related by long years of friendship, commingling, or working together.

Families, usually headed by the father, are generally large by Western standards. Many rural families are polygamous. The family is the nucleus and pillar of the community, as well as the source of individual strength, recognition, and social standing. Family events such as naming ceremonies (when a one-week-old baby is officially named) or weddings are cause for celebration by the entire village. The concept of marriage goes beyond two people to extend to the community, especially when a son marries and introduces his new wife to the family compound. Although urban women of the younger generation might work outside the home, most other women remain in the home. Women do household chores, though girls begin helping by age 5. Boys learn to work in the fields by age 10. Men provide the family income and are responsible for home and farm repairs.

Dating and Marriage. Young men and women normally do not socialize. "Boys with the boys and girls with the girls" is a popular Gambian phrase. Young men generally are not welcome to visit a young woman's house and can only court a girl with parental permission. Although dating is not accepted, some dating occurs at night without the knowledge of parents. This may include meeting at parties, soccer games, or on the street. Young people also meet at marriage ceremonies or school. It is not unusual for a young man to tell a young woman "I love you" at first sight. While the practice of arranged marriages is rapidly diminishing in urban areas, it is still common among rural families. Polygamy is uncommon in cities.

Weddings are very important and can take as long as three days to complete. For many groups, a groom pays a dowry (livestock or money) to a bride's family before he can marry her. Various parties come before the day when the bride travels from her village to the groom's village to symbolize her joining his family.

Diet. For breakfast, bread with butter or jam and hot tea are popular in urban areas. People also eat *rui* or *monno* (millet porridge), *churra gerte* (crushed peanuts and rice boiled together), or *accara* (fried bean flour). These breakfasts can be purchased from street vendors or prepared at home. Rice is the main staple and most Gambians eat rice and stew for lunch. The stew, which includes spices and sometimes vegetables (eggplant, cabbage, cassava, and/or okra), varies from a fish, chicken, or beef base to a peanut butter base. Other popular lunch dishes include *benachin* (jollof rice), *supakanja* (okra soup), and *domoda* (peanut butter stew). Dinner may be leftover rice from lunch, *chereh* (a form of millet), fried fish, beef sauce with bread, or salad with potatoes and chicken or beef. Gambians eat more fish than beef, but millet with a special beef sauce is popular for certain festivals. People might eat small bits of a habanero pepper, one of the hottest peppers in the world, with a bite of rice.

Recreation. Gambians spend their leisure time at festivals or ceremonies (weddings, burials, or namings). Dancing (mostly by women), drumming, and visiting friends are other favorite activities. Although The Gambia has beautiful beaches, most Gambians rarely use them, except for young men who may play beach soccer or go swimming. Men and boys play soccer; wrestling and track-and-field events are popular in school. Secondary school girls might play volleyball. Family outings are not common. Playing cards or checkers is popular. Television broadcasts are expanding. Movie theaters exist, but few people attend them; some watch videos at home.

The Arts. Gambians listen to reggae, *ndaga* music (Wolof music from Senegal), and *kora* music. A *kora* is an upright string instrument made from a gourd. Another popular instrument is the *djembe*, a large goatskin-covered drum. *Griots* (praise-singers, usually women) keep oral genealogies of villages and communities and recite or sing the histories of prominent local families. The National Museum in Banjul houses a sizeable collection of recorded oral histories, as well as native musical instruments and local handicrafts. The Gambian Craft Cooperative, sponsored by the government, promotes local folk arts. The Fula make elaborate beaded jewelry that denotes marital status.

Holidays. The Gambia's official public holidays include New Year's Day, Independence Day (18 Feb.), Easter (including

The Gambia

Good Friday), Labor Day (1 May), and Christmas. President Jammeh's 1994 coup is celebrated on 22 July. Most holidays, except Labor Day, are celebrated with festivals, which include ethnic dances, house parties, dances, and local wrestling competitions. Muslim holy days that also have official recognition include *Eid-el-Fitre*, or *Koritee* (three-day feast at the end of *Ramadan*); *Eid-el-Kabir*, or *Tobaski* (Feast of the Sacrifice, held in conjunction with the summer pilgrimage to Makkah, Saudi Arabia); and *Mauloud-el-Nabi* (Muhammad's birthday). Muslim festivals fall on different days each year because they are set by the lunar calendar.

Commerce. Offices are open from 8 a.m. to 4 p.m., Monday through Thursday. Small village shops remain open until 10 or 11 p.m. Businesses close on Friday by 1 p.m. for afternoon (Muslim) prayers. Outside of the Kombos, people shop mostly at weekly markets (*luumos*) that offer livestock, household goods, fabric, and food.

SOCIETY

Government. The president (currently Yahya Jammeh) is chief of state and head of government. The National Assembly has 53 seats; 48 are elected by popular vote and 5 are appointed by the president. Members serve five-year terms. The voting age is 18. The Gambia has five divisions (Lower River, Central River, North Bank, Upper River, and Western) and one major city, Banjul. Local power rests with the village chief (*Alikalo*), who settles disputes and makes village rules.

Economy. Agriculture employs 80 percent of the labor force, but most production goes toward subsistence rather than exports. The Gambia exports peanuts, cotton, and sesame. Rice, millet, maize, and sorghum are key domestic crops. Only men grow peanuts; women cultivate rice, millet, and sesame. Trade with neighboring countries, especially Senegal, is vital to economic growth. A growing number of people are involved in fishing, and seafood is exported to Europe. Peanuts, fish, and hides are processed on a small scale. Tourism is a vital source of revenue, and The Gambia is a favorite destination for Europeans who come for the beaches and pleasant weather. Young men often hope to meet and marry Europeans and leave The Gambia. Development and local initiative may be lacking because Gambians have come to rely on aid organizations to initiate projects or solve problems. Rates of unemployment and underemployment are extremely high. The currency is the *dalasi* (GMD).

Transportation and Communications. To travel short distances, people walk. Urban residents might also take a taxi. For longer distances, Gambians use donkey or horse carts, buses, or "bush-taxis," a network of crowded minibuses that travel on set routes without schedules. The South Bank Road is paved from the Kombos to Basse Santa Su. A paved road also runs along the north bank but not as far.

The Gambia has a modern telephone system, but most people do not own a phone. Public phones are available. There are several newspapers, a government-owned radio and television station, and a private radio station. In areas without electricity, televisions are sometimes run off car batteries. Many educated people listen to the British Broadcasting Corporation (BBC) on the radio. In rural areas, meetings or important news are announced by a man walking through the village beating on a drum and calling out the information.

Education. Although primary schooling is inexpensive, not all families send their children to school. The government offers financial assistance for girls, but boys are more likely to attend. Beginning at age seven, students spend six years in Lower Basic School. If they pass a leaving exam, they can attend Upper Basic School for three years. An entrance exam is required for admission to a four-year high school. Only about 20 percent of children move to this level, partly because of high fees, the distant location of schools, and a belief among some families that education is not useful for farming. Higher education is offered through the University of The Gambia, which was established in 1999.

Because students from different ethnic groups may be in the same class, teachers in the first few years of school struggle to bridge language barriers and introduce English. Children learn mostly by memorization, so learning to read in English can be hard for several years. Teachers often use local languages for the first three years before switching to English only.

Health. The healthcare system is heavily subsidized by international organizations. A female birth attendant and a village health worker of either sex are in every village, but they have limited training. A community health nurse is assigned to a group of villages to treat malaria and give shots. An area health facility has more staff; they provide more medicine and advanced care, and they visit health stations to give monthly immunizations. If they cannot care for a patient, he or she is sent to an urban hospital. Malaria and meningitis afflict many Gambians, especially children.

DEVELOPMENT DATA

Human Dev. Index* rank .... 155 of 177 countries
    Adjusted for women .... 125 of 144 countries
Real GDP per capita $1,690
Adult literacy rate .... 45 percent (male); 31 (female)
Infant mortality rate .... 73 per 1,000 births
Life expectancy .... 53 (male); 55 (female)

AT A GLANCE

Events and Trends.

- In January 2005, the nation's five main opposition parties announced plans to form a coalition and select a joint candidate to run against President Jammeh in 2006. The opposition's inability to unite was seen as a key factor behind Jammeh's reelection in 2001 and the continued dominance of his Alliance for Patriotic Reorientation and Construction (APRC) in the National Assembly.
- Newspaper editor Deyda Hydara was murdered in December 2004, prompting a demonstration by 300 journalists, who believe his death was politically motivated. Hydara was a critic of new media laws, which give six-month jail terms to journalists who write articles deemed libelous.

Contact Information. Embassy of The Gambia, 1156 15th Street NW, Suite 905, Washington, DC 20005; phone (202) 785-1399.

CultureGrams
People. The World. You.

ProQuest Information and Learning Company
300 North Zeeb Road, P.O. Box 1346
Ann Arbor, Michigan 48106 USA
Toll Free: 1.800.528.6279
Fax: 1.800.864.0019
www.culturegrams.com

CultureGrams World Edition 2006

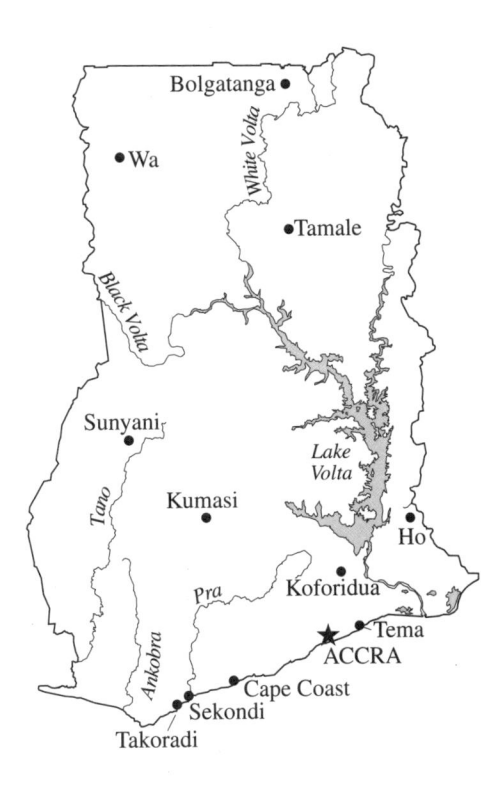

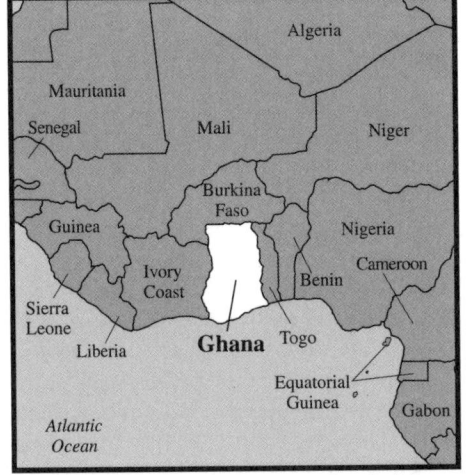

Republic of Ghana

BACKGROUND

Land and Climate. Covering 92,100 square miles (238,540 square kilometers), Ghana is about the same size as Oregon. Its three climatic zones include the southern forest belt (warm and humid), the coastal belt (warm and dry), and the northern grasslands (hot and dry). Forests and woodlands cover more than one-third of the total land area. A dam on the Volta River has created Lake Volta, the largest man-made lake in the world. Rain falls primarily between April and October. Ghana is hot and dry for the rest of the year; temperatures reach above 100°F (40°C). From late November to early January, hot, dry, and dusty harmattan winds blow across the north. Temperatures in the southeast range from 74°F (23°C) in October to 86°F (30°C) in June.

History. Ghana takes its name, though not its modern boundaries, from one of the great inland trading empires that flourished in West Africa from the fourth to the eleventh centuries A.D. The university city of Tombouctou (Timbuktu—now in Mali) was part of ancient Ghana.

Portuguese traders arrived in 1471. They mined gold and established headquarters for their slave trade. The area they controlled became known as the Gold Coast, and various European powers established forts there. In 1874, Britain took control of the Gold Coast and established Accra as the capital in 1876. After years of fighting with the Asante in the interior, the British gained control of present-day Ghana in 1901. Though the Asante were defeated, they still have a king who has some influence over local and regional politics.

The Convention People's Party (CPP), under the leadership of Kwame Nkrumah, won legislative elections in 1951, and for the first time the African majority controlled the government. On 6 March 1957, Ghana became the first Black African colony to gain independence from Britain. Three years later, the country became a republic and Nkrumah was elected president. Unfortunately, his socialist policies led to a significant drop in the standard of living. While he was on his way to Vietnam in 1966, Nkrumah was deposed by a military coup. Elections were held in 1969, but the military took over the government again in 1972.

In 1979, Flight Lieutenant Jerry Rawlings, with a group of junior officers and enlisted men, overthrew the government, arrested dozens of government officials, and executed eight of them (including three former heads of state). Rawlings drafted a new constitution, held elections, and in three months turned power over to a newly elected civilian government. However, Rawlings was not satisfied with government performance and again seized power in 1981. He outlawed political parties, suspended the constitution, and appointed a seven-member Provisional National Defense Council (PNDC).

In 1988, a national assembly was established, but members could not belong to political parties. The assembly was to represent different walks of life rather than political views. A constituent assembly, composed of elected and appointed officials, later helped draft a constitution to legalize political parties and provide for elections in 1992. Rawlings won the presidential race and began to improve economic conditions. He was credited with creating one of Africa's most stable economies, and his popularity allowed him to win a second (and, by law, final) term as president in 1996.

Rawlings's ruling National Democratic Congress (NDC) declared Vice President John Atta Mills its candidate for the 2000 presidential election. Mills lost to New Patriotic Party (NPP) leader John Kufuor, who became president in the first

Ghana

nonviolent transfer of power since Ghana's independence. Kufuor successfully reduced inflation and borrowing costs during his first term. Promising continued economic progress, he was reelected in December 2004.

THE PEOPLE

Population. Ghana's population of 20.8 million is growing at 1.4 percent annually. While 99.8 percent of the people are Black African, they are divided into more than one hundred ethnic groups, each with its own language and cultural heritage. Violence between these various ethnic groups is rare, although social interaction is limited and tension is sometimes significant. In many regions (especially the north), people who are not indigenous to the area live in separate sections of town called *zongo*.

The largest ethnic group is the Akan (44 percent), of which the major subgroups are the Asante (in Kumasi and the center of the country) and the Fante (in the center of the coastal region). Other major ethnic groups include the Ewe (in the Volta region to the east) and the Ga (in the coastal region surrounding Accra). The Adangme is the primary subgroup of the Ga. The Dagomba, Dagaaba, and Gonja ethnic groups live in the north. A few Europeans, Lebanese merchants, and some Indians and Chinese live in Ghana. The nation's two largest cities are Accra (two million residents) and Kumasi (one million). Together, Sekondi and Takoradi also have a large population. About 45 percent of the population lives in urban areas.

Language. English is Ghana's official language, partly because of the country's colonial association with Great Britain and partly because there are so many ethnic languages that no single one could effectively serve as the official language. English is used in school, business, and government. Many Ghanaians desire to make certain local languages official as well. Each ethnic group has a native tongue, the most significant of which include Akan (44 percent of all people), Dagomba (16 percent), Ewe (13 percent), and Ga-Adangme (8 percent). Akan has several dialects. Its Twi dialect is the most commonly used for communication between ethnic groups. Hausa, although native to only a few Ghanaians, is understood by many northern people and is their primary language for interethnic communication.

Religion. Although more than half of all Ghanaians belong to one of several Christian churches, and another 15 to 20 percent are Muslim, traditional African beliefs and practices play a major role in society and are retained regardless of any other religious affiliation. At least one-fourth of the population exclusively worships according to indigenous beliefs.

This traditional faith is characterized by a belief in a Supreme Being who has created all things and has given various degrees of power to all living (animate) and nonliving (inanimate) things. Out of respect for the Supreme Being, who cannot be approached directly, Ghanaians often communicate with him through intermediaries. Intermediaries can include animate or inanimate objects, as well as ancestor spirits. It is especially common for people to seek guidance through their ancestors. Accordingly, ancestor veneration is an important aspect of Ghanaian culture. These traditional beliefs are often referred to by outsiders as animism because of their emphasis on showing reverence for living things. Many Ghanaians would not accept the term *animism* to describe their worship. Traditional faith also includes a belief in wizards, witches, demons, magic potions, and other supernatural phenomena collectively known as *juju*.

Integral to traditional worship are various rites related to birth, puberty, marriage, and death. These are performed within the family. In addition, entire towns or regions celebrate seasonal festivals, through which people honor the dead or ask for blessings.

General Attitudes. Ghanaians are warm, extremely friendly, and sociable—even with strangers. They tend to be boisterous, which makes for animated arguments and celebrations. Ghanaians generally take life at a relaxed pace, viewing time as a series of events rather than a matter of hours or minutes. People are considered to be more important than schedules. Tolerance and acceptance are typical individual characteristics. Group (family, community) needs take precedence over personal desires. Ghanaians show great respect to the elderly, the well educated, the wealthy, persons with royal lineage, and persons who are noted for their hard work or integrity.

Ghanaians are proud of their status as the first sub-Saharan colony to gain independence from a European power. Although greatly influenced by Western civilization, the people are striving to develop a nation and culture that is uniquely African. Western visitors who act, or give the impression of being, superior because they come from economically advanced nations are offensive to Ghanaians.

Personal Appearance. Ghanaian dress is generally conservative. Nearly everyone considers it important to be clean and properly dressed in public. Casual attire is the rule for most occasions, although a suit and tie or dress is required for more formal instances. Shorts are not acceptable public attire. Western dress is standard in most areas, but officials often wear traditional clothing for ceremonial occasions. These outfits vary by region and ethnic group. For example, Asante, Fante, and Ewe men wear *kente*-cloth (colorful woven strips of cloth) robes. In the south, men may wear *ntoma* (long colored cloth wrapped around the body somewhat like a toga). Northern men wear a *smock* (long tunic made of wide strips of rough cotton cloth that are sewn together). Muslim men wear robes similar to those worn by Arab Muslims, except that the Ghanaian version is colorful. Regardless of what one wears, the design of the cloth can reflect one's status.

Women usually wear a traditional, long wraparound skirt; a separate top; and a headscarf. They wrap extra cloth at the hips or add it to the sleeves. A head cloth, if worn, generally matches a woman's dress. Women prefer bold colors and large prints.

CUSTOMS AND COURTESIES

Greetings. Because of pronounced differences between ethnic groups, greetings vary from area to area. A handshake is important when greeting most people, although Muslims avoid shaking hands with members of the opposite sex. Among some groups, male friends may shake hands first and, while pulling the palms slowly away, grasp each other's middle finger with a thumb and middle finger; then they snap the grasped finger. Regardless of the gestures or words used in greeting, the act of greeting another person is extremely important. To ignore a greeting or to fail to greet someone is a serious insult to most Ghanaians.

Before one begins a conversation, a general greeting such as *Good morning, Good afternoon*, or *Good evening* is necessary. When addressing a person of higher status, one follows the greeting with *Sir* or *Madame*. When greeting a respected elder or someone of royal descent, one often bows slightly with the left hand placed behind the back.

Most greetings are in the dominant local language and are followed by questions about one's health, family welfare, journey, and so forth. One addresses new acquaintances by title and family name. Friends and family members often use given names. Children refer to any adult who is well-known to the family as *aunt* or *uncle* (or *grandma* or *grandpa* for older people), even when they are not related. By the same token, adults of the same age might refer to each other as *brother* or *sister*, regardless of their relationship, and will use *auntie* and *uncle* for respected older people.

Gestures. Courtesy is important. Gesturing, eating, or passing items with the left hand is impolite. When yawning or using a toothpick, a person covers the mouth. Among Muslims, and some other groups who often sit on the floor, it is improper to allow the sole of one's foot to point at another person. Generally, a person does not place feet on chairs, desks, or tables—especially those being used by someone else. Knocking the hands together, palms up, in front of the body can mean "please" or "I beg of you" but can also convey thanks.

Ghanaians consider it impolite and defiant for a child to look an adult in the eye. Friends of the same gender may often and appropriately hold hands while walking or speaking. Members of the opposite sex might also hold hands, but showing any more affection in public is less acceptable. Personal space is rather narrow in Ghana and people stand close to one another when conversing.

Visiting. In a society where friendly social relations are important, visiting plays a key role in everyday life. Friends and relatives visit one another frequently, often unannounced, and appreciate the visits of others. In some areas, people prefer to dress up and visit on Sundays. Ghanaians work hard to accommodate their guests. Most visits occur in the home. Before entering a gate or door, one calls out *A-go*, instead of knocking, to announce one's presence. Guests might take a small gift for the children and sometimes the adults.

Some hosts prefer that guests remove their shoes when entering the home or certain rooms in the family compound. Guests are nearly always served water and often other refreshments. Refusing these offers is impolite. Visitors are usually welcome to stay as long as they wish. People generally avoid visiting during mealtime, but an unexpected guest would be invited to share the meal. When a visit is over, guests are accompanied to the bus stop or taxi stand or given a ride home. Leaving them on their own is considered impolite.

Eating. Ghanaians eat meals with their right hand. They wash their hands in a bowl of water before and after the meal. One scoops food and forms it into a ball with the right hand before eating it. Most Ghanaians prefer to eat at home, but they also enjoy eating at an open-air area with benches and tables where people make and sell inexpensive local foods.

LIFESTYLE

Family. In Ghana, the extended family is strong and vital. Some groups have a matrilineal family organization, in which inheritance is passed through the wife's family, and others are patrilineal. Regardless of how inheritance is passed, the oldest male leads most family organizations. He has financial responsibility for all who live with him. Extended families of three or four generations often share one household. A typical rural compound has a section of the house for the oldest male and sometimes his wife. If he has more than one wife, each will have one room for herself and her children. Additional rooms are reserved for members of the extended family. In farming families, everyone who is old enough helps raise the crops. Girls carry water, clean the house, take care of babies, and sometimes cook. Boys care for the family animals. Adult children care for elderly parents.

Elderly family members are deeply respected and exercise a great deal of influence on family decisions. Ghanaians normally sacrifice personal ambitions for the sake of the family unit. Funeral events are very important and can last from one to forty days, depending on the ethnic group and the status of the dead. Usually, there is one day set aside for the actual funeral, and then another one or more days reserved for mourning and for celebrating the deceased.

Dating and Marriage. Families still arrange many marriages, although children have the right to reject undesirable arrangements. A growing number of urban youth are adopting Westernized dating practices. Marriage in rural areas (and to some extent in urban areas) may also follow tradition, which allows a man to take more than one wife. Still, the Christian marriage with its monogamous restrictions is becoming prevalent. Traditionally, the groom gives the bride's family a dowry to indicate his responsibility for her. In northern areas, the dowry is often four cows (equal to about two years of salary for wage earners).

Diet. The Ghanaian diet consists primarily of yams, cassava, millet, maize, plantains, and rice. A typical southern dish is *fufu* (a doughlike combination of plantains and cassava). Also common is *ampesi* (boiled yams or plantains with sauce). In the north, the average family eats two or three daily meals with *tuo zaafi* (a thick porridge of corn or millet; often called "T.Z."). Ghanaians enjoy hot and spicy food, so most of their meals are accompanied by a pepper sauce. Soups and sauces are also made from palm or peanut oil. People enjoy meat, fish, or chicken with their meals, but these foods are too expensive for most people to eat regularly. Ghanaians supplement their diets with a variety of tropical fruits and vegetables.

Recreation. Most Ghanaians are highly devoted to soccer, the national sport. They are also fond of boxing, field hockey, and track-and-field. People enjoy the theater, movies, cultural presentations, and music and dance festivals, where available. Ghana has its own movie industry. Radio broadcasts are very popular and create a social gathering where electricity is not available (via battery-operated radios).

The Arts. The popular dance music known as *highlife* originated in Ghana and has since spread to many parts of Africa. Heavily influenced by jazz and other Western music, *highlife* typically is played by bands of guitars and horns. Traditional dance and music are performed at special festivals and funerals. Common instruments include wooden *atenteban* flutes, *balafon* xylophones, and various types of drums. Ghanaian textiles such as *kente*-cloth and *ntoma* (see Personal Appearance) have colorful geometric patterns and are considered to be among the most beautiful in Africa. Wood-carvers create pieces with intricate designs and inlaid bronze or bone.

Holidays. National public holidays include Independence Day (6 Mar.), Good Friday (Friday before Easter Sunday), Easter Monday, Republic Day (1 July), *Eid ul-Fitr* (the Muslim feast at the end of Islam's holy fasting month of *Ramadan*), *Eid ul-Adha* (the Muslim Feast of the Sacrifice), Christmas, and Boxing Day (26 Dec.). Boxing Day comes from the British tradition of giving service employees small boxed gifts. Today, people generally spend the day visiting friends and relatives.

Commerce. Daily commerce is mostly conducted in open-air markets ranging in size from a few dozen women selling crops

Ghana

in a village to large permanent complexes where thousands of vendors sell their various wares out of small booths. All types of food, clothing, fabrics, housewares, animals, jewelry, tailoring services, and more are found at these markets. Kiosks and roadside stands are also typical throughout Ghana. A common social gesture is the *dash*, whereby people show their appreciation for kindnesses rendered them (a market woman might add extra fruit to a purchase, or a consumer might give someone who was helpful or nice a few coins). Urban offices are open between 8 a.m. and 4:30 p.m., with a one- or two-hour lunch break.

SOCIETY

Government. Ghana is a multiparty democracy. The president (currently John Kufuor) is chief of state and head of government. Parliament has 230 seats. Direct popular elections for president, vice president, and members of Parliament are held every four years; the president and vice president are elected on the same ticket. The voting age is 18. Ghana is divided into 10 regions and 110 administrative districts. Although funding is controlled by the central government, these local districts have authority over education, health, agriculture, and social welfare. Local chiefs also have influence in traditional affairs. The Asante king (Otumfuo Osei Tutu II) has no constitutional authority, but his opinions are valued and sought.

Economy. The Ghanaian economy is based primarily on agriculture, which engages more than 50 percent of the labor force. Cacao (from which cocoa is made) is the most important cash crop, accounting for about 45 percent of exports. Other crops (corn, root crops, sorghum, millet, and peanuts) are produced for local consumption. Fishing, light manufacturing, and timber are key industries. Ghana also mines gold, bauxite, aluminum, and diamonds. World price fluctuations for these products can cause economic difficulties for Ghana, as can drought or other local events. Tourism is a significant source of foreign revenue.

Ghana has been privatizing and modernizing its economy for a number of years. Still, Ghana remains an essentially poor country. Corruption at the local level often hinders development, and income distribution is highly unequal. The currency is the *new cedi* (GHC).

Transportation and Communications. While Ghana's transportation system is underdeveloped, a rail system connects Accra with Kumasi and Takoradi. A fairly good system of buses connects major cities. Most people rely on public transportation, walking, or cycling. The *tro-tro* is a crowded, but efficient and inexpensive, minibus used for short-distance travel. In the north, bicycles and motorcycles are common means of transport.

Communications systems are limited, although the government is seeking to upgrade facilities and networks. Telephone service is only available in cities and towns. Ghanaians enjoy keeping up with local and international news via newspapers, radio, and television. Ghana has one national television station and several private regional stations. Mail and phone services are often unreliable, but the informal method of passing information works rapidly and well: letters or messages are passed to a driver or passenger traveling in the intended direction until they reach their destination. Internet cafés are popular in Accra and other cities.

DEVELOPMENT DATA
- Human Dev. Index* rank .... 131 of 177 countries
- Adjusted for women .... 104 of 144 countries
- Real GDP per capita $2,130
- Adult literacy rate .... 82 percent (male); 66 (female)
- Infant mortality rate .... 52 per 1,000 births
- Life expectancy .... 56 (male); 59 (female)

Education. Schooling in Ghana has been free, although parents now bear some of the cost of materials and supplies. Although a large percentage of Ghana's national budget is spent on education, efforts so far have not improved conditions of overcrowding or underfunding. Schools are organized on three levels: primary (six years), junior secondary (three years), and senior secondary (three years). Every administrative district has at least one high school. School is taught in English, so most children basically are learning in a foreign language. This keeps many children from progressing. The adult literacy rate is lower in rural areas. Qualified students may pursue a post-secondary education at one of Ghana's five universities, at teacher-training colleges, or at trade schools.

Health. Although the government is working to increase the quality and availability of medical care, facilities are limited or understaffed outside of major cities. Malaria and other tropical diseases and the lack of clean water or a modern sewer system are serious health threats even to urban residents. Almost half of all hospital admissions come from malaria. Intestinal disorders are common. HIV/AIDS and tuberculosis are growing problems. Many people rely on herbal medicine and traditional healing. Ghanaian law recognizes traditional healing and makes it a partner of Western medicine within the national health system. The infant mortality rate is lower than in the past but still high.

AT A GLANCE

Events and Trends.
- Voter turnout was more than 80 percent for December 2004 elections, in which President Kufuor won a second term by securing 53 percent of the vote. Kufuor's NPP won 129 of 230 parliamentary seats. During his first term, Kufuor introduced economic reforms that reduced inflation from about 40 percent to 12 percent and increased national income by 5 percent per year.
- A National Reconciliation Commission (NRC) established by President Kufuor investigated human-rights abuses and political killings that took place during the military government of former president Rawlings. The NRC submitted its final report in October 2004; its recommendations included reparations for roughly 3,000 victims.

Contact Information. Embassy of Ghana, 3512 International Drive NW, Washington, DC 20008; phone (202) 686-4520; web site www.ghana-embassy.org.

Republic of Guinea

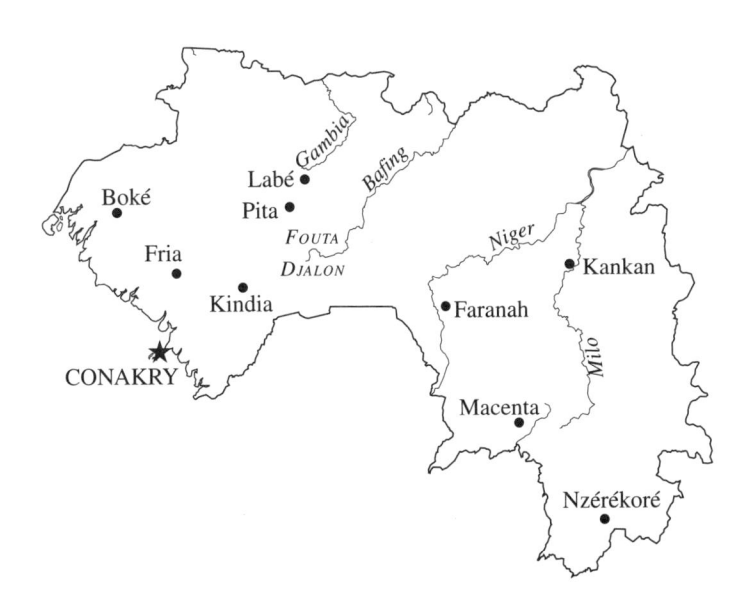

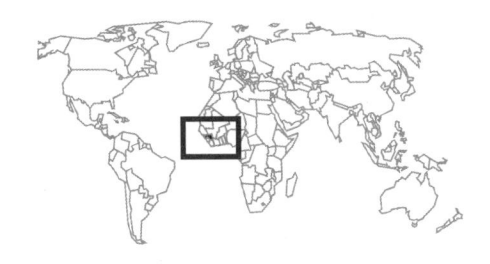

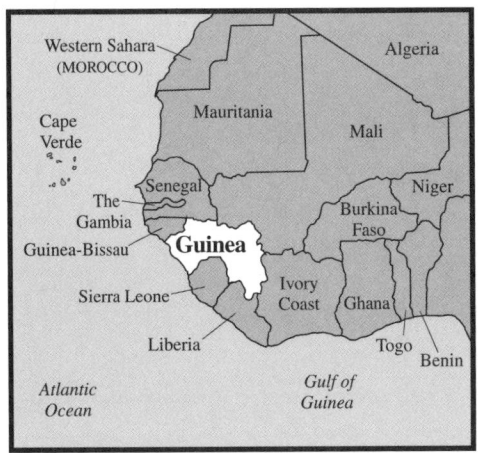

CultureGrams World Edition 2006

BACKGROUND

Land and Climate. Guinea covers 94,000 square miles (243,460 square kilometers) and is somewhat smaller than Oregon. The nation is divided into four geographical regions: the coast of lower Guinea; the central, mountainous Fouta Djalon; the savanna of upper Guinea; and the forest in the southeast. Numerous major rivers, including the Niger, Bafing, and Gambia, have their sources in Guinea.

Guinea has two distinct seasons: the rainy season (May–October) and the dry season (November–April). As much as 170 inches (432 centimeters) of rain may fall on the coast annually, while the savanna region receives about 60 inches (152 centimeters) each year. Average temperatures range from 80 to 90°F (26–32°C), but temperatures above 100°F (38°C) are not uncommon. Nighttime temperatures may fall to as low as 50°F (10°C) in the Fouta Djalon.

History. For thousands of years, various peoples populated Guinea. In the 10th century A.D., Soussou and Malinké (also called Mandingo or Maninka) groups began to move into the area, pushing the former inhabitants into smaller regions. Upper Guinea was part of the Ghana Empire in the 10th and 11th centuries, the Mali Empire until the 14th century, and then the Songhai Empire until the 19th century. People of the Fula ethnic group migrated into western Guinea in the 17th century, bringing Islam with them. They took control of the Fouta Djalon and established Islam as the state religion. Then they pushed the Soussou to coastal areas, where the Soussou established trade with Europeans. While not a major slave trade area, Guinea was affected by that trading as well as by disputes among European groups.

In the mid-1800s, El Hadj Umar Tall launched a *jihad* (holy war) in the region, establishing a state in parts of eastern Guinea and in parts of Mali and Senegal. He attracted many followers until he tried to impress the *Tijani* brand of Islam on the Fula and Malinké. They resisted and he eventually died (1864) fighting local peoples.

More successful at empire building in the 1800s was Samory Touré, a skilled Malinké warrior who quickly defeated various chieftaincies. Touré spread Islam and established a well-ordered society. His expanding empire soon met with French forces advancing from other African conquests. Touré's empire and French troops clashed throughout the 1880s and negotiated into the 1890s. The French finally captured Touré in 1898 and then completed their conquest of the area by 1904.

French rule brought private ownership of communal land and the expansion of commercial and service jobs. Although urban people who adopted the French language and culture evolved into an elite class, most people continued to live a subsistence agriculture lifestyle well after World War II.

After the war, several labor parties were established, including the *Parti Democratique de Guinée* (Democratic Party of Guinea) led by Ahmed Sékou Touré. He was a vocal supporter of autonomy. In 1958, his party organized support to vote against Charles de Gaulle's proposed French community and then declared independence. Guinea was the only French colony to vote "no" on the referendum that was to create the community. Thus, unlike other francophone African states, it was cut off from France's financial aid and other assistance programs. Guinea was also shunned by other Western nations and, in this relative isolation, developed a strong national identity.

Sékou Touré, once loved by the people for his leadership, never allowed elections and governed a capricious one-party

Guinea

state. He deteriorated into a brutal dictator and began facing opposition from various groups. Nevertheless, he remained in power until his death in 1984. Two weeks later, the military took control of the government and established the Second Guinean Republic under one of its officers, Lansana Conté.

In 1990, a committee began to oversee Guinea's transition to a multiparty system. A constitution providing for a democratic government was accepted in 1991. Presidential and parliamentary elections took place in 1993. Conté was declared president, although the results were disputed on many fronts. Elections held in 1998 brought the same result—victory for Conté—and the same criticisms that the vote was unfair.

Opposition parties boycotted a 2001 referendum that proposed eliminating constitutional restrictions on the number of terms the president could hold office. The referendum passed, allowing Conté to run for a third term in December 2003 elections. Believing the elections were rigged, the opposition again called on voters to stage a boycott, and Conté won with 95 percent of the vote.

THE PEOPLE

Population. Guinea's population of approximately 9.2 million is growing annually at a rate of 2.4 percent. The nation actually has a very high birthrate but its emigration rate keeps population growth low. About 44 percent of the population is age 14 or younger. Almost three-fourths of Guineans live in rural areas. More than one million live in the capital, Conakry. Another 250,000 live in each of the regional capitals of Labé, Kankan, and Nzérékoré.

Guinea's largest ethnic group is the Fula (also called Peuhl or Fulo, plural form Fulbe), which comprises 40 percent of the population and is concentrated in the Fouta Djalon. The other major groups are the Malinké (30 percent) in upper Guinea and the Soussou (20 percent) in the coastal regions. The Soussou are a collection of different ethnic groups that speak the same language. The Guerze, Kissi, and Toma inhabit the forest region. The country has numerous other ethnic groups, sometimes comprising only one village.

Language. French is the official language of Guinea, but most rural people do not understand it. Various African languages are spoken in different regions. On the coast, the most common language is Soussou; in the Fouta Djalon, it is Pular; in upper Guinea, it is Malinké; and in the forest, numerous languages intermingle, including Guerze, Kissi, and Toma. The few clerics with advanced Islamic education speak Arabic. Children learn a few Arabic verses from the *Qur'an* (Koran). Liberian and Sierra Leonean refugees introduced Krio, a language with both English and African elements.

Religion. Guinea's government promotes religious freedom. About 85 percent of the population is Muslim. Christians comprise 8 percent. Animism is still practiced by certain rural groups (7 percent). Some Muslims and Christians mix indigenous beliefs with their religion. For example, people buy *gri gri* (good-luck charms) for their children. Many animists living in the forest do not trust people of other religions or races because these groups have destroyed or otherwise violated sacred forests.

Devout Muslims follow the traditional worship practices of praying five times daily, avoiding alcohol, professing the name of and attributing all to *Allah* (God), fasting during the holy month of *Ramadan*, and giving alms to the poor. They accept the *Qur'an* as scripture that was revealed to Muhammad, Islam's last and greatest recognized prophet. Although they are devoted to Islam, Guinean Muslims are also highly tolerant of other faiths, and Christians enjoy full control over their religious affairs.

General Attitudes. Guineans identify strongly with their families and ethnic groups. Although various groups coexist without serious strife, there is a tendency to help and trust only one's own group. Tensions exist between ethnic groups, religions, and social classes in some areas, but they have not yet seriously threatened stability.

People speak often of religion in discussing how one should act. Most Guineans strongly believe that whatever happens is *Allah's* will, and they accept disappointment or sorrow with this attitude. Such an approach also means people live more for the present, assuming the future will take care of itself. Daily living and interpersonal relationships are often more important than material goods. The Guinean sense of time is relaxed, and people may arrive hours late for an appointment or event with little explanation.

Personal Appearance. Guineans wear Western styles as well as traditional Muslim and West African clothing. Men may wear a short-sleeved suit coat and matching pants to work, or they may wear a Western-style shirt, a tie, and pants. Muslim men may wear long robes called *boubous* over loose pants and a shirt. Women often wear brightly patterned, locally tailored blouses or Muslim-style robes called *petits boubous* with a matching *pagne* (length of cloth wrapped around the waist). Some women also wear Western-style dresses. Imported secondhand clothing is sold in city and village markets. No matter what style a person wears, Guineans consider it extremely important that clothing be clean, pressed, and in good repair.

CUSTOMS AND COURTESIES

Greetings. Greetings are an important part of everyday interaction. Failing to greet someone or skipping a greeting in favor of conversation is an insult. Guineans most often greet others in French or the language of the particular region or individual to whom they are speaking. *Bonjour* (Good day) and *Bonsoir* (Good evening) are the common French greetings, while *Salaam Alaikum* (Peace be upon you) is the preferred Muslim greeting. Greetings are usually followed by inquiries about the other person's family.

When walking along the road, a person might call out greetings rather than stop. Even strangers are greeted, including store clerks, taxi drivers, or anyone with whom one is about to interact. Upon arrival at a gathering, Guineans greet every person with a right-handed handshake. When the right hand is not clean, one extends a closed fist and the other person shakes the wrist. Raising both hands, palms out, is a common way to greet a larger group or someone who is a bit too distant for a handshake. Some older men also use this greeting rather than shake hands with women. If seated, a person shows respect by standing up to shake hands. Respect is also conveyed by grasping one's own right forearm with the left hand while shaking hands. Good friends who are parting for a long time might use a left handshake.

When addressing others, Guineans use titles, such as *Doctor, Madame* (Mrs.), or *Monsieur* (Mr.), instead of names. They also use familial titles, such as *frère, tante,* and *cousin* ("brother," "aunt," and "cousin"), with strangers as well as within the family. A younger man would call an older or more respected man "elder brother."

Gestures. Guineans hand objects to or accept them from others with the right hand or with both hands; using the left hand alone is considered rude. They beckon by waving all four fingers with the palm down. One hails a taxi by extending the arm, palm down, and waving the hand. A person may attempt to gain another's attention by puckering the lips and making a kissing sound. To show respect, one avoids eye contact, especially with older people. Men and women do not show affection in public, but friends of the same gender often hold hands or walk arm in arm. People avoid pointing the soles of their feet at others.

Visiting. To visit someone is to honor him or her, and Guineans are gracious hosts. They frequently invite friends over for a meal, but invitations are not necessary for one to visit. People sometimes visit simply to exchange greetings. To pass by a friend's home without stopping briefly is an insult. Proper greetings are exchanged at every visit, regardless of the purpose. A visitor usually does not bring a gift; rather, a visit is reciprocated with a return visit. However, a person returning or arriving from out of town often brings food (fruit, vegetables, or rice), fabric, or a specialty of that region.

Guests may be offered fruit or a beverage if the visit is not during mealtime, but otherwise they often are invited to eat. It is not impolite to say one has just eaten. However, the host usually insists the guest eat something, and it is rude to refuse entirely. Generally, the guest eats at least a small portion and thanks the host and the person who prepared the meal.

During visits, there often are several-minute gaps in conversation, filled only by a repeat of the greetings and inquiries about the family. When guests are ready to leave, they say they must go, shake hands, and thank the host and family for their hospitality.

Eating. Most Guineans eat with the right hand from a common platter that is often placed on the floor or a mat. In some families, people eat separately according to age and gender. Before and after any meal eaten with the hands, a bowl of water is made available for washing hands. Individuals eat only from the part of the dish that is immediately in front of them. The oldest person or the woman who prepared the meal may divide the meat and vegetables among those eating. Most Guineans do not drink during a meal because it implies the food is not good enough to satisfy the appetite. Most wait to drink water after the meal. Conversation is minimal, but guests always thank the host at the end of the meal. The host often replies with *Albarka*, an Arabic term used to credit *Allah* for providing the food.

Many Guineans living in nonagricultural settings eat the main meal around midday and another meal in the evening. Breakfast may include coffee and bread, as well as any leftovers from the previous day. In agricultural settings, people working in the fields eat a larger breakfast, which may include hot cereal. They then eat their main meal upon returning from the fields in the evening.

LIFESTYLE

Family. Extended families living together—and sharing child care, domestic chores, and meals—are common in rural areas. While extended families are also common in urban areas, the number of nuclear families living in individual homes is increasing. Obligations to one's extended family run deep and can involve giving money, lodging, or other favors to distant relatives. In general, a family's eldest male presides over the household.

Large families share a common compound with separate homes or rooms for individuals or nuclear family members. In rural areas, the most common type of dwelling is a sturdy, round home made of thick mud bricks and a thatched roof. The size of the home often reflects the importance of the owner in the community. For affluent villagers and urban residents, homes may be single- or multifamily cement block structures with cement floors, plywood ceilings, and corrugated tin roofs.

Dating and Marriage. Urban youth may date as in Western cultures, but they more often associate in groups. A person's family frequently influences the choice of a mate. Women usually marry before they are 20 and men usually wait until they are 25 or older. Traditionally, the man presents 10 kola nuts to the woman's family to propose marriage. The head of the woman's family cracks the nuts to signal his approval. Later, the groom offers fabric, jewelry, or cattle to the bride and her family. Muslim men are allowed to have more than one wife (as many as four total), but they must be able to financially support each one.

Diet. The main meal usually consists of rice with a sauce made from palm oil and tomato paste, peanut butter, or ground leaves. Meat or fish and vegetables, such as manioc, sweet potatoes, or squash, may be cooked with the sauce. Millet is a popular grain, particularly in the Sahelian region near Mali. The Malinké eat *too* (pronounced "TOE"), made from cassava or rice powder. In the Fouta Djalon region, soured milk over couscous is a favorite dish, especially at celebrations and large gatherings. Avocados, peanuts, mangoes, papaya, bananas, oranges, pineapples, and sometimes watermelon are eaten in season. Devout Muslims do not drink alcohol or eat pork.

Recreation. Soccer is by far the most popular sport in Guinea, although basketball and volleyball are also favorites. Although sports are mostly played by boys, urban girls participate through school. Many urban areas have facilities and organized sporting competitions.

Family gatherings, visits, and local festivals provide recreation for many people, especially in rural areas. Family celebrations held for Christian baptisms and traditional Muslim and Christian weddings are particularly important. It is customary at these events for *griots* (traditional singers) to sing about individual guests (their name, appearance, character), and the honored person is expected to give the *griots* a small sum of money in return.

The Arts. Although Guinea's urban youth prefer discos and Western music, traditional music remains popular in most parts of the country. Indigenous musical instruments include the *kora* (a lute-harp with metal or fiber strings stretched across half of a large gourd) and the *balafon* (a xylophone made of wood and gourd). The Malinké *djembe* (a drum with a narrow base and a goatskin surface) is one of a wide variety of Guinean drums and other percussion instruments. Dancing is popular at weddings and other celebrations.

Holidays. Guinean holidays include New Year's Day, Easter, *Tabaski* (an Islamic holiday commemorating Abraham's willingness to sacrifice his son to God), *Eid al Fitr* (a feast at the end of *Ramadan*, the month in which Muslims do not eat or drink from sunrise to sunset), Labor Day (1 May), *Mawloud* (the prophet Muhammad's birthday), Women's Day (27 Aug., celebrating a day in 1977 on which market women revolted against policies of forced collectivization), Independence Day (2 Oct.), All Saints' Day (1 Nov.), and Christmas. Islamic holidays involve people attending a mosque, visiting friends and family, and eating large meals. These holidays are determined according to the lunar calendar, which is shorter than the Western (Gregorian) year by about 11 days. Since dates are set

Guinea

according to the moon's phases, the Gregorian dates for these holidays differ from year to year. The period from Christmas to New Year's is a much-celebrated holiday season for all Guineans.

Commerce. Government offices and businesses are open from 8 a.m. to 4:30 p.m., Monday through Thursday. They close by 2 p.m. on Friday. Offices are closed Saturday and Sunday. Urban markets are open all day, every day, but many shops are closed on Friday afternoon and Sunday. In rural areas, market day may be only one day a week. Bargaining is expected. Business transactions can take some time to complete in Guinea, and patience and persistence are vital.

SOCIETY

Government. Guinea is officially a multiparty democracy consisting of 34 administrative regions. The president (currently Lansana Conté) is head of state and head of government. The president serves a seven-year term and appoints the prime minister (currently Cellou Dalein Diallo) and members of the Council of Ministers, an executive cabinet. The National Assembly has 114 seats. Its members are directly elected to five-year terms. The voting age is 18.

Economy. Guinea has abundant natural resources, including 25 percent of the world's known reserves of bauxite, along with diamonds, gold, and other metals. The country also has great potential for hydroelectric power. Bauxite and alumina are currently the only major exports. However, Guinea hopes to increase the mining of other resources. Other industries include processing plants for beer, juices, soft drinks, and tobacco.

Agriculture employs 80 percent of the nation's labor force. Under French rule, and at the beginning of independence, Guinea was a major exporter of bananas, pineapples, coffee, coca, peanuts, and palm oil. Unfortunately, isolation and insufficient capital caused these exports to decline under Sékou Touré.

Guinea is one of the poorest countries in the world, even though its real gross domestic product per capita is relatively high for the region. Most people do not earn a sufficient income, or they have no income at all. International aid is linked to economic reform. The government encourages a free-market economy, and a continued privatization effort is expected to help the economy and encourage more growth. The currency is the Guinean *franc* (GNF), which is not tied to any international currency and cannot be converted or taken out of Guinea.

Transportation and Communications. Guinea is working to pave roads that link major cities, but most roads are unpaved and not well maintained. Air Guinea airlines flies from Conakry to the regional capitals. An intercity bus service (*Sogetrag*) serves most of the nation's regions. Taxis and trucks are the main means of public transportation for most people, few of whom own cars. Many Guineans travel within their regions by motorcycle or bicycle. Short-distance travel is by foot.

The government sponsors a weekly newspaper, *Horoya* (*Liberty*), which is available in Conakry. Independent papers are published in French. National radio and television pro-

DEVELOPMENT DATA
Human Dev. Index* rank .... 160 of 177 countries
Adjusted for women........................NA
Real GDP per capita $2,100
Adult literacy rate .... 50 percent (male); 22 (female)
Infant mortality rate .... 92 per 1,000 births
Life expectancy................ 49 (male); 49 (female)

grams are broadcast from Conakry. A radio program in the local language is also broadcast in each region. Domestic and international telephone service is available, but most people do not have phones.

Education. Guinean education is based on the French system and includes six years of primary school, four years of middle school, and three years of high school. Students follow one of three tracks: social sciences, mathematics, or natural sciences. Passing national tests is required for graduation. Enrollment levels are low; only about one-third of all children attend primary school and the number drops to 15 percent for secondary school. Indeed, only about 15 to 30 percent of the population is functional in French, partly because school is sometimes taught in local languages rather than French. This is necessary because children begin school without knowing any French. French was not used as the language of instruction under Touré, but it was reintroduced in the Second Republic. Guinea has four universities and a number of trade and vocational institutions.

Health. Despite efforts to improve health conditions, the national healthcare system is chronically understaffed. Half of all doctors are in Conakry, so there is a shortage of doctors in the rest of the country. Only the wealthy can afford quality care. However, many *centres de santé* (health centers) are opening in rural areas, providing low-cost care and essential medications. Traditional healers practice in nearly every village and are often the first source of rural care. Maternal and infant mortality rates are extremely high. Childhood diseases and malaria are widespread. Waterborne diseases—as well as hepatitis, yellow fever, polio, typhoid, meningitis, and malaria—are common.

AT A GLANCE

Events and Trends.
- In January 2005, shots were fired at the motorcade of President Conté in what was described as an assassination attempt. The president was unhurt. At least 100 people were arrested, but later released, in connection with the shooting.
- For more than 15 years, Guinea has hosted refugees who fled wars in Liberia and Sierra Leone. With the end of the civil war in Liberia in 2003, efforts are underway to repatriate more than 100,000 remaining Liberian refugees to their homeland. Most Sierra Leonean refugees have returned since peace was established there in 2002.

Contact Information. Embassy of Guinea, 2112 Leroy Place NW, Washington, DC 20008; phone (202) 986-4300.

CultureGrams
People. The World. You.

ProQuest Information and Learning Company
300 North Zeeb Road, P.O. Box 1346
Ann Arbor, Michigan 48106 USA
Toll Free: 1.800.528.6279
Fax: 1.800.864.0019
www.culturegrams.com

© 2005 ProQuest Information and Learning Company and Brigham Young University. It is against the law to copy, reprint, store, or transmit any part of this publication in any form by any means without written permission from ProQuest. This document contains native commentary and original analysis, as well as estimated statistics. The content should not be considered strictly factual, and it may not apply to all groups in a nation. *UN Development Programme, Human Development Report 2004 (New York: Oxford University Press, 2004).

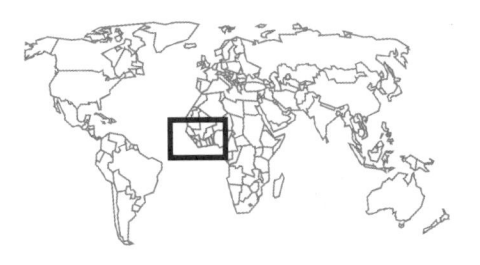

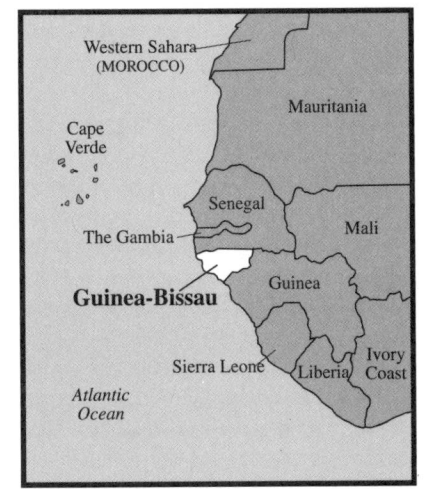

Republic of Guinea-Bissau

BACKGROUND

Land and Climate. Guinea-Bissau, a small West African country, covers 13,946 square miles (36,120 square kilometers). This area includes the Bijagos Archipelago and other offshore islands. The Bijagos and coastal regions feature canopied gallery forests and mangrove swamps. A low-lying coastal plain rises to savanna in the north. Three major rivers flow into the Atlantic Ocean. The climate is tropical and temperatures average near 80°F (27°C). The rainy season (May–October) is hot and humid. Rainfall amounts differ dramatically; the south receives twice as much as the north. The dry season (October–May) can be hot and dusty, but December and January are relatively cool and pleasant.

History. In the 15th century, the area now known as Guinea-Bissau was part of a vast empire centered in Mali. The Portuguese began exploring the region in the 15th century, first establishing themselves on the islands of Cape Verde, situated 350 miles (560 kilometers) northwest of Guinea-Bissau. They claimed the area around current Guinea-Bissau as Portuguese Guinea. The Portuguese established trading posts and in the 1600s began exporting slaves from the territory. As the slave trade diminished in the 1800s, Bissau became an important commercial center.

The Portuguese did not begin to conquer inland territory until the 20th century. Initially helped by Muslim groups with whom they traded, the Portuguese subdued animist groups and by 1936 had gained control of the entire area. In 1952, Portuguese Guinea became a province of Portugal. In 1955, a former colonial administrator, Amilcar Cabral, joined with other leaders to form the African Party for the Independence of Guinea and Cape Verde (PAIGC). It then led most ethnic groups in a guerrilla war against the Portuguese, beginning in 1961. By 1972, the PAIGC controlled most of the country (including the Cape Verde islands) and held national elections. It declared Guinea-Bissau's independence in September 1973. Portugal officially granted independence in 1974 when socialist António de Spínola took power in Portugal.

Guinea-Bissau's first president, Luís Cabral, was overthrown in 1980, and the union between Cape Verde and Guinea-Bissau dissolved. After the coup, João Bernardo Vieira assumed control of the PAIGC and led Guinea-Bissau as a one-party state until 1994. In 1990, a committee was formed to recommend changes in the constitution and electoral process so a multiparty system could be established gradually.

The nation's first free elections were held in 1994, but opposition parties, though active as early as 1991, were not well organized. As a result, the PAIGC retained its dominance. Vieira faced a closer race for president but won the election. In June 1998, General Ansumane Mane staged a coup against Vieira, which quickly escalated into civil war between forces loyal to Vieira and rebel army troops. The capital's 300,000 residents fled heavy fighting, which soon spread and involved troops from Senegal. Months of war destroyed most of the country's public infrastructure. A peace agreement was signed in November 1998. Accordingly, Senegalese troops withdrew, peacekeeping forces began to arrive, and an interim prime minister was installed in January 1999. Vieira remained president and elections were scheduled.

When Vieira's presidential guard refused to disarm, Mane's forces resumed the war and the capital was again subjected to heavy fighting and civilian panic. Within a month, nearly all of Guinea-Bissau's troops and citizens supported the rebels. The presidential guard surrendered in May 1999, and Vieira

Guinea-Bissau

was eventually allowed to leave the country to accept asylum in Portugal. Mane refused to take power and insisted that it remain with civilian authorities. Parliament chose an interim president, and peacekeeping forces withdrew in June 1999.

A multiparty presidential election was held in November 1999, followed by a runoff in January 2000. Voter turnout was extremely high, a sign that Guinea-Bissauans were looking for relief from a year of war. They elected Kumba Yallah president with 72 percent of the vote. He promised to stamp out corruption but soon arrested some of his critics. General Mane tried to overthrow Yallah in November 2000 but was killed when the coup attempt failed.

In November 2002, President Yallah dissolved the National People's Assembly, dismissed the prime minister, and installed a caretaker administration. International observers declared the moves unconstitutional. Opposition politicians, blaming Yallah for the nation's political and economic instability, called for his resignation. The military deposed Yallah in a bloodless coup in September 2003 and installed an interim civilian government to prepare the country for new presidential and parliamentary elections. However, political uncertainty still hampers the nation's progress.

THE PEOPLE

Population. Guinea-Bissau's population of 1.4 million is growing annually at a rate of 1.99 percent. Only 20 percent of Guinea-Bissauans live in urban areas, as most are farmers and fishing families living in small villages. More than 40 percent of the population is younger than age 15.

Guinea-Bissau has been described as a melting pot of West African ethnic groups, home to at least 13 major groups with distinct languages, customs, religious beliefs, and forms of social organization. The largest groups include the Balanta (27 percent), Fula (23), Mandinga (13), Manjaco (11), Papel (10), Beafada (3), Mancanha (3), and Bijago (2.5). The nation is also home to some Cape Verdeans, Senegalese, and Mauritanians. Bissau, the capital and largest city, is the most ethnically diverse; Bafatá and Gabú also have diverse populations. However, most small villages are ethnically homogenous.

Language. Although Portuguese is Guinea-Bissau's official language, it is rarely spoken by the average person. Government meetings, radio and television broadcasts, and certain other activities are conducted in Portuguese, but the language of daily interaction for most people is Kriolu or their own ethnic group's language. Kriolu is a mixture of Portuguese and several local indigenous tongues. Most urban residents speak Kriolu, but rural people may never learn it if they have no urban contacts. Still, its use is spreading to rural areas, especially among men.

Children learn to understand Portuguese because it is the language of school instruction. However, they usually fail to read, write, or effectively speak Portuguese because it is not well taught as a subject. Better-educated urban youth are beginning to speak a form of Kriolu that is moving closer to standard Portuguese. At the same time, some scholars are trying to introduce a standardized written form of Kriolu to schools, but Guinea-Bissauans consider Kriolu more of an oral language and have not embraced these efforts. A few people speak French because of contact with neighboring French-speaking countries.

Religion. While 30 percent of Guinea-Bissauans are Muslim and 5 to 8 percent are Christian, the rest follow traditional animistic beliefs. Religious preference is tied to ethnic grouping. The Fula, Mandinga, and Beafada, among others, are Muslims. The Balanta, Manjaco, Papel, Mancanha, Bijago, and others are animists.

Many animists believe in a creator-god that can be contacted only through other gods or supernatural beings (*iran*). The *iran* reside in shrines usually built near large trees. Persons considered "spiritual advisors" or intermediaries perform ceremonies to the *iran* and services for people (casting spells, telling fortunes, and treating illness). Certain animist rites of passage, such as circumcising young men after their elders teach them about becoming men, are performed in secret ceremonies.

Animists who convert to Christianity and Islam often mix their old and new beliefs rather than entirely abandon their animist traditions. For example, they may continue to seek advice from spiritualists and to use amulets and charms.

Muslims believe in the *Qur'an* (Koran) as the word of *Allah* (God) revealed to the prophet Muhammad. They show devotion through the Five Pillars of Islam: professing the name of *Allah* as the only God and Muhammad as his last and greatest messenger; praying five times daily; fasting during the holy month of *Ramadan*; giving alms (*zakat*) to the poor; and making a pilgrimage to Makkah (Mecca), Saudi Arabia.

General Attitudes. The people of Guinea-Bissau respect those who are peace-loving and nonaggressive. They generally try to avoid confrontation and therefore also refrain from making direct or assertive statements. Although some minor tensions exist between various ethnic groups, most groups are united because of their struggle for independence against the Portuguese. This feeling of unity has helped Guinea-Bissau avoid major internal conflict; even the 1998 to 1999 civil war was a political and not an ethnic conflict.

Generally friendly and hospitable, Guinea-Bissauans believe in mutual cooperation. Although the country is extremely poor, there are relatively few beggars or homeless people. People love to socialize with friends; a desire for privacy may be considered antisocial.

Most people believe that nature is controlled by gods and spirits and that people have relatively little power over nature. They tend to feel their individual conditions cannot or will not change. A common phrase is *Jitu ka ten* (There's nothing one can do). Such acceptance of life's difficulties reflects people's patience, perseverance, and even resignation. However, it also hinders progress. A more recent slogan has been used to combat this attitude: *Jitu ten ku ten* (There has to be a way).

Personal Appearance. Western-style clothing is typical attire for work and daily activities because it is inexpensive and readily available, shipped secondhand from Europe and North America. Adults value cleanliness and modesty. Locally made traditional clothing is more expensive and is reserved for special occasions. Some rural people still wear traditional clothing on a daily basis; styles vary by ethnic group and region. Many women wear long, colorful wraparound skirts with loose-fitting tops. Women enjoy intricately braided hairstyles, often done by weaving synthetic hair into their real hair. Schoolchildren wear short white robes over their clothing.

CUSTOMS AND COURTESIES

Greetings. Greetings are an important way to show respect for others. It is rude to start speaking without first greeting a person. A typical Kriolu greeting begins with *Kuma?* (How are you?); the response is *N sta bon* (I am fine). Later, one also might ask *Kuma di kurpu?* (How is your body?) or make other polite inquiries about the person's family and work. Greetings can last a long time, especially in rural areas, and cover a wide range of subjects.

People shake hands when they greet. Some hold on to the hand for a while after the initial handshake. One offers a closed hand if dirty so the wrist may be shaken. In urban areas, the Portuguese tradition of greeting by kissing alternate cheeks (first right, then left) is common. Except at large gatherings, it is polite to greet each individual in a group rather than the group as a whole. The same applies when a person leaves.

Good friends may call each other *primo* or *prima* (cousin) or *irmon/irma* (brother/sister); strangers often are addressed as *amigo* or *amiga* (friend). To address an older person, most Guinea-Bissauans use the term *tio* (uncle) or *tia* (aunt). Otherwise, people address each other by first name or nickname. Titles are reserved for formal occasions.

Gestures. One beckons by waving all four fingers with the palm facing down. Some rural Guinea-Bissauans may point directions with their tongues. Pointing at people with a finger is considered rude. Personal space is relatively small; people stand close together when conversing, and touching is an important part of communication. Friends of the same sex often walk hand in hand, but this does not suggest anything beyond friendship. It is impolite to stretch in public. To indicate "no," a person may wag an upright index finger from side to side or make two short clicking sounds in the mouth. To signify "yes," the person makes one clicking sound or lightly clucks the tongue.

Children are taught to show respect by not looking elders or superiors in the eye. Even Muslim elders often look sideways when conversing. Women are supposed to avoid eye contact with men unless they are romantically involved.

Visiting. Because visiting is considered a generous and thoughtful act, visitors are treated with great hospitality. Hosts nearly always offer guests water or something else to drink. If visitors arrive while the hosts are eating, tradition dictates that they must be invited to share the meal. It is rude to refuse this offer, even if a person is not hungry. Guests should at least take one bite before saying *N justa*, a Kriolu phrase meaning, "I've had enough."

It is not necessary to make appointments before visiting, although they are sometimes made in urban areas. Time is very flexible. Invited guests may arrive up to two hours late for a scheduled event without offending the hosts. Guests show appreciation to hosts with gifts of tobacco, kola nuts, bread, sugar, fruit, or *cana* (cane alcohol). It is inappropriate to criticize or joke about another person's ethnicity. Foreign guests should not inquire about the hosts' poverty, poor health, marital status, or educational background, as this would embarrass the hosts.

Eating. Most families eat three meals a day if they can afford it. During the rainy season (also called the "hungry season"), many eat only one or two meals. An urban breakfast might be eaten between 7 and 9 a.m., lunch between noon and 3 p.m. (including time for rest or a nap), and dinner between 8 and 10 p.m. Rural meal times vary by ethnic group, season, and personal habits. Breakfast is usually leftovers from the previous day, lunch is the main meal, and dinner is a lighter version of lunch. The main dish typically is served in large bowls placed on mats on the floor or ground. An older person usually divides the food into portions. Individuals eat only from the portion that is directly in front of them. It is impolite to move the bowl while others are eating. In many parts of the country, family members eat separately according to sex and age. Most Guinea-Bissauans eat only with the right hand; the left is used for personal hygiene. Spoons are more common in urban areas than in rural villages. The average person rarely eats at a restaurant.

LIFESTYLE

Family. The value placed on the extended family has a great impact on Guinea-Bissau's society and individuals. Conformity and contribution to the family are considered more important than individual interests. In return for conformity, individuals enjoy a sense of belonging and security. Most Guinea-Bissauans desire large families. Three generations usually share a household. Women are responsible for housework and child care, while men are expected to provide an income or food and clothing. Older siblings often care for younger children. Mothers carry young babies on their backs as they work. Most rural families engage in agriculture. Their basic living conditions do not include electricity, running water, or other modern conveniences. Urban families enjoy somewhat higher living standards.

Dating and Marriage. Dating habits vary widely. Muslims are generally stricter about moral behavior and interaction between boys and girls, but young women often marry in their teens. Arranged marriages are common in rural areas. Urban and animist social norms are less rigid, and urban youth often socialize and choose their spouses.

The birth of a child usually marks a couple as "married." The government does not recognize such unions, but fees and documentation requirements for a licensed marriage demand more money and time than the average person has, and so many couples live together without officially marrying. Even more costly, a prospective bride's family often requires the groom to provide expensive gifts or to farm family land for many years. The groom must also furnish a communal feast at the wedding. Many men put off getting married because they have to save money for the event.

Polygamy is common. Islamic law allows a man to have as many as four wives. Animists are not restricted in the number of wives they may have, but some urban people have begun to oppose the practice of taking more than one wife.

Diet. Guinea-Bissauans often say that if they haven't eaten rice at a meal, they haven't eaten at all. In rural areas, a main meal consists of rice or millet and some type of sauce (peanut, palm oil, sorrel and okra, or tomato) served with fish or meat, if available. Some groups only kill cattle for ceremonial feasts, although they do drink cows' milk. While fish is plentiful in coastal areas, people who live farther inland do not often eat it. Bay leaves, lemons, tomatoes, salt, and oil are common sauce ingredients. A popular dish is *chicken cafriela* (cooked in lemon, onions, and butter). Tropical fruits (mangoes, papaya, and bananas), vegetables (manioc, sweet potatoes, corn, and squash), and peanuts are eaten in season. Devout Muslims abstain from consuming alcohol and pork.

Recreation. Soccer is the nation's most popular sport. People take advantage of a short workday during the rainy season to attend local soccer matches. They also enjoying listening to radio broadcasts of soccer matches and other sporting events. Some urban residents enjoy basketball and tennis, while traditional wrestling (*luta livre*) is popular in rural areas. Most towns have a television and VCR set up in a theater format that people pay to watch. However, the most common leisure activity is sitting outside under a shady tree (in the day) or on a veranda (at night), chatting with friends and neighbors.

Guinea-Bissau

Guinea-Bissauans tell stories, sing songs, and gossip. In rural areas, people talk while sitting around the cooking fire.

The Arts. A popular musical rhythm in Guinea-Bissau is *gumbe*. Women dance to the music, while men keep the beat by hitting a water drum, a gourd that floats in water. During Vieira's dictatorship, *gumbe* musicians played an important role in challenging government authority. The *kora* (a stringed lute) is played solo or in arrangements of jazz or flamenco. The *bala* xylophone dates back hundreds of years to the Mali Empire. Cigarette paper is placed under the *bala* slats to produce a buzzing sound. Modern pop music is based on *fado*, a style of Portuguese folk singing.

Holidays. Guinea-Bissau's official holidays include New Year's Day, National Hero's Day (20 Jan.), Women's Day (8 Mar.), Easter (Friday–Sunday), International Worker's Day (1 May), Martyrs of Colonialism Day (3 Aug.), Independence Day (24 Sept.), Improvement of the State and Distribution of Equality and Opportunity for Guineans of all Origins Day (14 Nov.), and Christmas. *Carnaval* is usually held in February (before Ash Wednesday). Traditional dancing, parades, and papier-mâché masks are combined in several days of frenzied activity. Two holidays set by the lunar calendar are the feast to end the Islamic month of *Ramadan* (a month in which Muslims fast from sunrise to sundown) and *Tabaski* (Islam's Feast of the Sacrifice). In rural areas, various ethnic groups maintain their own calendars and holidays.

Commerce. During the rainy season, government offices are open from 8 a.m. to 3 p.m. This is a "short" schedule due to an increased demand for labor in the rice fields and because traveling on muddy roads is difficult. Dry season office hours are from 8 a.m. to noon and 3 to 6 p.m. Open-air markets and shops keep their own hours. Markets carry anything from food to clothing to electronics. Prices at market stalls are negotiable. Corner stores, found in larger cities, offer general goods and are usually owned by Mauritanians.

SOCIETY

Government. Under Guinea-Bissau's constitution, the president is chief of state and is elected by popular vote to a five-year term. Interim president Henrique Rosa currently holds office pending future elections. The prime minister (currently Carlos Gomes Junior) is head of government and is appointed by the president on recommendation of National People's Assembly's governing party. The National People's Assembly's 102 members are elected to four-year terms. All citizens are eligible to vote at age 18.

Economy. Guinea-Bissau is one of the world's poorest countries. About 85 percent of the labor force is engaged in agriculture. Most people do not earn a wage, being subsistence farmers, or their wages do not meet basic needs. Income is not distributed equally. Guinea-Bissau imports much of its food, fuel, and manufactured goods. It exports cashews, fish, peanuts, and palm products. Corruption, debt, low motivation, and other factors hinder efforts to implement land reform, tighten business regulations, promote self-sufficiency, and attract international investment. Guinea-Bissau uses West Africa's regional currency, the *CFA franc* (XOF).

Transportation and Communications. Unpaved roads make

DEVELOPMENT DATA
Human Dev. Index* rank .... 172 of 177 countries
Adjusted for women .... 141 of 144 countries
Real GDP per capita $710
Adult literacy rate .... 55 percent (male); 25 (female)
Infant mortality rate .... 109 per 1,000 births
Life expectancy .... 44 (male); 47 (female)

travel difficult during the rainy season. Rivers must be crossed by ferry. Only Bissau has buses and taxis. Many men in smaller cities ride bicycles to work. Between towns, people ride crowded *kandongas* (pickup trucks with seats and a roof for baggage). Otherwise, people walk. Guinea-Bissauans rely on radio broadcasts for news and information; families can transmit personal messages and announcements over the radio. Televisions are rare outside of Bissau. There is one national newspaper. Mail service does not extend beyond the Bissau post office. Rural people use a network of *kandonga* drivers, friends, and relatives to send messages.

Education. Guinea-Bissau lacks schools, teachers, materials, and money. Low attendance and high drop out rates are due in part to the use of Portuguese. Because children do not learn Portuguese at home, they are essentially taught in a foreign language. Written Kriolu materials are scarce and often not used. The national goal is to provide four years of compulsory education. Guinea-Bissau has secondary schools, but students must move to Bissau to complete their last two years. This is nearly impossible for many. The country has one school for teacher training. Teachers work long hours, are poorly paid, and often must strike to get their wages.

Health. Medical facilities are inadequate or absent in many areas. Life expectancy is low and the infant mortality rate is very high. Major causes of death include malaria, gastrointestinal infections, and AIDS. Bilharzia and tuberculosis are widespread. Malnutrition is a serious problem in many parts of the country. About one-half of all Guinea-Bissauans have access to safe water; one-fifth have proper sanitation.

AT A GLANCE
Events and Trends.
- In an October 2004 uprising, mutinous soldiers killed two high-ranking officers, including General Verissimo Seabre, the head of the military and leader of the September 2003 coup that deposed Kumba Yallah. The soldiers demanded back pay and better living conditions. The government ended the revolt by signing an agreement that included an amnesty for the troops.
- Henrique Rosa was sworn in as interim president following the September 2003 coup. The military made the appointment after agreeing with opposition groups on a plan for new elections. The former ruling PAIGC won parliamentary elections in April 2004, allowing party leader Carlos Gomes Junior to take office as prime minister.

Contact Information. Embassy of Guinea-Bissau, 15929 Yukon Lane, Rockville, MD 20855; phone (301) 947-3958.

CultureGrams™
People. The World. You.

ProQuest Information and Learning Company
300 North Zeeb Road, P.O. Box 1346
Ann Arbor, Michigan 48106 USA
Toll Free: 1.800.528.6279
Fax: 1.800.864.0019
www.culturegrams.com

© 2005 ProQuest Information and Learning Company and Brigham Young University. It is against the law to copy, reprint, store, or transmit any part of this publication in any form by any means without written permission from ProQuest. This document contains native commentary and original analysis, as well as estimated statistics. The content should not be considered strictly factual, and it may not apply to all groups in a nation. *UN Development Programme, Human Development Report 2004 (New York: Oxford University Press, 2004).

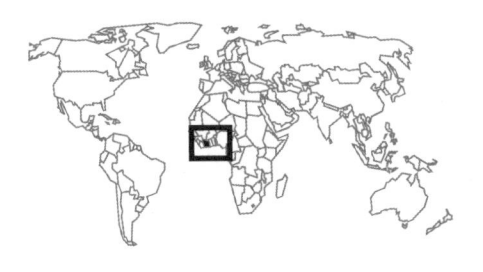

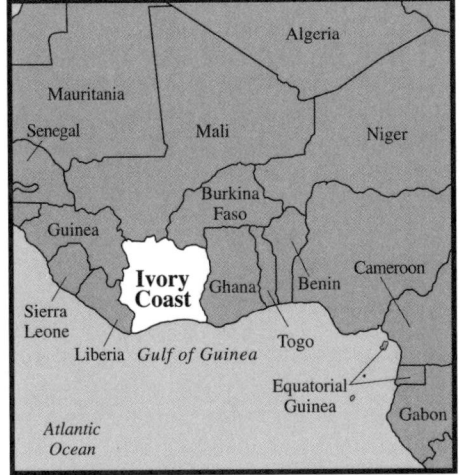

Ivory Coast

BACKGROUND

Land and Climate. Ivory Coast, also known as Côte d'Ivoire, is in West Africa, on the Gulf of Guinea. At 124,500 square miles (322,460 square kilometers), the country is slightly larger then New Mexico. Coastal lagoons and dense tropical forests in the south gradually give way to sandy-soiled grasslands in the central and northern parts of the country. The northwest has high mountain peaks, with Mount Nimba the highest at 5,748 feet (1,752 meters). Animal populations include elephants, antelope, monkeys, snakes, and crocodiles.

The climate is tropical in the south and semiarid in the north. Rainfall varies depending on the distance from the ocean. About 75 inches (191 centimeters) of rain falls each year along the coast, but only about 45 inches (114 centimeters) falls farther north. In the north, most of the rain comes in one season (May to November), while in the south there are two rainy seasons (May to July and October to November). The average annual temperature is 79°F (26°C).

History. Before European colonization in the 1400s, the Senufo and Malinke (both sometimes called Dyula), Yacouba (also called Dan), and Guéré (also called Wê) peoples interacted through marriage, cultural alliances, and trade. When the Europeans came, they hunted ivory until the area's elephant population nearly disappeared. The French built permanent settlements in the 1800s, and Ivory Coast became a French colony in 1893.

The French were harsh rulers. They imposed their government and language, manipulated tribal leaders, used forced labor, and levied taxes. After World War II, Ivorians began demanding more rights. In 1946, the French granted citizenship to colonial subjects. Ivorians were allowed political parties, free speech, and government jobs. The Ivory Coast Democratic Party (PDCI)—led by a southerner named Félix Houphouët-Boigny—became the most popular of numerous political parties. After World War II, independence movements emerged throughout Africa. A referendum in Ivory Coast led to its independence in 1960, but the country retained close economic and cultural ties with France. Meanwhile, opposition to Houphouët-Boigny's rule was growing.

Throughout the 1960s and 1970s, funds from exports of coffee and cocoa were used to develop the south; not as much was spent in the north. Strong development earned Ivory Coast the nickname "the economic miracle of West Africa."

A worldwide recession in the 1980s hurt coffee and cocoa prices, provoking a crisis in Ivory Coast. Crime, unemployment, and political scandals resulted. Opposition groups forced multiparty elections to be held in 1990; however, Houphouët-Boigny still won a sixth term. Three years later, he died and was replaced by his handpicked successor, Henri Konan Bédié. Bédié's tenure was marred by corruption and by an anti-foreigner ideology called Ivoirité, which blamed outsiders for economic problems. In December 1999, he was ousted in a coup led by General Robert Guei.

Guei claimed he would only hold power until fair elections could be held the next year. However, the 2000 elections were undemocratic by international standards. Also, many popular leaders—including Alassane Ouattara, a northern Muslim—were denied permission to run because one or both of their parents were not Ivorian. The result was that Guei declared himself president but was forced to hand over the presidency to Laurent Gbagbo after the elections were deemed fraudulent. Gbagbo continued promoting the Ivoirité ideology and treated northern ethnic groups poorly.

Ivory Coast

In September 2002, civil war broke out. Rebels from the Ivory Coast Patriotic Movement (MPCI) and the Movement for Justice and Peace (MJP) took control of areas in the north and west, demanding an end to discrimination. This event split the country along an ideological, ethnic, and political divide that had been building for 20 years. In 2003, northern rebels and other parties agreed to disarm in return for more political power and a compromise on presidential eligibility. Although the fighting did nearly stop, promises on both sides went unfulfilled. In 2004, parliament passed a law saying presidential candidates no longer needed both parents to be Ivorian. Talks held in South Africa in 2005 brought further progress, but the situation remains tense.

THE PEOPLE

Population. Ivory Coast's population of 17.3 million is growing at 2.11 percent annually. More than 60 ethnicities are traditionally grouped into the following large categories: Akan (accounting for 42.1 percent of the population) in the center and southeast; Mandé (26.5 percent) in the northwest; Voltaic (17.6 percent) in the northeast; and Kru (11 percent) in the southwest. Many residents belong to these ethnic groups but have migrated from other areas of West Africa. Other groups—including Europeans—make up 2.8 percent. About 45 percent of the population lives in urban areas. However, many people continue to live in small villages and maintain a traditional lifestyle.

Language. Because each ethnic group has its own language, the nation is linguistically diverse. The official language is French, but many residents also speak Dyula, a dialect derived from Arabic. Dyula is used in trade or when someone doesn't understand French. Agni is spoken in the east and Baoulé is spoken in the central part of the country. Mandé and Senufo are spoken across the north, but can be found in the south as well. Some people (especially the younger generation) speak Nouchi, a mixture of French and various African languages. There is no single commonly spoken African language. Arabic is taught at Qur'anic schools. French is taught in all other schools, and because males are more likely to have gone to school, they are more likely to speak French.

Religion. The population is divided into three main religious traditions: traditional animist religions (30–60 percent), Islam (20–30 percent), and Christianity (15–30 percent). Followers of indigenous religions typically worship their ancestors, use masks in their ceremonies, and believe that all objects have spirits. Muslims tend to live in the north. Christians—Catholics and Protestants, including numerous evangelical movements—tend to live in the south. Despite the general geographical separation of religious groups, the current conflict is not primarily religious. In fact, Ivorians tend to be religiously tolerant, and it is not uncommon for them to mix elements from two or more religious traditions.

General Attitudes. Ivorians respect those who are considerate, reliable, and capable. People who do not take life's troubles in stride are often ridiculed. Ivorians value a good sense of humor as well as the ability to tell stories and carry on long conversations. Their laid-back attitude is expressed in the saying *Ça va aller, Dieu est grand* (Everything will be all right, God is great).

The elderly and the wealthy are the most respected members of Ivorian society. Older Ivorians tend to value the extended family, tradition, respect, and loyalty, and many worry that a modern lifestyle will harm traditional morality. Young people put more value on the nuclear family and Western ideals such as romantic relationships, stable employment, and a comfortable lifestyle. Many residents of Abidjan think of themselves as cosmopolitan and liken their city to New York City.

Most Ivorians share pride in their national identity, pre-1980s stability, and relative economic prosperity. They want a full democracy and a transparent government but disagree over how to achieve these goals. Presidential eligibility has been a major issue. Southerners tend to think that both parents of candidates must have been born in Ivory Coast, while northerners believe that only the candidate must have been born in Ivory Coast. This conflict has aggravated interethnic regional conflicts and contributed to the outbreak of civil war.

Personal Appearance. Urban dwellers dress formally for public outings and family occasions. In rural areas, dress tends to be more casual. People wear their least valued clothing for manual labor. U.S. and European styles are popular in urban areas, but African dress is also popular. Men and women both wear *boubous* (embroidered robes worn over pants or a skirt). For special events in the south or west, people might wear intricately patterned *kita* or *kinte* cloths (brightly patterned woven fabric) tied around the body. Women tend to wear skirts or *pagnes* (colorful cloth wrapped around the waist) with a blouse. For formal occasions, they wear sandals or heeled-shoes; plastic flip-flops are fine for casual wear. Some women wear a head covering to indicate they are married. Professional men wear suits or a buttoned jacket with short sleeves and matching pants. Children's clothes are usually secondhand.

CUSTOMS AND COURTESIES

Greetings. Ivorians almost always give at least a brief greeting. Particularly in rural areas, ignoring someone is considered very rude. A traditional gesture used to show respect for a social superior involves shaking right hands while using the left hand to support the right elbow. Friends might nod, shake hands, or—especially among urban elites—exchange kisses on the cheek. People may then inquire about each other's welfare, family, or work. In French, the standard response to all of these questions is *Tout va bien* (All is well). Eventually, one person may ask *Quelle sont les nouvelles?* (What is the news?) At this point, one may discuss more serious concerns.

Gestures. A guttural sound and a head nod mean "yes," while shaking the head side-to-side means "no." Sucking air through one's teeth indicates disapproval. Friends of the same gender may hold hands, dance together, or engage in horseplay, but men and women do not publicly demonstrate affection. Sustained eye contact is acceptable in the south but not in the north, where people often look away during conversations with those they consider their social superiors. To catch someone's attention, one might call their name, wave, snap, raise a finger, or whistle through the teeth.

Visiting. Visiting and hospitality are highly valued. Visitors may drop by at any time during the day, but the usual visiting period starts after the evening meal. Hosts usually indicate a chair or mat where guests may sit and then serve them a glass of water. Visits tend to be long and casual, and attempting to shorten a visit is seen as rude. For important visits—such as meeting a village chief—the visitor might bring along a relative or friend of the host. At formal ceremonies in the north, people may exchange *kola nuts* (caffeine-containing tree nuts that have been traded for centuries) as a sign of respect.

Visitors may be invited to share a meal if they pass a group eating outdoors, but the visitor should decline if there is not enough food. Outside the family, women visit women, and men visit men. However, both sexes sometimes mix in open courtyards of homes. Dances, funerals, and weddings may last well into the night. Hosts show friendship by accompanying departing guests to the road (sometimes called *pushing*). At this point the guest may say *Je demande la route* (I ask for the road), and the host may respond *Je te donne la moité de la route*, short for "I give you half the road, (use the second half to come back)." In Dyula the guest asks for the road saying *Nbe sira dari*, and the host gives it by saying *Sira beyi*.

Eating. Hand washing is an important part of eating; everyone washes their hands before and after each meal. During the meal they eat only with their right hands because the left hand is traditionally used for personal hygiene. In rural or working-class areas, families gather around a communal bowl filled with ground cassava or grains, meat, and sauce. In some households, women, daughters, and young boys eat apart from husbands, fathers, and male guests. In upper-class urban households, men and women eat together at a table, using bowls and utensils. Children usually eat earlier in a less formal atmosphere. At the conclusion of the meal, everyone compliments the cook and thanks the host. Northerners might say *Barika* (A Dyula word meaning "strength," as in "May the Lord put strength in this meat"), while southerners might say *C'est doux* (It's sweet). Ivorians usually drink water after, not during, the meal.

Breakfast is usually served between 6 and 7 a.m., lunch at noon, and dinner between 7 and 8:30 p.m. Meals that are not eaten at home can be bought on the street. Street vendors sell fried plantains, peanuts, and yogurt. Outdoor restaurants called *maquis* sell alcohol and basic dishes.

LIFESTYLE

Family. Extended families remain strongly connected even when they are scattered across several villages. Everyone may gather in a single village for major events such as funerals or weddings. The father usually leads in the home, but the oldest woman in the family (called *la vieille*) may take charge if there is no male figurehead. Although some cultures are matriarchal and matrilineal, most are dominated by men. Problems within families are often negotiated through group meetings.

In urban settings, families have between two and five children, but in rural areas the number may exceed ten. Children are subordinate to adults and are expected to run errands, assist with household and farm tasks, and give respect to all their elders. Adult children usually care for elderly parents. Ivorians' sense of family is not limited to the nuclear family or blood relatives. Ivorians often refer to non-relatives they respect as *tante* (aunt), *tonton* (uncle), *grand frère* (big brother), *grande soeur* (big sister), *maman* (mom), or *papa* (dad). In addition, parents sometimes allow their children to be raised by wealthier relatives. City dwellers may house younger relatives who are attending schools nearby.

Dating and Marriage. Dating customs vary according to location. For example, casual dating is more prevalent in cities, where relationships are less controlled by family networks. Most men do not marry until they are economically stable, usually not before they turn 30. When weddings take place, religion plays a key role in customs. Muslim men may pay a bride-price before the ceremony, which takes place in a mosque. Christians may be married in a church or in a town hall. For both groups, the ceremony is usually followed by a celebration featuring food and dancing. Non-religious options include civil unions, cohabitation, or traditional ceremonies. In traditional societies, parents often arrange marriages. Once a girl reaches puberty (around age 12), she may become engaged—often to someone much older. The girl is dressed by the family of her husband-to-be before the marriage takes place in front of the whole village.

Polygamy is illegal, but it still occurs, especially in rural areas. There is a trend toward monogamous marriages, especially among the younger generation. However, adultery is common, particularly among men.

Diet. Imported sugar, salt, and canned goods supplement locally grown crops, which serve as the basis of most meals. Crops such as rice, cassava, and yams are served with a variety of sauces made of nuts, tomatoes, eggplants, okra, palm oil, and peppers. In southern areas, yams, cassavas, and plantains are pounded into a heavy paste called *futu*, or are boiled and then dipped into sauce. In the north, sorghum, millet, and corn flour are boiled with milk or water into a porridge called *tô*. For protein, Ivorians eat *groundnuts* (peanuts), beans, fish, cattle, lamb, chicken, goat, monkey, wild deer, and pork (except for Muslims). Seasonal tropical fruits (bananas, pineapples, star fruit, breadfruit, and mangoes) add variety to the diet. Malnutrition is widespread among women and children because they receive the smallest portions of protein-rich foods.

Recreation. *Football* (soccer) and *dame* (a form of checkers) are popular activities for males. Young girls get together in the evenings to gossip, sing, and talk. Young people gather to watch U.S., Chinese, and Indian films at video clubs. Most people enjoy listening to the radio and watching television; U.S. cartoons and Brazilian soap operas are popular. People may gather at *maquis* to eat *futu* and *alloco* (fried plantains), drink beer, and chat. Children may fashion toys out of sticks and broken bicycle parts.

The Arts. Traditional and modern arts can be found throughout the country. In the north, cotton is dyed with indigo and woven into blankets and clothing. Leather sandals are a popular craft in the southwest. The west is famous for its traditional masks, wood carvings, and music. Intricate *Kita* fabrics are most popular in the east, near Ghana.

Popular music styles throughout the country include reggae, African pop music, and French and U.S. rap. Ivory Coast has a strong local industry of pop and hip-hop musicians. *Zouglou* is a uniquely Ivorian music style with a fast beat and humorous lyrics. In the north, local bands play the drums and *balafon* (a xylophone made from calabash casings) at weddings, festivals, and other events. Groups achieve local popularity by playing traditional music all night long, many nights in a row, for religious holidays. Local dance troupes perform mask dances that require considerable acrobatic skill and strength.

Holidays. New Year's Day, Independence Day (7 Aug.), and National Day (7 Dec.) are celebrated throughout the country. Many people also celebrate Christmas and Easter. During Easter, which is called *Pakinou* among the Baoulé, families gather from around the country to celebrate. Muslims strictly honor religious holidays, including *Ramadan* (the holy month of fasting) and the feast at the end of Ramadan called *Eid al-Fitr*. During November in the region around Man, the people celebrate *Fête des Masques* (Festival of Masks) by competing in dances and honoring the spirits they believe live in wooden masks. In Gomon, the *Fête du Dipri* (Festival of the Dipri) is an overnight exorcism that takes place in the spring. In Senufo communities, male initiation rites called *Pôro* occur once every seven years. Female initiations include circumcision and

Ivory Coast

are kept secret, especially since they were outlawed by the government. Both types of initiations are often linked to celebrations in different societies.

Commerce. Business hours are 8 a.m. to 5 p.m., with a break between noon and 2:30 p.m. Markets are open during daylight hours. In rural communities, markets occur about once a week. In urban areas, markets are held every day, with the heaviest trade taking place once a week. Prices tend to be fixed for staple products, but negotiating is common on other goods. Most people use cash, though some sellers allow bartering.

SOCIETY

Government. The president (currently Laurent Gbagbo) heads a government supported by the National Assembly, a unicameral legislature with 225 seats. Representatives are elected locally and serve five-year terms. Gbagbo's Ivorian Popular Front (FPI) and Bédié's PDCI each have almost half the seats. The voting age is 18.

The coastal city of Abidjan was the capital until the 1970s, when President Houphouët-Boigny made Yamoussoukro—his hometown in the center of the country—the new capital. However, Abidjan is still home to most businesses and the National Assembly (though there are plans to move it to Yamoussoukro). Since the civil war started in 2002, the northern half of the country has been administered by a military coalition of three rebel organizations.

Economy. Ivory Coast is heavily dependent on export crops, particularly cocoa, coffee, timber, rubber, pineapples, and palm oil. Consequently, the Ivorian economy is sensitive to fluctuations in trade prices. Local economies depend on the cultivation of grains, produce, cotton, and tobacco. Much of the population is involved in agricultural production, especially in low-wage jobs on plantations in the southwest. Offshore oil and gas resources have yet to be exploited. More industries are being developed, with an emphasis on processing food, wood, oil, textiles, and fertilizer. About a third of the population lives below the poverty line, and foreign debt constitutes more than 80 percent of the GDP. The currency is the *CFA franc* (CFA or XOF).

Transportation and Communications. Most major roads lead to Abidjan and are paved but in poor condition. Roads and railways link Abidjan to Mali and Burkina Faso. The international airport in Abidjan was remodeled in 2001, but some major carriers (Air France, etc.) have discontinued service because of unrest. Transportation in rural areas involves walking or riding oxcarts, bicycles, mopeds, or minibuses (called *badjans*, *dynas*, or *gbakas*). Few rural Ivorians own a vehicle. Taxis are available in most cities and *wôro-wôros* (taxis that rent seats on fixed routes) are popular in Abidjan. City dwellers often use mopeds or motorcycles. Travel can be difficult and may involve long hours in buses on rough roads, especially in the north. Travelers must carry identification papers or risk a large fine.

Phone service is available in urban areas and cellular phones are increasingly popular. People sometimes create makeshift public phone services by renting out time on their personal cellular phones. Mail service extends to all urban areas but is often unreliable. People often pass news by word of mouth or by asking truck and bus drivers to deliver mail. Radio is the most popular medium, and there are several radio stations. Television stations are tightly controlled by the government. In the last five years, the internet has become increasingly available and affordable in large cities.

DEVELOPMENT DATA
- Human Dev. Index* rank .... 163 of 177 countries
- Adjusted for women .... 132 of 144 countries
- Real GDP per capita $1,520
- Adult literacy rate .... 60 percent (male); 38 (female)
- Infant mortality rate .... 97 per 1,000 births
- Life expectancy .... 42 (male); 41 (female)

Education. Students attend local primary schools, followed by regional high schools, and finally universities. Instruction is in French, which most students learn for the first time in school. Rural schools teach basic subjects, such as math and language, as well as agricultural information. If students successfully complete seven years of secondary school, they earn a certificate of completion called a *baccalaureat*. Students may then attend university, train to be a teacher, or learn a trade.

There is considerable gender discrimination in education (and in employment). Many believe that a boy who achieves an education will help his family more than a girl would, because she may marry into another family or drop out of school to have a baby. So girls may be kept out of school or only allowed to attend primary school. If parents cannot afford to educate all their children because of fees or the cost of supplies, they may send only their brightest children.

Health. The national health system lacks funding and resources. People often must pay for their treatment before receiving care, even during emergencies. Quality care is available at private hospitals, but these are too expensive for most Ivorians. Missionary clinics also provide some care. Neo-natal programs have led to a decline in infant mortality, but many children die once they stop breast-feeding and are exposed to contaminated water and inadequate diets. Instability in the north has led to malnutrition and outbreaks of disease. HIV/AIDS is a major health concern throughout the country, with up to 10 percent of the population infected.

AT A GLANCE

Events and Trends.
- Government troops bombed five opposition-controlled northern cities in November 2004. The French became involved when nine of their soldiers were killed in an air strike, but Ivorians protested French interference. The UN imposed an arms embargo in an attempt to quell the outbreak of violence.
- In April 2005, factions agreed to an immediate end of hostilities in a meeting negotiated by South African president Thabo Mbeki.

Contact Information. Embassy of Ivory Coast, 2424 Massachusetts Avenue NW, Washington DC 20008; phone (202) 797-0300.

© 2005 ProQuest Information and Learning Company and Brigham Young University. It is against the law to copy, reprint, store, or transmit any part of this publication in any form by any means without written permission from ProQuest. This document contains native commentary and original analysis, as well as estimated statistics. The content should not be considered strictly factual, and it may not apply to all groups in a nation. *UN Development Programme, Human Development Report 2004 (New York: Oxford University Press, 2004).

CultureGrams
People. The World. You.

ProQuest Information and Learning Company
300 North Zeeb Road, P.O. Box 1346
Ann Arbor, Michigan 48106 USA
Toll Free: 1.800.528.6279
Fax: 1.800.864.0019
www.culturegrams.com

Republic of Kenya

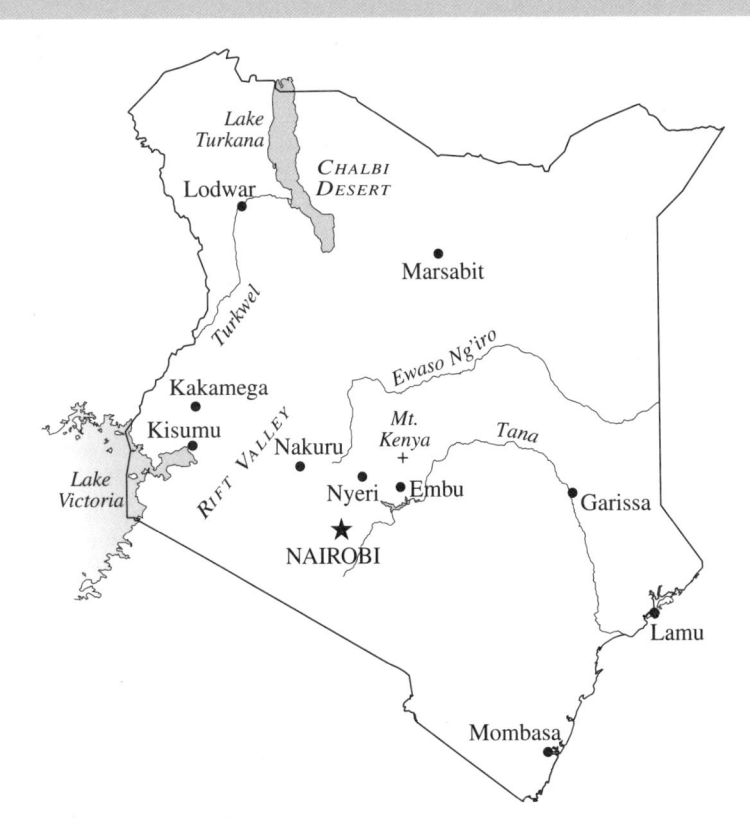

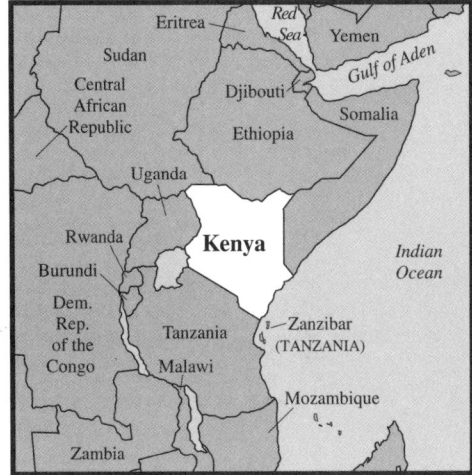

CultureGrams World Edition 2006

BACKGROUND

Land and Climate. Covering 224,961 square miles (582,650 square kilometers), Kenya is about the size of Texas. It is situated on the equator. The semidesert northern plains are hot and arid. The population in that part of the country usually practices nomadic pastoralism, moving from one area to another to take advantage of seasonal grazing patterns. In the southeast, near the coast, the tropical climate is hot and humid. The fertile Rift Valley bisects the western highlands. The climate is moderate in the rich agricultural highlands. Wildlife is abundant and diverse. Lake Turkana (Lake Rudolf) lies near the Chalbi Desert, and Lake Victoria overlaps the southwest border. Mount Kenya rises in the center of the country to 17,058 feet (5,199 meters). "Long rains" from April to June are usually reliable and heavy. They are followed by "short rains" from October to November. The country is generally dry and windy from December to March.

History. Kenya's first inhabitants were hunting groups (Dorobo) who lived on the area's vast plains. They mixed with Bantu peoples who had migrated from the south. By the 15th century the Bantu covered much of eastern Africa. More than half of Kenya's current ethnic groups have Bantu origins. Nilotic groups migrated from North Africa. Today's descendants of the Nilotic people are the Luo and Turkana. These mixed peoples eventually developed the Kiswahili language.

In 1498, Portuguese explorers established trading posts on the coast. Arabs drove out the Portuguese in 1729 and established their own trading posts. After 1740, Arabs ruled the Kenyan coast from the island of Zanzibar. In 1887, the British East Africa Company leased the coast from the sultan of Zanzibar. Kenya became a British protectorate in 1895 and was organized as a crown colony in 1920. The British introduced Christianity and brought people from India and other parts of its empire to work on large infrastructure projects, such as the railroad.

Following a period of violent partisan uprisings (the Mau-Mau Rebellion) in the 1950s, Great Britain granted Kenya independence in 1963. It remained in the Commonwealth as a sovereign republic. Jomo Kenyatta, leader of the independence struggle, served as the first president until his death in 1978. He formed a strong central government under one political party, the Kenya African National Union (KANU). He was followed by Daniel Toroitich arap Moi. In 1982, Moi declared KANU the only legal political party, citing a need to avoid having political parties based on tribes. All political candidates had to register with KANU to be eligible for office.

Under international pressure, Moi opened the country to multiparty democracy in 1992 and adopted a two-term limit for the president. A fragmented opposition failed to wrest power from KANU in 1992 and 1997, although most observers declared the balloting unfair due to vote rigging and political harassment. Politicians also stirred ethnic conflict as a means of intimidating voters. In the western Rift Valley alone, more than 1,500 people died as a result of ethnic violence.

In late 2002, Moi prepared to stand down as required by the constitution's term limit, but he forced KANU to select Uhuru Kenyatta (son of Jomo Kenyatta) as the party's candidate in the approaching presidential election. Controversy surrounding Moi's decision led to divisions within KANU. Many of its leaders joined with opposition parties to form the National Rainbow Coalition (NARC), which selected Mwai Kibaki as its candidate. In December 2002, Kibaki won the presidency with 62 percent of the vote. NARC enjoyed a landslide victory

Kenya

in parliamentary elections, ending four decades of KANU rule. Since taking office, Kibaki has sought to reverse the nation's economic decline, combat corruption, reduce unemployment, provide free public education, and improve roads and other infrastructure.

THE PEOPLE

Population. Kenya's population of 32.02 million is growing at 1.1 percent annually. Nairobi, the capital, is home to about 2 million people, but less than 25 percent of all Kenyans live in large urban areas. The population is concentrated in the southern two-thirds of the country, where the majority resides in rural towns and villages.

Although 99 percent of the population is African, it is divided among at least 47 distinct ethnic groups, which developed largely along linguistic lines. The largest of these groups include the Kikuyu (22 percent), Luhya (14), Luo (13), Kalenjin (12), Kamba (11), Kisii (6), and Meru (6). Smaller groups include the Embu, Maasai, Mijikenda, Samburu, Somali, Taita, Teso, Turkana, and others. About 1 percent of the population consists of Europeans, Asians, and Arabs.

Language. English and Kiswahili (also called Swahili) are Kenya's official languages. English is widely used in business, education, and government. Kiswahili was chosen as the national language over other native tongues because of its linguistic commonality with Kenya's other Bantu-based languages. Kiswahili is promoted to encourage national unity. Each ethnic group speaks its own native tongue and communicates with other groups in Kiswahili or English.

Religion. The majority of Kenyans are Christians. About 40 percent belong to various Protestant churches and 30 percent are Roman Catholic. Approximately 6 percent are Muslim. Most Muslims live along the coast and in the northeast. About 10 percent of the people follow indigenous belief systems or nontraditional Christian faiths.

General Attitudes. Kenyans are proud of their cultural heritage and their nation's accomplishments. They respect the national flag. When and wherever it is raised or lowered, people stop to observe the short ceremony before moving on. Kenyans are warm and friendly. The family is society's most important group, followed by the tribe. Failing to maintain close ties with the extended family is considered rebellious behavior. Family needs take precedence over personal interests. Individuals traditionally share their wealth with poorer family members. For instance, a man with adequate finances may be expected to pay school fees for his less-fortunate brother's children. Wealthier individuals are also expected to help their community. Unfortunately, with current economic strains and the loss of tradition, many middle-class people resent taking care of extended family members. Land ownership is a valued indicator of social status. For some groups, ownership of cattle, sheep, and goats is also an indicator of wealth.

Kenyans take pride in their efforts to preserve African wildlife. Thirty percent of Kenya's wildlife lives on several million acres of national reserves. Kenyan preservation values come from an ancient heritage that emphasized coexistence with animals. By the mid-1990s, the once-decimated elephant population had made a strong comeback and other animal groups were thriving. However, success has its drawbacks; elephants and other wildlife are increasingly responsible for crop destruction, human deaths, and other damage.

Personal Appearance. Kenyans dress conservatively, particularly in rural areas. Western-style clothing, with some African variations, is the norm. Imported secondhand clothing from Europe and North America is very popular and affordable; an entire commercial industry has developed around its trade. Light fabrics and short sleeves are common because of the warm climate. Sleeveless dresses or blouses are considered immodest.

Only children, tourists, and elderly men wear shorts. Women usually wear dresses, but many young urban women wear pants. Women often wear a *kanga* (long, colorful, cotton cloth) as a skirt, to cover their clothes, or to shield themselves from rain and wind. Mothers use a *kanga* to carry children on their backs. Rural and some urban women wear scarves. Small groups such as the Maasai, Samburu, and Turkana retain traditional dress.

CUSTOMS AND COURTESIES

Greetings. Each ethnic group generally uses a unique variety of salutations for different age groups and situations. However, a handshake is common and important throughout the country. Supporting the right forearm with the left hand while shaking shows special respect for a leader or elder. Kenyans are friendly and greet others with warmth and politeness. They often ask about each other's family and welfare. In coastal areas, a traditional Kiswahili greeting is *Jambo!* (Greetings!). *Habari gani?* (What is the news?) or just *Habari?* is common in noncoastal areas. The usual response is *Mzuri* (Good) or *Salama* (Peaceful). English greetings are also acceptable. Upon departing, Kenyans might say *Tutaonana* (We will see each other), or in the evening, *Lala salama* (Sleep peacefully). Maasai children greet elders with a slight bow; the elder responds by placing an open palm on the child's head.

Gestures. Kenyans pass and accept items with the right hand or both hands. Using the left hand alone is improper. The verbal "tch-tch" or a "tss-tss" sound expresses displeasure. Pointing at someone with the index finger is rude. One beckons by waving all fingers of the hand. People often point by extending the lower lip or nodding the head in the intended direction. Approval may be shown with both thumbs extended up. It is improper to touch an elder. It is often considered improper to photograph another person without permission. Public displays of affection (including holding hands) are not acceptable in most areas, although they are increasingly common in Nairobi. Eye contact is important, as people are more willing to trust a person who will look them in the eye.

Visiting. Because of strong family ties and friendships, visiting is a common activity among Kenyans. Sunday is a popular day for making visits. Most visits are unannounced; people often drop by for conversation and a cup of tea. No rules exist about how long a visit lasts, but it is impolite for a host to ask guests to leave. Hosts endeavor to make guests comfortable and they nearly always serve tea. Enjoying afternoon tea is a daily custom throughout the country.

Urban visitors might bring flowers and tea leaves to their hosts. Rural people bring edible gifts such as sugar, instant coffee, flour, or cornmeal. Such gifts are presented in a *kiondo* (Kikuyu word for a woven bag). The host returns the bag at the end of the visit, having placed in it gifts for the visitor. It is impolite to return an empty bag. It is also impolite to say good-bye at the door. Hosts commonly walk with departing visitors for some distance before returning home.

Eating. When guests are invited to dinner, they usually socialize with a host while final preparations are being made. After

Kenya

the meal, they stay for more conversation. Depending on the situation and family tradition, people may eat their meal with the right hand or with utensils. Rural Kenyans more often use their right hand, but urban residents do so only for certain foods. When diners use utensils, they hold a knife in the right hand and a spoon in the left. One washes one's hands before and after eating, often in a bowl at the table. In some traditional families, children do not eat with adults. Men are often served first. Among the Samburu, warriors avoid eating in the presence of women. European cuisine is prevalent in major cities, and Nairobi and Mombassa have restaurants with a wide variety of international cuisine.

LIFESTYLE

Family. The average family is very large. Kenyans are often close to their uncles, aunts, and cousins. Children in some ethnic groups call a maternal aunt *younger mother* or *older mother* depending on the aunt's age in relation to the child's mother. A paternal aunt is called *aunt*. Likewise, a paternal uncle is *younger father* or *older father*, while a maternal uncle is *uncle*. Urban families tend to be smaller, and nuclear-family households are becoming more common. Rural households usually contain more than one generation. The family's youngest adult son cares for aging parents. Because the family is a great source of pride, most Kenyans expect to marry and have children. Women care for the home, children, and garden. Most homes do not have modern appliances, so cooking can be a time-consuming chore; water and firewood must often be carried from long distances. Men do not do household chores, and they rarely cook.

An increasing number of educated women are choosing to avoid traditional roles for wives in favor of marriages in which both parents work. In such circumstances, the family will hire someone, often a young female relative, to take care of the children. Urban women comprise one-third of the labor force, one-third of college students, and as many as half of all graduate students. Rural women are responsible for most agricultural output but own very little land themselves.

Dating and Marriage. Dating starts at about age 18 in cities but is still rather uncommon in villages. Usually young people choose their partners, but some marriages are still arranged. Men and women usually marry in their early twenties. Wedding details are handled largely by the families. The groom's family pays the bride's family a dowry (traditionally livestock but now most often cash) as a way to thank them for raising the bride and to compensate them for losing her.

Diet. The most common meats in Kenya are goat, beef, lamb, chicken, and fish. Milk, *ugali* (a stiff dough made from cornmeal, millet, sorghum, or cassava), *uji* (porridge made from *ugali* ingredients), red bean stew, *mandazi* (a doughnutlike food), *githeri* (corn and beans), and *chapati* (a flat bread) are staple foods. *Sukuma wiki* (collard greens) is grown in nearly every garden and is a popular side dish to *ugali*. Abundant fruits include pineapples, mangoes, oranges, bananas, plantains, and papaya. Sweet potatoes, avocados, and cassava are also common.

Recreation. Soccer is the most popular team sport in Kenya. Soccer leagues exist throughout the nation. Highly organized but poorly equipped leagues operate in even the poorest areas. They are valued for giving youth a chance to develop discipline, teamwork, and physical skills. Track-and-field activities join soccer as Kenya's national sports. The nation has produced world-famous long-distance runners and other athletes.

Urban residents might play field hockey, cricket, or rugby. Many Kenyans enjoy a traditional strategy game (sometimes called *bao* or *ajua*) played with pebbles or seeds. Storytelling, riddles, and proverbs are also popular.

The Arts. Music in Kenya's cities is heavily influenced by Western imports, particularly gospel, as well as Congolese *lingala* music. One of the most popular locally-developed styles is the contemporary dance music known as *benga*. First popularized during the 1970s, *benga* fuses traditional rhythms of the Luo ethnic group with modern instruments such as the electric guitar. In rural areas, homemade drums and guitars commonly accompany dancing. The style of indigenous music and dance varies by region. *Taraab* music has Arab roots and developed in coastal areas. The Maasai are renowned for singing multipart harmonies. The Luo play the *nyatiti*, an eight-string lyre, to accompany lyrics about fables and legends. The Kenya National Theater in Nairobi offers drama, concerts, and dance programs.

Holidays. Kenyans celebrate New Year's Day; Easter (Friday–Monday); Labor Day (1 May); Madaraka Day (1 June), marking the birth of the republic; Kenyatta Day (20 Oct.), celebrating Jomo Kenyatta's arrest in 1952 for opposing British authorities; *Jamhuri* Day, or Independence Day (12 Dec.); Christmas; and Boxing Day (26 Dec.). Boxing Day comes from the British tradition of presenting small boxed gifts to service workers, tradesmen, and servants. It is now primarily a day for visiting family and friends. Parades, speeches, meals, and church services often mark official holidays.

For the Islamic population, the country also observes *Idul-Fitr*, a three-day feast at the end of the month of *Ramadan*. The first day is an official holiday for Muslims, but celebrations on the next two days occur after working hours. During *Ramadan*, Muslims do not eat or drink from sunrise to sunset, after which they eat meals and visit one another.

Commerce. Business and government hours are generally from 8 a.m. to noon or 1 p.m. and from 2 to 5 p.m., Monday through Friday. Some businesses are also open Saturday mornings. While prices are fixed in urban shopping areas, bargaining is common in rural markets and at roadside stands. Open-air markets operate twice a week, and roadside stands sell fresh fruits and vegetables every day.

SOCIETY

Government. Kenya is led by a president (currently Mwai Kibaki), who is head of state and head of government. The president is directly elected to a five-year term and selects a vice president (currently Moody Awori) from the 224 members of the National Assembly (*Bunge*). Members of the National Assembly also serve five-year terms. Voters directly elect 210 members, the president appoints 12 members, and two positions are reserved for the National Assembly's speaker and the attorney general. All citizens may vote at age 18. The nation is divided into eight provinces, each with a local government.

Economy. Kenya's economy has suffered badly in recent years from political turmoil, market reforms, global recession, rampant corruption, and other events. Although tight fiscal policies led to moderate economic growth in the 1990s, severe drought and a lack of foreign investment have caused increased unemployment and higher inflation. The nation is dependant on loans from foreign donor. The per capita gross domestic product is double what it was in the 1960s, but most people still struggle to meet basic needs.

Kenya

Kenya's economy is based on agriculture, which provides nearly 65 percent of all export earnings and employs 75 percent of the workforce. The chief cash crops are coffee, tea, and horticultural products. Other agricultural products include pyrethrum (a flower used to make insecticides), livestock, corn, wheat, rice, cassava, and sugarcane. Kenya traditionally has been self-sufficient in food production but recently has been unable to feed its population. Industries focus on small-scale manufactured items.

The tourist industry is a major contributor to the economy, but it has been negatively impacted by general insecurity in major towns and highly publicized attacks on tourists. Beach resorts and diverse wildlife are the primary attractions. The currency is the Kenyan shilling (KES).

Transportation and Communications. Kenya has good international and domestic air links. Travel by train or bus is slow and unreliable due to neglect of the nation's infrastructure. Most rural roads are unpaved. Large buses and *matatus* (small pickup trucks with cabs on the back) run throughout the country, but are often driven recklessly, with frequent accidents. Rural people rarely have cars, so for distances that they cannot walk they rely on *matatus*, which run on regular routes but without schedules. Taxis are plentiful in Nairobi. Traffic moves on the left side of the road. Mombasa is the primary shipping port, serving a number of East African countries.

Kenya has one of Africa's best telecommunications systems. The phone network is expanding, driven largely by mobile phone technology. Most Kenyans listen to radio broadcasts in both Kiswahili and English. The Kenya Broadcasting Corporation is a private corporation indirectly controlled by the government. Five private television and three private radio stations offer extensive programming. There are three daily national newspapers.

Education. Primary school is compulsory and free for ages six to fourteen. Secondary schooling lasts for four years. Most children are enrolled. In 2003, the new government began investing heavily to ensure adequate facilities for all primary-age children. Rural children are first taught in Kiswahili (or sometimes their native tongue). English is introduced in the first and second grades and is the language of instruction for all subjects (except Kiswahili language classes) after the third grade. Urban schoolchildren usually begin instruction in English.

Public schoolteachers are employed by the government. However, in recent years, schools in general (and especially rural schools) have suffered from considerable under-funding. Some teachers take second jobs to supplement inadequate salaries. Private schools are common; parents are often willing to pay to enable their children to get a better education. Attendance at boarding school is common, even from an early age. The hunt for schools in which to place one's children is a regular undertaking for parents. A university education is available to competent students and to those who can afford the tuition.

Health. Only about half of all Kenyans have access to basic health care. In rural areas, people often avoid government hospitals because they have inadequate medical supplies. A number of private facilities exist for those who can afford them.

DEVELOPMENT DATA
Human Dev. Index* rank . . . . 148 of 177 countries
   Adjusted for women . . . . 114 of 144 countries
Real GDP per capita $1,020
Adult literacy rate . . . . 90 percent (male); 79 (female)
Infant mortality rate . . . . 63 per 1,000 births
Life expectancy . . . . 44 (male); 46 (female)

Rural Kenyans continue to rely on traditional healing methods, although Western medicine is becoming more widely accepted. Infant mortality rates have dropped in recent years. Unfortunately, a high HIV infection rate and deaths occurring from AIDS have lowered overall life expectancy by nearly 20 years. Diseases such as malaria are prevalent in low-lying regions.

AT A GLANCE
Events and Trends.

- In October 2004, Kenyan ecologist Wangari Maathai became the first African woman to receive the Nobel Peace Prize. She was recognized for her commitment to the environment, sustainable development, and democracy. In 1977, Maathai founded the Green Belt Movement, which encouraged poor women to combat deforestation and desertification by planting trees.

- The draft of a new constitution was completed in March 2004. A constitutional review commission was to have finished the revision by 2003, but the process was delayed by disagreements over how much power the president should hold. According to the final version, the elected president will appoint a prime minister as head of government after the next elections in 2007. However, controversy surrounding the draft has delayed its implementation.

- In December 2004, 80 opposition members walked out of the National Assembly to protest the passing of a bill that would allow a simple parliamentary majority to amend the constitution. Prior to the bill, a two-thirds majority was required. The opposition believes the president will use the simple majority to weaken the prime minister's role under the new constitution.

- Although the December 2002 presidential and parliamentary elections were marred by some violence and ballot irregularities, observers declared the elections to be largely free and fair. The governing NARC coalition is comprised of the Democratic Party, the National Party of Kenya, the Liberal Party, and other parties.

Contact Information. Embassy of Kenya, 2249 R Street NW, Washington, DC 20008; phone (202) 387-6101; web site www.kenyaembassy.com.

© 2005 ProQuest Information and Learning Company and Brigham Young University. It is against the law to copy, reprint, store, or transmit any part of this publication in any form by any means without written permission from ProQuest. This document contains native commentary and original analysis, as well as estimated statistics. The content should not be considered strictly factual, and it may not apply to all groups in a nation. *UN Development Programme, Human Development Report 2004 (New York: Oxford University Press, 2004).

CultureGrams
People. The World. You.

ProQuest Information and Learning Company
300 North Zeeb Road, P.O. Box 1346
Ann Arbor, Michigan 48106 USA
Toll Free: 1.800.528.6279
Fax: 1.800.864.0019
www.culturegrams.com

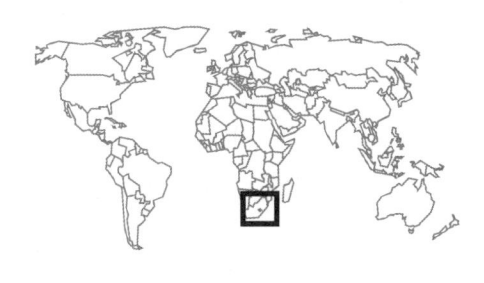

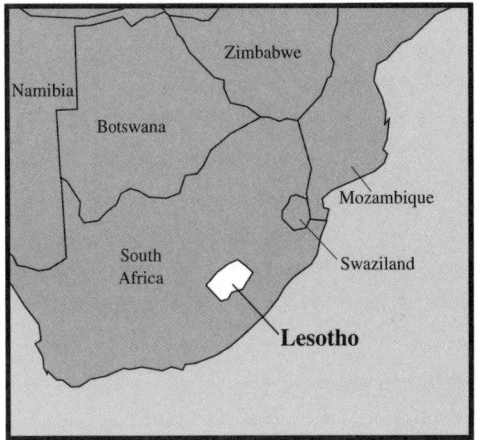

Kingdom of Lesotho

BACKGROUND

Land and Climate. Lesotho (pronounced "le-SUE-too") is a small, mountainous country slightly larger than Maryland and located in the east-central part of South Africa. Covering 11,718 square miles (30,350 square kilometers), it is completely surrounded by South Africa. Lesotho is divided into three basic geographic regions: the lowlands, at about 5,000 feet (1,500 meters) above sea level; the foothills; and the highlands, which include peaks of 11,000 feet (3,300 meters). Most of Lesotho's agricultural areas and the largest cities are located in the western lowlands. Mountains dominate the east. The Drakensberg Mountains in southeastern Lesotho border South Africa and are divided from the Maluti Mountains by the Orange River. The Caledon River forms much of the western border. Lesotho's waterways have potential for hydroelectric power and other economic development. A 30-year project (Lesotho Highlands Water Project) began in 1986. Six dams are being constructed to generate electricity, provide irrigation, improve highland access (with new roads), and store water that is sold to South Africa.

Because of its high elevation, Lesotho has a pleasant climate for most of the year. Its sunny skies (averaging three hundred days a year) are increasingly inviting to tourists. Summer extends from November to January, and winter is between May and July. Most rain falls from October to April. Lowland temperatures reach 90°F (32°C) in the summer and drop to 34°F (1°C) in the winter. The highlands are cooler, and mountains receive snow in winter.

History. The history of Lesotho, once called Basutoland, began when the Basotho nation was formed from the remnants of tribes scattered by Zulu and Matebele raids in the early 1800s. Moshoeshoe (pronounced "mo-SHWAY-shway") the Great united the people and ruled for almost 50 years (1823–70). During a series of wars with South Africa in the mid-1800s, Moshoeshoe lost considerable territory. After an appeal to Queen Victoria for protection against Boer (Dutch-origin farmers/settlers) advances, Britain annexed Basutoland as a territory in 1868.

In 1871, Basutoland was temporarily annexed by the Cape Colony (one of the four colonies that later became South Africa), but the people revolted and became a British crown colony in 1884. Even when South Africa formed in 1909, Basutoland remained with Britain. South Africa expected to someday annex the region but was never successful.

Internal self-rule was introduced in 1959 when a new constitution allowed for an elected legislature. In October 1966, Basutoland was granted full independence from Great Britain as the Kingdom of Lesotho. Upon independence, a constitutional monarchy was established with Moshoeshoe II as head of state and Chief Leabua Jonathan as prime minister.

In 1970, Jonathan suspended the constitution and dissolved Parliament to keep his ruling party (Basutoland National Party, or BNP) in power. Elections in 1985 were designed to favor the BNP and thus were boycotted by other parties. Jonathan's government was finally ousted by a bloodless coup in 1986. A six-man military council took over and technically vested power in the hands of the king. In reality, the king had little authority and the military junta ruled the country. After a power struggle, King Moshoeshoe II was forced into exile in 1990 and replaced by his son, King Letsie III, who was expected to be a puppet leader.

The junta promised to restore civilian rule by 1992. However, it took another power struggle to bring about democratic

Lesotho

elections the following year. The Basotholand Congress Party (BCP) heavily defeated the BNP. BCP leader Ntsu Mokhehle became prime minister.

Political stability remained elusive. Soldiers loyal to the BNP rioted in 1994. With military backing, King Letsie dissolved Parliament and the BCP government in August 1994. Intense pressure and domestic unrest forced him to reinstate Mokhehle's elected government a few weeks later. Letsie was able to have his father, Moshoeshoe II, who had returned to the country in 1993, reinstated as king in 1995. Moshoeshoe II died in a car accident in 1996. King Letsie returned to the throne under a pledge not to interfere with politics.

In 1997, Prime Minister Ntsu Mokhehle split with the BCP and created a new ruling party, the Lesotho Congress for Democracy (LCD). That party then went on to win national elections in May 1998, securing all but one seat in Parliament. Opposition leaders claimed elections had been rigged, but the king instructed the LCD to form a government. Mokhehle retired and Pakalitha Mosisili was named prime minister.

In September 1998, the army mutinied. Widespread protests by the opposition led to looting and violence that devastated Maseru. South Africa and Botswana intervened militarily to halt the revolt and destruction of property; their forces left the country in 2000. Since the end of the revolt, the nation has maintained political stability, though this is sometimes threatened by party disputes.

THE PEOPLE

Population. Lesotho's population of about 1.9 million is growing at an annual rate of 0.14 percent. The people of Lesotho are called Basotho (or Masotho for a single person). Their language is Sesotho. Between the 16th and 19th centuries, an influx of Sesotho-speaking peoples (refugees from tribal wars in surrounding areas) populated the region. This led to the development of the Basotho (or Sotho) ethnic group, giving Lesotho a fairly homogeneous population (nearly 80 percent Basotho). About 20 percent of the population is of Nguni origin (Xhosa and Baphuti tribes); some are San or Griqua. There are also small numbers of Europeans and Indians. About 37 percent of the people are younger than age 15. One-fifth of all people live in urban areas.

Language. Both English and Sesotho are official languages. Nearly all inhabitants speak Sesotho (also called Southern Sotho), a Bantu language written with Roman letters. English is used in business. It is also the language of school instruction after the fifth *standard* (grade). Many people can speak English. Zulu and Xhosa are also spoken by those who work in South Africa's mines or have contact with South Africa's Transkei region.

Religion. Nearly 80 percent of the population is Christian. Most people attend church weekly. The nation's three largest churches are the Roman Catholic Church, the Lesotho Evangelical Church, and the Anglican Church of Lesotho. Christian missions are scattered throughout the country. There is a small Muslim community in the north. About 20 percent of the population follows indigenous belief systems. Some Basotho Christians continue to practice some indigenous traditions or rites along with Christianity.

General Attitudes. The Basotho are a courteous, friendly people who are warm and hospitable to others. They laugh when embarrassed. Basotho avoid personal confrontation. Hence, they often say what they think another person wants to hear or what would please the listener, even if reality or intentions might be otherwise. Lesotho's citizens are proud of their independent nation, even if it is surrounded by a larger, more powerful country.

Individual shrewdness and independence are highly valued. Many have a strong entrepreneurial drive. Wealth is measured in cattle or sheep. People, especially in rural areas, tend to display a sort of passive optimism, believing that others will help them if they have trouble or that life will take care of itself. Except among the highly educated, one is considered to have reached one's potential upon fathering or bearing a child. The more children a man has, the more respected he is. People are proud of their families and treat the elderly with great respect.

Personal Appearance. The Basotho dress in conservative, Western-style clothing but often cover their clothes with a beautifully designed wool blanket, especially in rural areas. The blanket is used as a warm robe for cool evenings or to carry infants on their mothers' backs. Women tie it at the waist and men fold it on the shoulder when daytime temperatures warm up. Hats are common for men and women. People wear many types of hats, including baseball caps. Most hats are woven from straw. The *mokorotlo*, or *molianyeoe*, is the traditional hat of Lesotho; it is conical in shape, much like the roof of a rural home, and has an intricately designed knob on top. Women generally do not wear slacks or shorts. The people are clean, neat, and concerned with an orderly appearance. Shoes especially are kept neat and polished.

CUSTOMS AND COURTESIES

Greetings. Greetings tend to be somewhat formal in pattern. Upon shaking hands, two people greet by saying either *Lumela* (Hello) or *Khotso* (Peace be with you). This is followed by the phrase *U phela joang?* (How are you?). If acquainted, each makes polite inquiries about the other's family. They also typically ask *U tsoa kae?* (Where have you been?) and *U tsamaea kae?* (Where are you going?); an explanation is expected. The greeting process eventually evolves into a conversation. Greeting habits vary somewhat, depending on whether men, women, young adults, or children are involved. Personal space among Basotho tends to be close.

In farewells, the person leaving says *Sala hantle* (Stay well). The one staying says *Tsamaea hantle* (Go well). In very formal situations, one addresses others by title; otherwise one uses given names.

Gestures. Pointing with the index finger is impolite. One passes items with the right hand or both hands. It is common for friends of the same gender to walk down the street holding hands. Or if two people meet on the street and stop to shake hands and greet, they may hold the handshake throughout the conversation, regardless of their respective gender. Otherwise, members of the opposite sex do not touch or display affection in public. People use subtle movements of the head and eyes to convey positive or negative responses to something.

Visiting. The Basotho are hospitable hosts and enjoy having guests. Rural people usually visit without prior arrangement, as telephone and mail connections are not extensive. Upon arriving, a visitor knocks on the door and says *Ko ko* (Knock knock). The hosts usually can recognize the voice and know a friendly visitor is at the door; they say *Kena* (Come in), and the visitor may then enter the home. It is extremely discourteous to enter without announcing one's presence in this manner, even if the door is open.

When visitors arrive, even if unexpected, it is polite for the hosts to invite them to stay for something to eat. If visitors are far from home, the hosts offer them shelter for the night. Guests are nearly always served refreshments, such as tea and perhaps cookies or crackers. The Basotho customarily have tea and refreshments in the afternoon, and in rural areas afternoon guests are often served a full meal as well. Guests generally are not expected to bring gifts, but urban residents commonly will bring something to rural relatives.

Socializing among the Basotho takes place not only in the home but also at public places such as the market or *moreneng* (chief compound) during a *pitso* (town meeting). The local chief usually calls a *pitso* to share important news or discuss something. If the news is good, an impromptu party may occur.

Eating. When possible, people eat three meals a day. Breakfast often is eaten around 10 a.m. Lunch is the main meal and is eaten at midday. People in Maseru eat in the continental style; the fork is in the left hand and the knife remains in the right. In villages, people often eat with their right hand or use a spoon, depending on the food. When families are not able to sit down together for a meal, food is left simmering on the stove around mealtime. When individual family members are ready to eat, they serve themselves and eat alone. When the family or group does eat together, the men and/or any important guests of either gender are served first, and when they are satisfied, the women and children eat the remainder of the meal. Each person has a separate dish from which to eat. Finishing everything on one's plate is proper; men might have second helpings.

LIFESTYLE

Family. Lesotho has a strong patriarchal society centered on the family. However, because men often work outside the country during much of the year, women make many decisions and do most of the farm work. Women also work in road construction and in service occupations; they comprise about 45 percent of the labor force.

While the nuclear family lives alone in cities like Maseru, most rural extended families share a compound. It includes several buildings, a *kraal* (living space for animals), and a garden. The traditional *rondavel*, or *ntlo* (home), is built of stone and sticks held together with cow dung, which dries as hard as concrete and can be painted. Before it dries, people often draw intricate designs in it to beautify the home. Walls are thick, and the circular home is covered by a thatched roof. Windows are minimal to keep out cold. The diameter of the main home reflects the family's economic status—the wealthier the family, the larger the home. Its interior is not divided, so families usually have separate buildings for sleeping, cooking, storage, and so forth. Some homes are made of cement blocks.

Family members are expected to help one another. All those living in a compound contribute to its welfare by doing chores, cooking, minding the cattle, raising chickens, working for a wage and sharing part of it, and so forth. Children work hard and get up early to finish chores before going to school. If one person in an extended family falls on hard times, other family members are expected to help if possible. However, they are not expected to sacrifice their own needs to offer this help. When a man dies, his possessions are divided among his brothers and sons, who are expected to provide for his wife and any other women in his care.

Dating and Marriage. Young people meet through community activities, but Western dating is not common. Adult children usually remain with their parents until they marry, and often afterward. Families are heavily involved in marriage/wedding negotiations. The family of the groom is expected to pay a bride-price (in cattle or money) to the bride's family. When a woman marries, she moves to her husband's compound, which may be shared with his parents and others. Her in-laws may give her a new name reflecting the name of her firstborn, whom they will also name.

Diet. The Basotho diet consists of *mealie meal* (cornmeal), rice, potatoes, vegetables (cabbage, peas, etc.), and some fruits. *Papa*, a stiff cornmeal porridge, is eaten with every meal. Modern cold cereals are becoming popular for breakfast. Lunch traditionally consists of *moroho* (cooked vegetables) and *nama* (meat). The evening meal is around 7 p.m. and contains the same foods eaten at lunch. *Nama ea khomo* (beef), *nama ea khoho* (chicken), and *nama ea kolobe* (pork) are popular meats.

Recreation. Soccer is the most popular sport. Some urban residents play volleyball, netball (a basketball-like game for girls), and basketball. Visiting and holidays provide leisure and recreational opportunities. The Basotho like to sing and can harmonize with ease. Most social gatherings involve some sort of singing.

The Arts. The Basotho are proud of their native crafts, including pottery, leather work, tapestries, and weavings of straw or mohair. Straw *mokorotlo*, or *molianyeoe*, hats are one of Lesotho's most distinctive handicrafts. Artisans decorate woolen blankets with historical depictions. All of these items are displayed at the annual Maseru Cultural Festival each March.

Music and dance performances take place at informal gatherings and at special events such as marriages and funerals. Village and school choirs hold singing competitions as fundraisers; audience members pay to hear their favorite song from their favorite choir. A popular traditional instrument is the *lesiba*, a stringed reed often played by young men as a method of herding cattle. Contemporary music consists of singing accompanied by the piano, accordion, and drums.

Holidays. Lesotho's official holidays include New Year's Day, Army Day (20 Jan.), and Moshoeshoe's Day (12 Mar.). Tree Planting Day (21 Mar.) is important because Lesotho is subject to severe soil erosion and has virtually no forests. The government sponsors tree-planting projects to provide future building and fuel supplies and to guard against further erosion. Other national holidays include Family Day (first Monday in July), Independence Day (5 Oct.), and National Sports Day (first Monday in October). Easter (Friday–Monday) and Christmas are the most popular religious holidays. Boxing Day (26 Dec.) comes from the British tradition of giving small boxed gifts to service personnel and tradesmen. It is now usually a day spent visiting friends and relatives. Villages hold end-of-school "graduation" parties for schoolchildren.

Commerce. Businesses and government offices are open between 8 a.m. and 5 p.m., Monday through Friday. Some businesses open on Saturday until 1 p.m. More than 85 percent of the resident population is engaged in subsistence agriculture, so work schedules vary according to the season. As many as 250,000 men are gone at any given time to work in the mines or factories of South Africa. They may be in South Africa for several months each year or for several years. In Lesotho, the legal working age is 12.

SOCIETY

Government. Lesotho is a constitutional monarchy divided into 10 districts. King Letsie III is head of state but performs

Lesotho

mainly ceremonial duties. Most executive authority is vested in the prime minister (currently Pakalitha Mosisili). Parliament's lower house has 120 elected members; the upper house consists of 22 principal chiefs and 11 appointed members. The voting age is 18. Local authority is vested in the village chief.

Economy. Lesotho lacks abundant natural resources (except water) and relies largely on subsistence agriculture, which includes livestock raising. The economy also depends on wages earned by Basotho workers in South African mines. Unemployment can be as high as 50 percent at times. Poverty continues to affect about half of the population, and wealth is highly concentrated.

Grazing rights are communal, but arable land is allocated to individuals and families by local chiefs. Maize (corn), wheat, sorghum, peas, beans, and potatoes are the main crops. Nearly all food is consumed domestically, but asparagus and beans are exported along with wool, mohair, cattle, and hides. Industries include textiles, clothing, and light engineering. Native crafts are also important to the economy.

Tourism provides crucial foreign-exchange earnings. It is hoped that an eight billion dollar water project involving the construction of dams and reservoirs, and the subsequent sale of water to South Africa, will boost economic growth. Both the South African *rand* and the Basotho *loti* (plural is *maloti*) are acceptable currency in Lesotho. The *loti* (LSL) is backed by the *rand* (ZAR).

Transportation and Communications. Maseru is a small city, and it is easy to walk to its farthest points. A number of minibuses operate mostly along Maseru's main street and travel between cities in the lowlands. Other buses travel to eastern points. In keeping with British tradition, traffic moves on the left side of the road. Paved roads are generally in good condition, but most roads are unpaved. Domestic air travel links Maseru with some mountain cities; a few flights go to other African countries. Some areas of the country are accessible only by horse or foot. The Basotho pony is famous in southern Africa for its surefootedness. It has been bred over the years specifically for mountain transport. Many people in remote areas have never traveled outside of their area.

The communications system is improving, but interior mountain locations are often accessible only by radio. Telephone service outside Maseru is sporadic; mail is not always reliable. The government sponsors Radio Lesotho and two weekly newspapers. Several private newspapers also function. Television broadcasts are received from South Africa. For an hour each evening, Lesotho preempts the programming to show its own news and some entertainment. Most areas, except remote mountain locations, have access to television.

Education. Because boys often must tend flocks all day for months at a time when their fathers are working in South Africa, more girls are enrolled in school than boys. This has resulted in much higher literacy rates for women. Lesotho's educational system is administered largely by the three largest churches under the direction of the Ministry of Education. Influenced by the British colonial system, primary education consists of seven levels, called *standards*. At their completion, an exam is administered. If students pass and their family can afford tuition and board, they begin secondary education.

DEVELOPMENT DATA
Human Dev. Index* rank .... 145 of 177 countries
   Adjusted for women .... 117 of 144 countries
Real GDP per capita $2,420
Adult literacy rate .... 74 percent (male); 90 (female)
Infant mortality rate .... 85 per 1,000 births
Life expectancy .... 33 (male); 39 (female)

After completing another three years and passing an exam, students receive a Junior Certificate. Two more years in high school and completion of another exam enable students to attend the University of Lesotho. Vocational schools are also available. The Distance Teaching Centre provides basic education to those who do not or did not go to school.

Health. HIV/AIDS is Lesotho's greatest health concern. The nation has one of the world's highest rates of HIV/AIDS infection: 29 percent of the adult population. Because of Lesotho's elevation, many other diseases common to Africa are not found within the country. Water is generally safe in the capital. Each district has a government hospital in addition to church-sponsored hospitals. The level of health care available varies with location. Services are better in urban areas and near the borders. Those living near the border can seek care in South Africa. Traditional medicine is practiced in remote areas.

AT A GLANCE

Events and Trends.
- In an effort to provide more of Lesotho's homes with electricity, the government announced in 2004 that it would privatize the state-owned national utility company. Although the company was formed in the 1960s, less than 10 percent of the nation's 400,000 homes are currently connected to the electricity grid.
- The first phase of the Lesotho Highlands Water Project was officially opened in March 2004; two dams have been completed. Lesotho's government is pursuing charges of bribery against several foreign construction companies that sought contracts with the project. The Lesotho High Court convicted one company in September 2002 and another in August 2003. Both received heavy fines. The High Court also sentenced a project executive to a 15-year jail term for taking the companies' bribes. Officials hope the court decisions will reduce corruption in future government projects.
- Prime Minister Mosisili's LCD party won an overwhelming parliamentary majority in 2002. Although monitors declared the election to be fair, the opposition BNP claimed that the LCD had rigged the vote.

Contact Information. Embassy of the Kingdom of Lesotho, 2511 Massachusetts Avenue NW, Washington, DC 20008; phone (202) 797-5533.

© 2005 ProQuest Information and Learning Company and Brigham Young University. It is against the law to copy, reprint, store, or transmit any part of this publication in any means without written permission from ProQuest. This document contains native commentary and original analysis, as well as estimated statistics. The content should not be considered strictly factual, and it may not apply to all groups in a nation. *UN Development Programme, Human Development Report 2004 (New York: Oxford University Press, 2004).

CultureGrams
People. The World. You.

ProQuest Information and Learning Company
300 North Zeeb Road, P.O. Box 1346
Ann Arbor, Michigan 48106 USA
Toll Free: 1.800.528.6279
Fax: 1.800.864.0019
www.culturegrams.com

Libya
(Great Socialist People's Libyan Arab Jamahiriya)

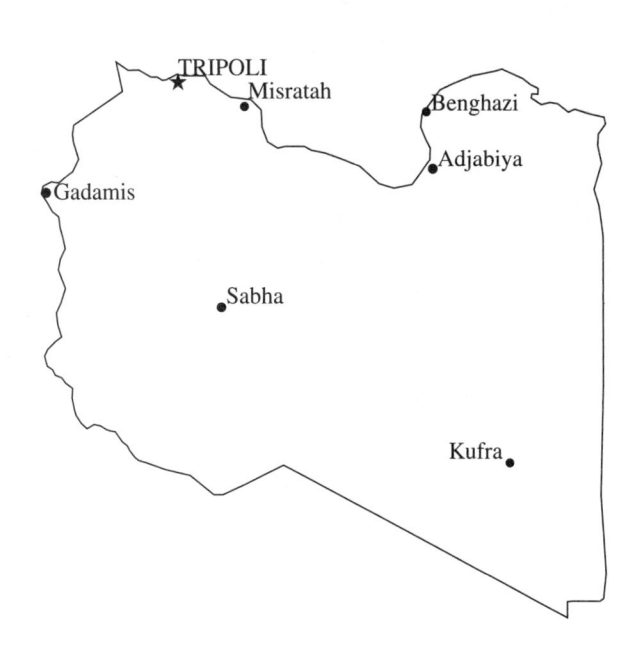

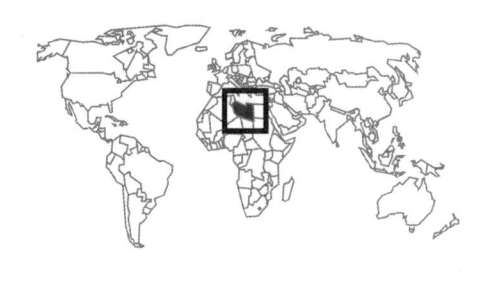

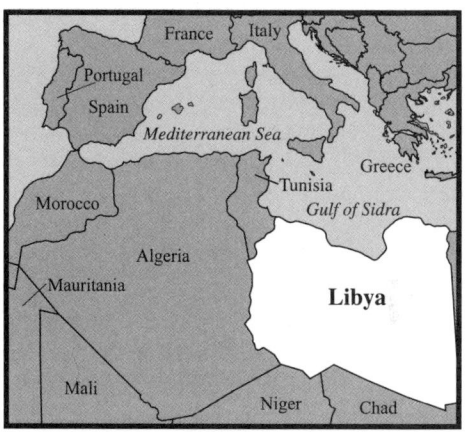

CultureGrams World Edition 2006

BACKGROUND

Land and Climate. The fourth largest country in Africa, Libya has an area of 679,362 square miles (1,759,540 square kilometers); it is larger than Alaska and Minnesota combined. Stretching south from the Mediterranean Sea, the rocky coast is bordered by a thin strip of farmable land and then the vast Sahara Desert, which covers 90 percent of the country. The landscape includes beaches, sand dune–filled deserts, oases, rocky hills, and mountains. Historically, the country had three regions: Tripolitania in the northwest, Fezzan in the southwest, and Cyrenaica in the east. The regions were joined in 1935, but they are still sometimes referred to today.

Near the coast, a Mediterranean climate provides warm summers, mild winters, and as much as 16 inches (41 centimeters) of rainfall per year. The rest of the country is much drier and hotter. Desert areas may receive only 1 inch (2.5 centimeters) of annual rain, and temperatures there may reach 120°F (49°C) during the summer. There are no permanent rivers, only *wadis* (dry riverbeds) that fill with water when it rains. A huge engineering project called the Great Man-Made River channels water from underground aquifers in the south to the north to use for drinking, irrigation, and industry.

History. Libya's first inhabitants were tribes called Imazighen, meaning "free men." Outsiders later came to call them "Berbers," a term many people still use. During the seventh century B.C., Phoenicians set up trading colonies in Libya. Three hundred years later, Greeks colonized the eastern coast. Then, in 146 B.C., Romans defeated the Phoenicians and took control of Libya. The area was subsequently invaded and ruled by Germanic Vandal tribes (beginning in 429 A.D.), the Byzantine Empire (533 A.D.), and Arabs (640 A.D.). Libya gradually became Arabized as thousands of Arabs settled there and absorbed or displaced the Imazighen. Muslim dynasties ruled until the 1500s, when the control of Libya passed between Spain, Malta, Barbary sea pirates, and finally the Ottoman Empire, which ruled from the mid-1500s to the early 1900s.

Beginning in the 1840s, members of the Islamic political *Sanusi* movement rose up against the Ottomans in North Africa. After defeating the Ottomans in 1911, Italy colonized Libya. At that point, the *Sanusis* began to fight the Italians. During World War II, Libya became a major battleground for the European powers, with *Sanusi* leader Mohammed Idris siding with Britain and the Allies. Upon defeat, Italy gave up control of Libya, which was briefly administered by the United Nations (UN). When Libya gained full independence in 1951, Idris became king and remained friendly with Western nations. He held nearly all political power and left the country's wealth in the hands of a few families.

This inequality worsened when oil was discovered in 1959. Libya went from being a poor agricultural country to a rich exporter of oil, and many Libyans wanted access to the new wealth. A group of junior military officers staged a coup in 1969. The group's leader, 27-year-old Muammar Qaddafi, began making changes immediately. Money from oil sales was used to build roads, hospitals, and schools. In addition, the agricultural sector grew and gave Libyans more access to food. Qaddafi came up with a governmental and economic system called *Jamahiriya* (nation ruled by the masses), which was meant to be an alternative to communism and capitalism. In theory, the system advocated a form of democracy, but in reality allowed Qaddafi full control.

Qaddafi exiled political opponents, shut down private newspapers, banned political parties, and replaced *Sanusi* clerics

Libya

with his supporters. On separate occasions, Qaddafi tried but failed to merge Libya with Egypt, Tunisia, Syria, and Chad. He led Libya into military conflicts with Egypt (1977), Uganda (1979), and Chad (1983–7). Libya was defeated in each case, but not before creating regional instability. In 1989, Libya reconciled with the Arab world (Egypt in particular) and formed an economic union called the Arab Maghreb Union with Tunisia, Algeria, Morocco, and Mauritania.

Meanwhile, Libya's relationship with Western nations deteriorated. In 1970, Qaddafi ordered the closure of U.S. and British military bases in Libya. He then offered support to militant groups such as the Palestinian Liberation Organization and the Irish Republican Army. U.S. and British diplomats were withdrawn in the early '80s. In 1986, two U.S. soldiers were killed in a Libyan-ordered bombing of a German nightclub. The United States responded by shelling Tripoli and other cities, killing dozens of Libyans. Then in 1988, Pan Am flight 103 exploded over Lockerbie, Scotland, killing 270 people. When Qaddafi refused to hand over the two Libyan suspects for international trial, the UN imposed sanctions on Libya.

In 1999, Qaddafi moved to have Libya rejoin the international community. He allowed the bombing suspects to be tried, and in 2001 the trial ended with one guilty verdict and one acquittal. In 2003, Libya agreed to compensate the families of the victims of Pan Am 103, after which the UN lifted sanctions. Later that year, Libya announced plans to get rid of all weapons of mass destruction. The United States responded in 2004 by lifting all remaining sanctions.

THE PEOPLE

Population. Libya's population of 5.63 million is growing by 2.37 percent annually. Almost 90 percent of the population lives in cities near the coast, with the largest urban areas being Tripoli (1.8 million) and Benghazi (950,000). About 97 percent of Libyans are of Arab ancestry; full-blooded Imazighen make up only a small minority. The Imazighen are tall and light-skinned, and they have their own language and customs. Though most have fully integrated into Libyan society, some small groups live in remote villages in the west. Tuaregs are another small group. These nomadic herders, who also have their own language, wear dark blue robes and migrate throughout North Africa. Because they are nomadic, some people consider them more African than Libyan. A large but unknown number of foreign workers has come to Libya from Egypt and Tunisia, sub-Saharan Africa, and the Middle East. There are also small groups of Greeks, Maltese, and Italians.

Language. Arabic is the official language and is spoken by nearly everyone, but it may take various forms. For example, Libyans read the *Qur'an* (Koran), school materials, and official documents in classical Arabic. However, they speak a Libyan dialect in daily conversation and usually understand at least some Modern Standard Arabic, which is used throughout the Arab world in written communication. Children grow up speaking the Libyan dialect, so the transition to classical and standard Arabic involves learning new words and a different accent. Imazighen speak Arabic and Tamazight. Tuaregs speak Arabic and Tamasheq. Second languages include English (most common), Italian, or French.

Religion. Islam is Libya's official religion, and Sunni Muslims make up more than 95 percent of the population. Other Muslim groups include *Sanusis*, Ibadhis (members of a branch of Islam), Sufis (Muslims who seek mysticism and a direct experience of Allah), Sharifs (who claim to be descendents of Muhammad), and *marabouts* (holy men who are considered teachers and leaders). Although some of Libya's laws are based on the *Qur'an*, Libya is more liberal than some Islamic states. For example, girls must receive education, and women may hold jobs and serve in the army.

Religion is a daily pursuit for Muslims. Like practicing Muslims everywhere, most Libyans pray five times a day, profess Allah as the only God and Muhammad as his prophet, help the poor, fast during the holy month of *Ramadan*, and make a pilgrimage to Makkah (Mecca) in Saudi Arabia at least once in a lifetime. Friday is the Muslim day of worship, when a sermon is given at the mosque during the noon prayer. Women may go to the mosque, but they usually worship at home.

General Attitudes. Libyans tend to value family and community more than individuality. They try to create unity by being hospitable and generous, even to strangers. For example, if a foreign visitor wanted an authentic Libyan meal, Libyans would go to great lengths to meet the request. Libyans are sensitive about how others view them, and they try to display high morals, maintain dignity, and keep promises. People value wealth and education but disapprove of showiness. Humor is appreciated, but some political jokes make people uneasy.

Most Libyans have a relaxed sense of time and do not consider punctuality a necessity. Older generations and rural Libyans value clan and tribal traditions. Younger, urban Libyans have begun to embrace modern culture, music, and sports figures. Less technology is available in rural areas. Many people believe showing off or giving too much praise can bring the "Evil Eye," or bad luck, so to ward it off, they may say *Ma' Sha' Allah* (As God wills it), burn herbs, and read passages from the *Qur'an*. Urban Libyans prize modern technology, such as satellite dishes, cell phones, and the internet.

Personal Appearance. How Libyans dress is a matter of personal preference, family influence, tradition, and location. In the past 20 years, Libyans have experienced both conservative and liberal influences regarding dress. On the one hand, Libyans have taken some modern style cues from Western television programs. On the other hand, workers from Egypt and Morocco living in Libya have exerted a conservative influence. In general, people may wear any clothes they wish, as long as they are not too revealing.

In cities, men and women often wear jeans and short-sleeved shirts at work or around town. Civil servants and businessmen may wear a suit and tie. Especially in rural areas, most women wear a long-sleeved blouse or jacket, floor-length skirt, and head scarf. In cooler weather, men and women may wear a long tunic (called a *hawli*). *Hawlis* are always white for men but may be any color for women. Older and rural men may wear the *hawli* with a vest and a cap, especially on Fridays. A few older, very conservative women may wear a white, sheet-like cover called a *farashiya*, which conceals the entire body, the head, and one eye. In rural areas, people tend to wear traditional clothing, and women nearly always wear a head scarf.

CUSTOMS AND COURTESIES

Greetings. Libyans consider the failure to welcome someone unkind. Even when entering a room full of strangers, it would be rude not to give a general greeting. A common saying is *Assalamu alikum* (I offer you peace), to which the response is *Wa Alikum Assalam* (I offer you peace, too). Another greeting is *Kayf halak?* (How are you?), to which the expected answer is *Al-hamdu lilah, bahi* (Praise to God, very well). Other greetings include *Sabah al-khayr* (Good morning) and *Masa' al-*

khayr (Good evening). People part by saying *Ma' al-salamah* (Go in safety). When Libyans meet friends, they shake hands, and women might embrace. Men don't shake hands with women unless the woman initiates the gesture.

Gestures. Libyans tend to gesture frequently during conversation, using hand movements for emphasis. For example, touching the tips of the fingers to the thumb can accentuate a point. However, some Libyans see excessive movement as a sign of lower social status. Like Muslims everywhere, Libyans use their right hand to eat.

It is improper for a man to touch a woman in public unless she is his wife or sister; however, women often hold hands with each other. Many people consider it improper to smoke or use coarse language in front of women or older men. It is considered rude for a woman to spit, cross her legs at the knee rather than the ankle, or stand with her hands on her hips.

Visiting. Libyans see visiting as an important way to show respect and maintain relationships. So, they visit each other often, especially on weekends and holidays. In rural areas, events such as births or weddings might involve the entire community. Whole families may visit each other, but men and women spend most of their time in separate rooms (children may be with either group). Guests are often invited, but unexpected visits are also welcomed.

Upon entering the home, guests are offered tea or coffee and food. Though guests may initially refuse, it is polite to accept at least a small portion. It is unthinkable for hosts to ask guests to leave. Even when the guests stand up to go, the hosts will say it is too early to leave. Hosts usually accompany guests to the gate of the house and may offer them a ride.

Eating. Libyans begin and end meals by washing their hands. Breakfasts are light, and the main meal is lunch. An afternoon snack and tea may precede a light dinner. Families eat together whenever possible. Most Libyans sit on cushions around a low table or a tablecloth spread out on the floor; some use a full-size table and chairs. Utensils are usually used, but some dishes (such as stews) are eaten using bread as scoops. Mealtimes are usually filled with conversation, but some people in the older generation prefer to eat in silence. Although there are quite a few restaurants (especially fast food establishments), most people dine out only occasionally. Young people see fast food as a rare treat. When one does dine out, a service charge is often added to the bill.

LIFESTYLE

Family. The most important unit in society is the family. Children are expected to obey and respect their parents and elders. Even small children help with simple chores. Young people usually live at home until they marry. A young man may move away to work or study, but it is socially unacceptable for a young, unmarried woman to live on her own. Adult children expect to care for their elderly parents.

Women are permitted to attend universities and to work; about 40 percent of urban women work outside the home in positions ranging from teachers to doctors. But even when women work in offices with men, there is still separation. For example, male and female teachers may have separate lounges where they can relax or grade papers. Also, even educated, Westernized women do not go to restaurants without a family member acting as a chaperon. Inside the home, women are responsible for children and household chores. Rural men usually take care of farming and other physical labor, but women occasionally help with these tasks, too.

Dating and Marriage. Libyans meet through relatives or friends, at college, or at work, but they do not usually date in the Western sense of the word. Instead, couples spend time together with family members or with a group of friends escorted by chaperones. Even if young people meet in college, marriages are usually coordinated through their families.

Traditional weddings are elaborate, lasting up to six days. Because of the time and expense involved in such an event, many modern Libyan weddings last from one to three days. Still, many customs have been retained, including signing a marriage contract; having families exchange gifts to demonstrate wealth and generosity; using henna dye to decorate the hands and feet of the bride and other females; and hosting large parties for both families. These parties often feature a great deal of food, music, dancing, and gifts. One-day weddings are most common in cities, where most of the wedding festivities take place in a hotel banquet room.

Diet. Breakfast consists of bread with jam and butter, cheese and olives, and tea or coffee. Popular dishes at other meals include *couscousi* (couscous, a hot sauce, and meat), *sharba libiya* ("Libyan soup," made of lamb and tomato stock, orzo pasta, chickpeas, cilantro, lemon, mint, and curry), *couscousi bil-bosla* (couscous with sautéed onions), *makaruna mbakbaka* (any pasta simmered in tomato and lamb stock with a mixture of spices), and *hassa* (gravy made of lamb, oil, crushed tomatoes, flour, and spices). Libyans enjoy various sweets, such as *baklawa* (a pastry filled with nuts and honey) and *magrud* (semolina cookies stuffed with dates and dipped in syrup). Libyans eat fresh fruits and vegetables, including dates, grapes, oranges, watermelon, potatoes, peas, and onions. Libyans generally avoid alcohol and pork because they are forbidden by Islamic and Libyan law. All meat must be *halal*, which means it is slaughtered according to Islamic tradition, including saying a prayer first.

Recreation. Libyans enjoy visiting each other and watching movies at home. The most popular sport is soccer (*football*), but only men attend professional matches. Young men also enjoy volleyball and basketball. Men go to cafés and play games like chess, cards, and dominoes. Some Libyans watch chariot and horse races. Women usually spend their leisure time socializing. They pay visits, have tea parties, and shop together. Young men and women stroll separately through town in the evening. On weekends, families may have picnics, and in the summer they go to the beach to swim, fish, or relax.

The Arts. Traditional folk dances where men and women dance separately are associated with each region. Dancing and singing take place at most celebrations, family parties, tribal meetings, and Sufi ceremonies. Popular instruments are the *oud* (lute), the *zokra* (similar to bagpipes), the *darbuka* (drum), and the *al-nay* (bamboo pipe). In some cases, traditional sounds have been blended with European pop styles to create a unique type of Libyan music.

Poetry recitation is popular, and Libyan poetry often includes themes of nationalism, religion, and love. Many Libyans make jewelry and weave fabric for shawls or carpets. Like other Muslims, Libyans avoid depicting people or animals in their art. Instead they use intricate patterns and elaborate calligraphy to decorate paintings and buildings.

Holidays. National holidays include People's Authority Announcement (2 Mar.), Evacuation of British Troops (28 Mar.), Student Revolution Day (7 Apr.), Evacuation of American Troops (11 June), and Qaddafi's Revolution Day (1 Sept.). Although national holidays take place on the same day

Libya

every year, religious holidays follow the Islamic lunar calendar and so fall on different days each year. One Islamic holiday is *Eid al-Fitr*, a three-day celebration following the holy month of *Ramadan*, when Muslims fast from dawn to dusk. Another holiday, *Eid al-Adha*, is a four-day holiday at the end of the pilgrimage to Makkah; also called Feast of the Sacrifice, it honors Abraham's willingness to sacrifice his son. Libyans also celebrate Islamic New Year and the Prophet's Birthday, for which many people light off fireworks.

Commerce. Civil servants work from 8:00 a.m. to 2:00 p.m., Saturday through Thursday. The weekend is only one day, the holy day of Friday. Shops open in the morning and close in early afternoon, then open again in the late afternoon. There are no regulations about hours of work; shopkeepers decide for themselves. Many people buy vegetables, fruits, meat, and poultry on the same day they plan to eat them. Despite government efforts to build them, large malls and supermarkets have not replaced local markets, which are still popular.

SOCIETY

Government. Based on Qaddafi's political ideas set forth in the *Green Book*, the country is divided into small localities, and each elects a committee. For two weeks each year, all the local committees gather to debate policies. The resulting resolutions are meant to influence the decisions of the Secretariat (cabinet) and Secretary (prime minister) of the General People's Committee.

Though Qaddafi has no official position and prefers to be called Brother Colonel or The Leader, he and a few associates control the government and military. Qaddafi delegates some tasks to a prime minister of his choosing (currently Shukri Ghanim).

Economy. Oil transformed Libya into one of Africa's wealthiest nations. Crude oil and refined petroleum products account for more than a third of GDP. Libya also exports natural gas and fruits, vegetables, grains, and cattle. However, the country still imports about two-thirds of its food.

The Libyan economy has also faced many challenges. For example, Qaddafi wanted employees to own their businesses, but the system crumbled because of mismanagement and corruption. The sanctions imposed on Libya by the UN were deeply damaging. Libya could not trade directly with Europe or the United States, so shortages in many goods occurred, inflation increased, and technology and infrastructure grew out of date. Many Libyans became bitter toward the nations that imposed the sanctions. The economy has improved since trade was normalized, but full recovery will take time. More products are now available, but they remain too costly for average Libyans. The economy, which has been controlled by the state, is gradually moving toward becoming more market-based. The currency is the Libyan *dinar* (LYD).

Transportation and Communications. Most highways are paved, but rural and desert roads are not. While many families have cars, buses are often used for travel between cities. Within cities, vans can be hired as taxis. Remote areas are accessed by four-wheel-drive trucks. Tripoli, Benghazi, and Sabhah have international airports.

All newspapers as well as radio and television stations are

DEVELOPMENT DATA

Human Dev. Index* rank . . . . 58 of 177 countries
    Adjusted for women . . . . NA
Real GDP per capita $7,570
Adult literacy rate . . . . 92 percent (male); 71 (female)
Infant mortality rate . . . . 26 per 1,000 births
Life expectancy . . . . 71 (male); 75 (female)

government-owned, and media coverage is tightly controlled. However, satellite dishes allow Libyans to see foreign programs. People without their own phones can use public phone offices to place calls. Internet use is on the rise, and major cities have internet cafés. The postal system is wide-ranging but service may be infrequent and inefficient.

Education. Education is mandatory for children ages 6 to 15. At all levels, boys and girls may attend classes together or separately. They receive comparable educations, including religious studies. After age 15, students may attend three years of high school or four years of vocational training. University study is available for all Libyans who complete high school, and all public education is paid for by the government. There are many public universities and several private ones, which are funded through tuition and investments. Today, many college graduates are unable to find jobs that match their qualifications, so they seek employment outside the country. Some older Libyans are illiterate because they never attended school, and children in remote areas don't always attend school because of transportation difficulties.

Health. Libyans receive free medical care, but many facilities, particularly in rural areas, lack basic supplies. For this reason, wealthier people seek care at private medical clinics in Libya or outside the country. Public facilities are better in major cities, where hospitals are linked to medical schools. Towns and villages are served by small hospitals and clinics. Despite government efforts to control diseases, there are occasional outbreaks of hepatitis A and polio. A social security system provides maternity leave, disability benefits, and pensions.

AT A GLANCE

Events and Trends.

- In December 2003, Muammar Qaddafi declared that Libya would terminate all its programs for developing weapons of mass destruction (WMDs). Libya agreed to get rid of the components of chemical weapons that it had, limit its missiles to those with a short range, and accept international inspections.
- In April 2004, the U.S. Department of the Treasury lifted a ban on U.S. citizens traveling to Libya and authorized the opening of a diplomatic mission in Libya. Later that year, the United States removed all sanctions against Libya. However, Libya remained on the State Department's list of countries that sponsor terrorism.

Contact Information. Libyan Liaison Office, 2600 Virginia Avenue NW, Suite 705, Washington, DC 20037; phone (202) 944-9601. Mission of Libya to the United Nations, 309 East 48th Street, New York, NY 10017; phone (212) 752-5775.

CultureGrams™
People. The World. You.

ProQuest Information and Learning Company
300 North Zeeb Road, P.O. Box 1346
Ann Arbor, Michigan 48106 USA
Toll Free: 1.800.528.6279
Fax: 1.800.864.0019
www.culturegrams.com

© 2005 ProQuest Information and Learning Company and Brigham Young University. It is against the law to copy, reprint, store, or transmit any part of this publication in any form by any means without written permission from ProQuest. This document contains native commentary and original analysis, as well as estimated statistics. The content should not be considered strictly factual, and it may not apply to all groups in a nation. *UN Development Programme, Human Development Report 2004 (New York: Oxford University Press, 2004).

CultureGrams 2006 World Edition
Republic of Madagascar

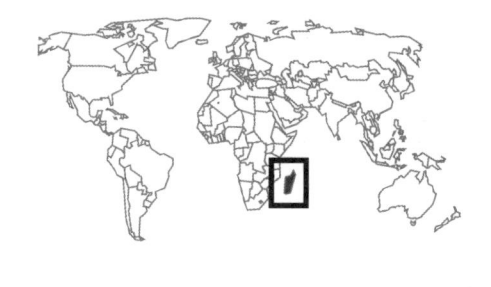

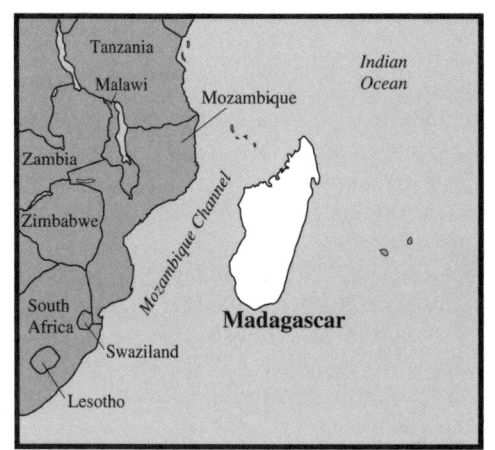

BACKGROUND

Land and Climate. Madagascar, situated off the southeast coast of Africa, is the world's fourth largest island. About the same size as Texas, it covers 226,656 square miles (587,040 square kilometers). A large central plateau rises to 4,500 feet (1,370 meters) in elevation. To the south and east lies a narrow coastal strip lined by rain forests. The west is hilly and dry, but the terrain flattens along the western coast. The country's major rivers drain west into the Mozambique Channel. The north features white beaches and the south has a desert-like landscape. The island's highest peak is Mount Maromokotro at 9,436 feet (2,876 meters).

The climate is tropical along the coast, temperate inland, and arid in the south. The hot and rainy season, with inland highs averaging 85°F (29°C), extends from September to April, interspersed with periodic cyclones. The dry and cool weather lasts from May to August. Only inland areas experience cold winters, with lows averaging 48°F (9°C).

Eighty percent of the island's flora and fauna are endemic to Madagascar. Its species include chameleons, tortoises, fossas (a catlike mammal), lemurs (a primate related to monkeys), and thousands of varieties of flowering plants. Medicinal plants such as the rose periwinkle (the source of two anticancer drugs) benefit not only local people but the entire world. Unfortunately, severe erosion and deforestation have endangered many species. International experts are working to learn from and preserve Madagascar's unique ecosystem.

History. Madagascar's first settlers arrived from Indonesia and Malaysia almost two thousand years ago. They are the ancestors of the island's highland tribes, primarily the Merina and Betsileo. Many Malayo-Indonesians also mixed with Arabs and Africans who came in later centuries, forming coastal tribes known collectively as Côtiers. The highland and Côtier peoples developed separately over time, with their respective kings, cultures, and dialects. Together, these peoples are called Malagasy.

After the Portuguese sighted Madagascar in 1500, European sailors and pirates visited often to trade guns and clothing for food and spices. Local hostilities and disease kept Europeans from having any real presence until the late-1800s.

In the 1790s, Merina king Andrianampoinimerina unified the highland tribes, establishing Antananarivo as his capital. His son, Radama I (1810–28), extended Merina domination to most other parts of the island. The Merina desire to unify the entire island collided with British and French colonial ambitions. The two powers had varying degrees of influence on Merina rulers until France finally took control of the island in 1896. The French sent Queen Ranavalona III into exile and battled nationalist movements into submission. After World War II, the Malagasy revolted against French rule (1947). French troops brutally suppressed the insurrection at a cost of as many as 80,000 lives. In 1958, the Malagasy overwhelmingly supported independence in a referendum. Independence was granted in 1960, though France retained a strong influence over politics and the economy.

Philibert Tsiranana was elected the first president of the Malagasy Republic. His close ties with France and a lack of political reform incited a rebellion in 1972, followed by military rule until 1975. Didier Ratsiraka was elected president; he severed most ties with the West and established a socialist system. Then followed several years of economic decline under relatively harsh rule. Calls for Ratsiraka's resignation mounted in the early 1990s and Albert Zafy defeated the incumbent in

Madagascar

the 1993 elections. However, Zafy's administration did not satisfy public demand for economic improvements, allowing Ratsiraka to capitalize on voter discontent and gain reelection in 1997.

Following a December 2001 election, neither Ratsiraka nor his main opponent, Marc Ravalomanana, gained the majority necessary to win the election outright. Ravalomanana accused Ratsiraka of vote rigging, and Ravalomanana supporters held mass protests in Antananarivo. Ravalomanana declared himself president in February, but Ratsiraka refused to relinquish power, establishing a rival government in Toamasina. Political violence threatened to escalate into civil war, but in April 2002, following a vote recount, Madagascar's high court declared Ravalomanana the election's winner. Ratsiraka went into exile. Political stability has returned under Ravalomanana, but the economy he inherited continues to struggle.

THE PEOPLE

Population. Madagascar's population of about 17.5 million is growing at an annual rate of 3.03 percent. The 18 Malagasy tribes continue to live in their historical lands. The largest tribe is the Merina, followed by the Betsileo. Other major tribes are the Betsimisaraka (east), Antandroy (south), and Tsimihety (north). Smaller groups include the Sihanaka, Bara, Antaisaka, Sakalava, and others. A small minority of Indo-Pakistani and Chinese merchants, as well as some Comorians, also live in Madagascar. Some tension and resentment exist between coastal and highland groups, as well as between immigrant and native peoples.

Language. Malagasy, an official language, is a unique mixture of Indonesian, African languages (mostly Bantu), Arabic, and some Malaysian. Written first in an Arabic-origin script called *Sorabe*, Malagasy was given its Latin script by British missionaries under commission from King Radama I. The alphabet does not contain the letters *c, q, u, w,* or *x*. Malagasy is derived primarily from the Merina dialect. People of other tribes speak their own dialects, although they also understand Malagasy and use it for written communication.

French is also an official language; it was used more than Malagasy in government, education, and business until 1972. Attempts to use Malagasy in school after 1973 were abandoned by 1991, partly because private schools continued to use French, and their graduates received the best jobs. Even today, Malagasy use many French words in daily speech or for science and technology.

Today, people speak a more common form of Malagasy than their ancestors. However, they retain traditional Malagasy oratory (*kabary*) and the use of proverbs. Malagasy proverbs store centuries of wisdom and culture. Nearly every conversation or speech contains a proverb or two. The right proverb can substitute for a more lengthy explanation.

Religion. About half of all Malagasy practice indigenous beliefs that acknowledge the existence of a supreme being, called *Andriamanitra* or *Zanahary*. *Razana* (ancestors) are considered intermediaries between the gods and the living. The living report their activities and needs to their ancestors, who provide directives and *fadys* (taboos). Zebus (oxen-like cattle, a traditional symbol of wealth) are sacrificed to *Andriamanitra* and ancestors, and food offerings are also presented in thanks or supplication.

Ancestor veneration is so rooted in the culture that even many Christians still practice it. One ceremony is the *famadihana* (turning of the bones), in which a family exhumes an ancestor's body to wrap it in a new *lambamena* (red cloth), a burial shroud. This is a joyous celebration with a zebu feast and traditional music; it represents the continuity of life. As one proverb explains: "Without ancestors, the living would not exist; and without the living, ancestors would be forgotten."

About 41 percent of the population is Christian. The London Missionary Society introduced Christianity in the 1800s. With their help, the first Malagasy Bible was printed in 1835. As French influence increased with colonization, Catholics came to outnumber Protestants, which include Adventists, Lutherans, Anglicans, Baptists, and others. About 7 percent of Malagasy (mostly Côtiers) are Muslims.

General Attitudes. Malagasy are deeply attached to their heritage. Parents and the elderly are respected and honored. Children rarely move far from their family. Malagasy are prone to share, no matter what little they have, according to the saying "Even one grasshopper is to be shared." Family needs have priority over individual desires. Years of corruption and growing poverty have strained these traditional values, but most people still adhere to them. People smile despite their everyday challenges.

Malagasy believe in *vintana* (destiny), which brings good or bad luck based on the time and date of a person's birth. If bad, it can be altered by an *ombiasy*, a person who heals or divines with charms and magic. People also consult a *mpanandro* (day-maker) for help in choosing the best day to get married, start construction, and so on. For other aspects of life, people accept *lahatra* (fate) as having control. Coastal people tend to prefer a more relaxed pace of life (*mora-mora*) than highland residents.

Personal Appearance. Most urban residents wear Western attire, although it may be secondhand or combined with traditional items. Rural people tend to wear traditional outfits more often than Western clothes.

Traditional highland attire includes the *lamba* (long white cotton wrap) for men and women, and *malabar* (long-sleeved striped or plaid shirt reaching to the knees and worn over pants) for men. Women drape the *lamba* over their shoulders; men wrap it at the waist. A red *lamba* is a sign of authority. Women braid or tie their long hair up to neck level.

A *lambaoany* (light, colorful wrap) is more common in coastal areas than the *lamba*, and men and women wrap these items differently according to gender and local tradition. Many men wear shorts under or instead of traditional wraps.

CUSTOMS AND COURTESIES

Greetings. Verbal greetings vary, but a common Malagasy greeting is *Manao ahoana tompoko?* (How are you, sir/madam?). One omits *tompoko* for a more informal greeting. Popular greetings in coastal areas are *Akory?* (How are you?), *Salama* (Peace), and *Arahaba* (Hello). In the north, the greeting *Mbalatsara?* (Doing well?) is common.

Courtesy requires one to greet an older or more superior person first, adding an appropriate title. That individual then chooses whether to offer a handshake. Men wait for women to put out their hand. To show respect, one gives a handshake using both hands or with the left hand holding the right elbow. To greet from a distance, people nod and remove hats or hold up the right hand.

After the initial greetings, people ask the question *Inona no vaovao?* (What is new?), to which the usual reply is *Tsy misy* (Nothing), especially if they do not intend to stop and talk. Except among close friends who use nicknames, people call each other by last or first names preceded by a title. Older relatives are addressed by relationship (grandfather, aunt, etc.) and spoken to with deference.

Gestures. "No" is indicated by shaking the head from left to right while saying *ahn-ahn-ahn*; "yes" is given with a nod and *uhn-uhn*. Public displays of affection between members of the opposite sex are not appropriate, but friends of the same sex commonly walk arm in arm. It is impolite to point with the finger, to put feet on furniture, or to step over someone's belongings. To pass in front of or between people, it is proper to offer apologies and/or bend slightly as if asking permission.

Visiting. Malagasy people like to visit each other often. Most visits, especially in rural areas, are unannounced. It is impolite to drop by at mealtime. Visits are prearranged for special occasions, to offer condolences, or to exchange New Year's wishes and gifts. People returning from a trip or visiting from out of town take *voan-dalana* (gifts from the journey) to their extended family.

In urban homes, guests are received in a *salon* (sitting room) and offered such refreshments as soda, peanuts, crackers, or cookies. Rural hosts set out new mats for guests and serve tea and *hanikotrana* (snacks such as cassava or sweet potatoes). In general, people serve what they have on hand or quickly send someone to a nearby store. One may decline refreshments if not staying long. Otherwise, guests are expected to eat what is served.

Eating. Families eat meals together, beginning with breakfast at 7 a.m. Lunch is at noon and dinner around 7 p.m. A snack is often eaten around 4 p.m. Urban highland Malagasy eat at a table. Invitations for lunch are more common than for dinner. When guests are present, children may eat separately. Guests leave a little food on their plate when finished to indicate the hosts have satisfied them. Friends or acquaintances leave shortly after the meal; relatives may stay a few hours. Rural and some urban coastal families eat on floor mats. Throughout the country, people eat with spoons and forks, but some coastal groups eat with the right hand.

Eating at a restaurant is considered a luxury. However, workers who cannot go home for lunch either go to a nearby *hotely* (inexpensive restaurant) or a *vary mitsangana* (outdoor vendor selling hot food to be eaten while standing). In Tana (the short name for the capital, Antananarivo), working mothers may take their own food to a downtown park, where their children can sometimes join them for lunch.

LIFESTYLE

Family. In a typical Malagasy household, the father is the provider and head of the family. The mother is the nurturer and homemaker. Children are to respect and listen to their parents and the elderly. When making important decisions, children are supposed to get their parents' blessings. Generally, they only leave home when they get married, and they later care for their aging parents. The traditional blessing parents give to newlyweds is for them to have seven boys and seven girls. This wish has changed somewhat with time, but children are still considered the ultimate riches.

Fihavanana (a well-maintained relationship) is valued above all else: "Better lose money than lose a relationship." This starts with the family and extends into community relations. Children are taught family unity with "Those who are united are as stone but those who are separated as sand." Economic hardships have forced many urban mothers to work outside the home, impacting family cohesion. Likewise, rural mothers work hard in the fields and often cannot provide enough care and nourishment to their children.

Urban families live in brick or cement houses. Rural two-story dwellings made of red adobe have mud floors. The first floor is for the kitchen and small farm animals (hens, ducks, geese); the second contains one or two bedrooms. Coastal rural huts are made of bamboo and straw.

Dating and Marriage. Traditional parents seek to arrange marriages for their children to spouses with a similar social status. The potential couple is free to decide whether to marry but does not usually reject their parents' opinions. Today, many urban youth find their mates in their neighborhood or through school or social activities. When dating, they go to dances and concerts, watch videos, and play sports or other games. Parents expect one-on-one dating to lead to marriage and for marriages to last.

Engagement is a formal affair. The man's family asks for the woman's hand at her parents' home. The two families carefully choose spokesmen well versed in *kabary*, who profusely apologize for their inadequacies before presenting the genealogy and history of the families and praising the bride and her family. After a formal speech of consent is delivered, the bride's family receives a *vodiondry* (literally, "lamb's rump" but meaning bride-price). A lamb is slaughtered for the occasion and a number of live zebus are given as a dowry. In highland areas, cash now takes the place of both zebu and lamb. After the adorned bride is formally given by her father to the groom, the couple must listen to advice by both sets of parents. Finally, the oldest and most respected family members give the couple their blessings.

While the bride's family pays for the engagement party, the groom's family finances the wedding. A civil wedding must first be performed at city hall. Religious weddings, usually on Saturdays, are followed by a feast and a dance.

Diet. A meal without rice is considered incomplete. Rice is served with *loaka* for lunch and dinner. *Loaka* can be anything from meat, fish, eggs, vegetables, or basic broth. One popular *loaka* is *ravitoto sy henakisoa* (ground manioc leaves with pork). Another is *ro mazava* (zebu stew with green leafy vegetables). *Sakay*, served on the side, is a mixture of jalapeños, ginger, and garlic. Served with the meal is *ranovola* (golden water), a drink made from water boiled in the browned rice that remains stuck to the bottom of the pan after cooking.

Seasonal fruits are served as dessert, including mangoes, litchis, pineapples, papaya, guava, strawberries, peaches, apples, oranges, and grapes. Bananas are found year-round. Manioc, sweet potatoes, and maize (corn) are served for breakfast, snacks, or other meals, especially in the countryside. An urban breakfast can include buttered *baguettes* (French bread) and jam.

Recreation. Soccer is the most popular sport among men. The entire family might watch the World Cup on television. Girls enjoy handball, and all Malagasy are fond of dance and music. The *fanorona* is a traditional game played by strategically placing small stones in hollows of a board or the ground. *Solitaire* is both a game and a decoration. It consists of a polished round wooden board laden with lustrous semiprecious stones in carved holes.

The Arts. Traditional *mpihira gasy* performers sing, dance, and play music in open-air concerts. An eloquent speech usually serves as introduction to their popular performances. Common instruments include accordions, violins, drums, flutes, and the indigenous *valiha* (a cylindrical harp-like

Madagascar

instrument). The guitar is a favorite among young people. The popular dance music called *salegy* combines East African guitar rhythms with local beats. Folk artists produce items for burial rituals. Tombs are decorated with tall wooden *aloalo* poles, in which artists carve figurative images and depictions of historical events.

Holidays. Madagascar's main holidays include New Year's Day, Martyrs' Day (29 March, honoring those killed in 1947), Labor Day (1 May), Independence Day (26 June), All Saints' Day (1 Nov.), Christmas, and the Anniversary of the Republic (30 Dec.). Schools and businesses observe Easter Monday, Pentecost Monday, and Ascension. Students have a holiday from July to October and around Christmas. New Year's Eve is a night for formal *bals* (dances) at fancy hotels or friends' houses. These parties bear a French influence but are opened with customary *afindrafindrao*, Malagasy line dancing: one couple leads off dancing and the other couples follow like a train.

Commerce. General business hours extend from 8 a.m. to 6 p.m. with a two-hour break for lunch, although banks and more stores are staying open through lunch as well. Small neighborhood stores often are run by non-Malagasy. Individual farmers sell their produce at open-air markets. Bargaining is common. Each market has a special day of the week during which more goods than usual are sold.

SOCIETY

Government. Madagascar is governed by a president (currently Marc Ravalomanana), who is the head of state. The president serves a five-year term and appoints a prime minister. Parliament is made up of a 90-member Senate and a 160-seat National Assembly. Local officials choose 60 senators, and the president selects 30. Members of the National Assembly are directly elected. Religious coalitions act as important pressure groups. The voting age is 18.

Economy. The Malagasy economy is based on agriculture, with 80 percent of people engaged in subsistence farming. Many farmers are also employed in an export-oriented agricultural pursuit. Cash crops include coffee, cloves, vanilla, sugar, and tobacco. Food crops include rice, cassava, cereal grains, potatoes, and corn. The primary livestock are zebus, pigs, goats, and sheep. Manufacturing, located mostly in Tano, focuses on textiles, timber, and food processing. The fishing industry has a high potential but is underexploited.

The skilled labor force is underemployed; college graduates have difficulty finding work in their fields. International donors are encouraging privatization and other economic reforms to help boost growth. Political instability, corruption, periodic natural disasters, and slumping world commodity prices have hindered progress. The currency is the *ariary*.

Transportation and Communications. Most people walk or ride a bus. Main cities have taxis. Used for hauling goods in Tana, a *pousse-pousse* (pedicab) is a common form of human transport in other areas. For intercity travel, people use *taxi brousse* ("bush-taxis," minivans with luggage racks). Many roads are not paved. A train runs between Tana and the southeast coast. Air Madagascar airlines offers domestic flights.

The postal system works relatively well and the telephone system in Tana is gradually being upgraded with digital technology. A cellular system is spreading outward from the capital, and internet access is available. Most rural areas lack telephone service. Most families have a radio and many own a television. One government television channel is joined by four private stations and satellite television.

Education. Many rural inhabitants lack full access to education. Although seven years of schooling is mandatory beginning at age seven, it is not widely enforced. Poverty has made it difficult for some parents to pay tuition or to lose the much-needed labor their children provide on the family farm in order for them to attend school. Still, education is very important and parents do whatever they can to give their children an education. The Malagasy say, "Foolish is he who is not better educated than his father." Private schools exist at all levels, and charitable organizations sometimes help pay tuition. Each province has a university; trade schools offer training in various fields. The wealthy can travel abroad for higher education.

Health. Madagascar's public health system includes hospitals, regional birthing hospitals, and clinics. Facilities are underfunded and underequipped. Patients must bring their own supplies such as cotton balls and syringes. Family members must take meals to patients. Basic maternal and child care are provided, but the infant mortality rate remains high. Private clinics offer modern care to those who can afford it. Employees of state companies are covered by national insurance; other employees buy private insurance. Malnutrition, diarrhea, cholera, malaria, and other diseases affect the population. Traditional medicines are still very valuable to most people, and medicine men are available in every town or village. Some 2,500 species of plants are used to treat ailments.

DEVELOPMENT DATA
- Human Dev. Index* rank .... 150 of 177 countries
- Adjusted for women .... 121 of 144 countries
- Real GDP per capita $740
- Adult literacy rate .... 74 percent (male); 61 (female)
- Infant mortality rate .... 79 per 1,000 births
- Life expectancy .... 52 (male); 55 (female)

AT A GLANCE

Events and Trends.
- Cyclones struck Madagascar in February and March 2004, leaving thousands of Malagasy homeless. More than 100 people died when their ferry was caught in a storm near the coast. The island is frequently hit by cyclones between December and March.
- The government replaced the Malagasy *franc* with the *ariary* (a precolonial currency) as the national currency in July 2003. The Malagasy *franc* will be exchangeable at banks until 2009. The decision was seen as an attempt to reduce the nation's ties to its French colonial past.

Contact Information. Embassy of Madagascar, 2374 Massachusetts Avenue NW, Washington, DC 20008; phone (202) 265-5525.

CultureGrams™
People. The World. You.

ProQuest Information and Learning Company
300 North Zeeb Road, P.O. Box 1346
Ann Arbor, Michigan 48106 USA
Toll Free: 1.800.528.6279
Fax: 1.800.864.0019
www.culturegrams.com

© 2005 ProQuest Information and Learning Company and Brigham Young University. It is against the law to copy, reprint, store, or transmit any part of this publication in any form by any means without written permission from ProQuest. This document contains native commentary and original analysis, as well as estimated statistics. The content should not be considered strictly factual, and it may not apply to all groups in a nation. *UN Development Programme, Human Development Report 2004 (New York: Oxford University Press, 2004).

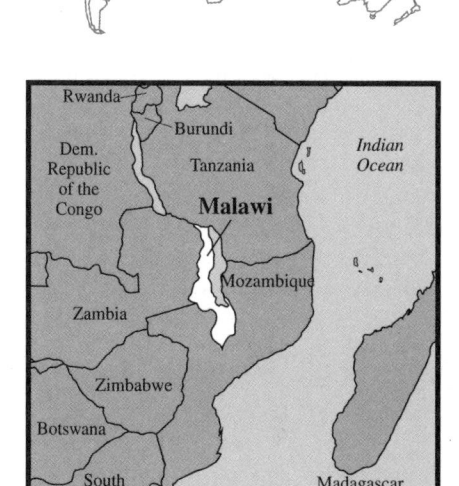

Republic of Malawi

BACKGROUND

Land and Climate. Malawi is a landlocked country that covers 45,747 square miles (118,484 square kilometers) in southeast Africa. Much of the east is dominated by spectacular Lake Malawi, which stretches 360 miles (570 kilometers) in length and varies in width from 10 to 50 miles (16–80 kilometers). Lake Malawi is the tenth largest body of freshwater in the world and the third largest in Africa after Lake Victoria and Lake Tanganyika. The East African Rift Valley, which forms the lake's trench, extends into Malawi from the north. The Shire River drains Lake Malawi and connects to the Zambezi River.

Dominated by the Nyika Plateau, rolling grasslands rise to 8,000 feet (2,500 meters) in the north. Mountains dot the central and southern agricultural plains. The southern region boasts the Zomba Plateau and Mount Mulanje, the tallest point (9,850 feet, or 3,002 meters) in southeastern Africa.

Malawi's subtropical temperatures and rainfall vary with elevation. The lakeshore and southern Shire Valley are the hottest and most humid areas. The higher agricultural plateau is more comfortable. The rainy season (November–April) brings 90 percent of Malawi's annual rainfall. Rains are often late or inadequate, causing hardship and drought. The hot, dry season (September–November) produces temperatures of 85 to 100°F (30–37°C). Temperatures during the cold season (May–August) cool to between 45 and 70°F (10–20°C). During July, the south may experience a damp fog or heavy cloud cover called *chiperoni* (a brand of blanket).

History. Early records identify the Kafula and Bantu speakers from Cameroon as the first ethnic groups to farm Malawi's fertile soil. Maravi people migrated from the Congo in the late 13th century, forcing the Kafula to flee to Zambia and Mozambique. The word *Maravi* (the origin of *Malawi*) means "the sun's rays." In the 15th century, the Maravi leader granted fertile land west of the lake to two groups who together became known as the Chewa. By the 18th century, more groups were migrating to Malawi, including the Tumbuka and Tonga in the northern and central areas, the Ngoni near Mzimba and Ntcheu, and the Yao in the south. The Yao cooperated with the Portuguese and Arabs in the slave trade, and they adopted aspects of the Arabs' language, appearance, and religion.

David Livingstone, a Scottish missionary and famous explorer, entered Malawi via the Shire River in 1859. The journey led him to Lake Malawi (which he named Lake Nyasa) and brought him face-to-face with the slave trade. European missionaries continued his early attempts to curb slavery, promote commerce, and Christianize the people.

British settlers arrived just after Livingstone. In 1891, Great Britain's political, economic, and strategic interests in southeast Africa prompted authorities to negotiate boundaries for, and claim the area as, the British Protectorate of Nyasaland. The British took the most productive agricultural areas, subdued local tribal authority, and made the native people tenants on their own land. In 1915, Reverend John Chilembwe, an educated Yao, encouraged a violent uprising to protest poor working conditions on farm estates. Chilembwe died in his attempt to kill British landlords. Today, he is regarded as the first martyr for Malawi's eventual freedom.

The Nyasaland African Congress (NAC) formed in 1944 among native associations and independent churches to counter British interests in Africa. Malawi's British leaders responded in 1953 by joining with other white settlers to form a federation with Northern and Southern Rhodesia (today's

Malawi

Zambia and Zimbabwe). In 1958, Hastings Kamuzu Banda, a physician, returned to Malawi after 40 years abroad to denounce the Federation of Rhodesia and Nyasaland. He became the NAC's new leader. In 1959, when Banda and other leaders of the NAC were jailed for their activities, he organized the Malawi Congress Party (MCP). An ensuing struggle with the MCP led the federation to dissolve. On 6 July 1964, Nyasaland became the Commonwealth of Malawi, with Banda as prime minister. Full independence was granted to the Republic of Malawi in 1966, and Banda became president.

Banda's methods of promoting development were not always popular with other Malawians. By 1992, Banda's one-party rule faced strong opposition from local Catholic bishops, the international community, and others over alleged human-rights abuses. In a 1993 national referendum, voters overwhelmingly supported a multiparty state, and the aging Banda lost the 1994 presidential election to Bakili Muluzi of the United Democratic Front (UDF). Muluzi was reelected in 1999. In accordance with the constitution, he stepped down at the end of his second term, and the UDF's Bingu wa Mutharika was elected president in May 2004.

THE PEOPLE

Population. Malawi's population of 11.9 million is growing at at a rate of 2.1 percent per year. More than 90 percent of the people are rural subsistence farmers. The population is concentrated in the fertile southern region, which suffers from extensive deforestation and overcultivation. Blantyre (the largest industrial city), Lilongwe (the capital since 1975), Mzuzu, and Zomba (the former capital) are crowded and burdened by squatter areas.

Although 99 percent of Malawians are African, they represent many ethnic populations. The Chewa, Tumbuka, and Yao are the largest groups. Smaller groups include the Nyanja, Lomwe, Sena, Tonga, Ngoni, and Ngonde. A few thousand Asians (mostly merchants) and Europeans live in Malawi.

Language. English, an official language, is used in government and business. Chichewa (also official) and Chitumbuka are the two most widely spoken languages. Banda, who was a Chewa, selected Chichewa as the main national language, and it is taught in schools along with English. Chichewa dominates in central and southern regions, while Chitumbuka is spoken mostly in the north. Smaller ethnic groups speak their own Bantu-related languages but usually know some Chichewa. These Bantu languages are melodic and expressive; every syllable ends in a vowel, though some are not pronounced.

Religion. Most Malawians are Christian. About 55 percent are Protestant and 20 percent Roman Catholic. Christians often mix their beliefs with local traditions. For instance, the *gule wamkulu* (great dance), popular in the central and southern regions, uses various masks representing ancestral spirits, people, and animals to tell stories and teach traditions. The different belief systems are not considered contradictory because each plays a role in people's daily lives. Muslims (20 percent) are concentrated in lakeshore areas. The remaining 5 percent of Malawians practice traditional indigenous beliefs through rituals, festivals, and dances.

General Attitudes. Malawians are proud of their nation's reputation as the "warm heart of Africa." The people are kind, courteous, and hospitable. They also describe themselves as friendly and trusting. Many Malawians, especially young people, are optimistic about building a democratic and progressive nation. Many older people remain unsure of democracy and would prefer a stronger leader. Some tension also exists between generations due to the influence of Western culture among the youth. Many people feel that Western influence threatens traditional ways of life. For others, the debate is irrelevant; they focus their efforts on housing and feeding their families. Material possessions are few but well cared for. Bicycles are prized, and it is quite an achievement to own a car.

In Malawian society, the family is considered a person's greatest asset. Parents fondly refer to children as "Firstborn," "Secondborn," and so on. Society is group oriented; individuals sacrifice their interests for the good of the family or community. They expect to share their incomes with poorer family members.

Personal Appearance. Although poverty prevents people from always looking their best, Malawians strive to be clean, neat, and modestly dressed in public. Western-style dress is common but may be combined with local fashions. Men wear pants, shirts, and often a suit jacket.

Women wear blouses, skirts, and dresses. They might also wrap a *chitenje* around their waist. This 7-foot-long (2-meter-long) African-print cotton fabric protects dresses from dust and dirt. The *chitenje* can also serve as a shield from wind and rain, as a baby carrier, or as a coiled support for baskets carried on the head. Major cities and tourist spots are the only places where women wear pants, shorts, and short skirts. Children are encouraged to wear school uniforms to help them develop a sense for "dressing smart" later in life.

CUSTOMS AND COURTESIES

Greetings. When meeting, Malawians shake right hands while placing the left hand under the right forearm. Showing both hands in this way demonstrates sincerity and trust. Women and men dip their knees slightly when exchanging greetings. If greeting elders or people of authority, they kneel down and clap their hands quietly two or three times. Women dip their knees whenever they meet someone, even if the person has lower status. Placing the prefix *a-* before a name or title shows respect. For example, *bambo* is the word for man, but usually one would address him as *abambo*.

People greet with an exchange of "Hello, sir!" (*Moni bambo!* in Chichewa; *Monire adada!* in Chitumbuka) or "Hello, madam!" (*Moni mayi!* or *Monire amama!*). This is followed by "How are you?" (*Muli bwanji?* in Chichewa; *Muli uli?* in Chitumbuka). The common response is "I am fine!" (*Ndili bwino!* or *Ndili makola!*). People also ask about each other's families.

Malawians rarely use first names. They address others as "Madam" or "Sir," followed by the surname. Informally, they use surnames alone. Persons in authority are addressed as *Bwana* (Boss). Young adults and teens may address each other as *chimwali* (sister) or *chimwene* (brother). Children are called *iwe* (you).

Gestures. Malawians give and receive items with both hands. Tossing food (such as fruit) is considered rude. A verbal "tss-tss" or "a-a-ah" expresses displeasure or disbelief. A loud and long hiss is used to get someone's attention from far off. When near, one says *Aisse* (Friend). Public displays of affection between men and women are not acceptable in most places. However, men may walk arm in arm or hold hands while laughing and exchanging stories; women will do the same. Hand gestures are dramatic and conversation is lively. Eye contact is important but direct gazes are limited, especially toward elders or persons of authority. The youth use the "thumbs up" gesture and *Sure!* (in English) in friendly exchanges. It is offensive to make the U.S. "OK" sign, with the thumb and index finger forming a circle. When describing a child's size to others, Malawians extend an upraised hand to the approximate height. Extending a level hand, palm down, is used only for animals.

Visiting. Strong family and community ties make visiting a common activity. Unannounced visits occur anytime, but especially on Sunday. Rather than knock at a door, Malawians call out *Odi! Odi!* until someone welcomes them in with *Odini!* A house with frequent visitors is highly regarded. The Chichewa proverb *Alendo ndi mame* (Visitors are like dew) means that a visitor's presence is short-lived and hence precious. Hosts automatically serve tea or water and refreshments to their guests; asking if a guest wants something is considered rude. Visitors customarily bring a small gift of money, tea, or sugar—especially if invited, visiting a new baby, or coming after a funeral. Attending funerals is extremely important, and people will travel great distances after the death of even distant relatives.

Eating. Malawians usually begin their day with corn porridge or a piece of bread and tea. They eat their main meal in the evening; lunch may or may not be available. There is a greater abundance of food after the April harvest. Women often cook meals over a fire, either in small mud-brick kitchens or over an open fire with three stones supporting a pot. Food is kept covered until it is ready to eat. Among some traditional families, women and children eat apart from men, who are served first. All wash their hands in a basin of water before and after eating. Most food is eaten with the right hand. *Nsima* (starchy porridge made of corn flour and water) is balled in the right hand, dipped in *ndiwo* (a sauce or condiment), and eaten. *Ndiwo* may be made of fish, meat, beans, greens, or other ingredients, depending on what is available. It is impolite to smell food or comment on the aroma of a meal. Leaving a small amount of food on the plate when finished assures the cook that a person has had enough to eat.

LIFESTYLE

Family. Malawians value large families; a typical household includes extended members, especially the husband's brothers. Most men assist with farming but may also hold jobs as teachers, health workers, fishermen, or general laborers, depending on where they live and their level of education. Some men practice polygamy, in which case they build a separate hut for each wife and her children.

Throughout Malawi, women raise the children, care for the home, cook, and farm. They teach children socially acceptable behavior, responsibility, respect for elders, and work skills. The elders of all ethnic groups reinforce these lessons.

Girls care for younger siblings, gather firewood, clean, and collect water. They often drop out of school to assume these responsibilities. Boys stay in school longer than girls but still assist with farming, sweeping, and other chores.

In rural areas, extended families live together in a compound of several huts, typically thatch-roofed, mud-brick dwellings with one or two rooms. A compound also includes a kitchen hut, a borehole or well, a *nkhokwe* (a structure for storing grain), and perhaps an enclosure for livestock. The family's fields are located nearby. Urban houses have electricity and running water and may be constructed of cinder block and tin roofs, though makeshift squatter areas are also common.

Dating and Marriage. Some ethnic groups celebrate the transition from youth to adulthood at about age 12 through initiation rituals. In such rituals, youth are prepared for their future roles as mothers and fathers; young men are circumcised—an increasing number have it done in hospitals.

There is little formal dating in Malawi; school dances are popular at secondary schools. In rural areas, a young man may notice a young woman's quiet manner and hardworking character. He must approach the girl's uncle to request marriage. Before the wedding, a group of elders meets with the couple to discuss marriage roles and responsibilities. In the north, the groom's family must pay a *lobola* (bride-price), usually in cattle or goats. Village weddings are less elaborate than urban celebrations. Typically, traditional dancing and food follow a church ceremony.

Diet. Malawians do not feel they have eaten unless they have had *nsima*. Rice is a more expensive, less filling alternative to *nsima*. Water is taken with meals. Malawians drink tea daily if they can afford it. Most Malawians do not consume enough calories to meet basic nutritional needs. Dried or fresh fish from Lake Malawi is the most abundant protein source. It is available in markets along with beef, chicken, and goat. But these foods are expensive. Alternative protein foods such as red beans and peanut flour are plentiful; insects such as grasshoppers and termite larvae are another source of protein. Locally grown fruits and vegetables include papaya, mangoes, bananas, tangerines, tomatoes, sweet potatoes, and avocados. Hawkers approach local buses to sell produce, dried fish (*nsomba*), and even roasted mice on a stick (*mbewa*). People of all ages like sugarcane for a snack.

Recreation. Soccer is the most popular national sport. Young boys create soccer balls out of plastic-bag scraps. Boys also make highly prized *magalimoto* (cars) out of scrap metal and bits of trash. Girls and boys play games like hide-and-seek (*kalondolondo*). Girls play netball, a game similar to basketball. People in a village, market, or at a bus stop gather around anyone playing *bao*, a strategy game with pebble or seed tokens on a carved-out board. Families enjoy church- and school-sponsored activities. Men often gather at local "bottle stores" to drink traditional beer or bottled soft drinks.

Recreational travel is rare, but urban dwellers may travel to home villages on holidays. Although Malawi has one television station, most people do not have access to a television set. In villages, someone who owns a television and VCR will charge people (mostly men) admission to watch videos. Action movies are the most popular.

The Arts. Song, dance, and drumming festivals are an integral part of social and religious life. For example, the *Ngwetsa* festival celebrates the harvest. The Chewa perform the *gule wamkulu* dance at celebrations, funerals, and initiation rites. Singing and drumming provide accompaniment. The *ingoma* is a dance that celebrates past victories of the Ngoni ethnic group; male dancers hold spears and shields and wear a traditional costume of animal skins. Unique Malawian instruments include the *zeze*, a one-string violin, and the *maseche*, a rattle attached to the legs and arms of dancers. Reggae and Congolese *kwasa kwasa* music are popular in bottle stores.

Holidays. Malawi's official holidays include New Year's Day; Chilembwe Day (15 Jan.); Martyrs' Day (3 Mar.), honoring those who gave their lives in 1963 in the quest for independence; Easter (Friday–Monday); Labor Day (1 May); Freedom Day (14 June); Independence Day (6 July); and Mother's Day (second Monday in October). Malawians celebrate Christmas Day (25 Dec.) and Boxing Day (26 Dec.). Boxing Day comes

Malawi

from a British tradition of giving small boxed gifts to service employees. It is now a time for visiting friends and relatives. Muslims observe *Idul-Fitr*, a three-day feast at the end of the month of *Ramadan*. During *Ramadan*, Muslims do not eat or drink from sunrise to dusk. During evening hours, people visit friends and eat.

Commerce. Urban businesses and government offices are open weekdays from 7:30 a.m. to 5 p.m. but close for one or two hours at lunchtime. Banks close at 3 p.m. but do not close for lunch. Food, baskets, bicycle parts, soap, traditional medicines, and used clothing are sold in open-air markets. City markets are open every day; rural villages have weekly market days. Bargaining is common in markets and at roadside stands. Prices are fixed at the People's Trading Center (PTC) and at grocery stores.

SOCIETY

Government. The Republic of Malawi is governed by a president (currently Bingu wa Mutharika) who functions as head of government and chief of state. The president is elected to a five-year term and appoints a vice president and a cabinet. The 193 members of the House of Parliament are elected by district constituents to five-year terms. All citizens may vote at age 18. The judicial system is modeled after British courts. A traditional authority system vesting power in village headmen and chiefs functions at the local level. The official courts respect the authority and decisions of these traditional leaders.

Economy. Subsistence agriculture, deforestation, and high unemployment reflect Malawi's fragile economic climate. Agriculture accounts for roughly two-thirds of Malawi's export revenue. Malawi is the one of the largest tobacco exporters in the world; U.S. manufacturers purchase much of the annual crop. Other exports are tea, sugar, coffee, peanuts, cotton, corn, and wood products.

Malawi relies on international aid for agriculture, health, education, and infrastructure development. The country has few natural resources other than its soil, and most workers are unskilled. Industry is underdeveloped, as is tourism. Many men work in South African and Zimbabwean mines. The currency is the *kwacha* (MWK).

Transportation and Communications. Malawians transport goods and passengers by road, air, water, rail, and even bicycle. Local buses are cheap but overcrowded, slow, and poorly maintained. Express buses are better but expensive. Small trucks and minivans reach rural and remote destinations; boats on Lake Malawi reach areas inaccessible by road. Only major roads are paved. The Lakeshore Road traverses the country from north to south. The Malawi Railways company ships exports to the Indian Ocean through Tanzania. It provides no passenger transport.

The postal system has been more reliable and private since the introduction of the multiparty system. Democracy has also encouraged the growth of newspapers and allowed for a more reliable and private postal system. Most homes lack phones, but post offices have them. Larger towns are equipped for electricity, which is not available in villages. The government operates two radio stations, and the country has one television station.

DEVELOPMENT DATA

Human Dev. Index* rank . . . . 165 of 177 countries
  Adjusted for women. . . . . 134 of 144 countries
Real GDP per capita $580
Adult literacy rate . . . . 76 percent (male); 49 (female)
Infant mortality rate . . . . 104 per 1,000 births
Life expectancy . . . . 38 (male); 38 (female)

Education. To improve Malawi's literacy rate for men and women, the government now provides free primary education for eight years beginning at age six. Teachers and facilities are in short supply, however. Only a small number of students move beyond a primary education. The government recently began a program to build new secondary schools and reach out to girls and rural children. National examinations are taken after grade eight, grade ten (*form* two), and grade twelve (*form* four). Secondary schools are supplemented by the Malawi College of Distance Education Centers. The University of Malawi enrolls about 3,500 students on five college campuses. There are two teacher-training colleges and several other technical schools.

Health. Serious health problems such as plague, tuberculosis, malaria, bilharzia, diarrhea, cholera, malnutrition, and respiratory infections are widespread in Malawi, which also has one of the world's highest rates of HIV/AIDS infection. An estimated one in seven Malawians are believed to be infected with the virus. Many families have lost both parents to HIV/AIDS, and households are often headed by older children or the elderly. The National AIDS Control Program cares for AIDS patients and orphans. Other urgent priorities include sanitation, immunizations, family planning, and maternal and child health care. The maternal death rate is high. Government efforts have increased access to free rural health centers or fee-based mission hospitals. Traditional healers (*Sing'anga*) are common and widely used. They prescribe roots, bark, and other plants for a variety of ailments. They also cast out demons or evil spells.

AT A GLANCE

Events and Trends.
- President Mutharika was chosen by the previous president and fellow UDF member Bakili Muluzi to represent their party in the May 2004 presidential election. However, two months after his victory, Mutharika sought to distance himself from Muluzi by levying corruption charges against senior members of his administration.
- A week prior to the May 2004 elections, the government announced a program to distribute free antiretroviral drugs to more than 30,000 Malawians infected with HIV/AIDS. The drugs prolong the lives of HIV/AIDS patients. An estimated 80,000 Malawians die each year of AIDS-related complications.

Contact Information. Embassy of the Republic of Malawi, 1156 15th Street NW, Suite 320, Washington, DC 20005; phone (202) 721-0274.

© 2005 ProQuest Information and Learning Company and Brigham Young University. It is against the law to copy, reprint, store, or transmit any part of this publication in any form by any means without written permission from ProQuest. This document contains native commentary and original analysis, as well as estimated statistics. The content should not be considered strictly factual, and it may not apply to all groups in a nation. *UN Development Programme, Human Development Report 2004 (New York: Oxford University Press, 2004).

CultureGrams
People. The World. You.

ProQuest Information and Learning Company
300 North Zeeb Road, P.O. Box 1346
Ann Arbor, Michigan 48106 USA
Toll Free: 1.800.528.6279
Fax: 1.800.864.0019
www.culturegrams.com

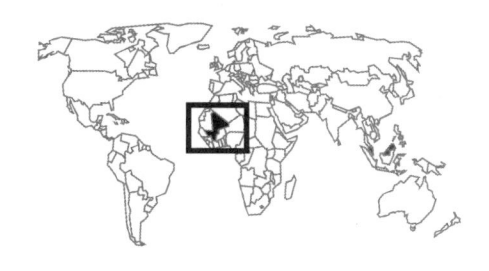

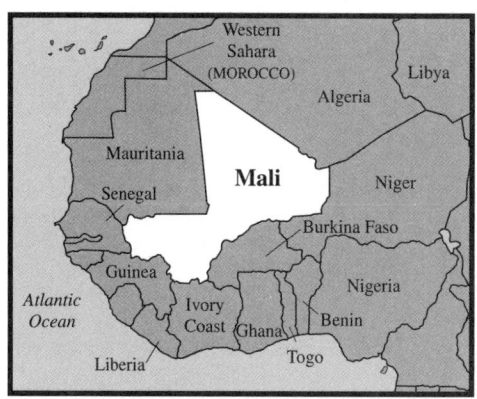

CultureGrams 2006 World Edition
Republic of Mali

BACKGROUND

Land and Climate. Mali, the seventh largest country in Africa, is about twice the size of Texas. It covers 478,764 square miles (1,240,000 square kilometers). Mali's north is in the southern Sahara Desert. Farther south is the semiarid Sahel with limited vegetation, mostly in the form of bushes and a few trees. Together, desert or semidesert regions cover 70 percent of Mali. Only in the deep south can one find abundant vegetation and mango groves. The fertile Niger River area is home to most of Mali's economic activity. The river's northern delta is submerged annually. Temperatures average 110°F (43°C) during the rainy season (June–September); humidity is lower but temperatures are higher in the north. Rain is minimal in the north. The "cold" season (October–February) is dry; temperatures average 85°F (30°C). In the hot season (March–May) daily highs reach well above 125°F (50°C).

History. From the seventh to the nineteenth centuries, parts of Mali were ruled by the kings of the Ghana, Malinke, Songhai, Bambara, and Toucouleur Empires. The Songhai Empire in the 15th and 16th centuries covered twice the territory of modern Mali. In the 14th century, Mali was the richest and largest West African empire. Tombouctou (Timbuktu) was a center of Islamic learning. Malians proudly remember this history through tale and song.

Colonialism came at the turn of the 20th century, and Mali was a French colony (Western Sudan) until 1960, when it gained independence under a socialist government led by Modibo Keita. In 1968, a military coup brought Moussa Traoré to power as president. In 1979, Traoré added civilians to his cabinet and formed a political party called the Democratic Union of the People of Mali (UDPM). Traoré continued as the country's president and general secretary of the UDPM. When popular demonstrations in 1991 were met with Traoré's orders to shoot civilians, Lt. Colonel Amadou Toumani Touré rebelled and arrested Traoré. The UDPM was disbanded and Traoré was convicted of ordering the deaths of the protesters. The popular Touré quickly worked to establish civilian rule through elections in 1992.

Voters approved a new constitution, elected a National Assembly, and elected Alpha Oumar Konaré as president. Student riots in 1993 threatened political stability, but Konaré negotiated with student leaders to end the crisis. Konaré also began negotiating with Tuareg rebels, who had long struggled to gain independence for their light-skinned ethnic group. The Tuaregs are nomads who follow their herds through Mali, Niger, and Mauritania, and who have fought all three governments. By 1998, fighting in Mali had all but ceased and international aid was sent to help solidify peace efforts.

In 1997, flawed legislative elections were annulled but rescheduled. Konaré's party, the Alliance for Democracy, won a majority in parliament. Konaré was reelected in 1997 to a second and final term. As Konaré stepped down in 2002, Touré was elected president in a hotly contested election. More than 24 candidates competed in the first round of voting, and some 47 counts of fraud and voting irregularities had to be resolved by a constitutional court before a winner could be announced. Touré, who ran as an independent candidate, won 64 percent of the vote in the election's final round, defeating the Alliance for Democracy candidate. Economic growth has contributed to the nation's recent political stability. The government's goals include increasing trade, improving the nation's roads, developing new industries, and broadening access to education and health care.

Mali

THE PEOPLE

Population. Mali's population of 11.96 million is growing annually by 2.8 percent. Nearly 90 percent of Malians reside in the fertile southern third of the country, while 10 percent (mostly nomadic people) live in the arid north. Seventy-five percent of all Malians live in rural areas. Of the country's 20 major ethnic groups, several comprise less than 1 percent of the population. The Bambara constitute the largest group (approximately one-third of the population) and generally populate the central and southern regions. The second largest group is the Malinke of the southwest and west. The Sarakole live in the northwest near Mauritania. The Fulani (also known as the Peul) are seminomadic herders who traditionally inhabit the northern desert and comprise some 17 percent of the population. Many Fulani migrated south and settled in the Mopti region due to deteriorating environmental conditions in the north. The Songhai live in the northeast along the Niger River, as do the Bozo, who earn their living from fishing in the Niger Delta. The Dogons live on and around the Bandiagara escarpment (also called the Dogon Cliffs). The Menianka and Senufou inhabit the southwest, along the border with Burkina Faso and Ivory Coast. The Tuaregs herd in the north.

Language. Mali's large number of languages and dialects reflects the ethnic diversity of the country. The official language, French, is spoken by government administrators and in urban areas and is the primary language of school instruction. However, the most widely spoken tongue is Bambara. Other languages include Fulfulde, Dogon, Senufou, and Jula. As is common in Africa, language is mainly oral. Books are published in at least four Malian languages, but history is transmitted by narration from generation to generation, from master to scholar, and from parent to child. A special caste called the *griot* has the responsibility to recount and sing the great past.

Religion. Ninety percent of all Malians are Muslim. Most of the rest, especially in the south and along the Dogon Cliffs, adhere to traditional religions, which usually emphasize animism. About 1 percent are Christian. The Peul, Sarakole, Moor, Songhai, and Tamashek have been Muslim for a long time. They honor Islam's Five Pillars of Faith by professing the name of *Allah* and declaring Muhammad to be his prophet; praying five times daily; fasting during the holy month of *Ramadan*; giving alms to the poor and *garabouts*, boys who attend *Qur'anic* (Koranic) schools and must beg for daily food; and making a pilgrimage to Makkah, Saudi Arabia. Some Muslims still practice aspects of their traditional faiths, such as using masks or totem animals and wearing *gri gri* charms (amulets used to protect a person from harm or illness). Ritual dances are performed to encourage rain for good harvests or for other events.

General Attitudes. Malians are usually polite and friendly. This congeniality helps ensure mutual respect among friends and strangers. If they feel slighted, Malians may make unexpected, teasing comments. These remarks are usually humorous and are regarded as attempts to be nice and not to offend. Malians often joke with other groups about family names or castes. These "joking cousin" remarks help maintain friendly ties and calm tensions between the many groups. Malians are rarely confrontational and will settle differences through a second party. Time is oriented more toward tradition and convenience than innovation or urgency. Muslims believe the "will of *Allah*" affects all events.

Between similar ethnic groups, caste membership determines one's relative social position. However, between dissimilar groups, such as the light-skinned peoples versus the dark-skinned sub-Saharan Malians, ethnicity is a distinguishing factor and cause of long-standing tensions. Traditional roles are often more important than assumed roles. A driver born as a "noble," for instance, may be more respected than a government official from a blacksmith family. However, wealth grants social status for any individual.

Traditional moral codes remain prevalent. For example, robbery may be a reason to beat a criminal, while embezzlement of public funds (a relatively modern crime) may be pardonable. General civic loyalties are shallow, but family needs come before individual wants.

Personal Appearance. Despite great poverty, physical appearance is of great importance to Malians. Western clothing is common in urban areas, although women tend to wear traditional clothing more often than men. Men wear trousers, not shorts, and a shirt. Wealthy men may wear a traditional *boubou* (long and flowing embroidered robe) over pants and shirt. Rural Muslim women wear long wraparound skirts, blouses, and sandals; animist women may omit blouses and shoes. Most women keep their hair covered. Among some ethnic groups, animist boys first wear pants after circumcision (5–12 years old). Neatness and modesty are valued throughout the country.

CUSTOMS AND COURTESIES

Greetings. Men and women either shake right hands or (sometimes when greeting a member of the opposite sex) clasp their own hands and bow slightly. A man of power (such as a village chief) will always initiate a handshake. Otherwise, a person joining a group or entering a room initiates a handshake with each adult in the room or area, beginning with the eldest or most senior. One may show special respect by touching one's own right elbow with the fingertips of the left hand while shaking right hands. One can also touch a right hand to the forehead or the heart after a gentle handshake.

Verbal greetings vary between ethnic groups. If a person's language is not known, one can greet that person in a commonly spoken language and the other will respond in his or her own language. For example, if one person uses the French *Bonjour* (Good day), the other might respond with the Bambara *I ni ce* (Hello). It is impolite not to greet someone when passing them on a path or street. Friends usually follow greetings with inquiries such as *I somogo be di?* (How is your family?) or *Here tilena wa?* (Did you have a good day?).

A family name provides information about a person's ethnicity, caste, and geographic origins. Depending on how much trust exists between greeters, Malians may or may not announce their family name to strangers. Rather, they will introduce themselves by their first name. Often, it is only when people are acquainted that they learn each other's family names. Friends generally address one another by given name.

Gestures. Because the left hand is considered unclean, it is disrespectful and unhygienic to take a Malian's left hand, offer the left for a handshake, offer food or money with it, eat with it, or accept anything with it. The only exception is when a close family member or friend leaves on a long trip, in which case the left hand is used in a handshake as a special gesture to indicate the two people will see each other again. Gesturing with the index finger is impolite; one points with the entire hand. Personal space is limited and people of the same sex often touch when conversing. One does not look an elder in the eye during conversation.

Visiting. Visiting plays an integral part in Malian society, as it is a way to maintain kinship bonds and friendships. Not visiting someone for an extended period of time reflects on the value of the relationship. Visits between rural friends and relatives occur often and usually unannounced, as making prior arrangements is difficult without telephones. Evening visits can last several hours. Houseguests may stay several weeks and will bring gifts of kola nuts (a traditional symbol of respect) and food from their home region.

Guests remove their shoes before entering a room or stepping on a mat. Hosts offer visitors water when they enter a compound and may give them the best seat. Hosts usually also serve refreshments, which the guests then offer to share with the hosts since eating in front of others is impolite. In villages, guests bring small gifts to their hosts, often including tea, sugar, or kola nuts. Hosts appreciate compliments on their home but deny them out of modesty. If visitors arrive while hosts are eating, they usually will be invited to share the food; unexpected guests might politely decline the meal. A tradition of tea drinking is common among older men. They brew three rounds of green tea mixed with sugar, and drink from a small shot glass. This procedure is repeated several times a day.

Visitors to a *dugutigi* (village chief) show him special respect. Those who do not speak the local language (such as government officials or foreigners) will not talk directly to the chief but to one or more translators and intermediaries.

Eating. Wealthy families eat their meals with a spoon and often other utensils, but eating food with the right hand is most common and traditional. Family members eat from communal bowls. The male head of the family determines which groups eat from one of several bowls. For example, men and boys may share one bowl, and small children and/or women share another. Marital status and age also determine eating patterns. Each person eats from the portion of the bowl that is directly in front of him or her. Adult men and women seldom eat from the same bowl.

LIFESTYLE

Family. Rural Malian families are large, but urban families are smaller. The infant mortality rate is high, and parents believe they must have many children to provide a posterity and sufficient hands for agricultural labor. Babies receive a lot of affection, but older children care for younger ones because parents are too busy working. Children assume chores by age five: girls make flour by pounding millet and corn; boys tend the livestock. Older boys work in the fields and older girls cook and care for younger siblings. Young women marry by the age of 18. The elderly enjoy great respect. The family or clan chief's authority is incontestable. Extended family members are obligated to help other family members in need, no matter how distant the relationship. The average wage earner cares for 10 people. Saving money is almost impossible.

For most, life functions at the subsistence level. Crops depend on sufficient rain, and food surpluses are rare. Houses are made of mud, rocks, and sometimes cement. Few households have electricity or running water. Even for city dwellers, these services are interrupted frequently.

Dating and Marriage. In urban areas, dating begins at about age 15, and promiscuity is widespread. In rural areas, rules differ according to the ethnic or social group. Individuals usually accept their families' judgment in the choice of a marital partner. Weddings involve many guests, much food, and dancing.

Marriage rules are influenced strongly by Islam, but the position of the woman is less dependent than in other Muslim countries since she can, under certain conditions, divorce her husband and rejoin her family. Polygamy is practiced (as allowed and controlled by Islamic law), but it is increasingly regarded as an economic burden. A Muslim man who wishes to take another wife usually seeks the approval of his first wife and then must provide for all wives (up to four) equally. Many urban women no longer accept the status of secondary spouse. Some rural women appreciate the extra help that multiple wives can provide.

Diet. The staples of a Malian diet are millet and corn. Flour is prepared as a thick porridge (*tô*) and dipped in a leaf or vegetable sauce. Popular is *tiga diga na* (peanut butter sauce); a meat sauce (goat, sheep, beef, or chicken) might be used on occasion. In the north, milk, dates, and wheat are important foods. Urban residents eat rice when possible. Malnutrition is widespread in Mali. During the "hungry season" (July–August), when food stores are depleted and new crops not ready to harvest, people rely on fresh mangoes for sustenance. Bananas and oranges are also available.

Recreation. The most popular sport in Mali is soccer. It is inexpensive, and as a spectator sport provides people with an opportunity to sit together and talk while watching the game. Also, informal peer groups, known as *groupe de grain*, often meet together to drink tea and socialize. In Bamako and other urban areas, wealthier people spend considerable time watching television and videos.

The Arts. The city of Djenné, built of dried bricks covered in mud-based plaster, is considered an architectural wonder. Such bricks are the primary elements of traditional Malian architecture, and mosques and homes are still made using this technique.

Music and dance are a fundamental part of daily life. Most players of traditional music belong to a caste called *jélé*. Many of Mali's musical forms come from the Malinke tradition, where women are often the singers. However, Malians have mixed traditional and Western forms of music, such as the blues and Latin rhythms, with great success. Malian musicians have become internationally renowned, many having relocated to France to sign with recording labels.

Carefully made designs and colors flavor the art of weaving, much of which is done by a weaver caste. Mud painted on specially primed fabric creates the *bogolan* (mud cloth). Villagers wear this fabric wrapped toga-like around the body. Wood carving is a prominent folk art, and Malians make exquisitely carved wooden masks. Although masks are used in some areas for animist traditions, they are primarily produced for the tourist market. Several organizations promote fine and traditional arts. The government encourages youth groups involved in theater, music, visual, and performance arts.

Holidays. National holidays include New Year's Day, Army Day (20 Jan.), Labor Day (1 May), and Independence Day (22 Sept.). The most important religious holidays are the feast at the end of *Ramadan* (when Muslims go without food and drink during the day but eat in the evenings) and *Tabaski* (feast of mutton, honoring Abraham for his willingness to sacrifice his son). The dates for these feasts change each year because Islam uses the lunar calendar. In cities, Christmas and Easter Monday are observed as days off from work. In animist areas, festivals associated with the seasons are celebrated with mask dancing.

Commerce. Government offices and larger stores remain open from 7:30 a.m. to 4:30 p.m., Monday through Saturday, except

Mali

Fridays, when they are open from 7:30 a.m. to 12:30 p.m. and from 4 to 7 p.m. Markets and street vendors are open until late into the evening and on Sundays. Open-air markets provide opportunities not only to buy basic goods but also to socialize.

Most Malians work in agriculture and are not normal wage earners. Wage earners usually are government employees, such as teachers. Because government wages are often unpaid, many civil servants must also work in agriculture to support their families. Urban unemployment can exceed 50 percent; many unemployed workers survive as street vendors.

SOCIETY

Government. Mali is a multiparty democracy. The president (currently Amadou Toumani Touré) is head of state; a prime minister (currently Ousmane Issoufi Maiga) is head of government. The president is elected to a maximum of two five-year terms and appoints the prime minister. Malians also elect the 147 members of the National Assembly to five-year terms. A Supreme Court is the final court of authority. The voting age is 21. Several political parties are active. Local decisions are made by village elders, who often consult under a tree until a consensus is reached. District chiefs are also elected.

Economy. Mali is one of the world's poorest countries, and most of its people have little ability to change their circumstances. Eighty percent of the labor force is employed in agriculture; however, most of the work is for subsistence. Mali's natural resources are limited to small deposits of gold, limestone, uranium, and other minerals. Harvests are often affected by drought, grasshoppers, and certain kinds of weeds. There is little industry, and the government and foreign corporations control most enterprises. Mali's main exports include cotton, cattle, gold, and peanuts. Small enterprises are growing, but the purchasing power of the domestic market is limited. Many small local efforts have succeeded in extending loans to women entrepreneurs and in raising revenue to build and staff primary schools. Mali lacks the necessary infrastructure (hotels, transport, services, etc.) needed to develop a viable tourist market. The country benefits from international aid and development projects. Mali uses the currency common to francophone African countries, the *CFA franc* (XOF).

Transportation and Communications. Travel by road is difficult, since the only paved road connects the regional capitals and most other roads are unpaved and passable only in the dry season. From August to December, the Niger River is usually navigable by larger ships. Canoes and small craft can use the river year-round. Commonly used is the *pinasse*, a covered motorized canoe. Buses link major cities, but outlying areas are usually only accessible by pickup trucks or vans that carry passengers and their cargo. People otherwise walk, ride bikes, or have mopeds.

Television broadcasts can be received in most regions, but access to a television and power source is limited in rural areas. Programs are mostly in French. Radio broadcasts are in local languages. For most people, the radio provides the primary source of news information. Numerous daily newspapers prosper in a free press. Telephone connections are generally good but not extensive. Most people go to a post office to make or receive calls. Mail is delivered to postal and government offices, not to homes. Rural people often send mail with travelers going in the letter's intended direction.

Education. A rising literacy rate is linked to higher rural enrollment (43 percent) in locally built primary schools. However, overall access to education is limited by school fees and the use of French as the language of instruction. Few adults read or write in French or Bambara. Professional training is relatively rare. Public schools, as well as Catholic, U.S., and French schools, serve urban areas. Rural Catholic or Protestant missions usually include a school. Many parents send their children (mostly boys) to *Qur'anic* schools and leave them in the care of the teacher. The University of Bamako offers bachelor degrees in a number of disciplines.

Health. Medical facilities and services are inadequate or nonexistent in much of the country. On average, there is only one doctor for every 17,000 people and one sickbed per 2,000 people. Clinics often are without staff or supplies. Hospitals in regional capitals have inadequate equipment. Widespread epidemics of malaria cause several thousand deaths each year. HIV/AIDS, influenza, dysentery, venereal disease, guinea worm, and German measles cause frequent sickness. Yellow fever, cholera, bilharzia, and rabies are also present. Blindness is common. Trachoma, a disease that can cause blindness, affects one-third of all children. Public hygiene is poor in urban areas, where sewage collects in open gutters. For most of the population, potable water is available only from deep, hand-powered pump wells.

DEVELOPMENT DATA
Human Dev. Index* rank . . . . 174 of 177 countries
   Adjusted for women. . . . . 142 of 144 countries
Real GDP per capita $930
Adult literacy rate . . . . 27 percent (male); 12 (female)
Infant mortality rate . . . . 118 per 1,000 births
Life expectancy . . . . 48 (male); 49 (female)

AT A GLANCE

Events and Trends.

- Prime Minister Ahmed Mohamed Ag Hamani resigned in April 2004 and was replaced by Ousmane Issoufi Maiga. President Touré had chosen Hamani in 2002, a surprise move given that Hamani held positions in the government of longtime ruler Moussa Traoré, whom Touré ousted in 1991. The new prime minister, Maiga, has been minister of finance and minister of sports. He also oversaw Mali's hosting of the African Cup of Nations in 2002.

- In September 2003, Alpha Oumar Konaré, Mali's president from 1992 to 2002, was made chairman of the African Union (AU), the 53-member regional body formed in 2002 to replace the Organization of African Unity (OAU). Among the goals of the AU are attracting foreign investment to Africa, spreading democracy, and establishing greater peace and security.

Contact Information. Embassy of Mali, 2130 R Street NW, Washington, DC 20008; phone (202) 332-2249.

CultureGrams
People. The World. You.

ProQuest Information and Learning Company
300 North Zeeb Road, P.O. Box 1346
Ann Arbor, Michigan 48106 USA
Toll Free: 1.800.528.6279
Fax: 1.800.864.0019
www.culturegrams.com

© 2005 ProQuest Information and Learning Company and Brigham Young University. It is against the law to copy, reprint, store, or transmit any part of this publication in any form by any means without written permission from ProQuest. This document contains native commentary and original analysis, as well as estimated statistics. The content should not be considered strictly factual, and it may not apply to all groups in a nation. *UN Development Programme, Human Development Report 2004 (New York: Oxford University Press, 2004).

CultureGrams™ World Edition 2006

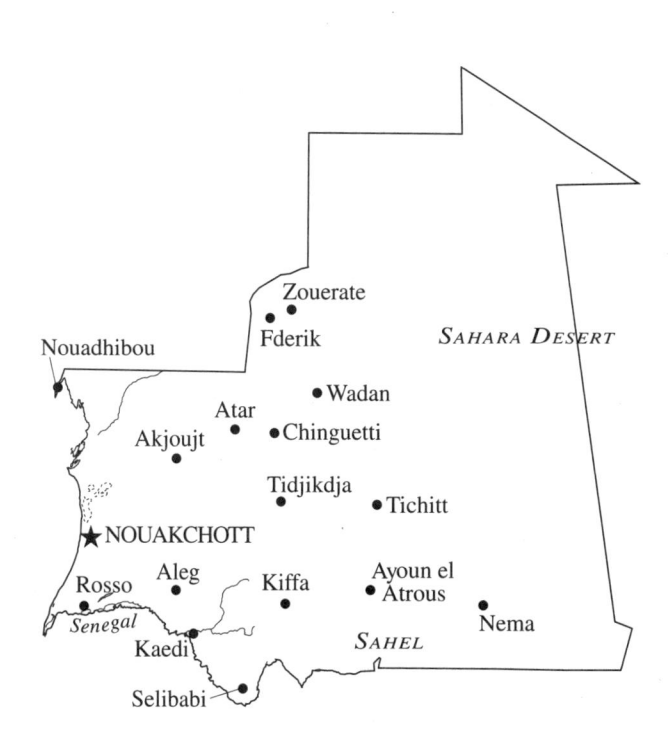

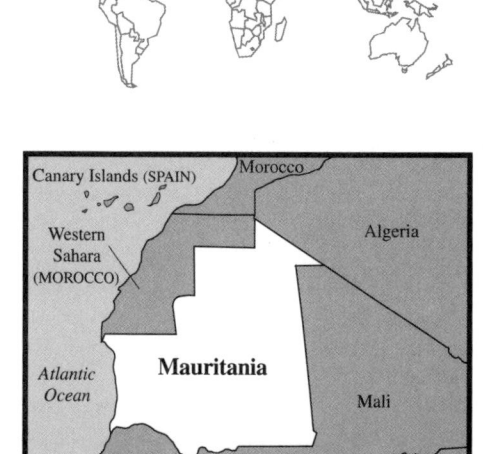

Islamic Republic of Mauritania

BACKGROUND

Land and Climate. The Islamic Republic of Mauritania covers 397,953 square miles (1,030,700 square kilometers) and is about the size of Texas, Oklahoma, and Kansas combined. Of the three main geographic regions (Sahara, Sahel, and Riverine), the Sahara takes up the northern two-thirds; it is characterized by shifting sand dunes, large rock outcroppings, little rain, and limited vegetation. The semiarid Sahel to the south supports savanna grasslands suitable for nomadic cattle and goat herds. The fertile soil of the Riverine region along the Senegal River supports rice, tropical vegetation, and crops for the country. Fishing grounds along the coast are among the richest in the world, and along with iron ore mined in the north, are one of the country's main natural resources.

Mauritania is hot and dry, although winter temperatures are somewhat cooler. During the hottest time of the year (which peaks in May), daytime temperatures reach well over 100°F (38°C), and dusty harmattan winds blow from the northeast. Desertification has intensified in the last 30 years, and the expanding desert threatens farms and the grasslands.

History. Moors from the north of Africa began migrating to the area in the third and fourth centuries. The term *Moor* was coined by the Romans and refers to people of mixed Berber and Arab bloodlines. In their own language, Moors call themselves Bidhane (Bidhany, singular), meaning "Bedouin." Their use of camels allowed for extensive trade by caravan. Traders carried West African slaves, gold, and ivory north to present-day Morocco and Algeria to exchange them for salt, copper, and cloth. Important trade towns were established in Chinguetti, Wadan, Walata, and Tichitt. Islam later spread through this vast network.

In the 10th century, the great Ghanaian Empire controlled much of the south. Arabs gained control in the 16th century. Islam flourished, Arabic spread, and the region became a center for *marabouts* (Islamic teachers and leaders) and learning.

With territories already in Algeria and Senegal, France established a protectorate over present-day Mauritania in 1903. France declared it a colony in 1920 but gained control only in 1934. Its minimal interest in Mauritania influenced its level of investment in the country. France granted complete independence in 1960, and the nation elected Moktar Ould Daddah as its president. Daddah held office for the next 18 years, during which time he nationalized the iron mines, took Mauritania out of the *franc* zone, and created Mauritania's own currency, called the *ouguiya*.

Daddah also acquired the southern third of Western Sahara (Morocco claimed the northern two-thirds) in 1975, after Spain withdrew from the territory. The Polisario Front, a guerrilla force favoring independence for Western Sahara, soon began attacking Nouakchott (the capital of Mauritania) and the country's railroad. Costs associated with the war, combined with severe droughts and lower global demand for iron ore, undermined Daddah's popularity. He was overthrown in 1978 and imprisoned until 1979, when he left the country and Mauritania relinquished its claim to Western Sahara.

Following a number of coups, Maayouia Ould Sid'Ahmed Taya came to power in 1984. Taya's initial actions proved popular: he normalized relations with Morocco, expressed neutrality in the ongoing Western Sahara conflict, and held elections for municipal councils. But in 1989, rising ethnic tensions along the Senegal River erupted into violence. Moors clashed with minority Black Africans over land, cattle, and other issues. As part of the overall dispute, race riots broke out

Mauritania

between migrant Mauritanian Moors and Black Africans in Senegal. In response, Taya's regime supported the killing or torture of Black Africans in the Riverine region. Because many of these native Mauritanians belong to ethnic groups that also inhabit Senegal, Mauritania began expelling tens of thousands of them (as if they were Senegalese) from their homeland. Others fled to Senegal to escape the violence.

By 1991, after Western governments threatened to cut off aid, Taya repatriated some of those who had been expelled. Taya sponsored democratic reforms and stood for elections in 1992, although opposition parties disputed his victory. Full multiparty elections were held for the National Assembly in 1996. Taya's Democratic and Social Republican Party (PRDS) won nearly every seat, and in December 1997 Taya was reelected president, capturing 90 percent of the vote (which was boycotted by major opposition groups). Taya won the 2003 presidential elections with 67 percent of the vote. Although opposition groups have made gains in recent parliamentary and municipal elections, the PRDS still dominates the political scene.

THE PEOPLE

Population. Mauritania's population of three million is growing at about 2.9 percent per year. Most people live in the coastal and Senegal River regions. About 600,000 reside in Nouakchott. Moors, many of whom still live in the desert as herders, make up the majority of the population. They are divided between White Moors (30 percent of the total population) and Black Moors (40 percent).

Black Moors descend from the sub-Saharan African slaves of the White Moors. Slavery has a long history in the Sahara, and Mauritania was the last country to formally abolish it in 1980. However, vestiges of the system remain in that some people are still kept as forced house servants or as traditional slaves. While slaves were indeed property to be bought and sold, they were taken into a family and treated as members of that family. Nevertheless, they were consigned to lives of heavy or menial labor without hope for freedom. Today, White and Black Moors share the same language, culture, and values, but they still are not well integrated with each other. Black Moors tend to live in poorer circumstances than Whites. However, they are represented in government and are working for greater equality.

Black African ethnic groups make up the remaining 30 percent of Mauritania's population. These include the Pulaar, Soninke, and Wolof. The Pulaar and a related group called the Halpular (or Toucouleur) form the nation's largest minority. The Pulaar are traditionally cattle herders and dairymen, but the Halpular are farmers. The Soninke are farmers and traders, who live primarily near the Mauritania-Senegal-Mali border. The Wolof inhabit the coastal areas and are reputable fishermen. Relations between the Moors and Black Africans are tenuous at best. The two groups are divided by history, language, and culture. For instance, Moors speak Arabic, but Black Africans speak their own tongue and usually French.

Language. The national language is Hassaniya, an Arabic dialect spoken by nearly 80 percent of the population. The Pulaar speak Pulaar (also called Fulani); the Halpular speak Fulfulde, a dialect of the same language. The Wolof speak Wolof and the Soninke speak Soninke. Most of these indigenous languages incorporate some French and Hassaniya terms. French and Arabic are the languages of business and higher education.

Religion. Essentially all Mauritanians are Sunni Muslims. Islam's seventh holy city is Chinguetti. *Islam* means "submission" and *Muslim* means "one who has submitted." Muslims surrender to the will of God (*Allah*) and keep the Five Pillars (or guiding principles) as defined by the *Qur'an* (Koran): professing one's faith; praying daily; fasting during *Ramadan*; giving alms; and making a pilgrimage to Makkah, Saudi Arabia. The phrase *Allah akbar* (God is great) calls faithful Muslims to prayer five times each day. Friday is the day of worship. During the holy month of *Ramadan*, Muslims fast between dawn and dusk every day. This observance commemorates the revelation of the *Qur'an* to the prophet Muhammad and is a time of purification and self-discipline.

Islam in Mauritania reflects the influence of indigenous African beliefs about the existence of ghosts, spirits, and supernatural powers. Some *marabouts* make charms (*gris-gris*) to ward off evil, curse someone, grant fertility, and so on.

General Attitudes. Moors tend to be stoic and reserved, while Black Africans are more animated and gregarious. All Mauritanians place high value on friendship, family ties, honesty, politeness, modesty, and respect for elders. In some areas, social rank is more important than material wealth. Rank is determined largely by family history and name.

The Moors are ordered by a caste system; *marabout* families have the highest rank and slaves the lowest. In between are various other castes, including warriors, herders, artisans, hunters and fishers, and so on. A similar system exists among Black Africans. More modern Mauritanians do not emphasize the caste system, especially if they belong to a less desirable caste.

A strong sense of loyalty to one's ethnic group is paramount. The needs of an individual are less important than those of the community. Poverty is a relative term, as the low standard of living is offset by sharing. Muslims accept life as being controlled by *Allah*, often saying *Inshallah* (God willing) to acknowledge that circumstances are beyond their control. This allows many to accept hardships in their lives. Many people associate modernization with Westernization, which older people see as a threat to traditional Islamic values.

Personal Appearance. Men typically wear a *boubou*, or *dara'a* (a long, draping robe in white or blue) over a *chia* (baggy pants). Turbans are wrapped in various ways about the head and/or face to protect against the sun and blowing sand. A *boubou* may be decorated with intricate embroidery. Black Africans are more likely to wear brightly colored clothing or even Western-style attire.

Moorish women wear a *mulafa*, a large piece of colored cloth that is wrapped around the body and draped over the head. A skirt and possibly a shirt are worn beneath the wrap but not seen in public. Black African women usually wear a *pagne* (wraparound skirt) along with a colorful *boubou* and head wrap. All women value and wear jewelry, especially gold. Many women decorate their skin with henna (a plant dye), which is also a status symbol.

CUSTOMS AND COURTESIES

Greetings. Mauritanian men shake hands with men but offer verbal greetings to women. Greetings can be lengthy, and men might hold hands while talking. After an initial greeting with an elder, one often touches one's right hand to the heart. The most common initial greeting is *Salaam alaykum* (Peace be with you), to which people reply *Wa alaykum salaam* (And peace be with you). Moors might also say *Iyak labass* (On you no evil), to which one responds *Labass* (No evil). In Soninke, this phrase is *An moho*; the response is *Jam*. For the Wolof, it is *Nanga def*, and the response is *Jam rekk*. Among Pulaar speakers, one says *M'bda* and is responded to with *Jam tan*. Throughout Mauritania, *Il humdu li'llah* (Praise be to God) is a standard response to good news.

In greeting an elder or social superior, a Moor may place the elder's right hand on his own head as an act of respect and submission. The elder gently tries to withdraw his hand from the person's head but eventually allows it to remain.

Gestures. Mauritanians use the right hand for making all gestures, eating, touching others, and passing objects. It is considered impolite to establish eye contact with an elder. A person makes a clicking sound with the tongue to show he or she is listening to or agrees with the speaker. To disagree, one sucks air through the teeth with the lips pursed. Public displays of affection are unacceptable, but friends of the same gender may hold hands. Married couples do not walk together in public. They are either entirely separate or the husband walks ahead of the wife.

Visiting. Paying frequent visits to friends and relatives is an important social obligation. Guests may drop by at any time and might stay several days. Mauritanians are generous to guests; wealthy hosts may even slaughter a goat for special visitors. People returning to a rural village are expected to bring back gifts, especially if they received a parting gift before taking their journey. Otherwise, visitors are only expected to bring news of their family and village.

When entering a house or tent, Mauritanians remove their shoes. Hosts offer guests something to drink, such as water, juice from a baobab tree, or *zrig* (milk, water, and sugar whipped together with a whisk). Later, they prepare mint tea. Guests arriving at mealtime are expected to stay and eat. After the midday meal, everyone usually takes a nap. Men lounge together on palm mats. Women are more likely to lounge with other women. Most visiting occurs outdoors because it is too hot inside.

Served among Moors in small glasses and sipped quickly, tea is offered to guests in three ceremonial rounds. With each round, more sugar and mint are added to symbolize three aspects of life: bitter like life, sweet like marriage, and sweetest like having children.

Eating. Meals usually are served at midday and in the evening. People may eat a light meal in the morning. Mauritanians eat with their right hand from a communal platter or bowl placed on the ground. Prior to eating, they wash their hands in a water basin. Men and women eat from separate platters and may even eat in separate rooms. Diners eat the portion of food directly in front of them but take meat from the center of the plate. They form balls of food in the hand before placing them in the mouth. Hosts often encourage guests to eat more. After the meal, people lick their fingers clean and then wash again in the water basin.

LIFESTYLE

Family. Extended families are very close and often live within the same compound surrounded by a high wall. Anyone with an income is expected to share earnings with the extended family. An urban wage earner might support an entire family in a remote village.

The father is the head of the family, followed by the eldest son. The father provides money, clothing, and other necessities. He often works away from the home village, and his family sees him only occasionally. Women care for the household and children. Parents strive to have as many children as possible, as numerous progeny brings them respect in the community and helps ensure they will be cared for in their later years. Young children help with chores, including caring for animals, tending a garden, or carrying water; urban children might sell candy or other small items.

Northern homes may be built of rock with a clay roof, but most homes are made of mud bricks and thatched roofs. Urban homes have more concrete. Nomadic families live in large camel-hair tents, which are elaborately decorated on the inside. In the south, Fulani herders live in *ruga*, temporary dome-shaped huts. The Halpular live in large compounds that house much of their extended family.

Dating and Marriage. Dating in the Western sense does not exist. If young people do meet, they keep it secret from their parents. Otherwise, families often arrange marriages. It is not uncommon for a couple to meet for the first time at their wedding. Celebrations can take as long as three days and involve feasting and dancing. The groom is expected to pay the bride's family a cash dowry according to his family's social rank and wealth. It is the bride's family's responsibility to give the couple furnishings. Islamic law allows men to have as many as four wives. Moor men have only one wife at a time, though divorce is common. Many Black Africans have two or more at a time.

Diet. Mauritanians eat rice and/or *couscous* on a daily basis. *Couscous* is made from sorghum flour carefully sifted and rolled into small balls and then steamed. *Idhin* is a kind of butter often poured on *couscous*. The southern diet also includes fish and millet. Corn and vegetables (carrots, lettuce, potatoes, and onions) are added in season. Bread is eaten in the morning or for snacks. People may eat porridge or bread and butter in the morning, rice with dried fish or a peanut or tomato sauce in the afternoon, and steamed millet flour with beans or milk in the evening. Along the Senegal River, mangoes are abundant in season; guavas, limes, and other citrus fruits are also seasonally available. Dates grow in northern oases.

Recreation. Men and boys play soccer, and men enjoy camel racing and card games. Women do not play sports but get together to do embroidery, have tea, or braid hair. Children often make their own toys, drum on pans and washtubs, sing, and dance. Mauritanians love to dance, particularly on special occasions. Families often come together in a circle to sing and dance. People may also gather together to listen to a visiting *marabout*.

The Arts. Because Mauritanian society is rigidly segmented, many of its arts reflect those same divisions. Special castes exist for artisans and musicians, who often have wealthy patrons. Poetry and song are believed to have special, sometimes magical, powers. Islamic holidays and celebrations are the most common venues for traditional music and dance. Instruments such as the *tidnit* (a four-string lute) and the *ardin* (harp) accompany vocalists in traditional musical performances. Orators known as *ighyuwa* or *griots* sing praises and recite oral histories and poetry. Another caste of artisans traditionally is involved in the production of art and handicrafts. Men are responsible for smithing (iron and gold or silver), woodworking, and leather working, while women make pottery, weave, and sew. Artisans sell and trade their wares in markets.

Holidays. Islamic holidays are set by the lunar calendar. The most important holidays include *El Fitr* (feast at the end of *Ramadan*), *Tabasky* (feast honoring Abraham's willingness to

Mauritania

sacrifice his son), and Muhammad's birthday. For *Tabasky*, Mauritanians dress in their finest clothes and feast on mutton.

National holidays include New Year's Day (1 Jan.), International Women's Day (8 Mar.), Labor Day (1 May), Islamic New Year, and Independence Day (28 Nov.). In the north, many people celebrate the harvest festival called *Getna* when the dates are ripe in July and August. Families feast on dates while camping among the date palms.

Commerce. Business hours are from 8 a.m. to 6 p.m. with a three-hour afternoon break from the heat. Some shops stay open late into the evening. Many women participate in commerce by making crafts or selling goods at open markets in larger villages and cities. The government sets prices for bread, tea, and sugar. In villages where cash and/or markets are not common, some people use payment-in-kind to obtain items they do not produce themselves.

SOCIETY

Government. Mauritania is a republic with a strong executive president (currently Maayouia Ould Sid'Ahmed Taya) who serves a six-year term of office and appoints the prime minister. The prime minister (currently Sghair Ould M'bareck) is head of government. Parliament consists of a 56-seat Senate (*Majlis al-Shuyukh*) and an 81-seat National Assembly (*Majlis al-Watani*). Senate members are chosen by local municipal councils and serve six-year terms, while National Assembly members are directly elected and serve five-year terms. The voting age is 18. The PRDS remains the most powerful party, but opposition parties have been legal since 1991. The first female member of parliament was elected in 1996.

Economy. Despite Mauritania's rich fishing grounds and iron ore deposits, the country remains one of the world's poorest. Most Mauritanians rely on subsistence agriculture and animal husbandry. Wealth is concentrated in the hands of a few. Livestock is the key measure of traditional wealth in Mauritania. The government is trying to overcome currency devaluation, foreign debt, and the inefficiency of state-run enterprises. Some industries are being privatized.

Mauritanians often work in other African nations as traders. With caravan trade a part of their heritage, many Moors buy goods from distant villages or countries and return to sell them in Mauritania's markets. Traders are esteemed over laborers, the latter being associated with lower castes and even slavery. This notion creates a glut of underemployed traders and a lack of skilled or motivated labor. Women often form cooperatives to make mats, grow gardens, and produce crafts. The Mauritanian currency is the *ouguiya* (MRO).

Transportation and Communications. Mauritania has several paved roads connecting major cities. Dirt roads are impassable in the rainy season. Although transportation is difficult, one can get most places by "bush-taxi," a network of crowded minibuses that travel on set routes with variable schedules. The railroad transports iron ore from Zouerate to Nouadhibou when sand is not covering the tracks.

Phones do not exist in many villages, and the postal service is unreliable, so traditional forms of communication are essential. Travelers are used as couriers to take news or tape-recorded messages to friends and relatives. Most people also listen to nightly radio transmissions for such news. Larger cities have phones and newspapers. The internet is available at internet cafés in Nouakchott. Newspapers are subject to government censorship. All broadcast media are state-owned.

Education. Mauritania's education system is based on the French model, which requires students to pass exams to advance. Young boys (younger than eight) often learn some math and Arabic by attending *Qur'anic* schools. After that, both boys and girls attend at least the first year of primary school. However, schooling is not mandatory, and some children stay home to help with family chores or because their parents distrust formal education. The language of instruction is either French or Arabic, depending on the decision of the individual village. Many villages lack schools or teachers. The few students who complete the primary level by age 13 may attend high school for another six years. It is split into junior and senior levels. The university in Nouakchott accepts high school graduates after they pass difficult entrance exams.

Health. Hospitals and clinics exist in larger cities, such as the 12 regional capitals, but they often lack supplies, electricity, water, and medicine. Clinics with foreign doctors are available only to the wealthy. Most outlying areas have no access to medical care. Many people suffer from the lack of fruits and vegetables in their diets. People along the Senegal River are especially at risk for malaria and guinea worm. Intestinal parasites are common throughout the country.

DEVELOPMENT DATA

- Human Dev. Index* rank .... 152 of 177 countries
- Adjusted for women .... 124 of 144 countries
- Real GDP per capita $2,220
- Adult literacy rate .... 52 percent (male); 31 (female)
- Infant mortality rate .... 72 per 1,000 births
- Life expectancy .... 51 (male); 54 (female)

AT A GLANCE

Events and Trends.

- In April 2005, President Taya decreed that weekends would be Saturday and Sunday instead of Friday and Saturday. Taya made the move to align the country with the other world markets. However, Friday is a holy day for Muslims, so many Muslims opposed the move.
- In January 2005, the UN's World Food Program announced that 400,000 people in Mauritania were in urgent need of food aid. The crisis was caused by a horde of locusts that swept through the country, devouring all plant life.
- After announcing that it had foiled several coup plots in 2003 and 2004, the Mauritanian government arrested several military officials. Former president Mohammed Ould Haidallah had already been arrested in 2003 for allegedly financing a coup. In February 2005, four soldiers were given life sentences for plotting coups. However, Haidallah was acquitted of financing revolutionary activities.

Contact Information. Embassy of Mauritania, 2129 Leroy Place NW, Washington, DC 20008; phone (202) 232-5700.

CultureGrams
People. The World. You.

ProQuest Information and Learning Company
300 North Zeeb Road, P.O. Box 1346
Ann Arbor, Michigan 48106 USA
Toll Free: 1.800.528.6279
Fax: 1.800.864.0019
www.culturegrams.com

© 2005 ProQuest Information and Learning Company and Brigham Young University. It is against the law to copy, reprint, store, or transmit any part of this publication in any form by any means without written permission from ProQuest. This document contains native commentary and original analysis, as well as estimated statistics. The content should not be considered strictly factual, and it may not apply to all groups in a nation. *UN Development Programme, Human Development Report 2004 (New York: Oxford University Press, 2004).

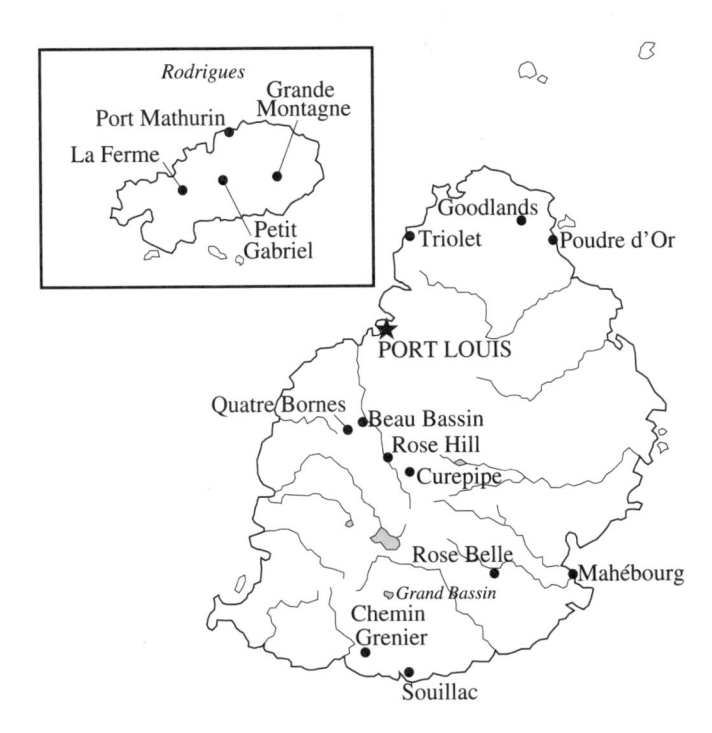

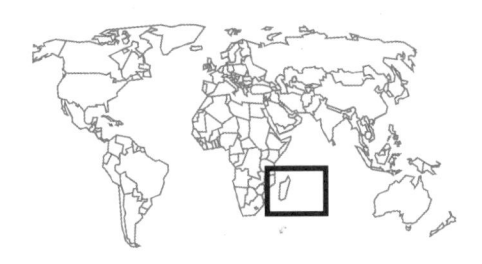

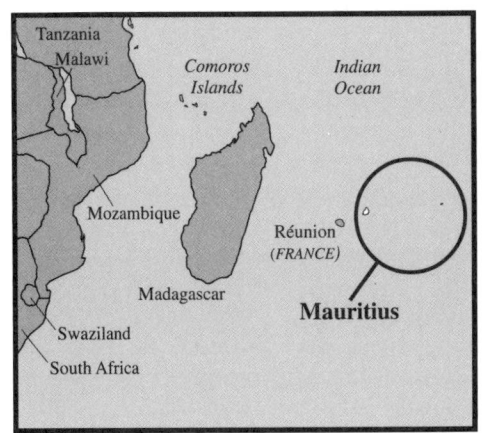

Republic of Mauritius

CultureGrams World Edition 2006

BACKGROUND

Land and Climate. Mauritius, a volcanic island in the Indian Ocean, covers 718 square miles (1,860 square kilometers) and lies 690 miles (1,110 kilometers) east of Madagascar. The country includes the islands of Mauritius, Rodrigues, and several smaller, uninhabited islands. Lush vegetation covers Mauritius throughout the year. The landscape is marked by impressive mountains that rim a central plateau, deep extinct volcanic craters, rivers, streams, and waterfalls. Surrounded almost entirely by coral reefs, Mauritius has a continuous belt of beaches with lagoons and clear waters that are perennially warm (70–80°F, or 21–27°C). Arable land is planted mostly with sugarcane. Forests are found in the southwest. Winter (May–November) is warm and relatively dry, while summer (November–May) is hot, wet, and humid. Cyclones are possible during much of the summer.

Mauritius is known for its many species of rare birds and plants, some of which exist nowhere else in the world. Scientists and bird watchers come from all over the world to try to see the Mauritian kestrel, the echo parakeet, and the pink pigeon—three of the world's rarest birds. All are nearly extinct, though captive breeding and release has begun to help the kestrel population. Mauritius is also known for being the home of the extinct (for more than three hundred years) dodo bird, a member of the pigeon family. The dodo is a popular theme for tourist souvenirs today. Several plant species unique to the islands are close to disappearing.

History. Malay and Arab sailors are thought to have visited the island in the 16th century. It appeared on a map as early as 1502. The Portuguese were the first Europeans to set foot on Mauritius. As a tribute to explorer Pedro Mascarenhas, the islands of Mauritius, Rodrigues, and French-owned Réunion are known as the Mascarene Archipelago. In September 1598, Dutch sailors arrived on the uninhabited island and named it Mauritius in honor of Prince Maurice of Nassau.

The Dutch began to settle the island in 1638, but they abandoned it in 1710 when sugarcane cultivation proved a failure. The Dutch are credited with introducing sugar (now a productive industry) and deer to the island, but they are also charged with causing the extinction of the dodo bird and destroying rich ebony forests.

Guillaume Dufresne d'Arsel claimed Mauritius for France in September 1715 and named it Isle de France. From 1735 to 1746, Mauritius flourished and developed under the direction of François Mahé de Labourdonnais. The British won Mauritius from France in 1810.

After the abolition of slavery in 1834, indentured laborers from India were brought to work in the sugarcane fields. While the British officially ruled Mauritius, they allowed French culture, language, and a Napoleonic law code to be maintained by the Franco-Mauritians, who remained the largest European ethnic group on the island. Mauritius gained independence in March 1968 through the leadership of Sir Seewoosager Ramgoolam, who became the nation's first prime minister. Mauritius retained its membership in the Commonwealth.

The 1980s and early 1990s were dominated by the leadership and coalition partners of the Militant Socialist Movement (MSM). MSM leader Sir Anerood Jugnauth was prime minister from 1982 to 1995. When he attempted to change the constitution in order to override a Supreme Court ruling, President Cassam Uteem dissolved parliament and held early elections in December 1995. Opposition candidate Navin Ramgoolam (son of Seewoosager Ramgoolam) won a landslide victory. A

Mauritius

coalition between his Mauritian Labor Party (MLP) and the Mauritian Militant Movement (MMM) completely dominated the balloting. The MSM gained no parliamentary seats at all.

Rivalries led Prime Minister Ramgoolam's coalition to collapse in June 1997. Deputy Prime Minister Paul Bérenger (the MMM leader) lost his ministerial post and became the opposition leader in parliament. Other MMM ministers also resigned and joined the opposition, but Ramgoolam's MLP remained the governing party.

In September 2000, an alliance of the MSM and MMM captured a decisive 54 of 62 contested seats in parliament, ousting Ramgoolam. Sir Anerood Jugnauth of the MSM was voted back as prime minister, and MMM leader Paul Bérenger again became deputy prime minister. In keeping with an agreement between the two ruling coalition parties, Jugnauth resigned in September 2003 (in the middle of his five-year term), allowing Bérenger to take the prime ministership. Jugnauth became president, a largely ceremonial role.

Because of its political stability, Mauritius has been able to better develop its health, education, and economic resources and strategically plan how it builds its infrastructure. Historically dependent on sugar production, the nation has successfully diversified its economy to now include major textile, tourism, and banking industries.

THE PEOPLE

Population. Mauritius has a population of about 1.2 million, growing annually at a rate of 0.8 percent. Approximately 40 percent of the population inhabits the urban area that stretches from Port Louis, the capital, to Curepipe.

About 68 percent of the nation's people are Indo-Mauritians, descendants of laborers brought from India to work on British sugar plantations. Another 27 percent are Creoles, descendants of Africans (from West and East Africa) brought by the French to the island as slaves. Sino-Mauritians (of Chinese origin) account for 3 percent of the population and Franco-Mauritians (of French origin) constitute 2 percent. About 10,000 foreign workers, mostly Chinese women, also reside in Mauritius. These diverse peoples live in relative harmony, but disruptions are not infrequent.

Language. English, the official language of Mauritius, is not spoken much in day-to-day communication. French and English are used almost exclusively in government and business. Road signs are in English, and most newspapers and media communications are in French. Television and radio programming is usually in French or Hindi and occasionally in English and Creole.

Creole, Bhojpuri, Hindi, Urdu, and Hakka (a dialect of Chinese) are the main languages spoken on Mauritius. Creole (spoken by 90 percent of the population) was developed in the 18th century by early slaves who used a pidgin language to communicate with each other and with their French masters, who did not understand the various African languages. The pidgin evolved in later generations to become a useful, casual language. Bhojpuri on Mauritius is a combination of the Bhojpuri Indian dialect and several other Indian dialects originally spoken by early Indian laborers. Most Mauritians are at least bilingual. Creole and Bhojpuri are rarely used in written form.

Religion. The world's four most widely-practiced religions—Christianity, Islam, Hinduism, and Buddhism—are all represented in Mauritius. Slightly more than half the population is Hindu. Although they are divided into two main sects (Sanathan Hindus and Arya Samajists), Mauritian Hindus generally share common beliefs, including the principles of reincarnation, the illusionary state of mortal life, and *karma* (the force generated by one's actions in the present life, which determines the quality of one's future life). Thirty percent of all Mauritians are Christians belonging to the Roman Catholic Church, the Anglican Church, or various other denominations. Seventeen percent of Mauritius's population is Muslim. Many Chinese are Buddhists.

General Attitudes. The Mauritian people are family oriented and religious. They are also optimistic, outgoing, intelligent, generous, and industrious. A generally relaxed attitude toward life is evident in Mauritians' casual approach to time schedules. People are considered more important than schedules, and being late for an appointment is not inappropriate. Mauritians have an ability to synthesize and adopt new ideas and cultures, combining Eastern philosophical values with a Western sense of rationalism and pragmatism. Although ethnic identity is strong, most Mauritians recognize the need for national unity.

Personal Appearance. Most Mauritian men wear conservative, Western-style clothing and wear traditional attire only on special occasions or holidays. For Hindu men, this would include a *langouti* (ankle-length cotton garment tied at the waist). Muslim men might wear a *salwaar-kameez* (broad pants that narrow at the ankle and a knee-length shirt).

Mauritian women also wear modest Western fashions but are more likely than men to wear traditional attire. For instance, Hindu women may wear a *saree* (a wraparound skirt with one end draped over the shoulder) and a *choli* (tight blouse). Muslim women may wear a *salwaar-kameez*. Many married Indo-Mauritian women wear a *tika* (a red dot made from vermilion powder) on their forehead to signify their husbands are alive.

CUSTOMS AND COURTESIES

Greetings. Mauritians usually shake hands when they meet. Adult men rarely shake hands with women, but handshakes between men and women are becoming more common with the younger generation. Close friends and relatives might kiss on both cheeks and/or hug when they meet.

Greetings are as varied as languages and situations. In formal settings, the French *Bonjour* (Good day) or the English *How are you?* is appropriate. Among Hindus, the *Namaste* is the traditional greeting. A person places the palms together (fingers up) in front of the chest or chin and says *Namaste*, sometimes bowing slightly. Muslims informally greet each other with *Salaam* (Peace). In Creole, one might say *Ki manière?* (How are you?) or *Causé!* (literally, "Speak," but meaning "How are you?"). In Bhojpuri, the standard greeting is *Kaisé ba?* (How are you?).

Adults of the same age generally address one another by first name, unless they are being formally introduced. Friends might call each other by nickname. Depending on the age difference between a person and an elder, the person appropriately addresses the older individual by familial titles such as brother, sister, uncle, aunt, grandfather, or grandmother (in either Creole or Bhojpuri). These titles are used for any elders, not just for relatives. Children never address an elder by name.

Gestures. It is not proper to pass or receive items with the left hand. Instead, one uses the right hand or both hands. Mauritians beckon by waving all fingers together with the palm down. People do not greet passing strangers.

Visiting. Visiting is a popular Mauritian pastime. It is common for people to visit friends and relatives unannounced. However, as telephones become more widely available, people are getting into the habit of calling ahead to make sure their intended hosts are at home. Sunday afternoon is the most popular time for visiting, as it is the time when people are least busy. Mauritians mostly socialize at home. Hosts usually serve tea with sugar and milk, often with *biscuits* (cookies), sweets, or other snacks. A host will insist that the guest accept food and drink. It is considered polite for the guest to accept and sample whatever is offered.

Guests are not expected to bring gifts, but they may give flowers to the hostess of a formal lunch or dinner. Among friends or family, guests often bring chocolate, sweets, pastries, or other small items to the children of the home. For the adults, visitors might bring something from their garden. In such a case, the hosts will give the guests something from their garden when the guests depart. Different fruits and vegetables grow in each region of Mauritius, so such garden exchanges allow people to share a variety of produce.

Eating. Mauritians eat three meals a day. The family tries to eat together whenever possible. Dinner usually is not eaten until around 7 p.m. Mauritians generally eat with a spoon, fork, and knife, but Indo-Mauritian families eat certain foods with the fingers of the right hand. A guest usually is given the option of using silverware or eating with the hand. An unexpected guest at dinnertime will be invited to share the meal.

Hindus do not eat beef. Muslims do not eat pork or drink alcohol. During the ninth lunar month, or *Ramadan*, Muslims do not eat or drink from sunrise to sundown.

LIFESTYLE

Family. Mauritian society places strong emphasis on family solidarity. It was once common for extended families—aunts, uncles, and other relatives—to live together. Today, however, the nuclear family household is most common. Still, people tend to build their homes close to other family members. The father is head of the family, which typically has two or three children. Parents work hard in caring for their children, and they strive to provide them with a solid education. Parents pay for any schooling costs, even at the university level. Mauritians have great respect for the elderly; it is the duty of their children to take care of them.

Dating and Marriage. Western-style dating is not common. Marriage is a strong tradition. Chastity is important, especially among Indo-Mauritian women. Many Indo-Mauritian families arrange marriages for their children, generally with the consent of the bride and groom. Sometimes, grooms in Muslim families give a dowry to the bride's parents.

A wedding is one of the biggest events for all Mauritian families, regardless of the ethnic group or religion. It tends to be a lavish and expensive affair. Wedding ceremonies are conducted along religious lines and vary accordingly. Among Hindus, for example, a bride and groom perform a ritual of walking around a fire during the *Vivaha* (marriage ceremony). As part of a Muslim ceremony, the bride and groom drink from a common cup to signify the beginning of their lives together. Women typically marry in their early twenties, while men usually marry when they are a few years older. Divorce is not well accepted and is relatively rare.

Diet. Rice is the main staple. *Roti* (Indian flat bread) is also a staple for many. French breads are immensely popular, especially at breakfast. Hindus prefer vegetarian dishes. Indian cuisine is most common, but Creole, Chinese, and spicy variations of all three are also available. Fresh seafood is popular. Some dishes include *faratas* (similar to pancakes), *briani* (rice and vegetables with a mixture of meat, chicken, or fish and a number of spices), *vanneyen* (chopped fish meatballs in a fish broth), *dohl pouri* (thin bread with meat and curry sauce inside), chicken curry, pickled vegetables, and seasoned squid. Most Mauritians drink tea with milk and sugar after meals. Fruits, Indian sweets, French pastries, and peanuts are popular snacks during the day and especially during afternoon tea.

Recreation. *Football* (soccer) is the Mauritian national sport. Horse racing is a popular spectator activity. People also enjoy swimming and water sports. Men are far more likely than women to play sports. Movies are the primary entertainment, along with informal social gatherings among friends and family. Young people like to listen to music and watch television. Playing cards and dancing the *séga* (a Mauritian dance) are especially popular in some parts of Mauritius. Bar cafés, where men gather to talk and drink, are found in both rural and urban areas. Wealthier Mauritians increasingly go to discos, casinos, and restaurants.

The Arts. The arts of Mauritius have benefited from a rich European legacy as well as the increasing influence of Creole culture. French is still the language of literature and dominates the work of poets, writers, and novelists. Creole is the medium of popular art, especially in music, theater, and dance.

Since the time of slavery, one of the primary artistic expressions of the Creole-speaking population has been the *séga* dance. *Séga* integrates Creole texts and modern percussion instruments with the rhythm of African, Caribbean, and Latin American pop music. The lively dance is accompanied by the *ravane* (a tambourine-like drum ringed with bells), the triangle, and the *coco* (similar to a maraca).

Mauritian architecture is characterized by Creole houses, distinct from more European buildings in their sharp roofs, geometric glass panes, and balcony or veranda. The making of woven cloth, baskets, hand-embroidered *sarees*, and woodwork is common in many areas.

Holidays. In addition to religious holidays for all major religions, there are a few national holidays. They include New Year's Day, Independence Day (12 Mar.), and Labor Day (1 May). With a large population of Christians, the nation celebrates Christmas and Easter. The Spring Festival (also called the Chinese New Year) and *Ching Ming* (when the dead are honored) are the two most important holidays for the Chinese. Two holidays significant to the Muslims are *Eid-ul-Fitr* (a three-day feast that commemorates the end of Ramadan) and *Eid-ul-Adha* (a feast that both honors Abraham for his willingness to sacrifice his son and marks the end of the pilgrimage to Makkah, Saudi Arabia).

Hindu festivals usually celebrate the victory of a god or principle. For example, *Divali* (Festival of Lights) focuses on the triumph of *dharma* over *adharma*, or light over darkness. The *Cavadee* celebrates the feat of Idoumban, who carried two mountain peaks on his shoulders. *Holi* is a time when people sprinkle each other with colored water in celebration of Prince Bhakta Pralad's defeat of the wicked Holika. During *Maha Shivaratree*, it is popular to dress in white and pour sacred water on a representation of Shiva, one of the three primary Hindu gods. The water is drawn from the Grand Bassin, a high-altitude lake located in a volcano crater. Special ceremonies take place at the lake on the Great Night of Shiva, which is during the summer festival.

Mauritius

Commerce. Businesses generally are open from 9 a.m. to 5:30 p.m., Monday through Friday. Many shops close on Thursday and Saturday afternoons; most close on Sundays and holidays. Most towns have an open-air market that might be open most days (as in the case of Port Louis) or one day each week. Prices in these markets are negotiable. In larger urban areas, supermarkets are replacing small local shops—traditionally a focal point for people to socialize, as well as to buy groceries and household items.

SOCIETY

Government. Mauritius is a parliamentary democracy. The president (currently Sir Anerood Jugnauth) is chief of state and the prime minister (currently Paul Bérenger) is head of government. The president's role is largely ceremonial and includes the provision that he or she must immediately resign from office if he or she refuses to sign a bill into law. In the 66-seat parliament, called the National Assembly, 62 members are elected by popular vote and 4 seats are appointed by the election commission. These appointed seats are reserved for smaller parties that have lost elections, which ensures that all ethnic communities or minorities have representation. Parliamentary elections are held at least every five years. The voting age is 18. Mauritius is divided into nine districts and three dependencies. Local councils govern in urban areas. The country has practically no army and has been politically stable since independence.

Economy. The sugarcane crop has dominated the Mauritian economy since the 19th century. The sugar industry accounts for 45 percent of all export earnings and employs more than 20 percent of the labor force. Grown on plantations and small farms, sugarcane covers 90 percent of the arable land. However, it has become less important in recent years due to an increase in earnings from textile exports (about 45 percent of export earnings) and tourism. Tea, grown in the highlands, is the second most important crop. All but a few staple foods are imported. Most exports go to nations of the European Union.

Manufacturing industries include textiles, electronics, gemstone cutting, knitted wear, and others. Mauritius successfully attracts foreign investment; its banking industry has made it an important regional offshore banking center. Tourism is one of the fastest-growing sectors of its economy and has been the key to Mauritius becoming less reliant on sugar and textiles. The government has also invested in the nation's technology infrastructure in an effort to attract high-tech firms.

Women earn only one-fourth of the nation's income; men generally have greater choices and opportunities for personal development than women. The Mauritian *rupee* (MUR) is the national currency.

Transportation and Communications. All areas of the island are accessible by road. Buses provide the main form of public transportation. Although crowded, they are reliable and fairly inexpensive. Taxis are available in most areas. Fares are negotiable and usually agreed upon in advance. Following the British tradition, traffic moves on the left side of the road. The national airline is Air Mauritius. Several international airlines fly to Mauritius. The telephone system services most of the island and is quite reliable. Most Mauritians read a daily newspaper. The majority of homes have telephones and televisions. Internet use is growing.

DEVELOPMENT DATA
- Human Dev. Index* rank . . . . 64 of 177 countries
- Adjusted for women . . . . 55 of 144 countries
- Real GDP per capita $10,810
- Adult literacy rate . . . . 88 percent (male); 81 (female)
- Infant mortality rate . . . . 16 per 1,000 births
- Life expectancy . . . . 68 (male); 76 (female)

Education. The government places great emphasis on education. Primary and secondary schooling are free and available to all. Families that can afford the fees send their children to private schools. Nearly all children are enrolled in primary school, which lasts six years, and two-thirds of them advance to secondary school. Only half of those complete secondary school. Secondary school finishers can pursue technical training at facilities run by the Industrial and Vocational Training Board. In addition, the University of Mauritius provides opportunities for higher education, emphasizing agricultural sciences and technology. The new University of Technology offers degrees that support the telecommunications, computer, and tourism industries for the island. Many Mauritians attend universities abroad, mainly in France, the United Kingdom, and India.

Health. The public healthcare system provides basic services to all citizens free of charge. The country's many qualified doctors are employed by the government or engaged in private practice. Private clinics provide more comprehensive medical care for those who can afford it. Health conditions are steadily improving, as all people have access to safe water, good sanitation facilities, and prenatal care for women. Nearly all infants receive their immunizations. Schistosomiasis and hepatitis are not uncommon.

AT A GLANCE

Events and Trends.
- In 2004, the Mauritian government began discussions that could lead to a formal claim of sovereignty over the Chagos Archipelago, a group of Indian Ocean islands belonging to the United Kingdom. The Chagos Archipelago was separated from Mauritius in 1965. The local population was removed between 1967 and 1973 to make room for a U.S. military base on the island of Diego Garcia. Mauritius believes the archipelago could be a source of revenue because of its tourism potential, its fishing resources, and the U.S. lease of Diego Garcia.
- When Paul Bérenger took office as prime minister in 2003, he became only the fourth person (and the first Franco-Mauritian) to serve in the position since Mauritius gained independence in 1968.

Contact Information. Embassy of Mauritius, 4301 Connecticut Avenue NW, Suite 441, Washington, DC 20008; phone (202) 244-1491.

Kingdom of Morocco

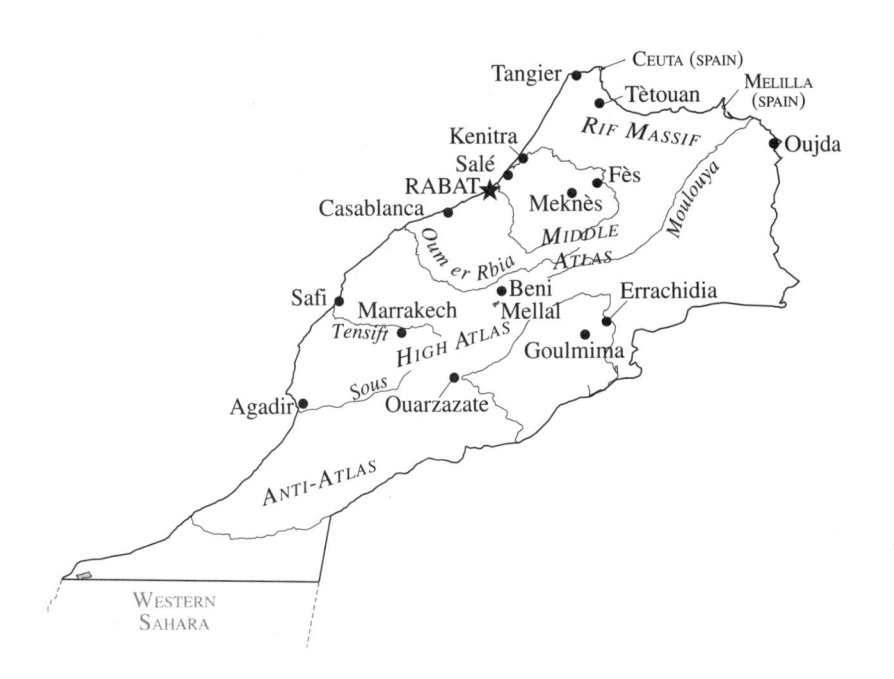

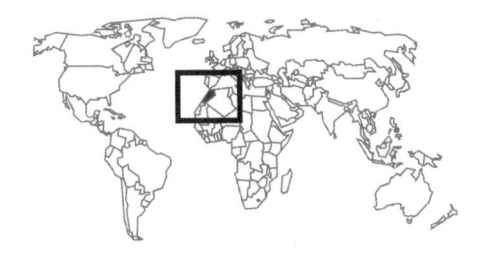

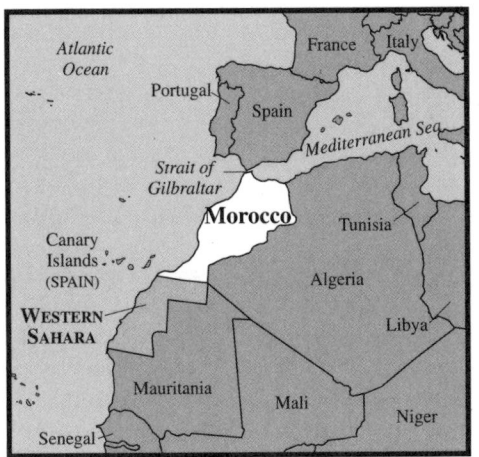

BACKGROUND

Land and Climate. Morocco lies on the northwest corner of Africa across the Strait of Gibraltar from Spain. About the size of California, Morocco covers 172,413 square miles (446,550 square kilometers). The Western Sahara, a disputed region which Morocco claims and administers, has 102,703 square miles (266,000 square kilometers). Spain controls two coastal enclaves (Ceuta and Melilla) in the north.

Traversing the middle of the country from north to southwest are two snowcapped mountain chains: the Middle Atlas and the High Atlas, which includes Mount Toubkal, North Africa's highest peak at 13,671 feet (4,167 meters). South of the High Atlas Mountains lie the Anti-Atlas Mountains. In the north, along the Mediterranean Sea, runs the Rif Massif range. Most of the country's agriculture is grown between the mountainous interior and the Atlantic coastal lowlands, into which flow the Oum er Rbia and Tensift Rivers.

To the south and east of the Atlas chains, the land becomes increasingly arid the closer it gets to the Sahara. The coastal north and west have mild winters and pleasant summers, while interior cities experience more extreme temperatures in both seasons. Winters in the mountains are cold and wet, but summers are pleasant. Towns closer to the Sahara can be hot in the summer and cool in winter.

History. The earliest known settlers of Morocco are believed to have come from southwestern Asia. Known collectively as Berbers, a more accurate indigenous term for them is Imazighen (meaning "free men"; Amazigh is the singular). Because of its strategic location, Morocco's history is replete with foreign invasion and rule, beginning with the Phoenicians in the 12th century B.C. and continuing with the Romans, Vandals, Visigoths, and Greeks.

The Arabs invaded in the seventh century A.D. and introduced Islam to Morocco. The Imazighen fought off direct Arab rule and established an independent kingdom in the eighth century. Two powerful Amazigh dynasties prospered until the 13th century, even expanding for a time into other regions. Following other invasions, the Alaouite Dynasty, which claims descent from the prophet Muhammad, took control in 1660. In 1787, Morocco signed a peace and friendship treaty with the United States. This treaty, which made Morocco one of the first independent nations to recognize U.S. sovereignty, is still in force.

European nations became involved in Morocco in the 19th century, and France made it a protectorate in 1912. The French ruled until Morocco's independence in 1956, when a constitutional monarchy was established. French and, secondarily, U.S. influence are still strong in Morocco. King Hassan II (who held power from 1961 to 1999) was a direct descendant of kings in the Alaouite Dynasty.

In 1975, Morocco occupied the Western Sahara and forced Spain to withdraw. Morocco began developing the region but was opposed by its neighbors, particularly Algeria, and other African states that recognized the Saharan Arab Democratic Republic (SADR) as the Western Sahara's government. The SADR's military arm, the Polisario Front, then waged an expensive and violent war against Morocco. Determined to retain the Western Sahara, Morocco built schools, hospitals, roads, and housing for the Saharan people.

Negotiations between King Hassan's government and the Polisario guerrillas opened in 1989 as part of a UN effort to solve the problem. A 1991 cease-fire ended 15 years of fighting and was to have preceded a UN-sponsored referendum in

Morocco

1992. In the vote, residents of the Western Sahara would be able to accept or reject annexation by Morocco. Unfortunately, the referendum has been repeatedly postponed because the sides cannot agree on who should be allowed to vote (i.e., all current residents or only those who were resident in 1974).

In 1996, a referendum in Morocco supported constitutional reforms that created a directly elected parliament and shifted some authority to local councils. Through elections in 1997, a Chamber of Representatives became Morocco's first freely elected legislative body. King Hassan II died in 1999; he was succeeded by his son, Muhammad VI, who has maintained royal authority and conservative values.

THE PEOPLE

Population. Morocco's population of about 32.2 million is growing annually at 1.6 percent. The population is composed of three main ethnic groups, the largest being the Imazighen and Arabs. Imazighen and Arabs interact, but generally not on an intimate level. The Haratin, descendants of slaves from West Africa, live throughout the southern part of Morocco. Among the Imazighen are a number of regional groups that call themselves by different names. For instance, people of the Rif refer to themselves as Irifin and people of the High Atlas refer to themselves as Ashilhayn.

About half of Moroccans live in urban areas, and urban migration is swelling city populations. Casablanca and the metropolitan area of Rabat and Salé account for more than one-third of Morocco's urban population. About one-third of Moroccans are age 14 or younger. The Western Sahara has an official population of about 260,000, most of whom are ethnic Sahrawi. These are nomadic peoples who live by animal husbandry and subsistence agriculture. Morocco includes them in their official statistics.

Language. The main official language is Arabic, although French also has official status. French is used widely in business, government, and higher education. Moroccan Arabic, called *Derija* (literally, "dialect"), is the most widely spoken tongue. Derija is quite different from the classical Arabic of the *Qur'an* (Koran), the scriptural text of Islam. Imazighen peoples, or some 60 percent of the population, speak Amazigh dialects in addition to Arabic. Prominent dialects include Tashilhayt (spoken in the High Atlas and Sous Valley), Tarifit (Rif region), and Tamazight (Middle Atlas region). Hasaniya, an Arabic dialect, is spoken around Goulmima and in the south, including Western Sahara. Spanish can still be heard in the north, which was formerly under Spanish control. English is gaining popularity.

Religion. Islam is the official religion of Morocco. The king is both the political and spiritual leader of his people. All ethnic Moroccans are Muslim. Conversion to another religion is not recognized by the state. Popular religion mixes aspects of various folk beliefs with traditional Islamic practices. Many Moroccans, most of them Amazigh, are Sufi Muslims. Some Christians and Jews live in Morocco: Jews are mostly native to the country, while Christians have European roots.

Muslims believe in a monotheistic god (*Allah*). They accept most biblical prophets but consider Muhammad to be the last and greatest prophet. Muslims believe he received *Allah's* revelations through the angel Gabriel and recorded them in the *Qur'an*. Religion is a matter of daily practice. The Five Pillars of Islam that Muslims strive to accomplish are to pray five times daily, profess *Allah* as God and Muhammad as his prophet, give of their income to help the poor, fast each day during the month of *Ramadan*, and make at least one pilgrimage to Makkah, Saudi Arabia. Friday is the Muslim day of worship, when a sermon is spoken at the mosque during the noon prayer. Women are not barred from going to the mosque, but they usually worship at home.

General Attitudes. Moroccan culture is deeply rooted in Islam. When people suffer misfortune, they tend to attribute the cause to *Allah*, and the phrase *Insha'allah* (If God wills) is frequently heard. This belief is strongest in rural areas. Urban Moroccans, especially the more educated, do not adhere to it as much. Moroccans value family, honor, dignity, generosity, hospitality, and self-control (particularly of one's temper). A calm attitude gains respect. Women traditionally are restricted to domestic roles, but in urban areas they receive more education and may work outside the home.

Personal Appearance. The national garment is the *djelleba*, a hooded, ankle-length article of clothing with long sleeves. The *djelleba* is worn by men and urban women. Although Western-style clothing is common throughout Morocco, many people still wear the *djelleba*—particularly for special occasions. Amazigh men also wear them, but Amazigh women's dress varies by region. Western attire is modest. Moroccans believe it is important to be neat, well-groomed, and appropriately dressed so one will be treated with respect. Women may cover their heads with scarves, but some do not. When entering a mosque, Moroccans wear clothing that covers the entire body (except the head and hands), and they remove the shoes. One does not wear shorts or other recreational attire in public; shorts are reserved for the beach.

CUSTOMS AND COURTESIES

Greetings. Moroccans generally shake hands when greeting. One might touch the heart after the handshake to express pleasure at seeing the other person or to show personal warmth. Rural children conventionally kiss the right hand of their parents or elders to show respect when greeting. People might greet close friends or relatives by brushing or kissing cheeks.

Assalam Oualaikoum (Peace be upon you) is commonly used as "Hello." People also use *Sbah al Kheir* (Good morning) and *Msa al Kheir* (Good evening). More formally, one might say *Ahlan Wasahlan* (Pleased to see you). Friends may exchange the phrase *Labess*, which means both "How are you?" and "Fine." Greetings between friends also include inquiries about each other's well-being and that of their families. Hosts often extend repeated enthusiastic phrases of welcome. Less fervent greetings might be considered rude. It is polite to greet an acquaintance when passing on an urban street, but people do not greet strangers. In rural areas, most people know one another, so men greet men and women greet women when passing on the street.

Moroccans always use titles in formal situations and to address acquaintances. Friends address each other by first name. Elders might be referred to by a title such as *hadj* (an honorable title for those who have completed a pilgrimage to Makkah) or the equivalent of "aunt" or "uncle."

Gestures. Moroccans pass items with the right hand or with both hands, not with the left alone. It is impolite to point at people and improper to let the bottom of the foot point toward a person. Moroccans generally consider it improper to cross their legs. Some might cross their legs at the knees but would not place an ankle over a knee.

Visiting. Frequent visits to friends and relatives are considered necessary to maintain strong relationships. Visiting is most popular on holidays but may occur at any time. Between family members, it is acceptable to visit unannounced. Whenever possible, friends make arrangements in advance. This is less common in rural areas, where telephones are not always available for calling ahead.

Moroccans are warm and gracious hosts. Social visits can last several hours. Guests invited for dinner in urban areas are not expected to take gifts. However, hosts will appreciate a gift of candy or a small toy for their children. If urban residents visit a relative or friend in a rural area, they are expected to take a gift (staple foods, clothing, household items). Guests invited to a wedding or special event may take gifts for the newlywed couple or person being honored.

Guests generally are offered refreshments. Refusing them is impolite, although guests sometimes give a token refusal before accepting the offered item. Milk and dates are served as a sign of hospitality. Mint tea is often offered to guests, business associates, or anyone with whom one might spend a few minutes during the day. It is considered a friendly, informal gesture that is affordable and easily prepared.

Guests please their hosts by complimenting them on their home. Men and women do not always socialize together. Rural couples more often socialize separately, while urban couples will socialize in mixed company. Men often associate in public coffeehouses, especially on weekends, holidays, or *Ramadan* evenings. At the end of *Ramadan*, heads of households give gifts of money or goods to the poor.

Eating. In most homes, the family eats the main meal of the day together. Before and after eating, people wash their hands. In rural areas, a basin of water is provided; urban residents wash in the sink. Moroccans eat with their fingers from a large communal dish, using the right hand only. Diners eat from the section of the dish directly in front of them.

Hosts encourage guests to eat as much as they like. If the hosts think guests have not eaten enough, they urge them to eat more. In traditional homes, it is impolite for guests to finish eating before the hosts, as this can imply the food did not taste good. Mealtime is an important time for conversation; guests who do not join the discussion embarrass the hosts. In restaurants, service typically is included in the bill, which usually is paid by the host.

LIFESTYLE

Family. Moroccan social life centers on the extended family. One's family is a source of reputation and honor, as well as financial and emotional support. It is considered one's duty to provide financial support to other members of the extended family when it is necessary or requested. Families may live in the same house or build an addition for a son when he marries. The tie between mother and son is the most important relationship. Men are very affectionate with children. Children, especially boys, are indulged but are also expected to contribute to the family by attaining a respectable position in society. Girls begin working in the house at a young age. Adult children are expected to care for their aging parents when it becomes necessary. Parents generally do not interfere with the domestic or private affairs of their children's families. Polygamy is legal but not frequently practiced. A man may have as many as four wives, but he must have permission from any wives he already has and must provide for each equally. Divorce, although frowned upon, is not uncommon.

Dating and Marriage. Dating in the Western sense does not occur in Morocco. In rural areas, young men and women often do not meet their mates until they are to be married. Urban couples meet in various situations, ask permission of their parents to marry, and have time to get acquainted before they get married. When a couple is engaged, the man pays the woman's father or eldest brother a sum of money to meet her wedding expenses. This payment sometimes inhibits a man from marrying because he cannot afford it. Women usually bring a dowry into the marriage. A woman is expected to be a virgin before marriage. Most women marry by their early twenties.

Weddings signify a new union between families and are celebrated as lavishly as possible. A wedding usually lasts two days. The first day is for the bride's female relatives and friends to come together and sing and dance. They decorate the bride's hands and feet with henna (a red plant dye). On the second day, the groom's family and bride's family celebrate the wedding together to show they are one family.

Diet. Mutton, beef, and chicken are the principal meats in the Moroccan diet. Popular dishes include *kefta*, ground beef or mutton seasoned and cooked over charcoal; *tajine*, a meat-and-vegetable stew; and *harira*, a tomato-based soup with beef or mutton, chickpeas, and lentils. *Couscous* (steamed semolina made from wheat) is usually eaten on Fridays. Coastal Moroccans cook fish in a variety of ways. Mint tea is the national drink. Islam prohibits the consumption of pork and alcohol. Although some men drink alcohol, it is not socially acceptable.

Recreation. Soccer is by far the most popular sport in Morocco. Many Moroccans also enjoy basketball and athletics; runner Hicham el Guerrouj set the world record in the mile in 1999. Leisure activities include visiting friends, relaxing at coffeehouses (men only), and going to the beach. Families or groups of girls or boys often take a stroll at dusk. Beach volleyball is gaining popularity.

The Arts. Forms of traditional music include Berber, Gnaouan, and Arab-Andalusian. Rhythmic Gnaouan music, originally from sub-Saharan Africa, features musicians that often do acrobatic crouching and whirling dances while playing. Arab-African *Raï* (opinion) music is an increasingly popular art form, especially among young people.

Morocco is famous for its pottery and ceramic tile. Artisans (especially Imazhigen) create silver jewelry, drums, carpets, hand-tooled leather, and wooden tables and boxes. Fine art forms such as painting and sculpture have developed significantly since Morocco gained independence in the 1950s.

Traditional literature includes histories, essays, and poetry, but other styles have been adopted. Poetry is often improvised and accompanied by a single-stringed instrument (*ribab* or *amzhad*) and a three-stringed banjo-like *lotar* or *kanza*.

Holidays. Each year, Muslims observe *Ramadan*, a month of fasting and prayer, when no eating, drinking, or smoking is permitted from dawn to sunset. In the evenings, families eat together and visit relatives or friends. Business is slower than usual during this month. Children, pregnant women, travelers, foreign visitors, and the ill are exempt from the fast.

Religious holidays include *Aid al Saghir* (the three-day feast at the end of *Ramadan*), *Aid al Kebir* (the feast at the end of the pilgrimage to Makkah), and *Mouloud* (celebrating the birth of Muhammad). Because Muslims use a lunar calendar (28-day months), the dates of these holidays constantly change in relation to the Gregorian calendar. In addition, numerous *Moussems* (religious festivals) are held throughout the year. Official public holidays include International New Year (1 Jan.), Throne Day (3 Mar.), Youth Day (9 July), Green March Day (6 Nov.), and Independence Day (18 Nov.).

Morocco

Commerce. A weekly *souk* (open-air market) is held in nearly every town. For rural residents, it is often the only source of basic foods, clothing, crafts, household items, and personal services such as haircutting. Urban residents have access to many shops and stores and can shop on a daily basis if necessary. A very basic convenience store called a *hanoot* is found in most areas. Almost all shops and offices close for about three hours during lunch. In the summer, government and bank offices often skip the three-hour break and close early to avoid the worst of the heat.

SOCIETY

Government. Morocco is a constitutional monarchy, but King Muhammad VI has broad powers as head of state. He appoints the prime minister (currently Driss Jettou) and retains authority to dissolve the legislature or revoke its decisions. The legislature has a 270-seat upper house (Chamber of Counselors) that can cast a no-confidence vote against the prime minister or overturn legislation from the 325-seat lower house (Chamber of Representatives). Counselors are indirectly elected to nine-year terms by an electoral college of local leaders and professionals. Representatives are directly elected to five-year terms. Elected regional councils have authority and funding to conduct some development projects. The voting age is 21.

Economy. Agriculture is the backbone of the economy, employing about 40 percent of the labor force. Most agricultural production is carried out by subsistence farmers, but a small modern sector produces enough food to account for 30 percent of all export earnings. Morocco has the world's third largest deposit of phosphate, which accounts for about 20 percent of export earnings. Other significant industries are food processing, leather goods, textiles, construction, and tourism. Morocco's small manufacturing sector is growing. Morocco has a small stock market, one of the first in the Arab world.

About 15 percent of the labor force works abroad, primarily in western European countries such as Belgium, France, and Spain. The money these workers send back to Morocco helps offset the country's foreign debt. Chronically high unemployment, illiteracy, a large government bureaucracy, and inefficient state-owned industries remain challenges to Morocco's economy. The currency is the Moroccan *dirham* (MAD).

Transportation and Communications. Paved roads connect all major cities and provide excellent access to the rest of the country. Public buses and interurban taxis are available almost everywhere. Rural people walk, ride bicycles or motorcycles, or use mules when carrying loads. Urban dwellers use the public transit system. Seven airports offer national service. A rail system connects the major cities of the north.

The government provides basic telegraph, telephone, and postal services throughout the country. Service is considerably better in urban areas than in rural regions. There are two television stations; the government-owned station broadcasts nationwide, while the private station serves major urban areas. Two national radio stations and eight regional stations serve the country as well. Newspapers are common, though several have been banned; the government tolerates little criticism of its policies. Many Moroccans use shortwave radios and satellite television to listen to news or watch shows from other countries. Internet access is growing; internet cafés are found in all major cities and some towns.

DEVELOPMENT DATA
Human Dev. Index* rank . . . . 125 of 177 countries
  Adjusted for women . . . . 100 of 144 countries
Real GDP per capita $3,810
Adult literacy rate . . . . 63 percent (male); 38 (female)
Infant mortality rate . . . . 43 per 1,000 births
Life expectancy . . . . 67 (male); 70 (female)

Education. Since the 1980s, the government has devoted considerable resources to improving Morocco's education system. And while the adult literacy rate is low, literacy among the youth (ages 15–19) is rising due to government efforts to build schools and train teachers. Still, less than two-thirds of all eligible children actually attend school. Many cannot afford it. Only 20 percent of rural women are literate. Girls and rural children are less likely than boys and urban residents to attend school. Of those who begin primary school, about 60 percent go on to secondary school. Preschool offers religious and patriotic instruction. The primary (six years) and secondary (seven years) levels are patterned after the French system; instruction is in Arabic. Private school instruction is usually in French. Students who complete secondary education may seek further education; there are 13 universities and many colleges and training institutes.

Health. Morocco lacks a comprehensive national healthcare system, but the Ministry of Health is trying to provide services to every region of the country. Each province has at least one hospital and some clinics, but these generally do not meet the needs of the entire population. Facilities are severely limited in rural areas. Rural women often will not go to a hospital or clinic because there are no female doctors or nurses. While water in urban areas is usually potable, rural water supplies are not as clean.

AT A GLANCE

Events and Trends.
- Reforms to Morocco's family law came into effect in 2004. Advocated by King Muhammad VI, the reforms include granting women greater property rights, raising women's legal minimum age of marriage from 15 to 18, making it easier for women to obtain a divorce, and increasing the stringency of the requirements that permit a man to practice polygamy.
- Islamic militants launched a series of suicide bombings in Casablanca in May 2003. The attacks killed 45 people, including 12 bombers. In the year that followed, the Moroccan government arrested an estimated two thousand people under anti-terrorism laws.
- A free trade agreement between Morocco and the United States came into effect in July 2004. The U.S. government also named Morocco as a major ally in its war on terror.

Contact Information. Embassy of Morocco, 1601 21st Street NW, Washington, DC 20009; phone (202) 462-7979.

CultureGrams™
People. The World. You.

ProQuest Information and Learning Company
300 North Zeeb Road, P.O. Box 1346
Ann Arbor, Michigan 48106 USA
Toll Free: 1.800.528.6279
Fax: 1.800.864.0019
www.culturegrams.com

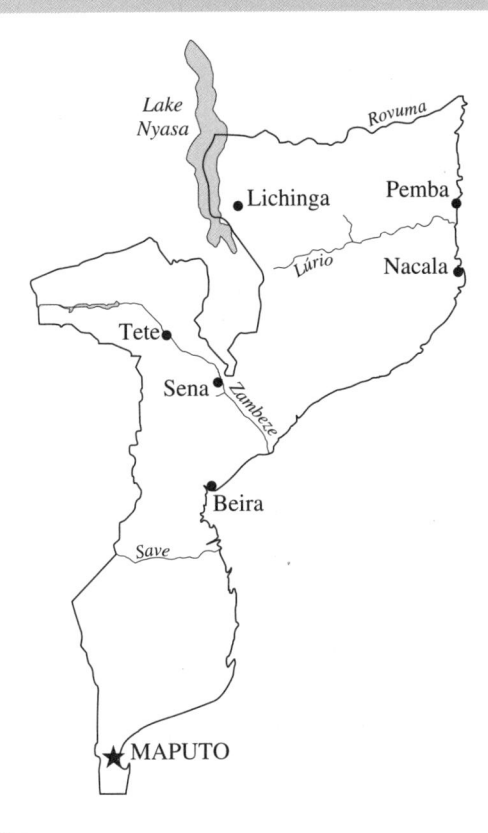

Republic of Mozambique

CultureGrams World Edition 2006

BACKGROUND

Land and Climate. Located on the southeast coast of Africa, Mozambique covers 309,574 square miles (801,590 square kilometers). It is nearly twice as big as California. Coastal plains cover some 44 percent of the territory. High plains (700–3,000 feet, or 200–900 meters) dominate the north and central regions. Mountains and very high plains above 3,000 feet cover 13 percent of the land. The highest peaks are Monte Binga (7,992 feet, or 2,436 meters), Monte Namuli (7,936 feet, or 2,419 meters), and Serra Zuira (7,470 feet, or 2,277 meters). Of the country's 60 or so rivers, the largest include the Zambeze, Rovuma, Lúrio, and Save. Only 20 of the nation's 1,300 lakes are larger than 6 square miles (10 square kilometers).

Mozambique has a tropical climate; the southern plains are the most humid. The Zambeze Valley is somewhat drier but still has a tropical climate. The north and center tend to be hotter than the south, where temperatures average 75°F (24°C). Above 3,000 feet, the average temperature falls to 64°F (18°C). The vegetation is mostly dense forest and savanna.

History. Mozambique's first inhabitants were the Khoi-khoi and the San. Very little is known about them except that they were hunters and gatherers. Sometime around A.D. 300, Bantu tribes migrating to the area brought agriculture and iron with them. Arab and Asian traders made contact with local groups as early as the seventh century; Arab trading posts flourished along the coast for many centuries.

By the 11th century, the Shona Empire (centered in present-day Zimbabwe) had established regional dominance. Their trading empire lasted until about the 15th century. The Maravi from the Great Lakes region invaded in the 13th century, and the Karanga Empire was established in the 15th century. New waves of immigration in the 18th century brought Tsongas, Yao, and Nguni to Mozambique. The Nguni came from the south and established the Gaza Empire. By the time Portuguese explorer Vasco de Gama reached the coast in 1498, Mozambique was home to various peoples with complex political, social, and economic systems.

By 1530, the Portuguese had expelled the Arabs from Sena and built various trading forts of their own; they made Mozambique a regular port of call for their ships. Most internal areas remained outside Portugal's control despite repeated incursions. Over time, Portuguese influence expanded to include political and economic control of these interior areas. In 1752, Portugal proclaimed Mozambique a colony and engaged in a flourishing slave trade. Many slaves, often sold by African tribal chiefs to Portuguese traders, were bound for plantations in Brazil.

Though outlawed in the 19th century, slave trading continued until 1912. Beginning in the late 19th century, the Portuguese shifted much of Mozambique's administration to private companies mostly controlled by the British. These companies enacted a policy of forced labor called *chibalo*. Workers were paid low wages and forced to work in fields to generate exports for the Portuguese; these workers were also required to build roads and railways to service Portugal's trade links.

Portuguese settlements expanded in the 1900s, especially after World War II. In 1960, during a protest in Mueda against *chibalo*, the provincial governor ordered soldiers to fire on the crowd. Six hundred people died and the massacre galvanized opposition to Portuguese rule. Several political groups organized under the banner of the Front for the Liberation of Mozambique (FRELIMO), led by Eduardo Mondlane. In 1964, FRELIMO began warring against Portuguese colonial

Mozambique

rule. Mondlane was assassinated in 1969 but remains an important national hero.

Portugal suffered heavy financial and troop losses fighting FRELIMO, and the war was partly responsible for the fall of Portugal's government in 1974. Portugal's new government negotiated the Lusaka Accords in 1974 with FRELIMO, which paved the way for independence in 1975. Ninety percent of the 200,000 or so Portuguese residents fled.

FRELIMO declared one-party Marxist rule under President Samora Machel. Civil war ensued. Southern Rhodesia and later South Africa supported the Mozambican National Resistance (RENAMO). The brutal war and then famine in the 1980s led to countless deaths and the destruction of Mozambique's economy.

Machel died in 1986 and was succeeded by Joaquim Chissano. Peace talks led to amnesty (1988) for RENAMO fighters and a cease-fire in 1990. Further negotiations led to a peace accord in 1992 between President Chissano and RENAMO leader Afonso Dhlakama.

Multiparty elections in 1994 gave Chissano the presidency by a thin margin over Dhlakama, and FRELIMO gained a narrow majority in the National Assembly. The government reformed its policies and embraced a market economy. Investment poured in from South Africa and elsewhere and people began to rebuild their country. Peaceful elections were held again in 1999 and again Chissano beat Dhlakama in the presidential race. After 18 years in power, Chissano declined to run for another term in 2004. He chose Armando Guebuza to succeed him as the FRELIMO candidate. Vowing to continue the economic reforms of his predecessor, Guebuza defeated Dhlakama in the December 2004 poll.

THE PEOPLE

Population. Mozambique's population of about 18.8 million is growing at 1.2 percent annually. The population is young; more than 40 percent is under 15 years old. Most people (80 percent) live in rural areas. Maputo, the capital and largest city, has about two million residents.

Nearly all Mozambicans are of African origin. The north is the land of the Makwa-Lomwé, who comprise about one-third of the population and follow a matrilineal social structure. Between the Zambeze and Save rivers are the Shona-carangas, divided into various subgroups. The Tsongas dominate southern Mozambique and have a patrilineal structure. Smaller groups include the Shangana, Chope, Manyika, and Sena; the Maravi in Tete; the Nguni in the south; the Makonde in the far north; and the Asians and Europeans, who control the formal economy.

Language. Portuguese is Mozambique's official language and is used in government, education, and business. English is also prominent in the business world. Most Mozambicans speak neither Portuguese nor English but communicate in their native languages, including Emakwa, Xisena, Xitsonga, Xitswa, Ciyao, Cishona, Chuwabo, Cinyanja, Shikamonde, Cinyungue, Cicopo, Bitong, and Swahili. Each of these Bantu tongues is very expressive and melodic; words end in a vowel. Many people speak more than one language to aid in cross-cultural communication.

Religion. Most Mozambicans adhere to indigenous animist beliefs, even if they also profess a major world faith. Islam is common in the north and along the coast, claiming membership among 20 percent of the total population. Some 30 percent is Christian. At least half of the people exclusively follow traditional practices, which include a belief in witchcraft and ancestor veneration. If a person becomes ill or has bad luck, the situation is often attributed to a lack of attention toward the ancestral spirits. *Regulos* (traditional chiefs) and *Nhangas* (traditional healers, or witch doctors) have great influence over people in local matters; witch doctors are called *Mukulukhana* in the north.

General Attitudes. Mozambicans respect people who are hospitable and kind. While most people have few material possessions, they consider themselves rich in family associations. The family is considered society's most valuable institution. Parents frequently refer to their children as "my first fortune" or "my second fortune," and so on. Parents hope to achieve a good education for their sons.

Even society is seen as a family, and concerns or needs of the group are more important than individual desires. A generation gap has formed with the spread of Western values through formal education, music, and media. Younger people think of older people as too conservative, and the older generation feels the youth have become alienated from their traditional or national values. South of the Save River, wealth is measured by the possession of cattle. Those who own cattle are greatly respected and admired. In the north, productive plantations are the symbol of wealth.

Personal Appearance. Mozambicans are clean and well-groomed in public. Women wear skirts and blouses or dresses, as well as jewelry such as bracelets and earrings (especially in the north). Married women usually wear a *capulana* (wrap-around skirt) tied about the waist and a head scarf. In the north, a man who cannot provide his wife with at least one *capulana* each year is not considered deserving of her respect. Northern women typically wear two *capulanas* with a matching blouse. The *capulana* (in the north and the south) not only protects against dirt and wind but is also a symbol of respect. Women use *muciro* (beauty cream), made from grated plant stems mixed with water, to cleanse and beautify their faces. Urban women may wear pants, shorts, and T-shirts, which is daily attire for men. In large cities, government and office workers may wear a suit or the more traditional *balalaica* (two-piece safari suit), *goiabeira* (square-cut, embroidered shirt that is not tucked in), or *bubu* (long, loose-fitting shirt with open collar, worn over pants).

CUSTOMS AND COURTESIES

Greetings. In formal settings, people greet one another with the Portuguese expressions *Bom dia* (Good day), *Boa tarde* (Good afternoon), and *Boa noite* (Good evening). They address others as *Senhor* (Mr.) and *Senhora* (Mrs.). If asked *Como está?* (How are you?), a person replies *Estou bem, obrigado* (Fine, thank you). For women, "thank you" is *obrigada*. Otherwise, people greet in their local languages according to situation and the relation between speakers. Men shake hands; close friends and women kiss each other on the cheek. When northern men and women meet each other, they clap hands three times before saying *Moni* (Hello). Urban youth greet informally with *Tudo bem?* (How's it going?) or a colloquial version of "Hi" (*Olá*, *Oi*, or *Alo*).

Rural people and even many urban residents often greet elders respectfully with *Bom dia mama fulana* (Good morning, dear Mother) or *Bom dia papa fulano* (Good morning, dear Father). In southern areas, greetings include inquiries about family, work, and other matters, and they may last several minutes. A younger person addresses an elder as *Tio* (Uncle) or

Tia (Aunt), even if they are not related. Peers call each other by first name or nickname.

Gestures. Generally, it is impolite to use the index finger for pointing. People receive and pass objects with both hands or the right hand alone. During conversation, Mozambicans do not place hands in pockets or look elsewhere. It is poor manners to speak to seated adults while standing. Young people may greet or say good-bye with the "thumbs up" gesture. An extended arm with the palm facing up is used to indicate the height of a person; a palm turned down indicates the size of animals. People nod to agree and shake their head to disagree. Public displays of affection are inappropriate, although friends of the same sex may hold hands while talking or walking.

Visiting. Families visit each other on weekends, particularly Sunday. Most casual visits are unannounced, and hosts expect to welcome anyone who comes by. However, in some cases a guest will announce a visit in advance so the hosts can prepare. Where phones are not available, a note or a child may be sent ahead to inform the hosts.

In northern rural areas, visitors approach a home and call out *Odi! Odi!* (May I come in?). They are welcomed with the answer *Héé!* The southern call is the same, but the answer is *Hoyo-hoyo!* (Welcome!). In cities, visitors knock on the door or ring the doorbell. Hosts offer their visitors something to eat and drink whenever possible. Guests bring gifts only for birthdays, a new baby, or some other festive occasion. For funerals, one takes money to help with family expenses. Funerals, weddings, and other major family events are extremely important and not to be missed.

Eating. Mozambicans start the day with *mata-bicho* (breakfast): tea with bread, sweet potatoes, manioc, or tapioca. If these are not available, they eat leftovers. Rural people eat with the fingers of the right hand. Urban people generally prefer to eat with utensils, although they may also eat certain foods with the hand. Families eat around a table or a mat. When working in the fields, men usually eat separately from women. If guests are present, they receive the first or best portions of food. Meals are prepared on wood or charcoal stoves in many areas, but gas and electricity are common in cities.

LIFESTYLE

Family. Extended families are usually very large and live together even if space and resources are limited. Family members rely on one another to share resources and to help in time of need. Children are taught to respect their elders. Men who practice polygamy are supposed to provide a separate hut for each wife and her children. In many cases, several wives will have their houses close together and will share household duties. Children may be disciplined by any adult family member. A man is head of a family and provides it with financial support. When a father dies, the oldest son is responsible for the family's welfare. A woman raises her children and oversees their education. She also cares for the household and garden. Girls help their mother with chores beginning at an early age; they are often promised in marriage by age 12 and can be married soon after that. Boys look after cattle and attend school. HIV/AIDS is widespread; children orphaned by the disease are cared for by their grandparents or oldest uncle.

Dating and Marriage. Dating is uncommon outside cities and is expected to lead to marriage. In most ethnic groups, young people pass to adulthood through initiation rituals, during which they are taught about their future roles as mothers and fathers.

Among groups in the south, a groom pays a *lobolo* (brideprice) in the form of cattle or cash to the parents of the bride before the wedding. This is to compensate them for raising her. If a *lobolo* is too high, a couple might live together in a de facto marriage without a formal ceremony, but such a union is not legally recognized. Traditional wedding celebrations include as much dancing and feasting as the families can afford. Christians often marry in a church. Muslims also have traditional ceremonies.

Diet. The staple foods for most Mozambicans are rice and a paste made from sun-dried cereals, usually cornmeal (called *upsa* or *xima*). Some people eat manioc meal as well. The country is rich in vegetables, which are eaten every day. Favorites include *cacana mboa* (pumpkin leaves), *nhangana* (leaves of *nhemba* beans), and *mathapa* (manioc leaves). Tropical fruits are abundant and eaten as snacks or desserts. Peanuts and coconuts are often served with vegetables. When possible, people include beef, fowl, fish, and seafood in their diet. In the north, beef and fish are often eaten dried. Traditional drinks are made with a fruit base, meal, and fermented sugarcane molasses.

Recreation. Both men and women enjoy sports in Mozambique, and soccer is by far the most popular sport. Rural children frequently lack access to a real soccer ball, but they play soccer with balls they can make from plastic material, sand, and/or old clothing. Many people enjoy basketball and volleyball, including beach volleyball. The wealthy may swim and play tennis. Some play roller hockey. Most Mozambicans like to go to the beach. *Ntchuva* and *murawarawa* are strategy games played on a board with 18 to 32 holes and two seeds in each. Rules differ, but the overall object of the games is to collect the most seeds.

Urban residents dance in discotheques. Men get together to drink at someone's home or a public bar. Women like to sing and dance; they may sing together when they do chores or cook. Traditional dancing provides amusement for everyone, and dance competitions are popular among different regions.

The Arts. Traditional arts vary by region and ethnic group. Music and dance are an integral part of most Mozambican communities' religious observances, festivals and celebrations, and entertainment. Artisans create ancestral masks and statuettes, often carved in ebony, for both decorative and religious purposes. Other folk arts include making clay sculptures and jewelry, and body tattooing.

The nation has produced a number of renowned artists. Painter Malangatana Valente Nguena helped preserve Mozambique's cultural identity throughout the struggle for independence and the civil war. He was instrumental in the establishment of the National Museum of Art and Center for Cultural Studies. Poet José Craveirinha was regarded as a national hero for his support of the independence movement and his efforts to promote African values and culture.

Holidays. Public holidays include New Year's Day, Day of Heroes (3 Feb.), Day of the Mozambican Woman (7 Apr.), Labor Day (1 May), Independence Day (25 June), Day of the Lusaka Accords (7 Sept.), Day of the Armed Fight (25 Sept.), and the Day of the Family (25 Dec.). People also celebrate local harvest festivals, at which the presiding elder calls on the ancestral spirits to bless all. Food and drink are symbolically offered to the spirits, and then everyone joins in a feast. Song and dance are always part of the event.

Commerce. Formal business is conducted Monday to Saturday, 8 a.m. to 6 p.m., except on Mondays, when most stores

Mozambique

open only in the afternoon. The official market, some grocery stores, and fish markets open Sunday mornings until 10 a.m. or noon. Rural villagers shop at open-air markets for basic goods.

SOCIETY

Government. The Republic of Mozambique is a multiparty democracy. Candidates are directly elected by popular vote. Coalition governments are formed when a party does not have a majority of votes in the legislature. The president (currently Armando Guebuza) is head of state and holds most executive authority. He appoints a prime minister (currently Luisa Diogo) from among members of the 250-seat National Assembly to serve as head of government. The president and members of the assembly serve five-year terms. The judicial branch consists of a Supreme Court and administrative, labor, customs, and maritime courts. The voting age is 18. Local leaders are village heads and appointed district administrators. Many cities also directly elect mayors.

Economy. More than 80 percent of Mozambicans are engaged in agriculture, especially farming and herding cattle. Fishing is also an important livelihood and industry. Export crops include cashews, tea, cotton, timber, copper, fish, and shrimp. Small-scale mining is found in some areas. Much industry centers on the processing of raw materials such as aluminum, iron, fertilizers, and cement. Sales of electric power generated by the Cabora Bassa Dam (one of the world's largest) are growing. After 1994, the government encouraged more private investment and foreign aid, and the government privatized more than nine hundred state institutions. Tourism, titanium and natural gas mining, and more hydroelectric projects are being developed. Challenges include expanding economic prosperity to areas other than around Maputo, relieving poverty, and curbing malaria and HIV/AIDS. Many Mozambicans work in South African mines and industry. The currency is the *metical* (MZM), a name derived from a gold measure used by Arabs before the colonial era.

Transportation and Communications. The average person travels on foot or by various forms of public transportation (buses, taxis, etc.). Only the wealthy own private cars. Traffic moves on the left. The existing highway system does not connect all regions of the country. Many roads are impassable every year in the rainy season. The best roads extend out from Maputo. Like the main roads, rail connections lead mostly to neighboring countries rather than to regions within Mozambique. Although the country has a long coastline with three major ports (Maputo, Beira, Nacala) and rich river basins, maritime and river transport are not well developed.

Two private television channels broadcast in Maputo, but public television reaches nearly every provincial capital. Broadcasts are in Portuguese. Radio broadcasts reach more people and use nearly all major languages as well as Portuguese. Provincial capitals and the main districts are connected by telephone via satellite. However, owning a phone is a luxury inaccessible to the majority of Mozambicans. People communicate via radio, letters, or word-of-mouth.

Education. Schooling is not mandatory. While two-thirds of eligible children enroll in elementary school, less than 10 percent pass to the secondary level. Fewer than one-third of adult women are literate; most rural women have no formal education. Urban children have greater access to schooling. Portuguese is the language of instruction in public schools. Since most rural children do not speak Portuguese when they begin school, it is difficult for them to learn fundamental skills in the early years. There are a growing number of private schools, mostly in Maputo, which are taught in English. Three universities and other advanced institutes provide higher education; they are concentrated in Maputo.

Health. A small fee is needed to access public health services. For those who can afford it, private service is available in public hospitals and at private clinics. Mothers and children receive free preventive care. Rural people may have to travel long distances to seek medical care. They turn to a traditional healer for many ailments.

Malaria, intestinal diseases, malnutrition, and tuberculosis are common. Leprosy and meningitis, as well as cholera, also threaten many people. More than half the population has no access to clean drinking water, so the government is working to turn water systems over to private management. One-fifth of all children die before they turn five. Mozambique has one of the highest rates of HIV/AIDS infection in the world; an estimated 12 percent of all Mozambican adults may be living with the disease.

DEVELOPMENT DATA

Human Dev. Index* rank .... 171 of 177 countries
Adjusted for women .... 139 of 144 countries
Real GDP per capita $1,050
Adult literacy rate .... 62 percent (male); 31 (female)
Infant mortality rate .... 137 per 1,000 births
Life expectancy .... 37 (male); 40 (female)

AT A GLANCE

Events and Trends.
- FRELIMO candidate Armando Guebuza won the December 2004 presidential election over opposition RENAMO leader Afonso Dhlakama with 64 percent of the vote. Dhlakama secured 32 percent. In the coinciding National Assembly elections, FRELIMO won 160 seats to RENAMO's 90. Guebuza is a popular figure in Mozambique, having been a leader of Mozambique's independence struggle as well as a key negotiator in the peace talks that ended Mozambique's long civil war in 1992.
- Hundreds of people gathered for the burial of poet José Craveirinha at a monument to national heroes in Maputo following his death in February 2003. A national day of mourning was declared.

Contact Information. Embassy of Mozambique, 1990 M Street NW, Suite 570, Washington, DC 20036; phone (202) 293-7146.

Republic of Namibia

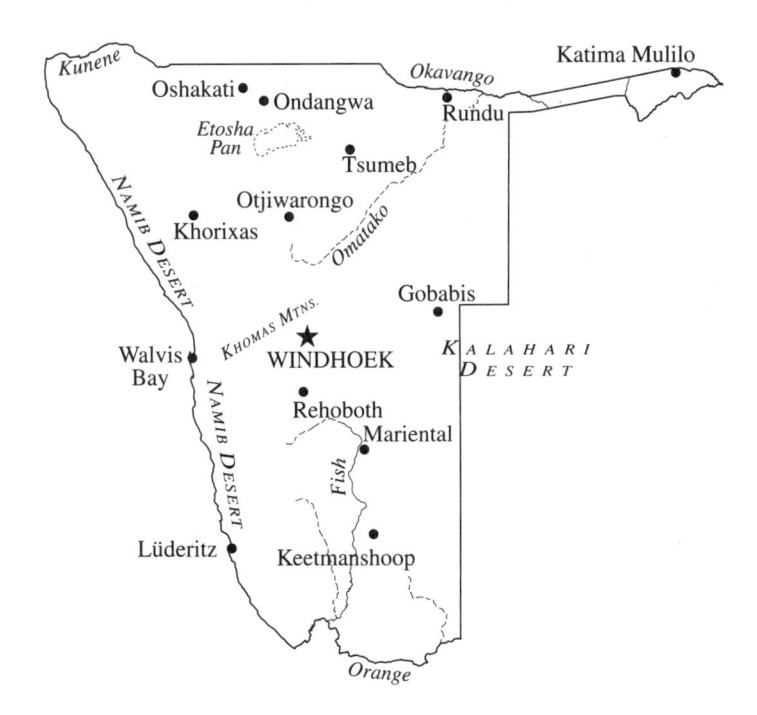

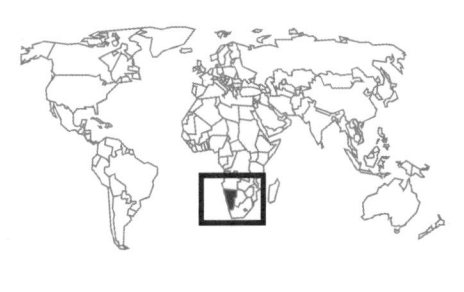

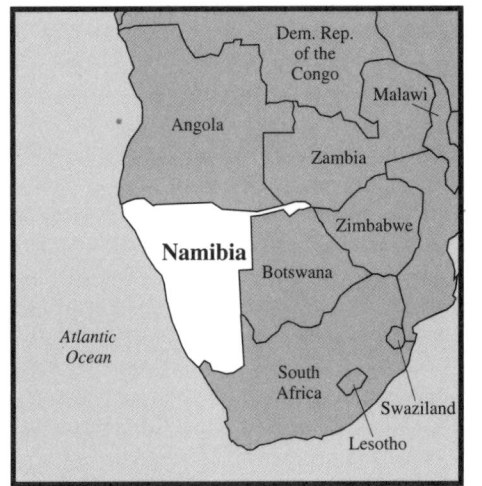

BACKGROUND

Land and Climate. Namibia, covering 317,816 square miles (823,144 square kilometers), is the driest country in sub-Saharan Africa. Two deserts flank its central plateau: the Kalahari to the east and the Namib along the western coast. The coast is usually foggy and cool because of the Benguela Current, a cold ocean current off the west coast of southern Africa. The central plateau covers about half of Namibia, rising abruptly from the desert to an elevation of over 3,300 feet (1,000 meters). The Fish River Canyon is among the largest canyons in the world. In the north, *iishana* (Oshiwambo word for temporary water holes caused by flooding in the rainy season; singular, *oshana*) support subsistence agriculture, livestock, and wildlife. Namibia's abundant wildlife population includes elephant, lion, giraffe, antelope, and rhinoceros. Etosha National Park encompasses the largest *oshana*, which covers some 1,900 square miles (5,000 square kilometers). *Omurambas* (dry riverbeds) are also a distinctive part of the Namibian landscape.

A short rainy season from mid-October to November is followed by a longer rainy season from January to April. Rains are sporadic and unpredictable. The rest of the year is extremely dry, with daytime temperatures around 104°F (40°C). Winter temperatures can get cold in central and southern regions but not below freezing. Temperatures in the north rarely reach below 50°F (10°C), and then only at night.

History. Several ethnic groups inhabited present-day Namibia before German colonization. Early nomadic tribes came under pressure from migrating Bantu-speaking peoples more than 2,300 years ago. Later migration waves of other groups from the north and south forced the earliest groups (Bushmen, Khoisan, and others) east toward the Kalahari. Descendants of these original inhabitants comprise five or six distinct tribal groups. Though once collectively referred to as "San" (a derogatory term) or "Bushmen," these people today prefer to be called by their specific tribal names. Other groups to settle in the region over the centuries include the Owambo, Herero, Nama, Damara, and Rehoboth Basters.

In 1884, Namibia became a German colony called South West Africa. Defeated in World War I, Germany lost authority over Namibia in 1920. The League of Nations gave Britain a mandate to prepare South West Africa for independence. The British turned administration over to South Africa. By 1946, South Africa claimed to annex the region and ignored UN protests. South Africa instituted apartheid (segregation) and confined each tribal group to a homeland or to "townships" on the outskirts of urban centers.

By 1957, the South West Africa People's Organization (SWAPO) had emerged as a leading multiracial force to oppose South Africa's occupation. SWAPO guerrillas began with isolated attacks in 1966, and fighting eventually (in the 1980s) became a large-scale war against South Africa's Defense Forces. Under pressure and upon losing key battles, South Africa withdrew in the late 1980s. It retained Walvis Bay, a deep-sea port, until March 1994. Independence was formally recognized on 21 March 1990.

Elections in 1989 gave SWAPO a mandate to form a new government, and SWAPO leader Sam Nujoma became Namibia's first president. The popular Nujoma won reelection in 1994 and secured a third term in 1999 after the legislature changed the constitution's limit on presidential terms from two to three. Nujoma stepped down prior to November 2004 elections, which SWAPO candidate Hifikepunye Pohamba won

Namibia

decisively. Pohamba took office in March 2005, widely expected to continue the policies of his predecessor in addressing the nation's key issues of poverty, unemployment, land reform, and a severe HIV/AIDS epidemic.

THE PEOPLE

Population. Namibia's population of more than 1.9 million grows by about 1.3 percent per year. Population density is very low, and more than half of all people live in the north. About 42 percent of the population consists of people younger than age 15. Windhoek, the centrally located capital, has about 200,000 residents. Less than 30 percent of the population lives in urban areas.

Namibia's many peoples were once classed into 11 ethnic groups, but many do not consider themselves part of their "assigned" category. The Owambo are classified as the largest ethnic group; statistics estimate they make up roughly half of the population. Other groups include the Kavango, Herero, Himba, Nama, Damara, Caprivians, Bushmen, and Khoisan. Rehoboth Basters descend from intermarriage between Europeans (mostly Germans) and Khoisan. White Namibians (10 percent of the population) are mostly Afrikaners (descendents of Dutch settlers) but also include persons of German, British, or Portuguese descent.

Language. To help unify Namibians, the government chose English as its official language and language of instruction, while recognizing 10 "national languages" spoken by the major ethnic groups. Most Namibians speak at least two indigenous tongues as well as English or Afrikaans, the official language before independence. The Owambo speak any of eight or more dialects of Oshiwambo. The Kavango speak five related languages; RuKwangali is the most dominant. The Herero and Himba speak Otjiherero. The Nama speak Nama and the Damara speak Damara, but these two are so closely related they are listed as Nama/Damara. The majority of Caprivians speak SiLozi, and the largest Bushmen groups speak Ju/'hoan. Nama/Damara and Ju/'hoan are Khoisan languages. Coloureds, Rehoboth Basters, and most whites speak Afrikaans. Many people speak German, especially in the city of Swakopmund.

Religion. German missionaries introduced Christianity in the 1800s and most people consider themselves Christian. However, traditional beliefs such as spiritual healing, witchcraft, magic, and ancestor veneration are still important in many people's lives. Indigenous beliefs coexist with Christian worship practices because they tend to apply to different aspects of a person's life. Lutheran and Catholic churches have the largest followings, but Anglican, the Seventh-day Adventist Church, and other congregations are also active. Most Afrikaners belong to the Dutch Reformed Church. Throughout the week, Namibians are openly religious: schools begin the day with prayer and hymn singing, and official ceremonies and meetings open and close with prayer.

General Attitudes. Because Namibia is a young and evolving nation, and because its citizens are of widely diverse ethnic and cultural backgrounds, it is difficult to describe general attitudes or shared attributes. Nevertheless, some common ground exists in important areas: most Namibians value family, education, good manners, hospitality, and hard work. Individual success (in higher education, government, business, etc.) brings honor to the entire family. Namibians respect high status, as defined by old age, wealth (often measured in livestock), political power, advanced educational degrees, and service to one's people. Government workers have high status, as do teachers and shop owners. In rural areas, clan names carry great weight. For many Namibians, it is improper to try to make oneself seem better than one's peers or family. It is better to allow praise to come from one's colleagues or family members. People avoid open confrontation.

Namibians have a strong capacity to forgive. A national reconciliation campaign helped heal the wounds of war, and people once on opposite sides of the war for independence live peacefully together in their communities. Namibians are more interested in forging a peaceful future than on gaining revenge for past wrongs.

Personal Appearance. Most Namibians wear Western-style clothing, although pan-African styles are becoming popular among the educated elite. Urban women wear skirts and trousers, but in rural areas long skirts are the norm. In both rural and urban areas, men usually wear trousers and dress shirts. It is important to have a clean and neat appearance. Clothes are ironed, with creased collars and pleats. Shirts are tucked in. Namibians dress up for Sunday church services. Children wear uniforms to school. Urban youth follow some U.S. fashion trends.

Herero women often wear Victorian-style dresses made with between 13 to 45 yards of fabric that form a large bell-like skirt over as many as nine underskirts. A shawl and a large matching hat complete the outfit. Some older Damara women wear a similar dress. German missionaries introduced the Victorian dresses to replace more revealing native attire.

CUSTOMS AND COURTESIES

Greetings. Greetings are essential to all human interaction. They show respect and recognize one's presence and value. To not greet someone is to disregard them. Men usually greet with a strong handshake. One always shakes with the right hand; the Owambo also place the left hand on the right elbow. Eye contact among equals shows sincerity. Women greet men and women by shaking hands, but they may kiss or hug close female friends.

There are as many different greetings as there are languages and situations. In one major Oshiwambo dialect, one says *Walalapo Nawa* (Good morning) and *Ngepi Nawa* (Good afternoon). *Moro* (Good morning) is the Otjiherero version of the Afrikaans greeting *Môre*. The Nama/Damara say *Matisa!* (How are you?).

One addresses a superior or high government official by title. Elders with high titles can be called *Sir* or *Madame*. Older Owambo are called *Meme* (for women) or *Tate* (for men). Individuals might be called by their family name; friends may use nicknames or first names.

Gestures. Namibians use hand motions for various reasons. For instance, a hitchhiker bends a hand up and down at the wrist to hail a ride. If a possible ride is full, the driver might pound a fist on the other hand or place a flat hand over a fist. Twirling a finger in a circle means the driver is not traveling far. A person forms a "V" with the middle and index fingers to show support for the Democratic Turnhalle Alliance (DTA), a political party. A right fist held up in the air is the symbol for SWAPO. Pointing two fingers to one's eyes is used when one wants the listener to pay attention. It is considered rude to point the sole of one's foot at someone or put one's hands in pockets while addressing an elder. Public displays of romantic affection are not common, but family members or friends of the same gender often hold hands in public.

Visiting. Visiting among family and friends is an integral part of life, even for relatives who live far apart. Frequent visits maintain friendships and are reciprocated. It is rarely necessary to prearrange informal visits. Punctuality is usually not strict. Hosts serve guests coffee, tea, or *cool-drink* (any soft drink or juice). Guests stay at least an hour. A rural visit often occurs outdoors, usually in the shade of a tree. If hosts offer food, it is impolite for guests to refuse it. Whole families participate in visiting, but children are sent away to play after they have greeted the adults. Sunday is the most important visiting day. Friends may visit after church, and relatives often gather for a hearty midday meal. Bad luck is expected to come to a family that is not sufficiently visited after the birth of a new baby or after a move to a new home.

Eating. Although urban residents eat with Western utensils, rural people more often eat with the right hand. This is especially true of children. Urban Namibians usually eat three meals a day. Businesses and schools often close for the lunch hour so people can eat at home.

In rural areas, people may eat only two meals a day. Breakfast might include bread and tea or coffee, or millet porridge. Namibians typically pray before midday and evening meals. Plates are prepared ahead of time in the kitchen and served all at once. Hosts give their guests the best treatment possible. Restaurants are too expensive for most Namibians. *Take-away* (take-out) food is reasonably priced and found in every town.

LIFESTYLE

Family. Rural Namibians live in extended family groups, often in the same village. Ties are strong, even though migration to urban areas has separated many families. All members must contribute to the betterment of the family through monetary support, good behavior, and even by having a baby. Adult family members work hard and give everything they can to the children for a good start in life. In turn, grown children are expected to support their elders. Families function as a group, even among urban residents, who tend to have nuclear households. Rural Namibians often visit urban relatives and may stay for long periods of time. It is common for a niece, nephew, or younger sibling to stay with an urban relative to attend a better school, look for work, or help care for small children. Urban families likewise try to visit their rural home often. As more people migrate to cities and stay with relatives, the tradition of wealth-sharing is coming under heavy pressure to change.

Both urban men and women often have jobs. Children live at home until married. Many children are raised by their grandparents or other relatives, especially as more women enter the workforce. Most rural women maintain traditional roles, which involve raising their children and farming or herding. Rural women have broad responsibilities, especially if their husbands have migrated to urban areas in search of work.

Dating and Marriage. Traditionally, a young man asked a young woman's parents permission to date her. However, urban young people now openly congregate in groups, and youth meet at dance clubs or school functions. In northern rural areas, girls and boys meet secretly. Among some groups, if a young couple is seen in public, they are assumed to be courting and are expected to marry. Rural women might marry younger than age 18, but most young people marry between the ages of 20 and 30. A married man often has one or more girlfriends. If he has a child by a girlfriend, it belongs to him and he usually gives it to his mother to raise.

Marriage customs are changing but some traditions remain strong. For some groups, a couple's parents must ritually agree to a proposed marriage; they will be called on to resolve future marital problems. In many Namibian cultures, the groom must pay *lobola* (bride-price) in the form of cattle or money to the bride's parents before a wedding can take place. Traditional wedding celebrations involve much dancing, a huge feast, and traditional music. Church weddings are followed by a reception at the bride's home or in a reception hall. Many couples have common-law marriages (no ceremony). Polygamy is acceptable in some rural areas.

Diet. Rural families grow their own staple crops such as maize, sorghum, and *mahangu* (millet). Rice is popular in urban areas among those who can afford it. Processed foods are imported from South Africa and are expensive. A typical meal includes *mealie meal* (cornmeal porridge) or *mahangu*, some sort of soup or sauce, and some meat when possible. Beef, chicken, and mutton are popular. People buy goats or sheep and slaughter them at home. *Biltong* is a jerky-like meat snack. Rural Namibians also eat seasonal wild fruits and nuts. *Braais* (barbecues) and *potjiekos* (pot food) are traditional ways of cooking. *Potjiekos* is any meal cooked in a three-legged cast-iron pot over a fire. Fish is available when the *iishana* flood, and boys use slingshots to bring down small birds. Tea and coffee are served throughout the day, when guests come, and with every meal.

Recreation. The most popular sport for men is soccer, followed for some by rugby, basketball, and track-and-field. Women play netball. This sport is similar to basketball except that dribbling the ball is not permitted, so the ball must always be passed up the court. Visiting and socializing are the most common leisure activities. An informal neighborhood *shabeen* (bar) is a popular spot for drinking beer, dancing, and listening to music.

The Arts. Namibian music differs according to ethnic group and region. *Lang Arm* (literally, "long arm"), or waltz music, was introduced to Namibia by the Germans and has become entwined in the traditions of the south. Northern music is more rhythmic in nature and involves African drums and three-part harmony singing. Music from other parts of Africa, such as Congolese-style *kwasa kwasa*, is also popular. Dance clubs can be found in all towns and in some rural areas. Children learn to sing early, and music plays a part in most aspects of life. Each ethnic group has its own traditional arts. Examples include Herero dolls, Owambo baskets, Caprivian wood carvings, and Nama ostrich shell jewelry.

Holidays. Holidays do not necessarily have the same meaning for all Namibians. For example, on Heroes' Day (26 Aug.) the Owambo mark the beginning of the armed resistance to South Africa, while the Herero honor ancestors killed by German colonizers. Public holidays include New Year's Day, Independence Day (21 March, celebrated with dance competitions, fireworks, and concerts), Easter, Workers' Day (1 May), Cassinga Day (4 May, honoring all SWAPO war dead and marking a massacre of eight hundred refugees during the war), Africa Day (25 May), Ascension, Human Rights Day (10 Dec.), Christmas, and Family Day (26 Dec.). The Day of the African Child (16 June) is not a public holiday but marks the 1976 slaying deaths of children in Soweto, South Africa.

Commerce. Private business hours vary. Urban banks usually are open from 9 a.m. to 4 p.m. and 9 a.m. to noon on Saturday. Urban Namibians shop at modern stores and supermarkets, but rural inhabitants have access to only a few basic goods. South

Namibia

African companies control most commerce and own most large businesses.

SOCIETY

Government. Namibia's president (currently Hifikepunye Pohamba) is head of state and head of government. The president appoints an executive cabinet, which is led by a prime minister. The legislature's upper house is the National Assembly, which consists of 72 elected representatives and 6 nonvoting representatives appointed by the president. The lower house is the 26-seat National Council, with two representatives from each of the country's 13 regions. The president and members of the National Assembly are elected to five-year terms. The voting age is 18.

Tribal chiefs, who are highly respected, are responsible for settling local disputes and allocating rural land use (tribal land cannot be owned). These local chiefs are very important, but their position relative to the central government can be a source of serious friction.

Economy. The government is the largest employer of wage earners, but most Namibians are subsistence farmers or work in agriculture and fishing. Namibia exports cattle and smaller livestock, fish, and *karakul* pelts (sheepskin). The mining industry exports diamonds, uranium, and copper. Tourism is a major growth industry with great potential. Namibia relies heavily on South Africa's economy, and the Namibian dollar (NAD) is tied to the South African *rand* (ZAR). Namibia has an open market, but nearly all goods are imported from South Africa. Wealth and land ownership are highly concentrated. White commercial farmers own most arable land. The relatively high gross domestic product per capita reflects wealth from diamonds and white-owned businesses; the average Namibian may earn a fraction of that.

Transportation and Communications. Most Namibians do not own cars. Buses and taxis are available in Windhoek. Private and public buses offer service from Windhoek to larger towns on the main north-south highway. People walk or bike short distances and *hike* greater distances. *Hiking* refers to hitchhiking or traveling by crowded minibuses called *combies* that make frequent stops on fixed routes without schedules.

Less than 10 percent of all homes have telephones, but the ratio climbs to half for urban areas. Post office phones accept prepaid phone cards. Radio broadcasts reach virtually all areas and are therefore more important than national television. Broadcasts are made in all major languages, and radio is the major source of news, sports, personal announcements, and music. Namibia has six major newspapers. Internet access is improving.

Education. Namibian children attend school year-round, with breaks in May, September, and December through January. Most schools board students in hostels and provide all meals at school. Fees can be expensive and therefore can prohibit attendance by the poor; many youth are not able to progress beyond primary school. English is the language of instruction in secondary schools; national languages are used at the primary level. To graduate, students must pass difficult exams in grades 10 and 12. Higher education is provided by the University of Namibia, three colleges of education, three agricultural colleges, a polytechnic school, and various vocational schools. Many of Namibia's professionals were educated abroad. To improve literacy, access to secondary education, and overcrowded rural schools, the government has allocated one-third of the national budget to education.

Health. Private hospitals are too expensive for most people, and government hospitals are understaffed and overcrowded. Clinics are found in most towns, although villages often share a clinic a few miles away. Clinics provide prenatal care, immunizations, checkups, and the diagnosis and treatment of disease. Rural clinics are staffed by nurses; doctors, mostly foreigners, are available primarily in urban areas. They visit small towns weekly to see patients with serious problems.

Namibia's HIV/AIDS infection rate is one of the highest in the world; more than one-fifth of the nation's adult population may be living with the disease. A high number of people die from malaria. Other diseases (river blindness, schistosomiasis, ringworm) are present in various regions. Malnutrition becomes most serious in times of drought.

DEVELOPMENT DATA

Human Dev. Index* rank . . . . 126 of 177 countries
Adjusted for women . . . . 101 of 144 countries
Real GDP per capita $6,210
Adult literacy rate . . . . 84 percent (male); 83 (female)
Infant mortality rate . . . . 70 per 1,000 births
Life expectancy . . . . 44 (male); 47 (female)

AT A GLANCE

Events and Trends.

- Backed by outgoing president Sam Nujoma, SWAPO's Hifikepunye Pohamba won the presidency in November 2004 with 76 percent of the vote. SWAPO also won 55 of 72 seats in the National Assembly. Pohamba's inauguration in March 2005 marked the first transfer of power in the nation's 15-year history, although Nujmoa will still have considerable influence as the head of SWAPO. The party's power is based among the Owambo, Namibia's largest ethnic group.
- A bridge across the Zambezi River between Namibia and Zambia was opened in May 2004. The bridge is expected to increase trade in the region by allowing a continuous thoroughfare from Namibia's port at Walvis Bay, through Zambia, to the Congolese city of Lubumbashi.
- In 2004, the German government issued an apology for the killing of tens of thousands of ethnic Herero after their rebellion against German rule in 1904. Germany has not offered financial reparations for the killings, which some Herero had demanded.

Contact Information. Embassy of the Republic of Namibia, 1605 New Hampshire Avenue NW, Washington, DC 20009; phone (202) 986-0540.

© 2005 ProQuest Information and Learning Company and Brigham Young University. It is against the law to copy, reprint, store, or transmit any part of this publication in any form by any means without written permission from ProQuest. This document contains native commentary and original analysis, as well as estimated statistics. The content should not be considered strictly factual, and it may not apply to all groups in a nation. *UN Development Programme, Human Development Report 2004 (New York: Oxford University Press, 2004).

CultureGrams
People. The World. You.

ProQuest Information and Learning Company
300 North Zeeb Road, P.O. Box 1346
Ann Arbor, Michigan 48106 USA
Toll Free: 1.800.528.6279
Fax: 1.800.864.0019
www.culturegrams.com

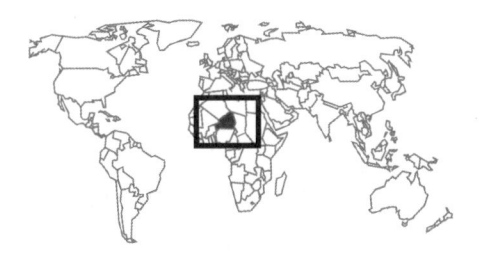

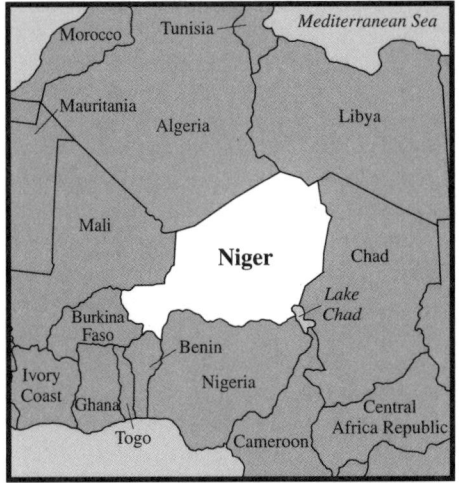

Republic of Niger

CultureGrams World Edition 2006

BACKGROUND

Land and Climate. Niger (nee-ZHARE), a landlocked country three times larger than California, covers 489,206 square miles (1,267,000 square kilometers). Four-fifths of it is part of the Sahara Desert. As the Sahara grows, droughts occur more frequently and last longer than in the past. Southern Niger is part of Africa's semiarid region called the Sahel, which receives rain and supports vegetation such as scrub brush and baobab trees. All of Niger's farming is done in the Sahel or near desert oases. The Niger River flows through the southwest, making this the most fertile region.

Niger is one of the hottest countries in the world, with average daily temperatures above 90°F (32°C) during the hottest months. From March to May, daytime highs soar above 110°F (43°C). It is a bit cooler in the rainy season (June–September). In the "cold" season (November–February), dry harmattan winds blow sand off the desert.

History. Nomads traversed Niger more than five thousand years ago, but little is known of their history. Tuaregs came from the north in the 11th century and established a sultanate in Agadez by the 15th century. Niger served as an important trading crossroads for mighty African empires, including the Songhai Empire of Gao in the 16th century. Even today, Tuareg caravans carry salt across the desert. In the 17th century, Djermas settled as farmers near present-day Niamey. Hausaland (southern Niger and northern Nigeria) became the site of a *jihad* (Muslim holy war) by the Fulanis in the early 19th century, which helped ensure Islam's presence in Niger.

Despite resistance by local groups (especially the Tuaregs) to French military incursions after 1890, Niger became a French colony in 1922. The French moved the capital from Zinder to Niamey in 1926. In the late 1950s, a fierce political struggle ensued over independence from France, which was finally granted in 1960. President Hamani Diori governed until he was ousted by a coup in 1974, when General Seyni Kountche assumed power. Kountche's regime was known for its stability and its success in reducing corruption.

With Kountche's death in 1987, Niger entered a lengthy period of political uncertainty under several successive national leaders. Kountche's Supreme Military Council first governed under General Ali Saibou. His rule proved unpopular and destabilizing, and a High Council of the Republic was convened by a national conference in 1991 to govern until 1993 elections.

The newly elected government under President Mahamane Ousmane faced a deteriorating economy, ethnic rebellions, and political rivalries. Elections in 1995 forced Ousmane to appoint his rival, Hama Amadou, as prime minister. Their rivalry paralyzed the government, leading to strikes and unrest. The military deposed both men and sponsored elections in 1996. Coup leader General Ibrahim Bare Mainassara was elected president by rigging the vote. His regime was known for corruption, repression, and incompetence. Protests, strikes, and even mutinies by unpaid soldiers plagued Bare. When he was assassinated by his own presidential guard in April 1999, no one protested.

Major Daouda Malam Wanka, head of the presidential guard, became president, lifted a ban on political activity, and announced elections for November 1999. In that vote, Mamadou Tandja was elected president. He was reelected in 2004 after becoming the first president to complete a full term in office since democratic elections were introduced in 1993.

Niger

THE PEOPLE

Population. Niger's population of 11.4 million is growing at 2.7 percent annually. More than 80 percent of Nigeriens live in rural areas. Niamey is the capital and largest city, with about half a million residents. About 56 percent of the population is Hausa. Other major groups include the Djerma (22 percent), Fulani (9), Tuareg (8), Kanouri (4), Toubou, and Gourmantche. The Hausa population centers on Zinder, although Hausaland stretches east nearly to Lake Chad and west nearly to Dosso. Djermas live mostly in the west, from Dosso to the coast. The Fulani and Tuareg tend to be seminomadic, though many Tuaregs can be found near Agadez and throughout the north. Prior to a 1995 peace accord, the Tuaregs waged a rebellion against several African states.

Language. French is the official language, but only about 10 percent of Nigeriens speak it. Many can speak Hausa, which is the primary language for communication and trade between ethnic groups in the east. In the west, Djerma and French serve this purpose. Ten languages have official recognition in Niger: Arabic, Boudouma, Djerma, Fulfulde, Gourmantchema, Hausa, Kanouri, Tamachek, Tasawak, and Toubou. Many people are multilingual.

Religion. More than 90 percent of Nigeriens are Muslim. They believe Muhammad was the last and greatest of history's prophets. The *Qur'an* (Koran), or scripture of Islam, is composed of revelations from *Allah* (God) to Muhammad. Muslims show devotion by following the Five Pillars of Islam: praying five times daily while facing Makkah, Saudi Arabia, giving money to the poor, fasting during daylight hours for the month of *Ramadan* (*Azumi* in Hausa), professing there is no God but *Allah*, and trying to make a once-in-a-lifetime pilgrimage (*hajj*) to Makkah. Men and sometimes women dress in white to visit a mosque on Friday afternoon to pray and worship. Women who go to mosque (usually elderly women) pray in a different area, but most pray at home or in the fields. Hausaland and the east are more conservative than the west. Children memorize Arabic verses written with charcoal on wooden boards at local *Qur'anic* (Koranic) schools. Islam plays a key role in major life events such as naming ceremonies (for seven-day-old babies) and funerals. Animist practices are often mixed with Islamic rites. A few cities have Christian churches.

General Attitudes. Nigeriens patiently accept life as it comes. They often end sentences with *Inshallah* (Arabic for "God willing") to indicate matters are out of their hands. This allows them to be stoic in the face of frequent hardships. Still, they laugh and joke often, and they rarely display real anger in public, especially when it involves personal matters. Proverbs are used in everyday conversation. People often encourage each other to "have patience" (*Sai hankuri* in Hausa). Time is flexible; events and appointments do not necessarily begin on time. Personal achievements are not emphasized in this group-oriented society. Nigeriens tend to identify first with family, followed by their village, ethnic group, and religion before the nation. Social status is based on age, wealth, or job title. Chiefs are accorded great respect in villages. Superiors can ask lower-status persons to run errands or do other favors for them.

Personal Appearance. A clean and modest appearance is extremely important to Nigeriens. Men wear *boubous* (long robes over drawstring pants) or a shirt-and-pant "suit" of matching material. Most men wear small embroidered caps. Formal dress usually includes a *boubou* with extensive embroidery. Tuareg men wear large indigo, green, or white turbans that cover the entire face except the eyes, while Tuareg women reveal their faces. Women wear a *pagne* (colorful wraparound skirt) with a matching tailored blouse and a headscarf. Married women wear an extra *pagne* around their shoulders or waist, and they may use it to carry children on their backs. Women elaborately braid their hair and wear jewelry. Some urban women wear Western-style clothing. Adults do not wear shorts. Many people wear secondhand clothing (such as T-shirts and jeans) from Europe or the United States. Young children or teens in various ethnic groups receive distinctive facial scars in elaborate ceremonies. The wounds are rubbed with ash to make them darker.

CUSTOMS AND COURTESIES

Greetings. Proper greetings come before any conversation, and it is rude to not greet someone—even a passing stranger. Initial phrases are followed by inquiries about health, family, work, or the weather. The greeting depends on the season and time of day. For example, in Hausa, *Ina kwana?* (How did you sleep?) is appropriate in the morning, but *Ina ini?* (How did you pass the day?) is for the afternoon. A response to either is *Lahiya lau* (In health). Responses are always positive; one admits to illness or bad times only after the greetings are over.

Nigerien men shake hands upon meeting and parting. The handshaking may continue until all greetings are exchanged. To show special respect, one might touch the upper chest with one's right hand and return to the handshake. It is polite to shake the hand of every adult at a small gathering. For large groups, one may instead raise the hands to chest level, palms out, and give a verbal greeting. Traditional Muslim men do not shake hands with women. Some urban Nigeriens may greet with a kiss to each cheek. In the east, Kanouris greet by shaking a closed fist at head level and calling *Wooshay! Wooshay!* (Hello! Hello!).

Nigeriens rarely call each other by given name. People can be addressed by job title. For example, a taxi driver would be called *mai mota* (person with the car). The elderly are called *tsohoa* (old woman) or *tsoho* (old man). A Muslim who makes a pilgrimage to Makkah earns the title of *el hadj* for men or *hadjia* for women. In most other settings, nicknames dominate. A nickname can be related to an event in a person's life, the day of week on which one was born (*Juma* is Friday), or one's relationship to another person (*Mamadou nya* is "Mamadou's mother"). Women cannot say their husband's name, even if referring to someone else with the same name, and adults do not address their in-laws directly. A deceased person's name is not spoken.

Gestures. Nigeriens eat or pass items with the right hand or both hands; the left hand alone is reserved for personal hygiene. Flicking the five fingers out in an openhanded gesture is insulting. To indicate "five," one brings all the fingertips of the hand together. To beckon, one waves the fingers of the right hand, palm facing down. One can also get a person's attention by snapping the fingers or hissing. Students snap their fingers rather than raise their hands to signal the teacher. One can point by puckering the lips in the indicated direction. To indicate approval or agreement, Nigeriens make a clicking sound deep in the throat or they may rapidly suck in air. Personal space is limited except between members of the opposite sex. Men and women do not hold hands in public or otherwise display their affection. However, male friends often hold hands. Traditionally, only people of equal social standing make extended eye contact. Younger people look down to show respect.

Visiting. Visiting someone's home is a sign of respect. Invitations are rarely issued; people are expected to drop in. When they approach a home, they signal their presence by clapping and calling out *Salaam Aleikum* (Peace to you). The hosts respond with *Amin Aleikum Salaam* (Come in peace) and the guests enter and remove their shoes. Hosts offer the best seat and something to drink. They usually also offer *hura*, a drink made of millet flour mixed with water and sometimes spices, milk, or sugar. Visitors bring gifts if staying the night. Typical gifts include *goro* (kola nuts), dates, peanuts, onions, fruit, or soap. Women and men socialize separately, even in the home. In public, women socialize at the market or the well, and men meet at the mosque or market.

Tea is an important custom for Tuaregs, Fulanis, and others. At least three rounds of tea are served. Sugar and mint are added each time to make the strong tea progressively sweeter. To describe the three rounds, Nigeriens use the phrase "Strong like life, subtle like friendship, sweet like love." Made in small blue teapots over coals, the tea is served in very small cups. Leaving before all rounds are finished is impolite. After a visit, it is polite for the host to accompany guests out the door a ways or even to walk them home.

Eating. Meals are served in a communal bowl and eaten with the right hand or a spoon. Nigeriens generally drink after, not during, the meal. The main meal, which may be in the afternoon or evening, often consists of *tuwo* (a thick, gelatinous millet paste) and a spicy sauce. Rural men and women eat separately, sitting on woven mats. Urban men and women eat together at a table. An urban breakfast may consist of bread and coffee, but a rural breakfast is generally leftovers from the day before. Snacks include peanuts, sugarcane, fruit, spiced cabbage or hibiscus leaves, and millet or bean cakes. People also chew kola nuts. No one eats in front of another person; food is always shared.

Restaurants vary from a table on a street corner to expensive indoor restaurants in large cities. Women usually prepare food sold on the street, but only men eat in public. Men selling cooked meat walk through the cities, balancing a tray on their heads. Women sit by open fires making *kosai*, a deep-fried bean cake, or doughnutlike *beignets*.

LIFESTYLE

Family. The family structure dominates Nigerien culture. Children must respect their parents. Older people are highly honored and must be obeyed by younger people. The elderly commonly live with their adult children. Children are seen as belonging to the entire community and they may be disciplined by neighbors or friends. Wealthier persons are expected to share with and help the extended family, no matter how distant their relationship.

Gender roles are rigidly defined. Women cook, clean, collect firewood, draw each day's water from the well, and care for the children. Both men and women work in the fields. Men maintain structures (homes, fences), provide food for the family, and buy clothing for them before major holidays. In areas where men cloister their wives (keep them from public view), the men shop in the market. The husband is the head of the family. Muslim men may have as many as four wives, and animists can take more. Each wife has her own hut within a walled family compound. The husband spends time with each wife in rotation. Wives take turns cooking for all. The more wives a man has, the more important he is considered to be. However, young men are moving away from this tradition because of the financial responsibility and other challenges. Polygamy is less common among the urban educated. Homes are thatched or made of mud bricks. Common family activities often take place under a thatched roof in a corner of the compound.

Dating and Marriage. Dating is not common in villages, though young people interact in the evening when girls dance in the village center. Urban youth may meet at social events such as dances or weddings. In rural areas, marriages are typically arranged by the family, but people can suggest their mate or decline a family's choice. The groom's parents pay an elaborate dowry to the bride's parents as part of the agreement. Village girls often marry in their teens (around 15) and boys between 18 and 25, while urban people marry later. It is not proper for a woman to be unmarried. Traditional weddings include feasting, dancing, and drumming. Various customs are employed to bring the bride and groom together. In some areas, the bride must identify (in the spirit of fun) one of two hooded men as her husband. In other places, a veiled bride is taken by camel to the groom's house. Elsewhere, a bride runs away the night before the wedding and must be retrieved from a friend's house by her future husband and his escorts. In divorce, children remain with the father.

Diet. Millet, sorghum, beans, and corn are staple foods throughout the country; rice and macaroni are additional staples in urban areas. All are eaten with sauces often made from okra, baobab leaves, peanuts, tomatoes, and spices. Yams, potatoes, lettuce, carrots, and tomatoes are available in the cold season. Fruits such as mangoes come in the hot season. Goat is the most common meat, but mutton, chicken, and camel are available. Meat is usually reserved for special occasions. *Hura* (millet drink) and *tuwo* (millet paste) are prepared daily. Most families drink *hura* for lunch and eat *tuwo* with a tomato or okra sauce for dinner. *Kilshi* (spiced beef or sheep jerky) and *brochette* (like a shish kebab) are popular foods. Food is scarcest in the rainy season before the new harvest.

Recreation. Traditional dancing, known as *tam-tam*, is popular in the villages; drummers play so that young women can dance. Spectators place coins on the foreheads of the dancers they prefer. The money drops to the ground and is swept up by the drummers' apprentice for their pay.

Women and men rarely spend leisure time together. For all Nigeriens, visiting is the most popular form of recreation. Women socialize when pounding millet, braiding hair, or (on special occasions) painting intricate designs on their hands and feet with henna. Boys like soccer. Men enjoy traditional wrestling. The Tuaregs have camel races. Urban men go to outdoor movie theaters to see karate and Indian romance films. Men have more leisure time and mobility than do women.

The Arts. Nigerien artisans carve animals, human figures, and kitchen utensils using materials from their surroundings, such as wood and cow horn. Stringed instruments, bowls, and containers are made from decoratively painted dried gourds. Textile arts also thrive, especially *kunta* (fabric strips sewn together forming geometric patterns) and *batik* (a resist-dye process). *Kunta* is often woven into blankets, which are given as wedding presents and kept as family heirlooms. A national cooperative has been formed to promote local artisans and their work. Tuaregs are noted for their exquisite silver jewelry. Many of these items are produced for the tourist market.

Holidays. Nigeriens celebrate New Year's Day, Reconciliation Day (24 Apr.), Independence Day (3 Aug.), and the Proclamation of the Republic (18 Dec.). For Independence Day, people plant trees to combat increasing desertification. School holidays are taken at Christmas and Easter.

Niger

The Islamic lunar calendar is used to set religious holidays, such as Muhammad's birthday (*Mouloud*). *Karamin sallah*, or "little feast," comes at the end of *Ramadan*, a month in which Muslims do not eat or drink during daylight hours. *Tabaski* (40 days after the *Ramadan* feast) commemorates Abraham's willingness to sacrifice his son. On *Tabaski*, also called *Babban sallah*, or "big feast," a sheep or goat is slaughtered and shared with friends. People dress up and visit family and friends, who thank the visitors with dates, nuts, or special candy.

Commerce. Business hours are from 8 a.m. to 6 p.m., but government and private stores close from noon to 3 p.m. for *sièste*, a break to escape the afternoon heat. Markets remain open during *sièste* and are themselves a social event; people dress up, meet friends, and chat at the market. In the evening, roadside tables offer everything from batteries to cookies. Store prices are fixed, but bargaining is expected in the market. Water is purchased daily from men who pass in the streets balancing large buckets on a pole across their backs. Village markets are held weekly, but women often sell food daily. Post offices provide banking services.

SOCIETY

Government. Niger's president (currently Mamadou Tandja) is chief of state and head of government. The president and members of the 83-seat National Assembly are elected to five-year terms. The prime minister (currently Hama Amadou) is appointed by the president. The voting age is 18. Men and women stand in separate lines; a husband may cast his wife's vote if she wishes. Most large cities, including Zinder, Tahoua, and Agadez, have sultans who hold office based on lineage. Villages often have a chief who is chosen by birth and ability. The central government ultimately makes most decisions, but on the local level the word of a sultan or chief carries great weight. Disputes are often resolved by going to a respected elder or chief. Villages have leaders for neighborhoods (in large villages), women, young men, the fields, and so on.

Economy. Niger is one of the world's poorest countries. Uranium accounts for 60 percent of all exports. Other industries, though minor, include cement, brick, textiles, chemical production, and slaughterhouses. About 90 percent of the population is engaged in subsistence agriculture and herding. Primary crops are millet, cowpeas, peanuts, sorghum, cassava, and rice. Animals raised include cattle, sheep, goats, camels, donkeys, horses, and poultry. Most wage earners work for the government, but they might go months without a paycheck because the government has so little money. The private sector is growing slowly as state enterprises are privatized. Young village men go to work for wages in neighboring countries (called *l'Exode*, or "exodus") and return to Niger during the rainy season. Niger receives international aid and imports most consumer items. It uses the currency common to francophone African countries, the *CFA franc* (XOF).

Transportation and Communications. Only major highways and city roads are paved. Highways connect Niamey to Nguigmi in the east and Agadez in the north. Only wealthy Nigeriens own cars. People often walk long distances to visit relatives and friends or to gather firewood and haul water. They may also use a motorcycle, moped, or bicycle, or ride a donkey or camel. A national bus line serves major routes, but most people cover large distances by "bush-taxis" (*taxis de brousse*). "Bush-taxi" cars carry 8 to 10 passengers (vans hold 17–25); they leave when full, so no schedule is definite. Every city has an *autogare*, a central gathering point for these taxis, usually near the market. Villagers ride "bush-taxis" to the weekly market, and the cars or vans often become loaded with livestock, grains, and other goods. During the taxis' frequent stops, vendors sell goods and snacks to passengers through the windows. Taxis also stop for prayer times.

Few Nigeriens have telephones, but they can communicate via word-of-mouth or radio. Television is often watched outdoors, where it is cooler, and is powered by car batteries in villages without electricity. A government newspaper and several independent papers operate.

Education. The school system is based on the French model. Students must pass difficult exams to advance from primary school to junior high and then high school, and they often must travel to larger villages to attend secondary schools. French is the language of instruction, which makes learning difficult for primary school children who have never spoken it before. Some alternative schools use local languages for instruction. Enrollment in primary school is mandatory, but only about one-fourth of students actually go. In rural areas, more boys than girls attend school. Teachers may strike for months when they are not paid. For many families, *Qur'anic* schools are a more vital part of education. There is a university in Niamey.

Health. Malnutrition, malaria, meningitis, and measles are all serious problems. Even "minor" problems like diarrhea may be deadly due to lack of proper medical care. Only the largest cities have hospitals, and there is a shortage of trained health-care workers. Larger villages may have a dispensary (clinic). Most people cannot afford the small fees and see the dispensary as a last resort anyway: they turn first to herbal medicine. Midwives attend village births.

DEVELOPMENT DATA

Human Dev. Index* rank . . . . 176 of 177 countries
  Adjusted for women . . . . 144 of 144 countries
Real GDP per capita $800
Adult literacy rate . . . . 25 percent (male); 9 (female)
Infant mortality rate . . . . 123 per 1,000 births
Life expectancy . . . . 46 (male); 46 (female)

AT A GLANCE

Events and Trends.

- In December 2004, President Tandja won a second term by taking 65 percent of the vote in a second-round election runoff against opposition candiate Mahamadou Issoufou.
- In 2003, the government of Niger refuted a claim made by the U.S. and British governments that Iraq had attempted to buy uranium from Niger for weapons production. The authenticity of documents that led to the controversial claim was later discredited.

Contact Information. Embassy of Niger, 2204 R Street NW, Washington, DC 20008; phone (202) 483-4224.

Federal Republic of Nigeria

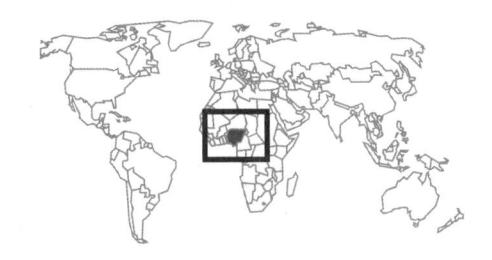

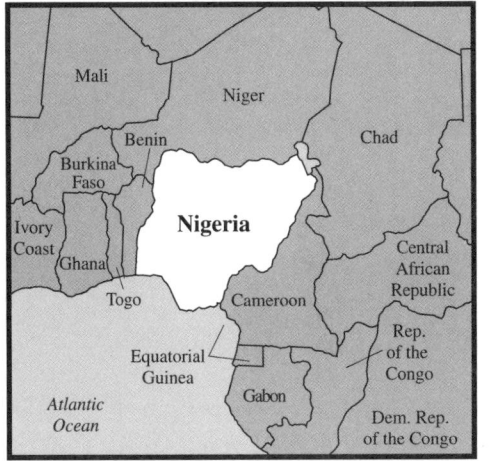

CultureGrams World Edition 2006

BACKGROUND

Land and Climate. Covering 356,668 square miles (923,770 square kilometers), Nigeria is about the same size as California, Nevada, and Utah combined. Its geography is as diverse as its people and culture. About 30 percent of the land is suitable for cultivation; 15 percent is covered by forests or woodlands. Desert areas are found in the far north. The country also features the grassy plains of the Jos Plateau in the north-central region, sandy beaches and mangrove swamps along the coast, and tropical rain forests and parklands in the central region.

Nigeria is divided into three areas by the Niger and Benue rivers, which meet and flow together to the Gulf of Guinea. These three regions (north, southwest, southeast) correspond roughly to the boundaries of the three largest ethnic groups (Hausa, Yoruba, Ibo). Where the three rivers flow into the Atlantic is called the Delta Region, the source of most of Nigeria's oil. The country's climate in the north is dry; the rainy season is from April to October. In the south, the climate is hot and humid year-round.

History. Nigeria, with its many ethnic groups, has a rich and diverse history that stretches back to at least 500 B.C., when the Nok people inhabited the area. Various empires flourished in different regions for centuries. The Hausa, who live in the north, converted to Islam in the 13th century and established a feudal system that was solidified over time. The Fulani built a great empire in the 1800s. In the southwest, the Yoruba established the Kingdom of Oyo and extended its influence as far as modern Togo. The Ibo, located in the southeast, remained relatively isolated.

At the end of the 15th century, European explorers and traders made contact with the Yoruba and Benin peoples and began a lucrative slave trade. The British joined the trade in the 1600s but abolished it in 1807. Most slaves taken from this region were shipped to North and South America as opposed to Europe. Although no European power had as yet colonized the area, British influence increased until 1861, when Britain declared the area around Lagos a crown colony. By 1914, the entire area had become the Colony and Protectorate of Nigeria.

When Nigeria became independent in 1960 (a republic in 1963), tensions began to rise among the various ethnic groups. After two coups and much unrest, the Ibo-dominated eastern region attempted to secede and establish the Republic of Biafra. Two and a half years of civil war (1967–70) followed, and the Ibo were forced back into the republic after more than one million people died.

National elections in 1979 established a representative civilian government, but it lasted only until late 1983, when a military coup gave General Mohammed Buhari control. He banned political parties. In 1985, Major General Ibrahim Babangida overthrew Buhari. He later promised civilian rule by 1992. Elections between two officially approved parties occurred in 1991. In preparation for democracy, the capital was moved from Lagos to Abuja in 1991.

National elections were held in June 1993. However, once it was apparent that Chief Moshood Abiola (a Yoruba) would win, Babangida refused to accept the results. He annulled the election and rioting broke out in many cities. After a power struggle, Babangida resigned. His rival, General Sani Abacha, seized power from the interim government.

Abacha dissolved democratic institutions and declared himself ruler of Nigeria. Human-rights abuses, corruption, and oppression became Abacha's hallmarks. Strikes and unrest failed to force him from power. International pressure even

Nigeria

failed to stop the 1995 execution of nine activists who had campaigned against oil industry damage to Ogoni lands. The Commonwealth suspended Nigeria's membership.

Abacha promised a return to democracy by the end of 1998 but allowed only five loyal parties to register in legislative elections. He then ordered all five parties to nominate him as their presidential candidate.

When Abacha died of a heart attack in June 1998, the nation celebrated and then waited to see whether his successor, General Abdulsalam Abubakar, would follow in his footsteps. Abubakar released political prisoners and fired Abacha loyalists. In July 1998, he agreed to release Chief Abiola and he reaffirmed his desire to eventually turn power over to a civilian government. Abiola died of a heart attack on the eve of his release. This prompted new chaos and ethnic-based violence. When calm was restored, opposition leaders renewed calls for the military to step aside in favor of civilian rule.

Unlike past military rulers, Abubakar kept his promise to hold free and fair elections beginning with local polls in December 1998. Legislative and presidential elections followed in February 1999. Olusegun Obasanjo, former military leader in the 1970s, was elected president and his People's Democratic Party (PDP) won a majority of parliamentary seats. A new constitution based on the 1979 constitution became law as Obasanjo took office in May 1999. The new president pledged to fight corruption, and the Commonwealth restored Nigeria's membership and lifted sanctions.

Unfortunately, the atmosphere of greater democracy unleashed simmering grievances between various regions, ethnic groups, and religions. Thousands have been killed in fighting between Christians and Muslims, between Yoruba and Hausa, and between ethnic groups in the Delta Region. Northern, Muslim-dominated states have enacted policies to implement *shari'a* (Islamic law) in order to enforce morality and other Islamic values, angering these states' Christian minority. Activists in the Delta Region often attack oil refineries and workers to demand a greater portion of oil revenue. Obasanjo, reelected in 2003, has been unable to reduce these long-standing tensions.

THE PEOPLE

Population. Nigeria's population of 137.3 million is growing at an annual rate of 2.5 percent. The country is home to more than 250 ethnic groups, the largest of which include the Hausa (21 percent of the population) and Fulani (9) in the north, the Yoruba (20) in the southwest, and the Ibo (17) in the southeast. Each ethnic group has a distinct cultural heritage. Other smaller groups, such as the Ogoni, comprise the remaining 33 percent of the population.

The primary groups in the Delta Region include the Ijaw, Itsekeri, and Urhobo. Ijaws and Itsekeris have been fighting violently over land rights and oil revenues, while they and others also target (with terrorism and kidnapping) Western oil companies and the government over the same issues. Under the 1999 constitution, a greater share of oil revenues is to remain in the region, and resources are to become more balanced on a national basis. Progress with these policies has prompted violence by groups that stand to lose influence and power with greater equality and democracy.

Language. More than 250 languages are spoken in Nigeria. English is the official language, although less than half the population can actually speak it. Many consider English a foreign language. Pidgin English (a combination of basic English and local languages) aids communication between people of different ethnic groups; it is often used in casual conversation. Each ethnic group has its own distinct language. Hausa, Yoruba, Ibo, and Fulani are widely spoken. In various regions, people speak their own ethnic language and then the language of the area's largest ethnic group. Educated Nigerians are often fluent in several languages.

Religion. Nigeria is divided primarily between Muslims and Christians. The north is mostly Muslim, and the southeast is primarily Christian. About half the residents of the southwest are Muslim; half are Christian. In all, about 50 percent of Nigerians are Muslim and 40 percent are Christian. Nigerians who follow traditional African belief systems exclusively (10 percent) are spread throughout the country. Many Christians and Muslims also incorporate indigenous African worship practices and beliefs into their daily lives.

Central to Muslims is their belief in the *Qur'an* (Koran) as the word of *Allah* revealed to the prophet Muhammad. They show devotion through the Five Pillars of Islam: professing that there is no God but *Allah* and Muhammad is his prophet; praying five times daily while facing Makkah, Saudi Arabia; giving money to the poor; fasting from dawn to dusk during the holy month of *Ramadan*; and making a pilgrimage to Makkah once in a lifetime, if possible.

As part of the 1999 constitution, the predominantly Muslim northern states have the option of establishing *shari'a* courts to handle certain cases. The states have interpreted that to mean *shari'a* can be the governing force in most local matters, a policy opposed by Christians and others.

General Attitudes. Individual Nigerians tend to identify first with their ethnicity, next their religion, and then their nationality. This helps explain the difficulty in uniting them or in solving disputes. Educated Nigerians avoid using the word "tribe," preferring "ethnic group"; however, the average person is not insulted by the word "tribe" when discussing ethnicity. People take great pride in their heritage. In addition to the Delta clashes, tensions exist between various groups due to their traditional spheres of influence, as well as past conflicts. For instance, the Ibo control some oil areas and are still bitter about the Biafra War; in 2000, some revived a call for independence. Yoruba tend to control the press and financial sector; they often led pro-democracy protests in the 1990s. The Hausa have held political and military control since independence. Obasanjo, a Yoruba, has his support base among the Hausa because of his past military ties.

Northerners tend to be quiet, reserved, and conservative in dealing with others. To them, raising the voice indicates anger. Southerners are more likely to be open and outgoing. They enjoy public debate and arguing. They may often shout to make a point or attract attention; shouting does not necessarily indicate anger. Daily life in Nigeria moves at a relaxed pace. Schedules are not as important as the needs of an individual.

Personal Appearance. Dress varies according to the area and culture, but dressing well is important for all Nigerians. Northern Muslims dress conservatively. Attire is more casual and more Western among the Ibo. Most people prefer traditional African fashions to Western clothing, although T-shirts and pants are worn in urban areas. Traditional men's clothing is loose and comfortable. Shirts typically extend to the knees. Women and young girls usually wear a long wraparound skirt, a short-sleeved top, and a scarf. Nigerian fabrics are known for their bright colors and unique patterns. Nigerian fashions are popular in other African countries.

Nigeria

CUSTOMS AND COURTESIES

Greetings. In Nigeria, greetings are highly valued among the different ethnic groups. Neglecting to greet another or rushing through a greeting is a sign of disrespect. Therefore, people are courteous and cheerful when exchanging greetings. Because of the diversity of customs, cultures, and dialects in Nigeria, English greetings are widely used throughout the country. Nigerians use *Hello* but perhaps not as often as *Good morning*, *Good afternoon*, and *Good evening*.

After the initial greeting, people usually inquire about each other's well-being, work, or family. The appropriate response is usually *Fine*, but one listens to this response before proceeding with the conversation. Personal space between members of the same sex is limited, and Nigerians may stand or sit very close when conversing.

Gestures. Because Nigeria is a multicultural nation, gestures differ from one ethnic group to another. Pushing the palm of the hand forward with the fingers spread is vulgar and should be avoided. Hausa do not point the sole of the foot or shoe at another person. Most people pass objects with the right hand or both hands but usually not the left hand alone. Yoruba often wink at their children if they want them to leave the room when guests are visiting. People beckon by waving all fingers together with the palm facing down.

Visiting. Visiting plays an important part in maintaining family and friendship ties. It is common for Nigerians to visit their relatives frequently. Unannounced guests are welcome, as planning ahead is not possible in many areas where telephones are not widely available. Hosts endeavor to make guests feel comfortable and usually offer them some refreshments. Invited guests are not expected to bring gifts, but small gifts are appreciated. For social engagements or other planned activities, a starting time may be indicated, but guests are not expected to be on time. Late guests are anticipated and they do not disrupt the event.

Eating. Eating habits depend on one's ethnic group and social status. Some Nigerians eat their meals with the hand (right hand only), while others use utensils. Hands generally are kept above the table. Families try to eat at least the main meal together, although in some traditional families men eat separately from women and children. Most people wash their hands before eating. Invited guests are expected at least to try any food that is offered. Eating while walking is considered rude. Tipping is common in restaurants and for most personal services.

LIFESTYLE

Family. The family is a source of strength and comfort for Nigerians. Extended family networks are very important. In general, Nigerian families are male dominated. However, women are active in politics and do earn nearly one-third of the nation's income. Polygamy is not uncommon. By Islamic law, a Muslim male can have as many as four wives with the consent of the other(s), provided he can care for each wife equally. Many non-Muslim Nigerians also practice polygamy. While the sheltered status of Muslim women in Nigeria is similar to that of other Islamic countries, most non-Muslim Nigerian women enjoy a great degree of freedom, both in influencing family decisions and in openly trading at the marketplace. About one-fifth of the labor force is female. Large families traditionally share the workload at home. Nigerians have deep respect for their elders. Children are trained to be unassertive, quiet, and respectful in their relations with adults.

Dating and Marriage. Western-style dating is uncommon in rural areas, but it is practiced by some urban youth. In Muslim areas, a person may be punished (flogged) for immorality. Marriage customs vary, but the payment of a bridal token or dowry is common throughout the country. The groom is expected to give money, property, or service to the family of the bride. Women usually marry by the time they are twenty and men marry in their midtwenties. Living together without a formal marriage ceremony is common and socially acceptable in the south. Many couples find a wedding to be too expensive. Some northern governments provide subsidies to help such couples have a wedding and avoid violating *shari'a*.

Diet. The mainstays of the Nigerian diet are yams, cassava (a starchy root), and rice. Yoruba are fond of hot, spicy food. Their meals normally are accompanied by a pepper sauce made with fish, meat, or chicken. Climatic conditions provide for a wide selection of fruits and vegetables to supplement the diet. Because of the tsetse fly, dairy cattle are scarce in coastal regions, but canned margarine, cheese, and powdered milk are used as dairy-product substitutes. The Fulani who herd cattle have dairy products, and they eat yogurt (and sell it mixed with millet and sugar).

Recreation. Nigerians primarily enjoy soccer, although the wealthy also like wrestling, polo, cricket, and swimming. Nigerians are extremely proud of their national soccer team, which has been successful in international competitions and won the gold medal in the 1996 Summer Olympics. Nigerians do not have access to working movie theaters, but they watch videos and television. U.S. productions are most popular. Live theater and art exhibits are well attended by the educated elite. Rural women have little time for recreation, but they socialize while doing chores or fixing hair. Men are more likely to spend time talking or drinking with one another. In many areas, visiting is the primary leisure activity. Nigerians also enjoy traditional music and dance.

The Arts. Nigerian music often combines Western and traditional elements. Derived from Ghanaian *highlife*, Nigerian *juju* incorporates guitars with the *dundun*, known as the "talking drum" because its tones can be understood as words. *Fuji* music has no guitars but uses several drums. Dancing commonly accompanies both *juju* and *fuji*.

Nigeria's painters and sculptors use modern techniques while drawing from indigenous themes. Among Nigeria's many folk arts are soapstone and wooden statuettes. Wooden masks are used in traditional religious ceremonies. Nigerian writers have received international recognition; among the most prominent are Chinua Achebe and Nobel Prize recipient Wole Soyinka.

Holidays. National holidays include New Year's Day, Labor Day (1 May), and National Day (1 Oct.). In addition, Christian and Muslim holy days are celebrated by the entire country. Muslim holidays are determined according to the lunar calendar, which is shorter than the Western (Gregorian) year by about 11 days. Since dates are set according to the moon's phases, the Gregorian dates for holidays differ from year to year. These holidays include *Maulid an-Nabi* (the prophet Muhammad's birthday), *Idul Fitr* (a three-day feast at the end of the month of *Ramadan*), and *Idul Adha* (the Feast of the Sacrifice). During *Ramadan*, families eat together in the evenings and visit friends. Christian holidays include Easter (Friday–Monday), Christmas, and Boxing Day (26 Dec.). Boxing Day is a day for visiting. It comes from a British tradition of giving small boxed gifts to service workers the day after Christmas.

Nigeria

Commerce. Most businesses are open from 8 a.m. to 1 p.m. and from 2 to 4 p.m., Monday through Saturday. Shops in the north close at 1 p.m. on Friday, the Muslim day of worship. Government offices usually close by 3 p.m. each day. Business is rarely discussed on the phone, and appointments are scheduled in advance.

SOCIETY

Government. The Federal Republic of Nigeria is composed of 36 states, each with elected governors and legislatures. The president (currently Olusegun Obasanjo) is head of state and head of government. According to the constitution, the president can serve a maximum of two four-year terms. Parliament consists of a 109-seat Senate (three seats for each state and one for the capital) and a 360-seat House of Representatives. Members of both chambers are elected to four-year terms. The voting age is 21.

Economy. Nigeria's economy is one of the largest in Africa and has great potential for high productivity, diversity, and vitality. Unfortunately, it has been battered by political turmoil, fluctuations in world oil prices, corruption, and poor central planning. Nigeria is one of the world's largest oil producers, but only a minority of the population actually benefits from oil revenue. Many Nigerians have no income or do not earn enough to meet their needs. Unemployment and inflation are high. Agriculture employs about 40 percent of the population. Nigeria is a major producer of peanuts. Other key crops include cotton, cocoa, yams, cassava, sorghum, corn, and rice. Rubber and cocoa are important exports. Petroleum accounts for 95 percent of all export earnings. In addition to oil-related and agriculture-processing industries, Nigeria has textile, cement, steel, chemical, and other industries. The currency is the *naira* (NGN).

Transportation and Communications. Nigerian cities are linked by roads, railroads, and air routes, but traffic is heavy on the roads, about half of which are not paved. People travel by bus in and between cities. Also common is the "bush-taxi," a crowded minibus that travels on a set route without a schedule. Nigeria's modern but poorly maintained telephone system is being expanded. Most newspapers are printed in English. There are several radio and television stations. Rural Nigerians rely on word-of-mouth and radio for information.

Education. Nigerians value education as the key to future success. Each of Nigeria's states provides primary and secondary education, and some offer higher education. While about 85 percent of all pupils complete the primary level, only 20 percent enroll in secondary school. This may be due to the fact that school instruction is in English. Children are required to grapple with a new language before they can even learn the skills they should acquire. By the time they are 12, most students perform poorly in both English and standard skills. A government program to promote the use of an area's dominant native tongue in primary schools was recently introduced in a few districts. The program is designed to give students basic skills first and introduce English later, but critics claim it will only add to ethnic tensions because not all of Nigeria's languages will be used in schools. In states with *shari'a*, boys and girls attend separate schools.

DEVELOPMENT DATA
Human Dev. Index* rank . . . . 151 of 177 countries
   Adjusted for women . . . . 122 of 144 countries
Real GDP per capita $860
Adult literacy rate . . . . 74 percent (male); 59 (female)
Infant mortality rate . . . . 70 per 1,000 births
Life expectancy . . . . 51 (male); 52 (female)

Although education for rural children is limited, government programs have doubled enrollment in some areas. Educational emphasis is on applied science and technology, with a goal to introduce more Nigerians into the skilled workforce. A considerable number of Nigerians attend universities around the world. Men are more likely to be literate than women.

Health. Less than 70 percent of the population has access to health care, and public hospitals are understaffed and poorly supplied. The best care is available at medical colleges. Private clinics are too expensive for most people. Facilities and care are inadequate in rural areas, and infant mortality remains relatively high. Twenty percent of all children die before they reach age five. Only two-thirds of all one-year-olds are immunized. Maternal mortality rates are among the world's highest. Tropical diseases present serious challenges for the people. AIDS takes more lives each year.

AT A GLANCE

Events and Trends.

- In February 2005, the Nigerian government initiated a program it hopes will triple the nation's cocoa production by 2008. Nigeria is currently the fourth-largest cocoa producer in the world. The program provides more than $1 million to establish more cocoa plant nurseries, buy farming chemicals, and encourage local cocoa processing.
- A longtime border dispute between Cameroon and Nigeria remains unresolved. A 2002 ruling by the International Court of Justice (ICJ) granted the oil-rich Bakassi Peninsula to Cameroon, but Nigeria failed to transfer the disputed region to Cameroon by the ICJ-mandated deadline in September 2004. The peninsula covers approximately 400 square miles (1,000 square kilometers) of territory in the Gulf of Guinea. Most of the roughly 300,000 residents want the area to remain part of Nigeria and have requested a referendum on the issue. Representatives of the two nations met in October 2004 but failed to reach agreement.
- President Obasanjo won a second term with more than 60 percent of the vote in April 2003 elections. His political party, the PDP, dominated parliamentary elections earlier that month, winning 73 seats in the 109-seat Senate and 213 seats in the 360-seat House of Representatives.

Contact Information. Embassy of Nigeria, 3519 International Court NW, Washington, DC 20008; phone (202) 986-8400; web site www.nigeriaembassyusa.org.

© 2005 ProQuest Information and Learning Company and Brigham Young University. It is against the law to copy, reprint, store, or transmit any part of this publication in any form by any means without written permission from ProQuest. This document contains native commentary and original analysis, as well as estimated statistics. The content should not be considered strictly factual, and it may not apply to all groups in a nation. *UN Development Programme, Human Development Report 2004 (New York: Oxford University Press, 2004).

CultureGrams™
People. The World. You.

ProQuest Information and Learning Company
300 North Zeeb Road, P.O. Box 1346
Ann Arbor, Michigan 48106 USA
Toll Free: 1.800.528.6279
Fax: 1.800.864.0019
www.culturegrams.com

Rwanda
(Rwandese Republic)

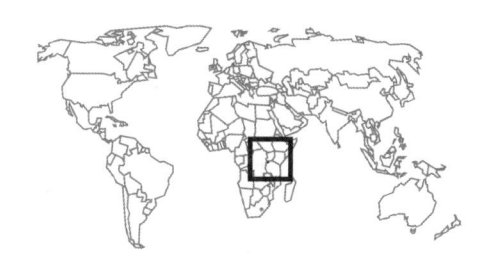

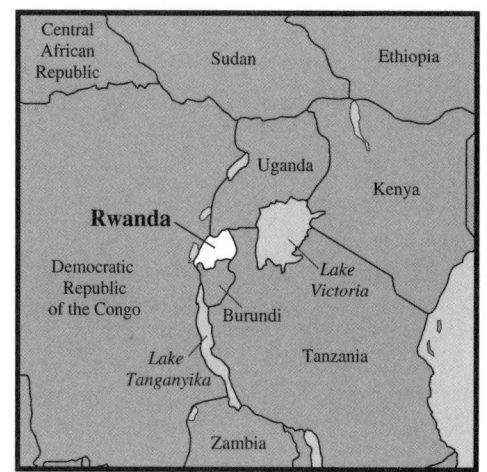

BACKGROUND

Land and Climate. Rwanda covers 10,170 square miles (26,340 square kilometers) of central Africa in the Great Lakes Region—named for lakes Victoria, Tanganyika, and Kivu. Often called the "land of a thousand hills," Rwanda is dominated by mountain ranges and highland plateaus. The highest point is Karisimbi peak (14,790 feet, or 4,507 meters) in the northwest Virunga range. These volcanic mountains are home to the mountain gorilla. East of the Virungas lies the populous central plateau. East of Kigali, the capital, the land becomes savanna grasslands and marshes. Virunga National Park and Nyungwe Forest are home to zebra, antelope, buffalo, impala, ape, crested heron, cormorant, fish eagle, and other species.

Rwanda's high altitude allows for a more moderate climate than its position just south of the equator would suggest. The average annual temperature of 66°F (19°C) varies little between rainy and dry seasons; rain falls mostly from February to May and September to December. The northwest tends to have a cooler climate, while the east is warmer.

History. Ethnic Twa were likely the original inhabitants of present-day Rwanda, with Hutu farmers firmly established by the 10th century and Tutsi pastoralists arriving after the 14th century. The Tutsi formed a monarchy by the 16th century and called the land Rwanda ("an extended or large country"). Social mobility and other factors kept race from becoming much of an issue before the 20th century, though class and clan affiliations did create divisions. Otherwise, Rwandans shared a common culture and language.

Germany colonized Rwanda in 1899, administering it indirectly through the existing *mwami* (king) system. During World War I, Belgium took control (1916) and received Rwanda as a League of Nations mandate in 1919. The Belgians continued indirect rule but restructured the system in a way that increased socio-economic divisions. Tutsi were openly favored over Hutu and Twa. In the 1950s, Hutu elite and the Catholic Church pressed for political reform, and limited elections were allowed in 1952. Still, Hutu leaders protested against the Tutsi monarchy and tensions mounted. Dissent erupted into violence in 1959 when Hutu began killing Tutsi after a Tutsi attack on a Hutu subchief. Violence spread rapidly; many Tutsi died or fled. Belgian troops intervened and, in a policy reversal, installed a Hutu-led administration. With democratization sweeping Africa, the monarchy was abolished in 1961 and full independence from Belgium followed in 1962.

However, independence did not change the culture of exclusion and suspicion that dominated Hutu-Tutsi relations. Tutsi exiles attacked government forces throughout the 1960s. The First Republic, headed by Gregoire Kayibanda, a Hutu, ended with a 1973 coup orchestrated by the Hutu Minister of Defense, Juvenal Habyarimana. Tutsi rebels in Uganda formed the Rwandan Patriotic Front (RPF) and invaded Rwanda in 1990. The conflict ended with a 1993 peace accord and power-sharing agreement. However, peace was shattered when Habyarimana's plane was shot down in April 1994 by Hutu extremists.

This attack marked not only the end of the Second Republic but the beginning of a 100-day, well-organized genocidal rampage in which hundreds of thousands of Tutsi and moderate Hutu were murdered. It is impossible to calculate the number of lives lost, but estimates reach close to one million. Two million refugees fled to neighboring Burundi, Tanzania, Uganda, and Zaire. Led by General Paul Kagame, the RPF fought back

Rwanda

and took over the capital on 4 July 1994. Within two weeks, Kagame established a Government of National Unity and named a moderate Hutu, Pasteur Bizimungu, president. Kagame took the vice president's role.

Hutu soldiers and others involved in the genocide fled the RPF advance, forcing a large part of the Hutu population to flee with them into Zaire. Tens of thousands died of disease in unsanitary camps. In 1996, Hutu refugees became targets for Tutsi violence. Hutu soldiers responded by attacking Tutsi, and Rwanda sent a militia to neighboring Zaire to defeat troops helping the Hutu. Most Hutu refugees were then sent back to Rwanda, although some guerrillas remained to launch attacks in northwest Rwanda.

The Rwandan militia soon allied with the forces of longtime Zairean rebel, Laurent Kabila. In 1997, Kabila's forces toppled Zaire's president, Mobutu Sese Seko, and renamed the country the Democratic Republic of the Congo. However, when Kabila failed to expel Hutu militias in eastern Congo, Rwanda switched its support to forces trying to overthrow Kabila. By the time a peace agreement was reached in 2002, the Congolese war involved six foreign countries and resulted in the deaths of an estimated three million people.

President Bizimungu resigned in March 2000, and parliament elected Kagame in April as Rwanda's first Tutsi president. In May 2003, Rwandans voted to approve a new constitution proposed by the Kagame administration to ensure ethnic balance in government. In August, Kagame won the first general presidential elections since the genocide, and the RPF won parliamentary elections the following month. Courts established in 1995 prosecute those accused of perpetuating the genocide. The legacy of genocide has left an indelible mark upon the people, but many Rwandans are optimistic that with these courts in place and a stable government in power, their path toward normalcy and reconciliation will continue.

THE PEOPLE

Population. Rwanda's 7.95 million inhabitants live in an area smaller than Maryland. The high population density is due partly to a tradition of large families, and partly to Rwanda's highland location as a place of refuge for people fleeing the colonial-era slave trade. The population is growing at an annual rate of 1.8 percent.

Reliable demographic data has long been unavailable because of politically motivated reporting, the civil war, and other factors. A government estimate indicates 80 percent of the population is Hutu. Tutsi comprise 19 percent and Twa 1 percent. Only 5 percent of Rwandans live in urban areas; the two largest cities are Kigali and Butare. The population, once decimated by genocide, has been replaced by large numbers of 1960s refugee families repatriating from Uganda, Tanzania, and elsewhere.

Language. French, Kinyarwanda, and English are Rwanda's official languages. English was added in 1995 to accommodate refugees repatriating from English-speaking nations. All Rwandans speak Kinyarwanda, but many also speak Kiswahili (Swahili), a trade language spoken in commercial centers. Kinyarwanda is the language of instruction in primary school; students begin learning French and English during their fourth year of primary school. French becomes the language of instruction in secondary schools. A growing number of secondary schools teach in English.

Kinyarwanda is a tonal language; it has the same alphabet as English except for the letters q and x. Small pronunciation differences are evident between regions but there are otherwise no major dialects.

Religion. Christianity was introduced in the early 20th century by European missionaries. Today, 65 percent of Rwandans are Catholic and 9 percent are Protestant. One percent of the population is Muslim. The remaining 25 percent practices indigenous beliefs exclusively. However, most Christians retain some traditional beliefs. Churches run schools and hospitals. They play a political role as well. While the Catholic Church supported Tutsi domination in the colonial era, it switched support to the Hutu in the 1950s. During the war, Catholic and some Protestant leaders remained allied with the Hutu government. Churches now work to promote reconciliation within and among congregations.

General Attitudes. Rwandans are often perceived as reserved and stoic. They are mindful of their public appearance and behavior. Rwandans value respect for others, especially elders and those in authority. Family ties are of utmost importance; a Rwandan will attend to a family matter at a moment's notice. In this oral culture, gossip is a custom, but people deplore lying or the inability to keep a secret. Fear and distrust are common after years of armed conflict and atrocities.

Rwandans must not only deal with the tragedies of the past, but also with present social change. With a new government, new national symbols, reformed social institutions, a new emphasis on English, and large numbers of Rwandans returning from a generation in exile, many people feel they are in a different country. These changes are difficult to assimilate in rural areas, where people are more conservative and traditional than in cities such as Kigali.

Personal Appearance. Conservative, Western-style dress is common, though it may be combined with traditional clothing. Rwandans strive to be neat and well dressed. They delight in occasions such as weddings and baptisms for which they can wear their finest traditional clothing. Women wrap themselves in a *pagne* (a wraparound skirt) and wear a headband symbolizing motherhood. Men may wear a special wrap and almost always a fedora. Some also wear a *boubou*, an adopted West African outfit of embroidered trousers and a long, loose top. For daily work, rural women wear a T-shirt, long skirt, and special wrap that can also serve as a head covering. Men wear a shirt and shorts or pants with the cuffs rolled up. Rural people may walk barefoot.

CUSTOMS AND COURTESIES

Greetings. Greetings are extremely important in Rwanda. It is impolite not to return a greeting or to start a conversation without a proper greeting. Younger persons must greet older persons first, and women greet men first. Upon seeing an acquaintance after a long while—which may be only as long as two days—Rwandans embrace in a semi-hug, first on one side and then the other. The longer the embrace, the deeper the emotions they feel. When being introduced for the first time or when greeting a professional colleague, Rwandans shake right hands and may place the left hand under the right forearm as a sign of respect. Some young urbanites "kiss the air" near each cheek while shaking hands.

Common verbal greetings include *Muraho* (Hello, it's been a while), *Mwaramutse* (Good morning), or *Mwiriwe* (Good afternoon/evening). The initial greeting is usually followed by *Amakuru?* (How's the news?) or, among close friends, *Bite se?* (How are things going?). The typical response is *Ni meza* (Fine) or *Ni meza cyane* (Very fine).

When referring to a family or household, Rwandans use last names: *kwa Kamanzi* (house of the Kamanzi family). When addressing individuals, they use first names, nicknames, occupational titles (teacher, nurse, carpenter), or even a person's child's name (*Mama Tatiana*, or "Tatiana's mother"). The friends of a boy named François would call his father *Papa François*. Elders are affectionately called *umusaza* (old man) or *umukechuru* (old woman).

Gestures. Body language, gestures, and facial expressions convey meaning, respect, or emphasis. One avoids eye contact with a superior or elder. The distance between people when they converse indicates their relationship: friends require little or no distance, while superiors must have more. Friends of the same sex often hold hands while walking or talking, but such public contact between members of the opposite sex is not appropriate. One passes an item to an older person with both hands. Rwandans toss their head to the side with a verbal *eh* to express disbelief, usually when they are listening to a personal experience. Hand gestures help tell a story, and a point may be emphasized by brushing the hands together almost as if clapping once. Pointing with the finger or hand is impolite; instead, the head is used, with the chin and mouth jutting in the direction indicated.

Visiting. Friends, neighbors, and relatives make and expect frequent impromptu visits. Visitors call out a greeting to announce their presence. They anticipate a response of *Karibu* (Kiswahili for "Welcome") or *Ninde?* (Who's there?). A host normally provides some refreshment, such as banana or sorghum beer or a soda. The lid of the drink is loosened in the presence of guests, not before. Sometimes tea is offered. On special occasions, visitors bring a gift of beer or food (potatoes, bananas, etc.). Rwandans gather the entire family to greet and talk with invited guests. In the Rwandan tradition, a conversation never ends; it is only postponed. At the end of a visit, the host accompanies guests to the fence or the road. If not, it is a sign the visit did not go well.

Eating. Many Rwandans begin their day with sorghum porridge or bread and tea. Most eat their main meal in the evening. Lunch may consist of bananas or leftovers from the night before. Some also drink a form of sour milk, similar to buttermilk. Although office workers and wealthy people have tea breaks, the high cost of sugar and milk make tea a luxury for many Rwandans.

Women cook over an open fire with three stones supporting a pot. Wealthier families have a houseboy or housegirl (often a distant relative) to cook and clean for them. Food is kept covered until ready to eat. Children usually eat separately from adults. Everyone washes their hands in a basin of water before and after eating, which is done with the right hand. Rural Rwandans sit around a common platter placed on a floor mat and eat the portion of food directly in front of them. One does not comment on the quality of a meal until it is gone. It is offensive to not eat with gusto or clean the platter. One may not sniff food or ask what someone else has eaten. It is impolite to remain silent or to leave before everyone has finished eating.

LIFESTYLE

Family. Large extended families are the norm in Rwanda. However, genocide and its repercussions (thousands in jail or living as refugees) have left the family unit somewhat disjointed. Most people are trying to rebuild their families, as evidenced by an increase in the number of weddings and an upsurge in the birthrate.

Rwandan women must show respect to their husbands, who have final authority over all family matters. Women typically raise the children, care for the household, and do the daily farming. Men assist with the construction of homes and the labor-intensive plowing and harvesting, and they carry out business dealings in the village and town centers. They may also be day laborers, watchmen, or tradesmen skilled in bicycle repair or carpentry. Those with more formal schooling are teachers and accountants. Girls care for younger siblings, fetch water and firewood, and clean the house. Boys look after the livestock. Boys stay in school longer than girls, although both may be kept home during peak agricultural periods.

Dating and Marriage. In rural areas, casual dating as couples is uncommon. Rather, young people build relationships by meeting at social gatherings, markets, school, and church. By tradition, a young man must ask a girl's father or uncle for permission to court her because he intends to marry her. He then presents gifts to her family (such as food or beer). Young urban people might date regardless of their parents' wishes, and a young man might date a succession of women until he finds one to marry. Both sets of parents must give their approval for a legal wedding to take place. Without it, the couple might pursue a common-law marriage, but they risk being rejected by one or both families.

Before a wedding, the groom's and bride's family negotiate the dowry (cows or cash), which is reimbursed if the girl breaks the engagement. If the bride's family demands too high a price, the couple might enter into a common-law relationship until the man can save enough for a dowry.

A committee of the couple's friends and relatives plans the wedding and reception; they are responsible for raising funds to pay for the events. The wedding day may include a dowry ceremony, a civil ceremony, a church ceremony, a reception, and a dinner. The reception features food, drink, and traditional dancing. Family members on each side make speeches of advice and best wishes.

Diet. Diet varies according to region, but beans are a staple in most areas. Kigali residents have access to a variety of food, but rural people eat what they grow. Wealthy people eat rice and meat (chicken, goat, or beef). Rural Rwandans consider meat a luxury for Sundays, holidays, or special events. Nearly everyone consumes *ubugali*, a thick, doughy paste made from corn, sorghum, or cassava flour. Formed into a ball, it is dipped into sauce made from beans, vegetables, or meat. Local fruits and vegetables include bananas, papaya, avocados, mangoes, sweet potatoes, passion fruit, tomatoes, cabbage, peas, and cassava leaves (made into a favorite dish called *isombe*). Rwanda imports food to meet basic needs. Products from Uganda are changing the way some people eat. For example, many now prefer English-style sliced bread to traditional French bread.

Recreation. Rwandans love soccer; children fashion soccer balls out of plastic bags bundled together with twine. They also make model cars and airplanes out of scrap metal. Other sports include basketball and volleyball. Girls jump rope or make traditional crafts such as baskets and wall hangings. Adults favor the traditional game of *igisoro*, in which small black seeds are placed strategically in hollows of a wooden board. Men socialize in local bars. Travel is usually limited to visiting relatives during the holidays.

The Arts. For many Rwandans, music is integral to daily life. Children learn songs and dances at school or in church or scout groups. Music competitions are a popular means of expressing

Rwanda

people's emotions. Dancers perform in a small group in which lead singers improvise and others clap hands. Traditional instruments accompanying them include *ingoma* (drums), *inanga* (harps), the flute, and the zither. Storytelling is important to all Rwandans. Tutsi oral literature, which recounts the history of the Tutsi monarchy, is both spoken and sung. Contemporary literature is written mainly in French. Traditional folk arts are utilitarian, including wood carving, basketry, and pottery.

Holidays. Official holidays include New Year's Day; Democracy Day (28 Jan.); Genocide Memorial Day (7 Apr.), commemorating the beginning of the 1994 genocide; Easter Monday; Labor Day (1 May); Ascension Day (21 May); Independence Day (1 July); Liberation Day (4 July), marking the end of the genocide; Assumption Day (15 Aug.); Republic Day (25 Sept.); Heroes Day (1 Oct.); Armed Forces Day (26 Oct.); All Saints' Day (1 Nov.); and Christmas. Muslims observe *Idil-Fitr*, a three-day feast at the end of *Ramadan*, their holy month of fasting.

Commerce. Offices are open weekdays from 8 a.m. to 5 p.m. but close for an hour or two at lunchtime. Some are open on Saturdays until 1 p.m. Banks close at 3 p.m. and are not open on Saturdays. Urban markets are open every day; rural areas have fixed market days. Roadside stands and kiosks, open daily, sell essential items such as soap, kerosene, sugar, tea, cooking oil, matches, and some fresh produce. Bargaining is common in markets and some shops.

SOCIETY

Government. Rwanda's president (currently Paul Kagame) is chief of state. The prime minister (currently Bernard Makuza) is head of government. The president appoints the prime minister and a Council of Ministers. Parliament consists of two chambers: an 80-seat National Assembly and a 52-seat Senate. According to the 2003 constitution, the president and the prime minister must belong to different political parties, and no party is allowed to hold more than half of the seats in the Council of Ministers. These measures are designed to prevent a single ethnic group from gaining too much power. The constitution also requires that women fill 24 seats in the National Assembly.

Economy. Agriculture dominates Rwanda's economy. Most people are subsistence farmers. Coffee and tea are the main export crops. Agricultural expansion is limited by the lack of fertile soil. Government commitment to economic reform has brought international aid that is fueling a growth in services and transportation, among other sectors. Significant economic challenges include rehabilitating infrastructure, the financial system, agriculture, healthcare facilities, and manufacturing plants. The currency is the Rwandan *franc* (RWF).

Transportation and Communications. The average Rwandan walks or rides a bicycle for local transportation. One can also hire a *taxi moto* (motorcycle taxi) or *taxi velo* (bicycle taxi). Urban taxicabs are expensive. Buses and minivans travel paved roads between major cities. Secondary roads are unpaved but still receive traffic. Many people hitchhike to travel long distances. Few Rwandans own cars, which are a status symbol, but those who do will offer rides to others.

DEVELOPMENT DATA
Human Dev. Index* rank . . . . 159 of 177 countries
  Adjusted for women . . . . 129 of 144 countries
Real GDP per capita $1,270
Adult literacy rate . . . . 75 percent (male); 63 (female)
Infant mortality rate . . . . 102 per 1,000 births
Life expectancy . . . . 38 (male); 39 (female)

Some urban residents and most government offices have phones; rural areas may have public phones at a post office or private kiosk. To keep in touch, Rwandans write letters and listen to the radio. Urban post offices function fairly well. In rural areas, people rely on hand delivery through friends and acquaintances. Numerous weekly and bimonthly newspapers are available. One television station broadcasts in Kigali.

Education. In theory, all Rwandan children, beginning at age seven, have access to seven mandatory years of primary schooling. In reality, family obligations and other factors force girls to drop out early and keep many children away. To enter secondary school, students must pass a national exam. There is fierce competition for places in private secondary schools. Rwanda's national university in Butare serves several thousand students.

Health. Kigali has two main hospitals, which are better supplied than hospitals in smaller cities. Rural Rwandans trust traditional healers over modern medicine and hospitals. The maternal mortality rate is high. Diseases such as malaria, tuberculosis, diarrhea, malnutrition, and respiratory infections are widespread, and Rwanda suffers from a severe HIV/AIDS epidemic.

AT A GLANCE
Events and Trends.
- In February 2004, the government began enforcing a provision in the constitution that requires all politicians and civil servants to declare their assets. The stipulation was included when the constitution was passed in 2003 in order to eliminate government corruption.
- In 2003, the International Criminal Tribunal for Rwanda (ICTR), which prosecutes people accused of perpetrating the 1994 genocide, began speeding up the number of cases tried. This resulted in a number of new convictions, alleviating the criticism that the tribunal was taking too long. However, the tribunal's defense lawyers have argued that they are not provided enough time to prepare the cases adequately. Thousands of people are still awaiting trial for crimes related to the genocide. Leaders who directed the massacres are being tried by the ICTR; individual participants are being tried by local courts.

Contact Information. Embassy of Rwanda, 1714 New Hampshire Avenue NW, Washington, DC 20009; phone (202) 232-2882.

© 2005 ProQuest Information and Learning Company and Brigham Young University. It is against the law to copy, reprint, store, or transmit any part of this publication in any form by any means without written permission from ProQuest. This document contains native commentary and original analysis, as well as estimated statistics. The content should not be considered strictly factual, and it may not apply to all groups in a nation. *UN Development Programme, Human Development Report 2004 (New York: Oxford University Press, 2004).

CultureGrams™
People. The World. You.

ProQuest Information and Learning Company
300 North Zeeb Road, P.O. Box 1346
Ann Arbor, Michigan 48106 USA
Toll Free: 1.800.528.6279
Fax: 1.800.864.0019
www.culturegrams.com

Republic of Senegal

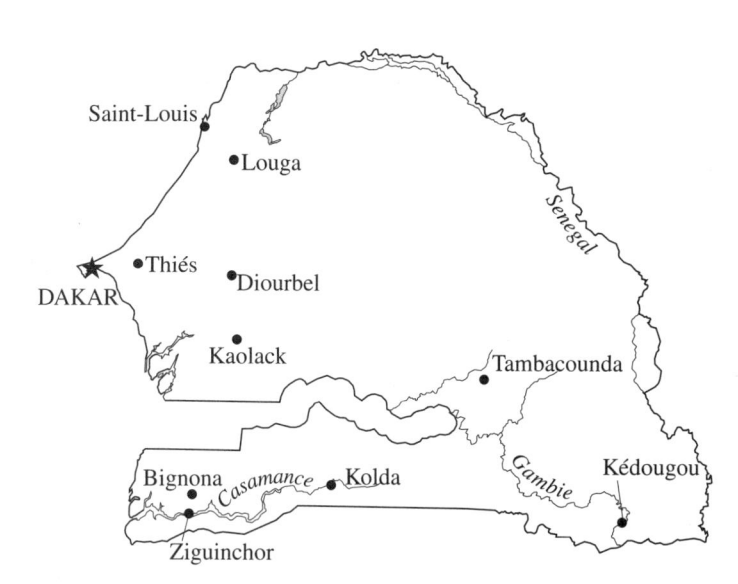

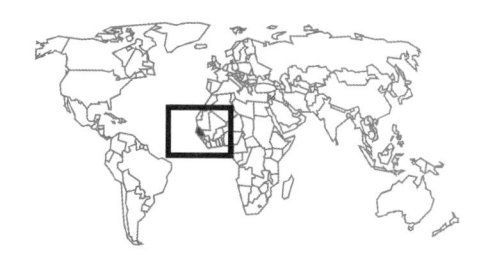

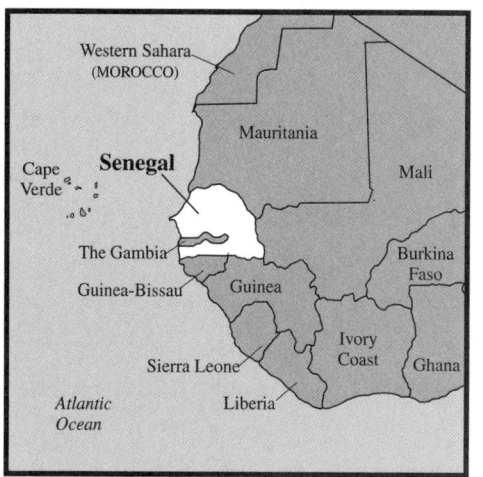

BACKGROUND

Land and Climate. Senegal lies in the westernmost part of Africa. Covering 75,749 square miles (196,180 square kilometers), Senegal is about the size of South Dakota. Most of the country north of The Gambia (a separate country that cuts through Senegal's southwest) is flat, with rolling plains and few trees. Part of northern Senegal lies in Africa's semiarid Sahel region and is subject to desertification. The southeast has plateaus over 1,600 feet (480 meters) high and the southwest consists of wetlands and forests. Much of Senegal is subject to drought, overgrazing, and deforestation. Four major rivers flow through the country from east to west. Dakar, the capital, is an important port for the region of West Africa.

Senegal has two distinct seasons: the sunny dry season (November–June), with moderate temperatures; and the hot, humid rainy season (July–October), with temperatures often above 90°F (32°C). Rains fall a bit earlier in the Casamance region, the section of Senegal below The Gambia. Dakar and other coastal areas are generally cooler than the rest of the country.

History. Black Africans historically have lived in the area now called Senegal. Great empires and independent kingdoms existed in the area from A.D. 300 to the 19th century. Islamic merchants from North Africa introduced Islam to the animistic peoples of the area in the 10th century. Portuguese sailors first traded with the people in the mid-1400s but were replaced by the French, English, and Dutch in the 1500s. The slave trade was established, and peanuts were introduced as a new crop to supply European demand. Several million West Africans were shipped to the Americas as slaves between the 16th and 19th centuries. Many were sold at an auction house that still stands on Goree Island (near Dakar).

By the 1800s, France began to dominate the area, conquering various kingdoms and establishing Senegal as one of several colonies in an administrative federation called French West Africa. Slavery was abolished in 1848, but French economic, educational, political, and judicial systems remained intact at the administrative level. After World War II, many residents began to demand independence. On 4 April 1960, the colony became a sovereign nation. France and Senegal still maintain close political, economic, and social ties.

In 1981, Senegal's constitution was amended to eliminate restrictions on various political parties. Abdou Diouf was elected president and his party, the Senegalese Socialist Party (PS), came to dominate parliament. Diouf was reelected in 1988 and 1993. When his party again dominated 1998 parliamentary elections, opposition groups refused to accept the results, claiming widespread fraud. Diouf reversed a vow to retire in 2000 by entering the electoral race for president in February of that year. After the second round of voting, his rival and five-time presidential candidate, Abdoulaye Wade of the Senegalese Democratic Party (PDS), was elected president. Diouf accepted the results and stepped down peacefully. Wade was inaugurated in April 2000.

Senegal has generally enjoyed good relations with other West African nations, though clashes along the Mauritanian border have not been uncommon. In 1989, for example, hundreds of people died when violence broke out between Moors (people of mixed Arab and Berber ancestry) living in Mauritania and Black Africans living in Senegal and Mauritania over a land and grazing dispute.

Senegal has also suffered the effects of a long-running separatist movement in the Casamance region. In 1982, groups

Senegal

among the region's majority Diola ethnic group launched a campaign for independence, claiming discrimination by the more numerous Wolof people of northern Senegal. More than two decades of violence cost an estimated 3,500 lives. Sporadic negotiations led to a peace deal between the government and rebels in December 2004, although talks must still resolve disagreements among rebel factions over the future of the region.

THE PEOPLE

Population. Senegal's population of approximately 10.9 million people is growing at 2.5 percent annually. About 43 percent of the population is younger than age 15, and roughly 50 percent lives in urban areas. Dakar has more than two million inhabitants.

The nation's major ethnic groups are Black African, including the Wolof (36 percent), Fulani (or Peul, 17), Serer (17), Toucouleur (9), Diola (9), and Mandingo (9). About 1 percent are European and Lebanese, and there are other smaller groups. The Lebanese have been in Senegal for many generations and form an influential merchant class.

Language. Although French is the official language of instruction, business, and government, six major local languages are spoken in Senegal. These include Wolof, Serer, Alpuular, Mandingo, Diola, and Bassari. Wolof, the native language of the dominant ethnic group, is most widely used. In fact, non-Wolofs north of The Gambia are bilingual in Wolof and their own ethnic language. Educated Senegalese also speak French. Some speak English, although it is not widely understood throughout the country. Senegalese languages are primarily oral. Attempts to create writing systems for these languages have met with some success. Many younger children now can write in their native language using a modified Latin alphabet. Muslims often use the Arabic alphabet to write in Wolof or one of the other local languages.

Religion. About 92 percent of Senegal's population is Muslim, 6 percent is animist or traditional, and 2 percent is Christian (mostly Catholic). The constitution guarantees freedom of religion and separation of church and state. Both Muslim and Catholic holy days are national holidays. In practice, however, Islam dominates social and political activities. The *marabouts* (Muslim religious leaders) influence voting patterns and economic practices. Their power has a strong impact on the country's development. The *marabouts* became powerful during the drive for independence. They were the movement's most vocal and supportive leaders and drew many animists to Islam because of their popularity.

Many Senegalese, especially in the south, combine their formal religion (Islam or Christianity) with indigenous animist practices and ceremonies. For instance, villagers believe in zombies, spirits, and genies. They often wear a *gri gri* (charm) around their arms, stomach, or neck. The *marabout* writes the charm in Arabic on paper and encases it in leather to be strung on a string. Some people are *Mourides*, Muslims who belong to a special brotherhood and practice a unique form of Islam developed in Senegal.

General Attitudes. Senegal has many diverse ethnic groups within its borders, each with its own history, language, and culture. Interactions between these groups and with non-African cultures have produced a multicultural people proud of their origins. Typically, a person's allegiances extend toward the family first, and then, in descending order, to an ethnic group, a religion, the home village, Senegal, the region of French West Africa, and finally, Africa. Personal relations, including doing favors and returning them, are extremely important in daily life. Sharing is also integral to good relations.

Concepts of time and distance are defined by a person's background. For example, a Senegalese farmer, whose way of life may not include motor vehicles, will consider a five-hour walk to another village a short trip. But an urban professional might drive rather than walk a short distance. Most other aspects of life are widely different between urban and rural classes. For instance, while wealthy and educated women may hold public office and be employed in important business positions in urban areas, rural women rarely have such opportunities. Throughout the country, women are responsible for the daily functions of the household. The Senegalese, urban and rural, are interested in domestic and world politics and appreciate exchanging ideas with foreign visitors.

Personal Appearance. Senegalese place great emphasis on their appearance and personal hygiene. Most bathe more than once a day, and perfumes or colognes are popular. Dressing well is important. Men do not go out in public without a shirt, and few women, with the exception of young, urban women, wear pants or shorts. Beggars might be barefoot in public. Revealing clothing is not appropriate in public. People wear beachwear only on the beach; shorts are for athletics.

Villagers and most adult urbanites wear traditional clothing. Young urban dwellers wear Western fashions until they get older. Traditional clothing for men includes loose-fitting cotton robes (*boubous*) worn over bouffant pants and a loose shirt. The amount or quality of embroidery can indicate one's level of wealth. Women wear a long robe over a long wraparound skirt (*sarong*); some skirts have multiple layers. A matching head wrap completes the outfit. Some ethnic groups have facial tattoos or ritual facial scarring.

Muslim women do not wear veils. Muslim women who have made a pilgrimage to Makkah, Saudi Arabia, wear a white scarf, while men wear a white headdress; these people are treated with great respect.

CUSTOMS AND COURTESIES

Greetings. In Senegal, courtesy is extremely important, so greetings should never be neglected. Senegalese greetings vary depending on the circumstances and how well people know each other. Shaking hands and kissing alternate cheeks three times (a French tradition) is common in urban areas. Rural Senegalese only shake hands, and social rules determine who may shake with whom. A minority of Muslim men do not shake hands with women. When joining or leaving a small group, one must greet each individual separately. Whatever greeting was used between two people is also used when parting. Upon parting, most Senegalese ask each other to extend best wishes to their families and mutual friends.

Gestures. Senegalese receive and give objects with their right hand or with both hands. Use of only the left hand is considered unclean. Public displays of affection are impolite, although some urban youth hold hands. It is inappropriate to eat while walking on the street. Senegalese tell street vendors they are not interested in their goods by motioning with a pushing back gesture and avoiding eye contact. They hail taxis by raising one arm. To get another person's attention, one might snap the fingers if close or hiss ("tsss") if farther away.

In traditional families, children and women respectfully curtsy to their elders when greeting or giving them water. People avoid eye contact with a member of the opposite sex or a person considered a superior (in age or status). Men and women keep their distance in public and are expected to be dignified and reserved around members of the opposite sex. More relaxed behavior is acceptable with members of the same gender, age, or status. Sharing a kola nut (which contains a mild caffeine stimulant) is a gesture of friendship.

Visiting. Senegalese enjoy visiting one another often in the home. Because most do not own telephones, dropping in uninvited is acceptable and appreciated. Still, uninvited guests try to visit before mealtimes, either in the late morning or early evening. Work, health, family matters, and mutual friends are briefly discussed before a visitor addresses the purpose of the visit. Guests may be treated to three rounds of tea, with more sugar added in each round. People remove their shoes when visiting a Muslim religious leader or entering a mosque; women cover their heads.

Senegalese are hospitable and can make a guest feel comfortable without expecting anything in return. However, friends will often bring gifts such as fruit or some cookies for the children. Hosts will offer a drink (usually nonalcoholic), but foreign visitors do not drink water unless it is bottled. To decline a drink, it is polite to say one has just finished drinking. It is impolite to refuse other refreshments. Although smoking is widespread among males, visitors to traditional Muslim homes avoid cigarette smoking until they leave. It is considered bad manners for women to smoke. It is considered bad luck to ask specific questions about children, such as when a baby is due, how many children one has, or what their ages are.

Eating. Generally, breakfast is between 6 and 9 a.m., lunch from noon to 1:30 p.m., and dinner from 8 to 9:30 p.m. In traditional homes, the sexes and different age groups eat separately. The main dish usually is served in large bowls placed on mats on the floor or ground, or on coffee tables. Several people eat from the same bowl using the fingers or a spoon, depending on personal habit, the occasion, and the dish. Proper etiquette for eating is stressed to children at an early age. It is important for diners to have clean hands, eat only from the portion of the communal dish directly in front of them, and avoid eye contact with persons still eating. One uses only the right hand to eat. The left can assist the right when one eats difficult foods, such as fruit or meat with bones. Occasionally, particularly when hosting Western visitors, some urban Senegalese follow French customs, eating at tables from individual plates with utensils.

LIFESTYLE

Family. In general, the family is a source of strength and pride for Senegalese. In most rural areas and among traditional urban families, extended families live together in compounds (with a separate dwelling for each nuclear family). But there is an urban trend for nuclear families to live in single households, often with relatives in the neighborhood. Rural family strength and unity are weakened as young men migrate to cities in search of work. Baptisms, circumcisions, marriages, funerals, and other important ceremonies are cause for elaborate celebrations. Most families live at subsistence levels as agricultural workers, although there is a growing middle class and a small wealthy elite. The elderly receive great respect and are cared for by their families.

Dating and Marriage. Western-style dating, where relative strangers go out with one another, is uncommon in Senegal. People tend to go out in groups or in couples with a person they and their families know. In fact, a couple's families tend to be heavily involved in courtship. Traditional families arrange marriages, but more urban residents are marrying according to their choice. Couples are often encouraged to marry young. However, it is acceptable for college students to wait until after they finish school. Many Muslims practice polygamy. Islamic law permits a man to have as many as four wives, but he must have the consent of the other wife (or wives), and according to the *Qur'an* (Koran), he must divide his resources and time equally among each wife's household. Half of households headed by men older than age 50 practice polygamy; by contrast, only 15 percent of men younger than age 40 take more than one wife.

Diet. Food preparation and presentation are skills that Senegalese females learn at an early age. Each ethnic group has its own traditional dishes, and some urban women also cook French meals. Many believe wealth is measured by body size, because the wealthier the family, the more oil and rice can be used in preparing dishes. Meals usually consist of one main dish of rice, millet, or corn, covered with a sauce composed of vegetables, meat (traditional Muslims do not eat pork), poultry, fish, beans, or milk and sugar. A dessert of fruit and/or yogurt might be served. One popular dish is *yassa*: rice and chicken covered with a sauce made of sliced onions and spices. Another is *thiebou dien*, a meal of fish and rice that is typically eaten for lunch. A traditional Wolof dish is *mbaxal-u-Saloum*: a sauce of ground peanuts, dried fish, meat, tomatoes, and spices served with rice.

Recreation. Traditional wrestling is Senegal's national sport. However, soccer is the most popular sport. Senegalese avidly follow international competitions. Other favorites include basketball, track-and-field, and jogging. Many urban residents enjoy movies and books. Concerts, discos, and videos are popular in areas with electricity. After the harvest, rural families visit relatives in urban areas. They also enjoy dancing. Family and village celebrations, as well as the weekly market, provide the main form of recreation for most rural people.

The Arts. Senegalese songs are usually unwritten, and certain instruments or music styles (such as *yela* music for women) are reserved for specific genders or age groups. In the past, only *griots* could perform music. Their traditional role was transmitting oral history, genealogies and social rankings, diplomacy, and storytelling. Today, *griots* continue to participate in naming ceremonies, weddings, and funerals.

Sabar (a set of five to seven tuned drums) are played by the Wolof people and accompanied by dancing. Another popular instrument is the *kora* (a 21-string harp made of the calabash gourd). *Mbalax* music began as a tribal style using *sabar* drums but now incorporates a mix of Afro-Caribbean pop; it is popular in many parts of Africa.

Senegal is a center of West African culture. The World Festival of Negro Arts was organized at Dakar in 1966, and the capital is seen as an important location for African literary expression.

Holidays. Senegal celebrates Islamic, Catholic, and national holidays, including New Year's Day, *Mawloud* (celebrating the prophet Muhammad's birth), Easter, Independence Day (4 Apr.), Labor Day (1 May), Ascension, and Whitmonday. On *Tabaski*, the head of each household sacrifices a lamb in honor of Abraham's willingness to sacrifice his son. *Korite* marks the end of *Ramadan*, the month of fasting when Muslims go without food or drink from sunrise to sundown each day. *Tamkharit*, the Islamic New Year, is also the day on which *Allah* determines people's destinies. Islamic holidays follow

Senegal

the lunar calendar and thus fall on different dates each year. All Saints' Day (1 Nov.) and Christmas are also celebrated.

Commerce. Government offices are open Monday through Friday, 7:30 a.m. to 4 p.m., with a short lunch break. Urban businesses follow the same general schedule, Monday through Saturday, but some stay open until 6 p.m. Rural Senegalese look forward to the weekly market day as a chance to dress up, see people from surrounding villages, and buy supplies. Also in villages, nearly everyone sells at least one product from home, whether it is salt, bouillon cubes, or another basic item.

Muslims do not schedule business meetings during prayer times, which take place five times each day. If a meeting runs into prayer time, it might be stopped so the people can pray, depending on the individuals and whether the area is traditional or Westernized.

SOCIETY

Government. Senegal's president (currently Abdoulaye Wade) is head of state and is limited to serving two five-year terms. The prime minister (currently Cherif Macky Sall) is head of government and appointed by the president. An appointed cabinet also aids the president. The *Assemblée Nationale* (National Assembly) has 120 seats. Its members are elected by direct popular vote to five-year terms. Local chiefs and religious leaders provide rural leadership and judicial services. To the average person, local authority is often more important than departments of the central government.

Economy. The majority (about 75 percent) of Senegal's labor force is engaged in agriculture. Since introduced by colonial powers, peanuts have remained the country's main cash crop and occupy about 40 percent of all cropland. Other agricultural products include millet, cassava, cotton, rice, poultry, and vegetables. Farmers depend primarily on rainfall to produce their crops, but a small number of projects are experimenting with irrigation techniques.

Senegal has one of the most developed manufacturing sectors in French West Africa. The most important industries include peanut oil extraction, tourism, phosphates, and food processing. Fish processing is the key component in Senegal's food industry. Senegal uses West Africa's regional currency, the *CFA franc* (XOF).

Transportation and Communications. Paved roads link major cities, while inland villages are connected by unpaved paths and waterways. An airline serves the northern and southern coasts. A railroad system extends from Dakar to the north and to Mali in the east. Most people do not own cars; they travel by public transport (buses, taxis, or a minivan system for longer distances), horse and buggy, bicycle, motorcycle, or on foot. The government sponsors a daily newspaper, other political parties sponsor weekly papers, and an independent daily paper is also available. While most urban residents have access to information through print or television, villagers rely more on radio because they lack electricity and local postal services. Most rural people have access to daily radio news broadcasts in local languages. Also, oral or written messages passed from person to person are an effective means of communication among villagers.

Education. Senegal's educational system is based on the French model. Classes are taught in French, so most of the literate population has learned to read and write in French. However, French typically is not spoken in the home, and most children do not speak it when they begin school; this hampers early learning. Officials hesitate to replace French because they fear most ethnic groups would resist an educational system based on a single ethnic language. In addition, they believe dropping French would isolate Senegal from the rest of the world.

Many Senegalese see school as being irrelevant to their daily activities, so they drop out early. Attendance is also affected by the need for children to work in the fields, a distrust of secular (versus religious) education, and other factors. About half of all students enter and complete a primary education, and about one-third of those go on to a secondary school. Children often attend *Qur'anic* schools, where they learn some Arabic and about Islam.

Health. Although health conditions are improving, diseases and infections continue to afflict many Senegalese, particularly those in rural areas who cannot afford or do not have access to modern medical treatment. Most physicians practice in Dakar. While Dakar doctors have access to modern facilities, rural healthcare facilities often lack equipment and medical supplies. Villagers rely on traditional healers and cures for many ailments.

DEVELOPMENT DATA

Human Dev. Index* rank . . . . 157 of 177 countries
Adjusted for women. . . . . 128 of 144 countries
Real GDP per capita $1,580
Adult literacy rate . . . . 49 percent (male); 30 (female)
Infant mortality rate . . . . 57 per 1,000 births
Life expectancy . . . . 51 (male); 55 (female)

AT A GLANCE

Events and Trends.
- In December 2004, Interior Minister Ousman Ngom and Casamance rebel leader Father Diamacoune Senghor signed a historic peace deal in Casamance's regional capital, Ziguinchor. If the peace holds, it would end one of Africa's longest-running conflicts. However, some rebel factions opposed the agreement because it preceded final discussions on how the politics and economy of the Casamance region will be shaped.
- A government-operated ferry traveling from Casamance to Dakar capsized off the Gambian coast in September 2002. As many as 1,800 people are believed to have died in the disaster; only 64 survived. Because the ferry was filled to more than three times its capacity and safety measures were not enforced, many Senegalese blamed government negligence for the capsizing.

Contact Information. Embassy of Senegal, 2112 Wyoming Avenue NW, Washington, DC 20008; phone (202) 234-0540. Senegal Tourist Office, 350 Fifth Avenue, Suite 3118, New York, NY 10118; phone (212) 279-1953.

CultureGrams World Edition 2006

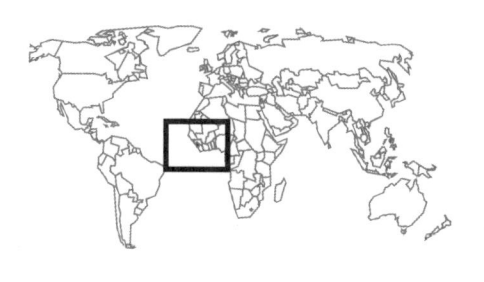

Republic of Sierra Leone

BACKGROUND

Land and Climate. Sierra Leone covers 27,699 square miles (71,740 square kilometers) of West Africa; it is about the size of South Carolina. The west coast is characterized by marshy inland waterways covered by mangrove swamps. The coast's 70-mile-wide lowlands are excellent for growing rice. To the east of these swamps, the land rises to a plateau of timber forests and mountain peaks. Near the capital city of Freetown, coastal cliffs extend from beaches up to 3,000 feet (900 meters). The drier north is mostly forested savanna. Tropical rain forests dot the south and east, but much of the land is used for agriculture.

The rainy season (May–October) is hot and humid; the heaviest rain falls between July and September. Most areas receive an average of 125 inches (318 centimeters) of rain. Daytime temperatures often reach above 90°F (32°C). The dry season (November–April) is noted for lower humidity, cool nights, and dusty harmattan winds out of the northeast (especially in December and January).

History. The land was on the periphery of the prosperous Mali Empire during medieval times. Inland Mande peoples began to migrate to coastal regions toward the end of the Mali Empire. Along the way, they mixed with other groups. Through intermarriage, indigenous peoples and the migrating Mande formed new ethnic groups, such as the Mende.

The Portuguese began exploring the coast in 1462, naming it Serra Lyoa ("Lion Range") for the thunderous roar of waves crashing into the steep peninsular mountains. The arrival of European explorers opened the region to missionaries, merchants, and slave traders. Many captives exported from Sierra Leone were destined for slavery in the United States.

Great Britain joined the lucrative slave trade and later (19th century) repatriated some slaves when slavery was abolished. British missionaries preached Christianity, and British traders began exporting timber, palm kernels, ginger, arrowroot, gum, ivory, hides, palm oil, and rubber. After diamonds and gold were discovered, Britain proclaimed a protectorate over Sierra Leone in 1896. During colonial rule, the influences of trade and missionary education altered traditional society.

Independence was secured in 1961 and Sir Milton Margai became the first prime minister. His half brother, Albert Margai, attempted to succeed him in 1967, but he lost the election; the military tried to keep him in power. The elected prime minister, Siaka Stevens, was able to take office in 1968. His party, the All People's Congress (APC), gained control of parliament by 1973, and Stevens ruled a one-party state until he retired in 1985. By 1990, opposition to APC rule was high. Captain Valentine Strasser led a coup in 1992, scheduled and later canceled elections, but then promised a return to civilian rule by 1996.

Election preparations were delayed by an intensification of a 1991 rebellion of the Revolutionary United Front (RUF), a violent group associated with warring Liberian factions. Despite help from Nigerian troops, Strasser was unsuccessful in defeating the RUF. The war devastated the economy, killed more than 10,000 people, and left thousands of others homeless and starving. Strasser's deputy, Brigadier Julius Maada Bio, deposed him in January 1996. Bio scheduled peace talks with the RUF and held multiparty elections in February.

Ahmad Tejan Kabbah was elected president. He signed a peace pact with the RUF, but fighting resumed in March 1997. To help the army fight the RUF, Kabbah came to rely on a civilian militia known as *Kamajors*. Insulted by this, and blaming

Sierra Leone

Kabbah for the collapse of peace, the army violently forced him from power in May 1997. Coup leader Johnny Paul Koromah declared himself head of state. RUF rebels then joined Koromah's forces. They looted Freetown, killing hundreds of civilians.

A Nigerian-led coalition of West African troops (called ECOMOG) led an assault on Freetown to restore Kabbah to power. Intense fighting and international pressure sent Koromah into hiding. President Kabbah returned to Freetown in March 1998. Koromah's troops and RUF forces fled into rural areas, killing and maiming civilians and forcing tens of thousands to flee to refugee camps. Nigerian troops and *Kamajors* remained to protect the president. Koromah was later captured, but the RUF continued a terror spree, displacing as many as two million people and killing thousands. The United Nations deemed Sierra Leone the most unlivable country in the world.

After more fighting and some negotiations, jailed RUF leader Foday Sankoh was released to engage in peace talks with the government. A peace agreement was signed in July 1999, granting the RUF positions in a transitional government. Sankoh became a vice president to Kabbah; Koromah returned to the army. For a time, the fighting subsided. However, the RUF violated elements of the peace accord at various times. The group refused to give up the country's valuable diamond mines, from which they had smuggled millions of dollars of diamonds to finance their war and enrich Liberia. In 2000, Sankoh refused to cooperate with the United Nations in disarming his group. By May, the RUF had begun killing and looting again, even capturing five hundred UN peacekeepers and holding them hostage. Sankoh tried to escape an angry Freetown mob but was eventually captured. The RUF went on the offensive, overrunning government and UN positions, and shattering the peace in June.

In March 2001, the RUF announced it would give UN peacekeepers access to its controlled territory provided that new elections were scheduled. The peacekeepers oversaw the disarmament of the RUF later that year, and peace was formally declared in January 2002. In May elections, voters overwhelmingly reelected Kabbah to another presidential term. The peace has endured, but Sierra Leoneans face the daunting task of rebuilding their devastated nation and economy after a decade of war.

THE PEOPLE

Population. Sierra Leone's population of about 5.9 million is growing at a rate of 2.3 percent per year. Eighteen ethnic groups comprise the population. The Mende (31 percent) and Temne (30 percent) are the two largest groups. Smaller groups include the Limba (8 percent), Fula, Kissi, Mandingo, Kono, and others. The Krios, descendants of returned slaves, live mostly in Freetown. The majority of the people (66 percent) live in rural areas, although cities are densely populated. Nearly all Sierra Leoneans are Africans. An entire Lebanese merchant class, which had lived in Sierra Leone since the early 1900s, fled after the 1997 coup.

Language. English is the official language and is used in government, but only the educated speak it. Krio, a mixture of primarily English, Yoruba, and other African languages, is the common language. Most people speak their native tongue and Krio. Mende dominates in the south and Temne in the north. French is taught in secondary schools because of the country's many francophone neighbors.

Religion. Both Christianity and Islam are practiced in Sierra Leone, but neither claims a majority of the population. Christianity was brought to Sierra Leone by returned slaves and gained converts through missionary schools. The fastest-growing religion is Islam. Most Sierra Leonean Muslims adhere to the Sunni branch of Islam.

Religious affiliation crosses ethnic and family lines. Sierra Leoneans of different faiths live in harmony because of their willingness to accept various beliefs as part of their eclectic (rather than exclusive) approach to religion. Most people believe in a supreme being, lesser deities, and a spirit world. Those who convert to a formal religion also usually retain traditional animist beliefs, especially because animism (the belief that spirits inhabit both living things and inanimate objects) is tied to daily life. Participation in secret societies, where socio-religious activities take place, is high—even among Christians and Muslims. For example, nearly all women participate in the secret *Bondo* society, where they dance, share lessons about womanhood, and initiate new members by circumcision and other rituals.

General Attitudes. Sierra Leoneans identify first with their ethnic group and then with Sierra Leone. Concerns are more provincial than national. People tend to be realistic and practical about their circumstances, which enables them to bear difficult situations. Two common Krio expressions are *Na so God say* (It is God's will) and *Ow fo do?* (What can you do?), to which the response is *Na fo biah* (You must bear it). Even from 1998 to 2001, with terrible atrocities occurring throughout the nation, people tried as much as possible to carry on a normal life with a desire to enjoy what pleasures the day could offer. Education is valued as the key to a better way of life. Urban people strive for material wealth because it is a sign of security. There is no strict social hierarchy, but members of a local chief's family are treated with great respect, as are the educated or wealthy.

Personal Appearance. Western-style clothing is nearly universal for men and boys. Women wear *lappas*, two yards of ankle-length cloth tied about the waist and topped with an African or Western blouse. Women's heads often are covered, wrapped with fabric that usually matches the *lappa*. *Lappas* commonly are made of brightly colored cotton cloth imported from Europe and Asia. Trousers are almost unheard of for women, as are shorts for anyone but young boys. Maintaining a good appearance, regardless of the weather or one's wealth, is a priority. On special occasions, people wear traditional clothing. For example, over a *lappa*, women wear matching long gowns made from *gara*, locally dyed cotton brocade. Men wear *gara* shirts with matching trousers. Around the shirt collar and pant cuffs is *planting*, fancy embroidery in a contrasting color.

CUSTOMS AND COURTESIES

Greetings. Greetings vary depending on the ethnic group, but one must greet another before beginning a conversation. An initial "Hello" (*Kushe* in Krio, *Bua* in Mende, and *Seke* in Temne) is acceptable in most situations. Men and women shake with the right hand. When meeting a person of high rank, one customarily supports one's right arm with the left arm—implying that the other's hand is of great weight. The Mende may touch their right hand to their heart after a handshake. When greeting, it is polite to ask "How are you?" (*Ow di bodi?* in Krio). A typical response is the equivalent of "I give thanks to God" (*A tel God tanki* in Krio). Good-bye might be said with *A de go* (I'm going) or *Nain dat* (That's all).

Sierra Leoneans often address others by the title *Mr.* or *Miss* followed by their first name. Other terms vary according to age relationship. For example, when one addresses someone of the same age, *brother* or *sister* is acceptable. One may use *auntie, uncle, ma,* or *pa* to address older people. Sierra Leoneans often address strangers as *padi* (friend).

Gestures. It is improper for a woman to whistle. Sierra Leoneans frequently hiss to get someone's attention and use the phrase *Ah sey!* (I say). To express displeasure in a rude way, Sierra Leoneans may "suck teeth" (make a sound by pulling air between pursed lips). People use only the right hand for passing items. They avoid pointing the soles of their feet at another person. Members of the same sex often hold hands or maintain close body contact while talking, but this is rare between members of the opposite sex.

Visiting. Friends visit, or *keep time*, with one another frequently. Men enjoy sitting in the evenings and drinking fresh palm wine. Women socialize at the cooking house of the family compound. Sierra Leoneans often tell friends in advance to expect a visit from them, but unannounced guests are also welcome. It is not necessary to bring a gift when visiting another's home. However, it is important to accept what the host offers—usually water or food. Honored guests may be given food upon departure. Although an event might have a designated starting time, guests can arrive up to two hours later. When guests leave, they are escorted at least to the edge of the host's property.

Eating. Traditional meals usually are served on a large platter with a bed of rice and a smaller amount of sauce in the center. The sauce is not mixed with the rice. Bones are left in the food; soft ones are eaten and harder ones are put aside. Eating practices vary according to locale and situation. In many homes, the husband may be served separately while the wife and children eat together. When visitors are present, adults eat from the common platter; children may be given spoonfuls of rice in their hands or a separate bowl. In villages, people eat with the right hand while squatting on the ground. In towns, spoons and chairs are more common. People drink only after the meal. At the end of a meal, a bowl of water is passed around for washing the face and hands.

Restaurants are uncommon, but urban residents can buy cooked rice at a *kukri*. Snacks (*street food*) such as bread and margarine, fried potatoes, fried plantains, fruit, roasted groundnuts (peanuts), homemade candies, and cookies are available in towns.

LIFESTYLE

Family. Extended families play an important role in the lives of Sierra Leoneans. Aunts may be addressed (and obeyed) as *mother*, and cousins are called *brother* or *sister*. Three to five generations may live within a family compound. This allows for care of both the young and old while the able-bodied work in the fields. Where there is more than one wife in the compound, wives share daily tasks and child rearing. This may not be the case for a paramount chief's wives, who may retain separate residences. Women generally take care of the compound, work in the garden and the market, and raise children, while men hunt, clear land, and do farm work. Men may also help with the upbringing of the children but to a lesser extent than women. Most women give birth to six or more children throughout life. *Fostering* is the custom of loaning a child to a childless woman to raise as one who will care for her in her old age; a child might also be shared with a wealthy person or relative who will educate and provide for him or her.

Dating and Marriage. Due to the coeducational system, relationships form early between boys and girls. Although parents try to discourage it, pregnancy among young girls is common. Dating without intending to marry is accepted in urban areas but not in villages. A date may be just a walk through the town or a chat on the veranda.

Marriage customs differ between urban and rural areas. In villages, a marriage may be arranged at any age, but it does not formally take place until the girl reaches puberty. The prospective husband agrees to pay the bride's parents a marriage payment after a great deal of negotiating and, sometimes, input from the whole village. It is the preparation for marriage, not the wedding itself, that is the event. After marriage, the woman lives in the husband's family's household. Polygamy is common. Western-oriented Sierra Leoneans choose their spouses.

Diet. Locally grown crops, such as cassava, are supplemented by imported items, such as tea, sugar, salt, and canned goods. The staple food is rice, eaten with a *plassas* (sauce) most commonly made from pounded cassava leaves, palm oil, and chili peppers. The diet also consists of groundnuts (peanuts), sweet potatoes, beans, fish, chicken, goat, small bush animals such as ground pigs (large rodents), *freetambos* (miniature deer), and an abundance of seasonal tropical fruit (bananas, plantains, pineapples, star fruits, breadfruit, papaya, oranges, grapefruit, mangoes, and coconuts). The Fulas herd cattle that are occasionally slaughtered and sold in the market. Meals tend to be unbalanced when the price of fish, beans, or groundnuts is high; then the diet consists mainly of rice and leaf sauces. Malnutrition is widespread among children because they receive the smallest portions of protein-rich foods (eggs and meat). Typically, a midday snack is followed by a large meal in the late afternoon; leftovers are put aside for the following morning's breakfast.

Recreation. Soccer is a popular sport and matches are usually well attended. Lack of resources and leisure time make other organized sports uncommon. However, schoolchildren compete in a variety of events (mostly track-and-field) during Sports Week. One event is the *paw paw* race, in which students run while carrying smaller students on their backs. Urban movie theaters usually show Indian, karate, and U.S. action films.

The Arts. Reggae music is widely popular. Disco dances that last until dawn accompany special events, even in towns without electricity, where a generator and sound system are rented for the occasion. Traditional music, dance, and theater play important symbolic roles in the lives of people, especially those living outside of the capital. Strangers are not permitted to attend certain events where traditional performances take place.

Sierra Leonean folk artists produce leather work, wooden carvings of human figures, and pottery with detailed designs. The dyeing of *gara* cloth is a popular handicraft. Artists apply wax designs to a fabric, place the fabric in a dye bath, and remove the wax to reveal the pattern. These fabrics are used for clothing, wall hangings, tablecloths, and other purposes.

Holidays. Sierra Leone's national days are Independence Day (27 Apr.) and Revolution Day (29 Apr.). Western and Christian holidays such as New Year's, Easter, and Christmas are celebrated universally, as is Pray Day, the last day of *Ramadan* (the Muslim holy month when worshipers fast each day from sunrise to sunset). The tradition surrounding New Year's and Easter is to have a party, sometimes with a sound system, at a

Sierra Leone

nearby river or beach. In towns with high hills, like Kabala, the New Year's tradition is to climb the mountain, taking along livestock to be slaughtered for a celebratory feast. Masquerades are a popular part of big celebrations: masked "devils," which often are associated with specific secret societies, entertain the people. On any holiday, children often go door-to-door asking for (and sometimes dancing and singing for) money.

Commerce. Sierra Leone's government offices and retailers are open primarily from 9 a.m. to 5 p.m. Open-air markets are active during daylight hours. Evenings bring out a different selection of goods: freshly cooked food and items such as cigarettes, soap, *mosquito coils* (repellent), and aspirin. Towns have a designated "market day," an expansion of the everyday market, when merchants from nearby villages sell more varied goods. Prices are fixed only in stores; bargaining is expected in markets.

SOCIETY

Government. The president (currently Ahmad Tejan Kabbah) is head of state and head of government. Voters directly elect the president, who is allowed to serve a maximum of two five-year terms. The legislative branch consists of a unicameral House of Representatives. Of its 124 members, 112 are elected to five-year terms. The remaining 12 seats are reserved for elected paramount chiefs. The voting age is 18.

Economy. Despite such natural resources as rutile and ilmenite (titanium ores), diamonds, gold, and bauxite, Sierra Leone remains a very poor country, with 75 percent of its people engaged in subsistence agriculture. A small wealthy class lives in the capital city.

The civil war destroyed many economic institutions. Sierra Leone relies on food subsidies from abroad and imports most manufactured goods. Export crops normally include palm kernels, coffee, cocoa, ginger, kola nuts, and piassava. Government corruption and smuggling have crippled the economy. If mineral resources were managed properly, the country would have a vast source of wealth. The currency is the *leone* (SLL), which is sometimes referred to in pounds. One pound equals two *leones*.

Transportation and Communications. Two paved roads link northern and eastern Sierra Leone with the capital. Most roads are unpaved. Common forms of transportation are taxis, mopeds, bicycles, and *poda-podas*. Small pickups fitted with seats and a roof, *poda-podas* carry people, goods, and animals. In rural areas, people generally walk, except when traveling extremely long distances or when transporting a large load (such as to or from the market). Freetown has a large natural harbor.

Postal service is fairly reliable, but rural delivery is unpredictable. Telephones are most common in Freetown but also operate in surrounding areas and larger *up-country* cities. The capital has several daily newspapers. The national radio broadcast can be picked up throughout much of the country, but television is limited mostly to Freetown and the surrounding area.

Education. Formal education is based on the British model. Schools often are run by missions. Classes are taught in English, although in rural primary schools instruction in local languages is common. Children may begin school at age five.

DEVELOPMENT DATA
Human Dev. Index* rank . . . . 177 of 177 countries
    Adjusted for women. . . . . NA
Real GDP per capita $500
Adult literacy rate . . . . 45 percent (male); 18 (female)
Infant mortality rate . . . . 145 per 1,000 births
Life expectancy . . . . 33 (male); 36 (female)

The dropout rate is high because of parents' inability to pay fees and other difficulties. About one-fifth of school-age children attend secondary schools. The curriculum often does not address the needs of rural people. The adult literacy rate is extremely low for women. Local education, "bush schools," or secret societies teach children skills and customs perceived as necessary by village elders. Such training prepares children to join society as adults. Sierra Leone has several teacher-training colleges and one university.

Health. Government-provided health care is inadequate. Most services, such as vaccinations, are provided by the World Health Organization and mission hospitals. Sierra Leoneans generally rely on a combination of traditional and Western medicines. Limited knowledge of nutrition and preventive care results in chronic illnesses such as anemia and gastrointestinal disease. Also prevalent are malaria, tuberculosis, schistosomiasis, typhoid, leprosy, and various skin lesions (attributable to nutritional deficiencies), which are slow to heal because of the climate. A high HIV infection rate is causing more AIDS deaths each year. Water is not potable. Goiter is endemic in the northeastern highlands, where the iodine content of the water is low.

AT A GLANCE
Events and Trends.

- In September 2004, UN peacekeepers turned over control of security in Freetown to local police. The move was part of the gradual withdrawal of UN troops from Sierra Leone.
- Sierra Leone's war crime court began hearing cases against former RUF leaders in July 2004. The United Nations and the Sierra Leonean government established the court to try those accused of atrocities during the civil war. The RUF was infamous for brutal campaigns that included cutting off the limbs of civilians. The head of the RUF, Foday Sankoh, died in a Freetown hospital in July 2003 while awaiting trial.
- President Kabbah won May 2002 elections with 70 percent of the vote. In parliamentary elections, Kabbah's Sierra Leone People's Party (SLPP) won 83 of 112 contested seats. The Revolutionary United Front Party (RUFP), the political party of the former RUF militia, was unable to win any parliamentary seats.

Contact Information. Embassy of Sierra Leone, 1701 19th Street NW, Washington, DC 20009; phone (202) 939-9261.

CultureGrams World Edition 2006

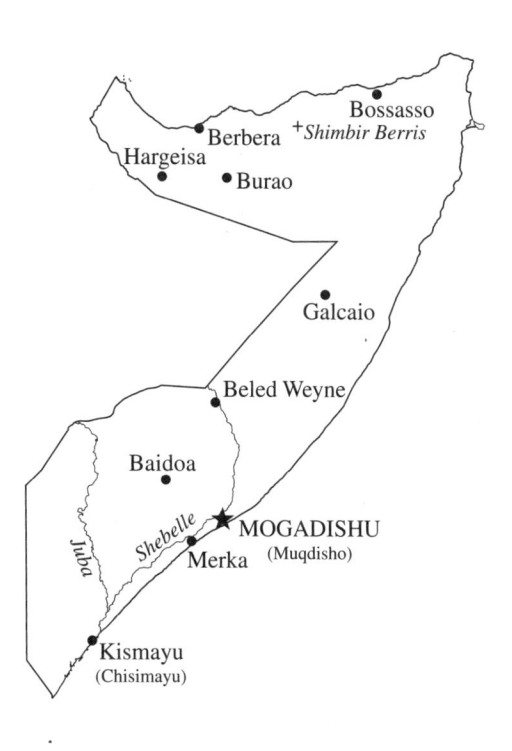

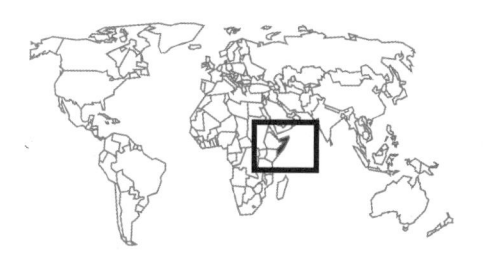

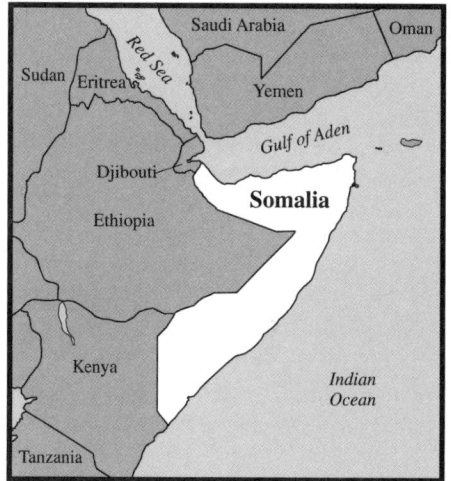

Somalia

BACKGROUND

Land and Climate. Somalia covers 246,300 square miles (638,000 square kilometers) on the Horn of Africa. The Guban is a hot, semiarid plain parallel to the Gulf of Aden. Shimbir Berris in the Oogo Mountains is the highest peak (7,900 feet, or 2,400 meters). The Hawd Plateau, grazing rangeland, covers most of the country's center. More fertile land lies between the Juba and Shebelle rivers, where crops are grown commercially. Lower Juba (south of the Juba River) is covered by thick bush but still supports some farming and livestock production. Drought and overgrazing have damaged much of Somalia's vegetation and wildlife.

Somalia's four seasons are *Gu* (heavy rains, March–June), *Hagaa* (dry, June–August), *Dair* (short rains, October–November), and *Jilal* (harsh, dry period, December–March). The climate is hot; some cities have average annual temperatures that exceed 88°F (31°C). Somalia's interior is arid, while coastal regions are more humid.

History. Somali have inhabited the Horn of Africa for centuries, occupying an area from near the Gulf of Aden, south to the Tana River in Kenya, and west to Harar in Ethiopia. Somali ivory, ostrich feathers, leopard skins, frankincense, and myrrh were carried as far away as China along early long-distance trade routes. While the Somali remained inland, the coast hosted settlers from India, Persia, Arabia, and Portugal. Their influence on architecture, clothing, language, and customs is evident today.

Islam was introduced in the ninth century by Arab sheiks who married into Somali families. Arabs controlled the southern coast between the ninth and nineteenth centuries; the sultan of Oman ruled as far south as Zanzibar until the Europeans began to compete for territory. In the 1880s, British Somaliland was established in the north, Italian Somaliland in the south, and French Somaliland around the present-day country of Djibouti.

Somali opposed colonialism and still have bitter feelings about the era. A rebellion launched in 1900 against Britain lasted until 1920; it failed, but it intensified Somali nationalism and eventually led to independence. In 1960, British and Italian Somalilands were united to form the Somali Republic.

Undermined by clan rivalries and corruption, the new parliamentary government never stabilized. Military leaders staged a successful 1969 coup. General Mohammed Siad Barre became president and suspended the constitution. He sought to reorder society and end tribal institutions by declaring Somalia a socialist state.

Due to the many ethnic Somali living in neighboring countries, clashes over borders were common for many years. During the Cold War, the Soviet Union and United States supplied arms to competing sides. The abundant weapons, controversial resettlement of refugees, corruption, and political repression all combined to spark a 1981 civil war in which the northern Isaak-led Somali National Movement (SNM) joined forces with the United Somali Congress (USC), composed mostly of Hawiye subclans, to fight the Darod-led government. In 1991, the Siad government collapsed and Somalia's political disintegration soon followed.

The SNM broke with the USC, denounced the 1960 union, and declared an independent Republic of Somaliland with Hargeisa as the capital. Somaliland, based on the borders of the old British Somaliland, is not internationally recognized, and it is opposed by some non-Isaaks in the north. However, it does have a functioning government with its own president.

Somalia

In the rest of Somalia, southern alliances dissolved in 1991 and Mogadishu was split between rival Hawiye subclans. The country plunged into anarchy. By 1992, famine, disease, and war threatened to engulf the population. A UN effort halted the famine but could not establish peace. Somali began to resent the international presence, anarchy returned, and foreign troops left in 1995. Somalia's various regions were claimed by rival warlords.

Various attempts to promote reconciliation failed, even when key clan leaders supported them. Opposing warlords in Mogadishu tried to manage public services as a joint venture in 1999, but the administration unraveled after only a few months. Also in 1999, arms began flowing into Somalia from a border war between Ethiopia and Eritrea. Each country sought allies among Somalia's rival factions, prompting an escalation in regional fighting. Some clans banded together to escape the anarchy of the late 1990s by declaring, like Somaliland, some form of autonomy. Northeastern clans joined in 1998 to establish Puntland ("Land of Frankincense") next to Somaliland. In 1999, the Rahanwayn Resistance Army announced a similar region centered in Baidoa.

Many of Somalia's clan leaders met in 2000 to establish a provisional government with jurisdiction over the entire country. They elected Abdulkassim Salat Hassan as president. Still, national reunification remained elusive because not all of Somalia's factions recognized the provisional government's authority. Peace talks repeatedly broke down, but in January 2004 warlords and politicians agreed to establish a new transitional parliament. The body was inaugurated in August 2004. Two months later it elected Puntland leader Abdullahi Yusuf Ahmed as president. The new government's challenges include fostering reconciliation among the clans and rebuilding the nation's infrastructure. However, after more than a decade of war and anarchy, many Somali remain pessimistic that a lasting peace can be achieved.

THE PEOPLE

Population. Somalia's population is estimated to be about 8.3 million, though taking an accurate census is impossible. Roughly 65 percent of the population lives in rural areas. About 45 percent is younger than age 15. Related to the Afar, Oromo, and other Cushitic peoples living on the Horn of Africa, Somali constitute 95 percent of the population. Minority groups include the Somali-speaking Hamari in Mogadishu; a related Arabic-speaking people living in other coastal cities; the Bajun, farmers and fishermen of Swahili origin; the Barawani, who speak a Swahili dialect; and other Bantu-speaking farmers living mostly along the Shebelle River.

Somali society is organized into large extended clan families, ranging in size from 100,000 to more than one million. There are six large clans (Darod, Isaak, Hawiye, Dir, Digil, and Rahanwayn) and a number of medium-to-small groups. Each of the larger families is further divided into lineage units that may range from 10,000 to 100,000 individuals. Additional divisions are made in these groups based on kinship alliances of smaller extended families. Once two people know each other's name and clan membership, it is possible for them to know how they are related, how they should address each other, and what level of respect they should give to each other. In rural areas, one can ask about another's lineage directly, but in an urban area it is more polite to identify it through indirect questions (about the person's home region, for example).

Language. The Somali language belongs to the Cushitic language family. It has three main dialects, each of which is difficult for speakers of the other two to understand. The dialects include Af-Maymay, spoken between the Shebelle and Juba rivers; Af-Benaadir, spoken on the coast from Mogadishu south; and standard Somali, spoken everywhere else. English, Italian, and Arabic are spoken by various educated Somali.

Until recently, Somali was an unwritten language; songs and poetry played a significant role in oral communication. In the 20th century, unique local scripts emerged and Latin alphabets were introduced by Westerners. By the late 1960s, more than 10 local scripts were being used in Somalia. Each script's usage depended on its usefulness, the clan to which its author belonged, and other factors. In 1972, the government adopted a Latin-based script and began to introduce it in schools and government documents. Literacy increased dramatically, due partly to a campaign to teach reading and writing in rural areas. Unfortunately, the script has yet to be fully standardized and uniformly adopted.

Religion. Nearly all Somali are Sunni Muslims. A small number are Christians. All towns have mosques; many on the coast are hundreds of years old, and some Mogadishu mosques are as many as one thousand years old. Muslims believe in a single god (*Allah*) and that Muhammad was his last and greatest prophet. Islamic scripture, the *Qur'an*, is believed to be the word of *Allah* as revealed to Muhammad. Muslims are taught to practice their religion through praying five times daily; giving alms to the poor; making a pilgrimage to Makkah, Saudi Arabia; abstaining from alcohol and pork; and attending to other duties.

General Attitudes. Most Somali in the interior have had little exposure to anything outside of Somalia. Even during the colonial era, European culture did not extend much beyond coastal cities. In the countryside, colonial powers were distrusted and disliked, and today's Somali view foreign assistance as having political motives. They may accept and be grateful for short-term assistance, but they sense paternalism quickly and may react violently to what they view as the belittlement of their culture or character. In addition, each person considers himself or herself to be equal among Somali, even though larger clans claim higher status. Somali consider themselves subservient to no one but *Allah*. Unlike in some Muslim countries, women can own property and manage businesses, even as they occupy a vital position in the extended family.

Somali cherish self-reliance, autonomy, and tradition. They value friendship based on mutual respect. Verbal gratitude is not often expressed, since giving obligates the receiver to reciprocate—unless the gift is charity, which is seen as an offering to *Allah* and requires no thanks.

Personal Appearance. Somali generally are tall and slender with narrow features. Urban men wear Western pants or a flowing plaid *ma'awiis* (kilt), Western shirts, and shawls. On their heads they may wrap a colorful turban or wear a *koofiyad* (embroidered cap). Rural men wear two 5-yard lengths of cloth—one wrapped around the waist to hang below the knees and the other wrapped around the upper body, or carried on the shoulder.

For northern women, the most fashionable dress is the *direh*, a long, billowing dress worn over petticoats. The southern favorite is the *guntino*, a 4-yard cloth tied over one shoulder and wrapped around the waist. Rural women wear sturdier varieties of the same clothing. All women wear shawls and headscarves. With the exception of a minority near the southern coast, women usually do not veil their faces. Women like sparkling, colorful touches in their everyday clothing. During religious holidays, children customarily receive new clothes if the family can afford it.

Somali bathe and wash often. They clean their teeth with sticks from a particular tree and polish them with powdered charcoal. Children wash their feet before going to bed. Women burn incense to perfume their bodies and homes. Henna gives women's hair and skin a glowing reddish tone.

CUSTOMS AND COURTESIES

Greetings. Somali greet each other by name or, in the case of relatives, by a word that shows their relationship (uncle, cousin, etc.). General greetings vary according to region and situation, but *Nabad* (Peace) is accepted nearly everywhere. The common southern variation is *Nabad miya?* (Is there peace?). Its equivalent in the north is *Ma nabad baa?* The Islamic greeting *Asalaamu aleikum* (Peace be upon you) is a common formal greeting, to which the response is *Aleikum ma salaam* (And peace be upon you). Such phrases are followed by inquiries about the general health and welfare of the individual and an exchange of information. *Iska warran?* (What's the news?) and *Maha la shegay?* (What are people saying?) are used as a "How are you?" in some parts of the country.

Men firmly shake hands with each other three times before putting that hand to their hearts. In some southern areas, women shake hands with each other and then kiss the hand they have shaken. Somali of the opposite sex who are not related usually do not touch when meeting.

Gestures. Somali use sweeping hand and arm gestures to dramatize speech. The eyes follow the direction of the hands, and the fingers may flutter. Many ideas are expressed through specific hand gestures. For example, placing both index fingers parallel to one another indicates "the same." A swift twist of the open hand and wrist means "nothing" or "no." A thumb under the chin indicates fullness. Snapping fingers may mean "long ago" or "and so on."

Visiting. Somali women socialize at home or at the market. Visitors need not take gifts or food to their hosts. Before entering a family compound, visitors announce their presence and wait a while in order not to surprise the family. Urban hosts serve guests sweet, spicy tea with milk and perhaps other refreshments. In rural areas, hosts offer tea or milk. A favorite time for urban visiting is late afternoon, when most of the day's work is done and the temperature is not too hot. In rural areas, night is better, as farm chores are completed and animals have settled down. When families socialize, men and women usually interact separately.

Tea shops, which often have tables outside, are centers for men to socialize and discuss current affairs. After lunch, men chew *khat*, a leafy green branch from a tree grown in the Ethiopian highlands and elsewhere. Women usually do not chew *khat*. After many hours of chewing, a mild high results; sustained use can lead to addiction.

Eating. When more than the immediate family is eating, men and women usually eat separately. In rural restaurants, women might choose to eat in rooms or areas separate from men. For the family meal, men usually are served first and the women and children eat later. Diners wash their hands in a bowl of water before and after the meal. On festive occasions, hands are also perfumed after the meal. When eating, people gather around a large common platter set on a table or on a mat on the ground. Diners eat with the right hand from the portion directly in front of them; guests usually are given larger servings. Young children are fed from the hand of the mother or a relative. The left hand usually does not have direct contact with food, as it is reserved for personal hygiene and prayer purification. Overeating is considered unacceptable.

LIFESTYLE

Family. Children inherit clan affiliation through their fathers. For some clans, a person's first name is a given name, second is the father's surname, and third is the grandfather's surname. A person's mother may be from another clan, and she retains her maiden name and position in her clan.

Family loyalty is important and families help one another in times of need. It is assumed that help will be reciprocated if needed in the future. Any good deeds bring honor to the family, clan, and society. The most fortunate members of a family feel especially obligated to help the others. Because resources are scarce, the hierarchy of who should be aided is clear. For instance, the extended family of the father's relatives has first priority. Aid can include such things as food, money, or shelter. Urban families might take in children of rural relatives and put them through school. War and repeated droughts have made it difficult for urban residents to provide this support, and many urban dwellers returned to their original rural areas as Somalia's clans intensified their divisions.

Dating and Marriage. Dating in the Western sense does not exist in Somalia, although it is common for young men and women to participate jointly in traditional dances. Virginity is valued in women prior to marriage. Divorce is legal and does occur. Arranged marriages are common; brides in these cases are often much younger than the grooms. Marriage to a cousin from the mother's side of the family (that is, of different lineage) has traditionally been favored as a way to strengthen family alliances, but this practice has been disrupted somewhat. Since 1991, Somali have tended to trust only members of their own clan for marriage. Weddings are celebrated by both families. Special foods such as *muqmad* (dried beef in clarified butter) and dates are served. In some areas, the couple is sequestered for a seven-day honeymoon.

Diet. Urban staple foods consist of locally produced meats and imported rice. In farming areas, sorghum, millet, corn, and sesame are common staples. Among nomads, milk from camels and goats is the main food available, supplemented with grains bought with money from the sale of animals. The milk is made into several varieties of yogurt.

Most urban people eat pancakes made from flour or millet for breakfast, rice or millet served with milk and *ghee* (clarified butter) for lunch and/or supper, and a small snack of milk or a bean dish in the evening. Nomads typically do not eat lunch when they are herding animals away from their homes. Vegetables gradually are being added to the diet, but they are still a novelty. Bananas, papaya, and mangoes are seasonal and plentiful. In some parts of the country, limes are always available, and grapefruit abound in season. Italian pasta has become popular in the cities as an alternative to rice. Fish is a staple in coastal towns.

Recreation. The youth enjoy soccer. Videos are popular in towns. Organized sports have all but been destroyed by war. However, cultural arts (primarily poetry, music, and dance) remain vital leisure and social activities.

The Arts. Somalia is viewed as a nation of poets. Today, poems and songs, parts of the oral culture that still flourishes, are recorded on cassettes and sent wherever Somali live. Many poems are about love, but others contain political commentary.

Somalia

This political poetry is called *gabay*. Common poetic metaphors known throughout society help unify Somali culture. People also perform plays and music. Accompanied by singing, stringed instruments (in the south), and drums, Somali dancers perform in two parallel lines of men and women or in circles. Artisans create intricately decorated wood carvings such as headrests, bowls, and vases. Carpets, baskets, pottery, and jewelry are other common handicrafts.

Holidays. Observed Islamic holy days include *Eid al Fitr* (three-day feast at the end of *Ramadan*), *Eid al Adha* (Feast of the Sacrifice, honoring Abraham's willingness to sacrifice his son), and *Mawliid*, the prophet Muhammad's birthday. Muslims fast from dawn until dusk each day of the holy month of *Ramadan*. Prior to the country's current instability, independence from Britain in the north was celebrated on 26 June and from Italy in the south on 1 July. The ancient Persian New Year (*Dab Shiid*, or "Starting Fire") is celebrated in many parts of Somalia.

Commerce. Organized commerce has been greatly disrupted. Open-air markets form the basis of daily commercial activity. Markets and commerce operate regularly in Somaliland and Puntland.

SOCIETY

Government. Somalia's government is led by a president (currently Abdullahi Yusuf Ahmed) as chief of state and a prime minister (currently Ali Muhammad Ghedi) as head of government. A 275-seat transitional parliament was established in 2004. The Darod, Hawiye, Dir, and Digil clans each have 61 seats in the body. The remaining 31 seats are divided among other clans.

Local and interclan affairs often are handled through traditional, male-dominated political structures and *shari'a* (Islamic law). For example, a *shir* is an open but not permanent deliberation forum of extended families or clan groups. *Shir* chiefs are appointed by kinsmen; decisions are made by consensus. A *shir* can declare war or peace, arbitrate family disputes, make policy for participating clans, and even dissolve itself if the alliance fails. Clans often make temporary agreements to solve specific problems, such as how to govern a region or town together.

Economy. Animal products account for the bulk of Somalia's limited exports. Meat (live sheep and goats) is shipped to Saudi Arabia and other markets; hides and skins are also exported. Somali sheep are especially prized in the Middle East. Most other production is for domestic consumption. Depending on the region, between 50 and 70 percent of the labor force is nomadic with camels, cattle, sheep, and goats. Remittances from Somali living abroad help support Somaliland's emerging economy.

Political instability, lack of a skilled labor force, poor land utilization, famine, disease, and other factors inhibit economic growth. However, Somalia could access marine and mineral resources. The currency is the Somali shilling (SOS), but U.S. dollars, British pounds, and other currencies are commonly accepted. Somaliland uses the Somaliland shilling.

Transportation and Communications. The system of roads in Somalia consists mostly of dirt tracks. It does extend between major cities, however, and large trucks with passengers and goods once traveled the routes. A system of minivans transports passengers between towns in times of peace. An international airport at Mogadishu, smaller airports in other towns, and dirt landing fields all exist in Somalia.

Somalia's telephone system is being rebuilt. Mobile phone systems are growing. Somalia's postal system does not function. Internet cafés operate in Mogadishu. Some warlords sponsor radio stations. Many Somali stay informed about international and some local events by listening to foreign radio broadcasts. Oral communication otherwise spreads news within Somalia.

Education. Somalia's formal education system, from primary levels through university, has been essentially destroyed by war. However, Somali value education, and many people have established private schools for the interim.

From the 1940s to 1972, the language of instruction was Arabic, English, or Italian. Traditional schools, where students learned the *Qur'an* in Arabic, served as kindergartens. The introduction of the written Somali script allowed the language to be used in school and in adult literacy programs. By 1975, nearly half of all Somali were literate in Somali and/or Arabic. However, initial gains did not last; by the 1980s, only one in ten children was able to attend school.

Health. Somalia has no real heathcare system and no modern hospitals. Primary-care clinics are run by or rely on international organizations, but violence has forced many to discontinue services. Malaria, tuberculosis, cholera, and other diseases are prevalent. Recent cholera epidemics have killed hundreds of people. Children, women of childbearing age, and the elderly suffer from unsafe water, poor nutrition, and a lack of medical services.

DEVELOPMENT DATA
Human Dev. Index* rank . . . . NA
    Adjusted for women . . . . NA
Real GDP per capita $500
Adult literacy rate . . . . 50 percent (male); 26 (female)
Infant mortality rate . . . . 119 per 1,000 births
Life expectancy . . . . 46 (male); 49 (female)

AT A GLANCE
Events and Trends.
- The tsunami that destroyed coastlines throughout southern Asia on 26 December 2004 also created large waves on Somalia's coasts, causing hundreds of reported deaths.
- Though not internationally recognized as a sovereign nation, Somaliland has a government led by President Dahir Riyale Kahin, who won multiparty presidential elections in April 2003.

Contact Information. Permanent Mission of Somalia to the United Nations, 425 East 61st Street, Suite 702, New York, NY 10021; phone (212) 688-9410.

CultureGrams™
People. The World. You.

ProQuest Information and Learning Company
300 North Zeeb Road, P.O. Box 1346
Ann Arbor, Michigan 48106 USA
Toll Free: 1.800.528.6279
Fax: 1.800.864.0019
www.culturegrams.com

© 2005 ProQuest Information and Learning Company and Brigham Young University. It is against the law to copy, reprint, store, or transmit any part of this publication in any form by any means without written permission from ProQuest. This document contains native commentary and original analysis, as well as estimated statistics. The content should not be considered strictly factual, and it may not apply to all groups in a nation. *UN Development Programme, Human Development Report 2004 (New York: Oxford University Press, 2004).

CultureGrams World Edition 2006

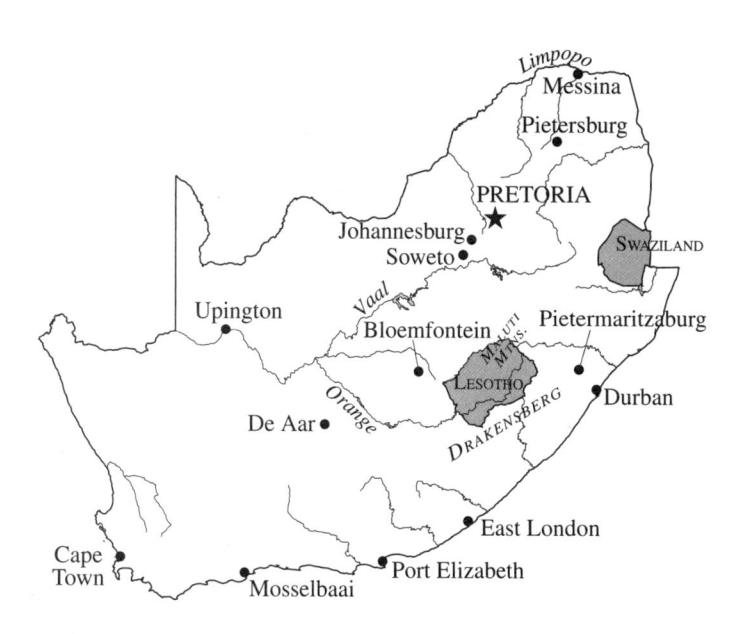

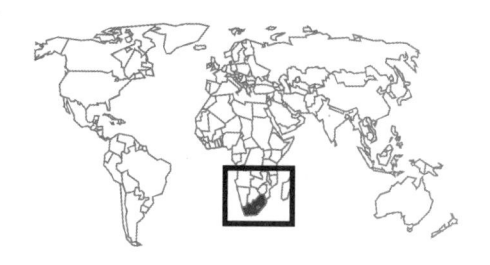

Republic of South Africa

BACKGROUND

Land and Climate. Covering 471,445 square miles (1,221,043 square kilometers), South Africa is slightly larger than Texas, New Mexico, and Oklahoma combined. The country's large interior plateau averages about 5,000 feet (1,500 meters) above sea level. Primarily savanna and semidesert, the plateau is rimmed by a narrow coastal belt, which is subtropical along the east coast and has a Mediterranean climate along the southwestern cape. South Africa's most important rivers are the Orange, Vaal, and Limpopo. Snow is confined to the Drakensberg and Maluti mountains in the east. Seasons run opposite those in the Northern Hemisphere. Humidity is generally low, except in the KwaZulu/Natal Province along the east coast. The country is noted for its long beaches, green forests, and rugged mountains. Diversity among plants and wildlife adds to its stunning scenic beauty. The Kingdom of Lesotho, surrounded by South Africa, sits on a high plateau. South Africa also nearly engulfs the Kingdom of Swaziland.

History. The Khoikhoi, San, and other indigenous Africans lived in southern Africa for thousands of years, although little is known of their history. In 1652, the Dutch established a provisions station at Cape Town. It supplied ships with fresh foods as they sailed around the tip of the continent. French Huguenot refugees joined the Dutch colony in 1688 and Germans came later. The colonists became known as *Boers* (farmers). They clashed at times with indigenous groups but stayed mainly in coastal areas. Britain gained formal possession of the Cape Colony in 1814. Dissatisfaction with British rule led many Boers to migrate to the interior between 1835 and 1848. Their migration, which they call the Great Trek, led to war with the indigenous Zulu, Xhosas, and other Africans. The Boers won most of the battles and took control of large tracts of land.

After the discovery of gold and diamonds in these Boer territories in the late 19th century, Britain annexed parts of the area. Tension erupted into the Boer War (1899–1902, also called the South African War), in which the Boers were defeated. In 1910, Britain combined its Cape and Natal colonies with the Boer republics of Orange Free State and Transvaal to create the Union of South Africa.

Following its election to power in 1948, South Africa's National Party (NP) devised the apartheid system that separated the country's population into racial groups: whites, blacks, coloureds (people of mixed race), and Indians. In 1961, the country gained independence from Great Britain and subsequently withdrew from the British Commonwealth over criticism of its racial policies. For the next three decades, South Africa was the scene of turmoil and violence. The African National Congress (ANC), first organized in 1912, was banned in 1960 for its communist views and antiapartheid activities. The ANC then launched, with other groups, an armed struggle against the government. Many ANC leaders, including Nelson Mandela, were jailed. In the 1970s and 1980s, international sanctions damaged the economy and isolated the country.

Frederik Willem (F. W.) de Klerk took office in 1989 and began to reform the government. He freed Mandela and other political prisoners, desegregated public facilities, and gave the ANC legal status. Mandela later suspended the ANC's armed struggle and dropped its socialist ideology. Violent clashes between rival African groups, among other factors, threatened progress toward greater political change. However, most apartheid provisions were abolished in 1991, and negotiations for a new constitution began in 1992. Mandela and de Klerk shared the Nobel Peace Prize in 1993.

South Africa

Despite sporadic violence, multiracial and multiparty elections were held peacefully in April 1994. Mandela was elected president. Mandela launched his *Masakhane* (Nguni for "Let us build together") campaign. In 1996, a new constitution was ratified. It has an extensive bill of rights guaranteeing equality for all who live in South Africa. In June 1999 elections, the ANC won all but one seat needed for a two-thirds (constitutional) majority, and Thabo Mbeki took over the presidency as Mandela retired.

The challenges facing South Africa are formidable: insufficient housing, high unemployment, violent crime, huge wealth inequality, and a high rate of HIV infection. Nevertheless, new health clinics and water systems have been built, homes are under construction, the unemployed are receiving training, and all children now have access to education.

THE PEOPLE

Population. South Africa's estimated population of 42.7 million is shrinking annually at a rate of 0.25 percent. The majority of the population (77 percent) is comprised of Africans, mostly from nine ethnic groups. The Zulus are the largest group (23 percent), followed by the Xhosas (18 percent), North Sothos, South Sothos, Tswanas, Shangaan-Tsongas, Swazis, Ndebeles, and Vendas. Each has its own cultural heritage, language, and national identity. Before migration patterns led groups to mix with one another, most lived in distinct areas of southern Africa. This division inspired the apartheid concept of "homelands," which was abolished in 1992.

People of mixed race (9 percent) are most often descendants of early white settlers, native Khoikhoi, and slaves imported from the Dutch East Indies during South Africa's colonial period. Indians (3 percent) are generally descendants of indentured laborers brought from India during the 19th century or of Indian immigrants who came between 1860 and 1911. Whites (11 percent) include English-speaking descendants of English, Irish, and Scottish settlers and Afrikaans-speaking descendants of Dutch, French, and German colonials. It is estimated that between two and four million illegal immigrants from neighboring African states also reside in South Africa.

Language. Sixty percent of all whites and most mixed-race people speak Afrikaans (a Dutch derivation). Other whites and Indians speak English. English is commonly used in business, between some ethnic groups, and as the primary language of instruction in secondary schools. The vocabulary and pronunciation of South African English reflects a unique relationship between English and other languages spoken in South Africa. English and Afrikaans are more common in urban areas than rural regions.

African languages are roughly divided into four families: Nguni; Sotho; Tsonga, or Shangana; and Venda. Most Africans speak a Nguni language: Zulu and Xhosa are most prominent, followed by Ndebele and Swazi. Sotho languages (South Sotho, North Sotho, and Setswana) dominate the central part of the country. Also, a few mixed languages have developed to facilitate communication between groups. Typical is a mixture of Zulu and Xhosa or Zulu and Sotho. People speak their original languages at home or within their own groups. Some whites are now learning a major African language to help them become more aware of their diverse culture.

Religion. More than half of Africans, most whites, and most mixed-race people are Christians. Some mixed-race people are Muslims. Afrikaans speakers belong primarily to the Dutch Reformed Church. English-speaking whites generally belong to Anglican, Lutheran, Presbyterian, Roman Catholic, Methodist, and other congregations. Africans typically belong to African Independent Churches—the largest of which is the Zion Christian Church—that combine Christian and traditional African beliefs in their worship patterns. As many as 20 percent of Africans adhere solely to indigenous belief systems. Most Indians are Hindus, although about 20 percent are Muslims and 10 percent are Christians. South Africa's Jewish community is small, but it has had a significant impact on the country's development.

General Attitudes. South Africa's complex transition from minority to majority rule has been painful at times, but the majority of citizens accept coexistence in a multiracial society. Nevertheless, a slow pace of change in some aspects of the transition has frustrated many people. Money is scarce to pay for textbooks that teach more African history. Some Africans complain of job discrimination, while many whites disagree with attempts to require companies to hire more Africans. Mixed-race people often express a feeling of being left behind or marginalized in new planning. And, even as some whites are reaching out to others by improving access to job training or land, integrating neighborhoods, or learning about indigenous cultures, others continue to fear majority rule and oppose reform efforts. At the same time, many Africans are angry that whites are not giving up more of their wealth or moving faster to integrate society.

Overall, however, people want to contribute their efforts to building a democratic society. Despite various setbacks, the majority of South Africans value their new economic opportunities and a renewed acceptance by the international community. They agree that South Africans must work together to achieve all the goals set forth in the constitution and to allow South Africa to capitalize on its natural wealth, its strong economy, and its diverse peoples.

Personal Appearance. Some rural Africans wear traditional clothing for special purposes or everyday attire. This may include a variety of headdresses and colorful outfits. They wear Western-style clothing on a daily basis, but women include a scarf or other headdress and wear either a dress or a blouse and skirt. Urban African men wear pants, shirts, and sometimes suits, but rarely shorts. African women wear both African and European fashions.

White South Africans wear Western-style clothing, usually made from lightweight cotton. They tend to be well dressed in public. Men wear suits or shirts and trousers. In rural areas, they may prefer shorts and kneesocks. Women generally wear comfortable dresses or modest pants. Many Muslim women wear head coverings and other traditional Muslim attire. Indian women often wear a *sari*, a wraparound-type dress.

CUSTOMS AND COURTESIES

Greetings. Of the numerous greetings used in South Africa, the English phrases *Hello* and *Good morning* are understood by most people. Afrikaans speakers say *Goeie môre* (Good morning). Young English speakers say *Howzit* (slang for "How are you?") to friends. A more formal *Good morning* or *Good afternoon* is common among adults. The Zulu and Swazis greet each other with *Sawubona* (literally, "I see you," meaning "Hello") or *Kunjani* (How are you?). An acceptable response to either is *Yebo* (Yes). The Xhosa greeting, *Molo*, and the Sotho phrase *Dumela* have similar meanings to *Sawubona*. On parting, most South Africans use a phrase that assumes a future meeting. In other words, people rarely say good-bye. Rather, one says *See you* in English, *Tot siens* (Till we see each other again) in Afrikaans, or something like the Sotho *Sala gashi* (Go well in peace).

South Africans shake hands when they greet, but the type of handshake differs between groups. Some use firmer, others lighter, shakes with one hand; many rural people use both hands. Close friends and relatives may hug. Sometimes African friends greet with an intricate triple handshake that involves interlocking the smallest fingers, clasping fists, and interlocking fingers again. African men may also hold hands when walking or conversing.

Although friends use first names and nicknames, South Africans generally do not address strangers or older people by their first name. Professional titles or the equivalents to "Mr.," "Mrs.," and "Miss" are preferred. It is polite to call an older African "father" (*Tata* in Xhosa, *Ntate* in SeSotho, or *Baba* in Zulu) or "mother" (*Mama* in Xhosa and Zulu or *Mme* in Sesotho). Afrikaans-speaking people, both white and of mixed race, refer to older males as "uncle" (*oom*) and older females as "auntie" (*tannie*).

Gestures. Africans and mixed-race people frequently use hand gestures in conversation. It is impolite to point at someone with the index finger, stand too close during conversation, or talk with one's hands in the pockets. Africans use the right hand for handshakes, to pass objects, or to gesture. Receiving an object with cupped hands is polite. Some young people express "hello" or "good-bye" by extending the thumb and little finger up (folding all other fingers against the palm) and rocking the hand from side-to-side. Whites tend to use minimal hand gestures and are comfortable passing items with either hand.

Visiting. Visiting is an important social activity for most of South Africa's groups. When possible, visits are arranged in advance, but unannounced visits among good friends or relatives are common, especially in areas where telephones are not accessible. South Africans are gregarious, hospitable, polite, and personally self-effacing. They enjoy conversing and socializing. Gender, ethnic, and age groups tend to socialize among themselves; association between such groups is more formal.

Etiquette varies widely between ethnic groups. Guests usually are served refreshments. In Indian homes, it is impolite to refuse these, and it is polite to accept second helpings if eating a meal. Among Africans, dinner guests are not expected to bring a gift. Whites will often bring something to drink (juice, wine, etc.). When guests leave, they usually are accompanied by their host to the gate, car, or street.

Eating. Whites generally observe the continental style of eating; the fork is in the left hand and the knife remains in the right. Africans more often eat meals with spoons or their fingers (depending on the food). It generally is not appropriate for adults to eat on the street unless eating ice cream or standing at a vendor's stand. Eating alone is also rare. Dinner, usually eaten after 6 p.m., is the main meal. All South Africans enjoy a *braai* (barbecue), especially on the weekend. Beef and *boerewors* (spiced sausage) are usually featured at a barbecue.

LIFESTYLE

Family. White families are small, live as a nuclear unit, generally are close-knit, and enjoy a good standard of living. Africans have strong extended family ties, even if nuclear units are not always able to live in the same household because of employment or education. Children are taught to respect their elders and obey their parents. Relatives play an important role in caring for children and providing aid to those in need.

Dating and Marriage. Dating habits vary between ethnic groups, but most South Africans plan on marrying and having children. For many ethnic groups, the groom must pay *lobola* (bride-price) in the form of cattle or money to the bride's parents before a wedding can take place. However, paying *lobola* can take years; a couple might have several children before it is paid. Traditional wedding celebrations involve much dancing and feasting. The law recognizes tribal weddings. Polygamy is more common in rural areas. Most white and mixed-race South Africans marry in a church or marry civilly. Indians have their own wedding traditions.

Diet. South Africans enjoy a wide variety of foods, from roast beef or roast lamb and potatoes, to various curries, to *boerewors* and pickled fish, grilled meats, stewed tomatoes, cabbage, pumpkin, and spinach. Wild game meats are also popular with many people. Corn, rice, beans, and potatoes are the staples for the rural majority. Africans eat *mealie meal* (cornmeal porridge, sometimes cooked with vegetables and meat) on a regular basis. Cooked in a three-legged cast-iron pot over a fire, *potjiekos* (pot food) is a popular meal among Afrikaans speakers for weekend social functions, festivals, and holidays. Fresh fruits and vegetables are abundant and often sold by farmers from roadside stands. *Biltong* is a jerky-like snack made from various types of meat. The *milk tart*, a custard-like pie, is a favorite desert. Wine, tea, coffee, beer, and *cool-drink* (any soft drink or juice) are common beverages.

Recreation. Soccer, rugby, and cricket are the most important sports in South Africa. Whites prefer rugby and cricket, while Africans mostly follow soccer. However, South Africans of all backgrounds cheer when fellow citizens win at international events. Many people enjoy tennis and swimming. Indeed, all ethnic groups value competitive sports, which are increasingly open to a broader population. Those who can afford equipment or club memberships participate in squash, lawn bowling, golf, field hockey, and sailing. Horse and car racing draw crowds. South Africans appreciate their many beaches and recreational facilities, including swimming pools, parks, libraries, and movie theaters. Dancing, playing music, attending festivals, and enjoying cultural events are popular activities throughout the year.

The Arts. South Africa boasts a diversity of musical styles. Choirs are common, and traditional folk songs have been integrated into choral music. The popular *mbaqanga* dance music originated in apartheid-era townships. *Kwaito* music, a favorite of young South Africans, mixes African melodies and lyrics with hip-hop and reggae. *Kwela* incorporates the distinctive penny whistle. South Africans are also devoted to the fine arts, and major cities host performances of the symphony, ballet, and opera. *Gumboot* dancing, developed by African gold miners, has become a popular performance art. Each ethnic group produces its own style of folk art, including basketry, beadwork, and soapstone carvings. South African authors of all races have dealt with controversial political and social themes, often writing in exile during the apartheid years. Nadine Gordimer, André Brink, and Es'kia Mphahlele are some of the most respected.

Holidays. The official holidays in South Africa include New Year's Day, Easter (including Good Friday and Family Day on Monday), Human Rights Day (21 Mar.), Freedom Day (27 Apr.), Workers' Day (1 May), Youth Day (16 June), National

South Africa

Women's Day (9 Aug.), Heritage Day (24 Sept.), Reconciliation Day (16 Dec.), Christmas, and Day of Goodwill (26 Dec.). Each religion also observes other important holidays.

Commerce. In general, businesses and shops are open from 8:30 a.m. to 5 p.m., Monday through Friday, and until 1 p.m. on Saturday. Shopping centers and supermarkets stay open into the evenings and on weekends. Banking hours are usually 9:00 a.m. to 3:30 p.m., Monday through Friday, and 8:30 to 11 a.m. on Saturday. Government offices are open from 8 a.m. to 4 p.m., Monday through Friday. Few businesses and shops are open on Sunday. *Pavement* (sidewalk) vendors offer various items, and small retail businesses (*spaza* shops) run from suburban homes sell goods to neighborhood residents.

SOCIETY

Government. South Africa's president (currently Thabo Mbeki) is chief of state and head of government. The president is chosen by an elected parliament on the basis of the majority party's recommendation. Parliament has two houses: a 90-member Council of Provinces and a 400-seat National Assembly. All members of Parliament are elected to five-year terms. Members of the National Assembly are elected directly by popular vote, while Council members are chosen by the nine provincial parliaments. The president serves a maximum of two five-year terms. All citizens are eligible to vote at age 18.

Economy. South Africa is the richest country in Africa, and whites generally enjoy a high standard of living. The relatively high per capita gross domestic product (GDP) reflects a wide gap between whites and others in terms of income because whites usually earn far more than Africans. Mixed-race people earn closer to the average national GDP. Women earn less than one-third of the nation's income.

More than half of all export earnings come from minerals and metals. South Africa is one of the world's largest producers of platinum and gold, and it also exports diamonds, chrome, and coal. Low gold prices on world markets have sometimes slowed that sector's growth. Wine and tourism are fast-growing industries. The industrial base is large and diversified, and new investment is allowing for growth. The government has privatized (in whole or in part) some of the largest state enterprises to improve market conditions and raise capital. Strong growth and investment will be necessary to reduce high unemployment and reduce poverty. The currency is the *rand* (ZAR).

Transportation and Communications. South Africa has the best-developed infrastructure in Africa. Railroads carry freight and passengers throughout the country; rail links with other southern African nations have been established, too. Air routes link major cities. South Africa's road system is well maintained and extensive. Traffic moves on the left side of the road. Many urban commuters take minibus *combies* to work.

The nation's advanced telecommunications system is also considered the best on the continent. Television is widely available, and four channels broadcast in English, Afrikaans, and the Nguni and Sotho language groups. One cable channel offers a mix of U.S. and British programming. Radio broadcasts are available in all of South Africa's languages.

Education. As in other areas of South African life, apartheid-

DEVELOPMENT DATA
Human Dev. Index* rank . . . . 119 of 177 countries
  Adjusted for women . . . . 96 of 144 countries
Real GDP per capita $10,070
Adult literacy rate . . . . 87 percent (male); 85 (female)
Infant mortality rate . . . . 62 per 1,000 births
Life expectancy . . . . 46 (male); 52 (female)

era segregation in public education has been dismantled. However, it will take some time before all children receive the same opportunities within a uniform system. Many schools are without adequate texts or supplies. Schooling is compulsory to age 15. Africans receive instruction in their native language until the seventh grade, and then they usually are taught in English after that. Afrikaans is also offered as a language of instruction. In urban areas, an increasing number of primary schools teach in English. There are 19 universities in South Africa.

Health. Medical services are socialized, but some private sector participation is also incorporated. Public hospitals and clinics are open to all citizens. Free care is given to all pregnant women and to children younger than age six. Disease and malnutrition are more common among blacks. South Africa is experiencing a devastating HIV/AIDS epidemic; it is estimated that roughly one-fifth of South Africa's adults are infected. Tuberculosis, malaria, and cholera are also serious problems. About half of South Africa's population lacks basic sanitation; almost one-third lacks access to adequate supplies of potable water.

AT A GLANCE
Events and Trends.
- In April 2004, President Thabo Mbeki secured a second five-year term when the ruling ANC party won nearly 70 percent of the vote in parliamentary elections. Factors contributing to the ANC victory included the stability of the economy and the party's efforts to increase the availability of housing and water.
- To counter the nation's HIV/AIDS epidemic, the Mbeki government made a decision in late 2003 to initiate a major HIV/AIDS program. The program includes the distribution of anti-retroviral AIDS drugs. The decision was made near the end of Mbeki's first term, during which he suffered widespread criticism for publicly questioning the causal link between HIV and AIDS.

Contact Information. Embassy of South Africa, 3051 Massachusetts Avenue NW, Washington, DC 20008; phone (202) 232-4400; web site www.saembassy.org. South Africa Tourism, 500 Fifth Avenue, Suite 2040, New York, NY 10110; phone (212) 730-2929; web site www.southafrica.net.

© 2005 ProQuest Information and Learning Company and Brigham Young University. It is against the law to copy, reprint, store, or transmit any part of this publication in any form by any means without written permission from ProQuest. This document contains native commentary and original analysis, as well as estimated statistics. The content should not be considered strictly factual, and it may not apply to all groups in a nation. *UN Development Programme, Human Development Report 2004 (New York: Oxford University Press, 2004).

CultureGrams™
People. The World. You.

ProQuest Information and Learning Company
300 North Zeeb Road, P.O. Box 1346
Ann Arbor, Michigan 48106 USA
Toll Free: 1.800.528.6279
Fax: 1.800.864.0019
www.culturegrams.com

CultureGrams World Edition 2006

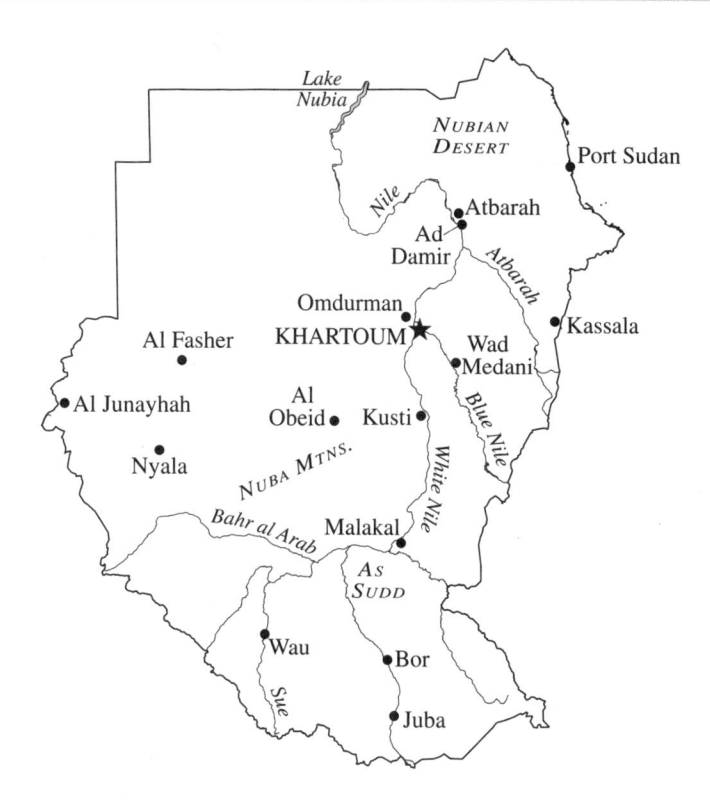

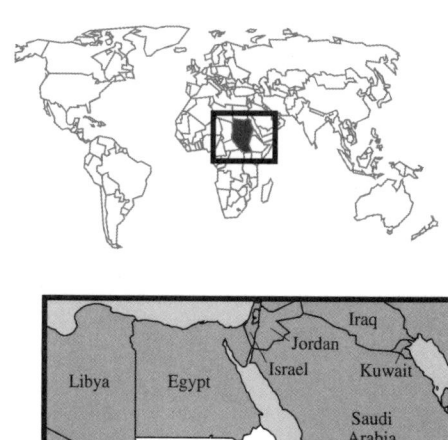

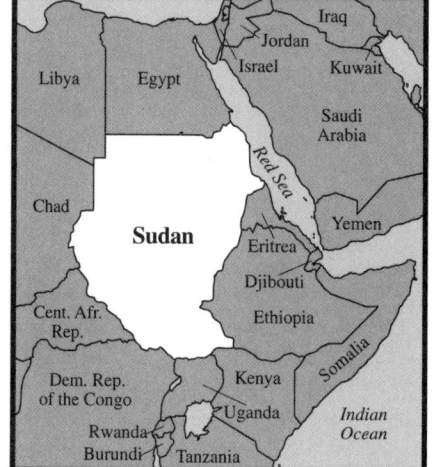

Republic of the Sudan

BACKGROUND

Land and Climate. With an area of 967,494 square miles (2,505,810 square kilometers), Sudan is the largest country in Africa and is almost one-third the size of the continental United States. Most of Sudan is a large plain. The Nubian Desert in the north is separated from the Red Sea by low coastal hills. Khartoum and surrounding areas are hot, arid, and subject to sandstorms. Hills and mountains run along the border with Chad. The White and Blue Nile rivers flow north, eventually converging to form the Nile River, which empties into the Mediterranean Sea. Southern Sudan has a tropical climate with open savanna grassland, large marshland (As Sudd in the Upper Nile region), and rain forests. Its climate and wildlife are similar to East Africa. A wide variety of wildlife can be found in eastern and southern Sudan, including elephants, lions, crocodiles, zebras, monkeys, boars, eagles, vultures, cranes, and more.

History. Contacts between Egypt and Cush (present-day Nubia) date back to several millennia B.C. The Nubians of Cush ruled northern Sudan between the eleventh and fourth centuries B.C. Cush also briefly ruled Egypt (713–671 B.C.). During the early Christian era, Sudan was part of Ethiopia's Kingdom of Aksum. When Arabs successfully invaded Egypt in the seventh century, a treaty with Nubia forbade Nubian settlement in Egypt and Muslim settlement in Sudan.

The area remained Christian until it fell under Egyptian domination in the 15th century. Still, Sudan continued to be semiautonomous for some time. Egypt (then a province of the Ottoman Empire) conquered Sudan in 1821, after which a joint Turko-Egyptian administration colonized the land. Between 1881 and 1885, Muhammad Ahmad Abdullah led a successful revolt against Egypt and the Ottomans. However, his Mahdia government fell in 1898 as British colonial interests in the region expanded. Egypt then ruled Sudan under British tutelage until after World War II. Two years after Egypt claimed sole ownership of Sudan, an agreement was reached (in 1953) with Britain to grant Sudan self-rule. The Sudanese people voted for and proclaimed (in 1956) an independent democratic state. Unfortunately, democracy did not last long.

Since 1958, when a military coup toppled the civilian government, control of Sudan has alternated between civilian and military governments. As each civilian government was unable to solve Sudan's many problems, including a civil war with the south, the military would take control. One such coup in 1969 brought Gaafar Nimeiry to power. In 1972, he recognized special autonomy for the south and ended the civil war. However, his program of Islamization in the 1980s, which sought to impose Islamic law (*shari'a*) on the whole country, rekindled the war and led to a coup in 1985. The officers involved sponsored free elections in 1986, but the new government under Sadiq al-Mahdi was unable to end the civil war or improve economic conditions. In 1988, when fighting prevented relief supplies from reaching drought-stricken areas, at least 250,000 people died. Al-Mahdi was overthrown in 1989 by Omar Hassan al-Bashir.

Al-Bashir suspended the constitution, dissolved parliament, and banned political parties. His regime focused on the war with the Sudan People's Liberation Movement (SPLM) and Army (SPLA). Seeking autonomy for the non-Muslim south, the SPLA's ability to fight was severely undermined by internal divisions between 1991 and 1996. Rival factions fought each other, destroyed villages, and terrorized their inhabitants. Hundreds of thousands of people became refugees, forced to flee either by drought or fighting. Today, many remain in camps in neighboring countries.

By 1996, Sudan had alienated its neighbors and faced international isolation. The SPLA resolved its major internal problems, united with the north's National Democratic Alliance (NDA, led from exile by Sadiq al-Mahdi and others), and began to launch major advances in 1998. Agreements between the Khartoum regime and rebel groups were signed to hold a referendum on self-determination for southern states. However, with no real timetable or specifics on how or where the referendum would take place, the fighting continued. Warring factions agreed in 1998 to not hinder international relief efforts striving to avert mass starvation. By 2000, pressure to end the war was mounting from within and without; al-Bashir pledged to make progress in negotiations.

A new constitution was passed in 1998. The following year, a power struggle emerged between al-Bashir and parliament speaker Hassan al-Turabi, who had long been considered the real political power in Sudan. Al-Turabi led an effort to curb al-Bashir's presidential authority by proposing laws to transfer certain powers to parliament. On the eve of the vote, al-Bashir dissolved parliament and declared a state of emergency. Al-Bashir then removed al-Turabi from his position as head of the ruling National Congress Party in May 2000. Al-Turabi responded by forming a new political group, but al-Bashir and the National Congress Party went on to win December 2000 presidential and parliamentary elections boycotted by the opposition. In 2001, al-Turabi and many of his supporters were arrested after his party signed a memorandum of understanding with the SPLA. He remained imprisoned until October 2003, when a ban on his party was lifted.

In 2002, after nearly two decades of civil war, the Sudanese government and the SPLA initiated a cease-fire and began peace negotiations. Although the cease-fire was repeatedly violated, negotiations continued over the next two years. In January 2005, the government and the SPLA signed a final peace treaty to end the long-running conflict.

Unfortunately, peace between the government and the SPLA has been overshadowed by a separate conflict in Darfur, a region of western Sudan. In 2003, the Sudanese military and the pro-government *janjaweed* militia responded to an uprising by Darfurian rebels, who claim the government oppresses Africans in favor of Arabs. Amid attacks by pro-government forces, huge populations of refugees fled into Chad. Widespread disease and malnutrition resulted. By 2005, the conflict had displaced an estimated two million people and claimed at least 100,000 lives. The Sudanese government denies links with the *janjaweed*, but the international community has widely condemned the government for supporting the militia's systematic killings, torture, and other atrocities.

THE PEOPLE

Population. Sudan's population of about 39.1 million is growing annually at a rate of 2.6 percent. Nearly 40 percent of the population is Arabic. Some Sudanese (such as the Fur) have African ancestry but follow Arabic customs; they live in the north or central regions. The Nubian minority (about 8 percent) is concentrated around the Nile in northern Sudan. They are not of the same ethnic group as the Nuba Mountain peoples of the south. The Beja (6 percent) live in the east. The Dinka, Funj, Nuer, Shilluk, and other African peoples of southern Sudan constitute half of the total population. Roughly 38 percent of all Sudanese live in urban areas. Khartoum's metropolitan area, including Omdurman, is home to more than four million people. Juba is the south's largest city, with approximately 100,000 people.

Language. Arabic is the official language of the entire country, but it is spoken by only about half of the population. Various dialects are found throughout the country; northern dialects are closer to classical Arabic than to southern dialects. Arabic Juba is a unique dialect used in southern urban areas for communication between ethnic groups. More than one hundred other languages are spoken, including Nubian, Dinka, Azande, Bari, Nuer, and Shilluk. Educated southerners speak English.

Religion. The majority (70 percent) of Sudanese are Sunni Muslim, living primarily in the north and central areas. The Christian population (5 percent) lives chiefly in the south. Other Sudanese follow indigenous (animist) beliefs.

Religious loyalties play an important role in Sudanese politics. For example, the Ummah Party is associated with the Mahdist movement of the 1880s. Mahdists accept Muhammad Ahmad Abdullah as a guide (*al-Mahdi*) sent to establish God's will on earth. His son created the Ummah Party and his great-grandson is Sadiq al-Mahdi, the party's current leader. Hassan al-Turabi is the nation's most powerful Islamic cleric. The animists are politically allied with the Christians in the SPLA.

Muslims believe in the *Qur'an* (Koran) as the word of *Allah* (God) revealed to the prophet Muhammad. They show devotion through Islam's Five Pillars of Faith: professing the name of *Allah* as the only God and Muhammad as his last and greatest messenger; praying five times daily; fasting during the holy month of *Ramadan*; giving alms (*zakat*) to the poor; and making a pilgrimage to Makkah, Saudi Arabia, if possible. Muslims are to abstain from consuming alcohol and pork.

General Attitudes. Northern Sudanese tend to be conservative, polite, expressive, and deliberate. They assess a situation carefully before acting. They believe strongly in accepting the challenges of everyday life because they view whatever happens as the will of God. Sudanese throughout the country appreciate good humor, chivalry, and strong families. Southerners generally are open, friendly, and hospitable.

Sudanese society is highly stratified. In addition to an underprivileged class, there is also a middle class (in cities) and a small upper class. All Sudanese respect wealth and power. Power may be defined as having a government position, being from a respected family, being a cleric or spiritual leader, or (in the south) being a local chief. Indeed, a chief commands great respect regardless of his skills or education. Rural wealth is measured by the size of one's herds (cattle among Africans; cattle, sheep, and camels for nomadic Arabs). Urban wealth is measured in terms of property and material possessions. Educated individuals command respect, as they are likely to work for the government or large businesses.

Personal Appearance. Urban men in the north wear Western-style clothing, although they might also wear the traditional *jalabia* (long white robes) and *imma* (turbans) that are prevalent in rural areas. Women wear traditional dresses and are required to be covered from head to ankle when in public. The covering is called a *hijab*. Women might also wear a *tarha* (veil). Nomadic people wear heavy robes for protection from the desert heat and blowing sand.

Southern men and women wear Western-style clothing. Women wear as much jewelry as they can afford. Wealthy women are easy to identify by the amount of expensive jewelry they wear. Most women wear less expensive locally made earrings and beads. All Sudanese dress conservatively in public.

CUSTOMS AND COURTESIES

Greetings. The northern Sudanese are more formal in their greetings than people in the south. Arabs give a gentle handshake to members of the same sex, and friends frequently embrace. A Muslim man generally will not touch a woman in public. The usual verbal greeting is *Salaam' alaykum* (Peace be upon you) or *Ahlan wasahlan* (Welcome), followed by *Kayf haalak?* or *Kayf innakum?* (both basically mean "How are you?"). Good friends may simply exchange a casual *Salam* (Peace). Friends, peers, and children are called by their given name or nickname. Relatives and older people are respectfully addressed by family title (uncle, aunt, etc.) or religious title (such as *hadji*, someone who has completed a pilgrimage) followed by their given name. Bureaucrats or professionals are addressed by title and surname.

In the south, old friends, relatives, or people who have not seen each other for a while will shake hands when greeting. Otherwise, a verbal greeting is sufficient for most situations. Both men and women shake hands with each other. Most people greet others with the local equivalent of the Bari phrases *Do pure* (Good morning), *Do parana* (Good afternoon), and *Gwon ada?* (How are you?). Workers address their superiors by title and surname. Friends and relatives may use nicknames. Married women rarely call their husbands by name.

Gestures. Sudanese consider it improper to gesture or eat with the left hand. One passes or accepts items only with the right hand or both hands, never with the left alone. Pointing with the finger is considered rude. In the north, it is offensive to allow the bottom of one's feet (or shoes) to point toward another person. Nodding the head down can mean "yes"; nodding up can mean "no." It is polite to stand when greeting someone.

Visiting. In the north, social visiting among friends and family members is very important to building and mending relations. Most visits occur in the home. Close friends and relatives may visit unannounced, while others are invited or make arrangements in advance. Religious holidays and special events (such as weddings) provide the best time for lengthy gatherings. Friday is the most popular day of the week for visiting, but visiting can be done on any day. It is most polite for guests to come in the midmorning or evening. At other times of day, people may be either eating or sleeping. Entire families visit, but men and women socialize separately. Children are expected to play away from the adults so as not to disrupt their conversation. Hosts serve tea, coffee, soft drinks, or water to their guests. First-time visitors only stay for a short time.

Southern Sudanese also place great value on visiting others. It helps maintain the extended family network. Hosts will prepare a meal of goat, sheep, or chicken for important guests. Otherwise, they serve light refreshments. Relatives, friends, and neighbors frequently exchange short casual visits without prior notice. For extended stays (of more than one day), persons need to make arrangements in advance. It is not uncommon for men and women to socialize together, especially at parties or other social functions.

Eating. Throughout Sudan, people eat two meals a day. Urban residents eat three meals when they can afford it. Dinner is the main family meal. Men and boys eat apart from women and girls. Everyone washes his or her hands before and after a meal, and each person eats with the right hand. If important guests are present, hosts serve more elaborate meals and special beverages. Families rarely eat at restaurants, but unmarried men and travelers do. Restaurant food is usually too expensive and of lower quality than what is prepared at home.

LIFESTYLE

Family. The Sudanese family is an extended, male-oriented organization. Three generations of males and their spouses and children often live in the same household or compound. Urban households tend to be more nuclear. Men are responsible for earning an income, herding livestock, and leading the family. They consider it their duty to raise many children, discipline them, find them good spouses, and keep the family free from scandal. Children who shame the family may be severely punished (in some areas, a girl who becomes pregnant out of wedlock may be killed by her family). Women cook, clean, care for the children, and help men with farming. They also collect firewood and complete other chores, depending on where the family lives. After giving birth, women customarily do not leave the house or do any work for 40 days. In general, southern women have more rights and freedom than northern women.

Dating and Marriage. Western-style dating does not occur in the north, where marriages are arranged (often between cousins) by families. A potential couple is usually allowed to reject the match. Grooms must pay the bride's family a dowry, usually in cash. Wedding celebrations may last for more than a day, and both families host feasts and parties. A festive procession of wedding guests takes the bride to the groom's home.

Southern youth meet at markets, dances, schools, and church functions. They are allowed to date. Parents of potential couples get involved when dating leads to engagement. Grooms pay a dowry in cattle or cash. As in the north, large parties celebrate the new union. In rural areas, guns are fired in jubilation. The divorce rate throughout Sudan is low.

Diet. Sudanese eat beef, chicken, goat, and mutton, though these foods are often unavailable. Sorghum, millet, and maize are the staple grains. In areas of substantial rainfall, people enjoy cassava, potatoes, peanut butter, mangoes, and papaya. Other local produce includes guavas, grapes, bananas, okra, carrots, tomatoes, onions, beets, cucumbers, oranges, and pineapples. *Kisra* (thinly layered food made from flour paste), *aseeda* (thick porridge), and *fatta* (bread, peas, tomatoes, cheese, lentils, and other ingredients) are common dishes. Although the government has prohibited the consumption of alcohol, southerners customarily drink a sorghum beer called *marisa*. Malnutrition is severe in some areas; relief efforts cannot adequately substitute for peace and good harvests.

Recreation. Soccer is Sudan's most popular sport, followed by basketball and volleyball. To a lesser extent, some men participate in running, swimming, wrestling, boxing, and traditional *stick* or *bracelet fighting*. In the north, women are not allowed to play any sport in the presence of men; there is no restriction in the south. In general, however, Sudanese women do not engage in sports. They tend to socialize in the home. Men belong to social clubs or go to coffee shops. Urban residents might enjoy an evening concert or movie. Many urban homes have televisions. Rural Sudanese might listen to the radio.

The Arts. Islam influences artistic expression in Sudan. Beautiful calligraphy of *Qur'anic* verses, accompanied by ornamental designs, adorns secular and religious buildings. Volumes of literature are devoted to the lives of religious men. Recitation of the *Qur'an* through dramatic songs is common in cosmopolitan regions.

Madeeh is Muslim gospel music sung to commemorate the prophet Muhammad and is the foundation of *haqibh*, chants and chorus accompanied by instruments such as the *tabla* (small hand drums) and the *oud* (Arabian lute). Each ethnic

Sudan

group has its own traditions of song and dance, but the ruling party has outlawed many public expressions. Sufi Muslims may dance and gyrate until they enter into a trance.

Pottery, basketry, beaded jewelry, needlework, and leather work are common Sudanese folk arts. Handicrafts are made of wood, ebony, ivory, and shells. Nomadic artisans create woven rugs or gold and silver jewelry. Nubians paint their houses bright colors; geometric patterns painted on the front often have religious significance. Some groups paint their bodies ornately, and the Nuba scar themselves in artistic patterns.

Holidays. National holidays are set by the Western (Gregorian) calendar. Islamic holy days are scheduled according to the lunar calendar, which is shorter than the Gregorian year by about 11 days. Since dates are determined according to the moon's phases, the Gregorian dates for holidays differ from year to year. The most important Islamic days are *Id al-Fitr* (a feast at the end of *Ramadan*), *Id al-Adha* (Feast of the Sacrifice, honoring Abraham for his willingness to sacrifice his son), and the prophet Muhammad's birthday. During the holy month of *Ramadan*, Muslims go without food or water from dawn to dusk. In the evenings, families eat together and visit friends and relatives.

Public holidays celebrated in the north include Independence Day (1 Jan.), Unity Day (3 Mar.), and Labor Day (1 May). The south celebrates New Year's Day and Independence Day together on 1 January. Southerners (including animists) also observe Christmas. They do not recognize Islamic holy days.

Commerce. Business hours are generally from 8 a.m. to 2 p.m., Saturday through Thursday. Friday is the day for Muslim men to go to mosque and pray. Most people buy their basic goods from neighborhood shops, open-air markets, and farmers' markets. Rural people produce most of their own goods.

SOCIETY

Government. Sudan is an Islamic state. President Omar Hassan al-Bashir is head of state and head of government. The president appoints a vice president (currently Ali Uthman Muhammad Taha). The 360-seat National Assembly has limited authority; laws are virtually made by decree and enforced by the military. Under the constitution, 270 of the National Assembly's members are popularly elected; the remaining 90 are elected by the National Congress Party, which controls all levels of central government.

Economy. Sudan's economy is based on agriculture, which employs 80 percent of the labor force. Nearly all rural people live in poverty as subsistence farmers. The gross domestic product does not reflect actual income, which is much lower. Grains (millet, sorghum, wheat, barley), cotton, peanuts, gum arabic, dates, and sesame are the main crops. Cotton is the primary export, accounting for almost half of total export earnings. Sudan is the world's principal supplier of gum arabic. Sesame, peanuts, and livestock are also exported. Industrial activities usually center on agricultural processing. Revenues from oil help support the economy, and the government has begun implementing privatization programs and other reforms designed to stabilize and liberalize the economy. However, debt, drought, war, and poor infrastructure all hinder economic growth. The currency is the Sudanese *dinar* (SDD).

DEVELOPMENT DATA
Human Dev. Index* rank .... 139 of 177 countries
    Adjusted for women .... 115 of 144 countries
Real GDP per capita $1,820
Adult literacy rate .... 71 percent (male); 49 (female)
Infant mortality rate .... 64 per 1,000 births
Life expectancy .... 54 (male); 57 (female)

Transportation and Communications. More than half of Sudan's roadways are unpaved and often in disrepair. Future road construction depends on war and the economy. The northern railway carries passengers and freight. The southern rail link has been shut down by the insurgency. Relatively few people own cars. Taxis and buses are available in Khartoum. The communications system is poorly maintained and barely adequate. There are five radio and two television stations.

Communications and other systems that rely on electricity suffer from severe power outages, especially in Khartoum. Since most electricity is generated by hydroelectric dams, its availability depends on water flow along the Nile.

Education. Nine years of education are compulsory, but this requirement often is not enforced. Facilities are generally inadequate, especially in rural areas. About half of school-age children in northern and central regions are enrolled at the primary level. Three-fourths of these pupils complete primary schooling, but only about one-fifth advance to the secondary level. The University of Khartoum is a four-year and graduate university. Arabic is the official language of instruction for all schools, but English is used in most southern schools.

Health. Sudan's public health system is not extensive. Urban facilities lack supplies and medicine. Rural clinics are all but nonexistent; only a few rural hospitals are operating. Southern facilities are either abandoned or destroyed. International relief agencies provide some basic services in war-torn areas and to internal refugees. Parasitic diseases are endemic, particularly in central and southern Sudan. Yellow fever, cholera, and malaria are active throughout the country. Malnutrition is widespread. Meningitis and other epidemics can be deadly.

AT A GLANCE

Events and Trends.
- In February 2005, leaders of several African nations met in Chad to discuss ways of ending the conflict in Darfur. A UN report issued the previous month stated that atrocities in Darfur could be categorized as crimes against humanity.
- The 2005 peace treaty between the government and the SPLA grants southern Sudan autonomy for six years, followed by referendum on secession. The treaty also gives the north and south equal shares of the nation's oil wealth.

Contact Information. Embassy of Sudan, 2210 Massachusetts Avenue NW, Washington, DC 20008; phone (202) 338-8565.

© 2005 ProQuest Information and Learning Company and Brigham Young University. It is against the law to copy, reprint, store, or transmit any part of this publication in any form by any means without written permission from ProQuest. This document contains native commentary and original analysis, as well as estimated statistics. The content should not be considered strictly factual, and it may not apply to all groups in a nation. *UN Development Programme, Human Development Report 2004 (New York: Oxford University Press, 2004).

CultureGrams
People. The World. You.

ProQuest Information and Learning Company
300 North Zeeb Road, P.O. Box 1346
Ann Arbor, Michigan 48106 USA
Toll Free: 1.800.528.6279
Fax: 1.800.864.0019
www.culturegrams.com

CultureGrams World Edition 2006

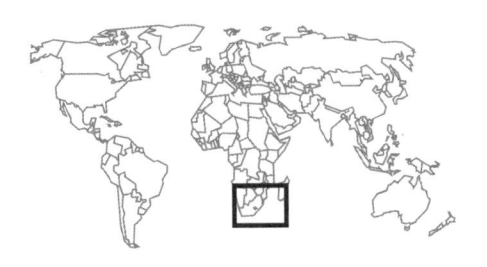

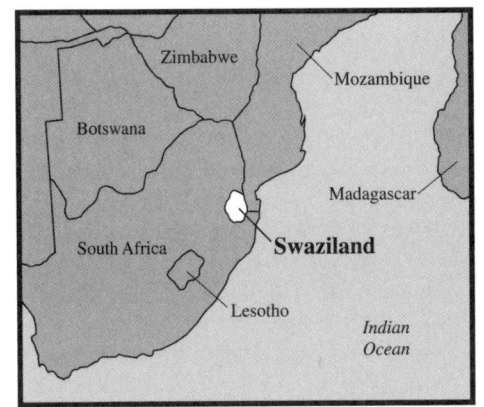

Kingdom of Swaziland

BACKGROUND

Land and Climate. With an area of approximately 6,704 square miles (17,363 square kilometers), Swaziland is about the same size as Massachusetts. Despite its small size, this landlocked country has four well-defined geographic regions that parallel each other and extend the length of the nation from north to south. The eastern Lubombo region (a 2,000-foot, or 600-meter, plateau and escarpment) is adjacent to the Lubombo Mountains and the border with Mozambique. Because of its rugged terrain, it is used mainly for cattle grazing. To the west, the Lowveld's fertile soil supports agriculture and some game farms. Irrigated farms support sugarcane, citrus, cotton, and corn. The remainder of the Lowveld is open savanna or dense African bush. The Midveld also supports considerable agriculture, including pineapples. Its hilly region gives way to the Highveld in the far west, where cattle grazing and commercial forestry are the principal economic pursuits. Most people live in the Midveld and Highveld regions.

Swaziland experiences four seasons. Frequent rains in the hot summer (October–February) are followed by a cooler fall (March–April) and a cold, dry winter (April–August). Warmer temperatures return in the dry spring (August–October). Swaziland's forests are mostly man-made; original woods can be found in the Jilobi and Siteki Forests.

History. In the mid-18th century, groups of Nguni tribespeople arrived in southern Swaziland from Mozambique by way of central Africa. Some of these early tribes successfully defended the area of present-day Swaziland from Shaka Zulu (the warrior-king of the Zulu people) and encroaching white immigrant farmers. In the early 1800s, under the leadership of the Dlamini clan, Sobhuza I was proclaimed king, and he began to unify the many Swazi clans; some surrounding Sotho and Tsonga peoples were also incorporated into the Swazi clans. But it was not until the 1840s in the reign of King Mswati II, who succeeded Sobhuza, that Swaziland became a nation. At about this same time, the first white traders settled near present-day Manzini.

When Mswati II died, a provisional government was formed among the Swazis, South Africans, and British. This brought British influence and settlement to Swaziland at the end of the 1890s. The kingdom soon became part of the British Empire. In 1921, King Sobhuza II was crowned *Ngwenyama* (Lion) of the nation. He is credited with buying back land (as much as half of today's territory) from white settlers and returning it to traditional local chiefdoms. His rule lasted until his death in 1982, which made him the longest-reigning monarch in modern Africa.

The British granted independence on 6 September 1968 under a constitution with a Westminster-style system (in which a chief executive is selected from the majority party in parliament). Unable to adapt to this style of government, Sobhuza dissolved Parliament, nullified the constitution, and assumed all powers for the throne in 1973. Sobhuza governed the rest of his life under a technical state of emergency.

Upon the death of Sobhuza II, the Queen Mother held the throne as regent until Sobhuza's son (Mswati III) turned 18. Throughout these years, a council of elders (*liqoqo*) governed by decree. King Mswati III was crowned in 1986. He led the country under the state of emergency until 1993, when parliamentary elections were held. Over the past decade, calls for further democratic reform have increased. However, with Parliament only an advisory body, King Mswati III has retained his far-reaching authority.

Swaziland

THE PEOPLE

Population. The 1.2 million Swazi people (called *emaSwati*, or "people of Mswati") are a mixture of several Bantu groups (Nguni, Sotho, Tsonga, and others). The population is growing at an annual rate of 0.6 percent. Tribes migrating to the region in the mid-1700s assimilated with those already present (*emaKhandza embili*). A few clans of the emaSwati claim kinship to prehistoric indigenous peoples who inhabited the region. Some African and non-African expatriates also live and work in Swaziland. Most people (77 percent) live in rural areas. Manzini and Mbabane are the two largest urban centers. About 41 percent of the population is age 14 or younger.

Language. SiSwati and English are the kingdom's official languages. SiSwati is a highly expressive language related to siZulu. The two are so closely related that when the British created an English name for the kingdom, they inadvertently used the siZulu pronunciation of *t* (sounds like *z*) in King Mswati II's name and devised the name *Swaziland* instead of the more accurate *Swatiland*.

English is the primary language of government and education. People often mix siSwati and English in informal conversation. SiSwati spelling is not yet uniform, but it uses the same basic alphabet as English. SiSwati also employs the click, a sound made by sucking the tongue back from the upper front teeth (like a "tsk-tsk" sound in English) or from the clenched side teeth (as if urging on a horse in English). There are four clicks, represented by the letters *c*, *q*, and *x* and by combinations like *ch*, *nq*, *ngc*, and others. SiSwati's tonality and stress are important to meaning. Proverbs, jokes, and U.S. and South African slang are ubiquitous.

Religion. Swazis are primarily Christians, but they freely mix indigenous beliefs and practices with formal Christianity. Many Western churches have congregations in Swaziland, the largest of which are Roman Catholic, Anglican, and Methodist. One of the country's largest churches, with more African than Western roots, is the Zionist Christian Church. Found throughout southern Africa, Zionists are known for holding festive worship services and wearing colored robes to church. The country's few Muslims are mostly Indians or Pakistanis.

Of the many traditional practices mixed with Christianity, consulting a *sangoma* for divination is quite popular. A *tinyanga* heals by faith or with traditional medicines. *Batsakatsi* (witches) can be paid to place or remove a *muti* (curse) on someone.

General Attitudes. Swazis tend to be warm and trusting, and they are highly respectful of elders. However, some distrust of foreigners and resentment of elders in the political hierarchy also exist. Personal space is very small; people stand close when conversing or lining up. Personal privacy is not considered very important. Swazis are group oriented and gregarious. Wanting to be alone or not discussing one's personal activities with neighbors is considered antisocial. Gender inequalities are extreme in Swaziland; women have very few rights in marriage and under the law. Swazis take great pride in the richness of their traditions. Swazis try to be as hospitable as their circumstances allow.

Personal Appearance. Swazis generally dress in Western-style clothing for business, recreation, and socializing. Schoolchildren wear uniforms; each school has specific colors. Traditionally, married women cover their heads in public, frequently with a brightly colored scarf. Young women are fond of elaborate styles of hair plaiting, and hair extensions are popular in urban areas. Some men, including the king, wear dreadlocks. Wearing pants is becoming more accepted for women; schoolgirls might wear athletic pants as a uniform during winter. Urban Swazis take pride in dressing well for shopping and social visits, and they are always neat and clean. Cleanliness extends to the home and possessions, too.

Traditional dress may be worn for ceremonial, casual, business, or formal settings. The *lihiya*, a single length of printed cloth, forms the basis of Swazi traditional dress for both men and women. *Emahiya* (plural of *lihiya*) are tied around the waist and over the upper body across one shoulder. Men add a *lijobo*, an animal skin worn at the waist, and a traditional club known as a *knobkerrie*. Both sexes wear beaded necklaces.

CUSTOMS AND COURTESIES

Greetings. Except in urban centers, it is extremely rude not to exchange greetings with passersby. Swazis shake right hands and exchange greetings when meeting friends, acquaintances, or strangers. One's left hand briefly supports one's own right forearm. When the left drops away, the speakers may continue to grasp right hands for a while. Friends make polite inquiries about health and family to begin a conversation.

The most acceptable initial greetings are *Sawubona* when addressing one person and *Sanibonani* when addressing more than one. Both literally mean "I see you." It is common for people to ask each other *Uphumaphi?* (Where have you come from?) and *Uyaphi?* (Where are you going?). Friends may ask *Kunjani?* (How are you?). To show respect, one adds a professional title or a social title like *make* (MAH-gay) for an adult woman, *babe* (BAH-bay) for an adult man, *sisi* for a girl, and *bhuti* for a boy. *Nkhosi*, the praise name for royalty, may be used when one is unsure of a person's title.

Gestures. Hand gestures have great significance to Swazis. Hands add emphasis and description to spoken words. Gestures alone may also be used, such as softly touching the mouth to indicate that the speaker should talk more loudly or placing an index finger against one's mouth to indicate a request for silence. Swazis always use the right hand to offer and receive a gift, to eat, and to greet another person. Using the left hand is extremely rude, as it is traditionally reserved for personal hygiene. SiSwati has no words for "right" or "left." So, in giving directions to go left, one refers to "the side of the hand with which you do not eat."

It is improper to point one's finger at another person, especially an elderly person. When motioning toward a person or a grave, one uses the fist as a sign of respect. A bent finger may sometimes be acceptable. To show respect during conversation, a Swazi will speak softly and/or avoid eye contact by looking down. Public displays of affection, even between spouses, are frowned upon. Swazis of the same sex may walk hand in hand. Swazis use a verbal click to express exasperation. To signify admiration of a woman's beauty and grace, men draw the index finger across the throat in a slashing motion.

Visiting. Swazis generally welcome both spontaneous and planned visits by family and friends on weekends, holidays, and during family celebrations. Family members are expected to stay in close touch through frequent visits, although that is changing as young urban Swazis find it expensive and time-consuming to travel often to their rural homesteads. Most visits of a few hours or even a day are spontaneous, while stays of a week or more usually are planned so that the host family can set aside housing and food and inform other members of the family who might wish to see the visitor.

The host family makes visitors comfortable and even sets aside an extra portion of each meal in the event that a guest may arrive. If no guest comes to eat the extra food, it is served at the following meal. Overnight visitors usually are offered accommodation in *endlini kaGogo* (grandmother's hut), the best and most highly respected place on the homestead. Guests generally do not bring gifts.

Eating. Traditionally there are two meals a day (morning and afternoon). Both consist of meat, vegetables, and *liphalishi* (a stiff porridge made from maize). In a rural homestead, males eat their meals in an enclosure near the entrance to the cattle *kraal* (corral), while females eat in the kitchen. The Swazi custom is for all men to eat from a common bowl using wooden spoons, unless meat is served. Meat is eaten with the hands. Men receive the choicest cut of meat (often the heart, liver, and intestines) and the head. Women also share a bowl, as do boys and girls, but they are unlikely to have spoons. In more modern rural and most urban families, each individual has a separate bowl, and both sexes eat under one roof.

LIFESTYLE

Family. Led by the oldest male, usually the grandfather, the extended Swazi family is close-knit. A homestead generally includes unmarried adult children and sometimes married sons and their families. Families have an average of six children. Important family decisions, such as the marriage or burial of a family member or the purchase of an expensive item, are made by consulting several relatives. In contemporary families with younger members living away from the homestead, family consultation can be complicated, but it continues to be the basis for decision making. Women are not as involved in these decisions until they are older or widowed. Women and girls are expected to obey and show deference to males at all times. Women have little control over family resources, make few decisions, and may need a male's permission to leave the homestead or pursue personal interests.

The nuclear family is increasingly common. Mothers primarily care for children, although older girls take care of younger siblings and do household chores. Because many men and women must seek employment away from the homestead, they often leave the children with their *gogo* (grandmother), who may be unable to give them adequate care. Fathers own all family assets, which usually pass to the eldest son when his father dies, subject to the family council's decisions. During the widow's two-year mourning period, she wears special attire and cannot remarry. The mourning period for widowers is three to six months.

Children take on chores at an early age. Boys usually herd the family's livestock. Cattle are an important status symbol for a family. Children are taught to respect all adults, not just their parents; this is especially true in rural areas. Children often make their own toys, but a boy's favorite is any ball with which he can play soccer. Boys and girls together play tag, hide-and-seek, cards, and word games. When a rural boy turns 18, he may build his own hut on the homestead.

A typical urban home is of masonry construction with a tile roof, an internal water system, and two to six bedrooms. A rural homestead consists of a *kraal* and three to eight single-room round or rectangular huts with thatched roofs. One hut serves as the kitchen. Water is carried from a well or river.

Dating and Marriage. Dating habits are mostly Westernized; couples attend movies and musical events. Young women usually marry before age 25 and men before age 30. Polygamy is legal for families who marry according to traditional law. Men wed under a more Western civil law cannot practice polygamy. Urban women prefer to be married under civil law.

The common factor in all marriages is the payment of *lobola* (bride-price) by the husband's family to the bride's parents as a sign of respect and gratitude for rearing the woman who will join his family. Most families find it impossible to pay the expected price of about 12 head of cattle. The first two head of cattle must be the family's two best cows—one to be given to the maternal grandmother and the other to the bride's father. It is possible to pay the two cows and then owe the rest after getting married. It may take a lifetime to pay *lobola*. One might also pay two cows plus a cash substitute for the rest. Another option is to promise that any *lobola* received by the new couple's first daughter belongs to that girl's maternal grandmother; this is sometimes wrongly interpreted as the girl belonging to her grandparents. Many couples simply live together and raise a family as if married until *lobola* can be paid.

Apart from the male homestead head, the bride's mother is given two cattle of her own as compensation owed her for the loss of her daughter. One of these cows is called the "wiper away of tears" (*insulamnyambeti*).

A traditional wedding is a two-day event. The bride's family brings her to the groom's home to begin the festivities. There is dancing, and two beasts are slaughtered. The following day is for eating, drinking, and giving gifts to the groom's family.

Diet. In addition to maize, basic foodstuffs include fruits (oranges, bananas, and peaches) and vegetables (cabbage, spinach, and lettuce). Meat is an important part of a Swazi meal, although poorer rural families may go weeks without eating it. Modern urban dwellers may eat traditional foods but are likely to replace the porridge with rice or mashed potatoes. Their meals may also contain fruits and beans, as well as some Western foods.

Recreation. Urban Swazis play soccer, tennis, squash, volleyball, and golf. Rural Swazis perform traditional dances and play soccer. Men and women perform traditional dances separately; such dancing usually accompanies most Swazi celebrations. Schoolchildren compete in track-and-field events, netball (similar to basketball, for girls), and soccer (for boys). Children hear few stories because of television and radio, but most are told tales of *Chakijane*, a rabbit trickster. Movie theaters and nightclubs are found only in urban areas, although even small communities frequently have a *take-away* (take-out) restaurant and bar for socializing. Musical events sometimes last all night. Swazis spend most vacations visiting family at the traditional homestead.

The Arts. Textiles are one of Swaziland's most distinctive folk arts. Artisans weave cotton, mohair, and angora into brightly patterned rugs and fabrics. Stylized pottery and soapstone carvings of wildlife and human figures are also popular.

Dance plays an important role in Swazi ceremonies. The Reed Dance, or *Umhlanga*, honors the Queen Mother. It has traditionally served as a display of marriageable girls. During the eight-day ceremony, the nation's young maidens wear elaborate costumes and perform dances and songs according to age group. A slow dance accompanies the moment when they bring bundles of reeds to the royal residence to build windbreaks. *Sibhaca* dancing is performed by groups of young men, who stamp their feet to the rhythm of music and chants.

Holidays. There are three major traditional Swazi events: *Lusekwane*, *Incwala*, and *Umhlanga*. For *Lusekwane* in late

Swaziland

December, young men bring branches of the *lusekwane* tree to the royal residence to build a cattle enclosure. *Incwala*, a few days later, is highlighted by the king tasting the new harvest's fruits. Lasting several days, it includes feasting, singing, dancing, and the slaying of a bull. *Umhlanga* takes place in late August or early September.

New Year's Day, Easter, Ascension, Christmas, and Boxing Day (26 Dec.) are all observed. Swaziland also marks Independence Day (6 Sept.) and National Flag Day (25 Apr.). Swazis celebrate the birthdays of King Mswati III (19 Apr.) and King Sobhuza II (22 July).

Commerce. General business hours are from 8 a.m. to 1 p.m. and 2 to 5 p.m., Monday through Friday. Government offices are closed on Saturday, but most businesses are open on Saturday morning. The government regulates certain dress standards for teachers and other civil servants.

SOCIETY

Government. Swaziland is an absolute monarchy with no written constitution. King Mswati III is the head of state and appoints a prime minister (currently Themba Dlamini). Parliament acts only as an advisory body. In the 65-seat House of Assembly, 55 members are elected representatives of each *inkhundla* (constituency or district). The king appoints the other 10 members of the House of Assembly, as well as 20 members (mostly chiefs) of the 30-seat Senate. Ten senators are chosen by the House of Assembly. There are no formal political parties. The judicial system balances traditional Swazi laws and customs with a version of Roman-Dutch law. The controversial Swazi Administration Act of 1998 gave chiefs extraordinary powers.

Economy. The sugar industry (production, refinement, and export) is vital to Swaziland's economy. The country also produces citrus fruits, canned fruits, cotton, vegetables, meat products, and timber. Asbestos, diamonds, and coal are mined. The government of Swaziland supports a system of free enterprise, protects against expropriation and industry nationalization, actively recruits foreign investment, and allows the free holding of industrial lands.

Most people are farmers. Wage earners also grow some staple crops such as maize. A growing number of women are becoming wage earners—mostly in the informal economy or in self-employed agricultural and handicraft enterprises. Expatriates once filled the bulk of skilled and managerial jobs, but Swazis now hold most of these positions. Wealth is highly concentrated and unequally distributed. The currency is the *lilangeni* (SZL).

Transportation and Communications. Most people travel on foot for relatively short distances. Buses provide public transportation within communities and between major population centers. Traffic moves on the left side of the road. Only about one-fourth of Swaziland's roads are paved, but secondary gravel roads are kept in good repair. Traffic accidents kill more Swazis each year than malaria or crime. The railway mainly transports cargo, but a passenger train that travels between Durban, South Africa, and Maputo, Mozambique, stops in Mpaka, Swaziland.

Radio and television broadcasts reach most of the country.

DEVELOPMENT DATA
Human Dev. Index* rank . . . . 137 of 177 countries
  Adjusted for women . . . . 109 of 144 countries
Real GDP per capita $4,550
Adult literacy rate . . . . 82 percent (male); 80 (female)
Infant mortality rate . . . . 68 per 1,000 births
Life expectancy . . . . 34 (male); 37 (female)

Programs are broadcast in both siSwati and English. In some areas, South African stations are also available. Daily newspapers are in both siSwati and English. The postal system is reliable. The telephone system is efficient, although many homes do not have telephones.

Education. Primary and secondary education are neither compulsory nor entirely free. About 25 percent of primary and secondary students do not attend school, in some cases because parents cannot afford the fees. Many capable young people find patrons to pay their fees or obtain scholarships in order to continue their schooling. Primary classes generally are taught in siSwati, but English is used exclusively from the secondary level onward. For higher education, which is free for qualified students, there are three campuses of the University of Swaziland, three teacher-training colleges, two nursing colleges, various vocational institutions, and the Swaziland College of Technology. The government provides adult education to improve literacy.

Health. Six full-service hospitals are linked in a network with numerous clinics, public health centers, and health outreach facilities, assuring that 80 percent of all Swazis live within an hour's walk of health care. Government programs combat infectious diseases, promote family planning, and provide immunizations to children. Traditional healing practices are common. HIV/AIDS is Swaziland's greatest health concern. The nation has one of the world's highest infection rates, with nearly 40 percent of Swazi adults infected. The disease has significantly reduced life expectancy rates.

AT A GLANCE

Events and Trends.

- In October 2004, the UN Convention on International Trade in Endangered Species lifted a ban on hunting Swaziland's roughly 60 white rhinos. Advocates of the move argued that revenue generated from trophy hunters could support conservation efforts, while opponents claimed that commercial interests were being placed ahead of long-term environmental concerns.

- In February 2004, Prime Minister Themba Dlamini declared a national emergency due to drought and the nation's AIDS crisis. He appealed to international donors for assistance. A series of droughts has caused severe food shortages. These have been worsened by the AIDS epidemic, which has left many Swazis without a family structure on which to rely for the sharing of resources.

Contact Information. Embassy of Swaziland, 1712 New Hampshire Avenue NW, Washington, DC 20009; phone (202) 234-5002.

CultureGrams™ World Edition 2006

United Republic of Tanzania

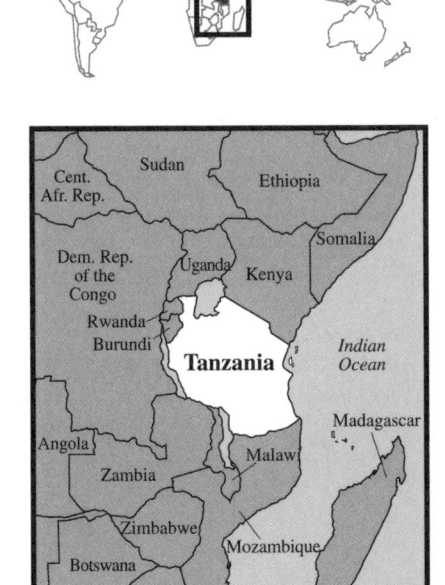

Boundary representations are not necessarily authoritative.

BACKGROUND

Land and Climate. The United Republic of Tanzania covers 364,899 square miles (945,090 square kilometers). It consists of mainland Tanganyika and three low coral islands that lie off the coast in the Indian Ocean: Mafia, Pemba, and Zanzibar. The combined size of these humid islands is about equal to that of Rhode Island. Tanganyika (about the size of Texas) is a land of great variation. It either shares or borders three of Africa's Great Lakes (Victoria, Nyasa, and Tanganyika). Most of the country is either low-lying coastal plain, upland plain (the Serengeti), or highland plateau. Mount Kilimanjaro, the highest point in Africa, rises to 19,340 feet (5,895 meters). Africa's lowest point is the floor of Lake Tanganyika at 1,174 feet (358 meters) below sea level. Tanzania's equatorial climate—hot, humid, and 90°F (32°C) on the coast—is tempered by inland elevations where temperatures are mild. Rains fall primarily from March to May and from October to December, with seasonal variations from north to south.

History. Various peoples inhabited the area now known as Tanzania for thousands of years before traders from southern Arabia began arriving in the eighth century. The Arabs founded the city of Kilwa as they began settling the coast. Over many generations, Arabs mixed with the local Bantu populations to produce both the Kiswahili language and the modern peoples of the coastal regions. The Portuguese arrived in the 15th century. They, together with Arabic overlords from Muscat and Oman, developed a series of populous and powerful trading cities and sultanates—particularly on the islands of Zanzibar and Pemba. The sultanate of Zanzibar firmly controlled both the islands and the mainland coast until the mid-1800s. In 1886, Tanganyika became a German protectorate. Zanzibar retained its independence but lost control over Kenya to the British. In 1920, Tanganyika fell under British rule as well.

In 1961, Tanganyika was granted independence, followed in 1963 by a fully independent Zanzibar. In 1964, the two nations merged to form Tanzania and became a socialist republic under Julius Nyerere. His party for the Revolution (CCM—*Chama Cha Mapinduzi*) worked to unite and develop a nation of many ethnic groups. Nyerere stepped down as president after constitutional reform in 1985 and chose Ali Hassan Mwinyi to succeed him. Mwinyi was reelected without opposition in 1990, but he promised to step down after democratic elections. Multiparty district and regional elections were held between 1992 and 1995, and full national elections were in 1995. Polling was chaotic and opposition groups charged fraud, but the independent judiciary ruled that the election results would stand. CCM candidate Benjamin Mkapa was elected president and the CCM maintained a majority in parliament. Mkapa won a second term in 2000.

For the most part, the union between Zanzibar and the mainland has been successful, although the Arab majority on Zanzibar desires more control over the island's economy and politics. Zanzibar maintains a semiautonomous status and elects its own president and legislature. Disputes surrounding Zanzibar's 1995 elections kept the government from functioning because opposition members of parliament refused to sit in session. A 1999 agreement brought the opposition back to their seats in parliament, but disputes continued. When the CCM candidate won Zanzibar's presidential election in 2000, the opposition Civic United Front (CUF) cited fraud and refused to recognize the results. Demonstrations on Zanzibar and Pemba turned into violent clashes with police in 2001. Dozens of CUF supporters were killed, and hundreds more

Tanzania

fled to Kenya. Talks between the CCM and CUF brought a resolution to the crisis later that year, and the two parties have implemented measures to promote reconciliation.

THE PEOPLE

Population. Tanzania's population of 36.6 million is growing at 1.95 percent annually. About one-third of Tanzanians live in urban areas. The largest city is Dar es Salaam, with about two million residents. Dodoma replaced Dar es Salaam as the nation's capital in 2000. About 44 percent of all Tanzanians are younger than age 14.

Ninety-nine percent of the population is African, coming from some 130 ethnic groups. Thirty of these groups are Bantu-speaking. The Nyamwezi-Sukuma (13 percent of the population) is the only group with more than one million members. There are three Nilotic ethnic groups, two Khoisan, and two Afro-Asiatic. The merchant/trader class is dominated by people of Lebanese, Palestinian, and Indian origin. Arabs are most numerous on Zanzibar. Refugees from neighboring countries live in border areas.

Language. Kiswahili (also called Swahili), the primary official language, developed along the coasts of Kenya and Tanzania as a trade language between Africans and Arabs. It is a mixture of various Bantu languages, Arabic, and English. Tanzanian Kiswahili follows a more traditional form than the Kiswahili spoken in Kenya. Zanzibar is considered to have the purest Kiswahili, which locals call *Kiunguju*. English, the second official language, is used in business, government, and higher education.

More than one hundred languages are spoken in Tanzania. Most people speak the language associated with their ethnic group, but they generally also speak Kiswahili. Nyerere made Kiswahili official at the time of independence to foster pride in the people's African identity. To help spread use of the language, he urged people to buy radios, and Radio Tanzania began broadcasting in Kiswahili. The language is still taught on the radio and it is still evolving.

Religion. On the mainland, more than one-third of the population is Christian. Another third is Muslim. On Zanzibar, nearly all inhabitants are Muslim. About one-third of the population follows indigenous beliefs, although many of these people have also accepted some Christian or Islamic beliefs. Muslims believe *Allah* (God) chose the prophet Muhammad and revealed the words of the *Qur'an* (Koran) to him through the angel Gabriel. As part of the practice of Islam, Muslims profess the name of *Allah* and proclaim Muhammad's calling. They pray five times daily and expect to make a pilgrimage to Makkah, Saudi Arabia, sometime in their life.

It is not unusual for professed Christians to mix their beliefs with local traditions. Thus, a local priest and a traditional healer might carry equal respect in a "Christian" village. The two belief systems are not considered contradictory because each has a place in the people's daily lives. The government is neutral in religious matters and has tried to promote religious tolerance throughout the country.

General Attitudes. Tanzanian social systems are group oriented, regardless of ethnic affiliation. Individuals are expected to put themselves second to group welfare. Consequently, Tanzanians are extremely polite and generous people, particularly in public. It is considered impolite to pass a person (unless in a large crowd) without showing a sign of recognition, even if only a smile. Tanzanians do not use obscene language of any kind, even mildly. Any kind of verbal abuse or criticism, especially in public, is a major offense that negatively reflects on the person's upbringing and background.

People often make requests without a "please." This is not considered impolite, as the word "please" is not native to the Bantu languages of East Africa. The Kiswahili equivalent, *tafadhali*, has actually been borrowed from Arabic but is still not integral to the culture. *Asante* (thank you) is also an adopted term. Whether spoken or not, thanks usually is shown with a returned favor or kindness. A deed is considered greater than verbal gratitude.

Personal Appearance. Urban Tanzanians dress conservatively and usually wear Western-style clothing. Shorts and other revealing attire are not proper, except in clearly defined work or recreational situations. In rural villages, many people wear traditional clothing associated with their specific ethnic group. Many also wear readily available secondhand clothing from the United States or Europe and imported clothing from China and India. Muslim men might wear a *kanzu* (long, embroidered cotton gown) with a matching skullcap or they may simply prefer Western-style clothing, with or without a skullcap. Some wear a *kanzu* only when going to the mosque. Muslim women might cover their hair but almost never their faces. They often wear *kangas* or *kitenge* (several pieces of colorful cotton wraparound fabric). Women on Zanzibar often wear a large black shawl called a *buibui*.

CUSTOMS AND COURTESIES

Greetings. Each region has a variety of non-Kiswahili greetings particular to the local ethnic groups, but Kiswahili is understood by the vast majority of Tanzanians. The most common Kiswahili greeting is *Hujambo* (or *Hamjambo* for more than one person), usually followed by a handshake. A more casual greeting is simply *Jambo*. A common response to *Hujambo* is *Sijambo* (I'm fine). *Hatujambo* means "We're fine." This exchange is followed by questions about one's home, family, work, or other activities. For example, one might ask *Habari za nyumbani?* (How are things at your home?). A common response is *Salama* (In peace, without problems). A typical greeting when approaching someone's home is *Shikamoo* (Is anyone there?), to which the response is *Karibu* ("Welcome" for one person) or *Karibuni* ("Welcome" for more than one person). Men and women shake hands with each other, although a man may wait for a woman to extend her hand before offering his. Mothers commonly are addressed by the name of their oldest son (or daughter until a son is born), rather than by their given name. Thus, the mother of Albert would be known as "Mama Albert."

Gestures. Tanzanians use the right hand or both hands to pass and accept items. To use the left hand alone, even in gesturing, is improper. The verbal "tch-tch" sound is considered an insult. In many cases, it is impolite to let the bottom of one's foot or shoe point at someone. Therefore, when sitting, one does not prop up the feet on chairs or tables but places them on the ground. It is impolite to photograph another person without permission; a person will rarely refuse but expects the courtesy of being asked.

Visiting. Among Muslims, visiting is an important social custom; friends and family visit often. All Tanzanians enjoy friendly social visits and enthusiastically welcome their visitors. Hosts do their best to make guests comfortable. Unannounced visits are common and warmly received. Most times of the day are acceptable for visiting except late in the evening (after 8 p.m. or so). A host also does not appreciate repeated visits at mealtime. Any guest arriving at mealtime, even if unannounced, will always be offered part of the meal. Not offering a meal would show a lack of hospitality, and refusing the offer is impolite. If a visit is arranged, a person does everything possible to keep the appointment. Not showing up for a scheduled visit is rude. It is polite for hosts to serve tea (often with milk and sugar), coffee, or another beverage. *Kitumbua* (a fried bread; plural is *vitumbua*) or *maandazi* (small doughnuts) may also be set out. Refusing these refreshments is considered impolite.

A first-time visitor customarily brings a small gift to the home. This may include sweets or cookies but not flowers. Flowers are used to express condolences. Guests of the opposite sex are entertained with the outside door open. When guests depart, hosts customarily accompany them part of the way (a few hundred yards) to see them off properly.

Eating. Throughout the country, people wash their hands in a bowl or basin of water before each meal. This practice is especially important because most meals are eaten with the hand. Even if diners use utensils, they wash the hands before eating. Because the left hand traditionally is used for personal hygiene, Tanzanians use only the right hand when eating without utensils. They might use the left to handle difficult foods, such as meat with bones, but never to take food from a communal bowl. Eating from a communal dish is common, especially when it contains *ugali* (a stiff porridge) or rice. Families on the Indian Ocean coast, as well as in villages and towns along the three lakes (Nyasa, Tanganyika, and Victoria), sit on woven mats on the floor to eat meals. Muslims tend to sit cross-legged on these mats, but others sit with one leg tucked and the other stretched out sideways away from the food. Among Muslims, as well as some rural non-Muslims, men and women often eat separately. When guests are invited, hosts usually serve dinner first and reserve socializing for afterward. Therefore, it is impolite for guests to leave a home immediately after a meal. During the Islamic holy month of *Ramadan*, Muslims do not eat or drink from sunrise to sunset; meals are served in the evening.

LIFESTYLE

Family. Tanzanian society emphasizes the principle of *ujamaa*, or "familyhood." The government encourages extended families to act as both economic and family units. A typical rural household is large. A family often lives with or near the father's brothers and their families. Less often, the family is joined by the mother's sisters and their families. Urban families are usually smaller and less cohesive than those residing in rural areas. Nationwide, the average number of children per family is five. The father is the traditional head of the household, but mothers wield substantial power as the day-to-day managers of the family. They oversee the child-rearing, farming, and cooking. Christian marriages tend to be monogamous. However, males in Muslim and traditional families may legally have as many as four wives. Polygamy is more common in rural areas.

Dating and Marriage. Western-style dating habits are uncommon among the majority of the people. Traditionally, marriages have been arranged, often within the extended family. Today, while individual preference is permitted, marriages between cousins are still encouraged—especially in rural areas. This practice is becoming less common in cities.

The husband's family normally gives a bride-price to the bride's family for two reasons. First, it is a way of showing respect for the bride's parents—of thanking them for raising the woman. Second, it helps compensate for the loss of a productive member of the bride's family. This is important especially in rural areas because extended families share work responsibilities. Because the bride-price can be very expensive, families often must ask for financial assistance from extended family members. The bride-price may consist of money, cattle, or crops, though it is not uncommon for it to be paid through "bride-service," in which the groom provides labor for the bride's family.

Diet. Tanzanians eat grains, fruits, and vegetables. Meat is served less often, the most common being chicken, goat, and lamb. It is often served as *nyama choma* (barbecued meat). *Kitumbua* is a popular snack or energy food, as is sugarcane. A daily staple is *ugali*, a stiff porridge made from maize (white corn), millet, sorghum, or cassava. Cooked bananas are a starch staple in much of northern Tanzania (particularly around Lake Victoria and in the foothills of Mount Kilimanjaro) and in the southwest around Mbeya and Lake Nyasa. Bananas are prepared in a variety of ways, including roasted, fried, or made into a paste and mixed with meat and gravy. Other fruits are mangoes, guavas, pineapples, jackfruit, breadfruit, and oranges.

Rice is the staple of much of the coastal area and is often cooked with a variety of spices (including cloves, curry, cinnamon, cumin, and hot peppers), which are mixed directly into the water as the rice cooks. This dish is called *pilau*. Dishes prepared as a relish to go along with the main starch food (*ugali*, rice, or bananas) are commonly meat stews, green leafy vegetables (cabbage, Swiss chard, spinach), and beans or cowpeas. Devout Muslims do not eat pork or drink alcohol.

Recreation. Soccer, track-and-field, and boxing are popular sports in Tanzania. The country is known for its world-class runners. Water sports are popular along the coast. Volleyball is a favorite among girls. People enjoy socializing at coffeehouses or at home. In their leisure time, men play *bao*, a strategy game for two in which each tries to earn his opponent's pebbles or seeds by moving them in a certain fashion around a board (or the ground). There are many variations, but the game is over when one player is out of playing pieces.

The Arts. Traditional *ngoma* music remains one of Tanzania's most popular styles. Dancers follow the rhythm of drums, accompanied by choral singing, xylophones, and whistles. Sung poetry called *taraab*, a product of Arab influence, has developed into a style of music and dance common on Zanzibar and along the mainland coast. Musicians in Dar es Salaam perform these local styles as well as jazz, gospel, and reggae. Tanzania's folk arts include the ebony sculptures of the Makonde people and baskets decorated with detailed geometric patterns. Intricate door carvings on Zanzibar combine Arabic and local motifs. *Tingatinga* artists paint animals and nature scenes using tiny, brightly-colored dots.

Holidays. Civic holidays include New Year's Day, Zanzibar Revolution Day (12 Jan.), Union Day (26 Apr.), Labor Day (1 May), *Saba Saba* (Farmer's Day, 7 July), *Nane Nane* (International Trade Day, 8 August), and Independence Day (9 Dec.). In addition to national holidays, Tanzanians honor Christian and Muslim religious holidays. Christians celebrate Easter (including Good Friday and Easter Monday) and Christmas. Islamic holidays are based on the lunar calendar and fall on different days from year to year. At the end of the holy month of *Ramadan*, a three-day feast is held to break the fast. The Feast of the Sacrifice, held 10 weeks later, honors Abraham

Tanzania

for his willingness to sacrifice his son. Muslims also mark the birthday of the prophet Muhammad.

Commerce. General business hours are from 8:30 to 11:30 a.m. and 2 to 6 p.m., Monday through Friday. Most businesses close by noon on Saturday. Government offices do not reopen in the afternoon; they close at 11:30 a.m. each day. The government regulates certain business dress standards. Most office workers wear Western-style clothing.

SOCIETY

Government. Tanzania is a democratic republic with a president (currently Benjamin Mkapa) as chief of state and head of government. The president is directly elected on the same ballot with the vice president (currently Ali Mohammed Shein) to a five-year term. The prime minister (currently Frederick Sumaye) is appointed by the president. The National Assembly (*Bunge*) has 274 seats, 42 of which are reserved for appointees or specific officials. Assembly members serve five-year terms. Zanzibar is a semiautonomous state with a separate parliament and elected president (currently Amani Karume). The voting age is 18. The CCM dominates politics, but opposition parties provide balance and pressure.

Economy. Although only about 4 percent of Tanzania's land is under cultivation, agriculture dominates the Tanzanian economy, employing 85 percent of the population and accounting for 85 percent of all exports. Key exports include coffee, cotton, sisal, cashew nuts, meat, tobacco, tea, cloves, coconuts from Zanzibar, and pyrethrum (a pesticide made from chrysanthemums). Tanzania also produces diamonds and other gems. Tourism is another key industry, with the nation's wildlife and natural beauty its primary attractions. Tanzania actively fights elephant poaching and ivory smuggling and has created game parks to protect endangered species.

Economic liberalization has encouraged private investment and the creation of new export products. Continued democratic reforms are expected to boost economic performance. However, corruption, mismanagement, and regional problems still hamper the economy. Progress has also been hindered by droughts and flood damage. The International Monetary Fund provides substantial loans and debt relief. Zanzibar's economy historically depended almost entirely on the export of cloves, but tourism has become the main source of income.

Tanzania ranks among the lowest countries in the world in terms of per capita GDP. To generate some cash income, a family will often run an informal shop (*duka*) that sells produce, soda, soap, and sundries. Or they may find odd jobs to supplement low-paying wage jobs. Tanzania's currency is the Tanzanian shilling (TZS).

Transportation and Communications. Most roads, especially in the rural interior, are not paved. People often travel on foot or by bicycle, ride on or carry loads with donkeys or oxen, or hitchhike. Buses, trains, and taxis are available in some cities, especially Dar es Salaam. Taxi fare is negotiated in advance. Trains and buses run between major cities. Between smaller towns, one can ride a small truck or van that has been converted into a passenger vehicle. Few Tanzanians own cars. Following the British tradition, traffic moves on the left side of the road. Telephone landlines are sparse in rural areas, but mobile phone networks are spreading. The internet is increasingly available in urban areas. The country is served by two daily newspapers.

Education. Primary school instruction is in Kiswahili, and English is the main language in secondary schools. About 70 percent of all school-aged children begin primary school, but less than 10 percent progress past the seventh grade. Education is highly regarded, but time in the classroom often comes at the expense of time in the fields, a sacrifice that many families cannot afford to make. Girls are valued because of their domestic roles, so boys are more likely than girls to get an education. As a result, there is a wide disparity between the male and female adult literacy rates. Because the distance between schools requires many students to live on campus, most secondary schools are boarding schools. All students wear uniforms. The University of Dar es Salaam emphasizes community service rather than strictly academic pursuits. Technical training is available at other institutions as well.

Health. In rural areas, malaria, sleeping sickness, bilharzia, hepatitis B, and a wide variety of intestinal parasitic diseases are common. Quality medical care is really only available in large cities, with the exception of a few remote, well-run mission hospitals. Rural clinics are available, but they often lack trained personnel and sufficient medical supplies. Tanzania has only one doctor for every 25,000 inhabitants. Cholera epidemics can kill scores of people and infect hundreds more. Such epidemics highlight the need for clean water, health education, and better medical care. Bad weather and crop failures put people at risk of malnutrition. About 8 percent of the adult population has HIV/AIDS.

DEVELOPMENT DATA
- Human Dev. Index* rank .... 162 of 177 countries
- Adjusted for women .... 131 of 144 countries
- Real GDP per capita $580
- Adult literacy rate .... 85 percent (male); 69 (female)
- Infant mortality rate .... 102 per 1,000 births
- Life expectancy .... 43 (male); 44 (female)

AT A GLANCE

Events and Trends.
- In November 2004, leaders from throughout Africa's Great Lakes region met with UN Secretary General Kofi Annan in Dar es Salaam for a summit on security and other issues. Representatives discussed ways to resolve the interrelated conflicts that have plagued the region for years.
- President Mkapa met with the presidents of Kenya and Uganda in March 2004 to sign a customs union agreement designed to eliminate tariffs and increase trade among the three nations. The union is a reestablishment of the East African Community, which collapsed in 1977.

Contact Information. Embassy of Tanzania, 2139 R Street NW, Washington, DC 20008; phone (202) 939-6125.

CultureGrams World Edition 2006

Togo (Togolese Republic)

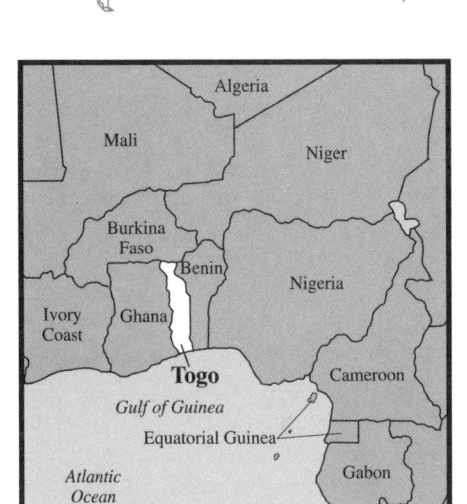

BACKGROUND

Land and Climate. Covering 21,930 square miles (56,790 square kilometers), Togo is a little smaller than West Virginia. From its Atlantic coast, Togo extends 350 miles (560 kilometers) to its northern border town of Sinkasse. Rolling savanna and a drier climate are prominent in the north, while the central hills and Atakora Mountains give way to a large southern plateau and narrow coastal plain. The maritime (coastal) region is hot and humid, and temperatures change only slightly between the dry seasons and the warmer rainy seasons (March–July, September–November). The average temperature is about 80°F (26°C). Central and northern temperatures can exceed 90°F (32°C) from February to April. Dry, dusty harmattan winds from the northeast are possible from January to March.

Togo was once covered with tropical forests. Unfortunately, the search for fertile land and the extensive use of firewood have decimated these forests. The areas protected as national parks have been cut from 200,000 to 100,000 hectares, although they still shelter buffaloes, antelopes, monkeys, and other wildlife.

History. It is believed that Togo was named after the small 15th-century lakeside village of Togodo (now called Togoville). In the Ewe language, *to* means "waters" and *godo* means "other side." Although little is known about Togo prior to the 15th century, the Kabyè and Lamba peoples were probably among the first to settle in the north between the 7th and 12th centuries. Others arrived later, fleeing wars in Dahomey (present-day Benin) and the Gold Coast (Ghana).

Tado, a village on the Mono River, had become a trading and cultural center for the Adja-Ewe ethnic groups. At the end of the 16th century, some of the Adja-Ewe left Tado for Atakpamé and Notsé. Then, in 1720, at odds with Notsé's King Agokoli, they left for various locations in the south and eventually founded Alomé (now Lomé).

From 1884 to 1914, Togo was a German colony called Togoland. It was then partitioned between France and Great Britain. Britain administered its smaller western portion as part of the Gold Coast. In a 1956 plebiscite, British Togoland voted to unite with the Gold Coast, which became Ghana upon independence in 1957. French Togoland gained independence in 1960 as the Republic of Togo.

The first president of Togo, Sylvanus Olympio, was assassinated in 1963 by rebel army officers who installed and later ousted Olympio's rival, Nicolas Grunitzky. Etienne Eyadéma, a colonel involved in both coups, became president in 1967. Eyadéma later changed his first name to Gnassingbé and his rank to general. In 1990, violent street riots and mass civil disobedience forced him to convene a national conference to form a transitional government. Eyadéma retained the presidency, but the conference chose Joseph Kolou Koffigoh, a lawyer and human-rights activist, as prime minister.

Elections set for 1992 were postponed after political violence forced 300,000 Togolese to seek refuge in Benin and Ghana. A general strike organized by trade unions and the opposition paralyzed economic activity. Opposition leaders were often harassed; many went into exile. When presidential elections were finally held in 1993, Eyadéma ran virtually unopposed and easily won.

Eyadéma ran against several candidates in 1998 elections. Unfortunately, charges of fraud and voter intimidation, as well as the suspension of vote counting, cast doubt on the election's fairness. Eyadéma declared victory. Supporters of his main

Togo

challenger, Gilchrist Olympio (son of Sylvanus Olympio), rioted in the capital's streets, and the head of the election commission resigned without publishing final vote tallies. Prior to 2003 presidential elections, Olympio, living in exile, was banned from running due to a law that requires candidates to maintain residency in the country. Eyadéma won reelection amid renewed charges of fraud.

After 38 years in power, Gnassingbé Eyadéma died in February 2005. The military appointed his son Faure Gnassingbé as president. When the appointment was condemned by other nations, Faure agreed to hold a presidential election. In April 2005, the poll took place amid protests and street violence, and Faure was declared the winner.

THE PEOPLE

Population. Togo's population of 5.6 million is growing at 2.3 percent annually. The largest city is Lomé, the capital, with more than one million inhabitants. Many Lomé residents live in slums or squatter settlements. About 70 percent of Togolese live in rural areas, but cities such as Kara, Sokodé, Atakpamé, and Dapaong are growing rapidly.

Togo is home to at least 37 tribal groups. Artificial European borders divided many ethnic groups, and the Togolese have as much or more in common with their ethnic kin in Benin and Ghana as they have with each other. Togo's largest groups are the southern Ewe and such related peoples as the Ouatchi, Fon, and Adja. They constitute about 39 percent of the total population. Next in size are the Kabyé (14 percent) and related Losso (6 percent) in the north. Other significant groups include the Mina, Kotocoli, Moba, Gourma, Akposso, Ana, Lamba, Ehoué, Konkomba, Solla, and Bassar. The northern peoples are of Sudanic origin; the southern groups are Bantu-speaking peoples.

Language. Togo's official language, French, is used in business and the media. On a daily basis, however, at least 36 languages and numerous dialects are spoken across Togo. Ewe dominates in the south and Kabyè in the north. Kotocoli is another common northern language. Mina is used throughout Togo for communication between ethnic groups. Anlo, Ouatchi, and others are considered dialects of Ewe. Dagomba, Gen, Hausa, Twi, Tem, Fon, Akposso, Anna, Bassar, and Lamba are spoken by their respective groups. Traders in major market towns often come from Nigeria or Ghana; they conduct business in Hausa or a mixture of pidgin English and French. Mina and Kotocoli are more common in rural markets.

Religion. Most Togolese (65–75 percent) maintain indigenous African religious beliefs. Even Christians (20–30 percent) often mix traditional ceremonies and rites with their Christian (mostly Catholic) worship. Between 5 and 10 percent of Togolese are Muslims. All groups venerate ancestors in daily rituals such as dropping the first morsels of food or sips of water on the ground as an offering.

Every village in Togo has its own gods and rituals, but the Togolese generally believe in a supreme being. Smaller gods serve as messengers to or links with this higher deity. Animal sacrifices and other rituals send the lesser gods off to, and welcome them back from, journeys to the heavens. Aného's local god is *Kpessou*. Every September, in a New Year celebration (*Kpessosso*), each resident enters blindfolded into *Kpessou's* house to retrieve a colored stone. The stone color is a personal omen: white predicts a year of peace; red can mean danger. In Notsé, a rite called *Agbogbozan* celebrates people's escape from the reign of King Agokoli and honors the local god, *Agbogbo*. Togo also has many harvest festivals to celebrate plentiful crops and the ancestors who brought them the good fortune.

General Attitudes. The Togolese are self-reliant, conservative, generous, and friendly. It is considered impolite to criticize others in public. As a general rule, most Togolese assess possible consequences before undertaking something new. In a tense political environment, individuals are more likely to remain silent than to endanger their families by pressing for reform. The Togolese favor tradition over change and trust the wisdom of their grandparents' generation. Technology and Western ways are more readily embraced by educated urbanites. The Togolese are proud of their society and do not appreciate foreign criticism of their way of life. They believe in destiny and in trusting God with the future. People adapt to difficult circumstances and get by on what they may have. Members of the same village often treat each other as family.

Personal Appearance. Togolese men usually wear Western-style pants and shirts. For formal or special occasions, they may wear a traditional *kente* (large wraparound cloth worn over shorts and a shirt) or an *agbada* (a long, flowing, cotton top). Women wear a blouse and a wraparound cloth (*avo tata* in the south; *bsawao* or *sata* in the north), the length of which depends on the wearer's age and marital status. A woman's hairstyle can also denote status, as elaborate designs are expensive. Some Togolese women cover their heads with scarves, though they are more common among Muslim women and northern women. Urban youth prefer African, European, and American fashions. Rural people wear traditional clothing more than Western attire.

Togolese like to be neat and clean and usually wash two or three times a day. To clean their teeth, people chew on a "chewing stick" that comes from specific trees considered to have medicinal value. Urban people might use toothbrushes and toothpaste instead of, or in addition to, the "chewing stick."

CUSTOMS AND COURTESIES

Greetings. Greetings carry tremendous significance in Togolese culture as demonstrations of friendship, solidarity, and concern. They are always necessary before beginning a conversation. Most greetings are lengthy and include inquiries about one's health, family, welfare, occupation, and so on. French greetings such as *Bonjour* (Good day) and *Bonsoir* (Good evening) are popular in urban areas, especially among the youth. In the south, Ewe speakers and others have adapted English greetings: *Moning* (Good morning), *Gudey* (Good afternoon), and *Gudivin* (Good evening). In Ewe, those same greetings are rendered *Ndi*, *Ndo*, and *Fye*. In Kabyè, they are *Nliwalè*, *Nya-na wysy*, and *Nya-na dhoo*.

Men shake hands to greet one another, often striking their thumbs and middle fingers together to make a light sound. They may greet adult women this way, but not superiors, young girls, or newly married women. When greeting a superior, a person waits for the superior to extend his or her hand first. A person kneels to greet elders or chiefs. The elder claps and offers a verbal response. This exchange also occurs the day after a funeral, as bereaved family members thank those who helped with the funeral.

The Togolese use titles and family names to introduce new acquaintances. Friends and family members address each other by first name or in terms of their relationship, such as "older brother's wife" or "mother-in-law." Adults refer to each other as "brother" or "sister." Children call their fathers *papa* (in French), *fo* (Ewe), *fofo* (Mina), or *tchaa* (Kabyè), and their mothers *maman* (French), *da* (Ewe), *dada* (Mina), or *n'na* (Kabyè). They call other adults "uncle," "auntie," *tantie* (derived from the German for aunt), *papa*, and *maman*, even if they are not related.

Gestures. Hand gestures often accompany verbal expressions, but they rarely replace them. It is impolite to gesture with or hand an item to a person with the left hand. People pass items to elders with both hands. Adults do not interrupt each other in conversation. Women are especially courteous to their husbands; traditional rural women kneel to speak to them. In general, only men engage in public discussion. If the discussion relates to the whole family, women and children may be present but cannot speak unless invited to do so. In some urban areas, however, women are beginning to talk and eat in the company of men. Young people may not burp or cross their legs in the presence of elders, nor may they sit in a chair reserved for, or just vacated by, an adult. One avoids eye contact with elders or superiors.

Visiting. The Togolese enjoy making and receiving unannounced courtesy visits. Visiting shows one's respect for the hosts. Friends and relatives visit often. They tend to visit at home, though men like to gather at local outdoor bars to drink *tchouk* (millet beer) and relax. Sunday is the most popular day for visiting and people dress in their finest clothing to socialize. Children enjoy spending time with their cousins and other relatives on these occasions.

Guests are typically served something to drink. Depending on the wealth of the host or the importance of the visitor, refreshments such as cookies, cakes, banana chips, peanuts, or cashews may also be offered. It is generally impolite to visit during mealtime, but if this occurs, guests are invited to eat with the family. In addition to friends, Togolese visit those who are sick, grieving, or celebrating a marriage or birth. Guests might take gifts to the hosts on special occasions. Departing guests are accompanied as far as a taxi station or even all the way home if appropriate.

Eating. Traditionally, Togolese men eat alone or with other men. Women sometimes eat with their children, sometimes alone, or if applicable, sometimes with their husband's other wives. They rarely eat with their husbands, although this is changing among young urban couples.

People generally eat with the right hand. Before the meal, everyone washes both hands in a bowl of water. Dishes are served in a communal bowl (*ewegba* in Ewe). Diners sit on a mat. Many urban dwellers now eat with utensils at a table. When eating meat, diners express satisfaction by breaking the bones and sucking out the marrow. Away from home, people frequent small food stands in the market; restaurants are not common.

LIFESTYLE

Family. Togo's society relies upon the strength of extended family ties, often within a polygamous system (although educated women avoid polygamous marriages). Hierarchy is important and elderly people are deeply respected. Because of their experience and wisdom, their advice and suggestions are sought before important decisions are made. Elders are also the custodians of traditions, which they strive to pass to the next generation.

A woman's primary role is to give birth to children and to raise and educate them while offering submission to her husband. Although men and women are technically equal before the law, men clearly dominate Togolese society. Still, a man's oldest sister has considerable authority in his family as his female representative. She intercedes for her nephews and nieces during traditional ceremonies, and she can bless or curse them as she sees fit.

Obligations within the extended family are many, but none perhaps are more significant than when a family member dies. All relatives are duty-bound to support and comfort the deceased person's immediate family. Funeral and burial practices vary by ethnic group, religion, and the type of death (natural, heroic, violent, or bad). Most funerals feature a wake, music, dance, and farewell ceremonies. In some cases, a *griot* (storyteller) recites the deceased's deeds and encourages relatives to follow his or her example. Traditional royalty are buried in secret. Their coffins are laden with useful items (such as money, weapons, food, clothing, and so on) that will command proper respect in the next life.

Special ceremonies are held for those who died violently (by accident, suicide, or murder) or badly (in illness or childbirth). Without the rituals, the soul is said to wander aimlessly forever. These persons are buried away from others at a site called a *zogbedji*, an Ewe word meaning "inhospitable land."

Dating and Marriage. Many young people are allowed to choose their spouses, but families often frown on unions outside of their ethnic group. Other families still arrange marriages, although the prospective couple is allowed to reject the match. Dating patterns depend on whether the match was arranged and whether the family is traditional or modern. Grooms must pay a dowry to the bride's family. Polygamy is legal and openly practiced, though Christians and some others may be discreet about it.

Diet. Togo's staple foods include maize, millet, yams, and rice. Beans, peas, groundnuts (peanuts), cassava, sweet potatoes, cocoyams, and plantains are also important to the daily diet. These foods might be boiled, fried, or pounded to make a soft dough or paste. *Pâte* (in French) or *akoumé* (in Ewe) is a stiff porridge made of cornmeal and water and served with a spicy sauce of okra, spinach, and fish or meat. Another typical meal is *fufu* (made of pounded yams, cassava, and/or plantains) with a sauce. Sauces vary by region, but *gombo* (made with okra, small fish, and baobab leaves) and *arachide* (peanut sauce) are common. Sauces may be served with meat (typically goat or beef), fish, or fowl. Many foods are prepared with palm, coconut, or peanut oil. On special occasions, Togolese prepare *dzèkounmè* (a cornmeal mixture stirred into boiling tomato sauce and eaten with fried meat, chicken, crab, or fish). Local produce includes oranges, grapefruit, limes, mangoes, pineapples, melons, and bananas. A typical diet varies little, but for special occasions the quality improves (more meat or special seasonings are added).

Recreation. For recreation, most Togolese look forward to market day. They can dress up, socialize, and enjoy a festive environment as they shop for needed items or food. Each village has a particular market day. People do not travel for pleasure, only out of need, so leisure excursions are mostly to local spots. Favorite indoor activities include storytelling and playing scrabble, *ludo* (a board game), and cards. Urban youth dance at nightclubs. Soccer is the most popular sport. People also like basketball, boxing, marathon racing, and bicycle racing. Sunday is the most popular day for song and dance festivals, visiting, and other recreational activities.

Each district usually has an annual festival. For example, the Kabyè hold *Evala* (traditional wrestling) matches to conclude

Togo

a complex adulthood initiation ceremony. Young men are taken by night to the forest to be taught important lessons of life. Access to their location is forbidden. Women may later watch the wrestling matches, urging the young wrestlers on by singing and dance-clapping.

The Arts. Music and dancing are prominent in Togolese celebrations. The most popular types of music are *soukous* (played with a high-pitched guitar), *highlife* (an upbeat dance style from Ghana), and Jamaican reggae. Different ethnic groups also perform their own types of drum-based music and dance. Togo's folk artists create pottery, textiles, and wooden sculptures of abstract human figures. The Ewe weave headdresses from natural vegetation for the yearly harvest festival. Many of these items are produced for Togo's limited tourist market.

Holidays. Togolese celebrate New Year's Day, Easter (Friday–Monday), and Christmas. Muslims celebrate *Aid el Fitr* (a feast at the end of the holy month of *Ramadan*) and *Aid el Adha* (or *Tabaski*, the Feast of Sacrifice, honoring Abraham's willingness to sacrifice his son). National holidays include Liberation Day (13 Jan.), Independence Day (27 Apr.), Workers' Day (1 May), and Togolese Martyrs' Day (21 June). This last date specifically honors villagers in Pya-Hodo who were killed for refusing to work. Today, the holiday also honors Togolese killed in the fight for human rights.

Commerce. Urban businesses are open on weekdays from 7:30 a.m. to 12:30 p.m. and from 2:30 to 6 p.m. Some are open on Saturdays and even on Sunday mornings. Cash is the usual means of payment. Shop prices are fixed. Young vendors hawk goods near taxi stands or wherever cars are stopped due to traffic, and stores may send their goods out to be sold on the streets. Most people, especially in villages, buy goods at open-air markets, where prices are negotiable.

SOCIETY

Government. Most executive authority in Togo resides with the president (currently Faure Gnassingbé), who controls the military and can dissolve the 81-seat National Assembly. Members of the National Assembly are elected by popular vote to five-year terms. The prime minister (currently Koffi Sama) is appointed by the president and has limited powers. The voting age is 18.

Economy. Togo's economy is based on agriculture and most people are subsistence farmers. Cash-crop production has been increasing since the early 1990s, and the income from cocoa, coffee, and cotton is important to the economy. Togo also exports *shea butter*, a fruit extract used in beauty products and foods. Phosphate is Togo's main export. Small-scale industries exist, but apart from agriculture, industry is based mostly on services. Strong economic growth is possible but hindered by political instability. Togo's real gross domestic product per capita reflects a widening gap between the wealthy and the poor. The currency is the *CFA franc* (XOF).

Transportation and Communications. Togo has no public transportation system. Private taxis and vans transport goods and passengers, while larger trucks take goods from Lomé's harbor to inland areas and neighboring countries. Many roads are impassable during the rainy season. A *zemidjan* (motorcycle with no sidecar) is a common form of local taxi. Some people own motorcycles; others have bicycles.

The postal system is not reliable, so people send letters or messages via the truck drivers' trade union or with a traveler going in the right direction. Towns with electricity generally have public telephones, but the high cost per minute does not permit regular use. Most rural villages lack electricity. Mobile phone use is increasing in urban areas. Most Togolese have a radio, which is the primary source of news.

Education. Nearly every village has its own primary school and most districts have a senior secondary school; junior secondary schools are distributed less equally. Children begin attending school at age six. Although students are technically required to attend until age sixteen, many students leave school before then, especially in rural areas. Student advancement is hindered by a lack of funding, poverty, overcrowding, and the distance secondary students might have to live away from home. Girls are less likely to advance because family resources go first to boys. French is the language of instruction, though teachers use local dialects in the first few years. Churches and the private sector also sponsor schools at all levels. Scores of new but unauthorized schools opened in the 1990s. Tuition is high, but parents are willing to sacrifice to give their children the better opportunities such schools provide. Lomé has a small university.

Health. The public health system is not well equipped or funded. Vaccination rates are below desirable levels and clinics are hard to find in rural areas. Economic progress may revive important government programs, but unreliable transportation and roads make it hard to distribute needed supplies. Malaria, intestinal worms, and other treatable ailments still cause a large number of deaths. No city has a fully functioning sewage system. Modern medical care is too expensive for most people. The majority rely on traditional medicine and herbs.

DEVELOPMENT DATA
Human Dev. Index* rank . . . . 143 of 177 countries
   Adjusted for women . . . . 119 of 144 countries
Real GDP per capita $1,480
Adult literacy rate . . . . 74 percent (male); 45 (female)
Infant mortality rate . . . . 68 per 1,000 births
Life expectancy . . . . 48 (male); 51 (female)

AT A GLANCE

Events and Trends.
- Faure Gnassingbé won the April 2005 presidential election with 60 percent of the vote; the opposition criticized the poll for voting irregularities and fraud.
- President Eyadéma approved the release of about five hundred prisoners in August 2004. The move was seen as an effort to show international donors that the government's human-rights record was improving. Three months later, the European Union announced that it would resume aid programs, which had been suspended since 1993.

Contact Information. Embassy of Togo, 2208 Massachusetts Avenue NW, Washington, DC 20008; phone (202) 234-4212.

CultureGrams
People. The World. You.

ProQuest Information and Learning Company
300 North Zeeb Road, P.O. Box 1346
Ann Arbor, Michigan 48106 USA
Toll Free: 1.800.528.6279
Fax: 1.800.864.0019
www.culturegrams.com

© 2005 ProQuest Information and Learning Company and Brigham Young University. It is against the law to copy, reprint, store, or transmit any part of this publication in any form by any means without written permission from ProQuest. This document contains native commentary and original analysis, as well as estimated statistics. The content should not be considered strictly factual, and it may not apply to all groups in a nation. *UN Development Programme, Human Development Report 2004 (New York: Oxford University Press, 2004).

CultureGrams World Edition 2006

Tunisia (Tunisian Republic)

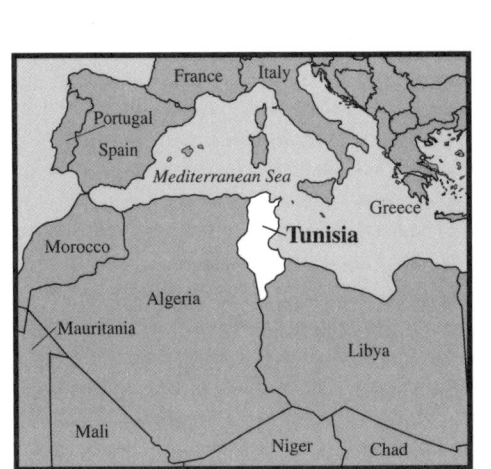

BACKGROUND

Land and Climate. Tunisia covers 63,170 square miles (163,610 square kilometers) and is slightly larger than the U.S. state of Georgia. Hundreds of miles of sandy beaches line Tunisia's Mediterranean coastline. The Atlas Mountains divide the more fertile north and east from the arid south. Tunisia's central region rises to a plateau and then gives way to the semidesert terrain of the Sahel. Further south, dry salt lakes and scattered oases border the Sahara Desert. About 19 percent of Tunisia's land is suitable for cultivation, and another 13 percent is used for permanent crops (such as citrus). Oranges and olives are two major agricultural products. Orange orchards are found in the Cap Bon (the northeastern peninsula). Olive groves are common from Tunis (the nation's capital in the north) to the central coastal city of Sfax, as well as on the island of Djerba. Tunisia's climate is mostly mild; average temperatures range from 52°F (13°C) in winter to 80°F (26°C) in summer. Toward the desert, temperatures are much hotter, especially when the south wind (sirocco, or *sh'hili*) blows. Sea breezes moderate the coastal climate. Winter nights can be cold in all parts of the country.

History. Throughout its history, Tunisia was a crossroads of many civilizations. Tunisia's indigenous inhabitants are known collectively as Berbers, but a more accurate indigenous term for them is Imazighen (Amazigh, singular). Phoenicians founded Carthage in 814 B.C. The Romans fought Carthage in three Punic Wars, eventually destroying it in 146 B.C.

The two major influences shaping modern Tunisian society are Islam and the remnants of French colonialism. Islam came with invading Arabs in the seventh century A.D. Indigenous groups gradually adopted the Arabic language and customs, and Tunisia became a center of Islamic culture. The Turkish Ottoman Empire ruled the area between 1574 and 1881. Economic difficulties and French colonial interests led to the Treaty of Bardo (1881), which made Tunisia a French protectorate. French culture soon became very influential, although it is less so today.

Tunisia was a major battleground during World War II. Before the war, many Tunisians had pressed for independence from France, and the movement picked up again after 1945. Independence was finally secured relatively peacefully in 1956. Habib Bourguiba, who had led the movement since the 1930s, became Tunisia's first president in 1957. Bourguiba was reelected every five years, always running unopposed, until he was named president for life in 1974. When he became too old to govern (in 1987), his prime minister, Zine El Abidine Ben Ali, legally removed him from power and took over as president. Bourguiba's 31 years in power left a strong imprint on Tunisia, his greatest achievements being in education, women's emancipation, and social modernization. He died in April 2000.

Ben Ali was formally elected in 1989 and reelected in 1994 and 1999. Other political parties have always been legal in Tunisia, but they have little power against the governing Constitutional Democratic Rally Party (RCD). Local elections in 2000 cemented the RCD's power further. Political parties of a religious or linguistic nature are illegal. Though accused of suppressing dissent, Ben Ali is credited with maintaining stability in an otherwise unstable region. He has associated Tunisia with the European Union and attempted to revive the Arab Maghreb Union (UMA), an organization aimed at regional cooperation in North Africa.

Tunisia

THE PEOPLE

Population. Tunisia's population of 9.97 million is growing at 1.01 percent annually. About 25 percent of the population is younger than age 15. Most people (98 percent) are of Arab descent. Others, mostly of European descent, live mainly in and around Tunis or on the island of Djerba. Two-thirds of Tunisians live in urban areas. Greatly influenced by the French, who ruled the country for more than 75 years, some urban Tunisians consider Tunisia the most Westernized state in the Arab world. Still, most Tunisians identify more with their "Arabness" than their "Westernness." People in small towns and villages tend to be more conservative than those in cities. Opportunities for personal advancement are expanding, as is the middle class: 80 percent of households own their own homes.

Language. Although Arabic is the official language, French is spoken in business and official circles. Urban Tunisians easily switch from one language to the other in the same sentence. Many high school students or graduates speak some English, since it is considered imperative to national and individual success. In 1996, primary schools began teaching English as well. Derija is the Arabic dialect spoken in Tunisia. Related to other North African dialects, it dominates in rural regions. Derija is a variation of the classical Arabic found in the *Qur'an* (Koran), but it is so different that a speaker of classical Arabic might not understand spoken Derija.

Religion. Islam is the official religion, and 98 percent of Tunisians are Muslim. The majority are Sunni Muslims of the Malikite tradition, as founded by Malik ibn Anas. He codified Islamic traditions and stressed the importance of community consensus (as opposed to Shi'ites, who emphasize the authority of Muhammad's descendants). Islam plays an important role in daily life, especially during family events such as births, circumcisions, weddings, and burials. Friday is Islam's holy day; government offices and many businesses close at 1 p.m.

Muslims accept the *Qur'an* as scripture, believing it was revealed by *Allah* (God) to the prophet Muhammad. Abraham is honored as the father of Muslims. Muhammad is considered the last and greatest prophet, although many biblical prophets are accepted as important messengers. In addition to attending Friday prayer services at the mosque, devout Muslims pray five times daily. However, most Tunisians do not strictly follow this practice. In villages without mosques, *zaouia* (small mausoleums built in memory of especially holy men) are the main centers for religious activity. One percent of the population is Christian and a smaller number is Jewish.

General Attitudes. Tunisians are a traditional, yet adaptable, friendly, and open people. They value hospitality, warmth, and generosity. Tunisians tend to act more formally with international visitors in order to give them the best impression of Tunisian culture. They might even take foreigners to their homes for a meal or to museums, cafés, or archaeological sites.

While Tunisians often are relaxed and informal with each other, they also emphasize showing respect for one another, especially their elders. Conformity to a group (family or community) and concern for its well-being are usually more important than individual desires. Still, social status and possessions are valued, especially by men. Tunisians tend to use phrases such as *Inshallah* (God willing) and *Allah ghalib* (God is stronger) to express hopes or intentions. Difficult times are explained as *maktoub* (fate), an attitude that provides comfort and encourages perseverance. A Tunisian's concept of time is loose; most people do not keep to a rigid schedule, and some things can take a long time to get done. "Tomorrow" can easily mean next week, and a meeting scheduled for 10 a.m. might not start until after lunch.

Personal Appearance. In Tunis and other large cities, fashion is influenced by western Europe, particularly Italy and France. However, most rural Tunisians still wear traditional North African clothing. Older women, both in the city and countryside, might wear a white *safsari* (rectangular piece of cloth that completely covers the clothing) while in public. Once worn mainly out of modesty, the *safsari* today also protects clothing from dust and rain. Older Amazigh women might wear a *futah*, a dark red wraparound dress. Shorts and bathing suits are not worn in public, except in resort areas. However, young urban women might wear short skirts, while their rural counterparts are sure to at least cover their knees and shoulders. Rural women wear their hair up and covered; they let it down for celebrations and special occasions.

CUSTOMS AND COURTESIES

Greetings. Greetings in Tunisia are an important and expressive part of personal interaction. Friends and family members often greet each other by "kissing the air" while brushing cheeks. Among strangers, both men and women, a handshake is the most common form of greeting. After a handshake, many rural people also kiss their right hand, then lay it flat on the heart to signify warmth or sincerity. Men might also shake hands when parting.

Standard greetings include *Ass'lama* (Hello), *Bisslama* (Good-bye), *Sabah El-Kheer* (Good morning), and *Tass'bah Ala Kheer* (Good night). Asking about someone's health and family is expected before further conversation. People say *Assalama Allekuhm* (Peace to you) when joining a group or entering a crowded room. When entering a store or office, a person greets the owner or staff. Neglecting to greet someone upon meeting is a serious oversight. Personal warmth is characteristic of all greetings.

Gestures. Hand gestures are vital to Tunisians in discussions and price negotiations. For example, the thumb and all fingertips pulled together and pointing up, while being waved toward the body, can mean "Good!" or "Wait!" depending on the context. One beckons by waving all fingers toward the body while the palm faces down. Using the index finger to point at objects is acceptable, but it is rude to point with the index finger at people. In general, it is better to place the index finger under the middle finger and point with both. Many Tunisians consider it inappropriate to wink at someone in public, but winking is fairly common among younger people.

Not all Tunisians subscribe to the tradition of avoiding the use of the left hand. Many urbanites use both hands freely. However, rural and some urban residents use only the right hand for shaking hands, passing objects, touching others, and eating. The left hand is reserved for personal hygiene. Like other Mediterranean peoples, Tunisians are spirited in conversational gestures and appreciate the same from visitors. Touching between members of the same sex is common to emphasize speech and communicate warmth. Friends of the same sex often walk hand in hand. However, men and women usually do not hold hands in public because public displays of affection are inappropriate.

Visiting. Family and friends visit each other frequently and unannounced—often in the late evening. Visits can last several hours, and guests usually are invited for a meal. It is especially important to visit neighbors and family on religious holidays.

Because hospitality is important, a host usually offers food and drink to guests. Such an offer is accepted, even if only for a taste. Invited guests might bring gifts of fruit to the host, but this is not expected. Unannounced guests do not typically bring a gift. Hosts commonly give first-time visitors a tour of the home, especially if a new room or new furniture has been added. On such an occasion, guests might congratulate the hosts with *mabrouk*, a congratulatory wish also used for weddings, graduations, or new employment.

Eating. Tunisians wash their hands before and after meals. Eating from separate plates with utensils is common among urban residents. Rural people often sit on the floor around a low, round, wooden table (*mida*) at mealtime. They eat with the hand or use bread as a scoop and customarily eat from a common plate or group of dishes. Tunisians do not like to eat alone. A host will often insist that guests have second or third helpings, and it is polite for guests to accept. When a person has eaten enough, he or she express the meal was satisfying by saying *Khamsa ou Khmis Aalik* (roughly meaning "You've done an excellent job") or *Hamdullah* (Thanks to God). Burping after a meal is considered rude.

LIFESTYLE

Family. Honor, reputation, and mutual support are the most important family values in Tunisia. The extended family is typically close-knit. By tradition, gender roles are clearly defined, with men the breadwinners and women responsible for the household and children. Today, however, many women (one-fourth of the labor force) also work outside the home. Tunisia is progressive among Muslim countries in its laws concerning women's rights at work and in matters of divorce and inheritance. However, attitudes are changing more slowly than the law. Polygamy has been outlawed since Tunisia's independence in 1956, even though Islamic tradition allows a man to have as many as four wives.

Dating and Marriage. Western dating practices were traditionally considered unacceptable, but attitudes are gradually changing. Rural marriages—sometimes between cousins—often are still arranged by parents, but urban youth have increasing opportunities to meet and get to know one another independently. Their parents still have a strong voice in whom they marry, but the couples have the final say. In all areas, weddings and social gatherings provide a chance for young people to meet. Tunisian men often delay marriage, as a man is expected to provide a considerable dowry to the bride's family before a marriage can take place.

Traditional weddings, particularly in rural areas, are celebrated over several days, even weeks, through ritualized ceremonies and parties. The most important festivities occur in the last few days before the wedding. Men and women have separate parties. In one (called *seqer* or *halwa*), the bride's body hair is "waxed" off with a sugar, water, and lemon paste. A henna party follows on the night before the wedding. Women invited to the bride's home apply patterns to her hands and feet using a paste made from henna leaves (the dried paste is removed after several hours, leaving patterns behind that last for several days). The bride also has her hair and makeup done. On her wedding day, a bride may change outfits several times, wearing one or two traditional dresses as well as a Western gown. After the ceremony, relatives and friends celebrate with dancing, music, and food.

Diet. *Couscous* is Tunisia's national dish; it is made of steamed and spiced semolina, topped with vegetables and meats. Appreciated for its delicacy and lightness, *couscous* is prepared in many ways. *Breek*, another favorite dish, is made of a thin fried dough stuffed with an egg, cooked vegetables, and tuna. *Tajine* is a crustless quiche of vegetables and meats. Tunisians frequently eat fish, lamb, and chicken. Tomatoes, potatoes, onions, olives, oil, and peppers are common to Tunisian cooking. A large variety of fruits are sold in the markets, including dates, oranges, apricots, watermelons, and nectarines. Cactus fruit (*hindi*), called the "sultan of all fruits," is widely available in the summer. *Tabuna* is a round bread baked in a cylindrical clay oven by the same name. Devout Muslims do not consume alcohol or pork, but alcohol is available in urban areas.

Recreation. Listening to music, watching videos or television, going to the beach, playing soccer and beach volleyball (mostly men), and visiting friends and relatives are among the most popular leisure activities in Tunisia. Soccer is the most popular sport. Most people enjoy chess and *shkubbah*, a traditional card game. Coffeehouses are extremely popular among men, who go there to play cards, discuss sports and politics, conduct business, and drink coffee. Women usually do not go to coffeehouses unless in the company of male relatives.

The Arts. Architecture and art from several ancient civilizations are ubiquitous. For example, the town of Dougga dates back to the Byzantine Empire. Roman mosaics are found everywhere. Tunisians are dedicated to preserving their rich heritage, for which the government provides financial support.

Modern culture is gaining increasing prominence; the Carthage Film Festival, held biannually, is a showcase for internationally recognized Tunisian films. Summer art festivals in Carthage and Dougga attract large crowds. Strongly associated with Tunisian national identity, *malouf* is a musical style played by small orchestras with instruments such as drums, lutes, sitars, and violins. Calligraphy and fine arts such as painting on glass and miniatures are deeply embedded in the nation's past and present. Painting often combines French and native influences.

Holidays. Although Tunisia's secular holidays follow the Western calendar, religious holidays follow the Muslim (lunar) calendar, so they fall on different days each year. The most important holiday period is *Ramadan*, a month of fasting and prayer. While Muslims do not eat, drink, or smoke from sunrise to sundown each day during *Ramadan*, they participate in lively evenings that involve special foods, carnivals, shopping, and festivals. Non-Muslims, while not expected to fast, should exercise good judgment about eating in public and taking part in the evening celebrations. *Aid El Seghir*, a two-day holiday, marks the end of *Ramadan*. People wear their best clothes to visit friends and relatives, and they trade presents of pastry. Other holidays include *Ras El Am El Hejri* (Islamic New Year), *El Mouled* (prophet Muhammad's birthday), and *Aid El Kebir* (commemorating Abraham's willingness to sacrifice his son). For *Aid El Kebir*, each household sacrifices a lamb at dawn and feasts on grilled lamb throughout the day as relatives visit one another.

Secular holidays include New Year's Day, Independence Day (20 Mar.), Martyr's Day (9 Apr.), Labor Day (1 May), Republic Day (25 July), Women's Day (13 Aug.), Evacuation Day (15 October, the day in 1963 when the last of the French troops returned to France), and the Second Revolution, or the day that Ben Ali assumed power from Bourguiba (7 Nov.).

Commerce. From September to June, business hours are Monday through Thursday, from 8 a.m. to 12:30 p.m. and 2 to 6

Tunisia

p.m. On Friday and Saturday, hours are from 8 a.m. to 1 p.m. Businesses are closed on Sunday, except in tourist areas. Many private companies, including banks, have slightly longer working hours during the week and are closed all day Saturday and Sunday. During July and August, most businesses operate Monday through Saturday, 7 a.m. to 1 p.m. During *Ramadan* banks and other businesses close in the early afternoon, then reopen after the breaking of the fast (after sundown) and usually stay open until late at night.

The weekly *souk* (market) is the focal point of local economic activity; people come to buy goods and produce, to trade, and to socialize. On the night of a *souk*, families often enjoy a meal of *couscous* topped with fresh vegetables. Urban markets are open throughout the week.

Tunisian businesspeople usually have tea or engage in small talk before discussing business, but this practice is disappearing among more Westernized Tunisians. Many details in business arrangements are not written down because the business environment does not always guarantee that such things as deadlines will be met.

SOCIETY

Government. Tunisia is a republic divided into 23 governorates. The central government is headed by a president (currently Zine El Abidine Ben Ali), who appoints a prime minister (currently Mohamed Ghannouchi) and a Council of Ministers. Members of the unicameral legislature, the 182-seat Chamber of Deputies (*Majlis al-Nuwaab*), are directly elected to five-year terms. All citizens may vote at age 20. The RCD is the dominant party. A number of independents and Islamists are represented in the legislature, and smaller political parties do function.

Economy. Agriculture, light industry, and services all play key roles in Tunisia's economy. Agriculture is especially important in the interior and along the Sahel coast; olives and dates are exported. Other agricultural products include olive oil, grain, dairy products, tomatoes, citrus fruit, beef, sugar beets, dates, and almonds. The textile industry (mostly for export) provides jobs for thousands of laborers, as does tourism, Tunisia's main source of hard currency. Remittances from Tunisian workers in France and income from oil, phosphates, and iron ore are also vital. Eighty percent of all exports go to Europe; most tourists come from Germany and France.

Tunisia's economy is shifting toward a free market, and economic growth has generally been high. The workforce is educated and productive. Inflation is low, but unemployment remains a significant problem with serious social implications. The currency is the Tunisian *dinar* (TND).

Transportation and Communications. A good network of paved roads and highways links all cities and towns. Major railroads serve northern and coastal areas. Tunis has an efficient light-rail system (*Métro Léger*). Buses are the most common form of public transportation. *Louages* (group taxis) run on set routes between cities and are faster than buses. Most families do not own cars. Motorcycles and bicycles are common. In rural areas, people may use donkey carts to transport goods and vegetables. There are airports in major cities.

Phone service is generally good, but it may be slow in summer because the shorter work schedule strains the system. Most people have telephones in their homes. Those who do not, have access to them at post offices. Mobile telephones are common among young urban Tunisians. The press is closely regulated by the government. There are four television stations. The radio is a state monopoly.

Education. Education has been an important element in Tunisia's development since independence. One-fourth of the government's budget is spent on education. This allows even the most remote regions to have free schooling. *École de Base* (Basic Education, grades 1–6) is compulsory and nearly all children are enrolled. Advancement depends on passing tests. About half of all students go on to the *Lycée* (grades 7–13). In 10th grade, students choose between two tracks: *Lettres* (humanities and social sciences) or *Sciences* (math and science). The rigorous Baccalaureate Exam is taken at the end of the 13th grade; successful students may go on to a university. A student's passing the test is a great source of pride for his or her parents. While classes are taught in French and Arabic, there is a trend to promote Arabic and the use of Arabic textbooks. Nearly half of all college students are women.

Health. The government provides free medical care to all citizens. Major cities have private clinics as well. Rural health care may be limited to clinics for child immunizations, family planning, and other basic services. Tunisia has made good progress in improving national health. For example, the infant mortality rate has dropped more than 85 percent since 1970.

DEVELOPMENT DATA
Human Dev. Index* rank . . . . 92 of 177 countries
Adjusted for women . . . . 77 of 144 countries
Real GDP per capita $6,760
Adult literacy rate . . . . 83 percent (male); 63 (female)
Infant mortality rate . . . . 26 per 1,000 births
Life expectancy . . . . 71 (male); 75 (female)

AT A GLANCE

Events and Trends.
- President Ben Ali unsurprisingly won reelection in October 2004, securing 94 percent of the vote. His RCD maintained its control of the Chamber of Deputies. The nation's main opposition party, the Democratic Progressive Party, boycotted the elections, alleging vote-rigging. A 2002 referendum had extended the president's term limit from three to five, allowing Ben Ali to run for a fourth term in 2004. The referendum passed with 99 percent of the vote.
- In January 2004, Tunisia won the prestigious African Cup of Nations soccer tournament, which it also hosted, by defeating Morocco 2–1 in the final game.
- Attributed to the al-Qaeda network, the 2002 bombing of a Jewish synagogue on the island of Djerba killed 19 people, most of them foreign tourists.

Contact Information. Embassy of Tunisia, 1515 Massachusetts Avenue NW, Washington, DC 20005; phone (202) 862-1850.

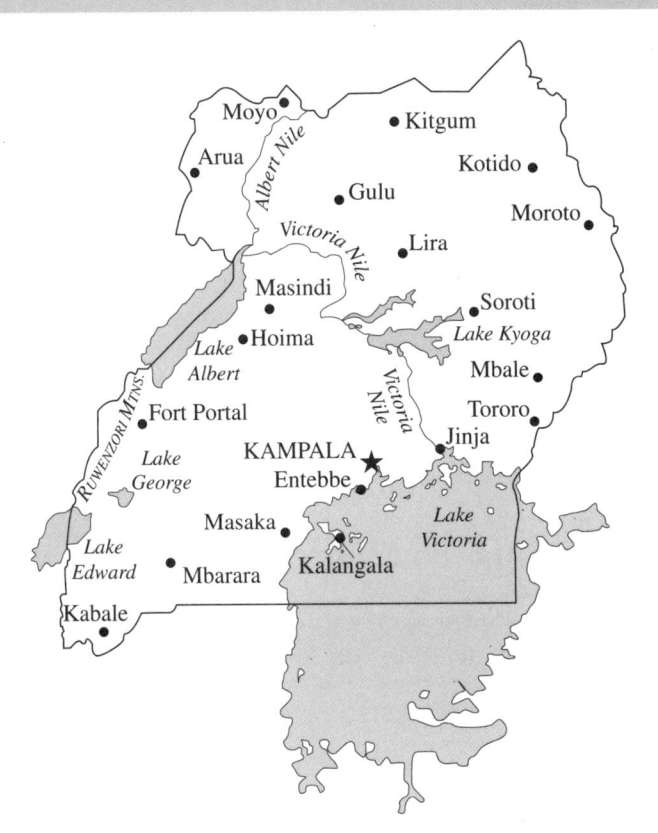

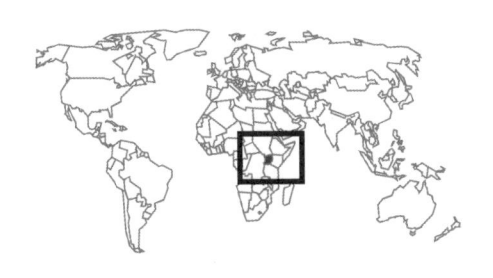

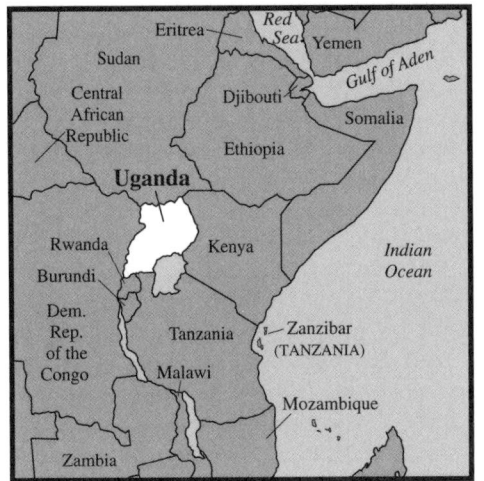

CultureGrams World Edition 2006

Republic of Uganda

BACKGROUND

Land and Climate. Known as the "Pearl of Africa" for the variety and beauty of its landscapes, Uganda covers 91,135 square miles (236,040 square kilometers), an area about the same size as Oregon. Roughly one-fourth of the land is arable; 12 percent is reserved for national parks and forests.

Uganda's climate is influenced by its proximity to the equator, mountains on the eastern and western borders, and large bodies of water. Uganda has two rainy seasons (March–July and September–October). The semiarid northeast experiences frequent droughts. Average temperatures range between 72 and 92°F (22–33°C) depending on the region and season. Areas around Lake Victoria tend to be cooler even in the dry season. The Ruwenzori Mountains and the Kigezi Mountains in southwest Uganda are cold and misty most of the year.

History. Farming and hunting groups, probably Bantus, lived in the Lake Victoria Basin by the fourth century B.C. These people could smelt iron and make a form of carbon steel. Smaller groups eventually came together, and by about A.D. 1000, the Buganda state emerged as the strongest kingdom among several Bantu and other kingdoms.

By the 1800s, the *Baganda* (people of Buganda), ruled by a *kabaka* (king), had a strong army and well-organized administration. However, European exploration and colonization collided with local politics, and Britain had established itself by about 1860. Christian missionaries soon followed, and the British East Africa Company laid claim to the territory in 1888. In reality, Britain had little control, and various religious groups fell to fighting one another. After an 1894 Protestant victory over Catholics and Muslims, the British expanded power and established Uganda as a protectorate. Britain signed a treaty in 1900 with Buganda before signing with three smaller kingdoms (Ankole, Toro, and Bunyoro). This treaty allowed the Baganda to become colonial administrators. They tended to impose their own culture on neighboring kingdoms, setting the stage for later conflicts.

At the same time, British authorities were bringing in white settlers, Indian laborers, and new cash crops. They built a railroad to improve movement of coffee and cotton. They drew borders that separated ethnic groups and put hostile ones together. Young, educated Baganda working for the British formed the Young Baganda Association in the 1920s and soon replaced older chiefs in the colonial administration.

Ugandans fought alongside the British during World War II, organized as the King's African Rifle (KAR). Baganda rioted over British economic policies after the war. England later began implementing policies to grant self-rule by 1961. Peaceful independence followed in 1962; Milton Obote of the Uganda People's Congress (UPC) served as prime minister and King Frederick Walugembe Mutesa II (*Kabaka Freddie*) as head of state. In 1966, Obote suspended the constitution and sent General Idi Amin Dada's army to seize the king's palace. In 1967, he abolished the kingdoms and introduced a new constitution that made Uganda a republic with a strong president.

Idi Amin Dada overthrew Obote in 1971, dissolved parliament, and named himself absolute ruler. Over eight years, he eliminated opposition, expelled Indian merchants, ruled with terror, and invaded Tanzania. The Uganda National Liberation Army (UNLA), comprised of Tanzanian troops and Ugandan exiles, fought back and captured the capital city of Kampala in 1979. Amin fled the country, which then experienced some instability prior to multiparty elections in 1980. Obote and the UPC returned to power in the balloting.

Uganda

Obote soon faced war with the National Resistance Army (NRA) under Yoweri Museveni. Some of Obote's officers rebelled in 1985, and he fled. Their attempts to establish a government failed, and the NRA took control of Kampala. Museveni's National Resistance Movement (NRM) reestablished political rule in 1986 and implemented some reforms. A 1995 constitution allowed for nonparty elections in 1996, through which Museveni was elected president. A referendum in June 2000 called on voters to choose between the existing NRM "movement" system and multiparty democracy. Opposition groups had little opportunity to campaign for a multiparty system, so the movement system was officially adopted. Museveni won reelection in 2001 with a large majority, though the opposition argued that fraud contributed to the victory.

The Museveni government's economic liberalization program is attracting new foreign investment, and privatization of state-owned industries is helping the economy to stabilize. Still, government corruption, rebel activity, and the loss of labor to AIDS all hinder expansion and productivity.

THE PEOPLE

Population. Uganda's population of 26.4 million is growing at 2.97 percent annually. Only 12 percent of the population lives in urban areas. More than half is age 14 or younger.

The nation's 48 distinct groups follow four main linguistic lines: Bantu, Nilotic, Nilo Hamite, and Sudanic. The largest Bantu group is the Baganda (13 percent) of central Uganda. Other major groups include the Bagisu, Banyankole, Basoga, Bunyoro, Batoro, and Banyarwanda. Among the Nilotics are the Acholi, Lango, Alur, and Jabwor. The Nilo Hamites are the Iteso and the nomadic, warrior Karamojong of northeast Uganda. Sudanic peoples in the West Nile region include the Lugbara, Kakwa, and Madi.

Language. English is the official language for government, education, and commerce. Baganda speak Luganda, a dominant language in the center and west, and Acholi and Lango speak Luo. Kiswahili joins Luo as prominent in the north. Generally, people speak their own native language or dialect first, a regional tongue, and then English if educated. Those who speak English well are highly respected. Most languages are named for the tribes that speak them (i.e., the Karamojong speak Akarimojong and the Iteso speak Ateso).

Religion. Most Ugandans are Christian; Catholics and Protestants comprise the largest denominations. Pentecostals and other smaller groups are growing. Sudanic peoples are mostly Muslim. Islam was introduced by Arab traders in the early 19th century, while Christianity came to Uganda in 1875. Most Christian churches built schools and health centers, so many people converted to Christianity even though they continued indigenous practices. Many Christians and Muslims today maintain indigenous beliefs, performing rituals for ancestors and gods at private shrines. Some people practice traditional rites exclusively. Regardless of one's religion, nearly all Ugandans have a high level of respect and fear for spirits, demons, and God.

General Attitudes. Ugandans treasure their heritage and place great importance on families and clans. In addition, they value economic prosperity, education, and spirituality. An educated man who speaks English well and owns a car and/or a house commands great respect. Western devices such as video cameras, mobile phones, and so forth are highly sought after symbols of wealth in urban areas. International travel is admired. A growing adoption of Western culture and individualistic habits disturbs many older people, who encourage schools to teach traditional values through song, dance, and drama.

In rural areas, appearing wealthy is also important, but the symbols are different: land, cattle, multiple wives, and bicycles. Everywhere, beauty is valued in women, and lighter skin is desired most. Ugandans admire a person who is generous, friendly, and willing to help others. It is considered immature to express anger or extreme negative emotions in public.

Personal Appearance. Ugandans wear Western-style clothing to offices or the market. Rural people reserve their best clothes for important days or visits. Imported secondhand attire from North America and Europe is very popular and dominates local markets. Revealing clothing such as miniskirts are considered a disgrace for women, but they are becoming common among young educated girls in Kampala. Traditional *gomesi* (a many-layered dress) and *kanzu* (a long, embroidered cotton gown for men) are worn mostly in central Uganda but also elsewhere. Many women wear wraparound skirts with blouses and shoulder wraps. The Karamojong wear traditional clothing unless traveling to other districts.

CUSTOMS AND COURTESIES

Greetings. Ugandans stand to greet elderly or high status persons who enter a room. Bantu girls kneel to greet elders. Women, too, greet men while kneeling. However, educated urban women are more likely to bend their knees rather than kneel. Initial verbal greetings are followed by several inquiries about family, work, and other matters. Actual greetings depend on the language but begin with some version of "How are you, sir/madam?" (in Luganda: *Musibityendo ssebo/ngabo?*), "How are the home people?" (Lysonga: *Koddeyo*?), or "How did you sleep?" (Luo: *Ibuto aber?*). The response is usually "Fine, and you?" (Luo: *Ber, ibuto aber?*). In Kiswahili, a casual "Hello!" is *Jambo!* Young Baganda might say *Ki kati?* (What's up?) and respond with *Ayendi, ki kati?* (I'm fine; what's up?). In Luo, such an exchange is *Kop ango?* (What issues?) and *Kop pe* (No issues).

Titles are used in offices and formal settings. Friends address each other by given name. They might also use nicknames or call someone by their child's name (*Mama Josephine,* or "mother of Josephine"). Young people call older people *auntie* or *uncle*, even if no family relationship exists.

Gestures. Ugandans greet, eat, and pass items with the right hand; using both hands to receive an item shows appreciation. People do not use the left hand alone. Ugandans usually point with the hand, but lips can also be used. One might show agreement by raising both eyebrows, but this gesture is not used with strangers. Sighing while visiting is impolite. When sitting, one's thighs should be covered. Ugandans gesture freely with their hands when talking to friends. Crossing one's arms at the chest can be seen as an act of defiance.

Visiting. Ugandans visit friends and relatives often and unannounced. It is a virtue to have many friends who make frequent visits. Upon entering a home, guests usually remove their shoes. Hosts almost always offer tea or food to guests, who are obliged to accept at least a taste if not an entire portion. Visitors receive the best seat and food. If chicken is served, an honored visitor receives the gizzard. If necessary, hosts will offer their own beds to overnight guests and sleep at a neighbor's. Guests might give hosts food (bread, sugar, salt, a live chicken, white ants, fresh produce) or other useful items, such as soap. Flowers are for people recuperating from illness or childbirth. Although people socialize at home, especially in rural areas, they also gather at parks, churches, soccer matches, or drinking places. At the end of a visit, hosts accompany guests part of the way home, or at least to their transportation.

Eating. Rural Ugandans eat two meals a day, in the morning and evening. People wash their hands in a basin before each meal; older children ensure younger ones have washed before sitting down. Ugandans generally eat outside, either on a veranda or under a shady tree.

Men usually are served first at a table or seated in chairs, followed by children and women seated on mats nearby. A boy's right to sit at a table depends somewhat on age but more on his level of acceptance in society. For example, a boy of 15 in secondary school may be granted a seat while a 17-year-old boy still in primary school will be on a mat.

Ugandans eat with their "natural fork" (the right hand), especially in rural areas. Rural people eat from a common platter, but urban residents more often use individual plates. Ugandans do not talk during a meal. Parents discourage talking so children do not choke or show food in their mouths and so they will get enough to eat from the common platter.

LIFESTYLE

Family. Most village families are large, especially when a man has multiple wives. Families in urban areas tend to be smaller. In times of need, Ugandans turn to the extended family for financial support or other assistance, even if it creates a burden for others. People who work away from their home districts are less likely to respond to such obligations. Ugandans pay particular attention to aging parents, who are provided for by the eldest or wealthiest son.

By custom, the father protects the family, buys clothing, pays school fees, tills the ground, and plants crops. Mothers make sure children are fed and clean. A woman keeps house and looks after her husband—preparing his meals, pressing his clothing, and finding water for his bath. Rural mothers weed gardens, harvest crops, and often sell produce in the market. Children begin chores as early as age three, often by rinsing dishes or sweeping. Older girls help their mothers care for younger siblings or work in the garden, while boys tend livestock, run errands, and help their fathers plant crops. Children legally belong to their father, even in divorce.

AIDS has been hard on Uganda's families, often leaving no one to support or care for children. Sometimes, the oldest child simply becomes head of the household over younger siblings. Such children are less likely to go to school, learn traditional values, or be safe from exploitation.

Urban homes are made of cement, have corrugated iron roofs, and contain two or three bedrooms. Rural homes have mud walls and thatched roofs. Northern and eastern groups smear their dirt floors periodically with a mixture of cow dung and soil, which they smooth out with stones to create a flat, hard surface. Karamojong live in walled communities called *manyattas* to protect their livestock and families from raids by rival groups.

Dating and Marriage. Young people meet in school, at church, or during festivals. Most have the freedom to date and select their own mate. Villagers often marry by age 18. Urban residents marry between 18 and 25 years.

Wedding ceremonies are increasingly held in churches, but only with written consent from the couple's parents. Consent is given after a bride-price has been paid in cash, livestock, or clothing and/or household goods. The purpose is to thank the girl's parents for raising her and to compensate them for losing her. A widow can be inherited by any of a man's surviving brothers. Wife inheritance, along with polygamy, is fading due to AIDS, difficult economic conditions, and exposure to Western culture.

A wedding is preceded by certain essential ceremonies. For instance, among Baganda, a prospective groom selects a spokesman from among his friends and they accompany him to present gifts to his girlfriend and her extended family in an "introduction ceremony." The paternal aunt who will coordinate wedding arrangements receives special gifts. If the gifts and entourage are accepted, the parties celebrate and begin planning the wedding.

Among the Acholi, Lango, and Alur groups, the man writes to the bride's parents expressing his intent to send representatives to an "asking for marriage ceremony." His spokesmen will negotiate the bride-price with the girl's brothers and uncles. The woman's family later visits the man's family for a "seeing the bride-price ceremony." If satisfied, they arrange for a ceremony in which to present the bride-price to the girl's father. Among the Karamojong, the prospective bride picks a strong man to throw a heavy club near the groom's family cattle. The distance the club travels along the herd marks how many cattle will be included in the bride-price. All ceremonies and negotiations can last for days and are cause for eating, drinking, and celebration. Traditionally, once a man sent someone to retrieve his wife from her home, they were considered married. Today, however, civil or church weddings are necessary to complete a union.

Diet. A typical breakfast may include tea and bread with margarine. Eggs, fried bananas, or fruit might also be served. For dinner, people eat a starchy staple with a meat stew or sauce and green leafy vegetables. *Matooke* (mashed bananas) steamed in banana leaves is a favorite dish. People also eat *kwon kaal* (millet bread), *chapati* (flat bread), *pasho* (maize paste), rice, cassava, and sweet potatoes. The most popular meats are beef, goat, and pork. Smoked meat in peanut butter and smoked fish in peanut stew are popular in some areas. Ugandans like citrus fruits, mangoes, watermelon, and papaya. Beans, cowpeas, and groundnuts (peanuts) are important sources of protein. Other delicacies include de-winged, salted, and fried white ants or grasshoppers, and meat steamed in a banana leaf.

Recreation. *Football* (soccer) is the most popular sport throughout Uganda. Urban residents might also play basketball, lawn tennis, cricket, rugby, and netball (a sport similar to basketball, played only by girls). People like to play cards or the traditional *omweso* (*coro* in Luo), a strategy board game played with seeds or stones. After work, men gather in small drinking places to talk about sports or politics. Women socialize at home, knitting or doing each other's hair while they chat and look after their children.

The Arts. Musicians throughout Uganda play drums, harps, xylophones, lyres, and thumb pianos (*okeme* in Luo). Instruments and musical styles may also be specific to a particular ethnic group. For example, Baganda play the *ngalabi* (long drum). The Acholi are known for their dance performances accompanied by the *gwata*, a half gourd struck with metal bicycle spokes. Folk art fulfills both aesthetic and functional purposes. Baskets, pottery, and wood carvings are the most common forms. The making of batik and bark cloth is typically reserved for women.

Holidays. Ugandans celebrate New Year's Day, Liberation Day (26 January, when the NRM came to power), Women's

Uganda

Day (8 Mar.), Easter (Friday–Monday), Labor Day (1 May), Martyrs' Day (3 June, the day in 1879 when 22 Christians were killed by Kabaka Muwanga), Independence Day (9 Oct.), Christmas, and Boxing Day (26 Dec.). Boxing Day comes from the British tradition of giving small boxed gifts to service workers or the poor. It is now simply a day to relax and visit friends and relatives. Muslims celebrate *Idd Fitr*, a three-day feast at the end of *Ramadan*, the holy month of fasting, and *Idd Adha*, the Feast of the Sacrifice. Ugandans travel to their home villages during Christmas for music, dance, and food. Christians attend church on Christmas Day and New Year's Day.

Commerce. Businesses are open weekdays from 8 a.m. to 5 p.m., with a lunch hour at 1 p.m. Banks close by 3 p.m. Urban stores close by 6 p.m. The post office and some businesses are open on Saturday morning. Rural people grow most of their food, but they buy supplies at open-air markets.

SOCIETY

Government. Uganda's president (currently Yoweri Museveni) is head of state and head of government. The prime minister (currently Apollo Nsibambi) heads the executive cabinet. The president is elected to a five-year term; the prime minister is appointed by the president. Members of the 303-seat unicameral National Assembly serve five-year terms. The counties directly elect 214 representatives. Seats are reserved for women (56), the army (10), the disabled (5), workers (5), and youth (5). The remaining eight seats are occupied by government officials. The voting age is 18. Uganda's 48 districts are divided into counties, subcounties, parishes, and villages. Elected local councils function at each level.

Economy. Agriculture is the mainstay of the economy. Most families rely heavily on subsistence farming for their livelihood; the bulk of this work is performed by women. Major cash crops include coffee and tea grown primarily in the western and central regions, and tobacco and cotton grown in the north and east. Uganda is one of the world's largest producers of raw coffee. Other crops include soybeans, maize, cassava, millet, and flowers. Fish from Lake Victoria is exported to Europe. The currency is the Uganda shilling (UGX).

Transportation and Communications. Uganda's transportation system is not well developed; the few paved roads outside of urban areas become impassable in heavy rains. Buses run between major towns. To reach "up-country" (rural) destinations, people ride aloft cargo in pickup trucks. Wealthier individuals own cars; traffic moves on the left. In cities, people take commuter taxis to work, ride bicycles, or walk. On water, people use canoes, boats, and ferries. In trading centers and smaller towns, people ride short distances on a *boda boda* ("bicycle-taxi" with a padded passenger seat over the rear wheel). Many families own at least one bicycle. Entebbe International Airport links Uganda to global destinations. Planes also fly to islands in Lake Victoria, remote areas, and small domestic airfields.

The public telephone system reaches the entire country but has too few lines to offer complete service. Mobile phones are filling the gap for businesspeople. Uganda's two daily newspapers enjoy wide circulation: the pro-government *New Vision* and the independent *Monitor*. The government operates tele-

DEVELOPMENT DATA
Human Dev. Index* rank . . . . 146 of 177 countries
    Adjusted for women . . . . 113 of 144 countries
Real GDP per capita $1,390
Adult literacy rate . . . . 79 percent (male); 59 (female)
Infant mortality rate . . . . 86 per 1,000 births
Life expectancy . . . . 45 (male); 46 (female)

vision and radio stations, but private broadcasters also have a voice in many locations.

Education. Children begin school by age six, attending primary school for seven years. About 40 percent of these students go on to secondary school ordinary level (senior 1–4), and some finish the advanced level (senior 5–6). After each division, students sit for a national exam to determine their advancement. The government pays school fees for four natural children in each family, but rural schools lack materials and facilities. Makerere University (est. 1922) is the most prestigious institution of higher education. Christians are more likely to have a formal education than Muslims, who often emphasize schooling that focuses on the study of the *Qur'an* (Koran).

Health. Immunization campaigns are combating diseases such as whooping cough, tuberculosis, diphtheria, measles, cholera, and polio, but malaria and intestinal diseases are still common in rural areas. AIDS is pervasive, and the many deaths caused by the disease have widespread social consequences. However, a national AIDS education effort has reduced rates of infection. Government hospitals exist in every district but are usually short of supplies and personnel. Each of the four major regions has at least one well-equipped mission hospital. Women, who bear an average of seven children, face a high maternal mortality rate.

AT A GLANCE
Events and Trends.
- The Museveni government and the Lord's Resistance Army (LRA), a rebel group in northeastern Uganda, agreed to a cease-fire in November 2004. Both sides expressed willingness to negotiate a peaceful solution to their conflict. The LRA has opposed the Museveni government since 1986. In that time, LRA attacks have killed thousands of people and displaced as many as 1.5 million people. The group is infamous for kidnapping children and forcing them to fight in battle.
- In November 2004, Uganda's Constitutional Court overturned the law that prevents political parties from participating in elections. If the ruling stands, parties will be able to take part in elections for president and the National Assembly scheduled for 2006.

Contact Information. Embassy of Uganda, 5911 16th Street NW, Washington, DC 20011; phone (202) 726-7100.

CultureGrams
People. The World. You.

ProQuest Information and Learning Company
300 North Zeeb Road, P.O. Box 1346
Ann Arbor, Michigan 48106 USA
Toll Free: 1.800.528.6279
Fax: 1.800.864.0019
www.culturegrams.com

© 2005 ProQuest Information and Learning Company and Brigham Young University. It is against the law to copy, reprint, store, or transmit any part of this publication in any form by any means without written permission from ProQuest. This document contains native commentary and original analysis, as well as estimated statistics. The content should not be considered strictly factual, and it may not apply to all groups in a nation. *UN Development Programme, Human Development Report 2004 (New York: Oxford University Press, 2004).

CultureGrams World Edition 2006

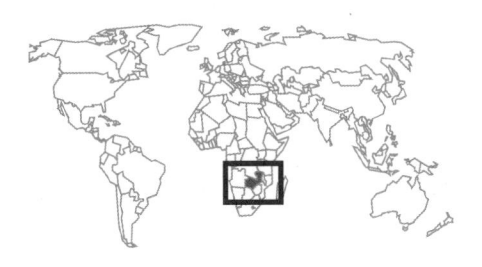

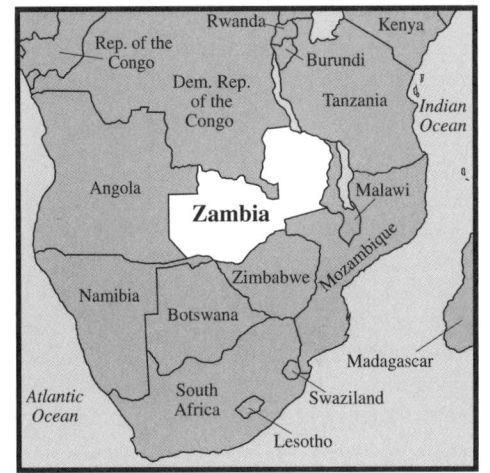

Republic of Zambia

BACKGROUND

Land and Climate. Zambia is a landlocked country covering 290,583 square miles (752,610 square kilometers) of south-central Africa. It is slightly larger than Texas. The plateau on which Zambia lies rises from 3,000 to 5,000 feet (900–1,500 meters) above sea level. The landscape consists largely of savanna, with some variation, such as the Muchinga Mountains in the northeast. Three large rivers, the Zambezi, Luangwa, and Kafue, flow through the country. The famous Victoria Falls are on the Zambezi. Except for the capital city of Lusaka, the most populous cities are in a region known as the Copperbelt, which lies along the northern border where the Democratic Republic of the Congo nearly bisects Zambia.

The cool, dry season is from April to August; the hot, dry season runs from August to October or November; the warm, rainy season is from November to April. Average daily high temperatures in Lusaka are 79°F (26°C) in January, 73°F (23°C) in July, and 88°F (31°C) in October. However, climate varies widely by region: the northwest receives the longest and heaviest rainfall, central Zambia is usually cooler than the rest of the country, and the east is typically hotter and drier. Vast areas of the country are designated as game parks, which contain lions, rhinos, elephants, hippos, a number of exotic bird species, and other diverse wildlife.

History. Between A.D. 300 and 1500, Bantu peoples replaced Zambia's original inhabitants and introduced their languages, culture, and institutions, including that of chieftainship, to the area. The 1800s brought Western missionaries and explorers, among them the Scottish missionary David Livingstone. In the 1890s, the British South Africa Company took control of Zambia, which became a British protectorate in 1924. The discovery of major copper deposits then led to the establishment of the Copperbelt and precipitated urbanization in that area.

In 1953, the area's European settlers formed the Central African Federation of Rhodesia and Nyasaland from Northern Rhodesia (now Zambia), Southern Rhodesia (now Zimbabwe), and Nyasaland (now Malawi). Northern Rhodesia gained independence when the federation was dissolved in 1963, and the country became known as Zambia in October 1964. Former African National Congress (ANC) official Kenneth Kaunda became president and head of the ruling United National Independence Party (UNIP). A one-party state was declared and all other political parties were banned in 1972. Kaunda united the country's many ethnic groups, built schools, and attempted to develop a healthcare system. However, the young nation continued to face economic problems.

In 1990, after severe food riots, Kaunda agreed to allow multiparty elections, which took place in October 1991 without violence or fraud. Kaunda lost the presidency to union leader Frederick Chiluba and peacefully accepted the election results. Although Chiluba won the election with 84 percent of the vote, he inherited a poor country and could not meet people's high expectations. His government was soon accused of being corrupt and unable to provide the nation with strong leadership. Under international pressure, Chiluba worked to privatize state industries and encourage foreign investment, but efforts dragged on for years and the transition to full democracy proved difficult. Widespread disillusionment, railway strikes, and economic woes plagued Chiluba's first term.

Kaunda came out of retirement to challenge Chiluba in the 1996 election, but Chiluba revised the constitution to require that presidential candidates' parents be born in Zambia (Kaunda's parents were born in Malawi). In protest, Kaunda's

Zambia

UNIP party boycotted the October 1996 balloting. Amid charges of fraud, Chiluba easily won. His party, the Movement for Multiparty Democracy (MMD), secured 130 seats in the 150-seat National Assembly. After quickly crushing an attempted coup in October 1997, Chiluba had Kaunda arrested as a possible conspirator and imposed a state of emergency until March 1998. Kaunda was released in June 1998.

Chiluba hoped to run for an unconstitutional third term in the 2001 election, but he withdrew his candidacy as public pressure against him increased. Levy Mwanawasa, Chiluba's former vice president, became the MMD candidate. Because opposition parties failed to unite behind one candidate, Mwanawasa faced 10 opponents and won with only 29 percent of the vote. Despite allegations of vote-rigging, he took office in January 2002. Mwanawasa inherited challenges that have faced Zambia for decades, including a struggling economy. He must also contend with the destructive social and economic impacts of one of the world's worst HIV/AIDS epidemics.

THE PEOPLE

Population. Zambia's population of 10.5 million is growing at an annual rate of 1.5 percent. Roughly 40 percent of the population lives in urban areas. Due in large part to HIV/AIDS, the nation has a very young population—less than half is younger than age 15. Close to 99 percent of Zambia's population is African. One percent is of European descent. A small Indian population forms an important urban merchant class. The Africans are divided into 73 ethnic groups. Most ethnic groups interact peacefully. They refer to one another as "cousin tribes" and may jokingly tease each other, but differences do not lead to violence.

Language. English is the official language of government, business, and education. It is more common in urban areas than in rural villages. There are as many languages spoken in Zambia as there are ethnic groups. Most people speak multiple ethnic languages, including at least one of several dominant regional languages. These regional languages include Bemba in the Copperbelt; Luapula in the Northern and Central Provinces; Nyanja in the Lusaka and Eastern Provinces; Tonga in the Southern Province and Kabwe rural areas; Lozi in the Western Province and Livingstone urban areas; and Kaonde, Lunda, and Luvale in the North-Western Province.

Religion. Many Zambians mix indigenous beliefs with their practice of Christianity or Islam. Because some sources do not include these people in their estimates, religion statistics vary widely. However, it is believed that roughly 80 percent of Zambians consider themselves Christian, and about 10 percent consider themselves Muslim. A number of Catholic, Protestant, and other Christian denominations are active in Zambia, and most Christians attend weekly services. Muslims live mostly in urban centers and near Zambia's eastern border. The majority of Indians living in Zambia are Muslim, although some Hindu Indians live in Lusaka. A small number of people practice indigenous beliefs exclusive of world religions. A belief in witchcraft remains strong, especially in villages.

General Attitudes. Most Zambians, especially those in rural areas, are patient and take life as it comes. In urban areas, where the pace of activities is faster, people are somewhat more conscious of time. The elderly, chiefs, and persons of high status are shown great respect. People consider caring for the elderly a privilege rather than a burden. In villages, certain people are expected to have a measure of wealth, but it is considered selfish or wrong for other individuals to try to seek to have more money or possessions than their neighbors. Bicycles, cows, radios, and televisions are signs of wealth. Society is community oriented, and individuals are expected to share with family. If one moves to the city to work, relatives may follow and expect financial support. The strain can force the person back into poverty and even back to the home village.

Personal Appearance. Zambians value a clean and neat appearance in public. Women take care to keep their family's clothes washed and ironed. Western-style clothing is common throughout Zambia. Men wear trousers or shorts and a shirt in rural and urban areas. Women wear a blouse with a skirt or dress. Most women also wear a colorful wraparound skirt (*chitenge*) as an apron-like covering to keep the skirt or dress clean. A mother may use a separate *chitenge* to carry a baby against her back. Girls and women fix their hair into tiny braids. While the process can take hours, it is considered an important way for women to look beautiful.

CUSTOMS AND COURTESIES

Greetings. Greetings vary according to the language and situation. For example, in Bemba, one might greet a peer with a respectful *Mwapoleni* (Welcome), but one would say *Mwapolenipo mukwai* (Welcome, very respectfully) to an elder. The *-po* suffix indicates added respect. Also in Bemba, a friend can ask *Muli shani?* (How are you?), but a subordinate will say *Bali shani* to a superior; the phrase has the same meaning, but with greater respect. In Lusaka, *Muli bwanji?* (How are you?) is a common Nyanja greeting; in the south, the preferred term is *Mwabonwa* (Welcome).

Adults respectfully address each other on formal occasions as "Mr.," "Mrs.," or "Miss" with their last names. All local languages have equivalent forms of these terms. People in most areas generally greet by shaking hands; the left hand supports the right to show respect. Kneeling down before the elderly or social superiors is common. Greetings that incorporate clapping and the gentle art of thumb squeezing are also practiced, especially by ethnic groups in the Western, North-Western, and Luapula Provinces. In most ethnic groups, parents also avoid physical contact with their children's spouses.

Friends or relatives are addressed by their oldest child's name. For example, if a woman named Beauty Kalungu has a daughter named Precious, Beauty's friends would call her *Ba na Precious* (mother of Precious), and Beauty's husband would be called *Ba shi Precious* (father of Precious).

Gestures. Zambians use handshakes widely as a gesture of thanks and friendship. Women commonly clap hands while conversing with others. Girls and women often kneel when addressing elders; men and boys curtsy slightly. Direct eye contact, embraces, and public displays of affection are avoided. Finger pointing is not acceptable. It is disrespectful to use the left hand to pass an object to someone. For example, if a person, intending to pay someone, is holding his or her money in the left hand, the person will transfer it to the right hand before giving it to the payee. People beckon by waving all fingers of the hand with the palm facing down, although this gesture is used for children and friends, not the elderly or chiefs.

Visiting. Official and business matters call for being punctual to appointments, especially in urban areas. In rural areas or traditional situations, however, people tend to be flexible about time, so allowance is made for delays. In fact, most people visit unannounced. An important exception is a visit with the local chief, when scheduling is always taken seriously. Because it is an honor to the family to have a visitor in the home, an unannounced visitor at mealtime is expected to share the food with the hosts. It is considered inappropriate for the host to have to invite the guest to partake of the food. It is also discourteous for the visitor not to join the hosts in eating the meal. Among friends, gift-giving is an accepted practice. One extends both hands when presenting and receiving a gift; kneeling when giving a gift is also customary in many parts of Zambia.

Eating. In rural areas, food is usually plentiful during harvest season, but it may be more scarce at other times of the year. Most people eat one main meal and various small snacks (pumpkin, sweet potatoes, peanuts, corn) throughout the day. Only the wealthy eat three meals a day. In most homes, families eat meals from communal dishes. One plate is provided for rice, potatoes, or *nsima* (a thick porridge; also called *nshima*), and another for sauces made of meat or vegetables. Zambians eat with the fingers of the right hand, never the left. They wash their hands in a common bowl before and after eating. Washing is done in a specific order: guests (if present) wash first, then the father, boys, girls, and finally the mother. Utensils are used in some homes, mainly with rice (but rarely with potatoes or *nsima*). Water is served with meals. In some areas, especially in villages, men eat in a place separate from women and children. All meals begin with a prayer said by the most important person—either the father or a guest, if present.

LIFESTYLE

Family. Extended families are important in Zambia, and they are often large. In the extended family, a father's brothers are also considered "fathers" and a mother's sisters are considered "mothers." Cousins are basically brothers and sisters. Other members of the same clan who are not actually blood relations may also be considered siblings. The father is the traditional head of the family, but women in rural areas head an increasing number of households, as men must frequently go to cities to find work. The HIV/AIDS epidemic has also forced the elderly or older children into the role of family head. In matriarchal families, the mother's brother has the greatest authority. Children obey their parents without complaint and show proper respect to anyone who is older. Traditionally, women were expected to be subservient to men and even submit to abuse, but there is an active movement to create gender equality in all aspects of life. Women care for the household, children, and garden. Girls begin helping their mothers at an early age. Most women in rural areas are mothers by the time they are 18. In urban areas, many women pursue education and careers before having families.

Dating and Marriage. Formal, traditional marriages take place soon after a girl matures. In most rural cases, couples marry without dating, but urban marriages are usually preceded by some dating. Many teenage couples choose to marry in informal unions, though in all cases, formal or informal, the blessing of the two families is required, elders are consulted, and negotiations are made for the *lobola* (bride-price). Church weddings are common, although some couples choose only to register at a district office. In cities, female friends of the bride have a "kitchen party," where the bride receives gifts for her kitchen, and older women teach the bride through songs and dances about what will be expected of her in marriage. Villagers cannot afford gifts or a party, but elder women do teach future brides how to please their husbands. Marriages are expected to be fruitful, and women bear, on average, six children—although not all live to maturity. Marital infidelity is common and culturally acceptable. This is a primary factor contributing to the nation's high HIV/AIDS infection rate.

Diet. *Nsima* is made from cornmeal and is the national food. It can also be made from cassava (in the north) or millet (near the Zambezi River). Zambians say that they have not eaten unless they have a meal with *nsima*. It is prepared as a dough or thick porridge and eaten with a sauce. People in rural areas make sauces from beans and vegetables. In cities, the sauce is made of a tomato- or oil-based soup combined with chicken, beef, or fish. Breakfast consists of tea with bread, sweet potatoes (when in season), or rice. Sometimes people will have a breakfast of leftover *nsima* from the night before. *Chibwabwa* (finely cut and boiled pumpkin leaves cooked with salt and oil) and *Ifisashi* (any green vegetable boiled and mixed with pounded groundnuts) are common foods. Fresh fruits and vegetables are abundant during and following the rainy season. Beer is heavily consumed, and many villagers brew their own.

Recreation. Soccer is the most popular sport for men and boys. Girls play netball, a game similar to basketball. Boys and girls enjoy checkers and *mankala*, a strategy game played with marbles or small stones. Rural families enjoy church activities, visiting, and traditional dancing. Men socialize and drink. Urban residents have access to basketball, discos, *ifisela* (drama), church activities, and social clubs. Women rarely have leisure time, but they do their daily chores with other women so they can sing and talk. Zambians do not typically travel for pleasure, only out of necessity.

The Arts. Many Zambians, particularly in rural areas, enjoy traditional music; common instruments are drums, xylophones, and the *kalimba*, which is played by using the thumbs to pluck small metal strips attached to a board. Urban music includes *kalindula*, a popular dance music, and *Zam-rock*, a form of rock with lyrics in local languages. Zambian artisans excel at creating wood carvings. Villagers create art that also fulfills everyday functions. They engrave intricate designs into dark brown pottery used for cooking and water storage.

Holidays. Public holidays include New Year's Day, Easter (Friday–Monday), Labor Day (1 May), Youth Day (19 Mar.), African Freedom Day (25 May), Heroes and Unity Day (first Monday and Tuesday in July), Farmers' Day (first Monday in August), Independence Day (24 Oct.), and Christmas.

Commerce. Business hours extend from 8 a.m. to 5 p.m., Monday through Friday, with a one-hour lunch break. Banks close by 2:30 p.m. Shops are open 8 a.m. to 6 p.m., Monday through Friday. They close on Saturday at 4 p.m. Sundays are devoted to church services and visiting family and neighbors. Rural commerce revolves around open-air markets and small village shops. Rural people might also barter for goods or sell beer to gain extra income. Door-to-door selling of goods is common. Women carry woven baskets with fresh vegetables and other foods to different houses. Men in rural areas buy clothing or other goods in town and transport it by bicycle to sell to other villagers.

SOCIETY

Government. Zambia's national government is directed by a president (currently Levy Mwanawasa), who is chief of state and head of government. Members of the National Assembly are elected by the general population to serve five-year terms. The voting age is 18. A chiefdom is a collection of small villages, locally governed by a chief. Representatives from each village choose successive chiefs after considerable debate. The chief's main power is land allocation within the chiefdom.

Zambia

Economy. Copper has long been the mainstay of Zambia's economy. During the 1970s, when copper prices were high, the copper industry constituted 90 percent of Zambia's exports. However, the world copper price plummeted in the 1980s, and privatization of the industry in the 1990s was hindered by corruption and mismanagement. As a result, many mines have closed. Although copper is still a major export, production is now only one-third of previous levels.

Corruption infects all levels of government and business, and the lack of credible institutions keeps foreign investors away. Poor harvests have had a devastating effect on the agricultural sector, where most workers are subsistence farmers. Outdated technology, poor transportation links, decreased productivity due to HIV/AIDS, and other problems hinder development of new industry. Economic growth has been low, and much higher levels will be required to lift people out of poverty. The currency is the Zambian *kwacha* (ZMK).

Transportation and Communications. The average Zambian travels on foot or by hitchhiking. A person can flag down a bus, car, truck, or even a bicycle. If given a ride, the passenger pays a reasonable fare to the driver. Buses, which are crowded and unreliable, travel between rural towns. Some urban Zambians own cars. Taxis are available in the cities. Vehicle breakdowns are a major problem due to poor roads and the expense of spare parts. Following the British tradition, traffic moves on the left side of the road. Zambia Airways airlines offers international and domestic flights. A rail line connects Livingstone in the south with Mufulira in the Copperbelt province. The Tazara (Tanzania-Zambia) Railway links Zambia to the Tanzanian port of Dar es Salaam.

Zambia's telephone system is unreliable; lines often do not function for weeks at a time. Several radio stations and a number of daily newspapers (two in English) serve all areas of the country. Television is available in urban areas and larger towns. Villagers receive news by radio and word of mouth. When teachers go to town for their paychecks, they often return with a newspaper for everyone to read.

Education. While Zambians value education and expect their children to do well when enrolled in school, families find it difficult to afford education costs. Although the government pays teacher salaries, families often cannot pay for the required books and uniforms. If they have enough money to send one child to school, they will send the oldest boy. English is the language of instruction in all schools, although most primary schools mix English with local dialects because few families speak any English in the home. Many students drop out or fail because they lack English skills. Only 20 percent of all children are educated in secondary schools and only 2 percent attend institutions of higher education. There are two universities, fourteen teacher-training colleges, and fourteen vocational and technical institutions.

An effort called Community Schools offers free schooling to children and is staffed with local volunteers. The teachers are not professionals and many do not have a higher education, but they receive some training and support. Another initiative, the Educational Broadcast System, is a radio schooling program for rural areas. It requires a volunteer to lead the students, but the class is run entirely over the radio. Both programs offer an alternative for disadvantaged children. Many of the students are children orphaned by HIV/AIDS.

DEVELOPMENT DATA
Human Dev. Index* rank . . . . 164 of 177 countries
Adjusted for women . . . . 133 of 144 countries
Real GDP per capita $840
Adult literacy rate . . . . 86 percent (male); 74 (female)
Infant mortality rate . . . . 98 per 1,000 births
Life expectancy . . . . 33 (male); 33 (female)

Health. Zambia's healthcare system is funded in part by outside sources. At the village level, a trained birth attendant delivers babies, and a community health worker treats minor ailments. More extreme cases are referred to a rural health center that has a nurse and clinical officer. To see a doctor, one must go to a district hospital. Young children go to Under-Five Clinics for checkups and vaccinations. Doctors are poorly paid, and clinics are not well staffed or supplied. The nation has 12 large urban hospitals.

Common childhood illnesses such as measles and diarrhea contribute to a high infant mortality rate. Most children suffer from malnutrition. Shallow latrines, open garbage pits, and polluted water create hygiene problems that allow for serious epidemics. Malaria, pneumonia, yellow fever, cholera, and tuberculosis are major health problems among adults. However, the HIV/AIDS epidemic is the nation's greatest health concern. Zambia has one of the world's highest rates of HIV/AIDS infection (more that one-fifth of the adult population) and, as a result, one of the world's lowest life expectancy rates.

AT A GLANCE
Events and Trends.
- President Mwanawasa fired his vice president, Nevers Mumba, in October 2004 for allegedly making accusations that the government of neighboring Congo provided financial support for the Zambian opposition. Mwanawasa was meeting with Congo's President Joseph Kabila at the United Nations when the comments were made.
- Former president Frederick Chiluba had more than eighty corruption charges against him dropped in September 2004, but six new charges were levied a few hours later. He is accused of stealing public funds during his 10 years in office. Although President Mwanawasa was Chiluba's handpicked successor (and widely expected to serve his interests), Mwanawasa distanced himself from Chiluba soon after taking office in 2002, stripping him of his immunity from prosecution.

Contact Information. Embassy of Zambia, 2419 Massachusetts Avenue NW, Washington, DC 20008; phone (202) 265-9717; web site www.zambiaembassy.org.

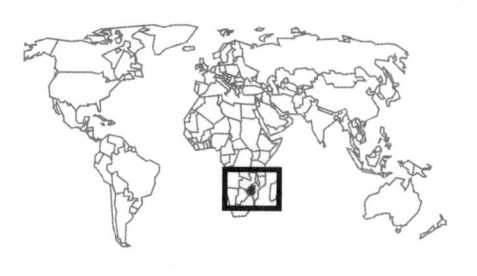

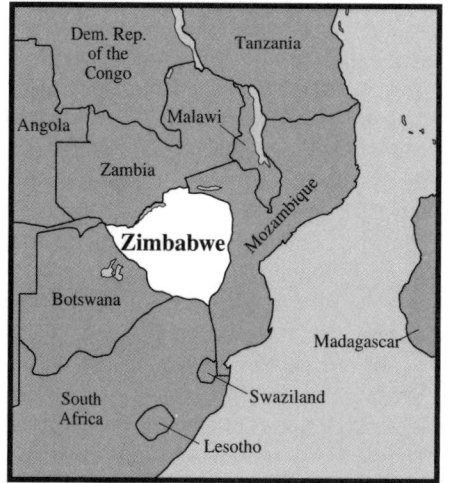

CultureGrams World Edition 2006

Republic of Zimbabwe

BACKGROUND

Land and Climate. Zimbabwe is a landlocked country located on southern Africa's Great Plateau. Covering 150,803 square miles (390,580 square kilometers), it is slightly larger than Montana. The Highveld, where most major cities are located, is a central plateau with altitudes over 5,000 feet (1,500 meters). The highest mountain peak is Inyangani (8,502 feet, or 2,592 meters). Typical to the Highveld but also found throughout the country are *kopjes*, huge granite rocks often resting on smaller formations. On both sides of the Highveld lies the Middleveld, which sends water from the Highveld into the Zambezi River (north) and the Limpopo River (south). Areas near each of these rivers are called Lowveld, where altitudes are below 1,000 feet (300 meters). Lush forests of the Eastern Highlands run along the border with Mozambique. Zimbabwe has a pleasant and mild climate, although temperatures increase as altitude decreases. Winter (May to August) highs average 55 to 73°F (13–23°C) and summer (November to March) highs range from 77 to 86°F (25–30°C). Summer is the rainy season. Some places in the Lowveld can reach above 100°F (38°C).

History. Bantu-speaking peoples who migrated from the north developed a strong presence in present-day Zimbabwe by A.D. 500, having replaced native San (Bushmen) tribes. Early Shona groups that began arriving in the 10th century established trade links on Africa's southeastern coast. They developed a major trading empire later called Great Zimbabwe (centered near Masvingo), which flourished until the 15th century. Powerful kings built stone fortresses and were rich in cattle, ivory, gold, and farmland. *Zimbabwe* means "stone houses" and implies power and permanence. Great Zimbabwe's granite ruins stand today as a national monument.

By the 16th century, Great Zimbabwe was in decline, and power splintered among several Shona states, most notably the Mutapa (north), Torwa (southwest), and later the Rosvi (south). Portuguese traders gained influence among the Mutapa but were eventually driven out. The Rosvi Dynasty declined in the early 1800s, and the Shona were subdued by the Ndebele (a branch of the Zulus) migrating from the south.

In 1888, Cecil John Rhodes formed the British South Africa Company (BSAC) and received in 1889 a charter from Britain's Queen Victoria to effectively colonize areas north of South Africa. Rhodes soon controlled Matabeleland (of the Ndebele) and Mashonaland (of the Shona), among other areas. Whites, mostly British, came searching for gold and farmland. These settlers voted in 1923 to become the British colony Southern Rhodesia, not a BSAC possession. In 1930, the Land Apportionment Act gave half of the country's land to whites and set up native reserves for blacks. The resulting inequality later fed the fire of rebellion and civil war.

In 1965, the white-minority government led by Ian Smith declared independence from Great Britain. That prompted UN sanctions and sparked several years of civil war. In 1979, a power-sharing agreement paved the way to multiracial elections in 1980. Zimbabwe was then internationally recognized as an independent republic. Robert G. Mugabe was elected prime minister.

Mugabe was reelected in 1985 as he worked to increase his power and curb opposition. In 1987, his Shona-dominated Zimbabwe African National Union (ZANU) reconciled with its rival, Ndebele-dominated Zimbabwe African People's Union (ZAPU), to form a strong ruling party called ZANU-PF (PF stands for Patriotic Front). The national constitution was

Zimbabwe

then amended to eliminate the office of prime minister and create a strong executive president (Mugabe).

In 1990, Mugabe was reelected in a landslide. Opposition to ZANU-PF began to grow but was disorganized and divided. Mugabe's government cracked down on dissent and controlled the 1995 elections. ZANU-PF received all but 3 of 150 parliamentary seats. In the 1996 presidential race, Mugabe was reelected unopposed, but voter turnout was very low. In 1997, economic and political troubles reached crisis proportions. Violent protests erupted at times over corruption scandals such as the looting of a war veterans' pension fund, economic mismanagement, land reform benefiting only government officials, and price hikes.

By 2000, Mugabe's attempts at land reform (promised since independence) had been largely unsuccessful. The government sponsored a referendum in February 2000 that would give it authority to acquire white-owned farms (covering 32 percent of all agricultural land) without compensation. To Mugabe's surprise, the referendum failed. Shortly thereafter, thousands of squatters invaded and occupied white-owned farms. Organized by the War Veteran's Association with Mugabe's backing, squatters demanded that white owners leave and sign over their property. More than one thousand farms were occupied. Several farmers were beaten, and a few were killed.

The unrest surrounding the land issue worsened Zimbabwe's economic crisis. Mugabe then made the unpopular and expensive decision to send troops into the civil war in the Democratic Republic of the Congo. In June 2000, these factors combined to produce the nation's highest voter turnout (65 percent) in parliamentary elections. Voters gave 57 seats to the opposition Movement for Democratic Change (MDC), slashing ZANU-PF's elected majority to 62. As presidential elections approached in March 2002, Mugabe tightened his control over the media and his party. He was reelected with 56 percent of the vote, although the opposition and the international community accused Mugabe and ZANU-PF of voter intimidation and electoral fraud.

In the years since the election, food shortages have been severe. While the government blames a lengthy drought for the shortages, Mugabe's critics point to mismanaged land reform as the key factor. The shortages, the land reform controversy, the economic crisis, and one of the world's highest rates of HIV have undermined the nation's former stability.

THE PEOPLE

Population. Zimbabwe's population of 12.7 million is growing at 0.7 percent annually. Ninety-eight percent of the population is African. The remaining 2 percent is comprised of people of European descent (mostly British), mixed heritage, and Indian descent. The largest African groups are the Shona (71 percent) and Ndebele (16 percent). Others include the Shangaan, Tonga, and Venda. The Ndebele mostly inhabit western regions and dominate in Bulawayo. The Shona are a combination of several groups, each with its own dialect. The largest of these are the Karanga, Zezuru, Manyika, Korekore, Rozwi, and Ndau. The Karanga dominated during the era of Great Zimbabwe. While urbanization has increased over the years, 65 percent of the people continue to live in rural settings. The largest cities are Harare and Bulawayo.

Race relations, though complex, were relatively peaceful after 1980. Because whites held land and wealth, most blacks acknowledged their important role in Zimbabwe. While whites had lost political power, they welcomed peace. Unfortunately, when the economy slumped and land reform did not progress, racial cooperation ended on many fronts.

Language. English is the official language and is spoken by most educated Zimbabweans. However, people in rural areas converse in their native languages. Shona and Ndebele are most common. Zimbabweans often speak more than one language, and many mix parts of several languages in daily speech. Both Shona and Ndebele are written languages and are taught in school. They are used for instruction in primary school but are being replaced by English in secondary schools. Because learning in English is hard for many students, some rural secondary teachers use indigenous languages to help teach important concepts.

Religion. Most Zimbabweans have a mixed belief structure. Various forms of Christianity predominate, but worship is combined with traditional practices and beliefs. These include consulting spiritual mediums or witch doctors (*n'anga*) and a strong belief in witchcraft, ancestor veneration, and clan affiliation with totems. A year or two after a family member dies, people of the Shona ethnic group hold a *kurova guva*, a weeklong party through which the departed spirit is united with the living. Forgetting a *kurova guva* invites bad luck. The Roman Catholic Church is the largest Christian church, but various Protestant and other denominations also have members. Attendance is high at church services, which are important social events for most rural people. Some Zimbabweans exclusively practice traditional beliefs. Muslims comprise less than 1 percent of the population.

General Attitudes. In urban areas, cosmopolitan ideals tend to prevail, while rural customs and attitudes are more traditional. Zimbabweans are generally friendly, cheerful, and courteous. While open and enthusiastic among friends, they are more cautious and reserved with strangers. Humility is esteemed. It is impolite to embarrass or shame someone in public. It is also considered impolite to convey unpleasant news, so conversation steps around it. Kinship, friendship, and extended family relations are very important.

Black Zimbabweans are individually polite and conciliatory toward whites but are often resentful because of continuing inequalities. Economic uncertainties have led many to develop a sense of "living for today," where money is quickly spent or borrowed and future consequences of current choices are considered less often. White Zimbabweans are proud of their heritage and connection to the soil. They value order and education. They believe land reform is necessary but should be conducted within the rule of law.

Personal Appearance. Wealth, or the appearance of it, is highly valued. For example, a protruding stomach is admired in a man because it means he can afford to eat meat every day. People bathe or wash daily, even in rural areas. Dressing "smart" in stylish, ironed, and clean clothing is important when not working in the fields. Ironing improves appearance and helps control *tumba* flies, which lay eggs on wet clothing; if eggs hatch, flies can burrow into the skin. Men prefer a suit for conducting business but otherwise wear a shirt and slacks. Women generally wear dresses that reach below the knee, or a wraparound skirt with a blouse. For significant rural gatherings, women also wear a *dhuku* (headscarf). Rural women rarely wear slacks, which are considered a sign of prostitution. Young urbanites wear modern fashions; children wear uniforms to school.

CUSTOMS AND COURTESIES

Greetings. Zimbabweans greet strangers with a single handshake but use a longer handshake with friends. As a sign of respect, one might support the extended right arm with the left hand. Rural Shona usually show additional respect with a series of slow, patterned hand claps. Common Shona greetings include *Mhoroi* (Hello), *Mangwanani* (Good morning), *Masikati* (Good afternoon), and *Manheru* (Good evening). However, a simple greeting is not sufficient. Inquiries about one's family follow. If asked *Makadii?* (Shona for "How are you?"), one replies *Tiripo kana makadiiwo* (We are fine if you are fine). The person is often answering for the family in this group-oriented society. In Ndebele, a typical response to the phrase *Siyabonga, linjani?* (Hello, how are you?) is *Sekona singabusalina* (I am fine).

Children are addressed by first name. Rural parents may be referred to by their oldest child's name: the prefix *Mai-* means "mother of" and the prefix *Baba-* means "father of." So the parents of Ngoni would be addressed as *MaiNgoni* (mother of Ngoni) and *BabaNgoni* (father of Ngoni). Parents are respected and obeyed. The elderly are addressed as "grandmother" or "grandfather." Any elderly person must be shown great respect, be greeted first, and be obeyed by children. Urban adults address each other by first and last name, adding a professional title if appropriate.

Gestures. Items are passed and accepted with both hands. Shona may clap hands as a gesture of gratitude or politeness. Women and girls, especially in rural areas, may add a curtsy. Respect is shown by physically lowering oneself, so people sit when they converse (women sit on floor mats; men are higher up on stools or chairs). One does not rise when an elder enters the room. Making direct eye contact with an elder is considered rude. Public displays of affection are inappropriate, but friends of the same sex may walk holding hands. Personal space is limited.

Visiting. The concept of time is more flexible in the village than in the city, where people generally expect guests to arrive on time. Unannounced visits are common in villages, but one first calls out a greeting and asks permission to enter the home. Zimbabweans strive to make guests comfortable. Hosts always offer refreshments, including soft drinks or tea and sometimes a snack. Refusing refreshments or meals is impolite. Hosts appreciate a small gift and may also give departing visitors a gift (like garden produce). Rural hosts accompany guests much of the way home. Urban hosts at least go to the front gate. Inviting friends or relatives for afternoon tea is popular, and people also enjoy having guests over for dinner.

Eating. Zimbabweans eat breakfast before work and their main meal in the evening. Lunch is usually light. While urbanites use Western utensils, rural residents normally eat with the fingers of their right hand. Everyone washes his or her hands before and after a meal, using a washbasin passed from person to person. It is customary that a younger person pours water for an older person. Rural families may eat from a communal dish, depending on the food. Rural families eat together, but children eat separately if guests are present. Only after all the food is eaten do Zimbabweans take drinks. Chicken is a favorite but expensive meat. Beef is more desirable but even harder to attain. When guests are present, they are served first and given some meat with their meal. One claps softly and says *Ndaguta* (I am satisfied) after a meal to show respect and indicate one has been well provided for. Rural families cook over a small fire or paraffin stove.

LIFESTYLE

Family. The mother exercises influence in the home, but the father is considered the head of the family, making all final decisions and financially supporting his family (including children, wives, and any mistresses). Polygamy, while practiced, is becoming less common. Women care for the children and household. They often sell produce or other items at roadside stands, and an increasing number hold professional jobs.

The extended family unit provides people with a social safety net. Relatives can expect financial support in hard times and must share in prosperous times. Borrowing (money or items) between relatives is common but is more like giving than lending. Urban families tend to be nuclear, whereas rural extended families often share a household. Children care for their parents when they get old, as the elderly are considered a family treasure. These networks of support are weakening due to urbanization and a severe AIDS epidemic. As adults die of AIDS, fewer people are left to care for children and the elderly. And as young adults move to the city, they participate less in the extended family network.

Dating and Marriage. Young Zimbabweans meet at school or social functions; dating is more common in cities. When a couple is ready to marry, a groom's representative visits the bride's family to negotiate gifts and a bride-price (*lobola* or *roora*). A traditional *lobola* involves cattle, but it is now more common to pay with cash. Virginity in women is valued and will bring a higher bride-price. As families demand higher prices, grooms are finding it difficult to pay the *lobola*. Traditional weddings can last more than a day and involve much feasting, dancing, and drinking. It is culturally acceptable for men to openly have extramarital affairs. Men consider this necessary to prove virility. However, it has contributed to a high HIV infection rate.

Diet. *Sadza*, a stiff porridge made from white cornmeal, is the staple food served at nearly every meal. *Sadza* is rolled into a ball and dipped in a sauce. A typical sauce is green, leafy vegetables cooked in oil with onions, tomatoes, and seasonings. Local vegetables include kale, spinach, and pumpkin. Stewed meat (particularly goat in rural areas) might also be used as a sauce for *sadza*. Protein can also come from fish or insects such as termites. In the cities, people tend to eat a more Western diet, including meat and potatoes or rice instead of *sadza*. Mangoes, tangerines, bananas, melons, guavas, and papaya (*pawpaws*) are enjoyed at various times of the year. Tea is popular with meals and in the office.

Recreation. Soccer is the nation's most popular sport. Basketball is gaining fans. Girls play netball. The wealthy enjoy tennis, swimming, boxing, rugby, cricket, polo, and other sports. Swimming can be hazardous in rivers and lakes, many of which contain the bilharzia parasite. People enjoy watching television and going to movies. Men frequent beer halls to drink, play games, socialize, and dance. Women get together in their homes. Vacations are rare and most often include visiting relatives; the wealthy might visit tourist attractions.

The Arts. Most Zimbabweans like to dance. Rural youth dance on Saturday nights to Zimbabwean music on the radio. Urban youth may prefer U.S. or British music, but they still appreciate local pop and traditional music. *Chimurenga*, one of the most popular local styles, combines traditional Shona music with electric instruments. First developed as songs of protest against the white-minority government, *Chimurenga* still draws from political and social themes. Also widespread is music played with the *mbira*, an instrument with small metal

Zimbabwe

strips plucked by the thumbs. *Mbira* music has been adapted to electric guitars in a style known as *jiti*.

Zimbabwean sculpture, which has roots in the stone carvings of Great Zimbabwe, experienced a revival in the 1950s. Often using mythology as their inspiration, sculptors create abstract forms of animal and human figures.

Renowned novelist and short-story writer Doris Lessing grew up in Southern Rhodesia and described the experiences of colonial white Africans. Other Zimbabwean authors such as Stanlake Samkange and Tsitsi Dangarembga have received international acclaim for their works.

Holidays. National holidays include New Year's Day, Easter (including Good Friday and Easter Monday), Independence Day (18 Apr.), Workers' Day (1 May), Africa Day (25 May), Heroes Day and Defense Forces Day (11–12 Aug.), Christmas, and Boxing Day (26 Dec.). Heroes Day honors casualties of the liberation struggle. Local religious celebrations are also held throughout the year.

Commerce. Urban offices, banks, and shops basically are open Monday through Saturday from 8 a.m. to 5 p.m., except Wednesday and Saturday afternoons. Small shops selling necessities and perishables are open longer and also on Sundays. Rural shops keep flexible hours. Women sell fresh produce at outdoor markets. Supermarkets are found in urban settings. Most people grow at least some of their own food; even urban people have gardens whenever possible.

SOCIETY

Government. Zimbabwe is a parliamentary democracy, although ZANU-PF controls most government offices. President Mugabe is chief of state and head of government. He appoints two vice presidents and a cabinet. Zimbabwe's unicameral parliament, called the House of Assembly, consists of 150 members. Of these, 120 members are directly elected, 12 members are appointed by the president, 10 are reserved for traditional chiefs, and 8 are reserved for provincial governors. The presidential term is six years; parliamentary elections are held every five years. The voting age is 18.

Economy. Agriculture employs about two-thirds of the labor force. Agricultural products such as tobacco and cotton account for 40 percent of all export earnings. Corn, tea, and sugar are other important products. Manufactured items, including footwear, furniture, and equipment, are key exports. Gold, nickel, coal, asbestos, and other mineral resources are mined. The economy depends heavily on the weather; droughts affect not only crops but also hydroelectric power output and thus industrial production. Corruption and mismanagement have damaged investor confidence, weakened public services, and crippled economic development. The currency is the Zimbabwean dollar (ZWD).

Transportation and Communications. Rural Zimbabweans travel mostly on foot, although daily buses provide transportation for longer distances. Urban residents also rely heavily on buses but have access to taxis and *kombis* (minivan taxis). Relatively few people own cars. A railway connects key cities. Zimbabwe trades through ports in South Africa and Mozambique. Zimbabwe's telecommunications system is relatively extensive, but rural people do not have easy access to a phone.

DEVELOPMENT DATA
Human Dev. Index* rank . . . . 147 of 177 countries
Adjusted for women . . . . 118 of 144 countries
Real GDP per capita $2,400
Adult literacy rate . . . . 94 percent (male); 86 (female)
Infant mortality rate . . . . 67 per 1,000 births
Life expectancy . . . . 34 (male); 34 (female)

Word of mouth transmits news in many areas. Zimbabweans often read newspapers, but they appreciate Western magazines that have less biased news than government-owned papers. The government operates the two television and four radio stations. Most rural areas lack electricity, but some people power televisions with car batteries. Nearly every home has a radio.

Education. Education is a high priority for Zimbabweans. Nearly all children attend seven years of primary school. About half pass to secondary school; poverty and language barriers keep many students from advancing. After four years of secondary school, students must pass national exams to qualify for two years of precollegiate schooling. They may otherwise pursue vocational training or end their studies. All schools charge fees and will not admit students who cannot pay. Private boarding schools offer the best and most expensive education. Mission schools are also good and less crowded than government-funded schools. Rural district schools, locally funded, are the most disadvantaged. The University of Zimbabwe in Harare is the premier institution of higher learning. Other universities, teacher-training colleges, and technical schools are located in major cities.

Health. Towns and cities usually have good plumbing and sanitation systems, but rural areas often lack them. Malaria, cholera, and bilharzia are widespread. Basic health services are free to the poor. Rural clinics, where available, are usually understaffed and poorly supplied. Mission hospitals and clinics offer better care. People often turn to traditional healers for help with certain types of illnesses, including AIDS. Zimbabwe has one of the world's highest HIV infection rates. With an estimated one in four adults infected with HIV, life expectancy rates are falling rapidly.

AT A GLANCE

Events and Trends.
- ZANU-PF secured a two-thirds majority in parliament by taking 78 of 120 contested seats in March 2005 elections. The MDC, which won 41 seats, accused the ruling party of fraud.
- In October 2004, MDC leader Morgan Tsvangirai was acquitted of a treason charge stemming from an alleged plot to assassinate Mugabe in 2002. Tsvangirai remains charged with calling for street protests against Mugabe in 2003. Both charges have been widely discredited as attempts by Mugabe to weaken the opposition.

Contact Information. Embassy of Zimbabwe, 1608 New Hampshire Avenue NW, Washington, DC 20009; phone (202) 332-7100.

CultureGrams™
People. The World. You.

ProQuest Information and Learning Company
300 North Zeeb Road, P.O. Box 1346
Ann Arbor, Michigan 48106 USA
Toll Free: 1.800.528.6279
Fax: 1.800.864.0019
www.culturegrams.com

© 2005 ProQuest Information and Learning Company and Brigham Young University. It is against the law to copy, reprint, store, or transmit any part of this publication in any form by any means without written permission from ProQuest. This document contains native commentary and original analysis, as well as estimated statistics. The content should not be considered strictly factual, and it may not apply to all groups in a nation. *UN Development Programme, Human Development Report 2004 (New York: Oxford University Press, 2004).

Country Data Tables

▼ **CAPITALS**
  POPULATION AND AREA
  DEVELOPMENT DATA

Nation or Territory	Capital	Nation or Territory	Capital
Afghanistan	Kabul	Finland	Helsinki
Albania	Tirana	France	Paris
Algeria	Algiers	French Polynesia	Papeete
American Samoa	Pago Pago	Gabon	Libreville
Angola	Luanda	Gambia	Banjul
Antigua and Barbuda	Saint John's	Georgia	Tbilisi
Argentina	Buenos Aires	Germany	Berlin
Armenia	Yerevan	Ghana	Accra
Australia	Canberra	Greece	Athens
Austria	Vienna	Grenada	Saint George's
Azerbaijan	Baku	Guam	Hagta
Bahamas	Nassau	Guatemala	Guatemala City
Bahrain	Manama	Guinea	Conakry
Bangladesh	Dhaka	Guinea-Bissau	Bissau
Barbados	Bridgetown	Guyana	Georgetown
Belarus	Minsk	Haiti	Port-au-Prince
Belgium	Brussels	Honduras	Tegucigalpa
Belize	Belmopan	Hong Kong	Hong Kong
Benin	Porto-Novo	Hungary	Budapest
Bhutan	Thimphu	Iceland	Reykjavk
Bolivia	La Paz	India	New Delhi
Bosnia and Herzegovina	Sarajevo	Indonesia	Jakarta
Botswana	Gaborone	Iran	Tehran
Brazil	Braslia	Iraq	Baghdad
Bulgaria	Sofia	Ireland	Dublin
Burkina Faso	Ouagadougou	Israel	Jerusalem
Cambodia	Phnom Penh	Italy	Rome
Cameroon	Yaoundé	Ivory Coast	Yamoussoukro
Canada	Ottawa	Jamaica	Kingston
Cape Verde	Praia	Japan	Tokyo
Central African Rep.	Bangui	Jordan	Amman
Chad	N'Djamena	Kazakstan	Astana
Chile	Santiago	Kenya	Nairobi
China	Beijing	Kiribati	Bairiki
Colombia	Bogot	Kuwait	Kuwait City
Comoros	Moroni	Kyrgyzstan	Bishkek
Congo, Dem. Rep. of	Kinshasa	Laos	Vientiane
Costa Rica	San Jos	Latvia	Rīga
Croatia	Zagreb	Lebanon	Beirut
Cuba	Havana	Lesotho	Maseru
Czech Republic	Prague	Libya	Tripoli
Denmark	Copenhagen	Liechtenstein	Vaduz
Dominican Republic	Santo Domingo	Lithuania	Vilnius
Ecuador	Quito	Luxembourg	Luxembourg
Egypt	Cairo	Macedonia	Skopje
El Salvador	San Salvador	Madagascar	Antananarivo
England	London	Malawi	Lilongwe
Equatorial Guinea	Malabo	Malaysia	Kuala Lumpur
Eritrea	Asmara	Mali	Bamako
Estonia	Tallinn	Malta	Valletta
Ethiopia	Addis Ababa	Marshall Islands	Majuro
Fiji	Suva	Mauritania	Nouakchott

Capitals

Nation or Territory	Capital
Mauritius	Port Louis
Mexico	Mexico City
Micronesia	Palikir
Moldova	Chisinau
Mongolia	Ulaanbaatar
Montserrat	Plymouth
Morocco	Rabat
Mozambique	Maputo
Myanmar	Yangon
Namibia	Windhoek
Nepal	Kathmandu
Netherlands	Amsterdam
New Zealand	Wellington
Nicaragua	Managua
Niger	Niamey
Nigeria	Abuja
Niue	Alofi
North Korea	Pyongyang
Northern Ireland	Belfast
Norway	Oslo
Oman	Muscat
Pakistan	Islamabad
Panama	Panama City
Papua New Guinea	Port Moresby
Paraguay	Asuncin
Peru	Lima
Philippines	Manila
Poland	Warsaw
Portugal	Lisbon
Puerto Rico	San Juan
Qatar	Doha
Romania	Bucharest
Russia	Moscow
Rwanda	Kigali
Saint Kitts and Nevis	Basseterre
Saint Lucia	Castries
Saint Vincent and the Grenadines	Kingstown
Samoa	Apia
Saudi Arabia	Riyadh
Scotland	Edinburgh
Senegal	Dakar
Serbia and Montenegro	Belgrade
Sierra Leone	Freetown
Singapore	Singapore
Slovakia	Bratislava
Slovenia	Ljubljana
Solomon Islands	Honiara
Somalia	Mogadishu
South Africa	Pretoria
South Korea	Seoul
Spain	Madrid
Sri Lanka	Colombo

Nation or Territory	Capital
Sudan	Khartoum
Suriname	Paramaribo
Swaziland	Mbabane
Sweden	Stockholm
Switzerland	Bern
Syria	Damascus
Taiwan	Taipei
Tajikistan	Dushanbe
Tanzania	Dodoma
Thailand	Bangkok
Togo	Lom
Tonga	Nuku'alofa
Trinidad and Tobago	Port of Spain
Tunisia	Tunis
Turkey	Ankara
Turkmenistan	Ashgabat
Tuvalu	Funafuti
Uganda	Kampala
Ukraine	Kyiv
United Arab Emirates	Abu Dhabi
United States of America	Washington, D.C.
Uruguay	Montevideo
U.S. Virgin Islands	Charlotte Amalie
Uzbekistan	Tashkent
Venezuela	Caracas
Vietnam	Hanoi
Wales	Cardiff
West Bank and Gaza	None
Yemen	Sana'a
Zambia	Lusaka
Zimbabwe	Harare

Nation or Territory	Population	Area (sq. mi.)	Area (sq. km.)
Afghanistan	28,513,677	251,773	652,090
Albania	3,544,808	11,100	28,750
Algeria	32,129,324	919,590	2,381,740
American Samoa	57,902	77	199
Angola	10,978,552	481,354	1,246,700
Antigua and Barbuda	68,320	170	440
Argentina	39,144,753	1,068,296	2,766,874
Armenia	2,991,360	11,506	29,800
Australia	19,913,144	2,967,892	7,686,850
Austria	8,174,762	32,375	83,850
Azerbaijan	7,868,385	33,436	86,600
Bahamas	299,697	5,353	13,860
Bahrain	677,886	240	620
Bangladesh	141,340,476	55,599	144,000
Barbados	277,264	166	430
Belarus	10,300,483	80,154	207,600
Belgium	10,348,276	11,780	30,510
Belize	272,945	8,866	22,963
Benin	7,250,033	43,482	112,620
Bhutan	2,185,569	18,147	47,001
Bolivia	8,586,443	424,165	1,089,581
Bosnia & Herzegovina	4,007,608	19,775	51,233
Botswana	1,561,973	231,800	600,370
Brazil	186,112,794	3,286,488	8,511,965
Bulgaria	7,517,973	42,823	110,910
Burkina Faso	13,574,820	105,869	274,200
Cambodia	13,363,421	69,900	181,040
Cameroon	16,063,678	183,567	475,440
Canada	32,507,874	3,851,788	9,976,085
Cape Verde	415,294	1,557	4,033
Central African Rep.	3,742,482	240,533	622,980
Chad	9,538,544	495,755	1,284,000
Chile	15,823,957	292,260	756,950
China	1,298,847,624	3,705,820	9,598,032
Colombia	42,310,775	439,773	1,138,910
Comoros	651,901	838	2,171
Congo, Dem. Rep. of	58,317,930	905,563	2,345,410
Costa Rica	3,956,507	19,730	51,100
Croatia	4,496,869	21,829	56,538
Cuba	11,308,764	42,803	110,860
Czech Republic	10,246,178	30,387	78,703
Denmark	5,413,392	16,629	43,070
Dominican Republic	8,833,634	18,815	48,731
Ecuador	13,212,742	109,483	283,560
Egypt	76,117,421	386,662	1,001,149
El Salvador	6,587,541	8,124	21,041
England	49,855,700	50,363	130,357
Equatorial Guinea	523,051	10,830	28,050

Nation or Territory	Population	Area (sq. mi.)	Area (sq. km.)
Eritrea	4,447,307	46,842	121,320
Estonia	1,341,664	17,462	45,226
Ethiopia	67,851,281	435,184	1,127,127
Fiji	880,874	7,054	18,270
Finland	5,214,512	130,127	337,030
France	60,424,213	211,208	547,030
French Polynesia	266,339	1,413	3,660
Gabon	1,355,246	103,347	267,670
Gambia	1,546,848	4,363	11,300
Georgia	4,693,892	26,912	69,700
Germany	82,424,609	137,803	356,910
Ghana	20,757,032	92,100	238,540
Greece	10,665,989	50,942	131,940
Grenada	89,357	131	339
Guam	166,090	212	538
Guatemala	14,280,596	42,043	108,890
Guinea	9,246,462	94,000	243,460
Guinea-Bissau	1,388,363	13,946	36,120
Guyana	705,803	83,000	214,970
Haiti	7,656,166	10,714	27,750
Honduras	6,823,568	43,278	112,090
Hong Kong	6,855,125	421	1,092
Hungary	10,032,375	35,919	93,030
Iceland	293,996	39,768	103,000
India	1,065,070,607	1,269,338	3,287,590
Indonesia	238,452,952	741,096	1,919,400
Iran	69,018,924	636,293	1,648,000
Iraq	25,374,691	168,754	437,072
Ireland	3,969,558	27,135	70,280
Israel	6,199,008	8,020	20,770
Italy	58,057,477	116,305	301,230
Ivory Coast	17,327,724	124,500	322,460
Jamaica	27,131,130	4,243	10,989
Japan	127,333,002	145,882	377,835
Jordan	5,611,202	35,475	91,880
Kazakstan	15,143,704	1,049,155	2,717,300
Kenya	32,021,856	224,961	582,650
Kiribati	100,798	313	811
Kuwait	2,257,549	6,880	17,820
Kyrgyzstan	5,081,429	76,640	198,500
Laos	6,068,117	91,430	236,800
Latvia	2,306,306	24,750	64,100
Lebanon	3,777,218	4,015	10,400
Lesotho	1,865,040	11,718	30,350
Libya	5,631,585	679,362	1,759,540
Liechtenstein	33,436	62	163
Lithuania	3,607,899	25,174	65,200
Luxembourg	462,690	998	2,586

Population and Area

Nation or Territory	Population	Area (sq. mi.)	Area (sq. km.)
Macedonia	2,071,210	9,928	25,713
Madagascar	17,501,871	226,656	587,040
Malawi	11,906,855	45,747	118,484
Malaysia	23,522,482	127,317	329,750
Mali	11,956,788	478,764	1,240,000
Malta	396,851	122	316
Marshall Islands	57,738	70	181
Mauritania	2,998,563	397,953	1,030,700
Mauritius	1,230,602	718	1,860
Mexico	104,959,594	761,602	1,972,550
Micronesia	108,155	270	700
Moldova	4,455,421	13,010	33,700
Mongolia	2,751,314	604,250	1,565,000
Montserrat	9,245	40	103
Morocco	32,209,101	172,413	446,550
Mozambique	18,811,731	309,574	801,590
Myanmar	50,100,500	262,000	678,500
Namibia	1,954,033	317,816	823,144
Nepal	27,070,666	54,362	140,800
Netherlands	16,318,199	16,036	41,532
New Zealand	3,993,817	103,737	268,680
Nicaragua	5,359,759	49,998	129,494
Niger	11,360,538	489,206	1,267,000
Nigeria	137,253,133	356,668	923,770
Niue	2,156	100	260
North Korea	22,697,553	47,250	120,540
Northern Ireland	1,702,600	5,482	14,199
Norway	4,574,560	125,182	324,220
Oman	2,903,165	119,498	309,500
Pakistan	159,196,336	310,410	803,940
Panama	3,000,463	30,193	78,200
Papua New Guinea	5,420,280	178,259	461,690
Paraguay	6,191,368	157,046	406,570
Peru	27,544,305	496,226	1,285,220
Philippines	86,241,697	115,830	300,000
Poland	38,626,349	120,728	312,685
Portugal	10,524,145	35,672	92,391
Puerto Rico	3,897,960	3,515	9,104
Qatar	840,290	4,416	11,437
Romania	22,355,551	91,700	237,500
Russia	143,782,338	6,592,734	17,075,200
Rwanda	7,954,013	10,170	26,340
Saint Kitts and Nevis	38,836	101	261
Saint Lucia	164,213	239	620
Saint Vincent & the Gr.	117,193	150	389
Samoa	177,714	1,133	2,934
Saudi Arabia	25,795,938	750,965	1,945,000
Scotland	5,057,400	30,421	78,789

Nation or Territory	Population	Area (sq. mi.)	Area (sq. km.)
Senegal	10,852,147	75,749	196,180
Serbia and Montenegro	10,825,900	39,518	102,350
Sierra Leone	5,883,889	27,699	71,740
Singapore	4,425,720	244	633
Slovakia	5,423,567	18,859	48,845
Slovenia	2,011,473	7,820	20,253
Solomon Islands	523,617	10,634	27,540
Somalia	8,304,601	246,300	638,000
South Africa	42,718,530	471,445	1,221,043
South Korea	48,598,175	38,023	98,480
Spain	40,280,780	194,897	504,782
Sri Lanka	19,905,165	25,332	65,610
Sudan	39,148,162	967,494	2,505,810
Suriname	481,146	63,039	163,270
Swaziland	1,169,241	6,704	17,363
Sweden	9,013,109	173,732	449,964
Switzerland	7,450,867	15,942	41,290
Syria	18,016,874	71,498	185,180
Taiwan	22,749,838	13,892	35,980
Tajikistan	7,011,556	55,251	143,100
Tanzania	36,588,225	364,899	945,090
Thailand	64,865,523	198,455	514,000
Togo	5,556,812	21,930	56,790
Tonga	110,237	277	718
Trinidad and Tobago	1,096,585	1,980	5,128
Tunisia	9,974,722	63,170	163,610
Turkey	68,893,918	301,382	780,580
Turkmenistan	4,863,169	188,500	488,100
Tuvalu	11,468	10	26
Uganda	26,404,543	91,135	236,040
Ukraine	47,732,079	233,090	603,700
United Arab Emirates	2,523,915	32,400	83,900
United States	293,027,571	3,618,765	9,372,558
Uruguay	3,399,237	68,039	176,220
U.S. Virgin Islands	108,775	135	349
Uzbekistan	26,410,416	172,740	447,400
Venezuela	25,017,387	352,143	912,050
Vietnam	82,689,518	127,243	329,560
Wales	2,938,000	9,018	20,769
West Bank and Gaza	3,636,195	2,367	6,130
Yemen	20,024,867	203,849	527,970
Zambia	10,462,436	290,583	752,610
Zimbabwe	12,671,860	150,803	390,580

Nation or Territory	Human Dev. Index Rank*	HDI Adjusted for Women*	Real GDP per Capita**	Adult Literacy	Literacy (Male)	Literacy (Female)	Infant Mortality (per 1,000 births)	Life Expectancy (Male)	Life Expectancy (Female)
Afghanistan	NA	NA	$700	36%	51%	21%	166	43	43
Albania	65 of 177	54 of 144	$4,830	99%	99%	98%	22	71	77
Algeria	108 of 177	89 of 144	$5,760	69%	78%	60%	32	68	71
American Samoa	NA	NA	$8,000	98%	98%	97%	9	72	79
Angola	166 of 177	NA	$2,130	42%	56%	28%	193	39	42
Antigua and Barbuda	55 of 177	NA	$10,920	86%	NA	NA	20	69	74
Argentina	34 of 177	36 of 144	$10,880	97%	97%	97%	16	71	78
Armenia	82 of 177	65 of 144	$3,120	99%	99%	99%	24	69	76
Australia	3 of 177	3 of 144	$28,260	99%	99%	99%	5	76	82
Austria	14 of 177	17 of 144	$29,220	99%	99%	99%	5	75	81
Azerbaijan	91 of 177	NA	$3,210	98%	99%	96%	82	69	75
Bahamas	51 of 177	46 of 144	$17,280	96%	95%	96%	17	64	70
Bahrain	40 of 177	39 of 144	$17,170	88%	92%	84%	18	72	76
Bangladesh	138 of 177	110 of 144	$1,700	41%	50%	31%	64	61	62
Barbados	29 of 177	27 of 144	$15,290	99%	99%	99%	13	74	79
Belarus	62 of 177	51 of 144	$5,520	99%	99%	99%	13	65	75
Belgium	6 of 177	7 of 144	$27,570	99%	99%	99%	5	76	82
Belize	99 of 177	80 of 144	$6,080	77%	77%	77%	26	70	73
Benin	161 of 177	130 of 144	$1,070	41%	55%	26%	86	49	53
Bhutan	134 of 177	NA	$1,969	42%	56%	28%	103	62	64
Bolivia	114 of 177	92 of 144	$2,460	87%	93%	81%	55	62	66
Bosnia & Herzegovina	66 of 177	NA	$5,970	95%	98%	91%	22	71	77
Botswana	128 of 177	102 of 144	$8,170	79%	76%	82%	70	40	42
Brazil	72 of 177	60 of 144	$7,770	87%	86%	87%	30	64	73
Bulgaria	56 of 177	48 of 144	$7,130	99%	99%	98%	21	67	75
Burkina Faso	175 of 177	143 of 144	$1,100	14%	19%	8%	99	45	46
Cambodia	130 of 177	105 of 144	$2,060	70%	81%	59%	74	55	60
Cameroon	141 of 177	111 of 144	$2,000	69%	77%	60%	69	46	48
Canada	4 of 177	4 of 144	$29,480	99%	99%	99%	5	77	82
Cape Verde	105 of 177	83 of 144	$5,000	77%	85%	68%	49	67	73
Central African Rep.	169 of 177	138 of 144	$1,170	50%	65%	34%	92	39	41
Chad	167 of 177	135 of 144	$1,020	47%	55%	38%	95	44	46
Chile	43 of 177	40 of 144	$9,820	96%	96%	96%	9	73	79
China	94 of 177	71 of 144	$4,580	91%	95%	87%	25	69	73
Colombia	73 of 177	59 of 144	$6,370	92%	92%	92%	22	69	75
Comoros	136 of 177	108 of 144	$1,690	57%	64%	49%	77	59	62
Congo, Dem. Rep. of	168 of 177	136 of 144	$650	63%	74%	52%	95	40	42
Costa Rica	45 of 177	44 of 144	$8,840	96%	96%	96%	10	76	81
Croatia	48 of 177	43 of 144	$10,040	98%	99%	97%	7	70	78
Cuba	52 of 177	NA	$5,259	97%	97%	97%	6	75	79
Czech Republic	32 of 177	32 of 144	$15,780	99%	99%	99%	4	72	79
Denmark	17 of 177	13 of 144	$30,940	99%	99%	99%	5	74	79
Dominican Republic	98 of 177	98 of 144	$6,640	84%	84%	84%	33	64	69
Ecuador	100 of 177	79 of 144	$3,580	91%	92%	90%	24	68	73
Egypt	120 of 177	99 of 144	$3,810	56%	67%	44%	34	67	71

*UN Development Programme, Human Development Report
**U.S. Dollars

Development Data

Nation or Territory	Human Dev. Index Rank*	HDI Adjusted for Women*	Real GDP per Capita**	Adult Literacy	Literacy (Male)	Literacy (Female)	Infant Mortality (per 1,000 births)	Life Expectancy (Male)	Life Expectancy (Female)
El Salvador	103 of 177	84 of 144	$4,890	80%	82%	77%	26	68	74
England	12 of 177	9 of 144	$26,150	99%	99%	99%	5	76	81
Equatorial Guinea	109 of 177	86 of 144	$29,780	85%	93%	76%	87	48	51
Eritrea	156 of 177	127 of 144	$890	57%	68%	46%	76	51	54
Estonia	36 of 177	33 of 144	$12,260	99%	99%	99%	12	66	77
Ethiopia	170 of 177	137 of 144	$780	42%	49%	34%	102	45	46
Fiji	81 of 177	69 of 144	$5,440	93%	95%	91%	13	68	71
Finland	13 of 177	10 of 144	$26,150	99%	99%	99%	4	74	81
France	16 of 177	15 of 144	$26,920	99%	99%	99%	4	75	83
French Polynesia	NA	NA	$17,500	98%	98%	98%	9	73	78
Gabon	122 of 177	NA	$6,590	64%	74%	53%	54	56	58
Gambia	155 of 177	125 of 144	$1,690	38%	45%	31%	73	53	55
Georgia	97 of 177	NA	$2,260	99%	99%	98%	19	69	78
Germany	19 of 177	19 of 144	$27,100	99%	99%	99%	4	75	81
Ghana	131 of 177	104 of 144	$2,130	74%	82%	66%	52	56	59
Greece	24 of 177	24 of 144	$17,740	98%	99%	96%	6	76	81
Grenada	93 of 177	NA	$7,280	94%	NA	NA	15	63	66
Guam	NA	NA	$21,000	99%	99%	99%	7	75	81
Guatemala	121 of 177	98 of 144	$4,080	70%	77%	63%	37	63	69
Guinea	160 of 177	NA	$2,100	36%	50%	22%	92	49	49
Guinea-Bissau	172 of 177	141 of 144	$710	40%	55%	25%	109	44	47
Guyana	104 of 177	81 of 144	$4,260	99%	99%	98%	37	60	66
Haiti	153 of 177	123 of 144	$1,610	52%	54%	50%	74	49	50
Honduras	115 of 177	95 of 144	$2,600	80%	80%	80%	30	67	71
Hong Kong	23 of 177	23 of 144	$26,910	94%	97%	90%	3	77	82
Hungary	38 of 177	35 of 144	$13,400	99%	99%	99%	9	67	76
Iceland	7 of 177	6 of 144	$29,750	99%	99%	99%	3	78	82
India	127 of 177	103 of 144	$2,670	58%	69%	46%	58	63	64
Indonesia	111 of 177	90 of 144	$3,230	88%	93%	83%	37	65	69
Iran	101 of 177	82 of 144	$6,690	77%	84%	70%	43	69	72
Iraq	NA	NA	$1,500	40%	55%	24%	53	59	62
Ireland	10 of 177	14 of 144	$36,360	99%	99%	99%	6	74	80
Israel	22 of 177	22 of 144	$19,530	95%	97%	93%	7	77	81
Italy	21 of 177	21 of 144	$26,430	99%	99%	98%	6	76	82
Ivory Coast	163 of 177	132 of 144	$1,520	49%	60%	38%	97	42	41
Jamaica	79 of 177	62 of 144	$3,980	88%	84%	91%	13	74	78
Japan	9 of 177	12 of 144	$26,940	99%	99%	99%	3	78	85
Jordan	90 of 177	76 of 144	$4,220	91%	96%	86%	18	70	72
Kazakstan	78 of 177	63 of 144	$5,870	99%	99%	99%	31	61	72
Kenya	148 of 177	114 of 144	$1,020	85%	90%	79%	63	44	46
Kiribati	NA	NA	$800	80%	80%	80%	50	58	64
Kuwait	44 of 177	42 of 144	$16,240	83%	85%	81%	10	75	79
Kyrgyzstan	110 of 177	NA	$1,620	98%	99%	96%	37	65	72
Laos	135 of 177	107 of 144	$1,720	67%	77%	56%	87	53	56
Latvia	50 of 177	45 of 144	$9,210	99%	99%	99%	10	65	76

*UN Development Programme, Human Development Report
**U.S. Dollars

Development Data

Nation or Territory	Human Dev. Index Rank*	HDI Adjusted for Women*	Real GDP per Capita**	Adult Literacy	Literacy (Male)	Literacy (Female)	Infant Mortality (per 1,000 births)	Life Expectancy (Male)	Life Expectancy (Female)
Lebanon	80 of 177	64 of 144	$4,360	87%	92%	81%	25	72	75
Lesotho	145 of 177	117 of 144	$2,420	82%	74%	90%	85	33	39
Libya	58 of 177	NA	$7,570	82%	92%	71%	26	71	75
Liechtenstein	NA	NA	$25,000	99%	99%	99%	5	76	83
Lithuania	41 of 177	37 of 144	$10,320	99%	99%	99%	7	67	78
Luxembourg	15 of 177	16 of 144	$61,190	99%	99%	99%	5	75	81
Macedonia	60 of 177	NA	$6,470	96%	97%	94%	12	71	76
Madagascar	150 of 177	121 of 144	$740	68%	74%	61%	79	52	55
Malawi	165 of 177	134 of 144	$580	63%	76%	49%	104	38	38
Malaysia	59 of 177	52 of 144	$9,120	89%	92%	85%	18	71	76
Mali	174 of 177	142 of 144	$930	20%	27%	12%	118	48	49
Malta	31 of 177	31 of 144	$17,640	93%	92%	93%	4	76	81
Marshall Islands	NA	NA	$1,600	94%	94%	94%	31	68	72
Mauritania	152 of 177	124 of 144	$2,220	42%	52%	31%	72	51	54
Mauritius	64 of 177	55 of 144	$10,810	85%	88%	81%	16	68	76
Mexico	53 of 177	50 of 144	$8,970	91%	93%	89%	22	70	76
Micronesia	NA	NA	$2,000	90%	91%	88%	31	68	71
Moldova	113 of 177	91 of 144	$1,470	99%	99%	99%	40	65	72
Mongolia	117 of 177	94 of 144	$1,710	98%	98%	98%	56	62	66
Montserrat	NA	NA	$3,400	97%	97%	97%	8	76	81
Morocco	125 of 177	100 of 144	$3,810	51%	63%	38%	43	67	70
Mozambique	171 of 177	139 of 144	$1,050	47%	62%	31%	137	37	40
Myanmar	132 of 177	NA	$1,027	85%	89%	81%	69	55	60
Namibia	126 of 177	101 of 144	$6,210	84%	84%	83%	70	44	47
Nepal	140 of 177	116 of 144	$1,370	44%	62%	26%	69	60	59
Netherlands	5 of 177	5 of 144	$29,100	99%	99%	99%	5	76	81
New Zealand	18 of 177	18 of 144	$21,740	99%	99%	99%	6	76	81
Nicaragua	118 of 177	97 of 144	$2,470	77%	77%	77%	30	67	72
Niger	176 of 177	144 of 144	$800	17%	25%	9%	123	46	46
Nigeria	151 of 177	122 of 144	$860	67%	74%	59%	70	51	52
Niue	NA	NA	$3,600	95%	95%	95%	29	69	71
North Korea	NA	NA	$1,300	99%	99%	99%	25	61	66
Northern Ireland	12 of 177	9 of 144	$26,150	99%	99%	99%	5	76	81
Norway	1 of 177	1 of 144	$36,600	99%	99%	99%	4	76	82
Oman	74 of 177	68 of 144	$13,340	74%	82%	65%	20	71	74
Pakistan	142 of 177	120 of 144	$1,940	41%	53%	29%	74	61	61
Panama	61 of 177	53 of 144	$6,170	93%	93%	92%	21	72	77
Papua New Guinea	133 of 177	106 of 144	$2,270	65%	71%	58%	53	57	59
Paraguay	89 of 177	75 of 144	$4,610	92%	93%	90%	27	69	73
Peru	85 of 177	74 of 144	$5,010	86%	91%	80%	33	67	72
Philippines	83 of 177	66 of 144	$4,170	93%	93%	93%	24	68	72
Poland	37 of 177	34 of 144	$10,560	99%	99%	99%	9	70	78
Portugal	26 of 177	24 of 144	$18,280	93%	95%	90%	5	73	80
Puerto Rico	NA	NA	$16,800	94%	94%	94%	8	73	82
Qatar	47 of 177	NA	$19,844	84%	85%	82%	19	70	75

*UN Development Programme, Human Development Report
**U.S. Dollars

Development Data

Nation or Territory	Human Dev. Index Rank*	HDI Adjusted for Women*	Real GDP per Capita**	Adult Literacy	Literacy (Male)	Literacy (Female)	Infant Mortality (per 1,000 births)	Life Expectancy (Male)	Life Expectancy (Female)
Romania	69 of 177	56 of 144	$6,560	97%	98%	96%	27	67	74
Russia	57 of 177	49 of 144	$8,230	99%	99%	99%	17	61	73
Rwanda	159 of 177	129 of 144	$1,270	69%	75%	63%	102	38	39
Saint Kitts and Nevis	39 of 177	NA	$12,420	98%	NA	NA	15	69	75
Saint Lucia	71 of 177	NA	$5,300	95%	NA	NA	14	71	74
Saint Vincent & the Gr.	87 of 177	NA	$5,460	83%	NA	NA	14	73	76
Samoa	75 of 177	NA	$5,600	99%	99%	98%	29	67	73
Saudi Arabia	77 of 177	72 of 144	$12,650	77%	84%	70%	14	71	74
Scotland	12 of 177	9 of 144	$26,150	99%	99%	99%	5	76	81
Senegal	157 of 177	128 of 144	$1,580	40%	49%	30%	57	51	55
Serbia and Montenegro	NA	NA	$2,200	93%	97%	89%	13	72	77
Sierra Leone	177 of 177	NA	$500	32%	45%	18%	145	33	36
Singapore	25 of 177	28 of 144	$24,040	93%	97%	89%	4	76	80
Slovakia	42 of 177	37 of 144	$12,840	99%	99%	99%	8	70	78
Slovenia	27 of 177	27 of 144	$18,540	99%	99%	99%	5	73	80
Solomon Islands	124 of 177	NA	$1,590	62%	68%	56%	22	68	71
Somalia	NA	NA	$500	38%	50%	26%	119	46	49
South Africa	119 of 177	96 of 144	$10,070	86%	87%	85%	62	46	52
South Korea	28 of 177	29 of 144	$16,950	98%	99%	97%	7	72	79
Spain	20 of 177	20 of 144	$21,460	98%	99%	97%	4	76	83
Sri Lanka	96 of 177	73 of 144	$3,570	93%	95%	90%	15	70	76
Sudan	139 of 177	115 of 144	$1,820	60%	71%	49%	64	54	57
Suriname	67 of 177	NA	$6,590	93%	95%	91%	24	68	74
Swaziland	137 of 177	109 of 144	$4,550	81%	82%	80%	68	34	37
Sweden	2 of 177	2 of 144	$26,050	99%	99%	99%	3	78	83
Switzerland	11 of 177	11 of 144	$30,010	99%	99%	99%	4	76	82
Syria	106 of 177	88 of 144	$3,620	83%	91%	74%	31	71	73
Taiwan	NA	NA	$23,400	95%	98%	92%	7	74	80
Tajikistan	116 of 177	93 of 144	$980	99%	99%	99%	112	66	71
Tanzania	162 of 177	131 of 144	$580	77%	85%	69%	102	43	44
Thailand	76 of 177	61 of 144	$7,010	93%	95%	91%	21	65	73
Togo	143 of 177	119 of 144	$1,480	60%	74%	45%	68	48	51
Tonga	63 of 177	NA	$6,850	99%	99%	99%	13	68	69
Trinidad and Tobago	54 of 177	47 of 144	$9,430	99%	99%	98%	25	69	75
Tunisia	92 of 177	77 of 144	$6,760	73%	83%	63%	26	71	75
Turkey	88 of 177	70 of 144	$6,390	87%	94%	79%	43	68	73
Turkmenistan	86 of 177	67 of 144	$4,300	99%	99%	98%	73	64	70
Tuvalu	NA	NA	$1,100	96%	96%	96%	21	65	70
Uganda	146 of 177	113 of 144	$1,390	69%	79%	59%	86	45	46
Ukraine	70 of 177	57 of 144	$4,870	99%	99%	99%	21	65	75
United Arab Emirates	49 of 177	NA	$22,420	79%	76%	81%	15	73	77
United States	8 of 177	8 of 144	$35,750	99%	99%	99%	7	74	80
Uruguay	46 of 177	41 of 144	$7,830	98%	97%	98%	12	72	79
U.S. Virgin Islands	NA	NA	$17,200	90%	NA	NA	8	75	83
Uzbekistan	107 of 177	85 of 144	$1,670	99%	99%	99%	71	67	72

*UN Development Programme, Human Development Report
**U.S. Dollars

Development Data

Nation or Territory	Human Dev. Index Rank*	HDI Adjusted for Women*	Real GDP per Capita**	Adult Literacy	Literacy (Male)	Literacy (Female)	Infant Mortality (per 1,000 births)	Life Expectancy (Male)	Life Expectancy (Female)
Venezuela	68 of 177	58 of 144	$5,380	94%	94%	93%	23	71	77
Vietnam	112 of 177	87 of 144	$2,300	91%	94%	87%	30	67	71
Wales	12 of 177	9 of 144	$26,150	99%	99%	99%	5	76	81
West Bank and Gaza	102 of 177	NA	$750	81%	89%	72%	22	71	74
Yemen	149 of 177	126 of 144	$870	50%	70%	29%	63	59	61
Zambia	164 of 177	133 of 144	$840	80%	86%	74%	98	33	33
Zimbabwe	147 of 177	118 of 144	$2,400	90%	94%	86%	67	34	34

*UN Development Programme, Human Development Report
**U.S. Dollars

Concepts and Terminology

The following is a list of some common concepts found in CultureGrams™. These are not necessarily definitions; they are explanations of how the terms are used in the series, what significance they hold in regard to understanding cultures, and often how they are calculated. For explanations of international organizations (United Nations, European Union, and others), please refer to reference sources in a library.

Cash Crops. A cash crop is an agricultural product that is grown for sale, not for the farmer's consumption. It is often a crop (coffee, cotton, sugarcane, rice and other grains) that requires manufacturing or processing. It may also be a crop (oranges, potatoes, bananas) that can be consumed upon harvest but is cultivated primarily to be sold. Cash crops are produced most effectively on a large scale, but they can be grown on small plots of land. When grown on a large scale, the crops are more likely to be exported than consumed locally, although small growers in developing countries may sell to a local buyer who then sells larger quantities domestically and abroad. The economies of many countries depend heavily on the sale of cash crops.

Diversified Economy. An economy is considered diversified if its stability relies on a variety of industries rather than one or two commodities. For example, oil-rich countries that rely almost solely on the petroleum industry for their income are vulnerable to changes in the price of oil on the world market. When the price drops significantly, the countries are suddenly unable to pay debts or finance social development projects. The same is true for countries that rely on agricultural products such as coffee or on minerals such as copper for their income. Countries whose economies are based not only on agricultural products but also manufacturing, services, technology, and so forth are better able to withstand global price changes. Thus, the more diversified a country's economic base, the better.

Foreign Language Phrases. Most CultureGrams contain phrases and words in the target culture's official or common language. In general, CultureGrams do not provide a pronunciation guide for these phrases, due to limited space. Also, including pronunciation and a translation tends to interrupt the flow of the text. CultureGrams are not designed to teach foreign languages. Rather, the phrases contained in CultureGrams are there to facilitate the description of how people interact with one another. Their translation often provides insights about the culture, but pronunciation is not necessary to gain that insight. In the few cases where pronunciation hints are provided, they are necessary for English speakers to properly pronounce a word. For instance, the country Lesotho is not pronounced as it would seem. Instead of saying "le-SO-tho," one should say "le-SUE-too."

Free and Compulsory Education. Most countries provide free education to their citizens, meaning the government operates a public school system open to all children who are in a certain age group. It does not necessarily mean there are no costs involved in attending school. Students may be required to wear uniforms (which must be purchased), might live far from the nearest school (and transportation must be paid for), or may need to supply their own books, pencils, and other basic items. In addition, having a child in school can cost a rural family one laborer on the family farm. This can become such a burden to poorer families that free education is still not accessible to them.

Compulsory education refers to the fact that the law requires children to attend school for a certain number of years. In many countries this rule is seldom enforced. Therefore, it may reflect the government's target for how long children should remain in school to obtain a basic education rather than how long they actually are required to attend. Compulsory education usually encompasses six to nine years, and optional schooling usually continues for three or more years.

Gross Domestic Product (GDP) Per Capita. This economic statistic refers to the value of all goods and services produced annually in an economy per person. Naturally, not every person produces goods and services, but the total is averaged for the entire population. If the term is expressed as "gross national product" (GNP), it is essentially the same statistic except for the addition of income earned abroad minus the income earned in the country by noncitizens. This is significant when part of the population works in other countries and sends back money to their families. It is also significant for countries that have substantial investments abroad. For most countries, the two statistics, GDP and GNP, are almost interchangeable.

In the past, GDP was calculated in terms of the U.S. dollar after conversion from the local currency at official exchange rates. This caused accuracy problems because of artificially set exchange rates and because a dollar may not buy the same amount of goods in the United States as it does in another country. Social scientists recently have developed the concept of Purchasing Power Parity (PPP), a measurement that tries to account for the inconsistencies of the past. When GDP is figured in terms of PPP, an international dollar not affected by exchange rates is used. Likewise, PPP attempts to express the relative ability of a person to purchase goods with the local currency. Therefore, measured with PPP, five hundred dollars will buy essentially the same things in the United States as it will in Brazil or Japan. For many countries, PPP data does not yet exist, and only estimates are available for others.

Most CultureGrams use PPP with GDP, as expressed by the phrase "real gross domestic product." When the word "real" is absent, only the GDP has been calculated. The real GDPs in CultureGrams usually are taken from the *Human Development Report* (New York: Oxford University Press). In cases where the real GDP is low (less than one thousand dollars, for example), one can assume that people have very little disposable income. But one should also remember that rural families may grow their own food and therefore need less disposable income

Concepts and Terminology

to meet basic needs. In other cases, such a low figure indicates people indeed may be without food, shelter, clothing, or other necessities.

Hard Currency. Many countries have currencies that are not acceptable as currency for international purchases or exchanges. These currencies are considered inconvertible (not a medium of exchange) outside of their sponsoring nation. Such countries must pay for imports with a convertible currency that is accepted as a medium of exchange among countries. A convertible currency often is called hard currency because it is worth something outside its own borders. The U.S. dollar, Japanese yen, British pound, European Union euro, and a few others are global hard currencies. The currencies of most advanced economies are also convertible. Regional hard currencies also exist, such as the *CFA franc*, a currency used in many West African nations (former French colonies) as both a domestic and regional exchange currency. However, the *CFA franc* would not be accepted as a global hard currency. Developing countries without convertible currencies use hard currencies to import goods and services. They obtain hard currency through their goods and services exports, their expatriate workers, tourism, and international lending or aid.

Human Development and Gender-Related Development Indexes. Originating with the United Nations Development Programme (UNDP), the human development index (HDI) and gender-related development index (GDI) attempt to compensate for the inability of traditional economic indicators to portray accurately the environment in which people live—whether that environment nurtures personal development or hinders it. The project functions under the assumption that human development is a process of "expanding [people's] choices to live full, creative lives with freedom and dignity." (UNDP 2003, 28). The three essential capabilities that people must have in order to expand their choices are "living a long and healthy life, being educated and having a decent standard of living." (UNDP 2003, 2). Accordingly, the basis of the HDI is statistics related to infant mortality, life expectancy, literacy, and real GDP. If people have access to adequate education, health care, and wages, they are more likely to be involved in community affairs, join the middle class, and contribute skills and time to society. Such societies are more often democratic and respectful of human rights.

Each country is ranked in relation to the others according to an index value that falls between 0 and 1. The HDI "shows how far a country has to travel to provide ... essential choices to all its people. It is not a measure of well-being. Nor is it a measure of happiness. Instead, it is a measure of empowerment" (UNDP 1995, 12). The GDI measures progress in the same way as the HDI, but it is adjusted to account for inequality between men and women. It is common for men to have access more quickly than women to the same basic resources and choices. Only 144 nations have been ranked for the GDI, whereas 175 have been listed for the HDI. Each CultureGram for which HDI and GDI data are available lists the country's rank. For more detailed analysis and additional data, refer to the entire *Human Development Report*, which is updated annually.

Income Distribution. This phrase generally is used in connection with the gap between what the poorest people in a country earn and what the richest earn. If income distribution is highly unequal, a small wealthy class generally controls the economy (and often the government) and owns most property. The much larger poor class is often landless, which is significant since the people are probably farmers who must rent property and receive only a small share of the benefits from their labor. An unequal, but not highly unequal, income distribution often indicates that a middle class is beginning to grow. When the distribution is fairly equal, as is the case in a minority of countries, it is due mostly to a large and prosperous middle class. However, it also can indicate the presence of a broad poor class and absence of a wealthy elite. Generally, having a highly unequal income distribution means the economy is unhealthy, whereas the existence of a strong middle (consumer) class is good for an economy.

Infant Mortality Rate. This statistic is expressed as the number of children per 1,000 live births who die before their first birthday. It is an important indicator of the overall health of a population, since infants who die at this age usually are subject to preventable diseases or birth defects related to the mother's health. Those who die at birth often do so because of a lack of prenatal care and medical attention at birth. People who have access to health care, clean water, nutritious food, and education are more likely to have a low infant mortality rate than people without such access. Industrialized countries generally have a low rate (fewer than 10 per 1,000), while developing countries usually have a higher rate (averaging more than 30). The poorest countries may have rates exceeding 100.

Life Expectancy. This measurement refers to how long a person can expect to live from birth if mortality patterns remain unchanged. Someone born today may be expected to live 80 years if living in some European countries but only 58 years if living in parts of Africa. However, since mortality patterns do change throughout a person's lifetime, the statistic is really a better reflection of how long an adult who is currently living can expect to live. So a person who is 50 today can expect to live until 80 in some countries or only a few more years in others. Women live longer than men in most countries, and people in industrialized countries live longer than those in developing countries. People in countries with high pollution have lower rates of life expectancy.

When a CultureGram lists only one average age, it is the average of the male and female averages. This statistic, like infant mortality, helps the reader understand the overall health of a population and whether the people have access to nutritious food, clean water, health care, and proper sanitation.

Literacy Rate. CultureGrams list a literacy rate for the general adult population. These data usually are taken from the *Human Development Report*, which defines adult literacy as "The percentage of people aged 15 and above who can, with understanding, both read and write a short, simple statement related to their everyday life" (UNDP 2003, 354). This is the global standard for reporting literacy, although a few countries will certify persons literate if they can write their name or if they have ever been enrolled in school. Most educational experts agree that such definitions are misleading, since being able to write a name or a short sentence does not imply a person can understand such things as a ballot, a newspaper, or work instructions. Were it possible to report functional literacy, many countries would have far lower literacy rates than are presented. But no uniform standard exists for reporting functional literacy. Therefore, readers should keep in mind that an

Concepts and Terminology

official literacy rate is only one indicator of a nation's overall educational level.

On the other hand, many developing countries report their literacy rates based on an official language that a majority or significant group of people does not even speak, let alone read. In these cases, people may be functional in a local language or an oral language but not functional in the "official" language. Although one cannot read and write an oral language, one can use it to recount history, calculate numbers, share information, relate instructions, and so on. In some areas, the ability to read may not be considered a necessary life skill. In other words, one cannot equate intelligence or skill with literacy.

Population and Population Growth Rate. The figure for population listed in each CultureGram is an estimate for the year previous to publication (i.e., 2003 population for text published in 2004). The estimate is based on the actual population at the last census, multiplied by an annual growth rate. The estimate may seem to conflict with other sources, since other sources often only print the population as of the latest census (whenever it may have been taken) or an estimate made in a base year (e.g., 2000).

CultureGrams estimates are in keeping with figures in U.S. government and UN publications, but they sometimes are modified by information from the target culture's government. Each population estimate is revised annually.

The population growth rate is an estimate based on the previous year's difference between births and deaths and the net number of migrants leaving or entering the country. The growth rate may change substantially in a single year if there is a large influx of immigrants, a massive emigration, a natural disaster, or an epidemic. Growth rates tend to be low in industrialized countries because families are small, averaging one or two children. Growth rates are generally high in developing countries, especially in areas where subsistence farming is the primary economic activity. These cultures require large families to help farm the land, but they often have a high infant mortality rate; many children are conceived to ensure that enough will survive into adulthood. In small nations, the growth rate may be low due to emigration, as people must go elsewhere to find work.

Poverty. Poverty is noted in CultureGrams in two ways. Sometimes poverty is described in general terms to indicate a low standard of living according to various governmental or societal criteria. Other references to poverty (those marked by an asterisk) are based on the Human Poverty Index (HPI) from the *Human Development Report 2003*. The HPI measures deprivation in three main areas—"a long and healthy life, knowledge and a decent standard of living" (UNDP 2003, 353). These figures, expressed sometimes as percentages and sometimes as fractions, indicate what portion of a population not only lives in poverty but also lacks access to adequate education, health care, safe water, and economic opportunity to escape the poverty they face.

Staple Food. Staple foods are those foods that supply the majority of the average person's calories and nutrition. A people's primary staple food is usually starchy, such as cassava (manioc), corn, rice, millet, or wheat. Staple foods also include any meats, fruits, and vegetables eaten frequently or in large quantities.

Subsistence Farming. Subsistence farming refers to farming as the main source of a family's livelihood. That is, a family will grow its own food, raise its own livestock, build its own home, and often make its own clothing. Members of such a family generally do not earn a wage by working at a job, but they usually are not entirely without a cash income. Family members might sell surplus produce or livestock, or make crafts or other items (blankets, baskets, etc.), in order to buy things they cannot provide for themselves. These usually include items such as sugar, cooking oil, clothing, rice or another staple food, and so forth. Subsistence farmers also may set aside part of their land to grow cash crops in order to earn money. Subsistence farmers generally do not grow an abundance of anything. They often live on small owned or rented plots of land, and they seldom enjoy the luxuries of running water or electricity.

Underemployment. Underemployment refers to when workers are not officially unemployed but either are unable to find enough work in their profession or are working in jobs below their skill level. For example, if a country's universities graduate many people in engineering or other professional fields but the economy is not diversified or well developed, those people may find themselves underemployed, working in jobs that do not take advantage of their skills, or only working part-time in their field of study. In the latter case, they may return to farming or local retailing. In too many cases, the most educated people simply emigrate to another country to find work, resulting in what is called a "brain drain."

Government unemployment figures generally do not include underemployment; it must be estimated. However, when unemployment is high (more than 10 percent), one usually can assume that underemployment affects at least as many or more workers. This condition reflects an economy that is not growing, and it can lead to social unrest. High underemployment (more than 40 percent) often leads to political turmoil and violence. Employing and paying people according to their skill level helps secure social stability and encourage economic growth.

Western/Western-style. This term usually refers to the dress, eating customs, culture, and traditions of Western Europe, the United States, and Canada. This culture often is referred to as Western because of its common ancient (primarily Greek and Roman) philosophical, legal, political, and social heritage. The term Western can also refer to cultures that have a Judeo-Christian value system and religious orientation.

© 2005 ProQuest Information and Learning Company and Brigham Young University. It is against the law to copy, reprint, store, or transmit any part of this publication in any form by any means without written permission from ProQuest. This document contains native commentary and original analysis, as well as estimated statistics. The content should not be considered strictly factual, and it may not apply to all groups in a nation. *UN Development Programme, Human Development Report 2004 (New York: Oxford University Press, 2004).

Glossary of Cultural Terms

This glossary lists key cultural terms used in CultureGrams™ texts. The text a term appears in (usually a specific country) follows in parentheses after the entry. However, since neither CultureGrams texts nor our glossary is intended to provide exhaustive information, note that the term might apply to other countries not listed. The spellings used are those given by our native writers and reviewers.

Aaaaall-right. "How are you?" (Trinidad and Tobago).
Aam. "Uncle." An Arabic term of address for an older man. (Syria).
Aamaa. The Nepali word for "grandmother." (Bhutan).
Aba. "The land" or "people of the land." (Kiribati). *See also* **Mane, Maneaba(s).**
Ab'a. (United Arab Emirates). *See* **Abaya.**
'Aba. A light wool cloak worn by laborers and village men. (Iraq).
Abaa. A hut made of bamboo and palm leaves where elderly men socialize and work on crafts. (Equatorial Guinea).
Abaaya. (Saudi Arabia). *See* **Abaya.**
Abambo. (Malawi). *See* **Bambo.**
Abaya. [NOTE: Spelling varies because it is a transliteration of Arabic.] A full-length black robe worn by women over their clothing. (Bahrain, Kuwait, Oman, Qatar).
'Abayah. (Iraq). *See* **Abaya.**
Abeer. A red liquid. Used along with water and powder by the Indo-Guyanese during **Phagwah**. (Guyana).
Abendbrot. A light evening meal commonly consisting of open-faced sandwiches. (Germany).
Abendessen. An evening meal. (Austria).
Abi. A Turkish term for "brother." Used to address an older man. (Turkey).
A bientôt. "See you soon!" A common French parting phrase, less formal then **Au revoir**. (France).
Abitur. An exam taken at the end of **Gymnasium**. Passing the exam is required for admittance to university. (Germany).
Abla. "Sister." A term added to the end of an older woman's name. (Turkey).
Abrazo. A hug often given when greeting close friends and family members. Characteristics vary depending on the country. (Bolivia, Chile, Colombia, Honduras, Panama, Spain, Uruguay, Venezuela).
Abu. "Father of." An Arabic title combined with a child's name to show respect. (Afghanistan, Bahrain, Iraq, Jordan, United Arab Emirates, West Bank and Gaza).
A buen tiempo. "You've come at a good time." A Spanish phrase used to invite guests or passersby to join the ongoing meal. (Dominican Republic). *See also* **Buen provecho.**
Abu ghayib. "Awaiting father." A respectful term used to address a man without children. (Iraq). *See also* **Um ghayib.**
Académie française France's official authority on the French language. It tries to keep the language pure. (France).
Accara. Fried bean flour. Can be eaten for breakfast. (Gambia).

Achachila. God of the mountains, part of traditional beliefs. (Bolivia). *See also* **Ch'alla, Pachamama.**
Achar. Chutney. (Nepal).
Achoura. [NOTE: Muslim holidays are set according to the lunar calendar.] A Muslim religious holiday celebrated one month after **Aid al Adha**. (Algeria).
Ackee. A rich red fruit often eaten at breakfast. (Jamaica).
Adab. "Hello." A common Hindu greeting. (Bangladesh).
Äddi. "Good-bye." A casual Luxembourgish parting phrase. (Luxembourg). *See also* **Au revoir.**
Äddi, bis mar. "Until tomorrow." A common Luxembourgish parting phrase used among friends and acquaintances. (Luxembourg). *See also* **Bis eng aner Kéier, Bis härno.**
A de go. "I'm going." A common Krio parting phrase. (Sierra Leone).
Adeus. "Good-bye." A common parting phrase. (Portugal).
Adharma. A Hindi term for "darkness." (Mauritius). *See also* **Divali.**
Adijo. "Adieu." A common phrase used when parting or exiting a room or an elevator, even if one does not know the others present. (Slovenia).
Adió. (Paraguay). *See* **Adiós.**
Adiós. (1) "Good-bye." A common term used in partings. In a few countries, such as Venezuela, the term is rarely used because it implies a more permanent farewell. Used in Spanish-speaking countries.. (2) A quick greeting on the street or in the countryside. Used in Latin American Spanish-speaking countries..
Adji. A mathematical and probability game. (Benin).
Adjö. The more formal Swedish word for "Good-bye." (Sweden). *See also* **Hej då.**
Adlea. Civil code. (Qatar).
Adobo. A stew made of chicken and pork in garlic, soy sauce, and vinegar. (Philippines).
Aezor. Long pants worn by women under a traditional dress (**Curta**). (Tajikistan). *Also called* **Pajomah.**
A fair go. "A fair chance." A phrase expressing the value that Australians place on fairness. (Australia).
Afé al hamdulilah. "Fine, praise be to **Allah**." The appropriate response to **Kaif al hal?** (Chad).
Afghani. Afghanistan's national currency. (Afghanistan).
Afindrafindrao. Malagasy line dancing. One couple leads off dancing and the other couples follow like a train. (Madagascar).
Afio mai. "Welcome" or "Come in." A respectful greeting. (American Samoa, Samoa).
Afiyet Olsun. "May what you eat bring you well-being." A Turkish phrase used to begin or to end a meal. (Turkey).
A fon dagbe a? "Did you wake up well?" A common Fon greeting. (Benin).
Aga. This term is added to a male senior acquaintance's name to show respect. (Turkmenistan). *See also* **Kaka.**

Glossary of Cultural Terms

Agai. "Older brother." A Kyrgyz title used to address a man older than the speaker. (Kyrgyzstan).

Agal. (United Arab Emirates). *See* **Ogal**.

Agama Djawa. Literally, "Javanese religion." This belief centers on the world of spirits, which need to be appeased with food sacrifices (**Sadjèn**). (Suriname). *See also* **Slametan**.

Agay. The Dzongkha word for "grandfather." (Bhutan).

Agbada. A top worn by men at formal occasions. (Benin, Togo).

Agbogbo. The local god in Notsé. (Togo).

Agbogbozan. A rite in the Notsé region that celebrates people's escape from the reign of King Agokoli and honors the local god, **Agbogbo**. (Togo).

Agha. "Older brother." A Kazak term added to the end of a name to show respect to an older man. (Kazakstan).

Aglipayan. The Philippine Independent Church. (Philippines).

A-go. An expression a vistor calls out to announce one's presence before entering a door. (Ghana).

Agouti. Sugarcane rat, a special delicacy. (Benin).

Aguayo. A woven square cloth worn by Bolivian women for a variety of purposes, such as carrying babies on their backs. (Bolivia).

Aguinaldos. Traditional Christmas songs. (Venezuela). *See also* **Gaitas**.

Agyz Acar. A three-day holiday celebrating the end of **Ramadan**. (Turkmenistan). *See also* **Aid al Fitr**.

Ah dey. "I'm alright." A typical Grenadian creole response to the questions **W'happen dey?** or **Hows tings?** (Grenada). *See also* **Just cool**.

Ahiga. Community hall. (Tuvalu). *Also called* **Maneapa(s)**. *See also* **Fakaala**.

Ahimaa. A Tahitian word for "ground oven." (French Polynesia). *Also called* **Umu**.

Ahimsa. The Jain practice of reverence for life. Literally means "nonviolence." (India).

Ahlan Wasahlan. (Morocco). *See* **Ahlan wa sahlan**.

Ahlan wa sahlan. An expression of welcome. Used in Arabic-speaking countries..

Ahn-ahn-ahn. Said while a person shakes his or her head from left to right to indicate "no." (Madagascar). *See also* **Uhn-uhn**.

Ah-nar-deh. The reluctance to bring about a loss of face or to cause trouble or inconvenience. Roughly translated as "having consideration for others." Often described as a Myanmar national characteristic. (Myanmar).

Ahoj. "Hi" or "Good-bye." Used casually in greeting or parting. (Czech Republic, Slovakia).

Ah sey! "I say." A Krio phrase used to get someone's attention. (Sierra Leone).

Aht Chabysh. Long-distance races on horseback. (Kyrgyzstan).

Ahu. Coconut candy, a dessert. (Guam).

Aib. "Shame." If guests visit without prior arrangement, it is considered an offense or *aib* not to invite them in for refreshments. (United Arab Emirates).

'Aid al Adha. (Egypt, West Bank and Gaza). *See* **Eid al-Adha**.

Aid al Adha. (Algeria). *See* **Eid al-Adha**.

Aid al Fitr. [NOTE: Spelling varies because it is a transliteration of Arabic. Also, Muslim holidays are set according to the lunar calendar.] A two- or three-day feast at the end of **Ramadan**. Celebrated in Muslim-populated countries. (Algeria, Chad, Egypt, West Bank and Gaza). *See also* **Aid al Saghir**.

Aid al Kebir. [NOTE: Spelling varies because it is a transliteration of Arabic. Also, Muslim holidays are set according to the lunar calendar.] Feast of the Sacrifice. A Muslim holiday that commemorates Abraham's willingness to sacrifice his son. (Morocco). *Also called* **Eid al Adha**.

Aid al Saghir. [NOTE: Spelling varies because it is a transliteration of Arabic.] A two- or three-day feast at the end of **Ramadan**. (Morocco). *Also called* **Aid al Fitr**.

Aid-e-adha. (Iran). *See* **Eid al-Adha**.

Aid-e-fitr. (Iran). *See* **Aid al Fitr**.

Aid-e-khadir. [NOTE: Spelling varies because it is a transliteration of Arabic. Also, Muslim holidays are set according to the lunar calendar.] Celebrates Muhammad's choosing of Ali (his son-in-law) as his successor. This holiday is celebrated by Shi'ite Muslims. (Iran). *See also* **Shi'i**.

Aid el Adha. (Togo). *See* **Eid al-Adha**.

Aid el Fitr. (Togo). *See* **Aid al Fitr**.

Aid El Kebir. (Tunisia). *See* **Aid al Kebir**.

Aid El Seghir. (Tunisia). *See* **Aid al Saghir**.

Aiga. Extended family or kinship group. (American Samoa, Samoa).

Aii. "Elder brother." A Lao term used to address a male with no specific title. (Laos).

Airag. Fermented mare's milk. (Mongolia).

Aish. Bread. Literally, the Arabic word for "life." (Egypt).

Aisse. "Friend." Used to get the attention of a nearby person. (Malawi).

Aitys. Singing debate. Two people sing their arguments and rebuttals, accompanied by music from a **Dombra**. (Kazakstan).

Aiya. "Older brother." A Sinhala term of address for a close male friend or relative. (Sri Lanka).

Ajsino oro. A folk dance. (Albania).

Ajua. A traditional strategy game played with pebbles or seeds. (Kenya). *Also called* **Bao**.

Ajvar. A pepper and tomato spread that Macedonians make in early October and eat with bread. (Macedonia).

Aka. "Big brother." An Uzbek term used to address male strangers. (Uzbekistan).

Akam jirta? "How are you?" An Oromifaa greeting. (Ethiopia).

Akaryna. A traditional ceramic flute. (Belarus).

Akimbo. Placing one's hands on one's hips. Can show defiance, anger, or frustration. (Barbados).

Akory. "How are you?" A Malagasy greeting, popular in coastal areas. (Madagascar).

Akoumé. The Ewe word for a stiff porridge made of cornmeal and water and served with a spicy sauce of okra, spinach, and fish or meat. (Togo). *Also called* **Pâte**.

Aksakal. A "white-bearded" elder. (Turkmenistan).

Aksanti. "Thank you" in Swahili. (Congo).

Alaja. A woven camel-hair talisman. It is often tied to the steering wheel for good luck. (Turkmenistan).

Alambamento. A ceremony in which the prospective groom offers a bride-price to the bride's family and conditions of the marriage are discussed. (Angola).

Alaps. Lords. A position in the traditional social system that is now incorporated into the formal government. (Marshall Islands). *See also* **Irooj, Rijerbal**.

Al-ardah. A sword dance for men. This national dance is accompanied by drums and a poet who chants verses. (Saudi Arabia).

Ala yeke senge? "Are you OK?" Part of a common Sango greeting, it usually follows the phrase **Bara ala** or **Bala mo** (Greetings to you!). (Central African Republic).

Alba-ca-Zapada. Snow White, the granddaughter of Santa Claus. (Moldova). *See also* **Mos Craciun**.

Al-Badiyah. The common name for the Syrian Desert. (Syria).

Albarka. An Arabic term that credits **Allah** for food. A host's reply to an appreciative guest. (Guinea).

Alcapurrias. Fried plantain dough with a meat filling. A locally prepared variety of **Frituras**. (Puerto Rico).

Alchiki. A game similar to marbles, but played with dried sheep bones. (Kazakstan).

Alendo ndi mame. "Visitors are like dew." A Chichewa proverb that means a visitor's presence is short-lived and hence precious. (Malawi).

Al-haj. (Jordan). *See* **Hadj**.

Al-hajjah. (Jordan). *See* **Hadjia**.

Al hamdo lellah. (Jordan). *See* **Al hamdu lillah**.

Al-hamdu lilah, bahi. Arabic phrase meaning "Praise to God, very well"; it is a common response to **Kayf halak?** (Libya).

Alhamdul'illah. (Comoros). *See* **Al hamdu lillah**.

Al hamdu lillah. [NOTE: Spelling varies because it is a transliteration of Arabic.] An Arabic phrase meaning "Praise be to God" or "Thanks be to God." Used by Arabic speakers. (United Arab Emirates).

Al-hamdu lillah, zein. "Praise to **Allah**, well." An Arabic response to the greeting **Kayf halak?** (Oman).

Alikalo. Village chief. Has local power and settles village disputes. (Gambia).

Aliki. Traditional chiefs. *Aliki* still play a significant role in influencing island events. (Tuvalu).

Alikum essalam. The usual response to the greeting **Assalam alikum**. (Bahrain).

Aling. (1) A Pilipino title for an unmarried woman. Added before her given name. (Philippines). (2) A Pilipino title added before an elderly woman's name. (Guam).

Al-Isra walmi'raj. [NOTE: Muslim holidays are set according to the lunar calendar.] A Muslim holiday celebrating the occasion of Muhammad's ascension to the sky. (United Arab Emirates).

Al-jil. Contemporary Egyptian pop music with a more-educated audience appeal. (Egypt). *See also* **Shaabi**.

Aljotta. Fish chowder. (Malta).

Allah. The Arabic word for "God." Used in countries with Muslims or Arabic speakers..

Allahaısmarladık. A parting phrase used to ask for blessings from **Allah**. (Turkey). *See also* **Güle güle**.

Allah akbar. "God is great." Used to call faithful Muslims to prayer five times a day. (Mauritania).

Allah ghalib. "God is stronger." An Arabic phrase used to express hopes or intentions. (Tunisia). *See also* **Inshallah**.

Al-lahjah Al-Ordoniah. The Jordanian dialect of Arabic. It is considered to be the closest to classical Arabic. (Jordan).

Alles goed? "Is everything all right?" A common Dutch greeting. (Netherlands).

Alloco. Fried plantains eaten as a snack food. (Ivory Coast).

Almacenes. A Spanish term for neighborhood shops. (Argentina). *See also* **Kioskos**.

Al-Mahdi. An Arabic word for "guide." (Sudan).

Al Mawlid. (Algeria). *See* **Mouloud**.

Al-Mawlid. (Egypt). *See* **Mouloud**.

Al-mizmar. A traditional dance that features the oboe-like *al-mizmar* instrument. (Saudi Arabia).

Almuerzo. The Spanish word for "lunch." (Cuba).

Al-nay. A simple bamboo pipe. (Libya).

Alo. "Hi." A colloquial greeting used among urban youth. Others include **Olá** and **Oi**. (Mozambique).

Aloalo. Tall wooden poles that decorate tombs with carved figurative images and depictions of past events. (Madagascar).

Aloha. A Hawaiian greeting. It has many meanings depending on usage. (United States of America).

Alpaca(s). An animal similiar to a llama. Its wool is used for textiles. (Peru).

Alright. A common informal greeting. (Antigua and Barbuda, Saint Lucia).

Alright alright. A common greeting, as if to bypass asking and responding to "How are you?" (Jamaica). *See also* **Whaapun?**

Al-Salaam 'Alaykum. (West Bank and Gaza). *See* **Assalaam alaikum**.

Al-salamu 'alaykum. (Iraq). *See* **Assalaam alaikum**.

Al Tarawiah. Special prayers offered during the Muslim holiday of **Ramadan**. (United Arab Emirates).

Alta velocidad. A high-speed train. (Spain).

Althingi. Iceland's national assembly, one of the world's oldest. (Iceland).

'Alu a. Literally "You go." A response to the parting phrase **Nofo a**. (Tonga).

'Am. (Iraq). *See* **Aam**.

Amakuru? "How's the news?" A phrase that usually follows the initial greeting **Muraho**, **Mwaramutse**, or **Mwiriwe**. (Rwanda).

Amala. Yam flour. Can be used to make a stiff porridge. (Benin). *Also called* **Loubo**.

Amarillo. "Traffic official" in Cuban Spanish. The literal Spanish meaning is "yellow." (Cuba).

Amca. "Uncle." A Turkish term of address for an older man. (Turkey).

Ami. "Uncle." A title used after a man's given name. (Azerbaijan).

Amiga. "Friend." A feminine term of address. (Guinea-Bissau, Panama). *See also* **Amigo**.

Amigo. "Friend." A masculine term of address. (Guinea-Bissau, Panama). *See also* **Amiga**.

Amin Aleikum Salaam. "Come in peace." A response to the phrase **Salaam Aleikum**. (Niger).

Amiwo. Corn flour. Used to make a stiff porridge. (Benin). *Also called* **Wo**.

Ammo. The Arabic word for a paternal uncle. (West Bank and Gaza).

Ampesi. Boiled yams, plantains, or other root crops with sauce. (Ghana).

Amshee afé. "Go in peace." An Arabic parting phrase. (Chad).

Amto. The Arabic word for a paternal aunt. (West Bank and Gaza).

Amzhad. A single-stringed instrument often used to accompany poetry. (Morocco). *Also called* **Ribab**.

Andriamanitra. A supreme being of Malagasy indigenous beliefs. (Madagascar). *Also called* **Zanahary**.

Anesaty. (Syria). *See* **Aneseh**.

Glossary of Cultural Terms

Aneseh. [NOTE: Spelling varies because it is a transliteration of Arabic.] "Miss." An Arabic title used with the last name. (West Bank and Gaza).

Angisa. A head scarf that accompanies the **Koto** dress. (Suriname).

Angkor Wat. A Khmer temple built in the 12th century. It is the world's largest religious building and a cherished national symbol. (Cambodia).

Angling. Fishing. (England).

Ang pow. A red envelope with money given on special occasions such as New Year's, weddings, etc. (Singapore).

Anh. "Brother." A Vietnamese term used to address a man the same age as one's brother. (Vietnam).

A ni sogoma. "Good morning." A common Dioula greeting. (Burkina Faso).

An moho. "On you no evil." A Soninke greeting. (Mauritania). *See also* **Jam.**

Annyong? [NOTE: Spelling varies because it is a transliteration of Korean.] "Are you at peace?" A common greeting among children. (South Korea). *See also* **Annyong haseyo?, Annyong hashimnikka?**

Annyong haseyo? [NOTE: Spelling varies because it is a transliteration of Korean.] "Are you at peace?" A common greeting between peers or to subordinates. (South Korea). *See also* **Annyong?, Annyong hashimnikka?**

Annyong hashimnikka? [NOTE: Spelling varies because it is a transliteration of Korean.] "Are you at peace?" A common greeting used to show respect to a social superior. (South Korea). *See also* **Annyong?, Annyong haseyo?**

Anong balita? "What's new?" A common Pilipino greeting used among friends. (Philippines). *See also* **Ayos ba tayo 'dyan?**

Antara. An assortment of vertically placed flutes tied together. Used to play traditional music. (Peru). *See also* **Charango, Quena.**

Anyong? (North Korea). *See* **Annyong?**

Anyonghaseyo? (North Korea). *See* **Annyong haseyo?**

Anyonghashimnikka? (North Korea). *See* **Annyong hashimnikka?**

Any time is Trini time. Refers to the fact that Trinidadians often arrive well after an event starts, and being late is not considered rude. (Trinidad and Tobago).

Ao dai. A long traditional dress with front and back panels worn by women over satin trousers on special occasions. (Vietnam).

Apa. "Older sister." A Bangla term used to address an older woman. Can be added as a suffix or used by itself. (Bangladesh).

Apa khabar? "How are you?" A common Malay greeting. (Malaysia).

Aparima. A slow hula performed by the bride for the groom at their wedding feast. (French Polynesia). *See also* **Tamaaraa.**

Api. A hot drink made of corn, spiced with sugar and cinnamon. (Bolivia).

Apinun. "Good afternoon." A common Melanesian Pidgin greeting for acquaintances. (Papua New Guinea).

Apinun kaikai. "Afternoon food." The Melanesian Pidgin word for dinner. (Papua New Guinea).

Aqal. A cord that holds a headscarf in place. (Iraq).

Arachide. Peanut sauce. (Togo).

Arahaba. "Hello." A common Malagasy greeting. (Madagascar).

Araijem. "See you later." A common Armenian parting phrase between friends. (Armenia).

Arak. A traditional strong liquor that is served with Middle Eastern foods, except among devout Muslims. (Lebanon).

Arback. Living ancestral spirits. Part of traditional Kyrgyz beliefs. (Kyrgyzstan).

Ardha. A traditional dance involving the use of the sword. Accompanied by drums and poetry reading. (Kuwait).

Ardin. A harp used to accompany vocalists in traditional musical performances. (Mauritania).

Arefa. [NOTE: Muslim holidays are set according to the lunar calendar.] Feast of the Sacrifice. A Muslim holiday that commemorates Abraham's willingness to sacrifice his son. (Ethiopia). *Also called* **Eid al-Adha.**

Arepa(s). A cornmeal pancake. (Colombia, Venezuela).

Arequipe. Caramel sauce. (Colombia).

Ariary. The national currency. (Madagascar). *See also* **Franc.**

Aright. A common Scottish greeting. (Scotland).

Armudi stakan. Small pear-shaped glasses used to serve tea. (Azerbaijan).

Arrivée de l'Evangile. Missionary Day. Celebrated on 5 March. (French Polynesia).

Arros negre. Rice with calamari ink. (Spain).

Arroz con gandules y pernil. Rice with pigeon peas and roasted pig. (Puerto Rico).

Arroz con menestra. Rice with spicy beans, barbecued beef, and refried plantains. (Ecuador).

Arroz con pollo. Rice with chicken. (Colombia, Costa Rica, Ecuador, Panama, Puerto Rico).

Arroz de coco. Rice pudding with coconut and rum. (Colombia).

Arroz y frijoles. Rice and beans. A traditional staple food. (Cuba).

Asado. (1) A Spanish term for barbecue, a popular social event. (Argentina, Paraguay, Uruguay). (2) A Spanish term for grilled beef. (Uruguay).

Asalaam alaikum. (Comoros). *See* **Assalaam alaikum.**

Asalaam alaykum. (Syria). *See* **Assalaam alaikum.**

Asalaamu aleikum. (Somalia). *See* **Assalaam alaikum.**

Asalaha Bucha. An important Buddhist holiday. Set according to the lunar calendar. (Thailand).

Asamblea General. Uruguay's General Assembly. It consists of two houses: a 30-seat Chamber of Senators and a 99-seat Chamber of Representatives. (Uruguay).

Asante. Swahili for "Thank you." An adopted form. (Tanzania).

Aseeda. A thick porridge. (Sudan).

Ashak. A pasta dish. (Afghanistan).

Ashi. (1) "So long." A common parting phrase. (Bangladesh). (2) Female royalty. (Bhutan).

Ashugh. (Armenia). *See* **Ashugs.**

Ashugs. Poet-singers. (Azerbaijan).

Ashura. [NOTE: Spelling varies because it is a transliteration of Arabic. Also, Muslim holidays are set according to the lunar calendar.] A holiday during which Shi'ite Muslims reenact the suffering of the martyr Hussain, the grandson of Muhammad. (Afghanistan, Iraq, Syria). *See also* **Shi'i.**

Assalaam alaikum. [NOTE: Spelling varies because it is a transliteration of Arabic.] "May peace be upon you." A common greeting. It is usually answered with **Waalaikum assalaam.** Used in countries with large or predominantly Muslim populations..

As-salaam aleikum. (Oman). *See* **Assalaam alaikum.**
Assalaam alikum. (United Arab Emirates). *See* **Assalaam alaikum.**
Assalaamu alaikum. (Bangladesh). *See* **Assalaam alaikum.**
As-Salaamu 'Alaykum. (Saudi Arabia). *See* **Assalaam alaikum.**
As-Salaamu Alaykum. (Kuwait, Qatar). *See* **Assalaam alaikum.**
Assalaamu alaykum. (Yemen). *See* **Assalaam alaikum.**
Assalama Allekuhm. (Tunisia). *See* **Assalaam alaikum.**
Assalam Alaikum. (Jordan, Singapore). *See* **Assalaam alaikum.**
Assalam alikum. (Bahrain). *See* **Assalaam alaikum.**
Assalam Oualaikoum. (Morocco). *See* **Assalaam alaikum.**
Assalamu alaikum. (Indonesia). *See* **Assalaam alaikum.**
Assalamu alikum. Arabic greeting meaning "I offer you peace." (Libya).
Assemblée Nationale. The French term for National Assembly. (Gabon, Senegal).
Assembleia Nacional. The National Assembly. (Angola).
Ass'lama. An Arabic term for "Hello." (Tunisia).
Assura. (Bahrain, Kuwait). *See* **Ashura.**
Atangas. A violet, bitter fruit about the size of a golf ball. (Gabon).
A tel God tanki. "I give thanks to God." A Krio response to the greeting **Ow di bodi?** (Sierra Leone).
Até logo. "See you soon." A common parting phrase. (Brazil).
Atenteban. A wooden flute. (Ghana).
Athletics. Track-and-field. (Grenada, Jamaica, New Zealand).
Atlas. Colorful patterned silk. (Uzbekistan).
Attan. Originally a Pashtun dance, now common throughout Afghanistan. Performed at feasts and other celebrations. (Afghanistan).
Attaya. Green tea with sugar. (Gambia).
Auf Wiedersehen. "Until we meet again." A common German phrase. (Switzerland).
Aunt(ie). A term a younger person uses to address an older woman, even if they are not related. (Barbados, Gambia, Ghana, Guam, Guyana, Saint Kitts and Nevis, Saint Lucia, Sierra Leone, Uganda). *See also* **Uncle.**
Au revoir. "Good-bye." A common French parting term. (Canada, France, Luxembourg).
Aurora borealis. The northern lights. (Norway).
Ausgleich. A compromise that led to the establishment of a dual monarchy with Hungary. (Austria).
Aussies. Australians. (Australia).
Autobahn. Expressway or freeway. (Germany, Liechtenstein).
Autogare. A central gathering point in each city for "bush-taxis." (Niger). *See also* **Taxis de brousse.**
Autonomie Interne. A holiday that celebrates Tahitian self-rule. Celebrated on 29 June. (French Polynesia).
Avo tata. A wraparound cloth worn by women. The term is used in the south. In the north the terms used are **Bsawao** or **Sata.** (Togo).
Awa in Majel. Marshallese time. A concept that interpersonal relations are more important than time. Meetings and appointments begin when they start and not always at a specific hour. (Marshall Islands).
Aw lafia. "Go in peace." A Sara parting phase. (Chad).
Ayatollah. (Iran). *See also* **Shi'i.**

Ayaz Ata. The Kazak name for Grandfather Frost. At the beginning of a new year, he delivers gifts to children. (Kazakstan). *See also* **Dyed Morosz, Zhanga Zhyl.**
Aye. (1) "Yes." (Scotland). (2) An expression of surprise or shock. One can also say **Mama.** (Central African Republic).
Ayendi, ki kati? "I'm fine, what's up?" A Luganda response to the greeting **Ki kati?** (Uganda).
A'y go. "It goes." A Sranan Tongo response to a greeting such as **Fa waka?, Fa'y tan?,** or **Fa'y go?** (Suriname).
Aynalayin. "Darling." Often used by elderly Kazaks to call to children. (Kazakstan).
Ayos ba tayo 'dyan? "Is everything all right?" A common Pilipino greeting used among friends. (Philippines). *See also* **Anong balita?**
Ayubowan. "May you be blessed with the gift of a long life." A Sinhalese phrase that accompanies the traditional greeting of placing one's palms together in front of the chest and bowing the head slightly. (Sri Lanka).
Ayurvedic. Traditional medicine that stresses the use of herbs and natural cures. (Sri Lanka).
Ayyalah. A popular traditional dance in which the dancers reenact a battle scene. (United Arab Emirates).
Azmaris. Traveling singers. (Ethiopia).
Azulejo(s). Glazed tile widely used to decorate the floors, walls, and facades of buildings. (Portugal).
Azumi. The Hausa word for **Ramadan.** (Niger).
Ba-. A prefix used when referring to more than one person. (Botswana). *See also* **Batswana, Mo-, Motswana.**
Baba. (1) "Father." An Arabic term of address used by children. (Qatar). (2) "Father." A Sango and Zulu term of address for older males. (Central African Republic, South Africa).
Babai. A taro-like, starchy root crop. (Kiribati).
Babban sallah. [NOTE: Muslim holidays are set according to the lunar calendar.] "Big feast." A Muslim holiday that commemorates Abraham's willingness to sacrifice his son. Celebrated 40 days after the **Ramadan** feast. (Niger). *Also called* **Tabaski.** *See also* **Eid al-Adha.**
Babe. A social title added to an adult male's name to show respect. Pronounced "BAH-bay." (Swaziland).
Babi-taxis. Three-wheeled motor scooters. (Bangladesh).
Babu. Lying down to converse and propping one's head with a large stone, coconut, or windowsill. (Marshall Islands).
Baby fathers. Men who have several children by different women. (Jamaica).
Baby mothers. Women who have children by different men. (Jamaica, Saint Lucia).
Bac. (1) The baccalaureate exam that is taken at the end of 13 years of education. (Gabon). (2) "Uncle." A term used to address a man the age of one's father. (Vietnam).
Bacalao. Dried fish, usually cod. (Dominican Republic).
Bacalao con viandas. Boiled cod with cassava and potatoes. (Puerto Rico).
Bacalhau. Codfish, usually dried and salted. (Portugal).
Baccalaureat. A certificate of completion that Ivorian students receive after successfully completing seven years of secondary school. After receiving the certificate, students may then attend university, train to be a teacher, or learn a trade. (Ivory Coast).
Bachata. A popular folk dance accompanied by accordions, drums, horns, and **Guayano(s).** (Dominican Republic).

Glossary of Cultural Terms

Bachillerato. Three years of education that prepare students for college. (El Salvador).

Backhendl. Fried, breaded chicken. (Austria).

Bac si. "Doctor." A Vietnamese title. (Vietnam).

Bad eye. Staring someone in the eye. The gesture is used to display anger. (Saint Vincent and the Grenadines).

Badjan. Minibus used in Ivory Coast. (Ivory Coast). *See also* **Dyna, Gbaka.**

Bagaimana kabarnya? "How is your news?" A common verbal greeting. (Indonesia).

Baganda. Historically, the people of the Buganda Kingdom. Today, a person belonging to the Buganda ethnic group. (Uganda).

Baguettes. French bread. (Madagascar).

Bahala na. "Accept what comes and bear it with hope and patience." A common Pilipino expression. (Philippines).

Bahasa Indonesia. Indonesian, the official language. (Indonesia).

Bahasa Melayu. Malay, the official language. (Malaysia).

Bahini. "Younger sister." A Nepali term of address. (Bhutan, Nepal).

Bah kut teh. Chinese pork soup. (Malaysia).

Baho. Meat, vegetables, and plantains. (Nicaragua).

Baht. Thailand's national currency. (Thailand).

Bai. "Younger brother." A Nepali term of address. (Nepal).

Baiga. Traditional horseback competitions. (Kazakstan). *See also* **Kokpar.**

Baikay. "Older brother." A Kyrgyz title used to address a man older than the speaker. (Kyrgyzstan).

Baile de las tijeras. The term means "dance of the scissors," and includes both the dance and the music that accompanies it. The dance originated among the mountain people of Peru. (Peru).

Bairn. A Gaelic word meaning "baby." (Scotland).

Baisakh. The first month in the Nepali calendar **Bikram Samvat.** (Nepal).

Baisakhi. The New Year celebration in northern India. Also, the start of Punjab's harvest season. (India).

Baiza. A form of Omani currency. One thousand *baiza* equal one **Rial Omani**). (Oman).

Baja mar. Spanish for "shallow sea." The name of the Bahamas originates from this phrase. (Bahamas).

Bajans. Barbadians, the people of Barbados. (Barbados).

Bajella. Boiled beans. (Bahrain).

Bake. A small, flat bread that is fried instead of baked. (Trinidad and Tobago).

Bakes. Fried flour dumplings. (Montserrat).

Bakhour. The Arabic word for "incense." (Bahrain, Qatar).

Bakkala. Small shops that contain basic goods. (Kuwait).

Baklava. A layered pastry with syrup and a nut filling. (Albania, Bosnia and Herzegovina, Bulgaria, Turkey).

Baklawa. (Libya). *See* **Baklava.**

Bala. A type of xylophone. (Guinea-Bissau).

Balafon. A type of xylophone. (Burkina Faso, Ghana, Guinea, Ivory Coast).

Balalaica. A traditional two-piece safari suit. (Mozambique).

Bala mo. "Greetings to you." A common Sango greeting. One can also say **Bara ala.** (Central African Republic).

Balboa. Panama's national currency. (Panama).

Balendėlai. Stuffed cabbage leaves. (Lithuania).

Bali shani. "How are you?" A Bemba greeting to a superior. Shows more respect than **Muli Shani?** (Zambia).

Baloncesto. The Spanish word for "basketball." (El Salvador).

Balot. A fertilized duck egg with an embryo, sold by street vendors. (Philippines).

Bals. The Malagasy word for "dances." (Madagascar).

Baltmaize. Latvian word for "white bread." (Latvia).

Balutan. A plate of food to take home. Offered to guests as they prepare to leave. (Guam).

Balzāms. A thick herb and alcohol mixture. (Latvia).

Bambo. "Man." Placing the prefix "a-" before the name, *abambo*, would show respect. (Malawi).

Bambuco. The national song and dance. Originated in the Andes Mountains. (Colombia).

Bami. A Javanese noodle dish. (Suriname).

Bammy. Cassava bread. (Jamaica).

Banca. A local outrigger boat. (Philippines).

Bandoneón. A musical instrument similar to an accordion. (Argentina).

Bands. Groups of people in brightly colored costumes. They participate in holiday celebrations. (Barbados).

Bandura. A stringed musical instrument. The Ukrainian national instrument. (Ukraine).

Bandy. A sport similar to hockey. (Sweden).

Banian. A sleeveless shirt, worn by men. (Sri Lanka).

Banitsa. A layered pastry. (Bulgaria).

Banners. Local fiefs. (Mongolia).

Bansh. A boiled dumpling stuffed with diced meat, onion, cabbage, garlic, salt, and pepper. (Mongolia).

Banya. The Russian word for "sauna." (Kazakstan).

Bao. A strategy game played with pebbles or seeds on a carved-out board. (Kenya, Malawi, Tanzania).

Bapak. "Father." A respectful Indonesian term of address for older men. (Indonesia).

Bara ala. "Greetings to you." A common Sango greeting. One can also say **Bala mo.** (Central African Republic).

Bara ala kwé. "Greetings, everyone." A common Sango greeting for a large group. (Central African Republic).

Bara brith. Currant cake. (Wales).

Baraholka. An open-air market where clothes, shoes, and household goods are sold. (Kazakstan).

Bara lawr. A mixture of seaweed and oatmeal that is fried and then served with bacon. (Wales). *Also called* **Laver bread.**

Barambo. The Sango word for "stool." (Central African Republic).

Barangays. A region similar to a county. (Philippines). *See also* **Barrios.**

Barbie. Barbecue. (Australia).

Barev. "Let good be with you." An Armenian greeting used as a casual "Hello." The plural form, **Barevdzez**, signifies more respect and formality. (Armenia).

Barevdzez. (Armenia). *See* **Barev.**

Barika. A Dyula, term meaning "strength," as in "May the Lord put strength in this meat." Ivorians might say it after a meal. (Ivory Coast).

Baris gede. A male military dance. (Indonesia).

Bariza. A Shingazidja word that can be used before anything to form a greeting. (Comoros). *See also* **Bariza hazi?, Bariza husha, Bariza masihu.**

Bariza hazi? "How is work?" A common Shingazidja greeting. (Comoros). *See also* **Bariza.**

Bariza husha. "Good morning." A common Shingazidja greeting. (Comoros). *See also* **Bariza.**

Glossary of Cultural Terms

Bariza masihu. "Good evening." A common Shingazidja greeting. (Comoros). *See also* **Bariza.**

Barong. An embroidered shirt worn by men that hangs over the pants. (Guam, Philippines).

Barov gnas. "Go with peace." A formal Armenian parting phrase used for long separations. (Armenia). *See also* **Barov mnas.**

Barov mnas. "Stay with peace." A formal Armenian parting phrase used for long separations. (Armenia). *See also* **Barov gnas.**

Barrios. (1) The Spanish word for "neighborhoods." (Dominican Republic). (2) Small villages or suburbs. (Philippines). *See also* **Barangays.**

Barščai. Beet soup. (Lithuania).

Basi. A ceremony involving offerings, food, rice wine, and religious chanting by a holy person. (Laos).

Basmachi. A resistance movement against the government of the Soviet Union in the early 20th century. (Uzbekistan).

Basmachi(s). Small bands of fighters that resisted the Soviets. (Turkmenistan).

Basturma. Salted beef with a spicy coating. (Armenia).

Bateys. Sugarcane villages where many Haitian workers live. (Dominican Republic).

Batidos de fruta. Fruit shakes. (Venezuela).

Batik. A traditional type of fabric with hand-colored patterns made using a hot-wax process on dyed cloth. (Indonesia, Malaysia, Niger).

Bâton de manioc. A dough-like paste made from cassava. (Gabon).

Batono. "Sir." A Georgian term of address used with the first name. (Georgia).

Batrana. Older rural women. (Moldova).

Batsakatsi. Witches. They can be paid to place or remove a curse on someone. A traditional practice. (Swaziland). *See also* **Muti, Sangoma, Tinyanga.**

Batswana. "Tswana people." Also, citizens of Botswana, regardless of ethnicity. (Botswana). *See also* **Ba-, Mo-, Motswana.**

Baurua. A traditional canoe made from driftwood lashed together with coconut fibers. (Kiribati).

Bayan. A traditional instrument similar to the accordion. (Belarus).

Bea bilong Solomons. "Beer of the Solomons." Betel nut chewed with pepper leaf and lime. It is mildly intoxicating. (Solomon Islands).

Beaucoup. A French term meaning "many" or "much." (Gabon).

Becak. A pedicab. (Indonesia).

Bedu. The Bedouin people. (Kuwait, United Arab Emirates).

Begena. A lyre, a musical instrument. (Ethiopia).

Beh-thwa-ma-lo-leh? "Where are you going?" A common Burmese greeting. (Myanmar).

Beignets. Deep-fried, doughnutlike food. (Gabon, Niger).

Beijinhos. "Little kisses." A small kiss on each cheek given at greeting and parting among relatives and friends. (Portugal).

Belarusian ruble. Belarus's national currency. (Belarus).

Belembaotuyan. A gourd with a long neck and one string; the musician strikes the string with a stick. A traditional musical instrument played by older men. (Guam).

Belo. The Melanesian Pidgin word for "lunch." (Papua New Guinea).

Belum. The Indonesian word for "not yet." (Indonesia).

Benachin. Jollof rice. (Gambia).

Bendición. A word used by children in asking blessings of their parents and other relatives. (Dominican Republic). *See also* **Dios te bendiga.**

Benga. A type of contemporary dance music. It fuses traditional rhythms of the Luo ethnic group with modern instruments such as the electric guitar. (Kenya).

Berbere. A red hot pepper that is often used to spice **Wat(s)** or served separately with raw meat. (Ethiopia).

Beretitenti. The Kiribati word for "president." (Kiribati).

Ber ibuto aber? "Fine, and you?" A Luo response to the greeting **Ibuto aber?** (How did you sleep?). (Uganda).

Beritta. A traditional Maltese cap. (Malta).

Beryani. Rice with meat, a common lunch item. (Bahrain).

Bes. The Arabic word for "enough." (Saudi Arabia).

Besa. "Sworn truce." Adherents believe family honor, hospitality, and a patriarchal order are the basis of successful relationships. (Albania).

Besbarmak. (Kazakstan). *See* **Beshbarmak.**

Beshbarmak. A dish of noodles and meat eaten with the fingers. (Kyrgyzstan).

Besht. (Bahrain). *See* **Bisht.**

Beso-beso. A kiss on each cheek, given in greeting. (Philippines).

Bey. A title used after a man's given name. (Azerbaijan, Turkey).

-bhabi. "Wife of older brother." A Bangla suffix used as a term of address. A man adds the suffix to the name of his friend's wife. (Bangladesh).

Bhaku. A wraparound jumper worn by married Tibetan women. (Nepal).

Bharata Natyam. A classical Indian dance. (Singapore).

Bhinneka Tunggal Ika. "Diverse yet unified." Indonesia's motto. (Indonesia).

Bhoot. The Nepali word for "ghost." The Nepalese believe *bhoot* can cause disease, crop failures, or accidents. (Nepal). *See also* **Bokshi, Graha dasha, Pret.**

Bhoto Jatra. A great festival that takes place around April or May. (Nepal).

Bhuti. A social title added to a boy's name to show respect. (Swaziland).

Bica. A strong espresso-type coffee. (Portugal). *Also called* **Cimbalino.**

Bidayuhs. Land Dayaks. An indigenous people in Malaysia. (Malaysia).

Bife à cavalo com fritas. Meat with egg and french fries. (Brazil).

Bigos. A common dish consisting of sausage, mushrooms, and pickled cabbage. (Poland).

Bigote para arriba. The gesture of placing the thumb and index finger on the upper lip in an upward "V." Literally, "upward mustache." The gesture means "Everything is all right." (Uruguay).

Big up. "Hello." An informal phrase used among friends. (Saint Vincent and the Grenadines).

Biharis. Muslims who immigrated to Bangladesh from Bihar, India. (Bangladesh).

Bikhair al-hamdu lillah. "Good, praise be to God." A common response to the greeting **Kaif halak?** (United Arab Emirates).

Bikkhu. A Buddhist priest. (Laos).

Glossary of Cultural Terms

Bikman. "Big man," or leader. There is one in each village. (Papua New Guinea). *Also called* **Kukurai.**

Bikram Samvat. Nepal's calendar. The New Year takes place in mid-April. (Nepal).

Bikutsi. An indigenous musical style. (Cameroon).

Bili-bili. Millet beer. (Chad).

Bilo. A coconut shell used to drink **Yaqona.** (Fiji). *See also* **Tanoa.**

Biltong. A jerky-like meat snack. (Namibia, South Africa).

Bilum(s). A woven string bag used by men and women. (Papua New Guinea).

Bin. "Son of." An Arabic title combined with the father's name. (Bahrain, Oman, Singapore). *See also* **Ibn.**

Bindi. A red dot worn on the forehead by Hindu women. (India).

Bint. (Oman). *See* **Binti.**

Bint-al-sahn. A popular festive bread cooked in layers and served hot with clarified butter and warm honey. (Yemen).

Binti. "Daughter of." An Arabic title combined with the father's name. (Malaysia, Singapore).

Birr. Ethiopia's national currency. (Ethiopia).

Birria. Goat soup. (Mexico).

Biryani. Rice with meat and spices. (Pakistan, United Arab Emirates).

Biscuits. Cookies. (Australia, England, Mauritius, New Zealand, Scotland, Wales).

Bis eng aner Kéier. "See you later." A parting phrase used between friends and acquaintances. (Luxembourg). *See also* **Äddi, bis mar, Bis härno.**

Bis härno. "See you later." A parting phrase used between friends and acquaintances. (Luxembourg). *See also* **Äddi, bis mar, Bis eng aner Kéier.**

Bisht. A robe worn on formal occasions over the **Dishdasha.** (Kuwait, Oman).

Bism Allah. [NOTE: Spelling varies because it is a transliteration of Arabic.] A Muslim blessing meaning "In the name of God." (United Arab Emirates).

Bismi Allah. (Algeria). *See* **Bism Allah.**

Bismilla. (Turkmenistan). *See* **Bism Allah.**

Bissimilai. A blessing often used over food. It can be used in a variety of situations. (Gambia).

Bisslama. "Good-bye." A standard parting phrase. (Tunisia).

Bissm Allah. (Jordan). *See* **Bism Allah.**

Bissm Allah arrahman arrahim. "By the name of God, most gracious and most merciful." A blessing said before a meal. (Jordan).

Bite se? "How are things going?" A phrase that follows the initial greeting **Muraho.** (Rwanda). *See also* **Amakuru?, Ni meza.**

Bit of a dag. A phrase meaning "a humorous character." (New Zealand).

Black buns. A fruit cake on a pastry base. (Scotland).

Black cake. A cake for special occasions made with fruit that is soaked in brandy. (Guyana, U.S. Virgin Islands).

Black pudding. Blood sausage. (Antigua and Barbuda, Saint Kitts and Nevis).

Blancos. "Whites." The name of the conservative landowners during the civil war, which lasted from 1839 to 1851. (Uruguay). *See also* **Colorados.**

Bless. "To be blessed." A phrase used to say "good-bye." (Iceland).

Bless Bless. (Iceland). *See* **Bless.**

Blockos. A street dance. (Grenada).

Bloco. The Portuguese word for "group." (Brazil).

Bloemkoel. Cauliflower. (Netherlands).

Bloke. An Australian colloquialism meaning "guy." (Australia).

Blynai. Pancakes. (Lithuania).

Bo. A term Grand Comorians use when calling out to someone. It precedes the addressee's name. (Comoros).

Boa continuação. A Portuguese parting phrase meaning "Have a nice day." (Angola).

Boa noite. "Good evening." A Portuguese greeting. (Mozambique, Portugal).

Board bus. A truck-turned-bus with a canvas top and wood sides that can be chartered for special events. (Grenada).

Boa tarde. "Good afternoon." A Portuguese greeting. (Mozambique, Portugal).

Bocadillo. A sandwich. (Spain).

Bocce. An Italian game similar to lawn bowling. (Italy).

Bocci. A traditional form of outdoor bowling. (Malta).

Bochas. Lawn bowling. Often played by older men. (Argentina).

Boda boda. A "bicycle-taxi" with a padded passenger seat over the rear wheel, used to travel short distances. (Uganda).

Bodegas. Neighborhood grocery stores. (Cuba).

Bodhrán. A traditional Celtic drum. (Ireland).

Boerewors. Spiced sausage. (South Africa).

Boer(s). Dutch and Afrikaans word meaning "farmer." White colonists primarily of Dutch descent in southern Africa. (Botswana, South Africa).

Bøf. Hamburger steak with a brown sauce and fried onions. (Denmark).

Bogadi. The bride-price paid by the groom's family to the bride's family. (Botswana).

Bogobe. Porridge. Made from sorghum, maize, or millet. (Botswana).

Bogolan. "Mud cloth." Specially primed fabric painted with mud. (Mali).

Bohz ooi. Round tents. (Kyrgyzstan).

Boilin'. Fish boiled with green bananas and vegetables. (Saint Vincent and the Grenadines).

Bok. "Hi." A common Croatian greeting. (Croatia).

Bokshi. The Nepali word for "witch." The Nepalese believe *bokshi* can cause disease, crop failures, or accidents. (Nepal). *See also* **Bhoot, Graha dasha, Pret.**

Bolas criollas. A popular game in Venezuela, similar to lawn bowling. (Venezuela).

Bolero. A popular dance. (Cuba).

Bolimbisi. "Please" in Lingala. (Congo).

Bolívar. Venezuela's national currency. (Venezuela).

Boliviano. Bolivia's national currency. (Bolivia).

Bollo(s). Corn mush that has been boiled in the husk. (Panama).

Bolludagurinn. Cream Puffs Day, celebrated on the third Monday in February. (Iceland).

Bom apetite. "Enjoy." A Portuguese phrase that allows visitors to politiely decline joining in a snack or a meal. (Brazil).

Bomba. A rhythmic dance with African influences. (Ecuador, Puerto Rico).

Bombachas. Loose-legged pants. A traditional piece of clothing worn by Argentine cowboys. (Argentina, Uruguay).

Bombilla. A metal straw that has a screen at the bottom. Used to drink **Mate** or other herbal teas. (Argentina, Paraguay, Uruguay).

Glossary of Cultural Terms

Bom dia. "Good day." A Portuguese greeting. (Angola, Mozambique, Portugal).

Bom dia mama fulana. "Good morning, dear Mother." A polite greeting used to respectfully greet one's female elders. (Mozambique).

Bom dia papa fulano. "Good morning, dear Father." A polite greeting used to respectfully greet one's male elders. (Mozambique).

Bon. A traditional belief that good and evil spirits animate nature. The beliefs include charms, astrology, offerings to spirits, and worship at small shrines. (Bhutan).

Bon appétit. A French saying that means "Good appetite." (Bolivia, Cameroon, Ecuador, Netherlands, Slovakia, Slovenia).

Bondo. A secret society for women where they dance, share lessons about womanhood, and initiate new members by circumcision and other rituals. (Sierra Leone).

Bonġu. "Good morning." A Maltese greeting. (Malta).

Boniatos. Sweet potatoes. (Cuba).

Bonjou kouman ou ye? "Good day, how are you?" The most common Haitian Creole greeting. (Haiti).

Bonjour. "Good day." A common greeting. Used in French-speaking countries..

Bonjour tout le monde. "Hello, everyone." A French greeting used at larger gatherings. (Gabon).

Bonnet. The hood of a car. (New Zealand). *See also* **Boot**.

Bonsoir. "Good evening." A common greeting. Used in French-speaking countries..

Bonswa. "Good evening." A common Maltese greeting. (Malta).

Booshiyya. A black veil that covers the face. Only the most conservative women wear these. (Bahrain). *See also* **Burqa**.

Boot. The trunk of a car. (New Zealand). *See also* **Bonnet**.

Bo pen nyang. "Never mind." A common expression that characterizes Lao feelings toward life. (Laos).

Bor. The Lao word for "not yet." (Laos).

Borsak. Fried dough. (Kyrgyzstan).

Borsch. [NOTE: Spelling varies because it is a transliteration of Russian.] Vegetable soup. (Belarus, Russia, Ukraine).

Borscht. (Israel, Latvia, Moldova). *See* **Borsch**.

Bosanski lonac. A stew with cabbage and meat. (Bosnia and Herzegovina).

Bosnjak. An old surname meaning "Bosnian." A nonreligious term referring to Muslims. (Bosnia and Herzegovina).

Botaki. A feast. Feasts are held at a **Maneaba(s)**. (Kiribati).

Botondi. "Thank you" in Lingala. (Congo).

Boubou(s). A long cotton robe or an outfit with trousers and a long, loose top. Worn in African countries..

Bouillie. A millet-and-peanut porridge flavored with lemon and sometimes sugar. (Chad).

Boule. A heavy porridge formed into a ball and dipped in sauce. Chad's national food. (Chad).

Boules. A form of lawn bowling. (Belgium).

Boul-joul. Salted codfish sautéed in olive oil with vegetables. (Saint Vincent and the Grenadines).

Boumba. A loose blouse worn by women with a **Pagne(s)**. (Benin).

Bounce. A colloquialism meaning "car accident." (Grenada).

Bouneschlupp. Bean soup. (Luxembourg).

Boutou. A word of West African origins meaning "insult." (Saint Vincent and the Grenadines).

Bowgee. Sister-in-law. (Trinidad and Tobago).

Box food. Food eaten out of a box when one is away from home. Generally consisting of fish, chicken, or goat served over rice and **Peas**. (Jamaica).

Boyo. A coconut flavored pastry. (Suriname).

Boza. A malt-based drink; a typical breakfast beverage. (Bulgaria).

Braai(s). Barbecue, a traditional way of cooking. (Namibia, South Africa). *See also* **Potjiekos**.

Bracelet fighting. A traditional Sudanese sport. (Sudan).

Brae. A hill. (Scotland).

Brahma. The creator. One of three supreme gods of Hinduism. (Nepal). *See also* **Shiva, Vishnu**.

Brahma Vihara. Buddhism's four pillars of virtue. (Laos). *See also* **Karunna, Metta, Mudhita, Uppekkha**.

Brahmin(s). The highest of the four Hindi castes. Composed of intellectuals and priests. Also used to refer to the people of the caste. (India, Nepal). *See also* **Chaturvarna Vyavasta, Kshatriya, Shudra(s), Vaishya**.

Brânza. Sheep cheese. (Moldova).

Brasa. (Suriname). *See* **Abrazo**.

Bratwurst. "Grilled sausage" in German. (Switzerland).

Brazilero. A language that is a mixture of Spanish and Portuguese. It is spoken in northern border towns. (Uruguay). *Also called* **Portuñol**.

Breek. A thin fried dough stuffed with an egg, cooked vegetables, and tuna. (Tunisia).

Briani. Rice and vegetables with a mixture of meat, chicken, or fish and a number of spices. (Mauritius).

Bringue. A weekend singing and drinking party that lasts until early morning. (French Polynesia).

Broadsheets. A type of newspaper that is more serious than a tabloid. (England).

Brochette. A type of food similar to a shish kebab. (Burkina Faso, Niger).

Broken English. An English-based creole. (Barbados, Grenada).

Brother. A term used to address males of the same age, regardless of relationship. (Ghana, Sierra Leone).

Brujería. Witchcraft. Practiced by small groups. (Cuba).

Bryndzové halušky. Small dumplings with processed sheep cheese. The Slovak national dish. (Slovakia).

Bsawao. A wraparound cloth worn by women. The term is used in the north. (Togo). *Also called* **Sata**. *See also* **Avo tata**.

Bua. "Hello." A common Mende greeting. (Sierra Leone).

Buai. Betel nut. (Papua New Guinea).

Bub. The Marshallese word for "pandanus." (Marshall Islands).

Bubu. A long, loose-fitting shirt with open collar, worn over pants. (Mozambique).

Bubuti. A verbal agreement or request that cannot be turned down. The word is never used lightly. (Kiribati).

Budoh mongoi. "Come and eat." A common greeting on the outer islands of Yap, Chuuk, and Pohnpei. (Micronesia).

¡Buenas! A common casual Spanish greeting. (Belize, Costa Rica, Guatemala, Panama).

¡Buenas noches! "Good evening." A common greeting. Used in Spanish-speaking countries..

¡Buenas tardes! "Good afternoon." A common greeting. Used in Spanish-speaking countries..

¡Buen día! "Good day." A popular Spanish greeting used in the morning. (Argentina, Uruguay).

Glossary of Cultural Terms

¡Buenos días! "Good day." A common greeting used in the morning. Used in Spanish-speaking countries..

Buen provecho. "Enjoy your meal." A Spanish phrase used to express appreciation or gratitude for the meal. Used in Latin American Spanish-speaking countries..

Buia. A raised platform with a thatched roof but no walls. Used to entertain visitors. (Kiribati).

Buibui. A large black shawl, worn by women on the island of Zanzibar. (Tanzania).

Buitenvrouw. "Outside woman." Surinamese men in common-law relationships often have a *buitenvrouw*, which may be a short-term mistress or a more formal partner (with children) over several years. (Suriname).

Bula! "Health." The most common way to say hello. Pronounced "MBOOLA." (Fiji).

Bumiputras. "Sons of the soil." A term to describe the Malays and indigenous groups together. (Malaysia).

Bună. "Good." A Romanian greeting used by women. (Romania).

Bunad. A traditional costume that is specific to each region. (Norway).

Bună dimineata. "Good morning." A common Romanian greeting. (Romania).

Bună seara. "Good evening." A common Romanian greeting. (Romania).

Bună ziua. "Good day." A common Romanian greeting. (Moldova, Romania).

Bundesrat. The Federal Council. The upper house in the legislature. (Austria, Germany).

Bundestag. The Federal Assembly. The lower house in the German legislature. (Germany). *See also* **Bundesrat.**

Bundesversammlung. The Austrian Parliament with two houses, the **Bundesrat** and the **Nationalrat**. (Austria).

Bunge. The National Assembly. (Kenya, Tanzania).

Bunraku. Japanese puppet theater. (Japan).

Buns. Cupcakes. (England).

Bun That Luang. A weeklong festival in November at a temple housing a relic of Buddha. (Laos).

Buonasera. "Good afternoon" or "Good evening." A common Italian greeting. (Italy).

Buongiorno. "Good morning." A common Italian greeting. (Italy).

Bure. The traditional Fijian home. It is usually built of local hardwood, a thatched roof, and woven floor covers. (Fiji).

Burek. (1) A meat pie. (Bosnia and Herzegovina). (2) A meat- or cheese-filled pie. (Macedonia).

Burékas. A pastry filled with cheese and spinach. (Israel).

Burkha. (Qatar). *See* **Burqa.**

Burns Suppers. Banquets that honor poet Robert Burns on his birthday, 25 January. (Scotland).

Burqa. [NOTE: Spelling varies because it is a transliteration of Arabic.] (1) A veil worn by conservative women that covers the bridge of the nose and cheeks. (Bahrain, Kuwait, Oman, Pakistan, United Arab Emirates). (2) A head-to-toe covering worn by women. (Afghanistan). *Also called* **Chadiri.**

Busetas. A Spanish term for minibuses used in rural areas of Ecuador. In urban areas they are called **Colectivos.** (Ecuador).

Bush gardens. A vegetable garden owned and worked by an entire family. (Niue).

Bushido. The Code of the Warrior, which stressed honor, courage, politeness, and reserve. (Japan).

Bush meat. Snake, monkey, porcupine, etc.; a delicacy in the south. (Cameroon).

Bush tea. An herbal tea. (Montserrat, Saint Kitts and Nevis, U.S. Virgin Islands).

Bush trucks. A colloquialism for "four-wheel-drive trucks." (Guyana).

Bush walking. A colloquialism for "hiking." (Australia).

Busi dresi. Forest medicines typically linked to traditional religious rituals. (Suriname). *See also* **Oso dresi.**

Buuz. A steamed dumpling stuffed with diced meat, onion, cabbage, garlic, salt, and pepper. (Mongolia).

Buzkashi. A game similar to polo. Played with a goat or headless calf. The teams try to carry the carcass from one spot to another and then back to the original spot. (Afghanistan, Tajikistan).

Bwana. "Boss." A term of address for persons in authority. (Malawi).

Byarozavik. Birch sap. A common drink. (Belarus).

Bye ch'nam, pram-bye kai, m'pai t'gnai. The three-year, eight-month, twenty-day rule of the **Khmer Rouge.** During this rule, nearly two million people were killed or died of starvation and disease. (Cambodia).

Byen mèsi, e ou? "Well, thank you, and you?" The proper creole response to the greeting **Bonjou kouman ou ye?** (Haiti).

Byolko. A dark, long loaf of bread. (Kyrgyzstan).

Byrek. A pastry with vegetables, cottage cheese, or minced meat. (Albania).

Bytromme. Town drum, a native musical instrument. (Denmark).

Byvai. "Bye." An informal Belarusian parting phrase. (Belarus).

Cabanes à sucre. Some Canadian maple-syrup farms are known by this name, which means "sugar cabins." (Canada).

Cabidela. Chicken with rice. (Portugal).

Cacana mboa. Pumpkin leaves. (Mozambique).

Cachupa. The Caboverdian national dish. A stew made of corn and meat or fish with manioc (cassava) that is cooked slowly in water. (Cape Verde).

Cadance. Lively dancing music from the French Antilles. (Saint Lucia).

Ca dao. Unaccompanied vocal Vietnamese music. (Vietnam).

Café com leite. Coffee with milk. (Brazil).

Cafézinho. Black coffee. (Brazil).

Cai luong. A type of musical comedy developed in the early 1900s. (Vietnam).

Cajón. An athletic dance performed in Lima by those of African descent. (Peru).

Caldeirada. Fish stew. (Portugal).

Caldo de bola. Plantain-based soup with meat and vegetables. (Ecuador).

Caldo verde. Soup made with potatoes, cabbage, and olive oil. (Portugal).

Caliente. The Spanish word for "hot." Refers to temperature rather than spiciness. (Mexico). *See also* **Picante.**

Callaloo. (1) A green, leafy plant similar to spinach. (Grenada). (2) A local plant that is cooked with coconut milk, pepper, and pumpkin. (Trinidad and Tobago).

Calling by. An Irish colloquialism for "visiting." (Ireland).

Call name. A colloquialism for "nickname." (Grenada).

Calulú A dish made of dried fish, vegetables, and palm oil. (Angola).

Glossary of Cultural Terms

Calypso. A form of social commentary invented in Trinidad and sung by performers called calypsonians. (Trinidad and Tobago).

Calypsonians. Performers of calypso music. (Trinidad and Tobago).

Cambute. A Costa Rican folk dance. (Costa Rica).

Cameros. The 15th-century Portuguese word for "prawns" and root of the word *Cameroon*. (Cameroon).

Camogie. The women's version of **Hurling**. A game played on a soccer-type field with wooden sticks and a small leather ball. (Ireland).

Campesino(s). A Spanish word meaning "farmers." Inhabitants of rural areas; often poor. (Bolivia, El Salvador, Panama, Paraguay, Peru).

Campo. The Spanish word for "countryside." (Dominican Republic).

Cana. Cane alcohol. (Guinea-Bissau).

Canadienses. A Spanish term for "Canadians." (Chile).

Cançoillotte. The French name for a type of soft cheese. The Luxembourgish term is **Kachkéis**. (Luxembourg).

Candombe. An African-influenced rhythm played with three drums. (Uruguay).

Canh ca. Fish and vegetable soup. (Vietnam).

Canteens. Cafés. (Ukraine).

Canton(s). (1) "County." Several villages led by a local traditional chief. (Chad). (2) A political region. (Luxembourg, Switzerland).

Capulana. A wraparound skirt worn by married women. It is a symbol of respect. (Mozambique).

Caribana. The local word for Carnival. (Antigua and Barbuda).

Carnaval. A three-to-five-day festival celebrated by parades, dances, and parties prior to Ash Wednesday. Celebrations are often marked by riotous excess in the days before Lent, a season of fasting and penitence. *Carnaval* is also spelled "carnival" in several countries. Celebrated in countries with high Roman Catholic populations..

Carnaval de Québec. A two-week period in February filled with activities. (Canada).

Carne guisado. A dish made of stewed meat with tomatoes and spices. (Panama).

Car park. A minibus station. (Guyana).

Carretas. Oxcarts. (Costa Rica).

Carry. A colloquialism for "bring." (U.S. Virgin Islands).

Căruță. Horse- or donkey-drawn carts. (Romania).

Casabe. Cassava baked into rounds of crisp cracker bread. (Dominican Republic).

Casă de piatră. "House of stone." A wish given to newlyweds, meaning a long and durable marriage. (Romania).

Casado. A meal of rice, beans, plantains, meat, and salad or eggs. (Costa Rica).

Casareep. A cassava extract. (Guyana).

Cassave. Bread made from manioc. (Haiti).

Castañuelas. Castanets. (Spain).

Castellano. Spanish. (Bolivia, Chile, El Salvador, Paraguay).

Catholicos. A supreme patriarch. The head of the Armenian Apostolic Church. (Armenia).

Čau. "Ciao." A common Czech parting phrase. (Czech Republic).

Causé! Literally, "speak." Mauritian Creole for "How are you?" (Mauritius).

Ça va? "How's it going?" or "Everything OK?" A common French greeting. (Canada, Central African Republic, France).

Ça va aller, Dieu est grand. French term meaning "Everything will be all right, God is great," it expresses the typically easy-going Ivorian attitude about life. (Ivory Coast).

Cavadee. A Hindu holiday that celebrates the feat of the god Idoumban, who carried two mountain peaks on his shoulders. (Mauritius).

Cavaquinho. The ukulele. (Cape Verde).

Cawl. A traditional Welsh soup. (Wales).

Cayes. Small islands. Pronounced "KEYS." (Belize).

Cazuela de ave. Chicken soup. (Chile).

Ceau. "Ciao." A Romanian greeting used among young people. (Romania).

Ceif. A common attitude. To act spontaneously for enjoyment and without regard for consequences like cost and time. (Bosnia and Herzegovina).

Ce mai facetz. "How do you do?" A Romanian greeting. (Moldova).

Cembalo. The Romanian term for "harpsichord." (Moldova).

Cena. The evening meal. Consists of a light snack. (Dominican Republic, Mexico).

Centres de santé. The French term for "health centers." (Guinea).

Cepelinai. Meat cooked inside a ball of potato dough, served with a special sauce. (Lithuania).

C'est doux. A French phrase meaning "It's sweet," some Ivorians might say this after a meal to compliment the cook and thank the host. (Ivory Coast).

Ćevapčići. Small elongated, minced meatballs eaten with chopped onions. (Serbia and Montenegro).

Ceviche. Raw fish seasoned with lemon and vinegar or lime. (Ecuador, Peru).

CFA franc. Communauté Financière Africaine franc (African Financial Community franc). The currency used in francophone African countries. (Benin, Burkina Faso, Cameroon, Central African Republic, Chad, Equatorial Guinea, Gabon, Guinea-Bissau, Ivory Coast, Mali, Niger, Senegal, Togo).

Chacabana. A white shirt, typically embroidered with four pockets. Worn over dark trousers. (Dominican Republic).

Chadiri. A head-to-toe covering worn by women. (Afghanistan). *Also called* **Burqa.**

Chador. A long dress worn over regular clothing by women in public. (Iran, Lebanon).

Chaebol. Huge conglomerates that dominate the South Korean economy. (South Korea).

Chai. Tea. (Afghanistan, Kyrgyzstan).

Chaihana. A building or tent used as a gathering place. (Azerbaijan).

Chakijane. A rabbit trickster who is the subject of children's stories. (Swaziland).

Chalga. A mix of Turkish, Romany, and Serbian music. (Bulgaria).

Ch'alla. Blessing of any material possession or event by offering symbolic articles and alcohol to **Pachamama** and **Achachila**. Part of indigenous beliefs. (Bolivia).

Chamorrita. An unaccompanied female chorus singing in harmony. (Guam).

Changua. Potato-and-egg soup. (Colombia).

Chao. "Hi." An informal French greeting. (Switzerland).

Glossary of Cultural Terms

Chao. (1) "Good-bye." A common Spanish parting phrase. (Chile, Colombia, El Salvador, Panama, Venezuela). (2) "Greetings." A common Vietnamese greeting. (Vietnam).

Chap. A Scottish term of address for males. (Scotland).

Chapan. A long coat worn by village men. Kept closed with a bandana-type tie around the waist. (Tajikistan). *Also called* **Joma.** *See also* **Chorsi.**

Chapati. Flat bread. (Kenya, Pakistan, Uganda).

Chapines. A colloquial term for Guatemalans as a group. (Guatemala).

Chaponlar. Long, open, quilted robes usually worn by older men. (Uzbekistan).

Charamuscas. Frozen fruit juice in plastic bags. (Honduras). *Also called* **Topogios.**

Charango. A musical instrument similiar to a guitar. (Bolivia, Peru).

Charreada. A Mexican form of rodeo. (Mexico).

Charshab. A long piece of cloth wrapped loosely around a skirt. A traditional piece of clothing worn by rural women. (Azerbaijan).

Chat. (Ethiopia). *See* **Khat.**

Chattel houses. Wooden homes set on coral stone 3 or 4 feet above ground for better air circulation. (Barbados).

Chaturvarna Vyavasta. The Brahmin classification philosophy. A four-class system. (India). *See also* **Brahmin(s), Kshatriya, Shudra(s), Vaishya.**

Chaty. The Czech term for "cottages." (Czech Republic).

¡Chau! "Good-bye." A common Spanish parting phrase. (Argentina, Bolivia, Uruguay).

Chau. "Nephew." A Vietnamese term used by a man to refer to himself when speaking to an older woman of his mother's generation. (Vietnam). *See also* **Co.**

Chau, chau. (Bolivia). *See* **¡Chau!**

Chaya. Traditional baggy drawstring pants with many extra folds between the legs that provide ventilation in the heat. Worn by Wolof and Fula men. (Gambia).

Check on. Dropping in at a friend's house to see how he or she is doing. (U.S. Virgin Islands).

Chee khel shoomo? "How are you?" A common Tajik greeting. (Tajikistan).

Cheers. A common parting phrase. (Scotland).

Chef. "Chief." A term of address for men, used to show respect. (Chad).

Chenchu'le. The Chamorro word for "support." People provide *chenchu'le* to family members in need. May take the form of money, time, or donations of food or drink. (Guam).

Cheongsam. (1) A traditional Chinese dress. (Singapore). (2) A traditional red and gold Chinese wedding dress. (Hong Kong).

Chereh. A form of millet **Couscous.** (Gambia).

Chévere. A Spanish colloquialism meaning "very well" or "cool." (Venezuela).

Chhetris. (India). *See* **Kshatriya.**

Chia. Baggy pants worn by men. (Mauritania).

Chibalo. A policy of forced labor. Workers were paid low wages and forced to work in fields to generate exports for the Portuguese. (Mozambique).

Chibuku. Bars that sell sorghum beer. (Botswana).

Chibwabwa. Finely cut and boiled pumpkin leaves cooked with salt and oil. (Zambia).

Chicha. (1) A fruit drink. (Chile, Panama). (2) A home-brewed alcoholic drink made from corn. (Bolivia).

Chicharias. Bars that serve **Chicha.** Indicated by a white flag hanging outside the establishment. (Bolivia).

Chicken cafriela. Chicken cooked in lemon, onions, and butter. (Guinea-Bissau).

Chicken souse. A spicy chicken stew. (Bahamas).

Chico. The Spanish word for "small." (Costa Rica, Mexico).

Chimurenga. Combines traditional Shona music with electric instruments. Draws from political and social themes. (Zimbabwe).

Chimwali. "Sister." A common Chichewa term of address among young adults and teens. (Malawi).

Chimwene. "Brother." A common Chichewa term of address among young adults and teens. (Malawi).

Chinellas. "Flip-flops." Worn by women and men, especially in rural areas. (Nicaragua).

Ching Ming. A festival that honors the dead. (Hong Kong, Mauritius).

Ching tzuo. "Please sit." A common Mandarin Chinese greeting. (Taiwan).

Chipa. Hard cheese bread. (Paraguay).

Chiperoni. A damp fog or heavy cloud cover. (Malawi).

Chips. French fries. (Australia, Montserrat).

Chirimía. The Spanish word for "oboe." (Costa Rica).

Chirmole. Soup. (Belize).

Chishlik. Skewered meat or fish. (Turkmenistan).

Chitenge. A colorful wraparound skirt. (Zambia).

Chitenje. A 7-foot-long African-print cotton fabric worn by women. Protects dresses from dust and dirt. Can also be used as a baby carrier or for a variety of other purposes. (Malawi).

Chivas. Minibuses. (Panama).

Chivito. Steak and egg with cheese and mayonnaise. (Uruguay).

Chocalat. A dark, gravy-like sauce made from **Odika.** Literally "chocolate" in French. (Gabon).

Choi. Tea. (Tajikistan, Uzbekistan).

Choihona. A tearoom or café. (Uzbekistan).

Choku. A religious ceremony. (Bhutan).

Choli. A tight blouse worn by Hindu women. (Mauritius).

Cholitas. Rural women. (Bolivia).

Cholo. A blouse worn by women. (Nepal).

Ch'ondogyo. An indigenous Korean religion. An eclectic combination of Buddhist, Confucian, and Christian beliefs. (North Korea). *Also called* **Tonghak.**

Choops. Sucking air through the teeth. Expresses irritation. (Antigua and Barbuda).

Choopsing. (Saint Lucia). *See* **Choops.**

Chops. Small engraved stamps. (Taiwan).

Chorba. A soup made with small pieces of meat and vermicelli. (Algeria).

Chorek. The traditional Turkmen bread, which is cooked in an outdoor clay oven. (Turkmenistan).

Chorsi. A bandana-type tie used as a belt. (Tajikistan). *Also called* **Meeyonband.** *See also* **Chapan.**

Chouriços. A salted or smoked sausage made from various meat pieces. (Portugal).

Chpabs. Moral proverbs that are passed down through oral recitations. (Cambodia).

Christian. A practicing member of a Protestant church. (Jamaica).

Glossary of Cultural Terms

Christmas Second Day. Boxing Day. Celebrated on 26 December. (U.S. Virgin Islands).

Chronia polla. "May you live many years." A traditional Greek holiday greeting. (Greece).

Chuch'e. The idea of self-reliance. (North Korea).

Chun Ben. An important Buddhist festival, during the last week of September, is marked on behalf of the dead and one's own salvation. (Cambodia).

Chung Yeung. A festival that honors the dead. (Hong Kong).

Chu nôm. A unique writing system developed using Chinese characters to write Vietnamese words. (Vietnam).

Chuños. Freeze-dried potatoes used in soups or side dishes when rehydrated. (Bolivia).

Chups. (Antigua and Barbuda). *See* **Choops.**

Chupse. (Barbados). *See* **Choops.**

Churra gerte. Crushed peanuts and rice boiled together. (Gambia).

Churrasco. (1) A barbecue with a variety of meats. (Brazil). (2) A piece of grilled chicken. Cooked on a charcoal stove at food stands. (Angola).

Churros. A batter made of flour, salt, and water, deep-fried, and sprinkled with sugar. (Spain).

Ch'usŏk. Harvest Moon Festival, held in the fall. Family members visit ancestral tombs to offer food in honor of the dead. (South Korea).

Chuups. (U.S. Virgin Islands). *See* **Choops.**

Chyny. The Kyrgyz word for "bowls." (Kyrgyzstan).

Chyr bau le meiyou? "How are you?" A common Chinese greeting. (Taiwan).

Ciamar a tha thu. "How are you?" A Gaelic greeting. (Scotland).

Čiao. "Hello" or "good-bye." A common Slovak greeting. (Slovakia).

Ciao. "Good-bye." A common parting phrase. (Bosnia and Herzegovina, Bulgaria, Italy, Luxembourg).

Ciaw. "Bye." A common parting phrase. (Malta).

Cibaeños. Residents of the Cibao Valley. (Dominican Republic).

Çiftelia. A type of mandolin with two strings. A unique Albanian instrument. (Albania).

Čika. "Uncle." A term of address used for older men who are not relatives. (Serbia and Montenegro).

Cimbalino. A strong espresso-type coffee. (Portugal). *Also called* **Bica.**

Cinco de Mayo. Celebrates an 1862 victory over the French. Celebrated on 5 May. (Mexico).

Cirene. Bulgarian feta cheese. (Bulgaria).

Ç' kemi? "What's up?" A common Albanian greeting. (Albania).

Clarsach. A small harp. (Scotland).

Co. "Aunt." A Vietnamese term used to address an older woman of one's mother's generation. (Vietnam). *See also* **Chau.**

Coal pots. Clay ovens. (Antigua and Barbuda).

Cobo. A gesture involving clapping cupped hands three or more times. Practiced when accepting a gift and on other occasions. Pronounced "THOMBO." (Fiji).

Cobra-Grande. A huge snake in Brazilian folklore. It lives in the Amazon and frightens people by changing shape. (Brazil).

Cobza. A short-necked lute. A folk instrument. (Romania).

Cocido. (1) A hot drink consisting of **Mate**, cooked sugar, and milk. (Paraguay). (2) Castilian soup. (Spain).

Coco. (1) A common term of address used for grandmothers. (Comoros). (2) A musical instrument similar to a maraca. Accompanies the **Séga** dance. (Mauritius).

Cocoa tea. Hot chocolate. (Saint Kitts and Nevis, Saint Lucia).

Cofradías. Religious fraternities dedicated to a particular saint. (Guatemala).

Co khoe khong? "How are you doing?" A popular Vietnamese greeting. (Vietnam).

Colada morada. A thick drink made with berries, sweet spices, and purple flour. (Ecuador).

Coladeira. A music and dance style that is upbeat and joyful. (Cape Verde).

Colcannon. A cooked mixture of potatoes and cabbage. A local delicacy. (Ireland).

Colectivos. Minibuses. (Colombia, Ecuador).

Colegios. Private schools. (Dominican Republic).

Collège. Junior high. (Chad, Comoros).

College. High school. (New Zealand).

Collèges. Secondary education. (France).

Colmados. Neighborhood markets. (Dominican Republic).

Colón(es). Costa Rica's national currency and El Salvador's former currency before switching to the U.S. dollar. (Costa Rica, El Salvador).

Colorados. "Reds." The name given to the urban liberals during the civil war from 1839 to 1851. (Uruguay). *See also* **Blancos.**

Comadre. A Spanish term of address used for women in the countryside. Literally it means "friend." (Dominican Republic).

Combies. Minibuses. (Botswana, Namibia, South Africa).

Come around. A colloquialism for "come over." (New Zealand).

Comersants. Traveling merchants. (Uzbekistan).

Comfort room. A colloquialism for "bathroom." (Philippines).

Com hare. "Come here" in the accent of a St. Thomian. (U.S. Virgin Islands). *See also* **Com heh, Com yah.**

Com heh. "Come here" in the accent of a Cruzian. (U.S. Virgin Islands). *See also* **Com hare, Com yah.**

Comida. The main meal of the day. (Cuba, Dominican Republic).

Comment allez-vous? "How are you?" A standard French greeting phrase. (France). *See also* **Ça va?**

Commune. A political division of a **Canton(s)**. (Luxembourg).

Como está? "How are you?" A Portuguese greeting. (Angola, Mozambique).

¿Cómo estai? "How are you?" An informal Spanish greeting used in Chile. (Chile).

¿Cómo estás? "How are you?" A common informal greeting. Used in Spanish-speaking countries..

Como estás? (Cape Verde). *See* **Como está?**

¿Cómo está (usted)? "How are you?" A common greeting. Used in Spanish-speaking countries..

¿Cómo has pasado? A los tiempos que nos vemos. "How have you been? It has been a long time." A Spanish greeting used after a long absence. (Ecuador).

¿Cómo le va? "How's it going?" A common Spanish greeting used among the youth. (Nicaragua).

Como vai? "How are you?" A common Portuguese greeting. (Brazil).

Compadre. A Spanish term of address used for men in the countryside. Literally it means "friend." (Dominican Republic).

Glossary of Cultural Terms

Compañero/Compañera. "Comrade." A Spanish term used to address strangers. Masculine *compañero*, feminine *compañera*. (Cuba).

Complet. Pants and a matching shirt jacket that buttons to the collar. (Central African Republic, Chad).

Complimento. A party that takes place at the bride's home after the wedding feast. (Guam).

Comptoirs Français du Pacifique franc. French Polynesia's national currency. (French Polynesia).

Com yah. "Come here" in the accent of a Cruzian. (U.S. Virgin Islands). *See also* **Com hare, Com heh.**

Confianza. The Spanish word for "trust." (Dominican Republic).

Congee. A porridge-like rice dish. (Hong Kong).

Congreso Nacional. The Honduran National Congress. (Honduras).

Conkies. Cornmeal, coconut, pumpkin, raisins, sweet potatoes, and spices steamed in a banana leaf. (Barbados).

Con permiso. A Spanish phrase meaning "with your permission," used to excuse oneself when passing between conversing individuals. (Argentina, Mexico, Venezuela).

Conquistadores. Spanish explorers who battled and conquered the indigenous people. (Honduras, Nicaragua).

Contribuição. A special celebratory meal at which guests are asked in advance to bring food or drinks (or money to pay for them). (Angola).

Cook-up rice. A dish with coconut milk, rice, meat or fish, and almost anything the cook has on hand. (Guyana).

Cook-ups. Informal get-togethers with friends. (Saint Vincent and the Grenadines).

Cool-drink. Any soft drink or juice. (Namibia, South Africa).

Coolin' out. Standing shoulder deep in the water and chatting with a group. (U.S. Virgin Islands).

Córdoba. The Nicaraguan currency. (Nicaragua).

Cornetto. A cream-filled croissant. (Italy).

Coro. A Luo term for a traditional strategy board game played with seeds or stones. (Uganda). *Also called* **Omweso.**

Corps de gars. An open-air structure where rural men socialize and work together. (Gabon).

Corrida de torros. A bull fight. (Spain).

Corridos. A traditional form of music in which the songs tell stories. (Mexico).

Corte. A wraparound skirt worn by rural Mayan women. (Guatemala).

Costa. The dry coastal plain. (Peru).

Costeños. Ecuadorian coastal inhabitants. Considered to be cosmopolitan, open, and liberal; generally are the businesspeople. (Ecuador). *See also* **Serranos.**

Cou cou. The Bajan national dish, made of cornmeal and okra. (Barbados).

Couscous. A pasta-like semolina often cooked with vegetables and meats. (Algeria, Burkina Faso, Mauritania, Morocco, Tunisia, West Bank and Gaza).

Couscousi. (Libya). *See* **Couscous.**

Couscousi bil-bosla. A dish consisting of pasta with sautéed onions. (Libya).

Cousin. A term of address used for relatives and friends. (Central African Republic, Guinea).

Cozido à Portuguesa. A mixture of meats with potatoes, rice, and vegetables. (Portugal).

Crab in a crab bucket. A phrase that compares a person to a crab trying to escape from a bucket but failing because other crabs keep pulling it down. The phrase relates to the tension between the desire to improve one's situation and the pressure from others not to act above one's station in life. (Bahamas).

Criollo. People who are of mixed indigenous and European heritage. (Bolivia).

Crook. A colloquialism used to describe a person who is unwell. (Australia).

Croque-monsieur. Toasted ham and cheese on bread. (France).

Crubeens. Pig feet; a local delicacy. (Ireland).

Crumbles. Fruit pies. (Scotland).

Csárdás. A courting dance that has two parts (slow then fast); the national dance. (Hungary).

Cuatro. A small guitar. (Venezuela).

Cueca. A traditional dance of courtship. It is the national dance of Chile. (Bolivia, Chile).

Cuisine. The French word for "kitchen." (Gabon).

Cumbia. A Latin dance. (Colombia, Costa Rica).

Cumpleaños de quince. A girl's 15th birthday. The most important birthday, celebrating the end of childhood. (Argentina).

Cum-rum. Small family-owned shops. (Grenada).

Curandeiros. Traditional healers. (Angola). *Also called* **Kimbondeiros.**

Curandero/a. (Peru). *See* **Curanderos.**

Curanderos. Native healers. The singular forms are masculine *curandero*, feminine *curandera*. (Dominican Republic).

Curta. Colorful traditional Tajik dresses. (Tajikistan).

Cusa. Squash filled with meat and rice. (Kuwait).

Cutarras. Leather sandals worn by men. (Panama).

Cutting down the tall poppies. A colloquialism for "bringing down people of power and influence to the common level." (Australia).

Cuy. Roast guinea pig. (Ecuador).

Cycles. Phases within primary and intermediate schools. (Bahrain).

Cymraeg. The Welsh language. (Wales).

Cześć. A common Polish greeting among friends. (Poland).

Da. An Ewe term children use to address their mothers. (Togo).

Dabkah. A traditional dance performed with handkerchiefs and accompanied by the pounding of feet. (Lebanon, West Bank and Gaza).

Dab Shiid. "Starting Fire." The ancient Persian New Year celebration. (Somalia).

Dacha(s). The Russian word for a "summer cottage." (Kazakstan, Kyrgyzstan, Russia, Ukraine).

Dada. (1) "Sister." A respectful term of address used to address an older female. (Benin). (2) A Mina term children use to address their mothers. (Togo). (3) A term Imazighen use to show respect to male elders, including siblings. (Algeria).

Daddy. A term of address a younger person will call an older man even if they are not related. (Saint Lucia).

Dagit. A skirt-and-blouse outfit worn by younger women. (Gambia).

Dahl. (1) Lentils. (Bhutan, Sri Lanka). (2) Curried chickpeas. (Grenada).

Dai. "Older brother." A term of address used instead of names or titles. (Nepal).

Dáil The Irish House of Representatives. (Ireland).

Dair. Somalia's season of short rains. Lasts from October to November. (Somalia).

Glossary of Cultural Terms

Dairies. Convenience stores. (New Zealand).

Daiza. "Aunt." A common term of respect added to a female formal acquaintance's name. (Turkmenistan). *See also* **Gelneje, Hanum.**

Daje. An Albanian term used for an uncle who is one's mother's brother. (Albania).

Daju. "Older brother." A Nepali term of address. (Bhutan).

D'akujem. A Slovak phrase used to express gratitude. (Slovakia).

Dal. A spicy soup. (Bangladesh).

Dalasi. The Gambia's national currency. (Gambia).

Dal bhaat. White rice and lentil soup. (Nepal).

Dalits. "Downtrodden." A collective group that is composed of two of India's classes, scheduled castes (SC) and scheduled tribes (ST). In the past, they were referred to as "untouchables." (India).

Damask. Woven textiles made in Damascus. (Syria).

Dame. A game similar to checkers, often played by Ivorian men and boys. (Ivory Coast).

Dan bau. A single-stringed instrument used to play traditional music. (Vietnam).

Dancehall. A popular form of Jamaican music that incorporates elements of reggae, disco, and rap. (Barbados, Jamaica, Saint Vincent and the Grenadines).

Danke, nein. "Thank you, no." A German phrase that allows a person to politely decline an offer. (Austria).

Dan tranh. A multiple-stringed instrument used to play traditional music. (Vietnam).

Dan vong co. A modified guitar used to play traditional music. (Vietnam).

Danwei. Mandarin Chinese for "work group." (China).

Danza puertorriqueña. A popular form of music for singing and dancing. (Puerto Rico).

Da pabachennya. "Good-bye." A formal Belarusian parting phrase. (Belarus).

Dara'a. (1) A long, draping robe in white or blue. (Mauritania). *Also called* **Boubou(s).** (2) A traditional dress. (Kuwait).

Dara surwal. Traditional Nepali attire worn by men. Includes tight, thin cotton pants and a flowing, knee-length cotton tunic. (Nepal).

Darbuka. An hourglass shaped drum. (Libya).

Dari mana? "Where are you coming from?" A phrase that usually follows an initial greeting. (Indonesia).

Dariy. "Nothing." A typical Yapese response to the greeting **Mogethin.** (Micronesia).

Dar vueltas. A Spanish phrase meaning "to take walks." Groups of youths in Bolivia walk around a central plaza while making eye contact and flirting as part of the initial dating process. (Bolivia).

Dasain. (Bhutan). *See* **Dashain.**

Dash. A common social gesture whereby people show their appreciation for kindnesses rendered them. For example, a market woman might add extra fruit to a purchase. (Ghana).

Dashain. [NOTE: Spelling varies because it is a transliteration of Nepali. Also, Hindu holidays are based on the phases of the moon.] A Hindu holiday that celebrates the inevitable triumph of virtue over evil. (Nepal).

Dashiti. A small top or short-sleeved shirt worn by rural men in casual settings. (Benin).

Dasho. A social rank comparable to that of a knight. (Bhutan).

Dastarkhan. "Spread." A table filled with food, candy, bread, drinks, and more. (Kazakstan).

Dav. A common Danish greeting. Pronounced "DOW." (Denmark).

Daw. "Aunt." A term used to address older women, regardless of relationship. (Myanmar).

Day does run 'til night catch it. A Bajan proverb meaning "Whatever you do will catch up with you in the end." (Barbados).

Dayi. "Uncle." A common Azeri term of address used after a man's given name. (Azerbaijan).

Ddok. Pounded rice cake. (South Korea).

Deara. A delicate cloth, worn by women at home, with holes for the arms and head, and a half-slip underneath. (Yemen).

Debka'. A group dance in which men hold hands in a circle and dance to the beat of a drummer and flute player. Traditionally performed at weddings. (Iraq). *See also* **Tabbal, Zummar.**

Debkah. Dances that are accompanied by a rhythmic stomping of feet. (Jordan).

Debs. An Irish graduation ball similar to the high school prom in the United States. (Ireland).

Dedo. Mush made of cornmeal, millet, or buckwheat. (Nepal).

Deel. A traditional Mongol gown or tunic worn by men and women. (Mongolia).

Deepavali. [NOTE: Spelling varies because it is a transliteration of Hindi. Also, Hindu holidays are set according to phases of the moon.] Festival of Lights, which celebrates the triumph of light over darkness. Celebrated in countries with Hindu populations. (Malaysia, Singapore).

Deepawali. (Sri Lanka). *See* **Deepavali.**

De facto marriage. A common-law marriage. (Australia).

Defunción. A three-day Fang celebration to honor the passing of the dead, which occurs four to six months after the death. (Equatorial Guinea).

Déjeuner. The French word for "lunch." (France).

Děkuji. The Czech phrase for "thank you." (Czech Republic).

Denar. Macedonian currency. (Macedonia).

Dendê. The Portuguese word for "palm oil." (Brazil).

Dendiko ba. Colorful traditional shirts worn by older women. (Gambia). *Also called* **Grandmbuba.**

Departamentos. Geographical and political regions similar to provinces or states. (Colombia, Honduras, Nicaragua, Paraguay, Peru, Uruguay).

Départements. Administrative divisions of France. Overseas divisions have representatives in the French government as well as some local autonomy. (France).

Derija. The Arabic word for "dialect." (Morocco, Tunisia).

Desayuno. The Spanish word for "breakfast." (Cuba, Dominican Republic).

Descanso. A midday break. (Bolivia).

Dessan. A mixture of poetry and singing that tells a story of a folk hero. (Turkmenistan).

Deus Volunte. "God willing." A parting phrase used by older or rural people. (Saint Kitts and Nevis).

Deutsche Mark. Germany's national currency prior to the euro. (Germany).

Devali. (Guyana). *See* **Deepavali.**

Dewan Negara. The Malay Senate. (Malaysia).

Dewan Perwakilan Daerah. The House of Regional Representatives. (Indonesia).

Glossary of Cultural Terms

Dewan Perwakilan Rakyat. The House of Representatives, Indonesia's unicameral parliament. (Indonesia).

Dewan Rakyat. The Malay House of Representatives. (Malaysia).

Dhal. Lentil soup with rice. (Fiji).

Dhananbaad. "Thank you." (Bangladesh, Fiji).

Dharma. (1) The Hindi word for "light." (Mauritius). (2) Buddhist doctrine. (Bhutan).

Dholak. A drum. (Pakistan).

Dhoti. A large piece of cloth wrapped around the waist. Traditional Indian attire worn by men. (India).

Dhow. Sailboat. (Bahrain, United Arab Emirates).

Dhuku. A headscarf worn by rural women. (Zimbabwe).

Dhul al-Hijjah. The month in the Islamic lunar calendar in which the **Hajj** to Makkah takes place. (United Arab Emirates).

Día de la Amistad. Friendship Day. Celebrated on 30 July. (Paraguay).

Día de la Raza. Day of the Race. Columbus Day. Celebrates the indigenous roots of Latin America. Celebrated on 12 October. (Chile, Colombia, Costa Rica, Guatemala).

Día del Mar. Sea Day. Celebrated on 23 March. (Bolivia).

Día de los Muertos. Day of the Dead. Celebrates life while honoring the dead. Celebrated 1 to 2 November. (Mexico).

Día de los Reyes. Day of Kings. Celebrated on 6 January. (Dominican Republic).

Dia Dhuit. "God to you." A typical Irish-language greeting. (Ireland).

Dia is Muire duit. "God and Mary to you." A typical Irish-language response to the greeting **Dia Dhuit**. (Ireland).

Di dau day? "Where are you going?" A common Vietnamese greeting used between friends. (Vietnam).

Didgeridoo. A 5-foot-long wooden Aboriginal instrument blown to produce a distinctive resonating sound. (Australia).

Didi. "Older sister." A term of address used instead of names or titles. (Nepal).

Did-o-bazdid. The Farsi term for "visiting." (Iran).

Diet. (1) The Japanese legislative power. (Japan). (2) The lower house of the Polish Parliament. (Poland). *Also called* **Sejm.**

Dimije. Long, wide, traditional Turkish pants. (Bosnia and Herzegovina).

Dim sum. Chinese dumplings. (Hong Kong, Malaysia, Singapore).

Dinar. The national currency of various countries. (Algeria, Bahrain, Jordan, Kuwait, Libya, Serbia and Montenegro, Sudan, Tunisia, West Bank and Gaza).

Dios le pague. "God will repay you." A common Spanish expression of thanks for an invitation or gift. (Ecuador).

Dios te bendiga. "May God bless you." A Spanish phrase. (Dominican Republic).

Director. A professional title, meaning "director," used to address strangers. Masculine *director*, feminine *directora*. (Chile).

Direh. A long, billowing dress worn over petticoats. (Somalia).

Dirham. Morocco and the United Arab Emirates's national currencies. (Morocco, United Arab Emirates).

Dirndl. A traditional dress with an apron. (Austria).

Dirndlkleider. Traditional dresses with gathered waists and full skirts, worn with an apron. (Germany).

Dishdasha. A long robe worn by men. (Iraq, Kuwait, Oman, United Arab Emirates). *Also called* **Kandurah.**

Divali. (Mauritius, Trinidad and Tobago). *See* **Deepavali.**

Dīvāns. A living room couch that folds out into a bed. (Latvia).

Diwali. (Bhutan, Fiji, India). *See* **Deepavali.**

Diwaniyah. A separate part of a house or compound where the male host and his male guests relax, converse, eat, drink tea or coffee, watch television, and listen to music. The term may also refer to a large gathering hosted by a political candidate at which he outlines his platform. (Kuwait).

Diyan lang. "There, only." A typical Tagalog response to the greetings **Saan ka pupunta?** and **Saan ka galing?** (Philippines).

Djambia. A curved dagger. (Yemen).

Djedje? "How? How?" A common informal greeting used on the island of Anjouan. (Comoros).

Djeli. Praise singers. (Burkina Faso). *Also called* **Griots.**

Djelleba. The national garment. A hooded caftan worn by men and urban women. (Morocco).

Djembe. A large goatskin-covered drum. (Gambia, Guinea).

Djerma. A textile art that has fabric strips sewn together forming geometric patterns. (Niger).

Doamna. "Mrs." A Romanian title used by adults for all but close friends and relatives. (Moldova).

Dobar dan. "Good day." A common Serbo-Croatian greeting. (Bosnia and Herzegovina, Serbia and Montenegro).

Dober dan. "Good day." A common Slovene greeting. (Slovenia).

Dober den. "Good day." A Bulgarian greeting. (Bulgaria).

Dober tek. "Good appetite." A Slovene wish made before eating. (Slovenia).

Dober večer. "Good evening." A common Slovene greeting. (Slovenia).

Dober vetcher. "Good evening." A Bulgarian greeting. (Bulgaria).

Dobra dan. "Good day." A common Croatian greeting. (Croatia).

Dobra vecer. Macedonian for "Good afternoon." (Macedonia).

Dobra večer. "Good evening." A common Croatian greeting. (Croatia).

Dobro jutro. "Good morning." A common Serbo-Croatian and Slovene greeting. (Bosnia and Herzegovina, Croatia, Slovenia).

Dobro utro. "Good morning." A common greeting. (Bulgaria, Macedonia).

Dobro vecer. "Good evening." A common Serbo-Croatian greeting. (Bosnia and Herzegovina).

Dobroye utro. "Good morning." A common Russian greeting. (Russia).

Dobrú chut. "Good appetite." A Slovak wish made before a meal. (Slovakia).

Dobrý deň. "Good day." A formal Slovak greeting. (Slovakia).

Dobry den. "Good day." A common Czech greeting. (Czech Republic).

Dobry dien. "Good day." A common Russian greeting. (Russia).

Dobry dzen'! Yak spravy? "Hello! How are you?" A common Belarusian greeting. (Belarus).

Dobryj den'. "Good day." A common Ukrainian greeting. (Ukraine).

Dobry vecher. "Good evening." A common Russian greeting. (Russia).

Dobry wieczór. "Good evening." A common Polish greeting. (Poland).

Doce de coco. A snack made of coconut and sugar. (Cape Verde).

Doce de leite. A snack made of milk, sugar, and lemon. (Cape Verde).

Doganym. "Sibling." A term of address used with equals and younger acquaintances. (Turkmenistan). *See also* **Jigim**.

Dohl pouri. Thin bread with meat and curry sauce inside. (Mauritius).

Doi moi. The Vietnamese economic policy of "renovation." Characterized by economic restructuring, more private enterprise and other market-oriented policies, and more open international trade. (Vietnam).

Doira. A drum-like tambourine. A traditional Uzbek musical instrument. (Uzbekistan).

Dollard Des Ormeaux. Many French-speaking Canadians celebrate this holiday instead of Victoria Day on the third Monday in May. While Victoria Day honors England's Queen Victoria, *Dollard Des Ormeaux* celebrates a battle hero from Québec's early days. (Canada).

Dolma. Grapes or cabbage leaves stuffed with meat, cracked wheat, greens, and spices. (Armenia).

Dolmuşes. Shared taxis. (Turkey).

Dolo cabarets. Local beer stands where both men and women gather for drink, food, and conversation. (Burkina Faso).

Doma. Betel nut. (Bhutan).

Dombra. A two-stringed instrument similar to a mandolin. (Kazakstan).

Dominsoara. "Miss." A Romanian title used with the family name for all but close friends and relatives. (Moldova).

Dom kultury. "House of culture." A community recreation center. (Russia).

Domnul. "Mister." A Romanian title used with the family name for all but close friends and relatives. (Moldova).

Domoda. Peanut butter stew. (Gambia).

Don. (1) A Spanish title used with a male's first name to show respect. Used in Spanish-speaking countries.. (2) A robe. (Turkmenistan).

Doña. A Spanish title used with a female's first name to show respect. Used in Spanish-speaking countries..

Dona. "Lady." A term of address used as a sign of respect. (Cape Verde).

Dong. Vietnam's national currency. (Vietnam).

Doo doo. Someone who looks good. (Trinidad and Tobago).

Do parana. "Good afternoon." A common Bari greeting. (Sudan).

Do pure. "Good morning." A common Bari greeting. (Sudan).

Dorood. "Greetings." A typical Farsi greeting. (Iran).

Dorood-bar-to. "Greetings to you." The proper response to the Farsi greeting **Dorood**. (Iran).

Doručak. The Serbian word for "breakfast." (Serbia and Montenegro).

Dost. The Uzbek word for "friend." Specifically, a very close friend. (Uzbekistan).

Do svidaniya. "Good-bye." A formal Russian parting phrase. (Belarus).

Dot. Gifts that a groom must give to the bride's family when they get engaged and when they marry. (Gabon).

Do te shihemi. "See you later." A common Albanian parting phrase. (Albania).

Dóttir. The Icelandic word for "daughter." (Iceland).

Doubles. Popular fast-food Indian dish which consists of fried dough stuffed with chickpeas and hot sauce. (Trinidad and Tobago).

Doucana. A dish with coconut, sweet potatoes, flour, sugar, and spices, served with spicy **Saltfish**. (Antigua and Barbuda).

Dovga. Rice mixed with yogurt and herbs. (Azerbaijan).

Do videnia. "Good-bye." A formal Slovak parting pharse. (Slovakia).

Do vidjenja. "Good-bye." A Croatian parting phrase. (Bosnia and Herzegovina, Croatia).

Dovijdane. "Till I see you again." A common Bulgarian parting phrase. (Bulgaria).

Do widzenia. "Good-bye." A common Polish parting phrase. (Poland).

Drachma. Greece's national currency prior to the euro. (Greece).

Drago mi je. "I am pleased." A Serbian expression used upon introduction. (Serbia and Montenegro).

Dragstors. The Serbian word for "drugstores." (Serbia and Montenegro).

Dram. Armenia's national currency. (Armenia).

Dramnyen. A lute. (Bhutan).

Draughts. A game similiar to checkers. (Antigua and Barbuda, Barbados, Grenada).

Dreamtime. According to Aboriginal belief, the time when ancient ancestors created the land and living things. (Australia).

Dreich. A word for "dull." (Scotland).

Dressers. People who staff dispensaries and provide first aid. (Tuvalu).

Driglam namzha. A traditional code of etiquette. (Bhutan).

Droog. The Russian word for "friend." Specifically, a very close friend. (Uzbekistan).

Drug. "Comrade." A Serbo-Croatian term of address for men. (Bosnia and Herzegovina).

Drugarice. "Comrade." A Serbo-Croatian term of address for women. (Bosnia and Herzegovina). *See also* **Gospodijica, Gospodin, Gospodja.**

Du. The familiar "you" form of address in German. (Liechtenstein).

Dub. A style of music in which disc jockeys rap street poems. (Grenada, Montserrat, Saint Lucia).

Duduk. An oboe carved from apricot wood. The Armenian national instrument. (Armenia).

Duendes. According to legend, little elves that live in the jungle and play tricks on people. (Guam).

Duff. Pudding. (Bahamas).

Duglas. A group of people descended from East Indians and Africans. (Grenada).

Dugutigi. A village chief. (Mali).

Duka. An informal shop. (Tanzania).

Dulceaţă. Fruit preserves. (Romania).

Duma. A 450-seat house in the Federal Assembly. (Russia).

Dumela. Literally, "I see you." A Sotho greeting meaning "hello." (South Africa).

Dumela Rra/Mma, O tsogile jang? "Greetings, sir/madam, how did you wake?" A common adult Setswana greeting. (Botswana).

Dundun. The "talking drum." Its tones can be understood as words. (Nigeria).

Glossary of Cultural Terms

Dupalar. Squarish hats with a traditional design that identifies the wearer's home region. (Uzbekistan).

Dupatta. A scarf worn by women. (Pakistan).

Durbakkah. An earthenware drum. (Jordan).

Durchlaucht. "Your Serene Highness." A German phrase used to address the Liechtenstein prince. (Liechtenstein).

Dussehra. A Hindu holiday that celebrates the triumph of good over evil. (India).

Dvorets kultury. "Palace of Culture." A community recreation center. (Russia).

Dyed Morosz. The Russian name of Grandfather Frost. At the beginning of the year, he delivers gifts to children. (Kazakstan, Russia). *See also* **Ayaz Ata, Noviy Gohd, Zhanga Zhyl.**

Dyna. Minibus used in Ivory Coast. (Ivory Coast). *See also* **Badjan, Gbaka.**

Dzèkounmè. A cornmeal mixture stirred into boiling tomato sauce and eaten with fried meat, chicken, crab, or fish. (Togo).

Dzhorgosalysh. Horseback races characterized by the gait known as a pace. Popular for betting. (Kyrgyzstan).

Dziękuję. The Polish phrase for "thank you." (Poland).

Dzień dobry. "Good day." A common Polish greeting. (Poland).

Dzongda. A person who has broad authority to implement and enforce government programs at the district level. (Bhutan).

Dzongkhag. A district in the Bhutanese government. (Bhutan).

Dzongs. Monastic fortress complexes built in the 17th century. Today they serve as government centers. (Bhutan).

E aa koe na? "What are you doing?" or "How are you?" A casual Tuvaluan greeting. (Tuvalu).

Eba. Gari boiled in water and served as a side dish. (Benin).

Echar una zorrita. (1) A Spanish phrase meaning "to throw a little fox." (2) A Venezuelan colloquialism that means "to take a nap." (Venezuela).

École de Base. Basic Education, grades 1 to 6. (Tunisia).

École primaire. French for "primary school." (Comoros).

Ecuavolley. Ecuadorian volleyball. Played with a heavy ball and three players on each side. (Ecuador).

Edep. A quality referring to politeness, graciousness, modesty, hospitality, respect toward elders and guests, and responsibility toward family. (Turkmenistan).

Edje. "Hello." A Shingazidja greeting used between social equals. (Comoros).

Educación básica. "Basic education." A three-year program following elementary school for youth ages 12 to 15. (El Salvador).

Eduskunta. The Finnish Parliment. (Finland).

Eet smakelijk. "Eat deliciously." An expression used to begin a meal. (Netherlands).

E fano koe ki fea? "Where are you going?" A common Tuvaluan greeting. (Tuvalu).

Efes. The Turkish name for the city of Ephesus. (Turkey).

Eh. (1) A Canadian phrase used in similar ways to the phrases "Ya know" and "Isn't it?" (Canada). (2) Expresses disbelief when used with the gesture of tossing one's head to the side. (Rwanda).

Ei. "Hi." A Tahitian greeting used when passersby are not close enough for a handshake. (French Polynesia).

Eid al Adha. (Bahrain, Oman, Saudi Arabia, Somalia). *See* **Eid al-Adha.**

Eid al-Adha. [NOTE: Spelling varies because it is a transliteration of Arabic. Also, Muslim holidays are set according to the lunar calendar.] Feast of the Sacrifice. A Muslim holiday that commemorates Abraham's willingness to sacrifice his son. Celebrated in predominantly Muslim countries. (Iraq, Jordan, Kuwait, Libya, Qatar, Syria, United Arab Emirates, Yemen). *Also called* **Aid al Kebir, Eid Arafat.**

Eid al-Fitr. (Iraq, Ivory Coast, Jordan, Kuwait, Libya, Qatar, Syria, United Arab Emirates, Yemen). *See* **Aid al Fitr.**

Eid al Fitr. (Bahrain, Guinea, Oman, Saudi Arabia, Somalia). *See* **Aid al Fitr.**

Eid Arafat. Feast of the Sacrifice. A Muslim holiday that commemorates Abraham's willingness to sacrifice his son. (Yemen). *Also called* **Eid al-Adha.**

Eid el Adha. (Eritrea). *See* **Eid al-Adha.**

Eid el Fitr. (Eritrea). *See* **Aid al Fitr.**

Eid-el-Fitre. (Gambia). *See* **Aid al Fitr.**

Eid-el-kabir. (Gambia). *See* **Aid al Kebir.**

Eid-i-Milad-un-Nabi. (Pakistan). *See* **Mouloud.**

Eid Milad el-Nabi. (Eritrea). *See* **Mouloud.**

Eid-ul-Adha. (Mauritius). *See* **Eid al-Adha.**

Eid ul-Adha. (Ghana, Lebanon). *See* **Eid al-Adha.**

Eid-ul-Azha. (Bangladesh, Pakistan). *See* **Eid al-Adha.**

Eid-ul-Fitr. (Bangladesh, Mauritius, Pakistan, Trinidad and Tobago). *See* **Aid al Fitr.**

Eid ul-Fitr. (Ghana, Lebanon). *See* **Aid al Fitr.**

Ei Iaora. "Hi." A Tahitian greeting used when passersby are not close enough for a handshake. (French Polynesia).

Eingyi. A short-collared shirt worn by Burmese men. Accompanies a **Taikpon** and a **Longyi.** (Myanmar).

Eisteddfod. A national Welsh festival held the first week of August. It features competitions in music, drama, literature, and art. (Wales).

Ejay. "Older sister." A Kyrgyz title used to address a woman older than the speaker. (Kyrgyzstan).

Ekalesia Niue. A local denomination related to Congregationalism; an offspring of the London Missionary Society. (Niue).

Ekalesia Tuvalu. The Christian Church of Tuvalu. (Tuvalu).

E karo. "Good morning." A common Yoruba greeting. (Benin).

Ekushe. A political holiday on 21 February that honors six people killed in a 1952 political protest. (Bangladesh).

El Congreso Nacional. The Bolivian National Congress. (Bolivia).

El desayuno. Spanish for "breakfast." (Spain).

El Fitr. (Mauritania). *See* **Aid al Fitr.**

El gaucho Martín Fierro. Argentina's national epic poem. Describes the life of a cowboy. (Argentina). *See also* **Gaucho(s).**

El hadj. (Niger). *See* **Hadj.**

Elhamduli Allah. (Algeria). *See* **Al hamdu lillah.**

Elinize sağlik. "Bless your hand." A Turkish phrase used to compliment the cook. (Turkey).

El Intelaka. A Muslim holiday that celebrates the anniversary of the first day of Fatah resistance. (West Bank and Gaza).

El interior. "The interior." The area of land located outside the Panama Canal Zone. (Panama).

El Loco. "The Madman." A nickname for Abdalá Bucaram because of his flamboyant personality. He won the 1996 presidental elections. (Ecuador).

El Mouled. (Tunisia). *See* **Mouloud.**

El pato. A Spanish word meaning "the duck." Argentina's national sport is nicknamed el pato because the ball game used to be played with a leather stuffed duck. (Argentina).

El pesebre. The Spanish phrase for "the nativity." (Colombia).

Glossary of Cultural Terms

El Shabka. "Big Feast." A wedding celebration held at hotels or large homes. (West Bank and Gaza).

El trópico. Wet, hot, forested lowlands found in the east and northeast of Bolivia. (Bolivia). *Also called* **Llano(s).**

Ema datsi. A hot curry of red chilies and farmer's cheese. (Bhutan).

Emahiya. (Swaziland). *See* **Lihiya.**

EmaKhandza embili. Tribes present in the region now known as Swaziland when the Swazi people migrated there in the mid-1700s. (Swaziland).

EmaSwati. "People of Mswati." The Swazi people. (Swaziland).

Empanadas. Meat, vegetable, or cheese turnovers. (Argentina, Chile, Colombia, Costa Rica, Ecuador, Paraguay).

Empanadas de horno. Meat turnovers with beef, hard-boiled eggs, onions, olives, and raisins. (Chile).

Enah. "Yes." Meaning "hello." A Machushi response to the greeting **Morogeh koman honah.** (Guyana).

Enchiladas. Tortillas filled with meat and covered in a chile sauce. (Mexico).

Endemin neh? "How are you?" An Amharic phrase used to greet males among friends and peers. (Ethiopia).

Endemin nesch? "How are you?" An Amharic phrase used to greet females among friends and peers. (Ethiopia).

Endlini kaGogo. "Grandmother's hut." The best and most highly respected place on the homestead, usually offered to overnight guests. (Swaziland).

E noho ra. "Stay well." A Maori expression commonly used to reply to the phrase **Haere ra.** (New Zealand).

Ensalada chilena. Tomato-and-onion salad served chilled. (Chile).

Entrik. The Armenian word for "dinner." (Armenia).

Epos. Tajik historical or legendary poems. (Tajikistan).

Equib. A savings club. (Ethiopia).

Erythrea. The Greek word for "red" from which Eritrea derived its name. (Eritrea).

Escabeche. Onion soup. (Belize).

Escudo. Cape Verde's national currency. (Cape Verde).

Esh. Boiled millet flour. (Chad).

Esha. The Arabic word for "supper." (Bahrain).

Eshloanak. "How are you?" A common Arabic phrase used to greet men. (Bahrain, Kuwait).

Eshloanich. "How are you?" A common Arabic phrase used to greet women. (Bahrain, Kuwait).

Español. The Spanish word generally used for the Spanish language. In some countries, however, Spanish is called **Castellano.** (Paraguay).

Estadounidense. A Spanish word for U.S. citizens. (El Salvador).

Está en su casa. "You are in your house." A traditional Spanish greeting used to welcome visitors to one's home. (Peru).

Estar limpio. (1) To be clean. A Spanish phrase. (Venezuela). (2) To be out of money. A Venezuelan colloquialism. (Venezuela).

Estar pelado. (1) To be bald. A Spanish phrase. (Venezuela). (2) To be out of money. A Venezuelan colloquialism. (Venezuela).

Está servido? "Will you join me?" A Portuguese expression used to invite guests to join in a meal or a snack. (Brazil).

Estilo manabita. A Spanish phrase for "common-law marriages." (Ecuador).

Estou bem. "I am fine." A Portuguese response to the greeting **Como está?** (Cape Verde).

Estou bem, obrigado. "Fine, thank you." A Portuguese response to the formal greeting **Como está?** (Mozambique).

Estoy lleno. "I am full." A Spanish phrase. (El Salvador).

Etrennes. A New Year's gift. (France).

Evala. Traditional wrestling. (Togo).

Evangélicos. Evangelical protestants. (Bolivia, Guatemala, Honduras).

Ewegba. An Ewe term for a communal bowl that meals are served in. (Togo).

Fa'alupega. The official list of names and ranks of each village's chiefs and orators. (American Samoa). *See also* **Matai, Tulafale.**

Faamu. Adoptive parents. (French Polynesia).

Faano. Traditional skirts worn by older women. (Gambia).

Faapu. The family garden. (French Polynesia).

Fa'a Samoa. "The Samoan Way." A casual way of life that is careful to respect and preserve tradition. (American Samoa, Samoa).

Faatele. A traditional Tuvaluan dance. (Tuvalu).

Fado. A style of Portuguese folk singing that has influenced Guinea-Bissauan pop music. (Guinea-Bissau).

Fadys. The Malagasy word for "taboos." (Madagascar).

Fafa. A type of spinach. (French Polynesia).

Fafaru. "Smelly fish." Fish that is fermented in seawater for several days. (French Polynesia).

Fa fu den sama? "How is your family?" A Ndyuka greeting. (Suriname).

Fahu. The leader over the nuclear family in the highly organized extended family system; usually the father's eldest sister. (Tonga). *See also* **Mehikitanga.**

Fa'i. Green bananas. (Samoa).

Faikai. Chunks of fish marinated in coconut cream. (Niue).

Faikava. The dating practice of making **Kava**; a boy may ask a girl to have a *faikava* at her home. (Tonga).

Faja. A woven belt worn by men and women. (Guatemala).

Fakaala. The Tuvaluan word for "feast." (Tuvalu).

Fakaalofa atu. "Love be with you." A Niuean greeting. (Niue).

Faka Tonga. "The Tongan Way" of life. Characterized by being easygoing and relaxed. (Tonga).

Falafel. Pita bread filled with fried balls of crushed garbanzo beans. (Israel, West Bank and Gaza).

Falaninii. Sleeping mats. (Samoa).

Fale. A house or shelter. (Niue, Tonga, Tuvalu).

Fale Alea. The Tongan Legislative Assembly. (Tonga).

Fale fono. Village council house. (American Samoa).

Fale telefoni. Telephone house, where the telephone for the village or several villages is kept. (Tonga).

Famadihana. "Turning of the bones." An ancestor veneration ceremony in which a family exhumes an ancestor's body to wrap it in a new burial shroud. (Madagascar). *See also* **Lambamena.**

Fandango. A large party. (Guam).

Fanmi Lavalas. A political party in Haiti named after the Lavalas family. (Haiti).

Fanorona. A traditional game played by strategically placing small stones in hollows of a board or on the ground. (Madagascar).

Farakha. A wavy, knotted tassel worn at the neck by men. (Oman). *Also called* **Kashkusha.**

Glossary of Cultural Terms

Faranji. A head covering worn by rural women. (Tajikistan).
Farashiya. A garment worn by older, traditional women in Libya; it is a white, sheet-like cover that conceals the entire body, the head, and one eye. (Libya).
Faratas. A food similar to pancakes. (Mauritius).
Fårikål. Cabbage and mutton. (Norway).
Farmhouse restaurants. Irish restaurants that feature traditional recipes. (Ireland).
Fasching. A German word for Carnival. (Austria, Germany).
Fasika. Easter. (Eritrea).
Fasnacht. A German word for Carnival. (Liechtenstein).
Fastelavn. A Danish holiday marked by public celebration and games. (Denmark).
Fasule. Boiled dried beans. (Albania).
Fat cakes. Deep-fried dough. (Botswana).
Fatta. A dish made of bread, peas, tomatoes, cheese, lentils, and other ingredients. (Sudan).
Favelas. Shantytowns located on the outskirts of urban centers. (Brazil).
Fa waka? Literally, "How are you walking?" A Sranan Tongo greeting meaning "How are you?" (Suriname). *See also* **Fa'y go?, Fa'y tan?**
Fa'y go? Literally, "How are you going?" A Sranan Tongo greeting meaning "How are you?" (Suriname). *See also* **Fa waka?, Fa'y tan?**
Fa'y tan? Literally, "How are you staying?" A Sranan Tongo greeting meaning "How are you?" (Suriname). *See also* **Fa waka?, Fa'y go?**
Fedayeen. Palestinian resistance members. (Jordan).
Fedoras. Fur caps worn by men. (Lithuania).
Fefe hake? "How do you do?" A Tongan greeting used upon introduction. (Tonga).
Feijoada. Black beans with beef, pork, sausage, and sometimes a pig's ears, feet, and tail. (Brazil).
Feiticeiros. Witches. People believe that witches can free them from a problem or help them obtain wealth, usually at the expense of others. Deaths or accidents are often attributed to witchcraft. (Angola). *Also called* **Macumbeiros.**
Feliz Arabia. "Happy Arabia." The name the ancient Romans gave to Yemen because of its people's hospitality and strong society. (Yemen).
Feliz noite. A Portuguese parting phrase meaning "Good night." (Angola).
Fenkata. Stewed rabbit. (Malta).
Ferias. Traveling markets or fairs. (Chile, Venezuela).
Festa(s). Feast Day. A holiday that honors a local patron saint. (Malta).
Festival. Fried dough. (Jamaica).
Fête. A party. (Saint Lucia).
Fête de Mouton. [NOTE: Muslim holidays are set according to the lunar calendar.] A Muslim holiday that commemorates Abraham's willingness to sacrifice his son. (Cameroon, Gabon). *Also called* **Eid al-Adha.**
Fête de Notre Dame. A very large festival generally held in August. (Haiti).
Fête des Masques. The "Festival of Masks" is an event that takes place in the region around Man every November. During the festival, local people compete in dances and honor the spirits they believe live in large wooden masks. (Ivory Coast).
Fête des Mères. Mother's Day. Celebrated at the end of May. (Central African Republic).

Fête Dieu. A Haitian celebration held the first Thursday in June. The festivities mark the institution of the sacrament or communion. (Haiti).
Fête du 3 janvier. A holiday in commemoration of the 3 January 1966 uprising. (Burkina Faso).
Fête du Dipri. The "Festival of the Dipri" is an overnight exorcism event that takes place in Gomon during the spring. (Ivory Coast).
Fête du Ramadan. The feast celebrated at the end of the month of **Ramadan**. (Cameroon).
Fête du Travail. Labor Day or May Day. Celebrated on 1 May. (Central African Republic, Gabon).
Fête National. A holiday that commemorates independence. Celebrated on 17 August. (Gabon).
Fetes. (1) Fund-raising parties. (Montserrat). (2) Parties. (Barbados).
Fèt Gede. A holiday that honors the dead. (Haiti).
Fiafia. A party. (Niue, Samoa).
Field trip. Ships that transport passengers and supplies to and from outer islands. (Micronesia).
Fiereljeppen. Pole-vaulting for distance. (Netherlands).
Fiestas. The word for "parties." Used in Spanish-speaking countries..
Fietspaden. The Dutch word for "bike paths." (Netherlands).
Fihavanana. A well-maintained relationship. (Madagascar).
Fil. A kind of yogurt. (Sweden).
Finadene. A sauce made of soy sauce, lemon juice, hot peppers, and onions. (Guam).
Finants. The Estonian word for "finance." (Estonia).
Fincas. Agricultural plots in the forest. (Equatorial Guinea).
Fin du Ramadan. The feast celebrated at the end of the month of **Ramadan**. (Gabon). *Also called* **Aid al Fitr.**
Fine'eiki. "Mrs." A Tongan title. (Tonga).
Finmark. The name of the former Finnish national currency. (Finland). *Also called* **Markka.**
Fish-and-chips. Fish and french fries. (England).
Fish suppers. Fish and chips seasoned with salt and vinegar. (Scotland).
Fish water. Fish stew. (Antigua and Barbuda).
Fisting. Hitting fists together. Often replacing a handshake or embrace between friends when coming or going. (Saint Vincent and the Grenadines).
Fit fit. Bits of bread. (Eritrea).
Fit like. A Scottish colloquialism for "How are you?" (Scotland).
Flats. Apartments. (England, Ireland, Scotland, Singapore, Wales).
Fo. An Ewe term of address children use for their fathers. (Togo).
Fofo. (1) A Mina term of address children use for their fathers. (Togo). (2) "Brother." A respectful term of address used to address an older male. (Benin).
Föhn A warm southerly wind. (Liechtenstein).
Folkeshøjskole. The Danish word for "community college." (Denmark).
Folkeskole. Literally, "people's school," it is a primary school. (Denmark).
Folketing. The Danish Parliament. (Denmark).
Fondue. A traditional dish in which pieces of bread are dipped in melted cheese. (Switzerland).

Glossary of Cultural Terms

Fono. (1) Village council. (American Samoa, Samoa). (2) Legislative Assembly. (Samoa).

Fonopule. Island councils that manage local government. (Tuvalu).

Football. The game people in the United States call "soccer." A term used outside the United States..

Footy. An Australian colloquialism for Australian-rules football. (Australia).

Foreninger. Local community clubs. (Denmark).

Form. A grade in school. (England, Guyana, Lithuania, Malawi, Montserrat).

Fostering. The custom of loaning a child to a childless woman or a wealthy person. (Sierra Leone).

Fou. Flower garlands that are worn in the hair on festive occasions. (Tuvalu).

Foul. (Egypt). *See* **Ful.**

Foutour. The Arabic word for "breakfast." (Bahrain). *Also called* **Iftar.**

Franc. (1) The national currency of various countries. (Comoros, Congo, Guinea, Liechtenstein, Rwanda, Switzerland). (2) The former national currency. (France, Madagascar).

Frau. "Mrs." or "Miss." A German title used with the last name. (Austria, Germany).

Freetambos. Miniature deer. (Sierra Leone).

Frère. "Brother." A familial title used with strangers as well as family. (Guinea).

Frijoles. Red beans. (El Salvador).

Frijoles con chicharrón. Pork and beans. (Colombia).

Frikadeller. Danish meatballs. (Denmark).

Fritada. Fried pork. (Ecuador).

Frittatensuppe. Soup with shredded crêpes. (Austria).

Fritten, Ham an Zalot. French fries, ham, and salad. (Luxembourg).

Frituras. Foods fried in oil. (Puerto Rico).

Frokostbord. A cold buffet of many different foods. (Denmark).

Fuaga mei. Breadfruit. (Tuvalu).

Fualah. A ritual meal of sweets and fruits. Provided to first-time visitors. (United Arab Emirates).

Fufu. A stiff paste made by boiling flour. (Cameroon, Ghana, Togo).

Führer. The German word for "leader." (Germany).

Fuji. Nigerian music that has several drums but no guitars. Dancing will often accompany the music. (Nigeria).

Ful. Spicy beans. (Yemen).

Funáná. A lively and popular form of dance music with a strong beat. (Cape Verde).

Fundi. A title for a teacher or craftsman. (Comoros).

Funge. A paste of ground cornmeal, similar to thick porridge. A staple food at lunch and dinner. (Angola).

Fungee. A soft bread made with cornmeal and okra that is baked in a bowl. (Antigua and Barbuda).

Fungi. Cooked cornmeal with okra. (U.S. Virgin Islands).

Funkasunntig. Bonfire Sunday. A holiday with folk and pagan origins. (Liechtenstein).

Fürst. The ruling prince. (Liechtenstein).

Fusi. A co-op store that carries staple foods and sundry items. (Tuvalu).

Fußball. The German word for "soccer." (Germany).

Fustanelle. A full, colorful wool skirt, part of a traditional outfit. (Albania).

Futah. (1) A dark wraparound dress worn by older Amazigh women. (Tunisia). (2) A patterned cotton cloth wrapped around the lower part of the body. Worn by men. (Yemen).

Fútbol. The word for "soccer." Used in Spanish-speaking countries..

Futebol. The Portuguese word for "soccer." (Brazil, Cape Verde).

Futi. Plantains or cooking bananas. (Tuvalu).

Fu true. A common Montserratian phrase used to add emphasis. (Montserrat).

Futu. A heavy paste made of pounded yams, cassavas, and plantains; southern Ivorians make this dish, often dipping it in sauce. (Ivory Coast).

Futur. Breakfast. (Iraq). *Also called* **Riyuq.**

Fye. "Good evening." A Ewe greeting. (Togo).

Fylker. The Norwegian word meaning "province." (Norway).

Ga'at. A thick barley porridge. (Eritrea).

Gabay. Political poetry. (Somalia).

Gaboot. Raisin-filled dumplings in a meat stew. (Kuwait).

Gado-gado. A dish of vegetables and tofu topped with peanut sauce. (Indonesia).

Gaelic football. A sport played with a round ball. Combines elements of soccer and basketball. (Ireland, Northern Ireland).

Gagaku. Japanese music played with string and wind instruments and drums. (Japan).

Gagimarjos. "Hello." An informal Georgian response to the greeting **Gamarjoba**. (Georgia).

Gahwa. Coffee flavored with cardamom. (Kuwait).

Gaida. A bagpipe. A traditional musical instrument. (Bulgaria).

Gaines. A caste of professional singers that perform Hindu songs and tell stories. (Nepal).

Gaita. A type of accordion. (Cape Verde).

Gaitas. (1) Bagpipes. (Spain). (2) Traditional Christmas music. (Venezuela). *See also* **Aguinaldos.**

Gajda. A type of bagpipe. Used in the traditional music that accompanies folk dances. (Macedonia).

Gajde. A type of bagpipe. (Albania).

Gala. The Latvian word for "meat." (Latvia).

Gallebeyya. A long dress-like robe worn by rural men. (Egypt).

Gallo pinto. A dish of rice and beans fried together. (Costa Rica, Nicaragua).

Gallos. Tortillas with meat and vegetable fillings. (Costa Rica).

Galyn. Bride-price. (Turkmenistan).

Gaman. "Enduring patience," a respected Japanese trait. (Japan).

Gamarjoba. "Hello." A Georgian greeting. Literally, "Let you win." (Georgia).

Gamelan. A traditional music orchestra with gongs, xylophones, drums, and other percussion instruments. (Indonesia, Malaysia, Suriname).

Ganoon. A charcoal basket used for cooking. (Chad).

Gara. Dyed fabrics. Artists apply wax designs to the fabric, place it in a dye bath, and remove the wax to reveal the pattern. (Sierra Leone).

Garabouts. Boys who attend **Qur'anic** schools and must beg for food daily. (Mali).

Garamut. A traditional musical instrument. A log with a small hollowed-out portion where a stick is rhythmically beaten. (Papua New Guinea).

Garçom. Literally, "boy." A French term used to call a waiter. (Brazil).

Glossary of Cultural Terms

Garçon. A greeting used among male peers that is equivalent to "man" or "dude." (Saint Lucia).

Gari. A type of grits made from cassava. (Benin).

Garinagu. People of mixed Caribbean and African descent. (Belize).

Garnaches. Fried tortillas with beans, cheese, and sauce. (Belize).

Garri. Grated cassava that is dried over a fire until light and flaky. (Cameroon).

Garrison constituencies. Communities over which political parties strive to maintain control. Parties have joined with urban gangs to force citizens to vote in certain ways. (Jamaica).

Garrobo. Iguana soup. (Nicaragua).

Gasabah. Cane flute. (Jordan).

Gaspa. A long bamboo flute. (Algeria).

Gasthaus. A pub. (Austria).

Gate jo-ni mo? "Where are you going?" A common Dzongkha greeting to passersby. (Bhutan).

Gaucho(s). The Spanish word for "cowboy" or "herdsman." (Argentina, Uruguay).

Gaung-baung. A round cap of pink or yellow silk stretched over a rush frame. Worn by Burmese men on the most formal occasions. (Myanmar).

Gazpacho. Cold vegetable soup. (Spain).

Gbaka. Minibus used in Ivory Coast. (Ivory Coast). *See also* **Badjan, Dyna.**

Gebetta. A strategy game played with pebbles on a playing surface that is created by making depressions in the ground. (Eritrea).

Geduk. A short drum made from a hollow tree trunk. (Malaysia).

Gefilte. A dish of baked or stewed ground fish. (Israel).

Gekookte aardappelen. Boiled potatoes. (Netherlands).

Gelneje. "Sister-in-law." A common term of respect added to a female formal acquaintance's name. (Turkmenistan). *See also* **Daiza, Hanum.**

Gemütlichkeit. A relaxed and happy approach to life; an Austrian trait. (Austria).

Gena. A rural sport similar to field hockey. (Ethiopia).

Genji. A sleeveless vest worn by rural men. (Bangladesh). *See also* **Lungi.**

Genkan. A small hallway between the door and living area, where one stands to remove one's shoes. (Japan).

Genki? "How's it going?" A common casual greeting used among the youth. (Japan). *See also* **Ohayou.**

Gerobak jualan. A mobile eatery. The vendors are called **Kaki lima**. (Indonesia).

Ger(s). A wooden tent covered in sheep-wool felt and a white cloth. (Mongolia).

Getna. A holiday celebrated when the dates are ripe. (Mauritania).

Gezondheid. The Dutch equivalent of saying "Bless you." One can also say **Proost**. (Netherlands).

Gezuar. "Cheers." An Albanian phrase used by vistors before drinking. (Albania).

Ghada. The Arabic word for "lunch." (Bahrain).

Ghana. A type of Maltese music that incorporates both Arabic and Italian influences. Pronounced "ah-nah." Performed by **Ghannejja**. (Malta).

Ghannejja. Singers. (Malta). *See also* **Ghana.**

Gharara. A long blouse worn over a long skirt with a matching shawl. (Suriname).

Gharbata. Tea. (Belarus).

Ghatak. A matchmaker. (Bangladesh).

Ghee. Clarified butter. (Nepal, Somalia).

Ghidaa'. Lunch. (Iraq).

Ghishwa. A face veil worn by conservative Muslim women. (United Arab Emirates).

Gho. A long-sleeved, ankle-length robe that is hoisted to knee level and belted tightly so that it forms pleats in the back and a deep pocket at the belly. Traditional attire worn by men. (Bhutan).

Ghozi. A whole lamb or kid goat stuffed with seasoned rice. (Qatar). *Also called* **Kubsa.**

Ghutra. (Qatar, Saudi Arabia). *See* **Gutra.**

Gidday. A colloquialism for "Good day." An informal greeting. (New Zealand).

Gimnazija. General education high school that prepares students for university studies. (Macedonia).

Githeri. A dish of corn and beans. (Kenya).

Gjelle. A dish of boiled beans or vegetables with meat. (Albania).

Gjithe te mirat. "All the best." A typical Albanian parting phrase. (Albania).

Glamorgan sausages. A meatless dish made with cheese, bread crumbs, herbs, and leeks. (Wales).

Glasnost. The Russian policy of openness. (Latvia, Russia).

Glens. Valleys. (Scotland).

Goat water. A spicy stew made with goat meat. (Antigua and Barbuda, Montserrat, Saint Kitts and Nevis).

Goddag. "Good day." A Danish greeting. (Denmark).

God dag. "Good day." A Norwegian and Swedish formal greeting. (Norway, Sweden).

God morgon. "Good morning." A formal Swedish greeting. (Sweden).

Godo. "Other side." An Ewe term. Combined with **To**, "waters," it forms the name of the lakeside village of Togodo, for which Togo is named. (Togo).

Goedemorgen. "Good morning." A common Dutch greeting. (Suriname).

Goeiedag. "Good day." A Dutch greeting. (Belgium).

Goeie môre. "Good morning." An Afrikaans greeting. (South Africa).

Gogo. (1) A traditional music rhythm. (Benin). (2) The siSwati word for "grandmother." (Swaziland).

Goiabeira. A square-cut, embroidered shirt worn by government and office workers. (Mozambique).

Golubtsy. Stuffed cabbage leaves baked with tomato sauce and eaten with sour cream. (Russia).

Gombo. A sauce made with okra, small fish, and baobab leaves. (Togo).

Gomesi. A many-layered traditional dress. (Uganda).

Goombay. A type of island music created with goatskin drums, saws, and maracas. (Bahamas). *See also* **Rake n' scrape.**

Gordita. A Spanish word meaning "little fat one." In some places, it is not considered rude to comment on such physical attributes. (Argentina).

Goro. Kola nuts. (Niger).

Gospa. "Madam." A Slovene title used to show respect. (Slovenia).

Gospod. "Sir." A Slovene title used to show respect. (Slovenia).

Glossary of Cultural Terms

Gospodična. "Miss." A Slovene title used to show respect. (Slovenia).

Gospodijica. "Miss." A Serbo-Croatian title. (Bosnia and Herzegovina).

Gospodin. "Mister." A Slavic title. (Belarus, Bosnia and Herzegovina, Bulgaria, Macedonia, Russia, Serbia and Montenegro).

Gospodine. "Mister." A Croatian title. (Croatia).

Gospodja. "Mrs." A Serbian title. (Bosnia and Herzegovina, Serbia and Montenegro).

Gospodjice. "Miss." A Croatian title. (Croatia).

Gospodjo. "Mrs." A Croatian title. (Croatia).

Gospogja. "Mrs." (Macedonia).

Gospogjica. "Miss." (Macedonia).

Gospozh. (Belarus). *See* **Gospozha.**

Gospozha. "Mrs." A Bulgarian and Russian title. (Bulgaria, Russia).

Gospozhitsa. "Miss." A Bulgarian title. (Bulgaria).

Gostilne. Local inns. (Slovenia).

Góðan daginn. "Good day." An Icelandic greeting to a stranger. (Iceland).

Go to the loo. A colloquialism for "go to the bathroom." (New Zealand).

Gourde. Haiti's national currency. (Haiti).

Gozinaki. A honey-and-walnut confection. (Georgia).

Gozo. A thick paste made by soaking cassava root in water, drying it in the sun, grinding it into flour, and boiling it. (Central African Republic).

Grabar. The Armenian word for "standard." (Armenia).

Gracias. The Spanish word for "Thank you." (Bolivia, Mexico).

Graha dasha. A traditional Nepali belief in which a bad position of the planets can cause disease, crop failures, or accidents. (Nepal). *See also* **Bhoot, Bokshi, Pret.**

Gran Colombia. A federation, including parts or all of present-day Colombia, Panama, Venezuela, and Ecuador. Led by Simón Bolívar, it was later dissolved. (Colombia, Ecuador).

Grand boubou. A robe that reaches a man's knees or feet. (Central African Republic). *See also* **Boubou(s).**

Grandes Ecoles. French schools to study for careers in government, the military, education, and industry. (France).

Grande soeur. French term meaning "big sister." Ivorians may call each other by familial names to show respect and affection even if they are not related. (Ivory Coast).

Grand frère. French term meaning "big brother." Ivorians may call each other by familial names to show respect and affection even if they are not related. (Ivory Coast).

Grandma. A term of address used by children for any older women. (Ghana).

Grandmbuba. Colorful traditional shirts worn by older women. (Gambia). *Also called* **Dendiko ba.**

Grandpa. A term of address used by children to address older men. (Ghana, Guyana).

Grannie. A term of address used by children to address older women. (Guyana).

Gratin. Potatoes sliced and baked with white sauce and cream. (Switzerland).

Green Book. Book in which Libyan leader Muammar Qaddafi explains his concepts about creating a direct democracy and new economy; however, the book does not include plans for implementation. (Libya).

Greenies. Environmentalists. (Australia).

Griessnockerlsuppe. Soup with small semolina dumplings. (Austria).

Gri gri. Good-luck charms. (Guinea, Mali, Senegal).

Grillad lax med spenat, citron och potatis eller ris. A dish of grilled slices of salmon with spinach, slices of lemon, and potatoes or rice. (Sweden).

Griots. Orators. (Burkina Faso, Gambia, Guinea, Mali, Mauritania, Senegal, Togo).

Gris. Coconut water. (Papua New Guinea).

Gris-gris. Charms. (Burkina Faso, Chad, Comoros, Mauritania).

Grita. A personally styled yell used to express friendship, break the monotony of fieldwork, and show joy at **Fiestas**. (Panama).

Gritería Day A holiday that celebrates Christ's conception. The Virgrin Mary is especially celebrated at this time. (Nicaragua).

Groentesoep. Vegetable soup. (Netherlands).

Grogue. Strong rum made from sugarcane; the national drink. (Cape Verde).

Groundnuts. A term for peanuts. (Ivory Coast).

Ground provisions. Root crops such as sweet potatoes and yams. (Guyana, Montserrat, Saint Lucia).

Groupe de grain. Informal peer groups. (Mali).

Grüezi. "Greetings." A Swiss German phrase used to greet strangers. (Liechtenstein).

Grundtvigianism. "The happy Lutheranism." A Danish movement. (Denmark).

Grüß Dich. "Greetings to you." A casual German greeting. (Austria).

Grüss Gott. "Greetings." A German phrase used to greet strangers. (Liechtenstein).

Grüß Gott. (Austria, Germany). *See* **Grüss Gott.**

Grütsie. "Hi." A typical Swiss German greeting. (Switzerland).

Gu. Somalia's season of heavy rains. Lasts from March to June. (Somalia).

Guacho. Rice soup. (Panama).

Guagua. A van or bus used as a taxi that runs a long fixed route. (Dominican Republic).

Guai. A Mongol term of address used to show honor to an elder or someone of higher status. (Mongolia).

Guampa. A container, usually made of wood, cattle horns, or gourds, used to drink tea. (Paraguay).

Guanacasta. A large fast-growing tree found in Central America. (Belize).

Guanxi. A principle that commits friends and associates to do what they can for each other when called upon. (China).

Guaraní. Paraguay's national currency. (Paraguay).

Guava cheese. A chewy dessert made by boiling and puréeing guavas before mixing them with sugar. (Grenada, Saint Kitts and Nevis).

Guayabera(s). A traditional, embroidered dress shirt worn by men. (Belize, Cuba, Honduras, Nicaragua, Panama, U.S. Virgin Islands).

Guayano(s). A scraping percussion instrument. (Dominican Republic).

Gud aftanun. "Good afternoon." A common Solomon Island Pijin greeting. (Solomon Islands).

Gudden Owend. "Good evening." A common Luxembourgish greeting. (Luxembourg).

Gudey. "Good afternoon." An English greeting adapted by the Ewe. (Togo).

Glossary of Cultural Terms

Gudivin. "Good evening." An English greeting adapted by the Ewe. (Togo).

Gud mone. "Good morning." A common Solomon Island Pijin greeting. (Solomon Islands).

Gud naet. "Good night." A common Solomon Island Pijin greeting. (Solomon Islands).

Guilder. The former currency of the Netherlands, before the euro was adopted in 2002. This currency was also known as the *florin*. (Netherlands).

Guiso. A dish made of ground beef with rice, onion, egg, etc. (Uruguay).

Guitarra. A cittern-like instrument. (Cape Verde).

Guitarrón. A 25-string guitar. (Chile).

Güle güle. "Good-bye." The response to the phrase **Allahaısmarladık**. (Turkey).

Gule Wamkulu. "Great Dance." Incorporates symbolic masks to tell stories and teach traditions. (Malawi).

Gulyás. "Goulash." A soup of meat, potatoes, onions, and paprika. (Hungary).

Gumbe. A popular musical rhythm. (Guinea-Bissau).

Gumboot. A popular dance developed by Black African gold miners. (South Africa).

Günaydin. "Good morning." A Turkish greeting. (Turkey).

Guntino. A 4-yard cloth worn by women; tied over one shoulder and wrapped around the waist. (Somalia).

Gurban Bayramy. A one-day festival commemorating Abraham's willingness to sacrifice his son. (Turkmenistan). *See also* **Eid al-Adha**.

Guriltai shul. Mutton-and-noodle soup. (Mongolia).

Gusle. A single-stringed instrument. (Bosnia and Herzegovina, Serbia and Montenegro).

¡Gusto de verte! "Nice to see you." A traditional Spanish greeting. (Chile).

Guten Abend. "Good evening." A common German greeting. (Austria, Switzerland).

Guten Morgen. "Good morning." A common German greeting. (Austria, Switzerland).

Guten Tag. "Good day." A common German greeting. (Austria, Germany, Switzerland).

Gutnait. "Good evening." A common Melanesian Pidgin greeting for acquaintances. (Papua New Guinea).

Gutra. A light cloth headdress worn by men. (Bahrain, Kuwait).

Guugs. Horse racing. (Ethiopia).

Gwata. A musical instrument played by the Acholi to accompany dance performances. A half gourd struck with metal bicycle spokes. (Uganda).

Gwon ada? "How are you?" A common Bari greeting. (Sudan).

Gyalpo. The Bhutanese king. (Bhutan).

Gymnasia. High school. (Switzerland).

Gymnasio. The level of schooling after elementary school. (Greece).

Gymnasium. A high school that prepares students to attend a university. (Bosnia and Herzegovina, Germany, Slovenia).

Habari? "News?" A common Swahili greeting. (Comoros, Kenya).

Habari gani? "What is the news?" A common Swahili greeting. (Kenya).

Habari za nyumbani? "How are things at your home?" A common Swahili phrase used to inquire about family. (Tanzania).

Habichuelas. Beans. (Dominican Republic).

Habichuelas con dulce. A dessert similar to rice pudding but made from beans. (Dominican Republic).

Hackbrett. A hammered dulcimer. A common Austrian folk instrument. (Austria).

Hadith. The Islamic prophet Muhammad's compiled sayings. (Oman, Qatar).

Hadj. [NOTE: Spelling varies because it is a transliteration of Arabic.] An Arabic title for Muslim men who have completed the pilgrimage to Makkah, Saudi Arabia. (Morocco).

Hadji. (Sudan). *See* **Hadj**.

Hadjia. An Arabic title for Muslim women who have completed the pilgrimage to Makkah, Saudi Arabia. (Niger).

Hadjilidj. A type of nut offered to favored guests. (Chad).

Ha-dudu. A sport played by village boys where two teams try to eliminate all the other team's players. One player will enter the other team's zone while holding his breath. He will try and touch the other players and make it back to his own zone. If he makes it back to his side while still holding his breath, the players he touched will be out. Otherwise, he is out. (Bangladesh). *Also called* **Ka-baddi**.

Haere ra. "Farewell." A common Maori parting phrase. (New Zealand).

Hafa adai. "Hello." A common Chamorro greeting. (Guam).

Hafa tatatmanu hao? "How are you?" A common Chamorro greeting. (Guam).

Hagaa. Somalia's dry season. Lasts from June to August. (Somalia).

Hagelslag. Chocolate sprinkles. (Netherlands).

Haggis. Ground sheep entrails that are mixed with oats and spices, tied in a sheep's stomach, and cooked. (Scotland).

Hai hau ma? "Is everything okay?" A common Mandarin greeting. (Taiwan).

Hailing. (Belize). *See* **Hail(s)**.

Hail(s). To greet. (Belize).

Hairouna. "Home of the Blessed." The Carib name for Saint Vincent. (Saint Vincent and the Grenadines).

Haj. (Oman, Pakistan). *See* **Hajj**.

Haji. (Afghanistan). *See* **Hadj**.

Hajimemashite. "Nice to meet you." A Japanese greeting used in formal situations. (Japan).

Hajj. [NOTE: Spelling varies because it is a transliteration of Arabic.] One of the Five Pillars of Islam, the *Hajj* is a pilgrimage to Makkah, Saudi Arabia. A religious practice followed in Muslim-populated countries.. *See also* **Salat, Saum, Shahada, Zakat**.

Hajoghootiun. "Good luck." A common Armenian parting phrase. (Armenia).

Haka. A Maori war dance. (New Zealand).

Hakkebøf. A Danish hamburger. (Denmark).

Hala. "Aunt." A common Azeri term of address used after a woman's given name. (Azerbaijan).

Haladnik. Cold vegetable soup. (Belarus).

Halal. A Muslim requirement that meats should prepared according to Islamic law. This includes not eating pork and having the animals slaughtered humanely by a butcher who has first said a prayer. (Libya, Singapore).

Halászlé. Fish soup. (Hungary).

Halk Maslahaty. The People's Council. Members offer advise and recommendations to the national government. (Turkmenistan).

Glossary of Cultural Terms

Hallå. "Hello." A Swedish greeting used to answer the phone. (Sweden).

Hallacas. A thick, deep-fried pancake stuffed with stewed meat, potatoes, olives, raisins, and other spices. Similar to **Arepa(s)**. (Venezuela).

Halle. An Albanian word for "aunt," specifically the father's sister. (Albania). *Also called* **Teto.**

Halling. A well-known Norwegian folk dance in which male dancers perform challenging kicks and leaps. (Norway).

Hallo. "Hello." A common greeting. (Belgium, Germany).

Halló. "Hello." A casual Icelandic greeting. (Iceland).

Halo. "Hello." A casual greeting. (Malaysia, Solomon Islands).

Haló. "Hello." A common Hungarian phrase used for greeting and parting. (Hungary).

Halo-halo. A drink made from sweetened beans, milk, and fruits, served with crushed ice. (Philippines).

Halvo. A paste of sugar and oil. (Tajikistan).

Halwa. (Tunisia). *See* **Seqer.**

Halwa. A starch pudding mixed with crushed cardamom seeds, saffron, sugar, and fat. (Bahrain).

Hamdellah. (Eritrea). *See* **Al hamdu lillah.**

Hamdullah. (Tunisia). *See* **Al hamdu lillah.**

Hamjambo. A casual Swahili greeting used when addressing two or more people. (Tanzania).

Ha na? "How are you?" An informal Pidgin English greeting. (Cameroon).

Hanbok. Traditional attire that is reserved for special occasions. For women, this is a long two-piece dress that is often very colorful. For men, this includes trousers and a loose-fitting jacket or robe. (North Korea, South Korea).

Hangi. A dish composed of meat, seafood, potatoes, sweet potatoes, carrots, and other vegetables all cooked in wire racks lined with cabbage leaves. (New Zealand).

Hangikjöt. Smoked mutton. (Iceland).

Hanikotrana. Snacks such as cassava or sweet potatoes. (Madagascar).

Hanim. A Turkish title following a woman's given name. (Turkey).

Hanoot. A basic convenience store. (Morocco).

Hant. A rummy-like card game. (Macedonia).

Hanukkah. Festival of Lights, a Jewish holiday. (Israel).

Hanum. (1) "Miss" or "Mrs." An Azeri title used after a woman's given name. (Azerbaijan). (2) "Lady." A term of respect added to a female formal acquaintance's name. (Turkmenistan). *See also* **Daiza, Gelneje.**

Hao jiu bu jian le. "Long time no see." A Mandarin Chinese phrase used between acquaintances who have not seen each other in a long time. (China).

Haqibh. Chants and chorus accompanied by instruments such as the **Tabla** and the **Oud**. (Sudan). *See also* **Madeeh.**

Harees. A blend of wheat and meat cooked until mushy, with butter melted over the top. (Bahrain, Kuwait).

Harina de maíz. Cornmeal. (Cuba).

Harira. A tomato-based soup with beef or mutton, chickpeas, and lentils. (Morocco).

Hari Raya Haji. [NOTE: Muslim holidays are set according to the lunar calendar.] Feast of the Sacrifice. A Muslim holiday that celebrates Abraham's willingness to sacrifice his son. Celebrated at the end of the pilgrimage to Makkah, Saudi Arabia. (Malaysia, Singapore). *Also called* **Eid al-Adha.**

Hari Raya Puasa. [NOTE: Muslim holidays are set according to the lunar calendar.] A three-day feast celebrated at the end of the month of **Ramadan**. (Malaysia, Singapore). *Also called* **Aid al Fitr.**

Harisa. A dish of wheat and chicken cooked in large pots for several days. (Armenia).

Här Minister. "Mr. Minister." A Luxembourgish title. (Luxembourg).

Hashi. The Japanese word for "chopsticks." (Japan).

Hassa. Libyan gravy made of lamb, oil, crushed tomatoes, flour, and spices such as garlic, cilantro, and mint. (Libya).

Hasta luego. "Until later." A common parting phrase. Used in Spanish-speaking countries..

Hasta mañana. "Until tomorrow." A common Spanish parting phrase. (Bolivia).

Hat bo. Traditional Chinese opera. (Vietnam).

Hat boi. Traditional Chinese opera. (Vietnam).

Hat cheo. Vietnamese operettas. (Vietnam).

Hatte. A blouse that leaves the midriff bare. (Sri Lanka).

Hat tuong. Traditional Chinese opera. (Vietnam).

Hatujambo. "We're fine." A common Swahili response to the greeting **Hamjambo**. (Tanzania).

Hau. "Temporal Ruler," an office created by the Tongan monarchy in 1470. (Tonga).

Havli. Compounds of mud-brick structures of several rooms, surrounded by high mud walls that provide security, protect gardens, and keep animals inside. (Tajikistan).

Hawli. A long tunic worn by Libyan men and women during cooler weather. It is always white for men but may be any color for women. (Libya).

Hawn kif aħna. "Hi. How are you?" A Maltese greeting. (Malta).

Haya Kala? "How are you?" A common Arabic greeting. (Qatar).

Hayeren. The Armenian language. (Armenia).

Hœ. "Hi." A casual Icelandic greeting. (Iceland).

Head isu. "Good appetite." An Estonian phrase used at the beginning of a meal. (Estonia).

Headman. An elder appointed by the village chief. The plural form is *headmen*. (Botswana).

Headmen. (Botswana). *See* **Headman.**

He done reach. "He has arrived." An example of the Bahamas's unique idioms. (Bahamas).

Héé. A welcoming answer to visitors who call out the phrase **Odi! Odi!** (Mozambique).

Hegira. [NOTE: Spelling varies because it is a transliteration of Arabic.] The Islamic New Year. The migration of Muhammad from Makkah to Al Medina in the seventh century. (Saudi Arabia).

Hei. "Hi." A common greeting. (Finland, Norway).

Heilige Drei Könige. Holy Three Kings. Celebrated on 6 January. (Austria).

Heiliger Abend. Holy Evening. Christmas Eve. (Austria, Germany).

Heisei. "Achievement of universal peace." The Japanese name referring to the reign of Emperor Akihito. (Japan).

Heiva Taupiti. A season of celebrations that culminates with **Tiurai**. (French Polynesia).

Hej. "Hi." A common greeting. Pronounced "HEY." (Denmark, Sweden).

Glossary of Cultural Terms

Hej då. "Good-bye." A casual Swedish parting phrase. (Sweden). *See also* **Adjö**.

Heladería. An ice cream shop. (Argentina).

Here tilena wa? "Did you have a good day?" A greeting used between friends. (Mali).

Hermano/a. "Brother" or "sister." A Spanish term often used as a term of address. Masculine *hermano*, feminine *hermana*. (Panama).

Herr. "Mr." A German title used with the family name. (Austria, Germany).

Hetman. Military chieftain. (Ukraine).

Hexagone. Another name for France. (France).

Hey de mon, leh we go limin. A typical Creole invitation between male friends to go out on the town. (U.S. Virgin Islands).

Hey how? A common greeting between acquaintances. (Belize).

High. A type of island characterized by volcanic peaks, fertile valleys, lush tropical forests, rushing streams, waterfalls, and white-sand beaches. (French Polynesia). *See also* **Low**.

Highlife. Popular Ghanaian dance music. (Ghana, Nigeria, Togo).

Hijab. A scarf worn by Muslim women to cover their hair. (Bahrain, Iraq, Kuwait, Lebanon, Qatar, Sudan).

Hijra. (United Arab Emirates). *See* **Hegira**.

Hijri. The Islamic lunar calendar. (Bahrain).

Hike. (Namibia). *See* **Hiking**.

Hiking. Hitchhiking or traveling in crowded **Combies**. (Namibia).

Hin. A curry dish, usually of fish, chicken, or shrimp. Served with rice. (Myanmar).

Hindi. Cactus fruit. (Tunisia).

Hindi-pop. A blend of East Indian music, traditional Creole music, European pop, and Caribbean rhythms. (Suriname).

Hinna. A party held with family at the bride's home the night before her wedding. (West Bank and Gaza).

Hiragana. A Japanese phonetic alphabet. (Japan). *See also* **Kanji, Katakana, Romaji**.

Hiva kakala. Love songs accompanied by a guitar or ukulele. (Tonga).

Hneh. A type of oboe. (Myanmar).

Hochdeutsch. High German; it is the standard form of German used in written material in Switzerland. (Switzerland).

Hoe gaat het? "How are you?" A common Dutch greeting. (Netherlands, Suriname).

Hogmanay. New Year's Eve. (Scotland).

Hogy vagy? "How are you?" A Hungarian phrase that often follows the initial greeting. (Hungary).

Hoi. A casual greeting used among friends. (Liechtenstein).

Hojatolislam. A Muslim religious title. (Iran).

Hola. "Hi." A casual greeting. Used in Spanish-speaking countries..

¡Hola! ¿Cómo estás? "Hi. How are you?" An informal Spanish greeting. (Paraguay).

Holi. A holiday that is celebrated by people throwing colored water on passersby. (India, Mauritius, Nepal).

Holi Phagwah. (Suriname). *See* **Phagwah**.

Holodomor. The Ukrainian word for "famine." (Ukraine).

Holubtsi. Cabbage leaves stuffed with ground meat and rice. (Ukraine).

Hongi. A traditional Maori greeting where people press noses together with their eyes closed. (New Zealand).

Hopak. A showy Ukrainian folk dance in which men jump, twirl, and kick; the women perform simpler movements. (Ukraine).

Hosselen. The informal selling of goods and services. Many Surinamers maintain a formal job for its pension and health benefits, while relying on *hosselen* to earn extra money without the interference of a boss or the government. (Suriname).

Hotely. An inexpensive restaurant. (Madagascar).

Housecker. St. Nicholas's helper who brings birch twigs to bad children. (Luxembourg).

How! "But of course!" A phrase used in the Antiguan English dialect. (Antigua and Barbuda).

Howa, gowy Allaha shukur. "Yes, thank God." (Turkmenistan). *See also* **Howa, yakshi Hudaya shukur**.

Howa, yakshi Hudaya shukur. "Yes, thank God." (Turkmenistan). *See also* **Howa, gowy Allaha shukur**.

Hows tings? "How are things?" A casual Grenadian creole greeting. (Grenada).

How things? An informal greeting used between friends. (Saint Vincent and the Grenadines).

How ya gine? "How are you doing?" An informal Bajan greeting used between young people. (Barbados).

How you do? An informal greeting used between friends. (Saint Kitts and Nevis, Saint Vincent and the Grenadines).

Howzit. "How are you?" A slang expression used among young English speakers. (South Africa).

Høyesterett. The Norwegian Supreme Court. (Norway).

Hoyo-hoyo! A welcoming answer to visitors who call out the phrase **Odi! Odi!** (Mozambique).

Hryvnia. Ukraine's national currency. (Ukraine).

Hsien. The Taiwanese word for "counties." (Taiwan).

Htamin. Rice. Eaten with every lunch and dinner meal. Synonymous with the word for "food." (Myanmar).

Huan Ying. "Welcome." A Mandarin greeting used by shopkeepers to passersby. (China).

Huasos. Cowboys. (Chile).

Huayno. (1) A type of music from the mountains. (Peru). (2) A dance with many jumps. (Peru).

Hui. Important family meetings. (New Zealand).

Huipil. A Mayan blouse. Its design identifies a woman's social position and hometown. (Guatemala).

Huisarts. The family doctor. (Netherlands).

Hujambo. A casual Swahili greeting used when addressing one person. The plural form is **Hamjambo**. (Tanzania).

Hujra. A special room where male hosts receive male guests. (Afghanistan).

Hura. The Hausa term for a drink made of millet flour mixed with water and sometimes spices, milk, or sugar. (Niger).

Hurling. A sport played on a soccer-type field with wooden sticks and a small leather ball. (Ireland, Northern Ireland).

Hurtitruten. Coastal steamboats. (Norway).

Hush Kalipsis. "Welcome." An Uzbek greeting to visitors. (Uzbekistan).

Hussars. Fifteenth-century light cavalry who were famous for their horsemanship. (Hungary).

Huushur. A fried dumpling stuffed with diced meat, onion, cabbage, garlic, salt, and pepper. (Mongolia).

Hwan'gap. A celebration commemorating a family member's 60th birthday. (South Korea).

Hyvää huomenta. "Good morning." A Finnish greeting. (Finland).

Glossary of Cultural Terms

Hyvää päivää. "Good afternoon." A typical Finnish greeting. (Finland).
Ia orana. A polite and formal Tahitian greeting used by everyone. (French Polynesia).
I baii? "How are you?" A Sara greeting. (Chad).
Ibans. Sea Dayaks. An indigenous people that live in Malaysia. (Malaysia).
Ibbi jay. "They are fine; they are there." A customary response to the Mandinka greeting **Summo lay?** (Gambia).
Ibe. Mats made of pandanus leaves. (Fiji).
Ibn. "Son of." An Arabic title combined with the father's name. (Bahrain). *See also* **Bin.**
Ibtida'i. Primary school. (Saudi Arabia).
Ibu. "Mother." An Indonesian term of address used to show respect to older women. (Indonesia).
Ibuto aber? "How did you sleep?" A common Luo greeting. (Uganda).
Id al-Adha. (Afghanistan, Ethiopia, Sudan). *See* **Eid al-Adha.**
Id-al-Adha. (Comoros). *See* **Eid al-Adha.**
Id al-Fatar. (Ethiopia). *See* **Aid al Fitr.**
Id-al-Fitr. (Comoros). *See* **Aid al Fitr.**
Id al-Fitr. (Afghanistan, Sudan). *See* **Aid al Fitr.**
Idd Adha. (Uganda). *See* **Eid al-Adha.**
Idd Fitr. (Uganda). *See* **Aid al Fitr.**
Idhin. A kind of butter often poured on **Couscous.** (Mauritania).
Idil-Fitr. (Rwanda). *See* **Aid al Fitr.**
Id-i-Navruz. The Islamic New Year. (Tajikistan). *Also called* **Hegira.**
Id-i-Qurbon. Feast of Sacrifice. A Muslim holiday honoring Abraham's willingness to sacrifice his son. (Tajikistan). *Also called* **Eid al-Adha.**
Idir. Local burial society meetings. (Ethiopia).
Id-i-Ramazon. A feast at the end of **Ramazon**, the Muslim holy month. (Tajikistan). *Also called* **Aid al Fitr.**
Idul-Adha. (Indonesia). *See* **Eid al-Adha.**
Idul Adha. (Nigeria, Sri Lanka). *See* **Eid al-Adha.**
Id ul Azha. (Guyana). *See* **Eid al-Adha.**
Id-ul-Fitr. (India). *See* **Aid al Fitr.**
Idul-Fitr. (Kenya, Malawi). *See* **Aid al Fitr.**
Idul Fitr. (Nigeria, Sri Lanka). *See* **Aid al Fitr.**
Id ul Fitr. (Guyana, Suriname). *See* **Aid al Fitr.**
Idul-Fitri. (Indonesia). *See* **Aid al Fitr.**
Ietoga. Fine mats; offered by the bride's family to the groom's family after a wedding reception. (Samoa).
Ifil. A slow-growing tropical tree. Guam's official tree. (Guam).
Ifisashi. Any green vegetable boiled and mixed with pounded groundnuts. (Zambia).
Ifisela. Drama. (Zambia).
Iftar. (1) The Arabic word for "breakfast." (Bahrain). *Also called* **Foutour.** (2) Special snacks eaten at night to break the fast during **Ramadan**, the Muslim holy month. (Bangladesh).
Igal. A braided black cord that holds in place the **Ghutra.** (Saudi Arabia).
Ighyuwa. Performers that sing praises and recite oral histories and poetry. (Mauritania). *Also called* **Griots.**
Igisoro. A traditional game in which small black seeds are strategically placed in hollows of a wooden board. (Rwanda).
Igneri. A name that means "Ancient Ones." The Igneri were the first known inhabitants of what are now the U.S. Virgin Islands. (U.S. Virgin Islands).
Igra oro. Folk dances. (Macedonia).

Ihram. A white, two-piece, towel-like garment worn by men during the **Hajj.** (Saudi Arabia).
Iishana. Oshiwambo word for temporary water holes caused by flooding in the rainy season. The singular form is **Oshana.** (Namibia).
Ikat. A common handwoven textile involving an intricate dye process. (Laos).
Ikebana. Flower arranging. (Japan).
Iki. "Later." An informal Lithuanian parting phrase used between friends. (Lithuania).
Il humdu li'llah. (Mauritania). *See* **Al hamdu lillah.**
Ilienden. A holiday on 2 August that celebrates the uprising against the Ottoman Turks in 1903. (Macedonia).
Il-Maltija. The national dance. (Malta).
Imams. (1) Muslim religious leaders. (Oman). (2) Holy men revered by Shi'ite Muslims as the descendents of Fatima, the prophet Muhammad's daughter, and her husband, Ali. Shi'ites believe the *Imams* disappeared but will reappear in the future to guide Muslims to their destiny. (Azerbaijan, Iran).
Imenden. A person's name day. Commemorates the saint after whom a person is named. The person throws a party and receives gifts from friends and family. (Macedonia).
Imma. The traditional turban. (Sudan).
Immen den. Name days, which are celebrated with a family meal. (Bulgaria).
Imqaret. A pastry filled with dates. (Malta).
Ina ini? "How did you pass the day?" A Hausa greeting used in the afternoon. (Niger).
Ina kwana? "How did you sleep?" A Hausa greeting used in the morning. (Niger).
Inanga. Harps. (Rwanda).
Inchpes ek? "How are you?" A formal Armenian phrase used after an initial greeting. (Armenia).
Incwala. A celebration that includes feasting, singing, dancing, and the slaying of a bull. The highlight is the king tasting the new harvest's fruit. (Swaziland).
Indianista. An Indian novel genre that focuses on indignities suffered by native peoples. (Peru).
Indígenas. The Spanish word for "indigenous." A term collectively referring to indigenous peoples. (Guatemala).
Ingeniero/a. A Spanish title used to address a person with a bachelor of science degree. Masculine *ingeniero*, feminine *ingeniera*. (Panama).
Ingera. Sour bread made of **Teff**, millet, or corn flour fermented in water. (Eritrea). *Also called* **Taitah.**
Ingoma. (1) A dance that celebrates past victories of the Ngoni ethnic group. (Malawi). (2) Drums. (Rwanda).
Ingrato. "Ungrateful." A term used to describe those who fail to show respect for friends and acquaintances. (Cape Verde).
I ni ce. "Hello." A Bambara greeting. (Mali).
Injera. Bread made from a native grain known as **Teff.** (Ethiopia).
Inkhundla. A constituency or district. (Swaziland).
Inona no vaovao? "What is new?" A common Malagasy phrase asked after the initial greeting. (Madagascar).
Inset. A plant from which the stem is used to make **Koocho** bread. (Ethiopia).
Insha'Allah. [NOTE: Spelling varies because it is a transliteration of Arabic.] "God willing." An Arabic phrase used to acknowledge God's hand in a person's life. Used in Muslim-populated countries. (Comoros, Egypt, Morocco).

Glossary of Cultural Terms

Inshallah. (Mauritania, Niger, Pakistan, Tunisia). *See* **Insha'Allah.**

Insh'allah. (Qatar). *See* **Insha'Allah.**

In shallah. (United Arab Emirates). *See* **Insha'Allah.**

Inside. A word called out by visitors as they approach a person's gate. (Antigua and Barbuda).

Insulamnyambeti. A siSwati phrase meaning "wiper away of tears." This refers to one of two cows that a bride's mother receives as part of the bride-price. (Swaziland). *See also* **Lobola.**

Intifada. An uprising of Palestinian Arabs against the Israelis. Palestinians have waged two uprisings, the first breaking out in 1987, the second in 2000. (Israel, West Bank and Gaza).

Inti Raymi. Festival of the Sun. Celebrated at the Incan ruins near Cuenca. (Ecuador).

Intshwarele. "Excuse me." A Setswana phrase used when passing between two conversing individuals. (Botswana).

Ipelegeng. The Setswana word for "carry yourselves." Reflects the Batswana attitude toward community self-help. (Botswana).

¡Iporã! "Just fine." A Guaraní phrase used to respond to the greeting **¿Mba'eichapa?** (Paraguay).

Iran. Supernatural beings. (Guinea-Bissau).

Irasshaimase. "Welcome." A greeting used by a worker to a customer. (Japan).

Irie. "Everything is cool." (Grenada).

Irma. "Sister." A Kriolu term of address used between good friends. (Guinea-Bissau). *See also* **Irmon.**

Irmon. "Brother." A Kriolu term of address used between good friends. (Guinea-Bissau). *See also* **Irma.**

Irooj. Land-owning chiefs. A position in the traditional social system that is now incorporated into the formal government. (Marshall Islands). *See also* **Alaps, Rijerbal.**

Iroojlaplap. Paramount chief. (Marshall Islands).

Irxoxt. The Maltese word for "Risen Christ." (Malta).

'Isha'. Dinner. (Iraq).

Ishkhan. The Armenian word for "prince." (Armenia).

Ish mwe. "My child." A Saint Lucian creole phrase used by adults to address children. (Saint Lucia).

I siibi mooi? "Did you sleep well?" A Ndyuka greeting. (Suriname).

Iska warran? "What's the news?" A Somali phrase used to mean "How are you?" (Somalia).

Islam. A religious faith, *Islam* literally means "submission." A **Muslim** is one who submits to the will of **Allah**. (Bahrain, Mauritania).

Isombe. A favorite dish made from cassava leaves. (Rwanda).

I somogo be di? "How is your family?" A Bambara inquiry that follows an initial greeting. (Mali).

Ita. "Brother" or "sister." A Sango term of address used for a close friend. (Central African Republic).

Ita ti mbi. A Sango term that can mean "brother," "sister," "half brother," "cousin," or "close friend." (Central African Republic).

Itau. A traditional friendship. (Fiji).

-ito. A Spanish suffix that is used to form a diminutive. Masculine *-ito,* feminine *-ita.* (Chile).

Itok im moña. "Come and eat." A common Marshallese greeting. (Marshall Islands).

Iu bin stap long wea? "Where are you coming from?" A Solomon Island Pijin greeting. (Solomon Islands).

Iu go long wea? "Where are you going?" A Solomon Island Pijin greeting. (Solomon Islands).

Iwe. "You." A term of address for children. (Malawi).

Iyak labass. "On you no evil." A Hassaniya greeting used by Moors. (Mauritania). *See also* **Labass.**

Iyi günler. "Have a nice day." A Turkish greeting used when one enters a room. (Turkey).

Iyiyim, teshekur ederim. "Fine, thank you." A typical Turkish response to the greeting **Nasisliniz?** (Turkey).

Jaajmi. Raw fish. (Marshall Islands).

Jaanipäev. Midsummer's Day. Marks the beginning of the summer's "white nights," when the sun sets for only a few hours. (Estonia).

Jakaro. Coconut sap. (Marshall Islands).

Jaki. Mats woven from pandanus leaves. (Marshall Islands).

Jakshi baringiz. "Go well." A Kyrgyz parting phrase used by a host as guests depart. (Kyrgyzstan).

Jakshi kalingiz. "Stay well." A Kyrgyz response to the parting phrase **Jakshi baringiz.** (Kyrgyzstan).

Jalabas. [NOTE: Spelling varies because it is a transliteration of Arabic.] Long robes worn by men. (Syria).

Jalabia. (Sudan). *See* **Jalabas.**

Jalabiyas. (Eritrea). *See* **Jalabas.**

Jam. (1) "Fine." A Fulfulde response to the greeting **Jam na?** (Cameroon). (2) "No evil." A Soninke response to the greeting **An moho**. (Mauritania). (3) A greeting in which men lightly touch closed fists. (Saint Lucia).

Jamahiriya. The official term describing nature of the state of Libya, it means a nation governed by the masses. (Libya).

Jambo. (1) "Hello." A common Swahili greeting. (Congo, Kenya, Tanzania, Uganda). (2) The Marshallese practice of wandering around to visit and chat. (Marshall Islands).

Jameed. Yogurt sauce. (Jordan).

Jamhuri Day. Independence Day. Celebrated on 12 December. (Kenya).

Jam na? "How are you?" A Fulfulde greeting. (Cameroon).

Jam puffs. Jam-filled sourdough pastry. (Barbados).

Jam rekk. "No evil." A Wolof response to the greeting **Nanga def.** (Mauritania).

Jam sukaabe? "How are the kids?" A Fulfulde greeting. (Burkina Faso).

Jam tan. "No evil." A Pulaar response to the greeting **M'bda**. (Mauritania).

Jam waali. "Good morning." A Fulfulde greeting. (Burkina Faso).

-jan. "Dearest." An Armenian suffix added to a person's first name as a sign of affection between close friends.

Jandals. Rubber flip-flops. (Samoa).

Jāņi. Midsummer's Day. Marks the beginning of the summer's "white nights," when the sun sets for only a few hours. (Latvia).

Jan mashtami. A Hindu festival celebrating the birth of Lord Krishna. (India).

Jarabe tapatio. The Mexican Hat Dance. (Mexico).

Jash. The Armenian word for "lunch." (Armenia).

Jatakas. Stories of the Buddha's previous lives. (Cambodia).

Jatiya Sangsad. Bangladesh's National Parliament. (Bangladesh).

Jaunkundze. "Miss." A Latvian title added after the surname. (Latvia).

Jause. Afternoon coffee. (Austria).

Glossary of Cultural Terms

Je demande la route. French phrase meaning "I ask for the road." Guests may say this to hosts after they accompany each other to the road at the end of a visit. (Ivory Coast).

Jeepney(s). A decorated minibus built on the frame of an old military jeep. (Philippines).

Je Khenpo. The Buddhist chief abbot. (Bhutan).

Jélé. A caste whose members are players of traditional music. (Mali).

Jerk. Spicy barbecued pork or chicken. (Jamaica).

Je te donne la moité de la route. French phrase meaning "I give you half the road (use the second half to come back)." Hosts may say this to guests after they symbolically accompany each other to the road at the end of a visit. (Ivory Coast).

-ji. A suffix used with the last name to show respect. (India).

Jiaozi. Chinese dumplings. (China).

Jigim. "Sibling." A term of address used with equals and younger acquaintances. (Turkmenistan). *See also* **Doganym.**

Jihad. A Muslim holy war. (Guinea, Niger).

Jikhalsi. Special cities. (South Korea).

Jilal. Somalia's harsh and dry season. Lasts from December to March. (Somalia).

Jimbôa. A cooked leafy vegetable similar to spinach. (Angola).

Jindungo. Small, hot peppers frequently added to meals. (Angola).

Jirga. The village council. (Afghanistan).

Jiti. A style of music in which **Mbira** music has been adapted to the electric guitar. (Zimbabwe).

Jitney. A small bus holding up to 25 passengers. (Bahamas).

Jitu ka ten. "There is nothing one can do." A common Kriolu phrase. (Guinea-Bissau).

Jitu ten ku ten. "There has to be a way." A new Kriolu slogan. (Guinea-Bissau).

Jó estét kívánok. "Good evening." A polite Hungarian greeting. (Hungary).

Jó étvágyat. "Good appetite." A Hungarian phrase used before eating or when entering a room where someone is eating. (Hungary).

Joget. A popular Malaysian dance. (Malaysia).

Jogorku Kenesh. The Kyrgyz Supreme Council. (Kyrgyzstan).

Johnnycakes. Sweet fried dumplings. (Antigua and Barbuda, Saint Kitts and Nevis, U.S. Virgin Islands).

Joie de vivre. A French phrase meaning "joy of living." (French Polynesia).

Jolok bod. "Excuse me." A Marshallese phrase used when passing between people who are conversing. (Marshall Islands).

Joma. A long coat worn by village men. Kept closed with a bandana-type tie around the waist. (Tajikistan). *Also called* **Chapan.** *See also* **Meeyonband.**

Jó napot kívánok. "Good day." A polite Hungarian greeting. (Hungary).

Jó reggelt kívánok. "Good morning." A polite Hungarian greeting. (Hungary).

Joropo. The traditional music of Venezuelan cowboys. (Venezuela). *See also* **Llaneros.**

Jota. A soup of kidney beans, sauerkraut, and bacon. (Slovenia).

Jounet Creole. Creole Day. A local festival celebrated on 31 October. (Saint Lucia).

Jour de l'An. New Year's Day. (Gabon).

Jour de l'an. A French phrase meaning "New Year's Day." (France).

Jouvert. A street parade during Carnival that begins at sunrise with bands and costumed marchers. (Saint Lucia).

Judd mat Gaardebounen. Smoked collar of pork with broad beans. (Luxembourg).

Jug-jug. Sorghum and green pigeon peas. (Barbados).

Juju. (1) Nigerian music that incorporates guitars with the **Dundun.** (Nigeria). (2) Supernatural phenomena. (Ghana).

Juku. Private, after-hours Japanese schools that help students "cram" for exams. Students attend these schools after a full-day spent at their regular private or public schools. (Japan).

Jul. The Swedish word for "Christmas." (Sweden).

Julenisse. Father Christmas. (Norway).

Jultomte. (1) The name of the Swedish Santa Claus. (Sweden). (2) A Christmas gnome who lives under the house. (Sweden).

Juma. The Arabic word for "Friday." (Niger).

Jum'a. (Egypt). *See* **Ju'mma.**

Jumbie. Unpleasant spirit or ghost. (Trinidad and Tobago).

Jumbos. Motorized tricycles. (Laos).

Ju'mma. [NOTE: Spelling varies because it is a transliteration of Arabic.] Muslim prayer services held midday on Fridays. (Bangladesh).

Jumpers. An Australian term for "sweaters." (Australia).

Jumpups. Block parties that involve street dancing. (Montserrat).

Junta local. A town council. (Panama).

Just cool. "Everything is fine." A typical Grenadian creole response to the questions **W'happen dey?** or **Hows tings?** (Grenada). *See also* **Ah dey.**

Jutho. The Hindu principle of ritual impurity. (Nepal).

-jye. A Nepali suffix used with the last name, to be polite. (Nepal).

-jyu. (Nepal). *See* **-jye.**

Ka. The Fang word for "no." (Equatorial Guinea).

Ka'abah. The cube-shaped stone building in Makkah, Saudi Arabia, that all Muslims in the world face during their daily prayers. (Saudi Arabia).

Kaatsen. A team sport similar to baseball in which players hit a small soft ball with the hand. (Netherlands).

Kabaddi. A type of wrestling. (Pakistan).

Ka-baddi. A sport played by village boys where two teams try to eliminate all the other team's players. One player will enter the other team's zone while holding his breath. He will try and touch the other players and make it back to his own zone. If he makes it back to his side before taking a breath, the players he touched will be out. Otherwise, he is out. (Bangladesh). *Also called* **Ha-dudu.**

Kabaka. The Luganda word for "king." (Uganda).

Kabary. Traditional Malagasy oratory. (Madagascar).

Ka'been. Marriage registry. (Bangladesh).

Kabne. A ceremonial shawl for men and a scarf for women. (Bhutan).

Kabsa. [NOTE: Spelling varies because it is a transliteration of Arabic.] Rice mixed with meat. (United Arab Emirates).

Kabsah. (Saudi Arabia). *See* **Kabsa.**

Kabuki. Highly stylized drama that blends dance, music, and acting. Known for its spectacular sets and costumes. (Japan).

Kachkéis. A soft cheese. (Luxembourg).

Kackavall. A type of cheese. (Albania).

Kadaif. A special dessert in syrup, eaten on New Year's Eve. (Albania).

Glossary of Cultural Terms

Kadaw. A gesture made by kneeling and touching the forehead and both palms to the floor three times. Customary when a person takes leave from a monk. Respect is paid to images of Buddha in the same way. (Myanmar).

Kadri. Celebrated on 25 October. A day for children to go to neighbors' houses, sing special national songs, dance, and ask to be let in out of the cold. The children are given candy and fruit. (Estonia).

Kafel. "It was good." A Yapese greeting or parting phrase. (Micronesia).

Kaffee-trinken. Afternoon coffee. (Germany).

Kaffiyah. A checkered headscarf worn by men. (Iraq). *See also* **Yashmagh.**

Kaftans. Long tailored robes worn by older men. (Gambia).

Kaganat. The Kyrgyz word for "kingdom." (Kyrgyzstan).

Kahve. A thick brew of coffee served in very small cups with nearly every meal. (Turkey).

Kaif al hal? (Chad). *See* **Kaif halak?**

Kaif halak? [NOTE: Spelling varies because it is a transliteration of Arabic.] "How are you?" A common Arabic greeting. (United Arab Emirates).

Kaiga i taeao, inuti. The Tuvaluan word for "breakfast." (Tuvalu).

Kaiga i tuutonu. The Tuvaluan midday meal. A major occasion on Sundays. (Tuvalu).

Kaimen Pugar. "Peace be with you." A Wapisiani greeting. (Guyana).

Kaimoana. The Maori word for "seafood." (New Zealand).

Kaisé ba? "How are you?" The standard Bhojpuri greeting. (Mauritius).

Kaiu. The Tuvaluan word for "stingy." (Tuvalu).

Kai yang. Barbecued chicken. (Laos).

Kajmak. A cheese that consists of the accumulated skim of boiled milk. (Serbia and Montenegro).

Kaka. Father. This term is added to an elder male relative's name to show respect. (Turkmenistan). *See also* **Aga.**

Kak dela? "How are you?" A common Russian greeting between friends. (Russia, Tajikistan).

Kaki lima. Street vendors selling food. Literally "five feet" in Indonesian, meaning two of a man and three of a cart. (Indonesia).

Ka kite ano. "See you later." A Maori parting phrase that is common and informal. (New Zealand).

Kako e semejstvoto? Macedonian for "How is your family?" (Macedonia).

Kako se imaš? "How are you?" An informal Slovene greeting. (Slovenia).

Kako se imate? "How are you?" A formal Slovene greeting. (Slovenia).

Kako si? An informal way of saying "How are you?" in Macedonian. (Macedonia).

Kako ste. A formal way of saying "How are you?" in Macedonian. (Macedonia).

Kak si? "How are you?" An informal Bulgarian greeting used between friends and family. (Bulgaria).

Kak ste? "How are you?" A standard Bulgarian greeting. (Bulgaria).

Kalbatono. "Madame." A Georgian term of address. (Georgia).

Kalbi. Marinated short ribs. (North Korea, South Korea).

Kalevala. Finland's national epic. A compilation of folk songs and stories. (Finland).

Kalevipoeg. "Son of Kalev." The Estonian national epic. (Estonia).

Kalimba. A traditional instrument played by plucking small metal strips with the thumbs. (Zambia).

Kaliméra sas. "Good morning." A Greek greeting. (Greece).

Kalindula. A popular dance music. (Zambia).

Kalispéra sas. "Good evening." A Greek greeting. (Greece).

Kallaloo. A stew traditionally made with pig tail, conch, blue fish, land crab, salt beef, or oxtail. (U.S. Virgin Islands).

Kalojam. Dough boiled in syrup; a popular sweet. (Bangladesh).

Kalondolondo. Hide-and-seek. (Malawi).

Kalym. A large sum of money given to the bride's parents to solidify the engagement. (Kyrgyzstan).

Kamaimai. Boiled toddy (coconut sap) that forms a thick, sweet molasses. (Kiribati). *See also* **Kaokioki.**

Kamanche. A spiked fiddle; a traditional Iranian instrument. (Iran).

Kamelaha? "How are you?" A Tigrinya greeting to a man. (Ethiopia).

Kamelehee? "How are you?" A Tigrinya greeting to a woman. (Ethiopia).

Kamisa. A cotton loincloth worn by Amerindian men. (Suriname).

Kamma. A round embroidered hat worn by men. (Oman).

Kamoolal. Thanksgiving Day. Celebrated the first Friday in December. (Marshall Islands).

Kanda. Meat, fish, fruit, or termites wrapped in a leaf and steamed. (Central African Republic).

Kandaisiz? "How are you?" A common Uzbek greeting. (Uzbekistan).

Kan dikdik kan in yokwe. "Little food with lots of love." A common Marshallese expression. (Marshall Islands).

Kandongas. Pickup trucks with seats and a roof for baggage. Used to travel between towns. (Guinea-Bissau).

Kandu. A traditional white robe worn by elders, rural men, and urban men going to a mosque. (Comoros).

Kandurah. A white robe worn by men. Worn with an **Agal** and **Kitra**. (United Arab Emirates). *Also called* **Dishdasha.**

Kang. The Thai word for "curry." (Thailand).

Kanga(s). Colorful cotton cloth worn by women. (Kenya, Tanzania).

Kanji. The Japanese writing system based on Chinese characters. (Japan). *See also* **Hiragana, Katakana, Romaji.**

Kannan. A wooden stringed instrument similar to the zither. The Estonian national instrument. (Estonia).

Kantele. A stringed instrument played with the fingers; it is also the Finnish national instrument. (Finland).

Kantsi. An embroidered deer, bull, or goat horn. (Georgia).

Kanza. An instrument similar to a three-stringed banjo. (Morocco). *Also called* **Lotar.**

Kanzu. A long, embroidered cotton gown worn by men. (Tanzania, Uganda).

Kao. The Thai word for "rice." Usually a long-grained jasmine rice. (Thailand).

Kaoha. "Hi." A common greeting used in the Marquesas Islands. (French Polynesia).

Kaokioki. Fermented toddy (coconut sap); an alcoholic drink. (Kiribati). *See also* **Kamaimai.**

Kapelica. Small shrines. (Slovenia).

Glossary of Cultural Terms

Kapiteins. Maroon and Amerindian chiefs who receive public salaries and have authority over some local matters. (Suriname).

Kāpostu zupa. Cabbage soup. (Latvia).

Karagöz. A shadow play created by casting shadows of puppets on a curtain. (Turkey).

Karai. A term of address for men that is followed by the first name. Used in rural areas. (Paraguay).

Karakul. Sheepskin. (Namibia).

Karakuli. A fez-type hat. (Pakistan).

Karamin sallah. "Little feast." A celebration at the end of the month of **Ramadan**. (Niger).

Karavay. A traditional wedding pie. Includes honey and vodka to make the future life of the couple sweet and merry. (Belarus).

Karbonade. Pork chop. (Netherlands).

Karbonāde. Pork steak. (Latvia).

Kare-kare. A stew of meats and vegetables served in a peanut sauce. (Philippines).

Kargad ikavit. "Bye, take care." A Georgian parting phrase. (Georgia).

Karibu. "Welcome." A Kiswahili response to visitors who announce their presence. (Rwanda, Tanzania).

Karibuni. "Welcome." A Kiswahili response to visitors who announce their presence. This term is used when responding to more than one person. When responding to an individual, the term **Karibu** is used. (Tanzania).

Karma. A force, generated by one's actions in the present life, that determines the nature of one's next life. A Buddhist and Hindu belief. (Bhutan, Mauritius, Myanmar, Nepal).

Kartor. The Lao national game in which players try to keep a rattan ball in the air without using their hands. (Laos).

Kartupeli. Potatoes. (Latvia).

Karunna. Compassion. One of Buddhism's pillar virtues. (Laos). *See also* **Brahma Vihara**.

Karutsa. Horse-drawn carts. (Moldova).

Kaseko. A musical style that combines traditional Creole music and Caribbean rhythms. Uses call-and-response singing and percussion instruments such as the **Skratsji**. (Suriname).

Kaselaleliah. "Hello." A Pohnpei greeting. (Micronesia).

Kasha. Cooked or baked cereal. (Belarus, Moldova, Ukraine).

Kashkaval. A yellow cheese. (Macedonia).

Kashkazi. The hot, humid rainy season. Runs from November to March. (Comoros). *See also* **Kusi**.

Kashkusha. A wavy, knotted tassel worn at the neck by men. (Oman). *Also called* **Farakha**.

Kashrut. Jewish dietary laws. (Israel).

Käsknöpfle. A pasta with sharp cheese. (Liechtenstein).

Katakana. A Japanese phonetic alphabet. (Japan). *See also* **Hiragana, Kanji, Romaji**.

Katei ni Kiribati. "The Gilbertese way." The attitude that the future will take care of itself. (Kiribati).

Kathakali. A mimed dance that traditionally lasts all night. (India).

Katta sambol. A spicy mixture of fried onions and chilies. (Sri Lanka).

Kaukau. Sweet potato. (Papua New Guinea).

Kava. (1) A mildly narcotic, nonalcoholic beverage made from the crushed *kava* root, a shrub in the pepper family. (American Samoa, Fiji, Samoa, Tonga). (2) Coffee. (Belarus).

Kaval. A type of flute; a traditional instrument. (Bulgaria).

Kawanatanga. Maori word for "governance." (New Zealand).

Kawiarnia. Polish word for "café." (Poland).

Kayfak? "How are you?" A common Arabic greeting. (Qatar).

Kayf haalak? (Sudan). *See* **Kaif halak?**

Kayf halak? (Libya, Oman, Qatar). *See* **Kaif halak?**

Kayf innakum? "How are you?" A common Arabic greeting. (Sudan).

Każini. Pubs. (Malta).

Kde Slovák tam spev. "Wherever there is a Slovak, there is a song." A Slovak saying. (Slovakia).

Kebab. Skewered meat. (Israel).

Kebaya. A traditional Malay dress. (Singapore).

Kebbeh. Spiced meatballs. (Syria).

Kebero. A drum. (Ethiopia).

Kecap manis. A sweet dark sauce. (Indonesia).

Keef haalak? (Syria). *See* **Kaif halak?**

Keef halak? (Lebanon). *See* **Kaif halak?**

Keef halik? "How are you?" A common Arabic greeting used when addressing women. (Lebanon).

Keep time. A colloquialism meaning "to visit." (Sierra Leone).

Kefelhal? (Eritrea). *See* **Kaif halak?**

Keffiyah. A head covering worn by Bedouin men. (Syria).

Kefir. Fermented cow's milk. (Belarus).

Kefta. Ground beef or mutton that is seasoned and cooked over charcoal. (Morocco).

Ke itumetse. "I am pleased." A Setswana phrase to thank the host after a meal is completed. (Botswana).

Kelaguen. Grilled chicken mixed with lemon juice, green onions, hot peppers, and grated coconut. (Guam).

Kemem. Marshallese word for "feasts." (Marshall Islands).

Kena. "Come in." The host's response to **Ko ko**, the visitor's announcement of his or her arrival. (Lesotho).

Kendo. The sport of fencing with bamboo poles. (Japan).

Kente. Colorful woven cloth; used for robes worn by men. (Ghana, Togo).

Kerekere. A custom that allows a relative or neighbor to ask for something that is needed. It must be given willingly, without expectation of repayment. (Fiji).

Ke teng. Literally, "I am here," meaning "fine." A Setswana reply to the greeting **O kae?** (Botswana).

Ke tsogile sentle. "I awoke well." A Setswana reply to the greeting **Dumela Rra/Mma, O tsogile jang?** (Botswana).

Kezét csókolom. "I kiss your hand." A formal Hungarian greeting used to address older women. (Hungary).

Kgotla. A meeting place where neighborhood and village decisions are made. (Botswana).

Khadag. A blue silk bag filled with **Airag** that can be presented to an elder or a person of higher social rank as a sign of deep respect and well-wishing. (Mongolia).

Khadi. A Muslim religious leader who performs weddings. (Israel).

Khaen. A type of bamboo flute used to play Lao folk music. (Laos).

Khair. "Good-bye." A common Tajik parting phrase. (Tajikistan).

Khalah. (Iraq). *See* **Khaleh**.

Khaleh. "Aunt." An Arabic term of address for an older woman. (Syria).

Khalo. The Arabic word for a maternal uncle. (West Bank and Gaza).

Glossary of Cultural Terms

Khalto. The Arabic word for a maternal aunt. (West Bank and Gaza).

Khamari. A dance performed at weddings and other social gatherings by women. (Kuwait).

Khamasiin. A hot, driving, dusty wind that blows in the spring. (Egypt).

Khamauk. A conical bamboo hat worn by farmers. (Myanmar).

Khamsa ou Khmis Aalik. A phrase used to express that a meal was satisfying. Roughly means "You've done an excellent job." (Tunisia).

Khan. "Sir." An Arabic title. (Afghanistan).

Khana khanu bajou. "Have you eaten your rice already?" A Nepali greeting used to mean "How are you?" (Nepal).

Khanjar. An ornamental dagger. (Iraq, Oman).

Khash. Cow's feet that are cooked all night and often served at sunrise on winter weekends. (Armenia).

Khat. A leafy plant that produces a mildly stimulating effect when chewed. (Somalia).

Khatchapuri. Cheese-filled cookies. (Georgia).

Khatchkars. Decorative stone monuments. (Armenia).

Kheer. A type of rice pudding. (Pakistan).

Khleb. Coarse, Russian-style bread. (Turkmenistan).

Khmer Rouge. "Red Khmer." This radical communist organization began a violent restructuring of the entire society that killed nearly two million people through violence, starvation, and disease. The educated and business classes were all but eliminated and the economy was completely destroyed. (Cambodia). *See also* **Bye ch'nam, pram-bye kai, m'pai t'gnai.**

Khoda hafiz. [NOTE: Spelling varies because it is a transliteration of Arabic.] "Good-bye" or "May God be with you." A common Arabic parting phrase. (Afghanistan, Bangladesh, Iran).

Khodha haafis. (Pakistan). *See* **Khoda hafiz.**

Khon. Masked plays that feature ornate costumes. (Thailand).

Khorovats. Marinated meat placed on sticks and cooked over coals by men. (Armenia). *Also called* **Kyabab.**

Khoskap. "Tying of Promise." An event at which the groom presents a ring to his intended bride as a promise to marry. (Armenia).

Khotso. "Peace be with you." A formal Sesotho greeting. (Lesotho).

Khubus ti? "How are you?" A common Dari greeting. (Afghanistan).

Khubz. Flat bread. (Iraq).

Khumiss. Fermented mare's milk. (Kazakstan).

Khun. A respectful Thai title used with the first name. (Thailand).

Khuru. A game similar to lawn darts. (Bhutan).

Kia ora. "Be well." A Maori phrase that can mean "hello" or "thank you." (New Zealand).

Kibare. "Hi." A common Mooré greeting. (Burkina Faso).

Kibba. A fried cracked wheat dough stuffed with meat or vegetables. (Iraq).

Kibbeh. A popular beef dish that can be baked, fried, or eaten raw. (Lebanon).

Kibbutz. A place where families live and share the land, work, food, and dining hall equally. They concentrate on agriculture and technology. (Israel). *See also* **Moshav.**

Kiekie. A traditional skirt made from pandanus leaves and woven into different designs that hang as strips from the waist. It is still sometimes worn over skirts, dresses, and **tupenus**. (Tonga).

Ki kati? "What's up?" A Luganda greeting used among young Baganda. (Uganda).

Kilshi. Spiced beef or sheep jerky. (Niger).

Ki manière? "How are you?" A common Mauritian Creole greeting. (Mauritius).

Kimbondeiros. Traditional healers. (Angola). *Also called* **Curandeiros.**

Kimch'i. A spicy pickled cabbage. (North Korea, South Korea).

Kimeshek. A Muslim-style head wrap worn by older Kazak women. (Kazakstan).

Kimono(s). A long traditional robe with long sleeves and tied closed with a special sash. (Japan). *Also called* **Wafuku.** *See also* **Obi.**

Kina Gecesi. "Henna evening." An event for women at which the hands and fingers of the bride are decorated with henna leaf dye. The beginning event of a traditional Turkish wedding. (Turkey).

Kindy. An Australian colloquialism for "kindergarten." (Australia).

Kinh. The Vietnamese ethnic group. (Vietnam).

Kin khow leo bor? "Have you eaten?" An informal Lao greeting. (Laos).

Kinte. Colorful, intricately patterned cotton fabric wrapped around the body as clothing; worn for special events in the southern Ivory Coast. (Ivory Coast). *Also called* **Kita.**

Kiondo. Kikuyu word for a woven bag used to bring gifts. (Kenya).

Kioskos. Small neighborhood shops. (Argentina). *See also* **Almacenes.**

Kiosks. Small newsstand shops that offer a variety of goods. (Poland).

Kip. Laos's national currency. (Laos).

Kippah. An embroidered cap worn by men. (Israel). *Also called* **Yarmulke.**

Kira. The traditional Bhutanese outfit for women. A large rectangular cloth wrapped from ankle to bodice and belted at the waist; it is fastened at the shoulders and worn under a jacket. (Bhutan).

Kirikiti. Samoan cricket. (American Samoa, Samoa).

Kisel. A fruit puree. (Belarus).

Kisra. Thinly layered food made from flour paste. (Sudan).

Kissar. A light sourdough crêpe. (Chad).

Kita. Colorful, intricately patterned cotton fabric wrapped around the body as clothing; worn for special events in the southern Ivory Coast. (Ivory Coast). *Also called* **Kinte.**

Kitandeiras. Women who sell fruit and other goods on street corners or by walking through the city carrying their products on their heads. (Angola). *Also called* **Zungueiras.**

K'itcha. Unleavened bread. (Eritrea).

Kitchen gardens. Small plots of land that produce various fruits, **Ground provisions**, and herbs for tea. (Montserrat).

Kitenge. Several pieces of colorful cotton wraparound fabric used as clothing. (Tanzania). *Also called* **Kanga(s).**

Kitfo. A finely chopped, raw red meat mixed with butter, cheese, and cabbage. Served with the bread **Koocho**. (Ethiopia).

Kitra. (United Arab Emirates). *See* **Gutra.**

Kitumbua. Fried bread. The plural form is *vitumbua*. (Tanzania).

Glossary of Cultural Terms

Kiunguju. The word for "Kiswahili" on the island of Zanzibar. (Tanzania).

Kiyit. A wedding custom in which relatives of the bride and groom exchange clothes. (Kyrgyzstan).

Kizomba. A popular musical style. (Angola).

Kkoktukaksi. Puppet theater. (South Korea).

Klambi koeroeng. A tight-fitting jacket worn with a **Sarong** and **Slendang**. (Suriname).

Kleeschen. The Luxembourgish name for "St. Nicholas." (Luxembourg).

Klibbere goen. An Easter tradition where young boys announce church services with rattles because, according to legend, all church bells leave and go to Rome, Italy, for confessional. When the bells return on the Saturday before Easter, the children collect money and Easter eggs from each home as their reward. (Luxembourg).

Klompen. Dutch wooden shoes or clogs. (Netherlands).

Klongs. Canals that are often used for transportation in rural and some urban areas. (Thailand).

Knäckebröd. Crisp bread. (Sweden).

Knedlo, vepřo, zelo. A meal of sauerkraut, pork roast, and dumplings. (Czech Republic).

Knesset. The Israeli Parliament. (Israel).

Knobkerrie. A traditional club. Part of male traditional dress. (Swaziland). *See also* **Lihiya, Lijobo.**

Knock-it. A greeting in which friends (particularly men) lightly touch closed fists. (Belize).

Knödel. Moist dumplings. (Austria).

Ko. "Big brother." A term used to address young men, regardless of relationship. (Myanmar).

Koba. The Marshallese equivalent to living in a common-law marriage. (Marshall Islands).

Kobouz. Unleavened bread. (Bahrain).

Kobuz. A stringed instrument that **Ashugs** use to accompany their performances. (Azerbaijan).

Koddeyo. "How are the home people?" A Lysonga greeting. (Uganda).

Koe kia. "Good-bye." A Niuean parting phrase. (Niue).

Kofia. An embroidered cap worn by men. (Comoros).

Koha. A gift of money one leaves when welcomed on a **Marae**. The *koha* is a donation toward the cost of hospitality. (New Zealand).

Koka'anga ngatu. Parties in which women make **Tapa**. (Tonga).

Ko ko. "Knock knock." A phrase used to announce one's presence when visiting a home. (Lesotho).

Kokoko. A phrase visitors use to announce their presence. (Gabon).

Kokoretsi. Liver, lungs, and spleen wrapped in intestines and roasted on a spit. (Greece).

Kokpar. A traditional horseback competition in which opposing teams try to move a goat's carcass to a central goal. (Kazakstan). *See also* **Baiga.**

Koláč. Nut or poppy seed rolls. (Slovakia).

Kolah. A turban cap. The color and design are distinctive to the wearer's ethnic background. (Afghanistan).

Kola nuts. Caffeine-containing tree nuts that have been traded in West Africa for centuries; these are sometimes exchanged as a sign of respect at formal ceremonies in the north. (Ivory Coast).

Kolatsche. A Bohemian pastry made out of yeast dough. (Austria).

Koliadki. Christmas carols. (Ukraine).

Koline. A seasonal holiday celebrating the new harvest. Farmers celebrate by sharing newly butchered pork and special sausages with neighbors. (Slovenia).

Kolo. A folk dance. Characteristics may vary depending on the country. (Bosnia and Herzegovina, Croatia, Serbia and Montenegro).

Kolokolo. Coconut fiber string. Made by elderly men for use around the home. (Tuvalu).

Kolpak. A traditional white wool pointed hat worn by men for protection against the elements and as a sign of patriotism. (Kyrgyzstan).

Kombis. Minivan taxis. (Zimbabwe).

Komšija. "Neighbor." A Serbian title used with the last name. (Serbia and Montenegro).

Komsija. Serbo-Croatian word for neighbor. (Bosnia and Herzegovina).

Komuz. A three-stringed instrument similar to the guitar. Used to play traditional music. (Kyrgyzstan).

Ko naera? "Where are you going?" An informal Kiribati greeting. (Kiribati).

Konjak. A strong alcoholic drink. (Albania).

Konnichiwa. "Hello." A standard Japanese greeting. (Japan).

Konpa. A style of music especially popular in urban areas. The music is related to big band music played in the United States during the 1940s. (Haiti).

Koocho. A bread prepared from the stem of a plant called **Inset**. Served with **Kitfo**. (Ethiopia).

Koofiyad. An embroidered cap. (Somalia).

Koopkari. A traditional polo-like sport in which participants on horseback attempt to carry a sheep carcass to a central goal without having it taken away by their competitors. (Uzbekistan).

Kop ango? "What issues?" A Luo greeting. (Uganda).

Kopjes. Huge granite rocks that often rest on smaller formations. (Zimbabwe).

Kop pe. "No issues." The Luo response to the greeting **Kop ango?** (Uganda).

Kora. A traditional stringed instrument made from a gourd. (Gambia, Guinea, Guinea-Bissau, Senegal).

Korfbal. A sport played on a grass field or indoors that combines elements of soccer and basketball. (Netherlands).

Korite. [NOTE: Spelling varies because it is a transliteration.] A feast that marks the end of the Muslim holiday **Ramadan**. (Senegal).

Koritee. (Gambia). *See* **Korite.**

Korjaals. Motorized river canoes used to access Suriname's interior villages. (Suriname).

Korpacha. Mats that are used for sitting. (Uzbekistan).

Koruna. The Czech Republic and Slovakia's national currencies. (Czech Republic, Slovakia).

Kosai. A deep-fried bean cake. (Niger).

Košava. Strong winds. (Serbia and Montenegro).

Kosh bogula. "Good-bye." A common Kyrgyz parting phrase. (Kyrgyzstan).

Kosilo. Slovene word for the main meal of the day. Eaten in the midafternoon or after work. (Slovenia).

Kosu. The Saramaccan term for a traditional wraparound dress. (Suriname). *Also called* **Pangi.**

Glossary of Cultural Terms

Kota. "Elder." A term used to address older men. (Angola).

Koto. A Creole dress consisting of many layers of colorful fabric; it is accompanied by a head scarf (**Angisa**). (Suriname).

Köttbullar med kokt potatis, brun sås och lingonsylt. Meatballs with brown sauce, boiled potatoes, and lingonberry jam. (Sweden).

Kozaks. Zaporozhian Cossacks. (Ukraine).

Kpessosso. The New Year celebration in Aného. Each resident enters blindfolded into the house of **Kpessou** (Aného's local god) to retrieve a colored stone. The color of the stone is a personal omen. (Togo).

Kpessou. Aného's local god. (Togo).

Kpu. A contraption similar to a mortar and pestle, used to grind leaves and prepare many other foods. (Central African Republic).

Kraal. An animal corral. (Lesotho, Swaziland).

Krama. A large scarf that may be used in a variety of ways, including a hat, small blanket, and baby carrier. (Cambodia).

Krapfen. A type of doughnut. (Austria).

Kravata. Croatian word for "tie." (Croatia).

Krentenbollen. Raisin rolls. (Netherlands).

Kresovanje. Midsummer's Night Eve. (Slovenia).

Kroket. A deep-fried sausage. (Netherlands).

Krona. Sweden's national currency. (Sweden).

Króna. Iceland's national currency. The plural form is *krónur*. (Iceland).

Krone. Denmark's national currency. (Denmark).

Kroner. Norway's national currency. (Norway).

Krónur. (Iceland). *See* **Króna**.

Kroon. Estonia's national currency. (Estonia).

Kshatriya. The Hindu caste composed of rulers and warriors. (Nepal). *See also* **Brahmin(s), Chaturvarna Vyavasta, Shudra(s), Vaishya**.

Kubsa. A whole lamb or kid goat stuffed with seasoned rice. (Qatar). *Also called* **Ghozi**.

Kučios. Christmas Eve. (Lithuania).

Kuduro. A popular musical style, heavily influenced by rap and rhythm and blues. (Angola).

Kuftal. Pounded, boiled meat. (Armenia).

Kufteta. A fried meat patty with bread crumbs. (Bulgaria).

Kugelis. Potato pudding with a sour cream sauce. (Lithuania).

Kuidas elate? "How's life?" An Estonian phrase used to begin a conversation. (Estonia).

Kuidas läheb? "How is it going?" An Estonian phrase used to begin a conversation. (Estonia).

Kūkas. Cakes. (Latvia).

Kuk Hoe. The South Korean National Assembly. (South Korea).

Kukri. A place where urban people can buy cooked rice. (Sierra Leone).

Kukurai. "Big man" or leader. There is one in each village. (Papua New Guinea). *Also called* **Bikman**.

Kuma? "How are you?" A typical Kriolu greeting. (Guinea-Bissau).

Kuma di kurpu? "How is your body?" A polite Kriolu inquiry. (Guinea-Bissau).

Kumara. Sweet potatoes. (New Zealand, Solomon Islands).

Kumari. A title used with the last name of an unmarried woman to show respect. (India).

Kumiss. Fermented mare's milk. (Kyrgyzstan).

Kumu. Greens of any kind. (Papua New Guinea).

Kumusta ka na? "How are you doing?" A formal Tagalog greeting. (Philippines).

Kuna. Croatia's national currency. (Croatia).

Kundu. A traditional drum that is hourglass-shaped and covered with lizard skin. (Papua New Guinea).

Kundze. "Mrs." A Latvian title added after the name when an introduction is made. (Latvia).

Kungs. "Mr." A Latvian title added after the name when an introduction is made. (Latvia).

Kunjani? "How are you?" A common Zulu and Swazi greeting. (South Africa, Swaziland).

Kunta. Fabric strips sewn together to form geometric patterns. Often woven into blankets given as wedding presents and kept as family heirlooms. (Niger).

Kurban Ait. [NOTE: Muslim holidays are set according to the lunar calendar.] Day of Remembrance; a Muslim holiday. (Kyrgyzstan).

Kurban Bairam. [NOTE: Spelling varies because it is a transliteration. Also, Muslim holidays are set according to the lunar calendar.] Feast of the Sacrifice. A Muslim holiday commemorating Abraham's willingness to sacrifice his son. (Albania, Bosnia and Herzegovina, Croatia). *Also called* **Eid al-Adha**.

Kurban Bairami. (Azerbaijan). *See* **Kurban Bairam**.

Kurban Bayramı. (Turkey). *See* **Kurban Bairam**.

Kurent. A demon figure who chases away the winter. (Slovenia). *See also* **Kurentovanje**.

Kurentovanje. The evening before **Pust** when **Kurent** chases away winter. (Slovenia).

Kures. The Kazak form of wrestling. (Kazakstan).

Kurja obara. Chicken stew with buckwheat groats. (Slovenia).

Kurova guva. A weeklong party held a year or two after a family member dies. At this time the departed spirit is united with the living. (Zimbabwe).

Kurpacha. Thick cushions that are spread on the floor and used for sitting. (Tajikistan).

Kurta surwal. Colorful pants, tight from the calves down, with a matching, knee-length tunic. Worn by unmarried girls and women in Terai. (Nepal). *Also called* **Punjabi**.

Kushe. "Hello." A common Krio greeting. (Sierra Leone).

Kusi. The pleasant season with warm, clear, breezy days and cool nights. Lasts from April to September. (Comoros). *See also* **Kashkazi**.

Kutyapi. A two-stringed lute. (Philippines).

Kuzuzangpo? "Is your body well?" A common Dzongkha greeting and parting phrase. (Bhutan).

Kuzuzangpo la dasho. A Dzongkha title used to address superiors. (Bhutan).

Kvass. A tangy Russian juice made from dried bread. (Kazakstan).

Kwacha. Malawi and Zambia's national currencies. (Malawi, Zambia).

Kwaito. A popular style of music that mixes African melodies and lyrics with hip-hop and reggae. (South Africa).

Kwanjin. Breadfruit baked on coals and then scraped. (Marshall Islands).

Kwanza. Angola's national currency. (Angola).

Kwasa kwasa. A Congolese style of dance music. (Botswana, Congo, Malawi, Namibia).

Kwela. (1) A style of music that incorporates the distinctive penny whistle. (South Africa). (2) The Kimbundu term for a

Glossary of Cultural Terms

strategy game played with beads or seeds placed in holes on a wooden board or in the ground. (Angola). *Also called* **Wela.**

Kwezi. Part of a child's greeting to an elder. A child will cup both hands and extend them while saying *Kwezi*. (Comoros).

Kwon kaal. Millet bread. (Uganda).

Kyabab. Marinated meat placed on sticks and cooked over coals by men. (Armenia). *Also called* **Khorovats.**

Kyat. Myanmar's national currency. (Myanmar).

Kyeshki as. Kazak word for a light evening meal. (Kazakstan).

Kygyzcha. A style of eating without utensils. (Kyrgyzstan).

Kýna. Papua New Guinea's national currency. (Papua New Guinea).

Kyrk. The Kyrgyz word for "forty." (Kyrgyzstan).

Kyz. The Kyrgyz word for "girls." (Kyrgyzstan).

Kyz Dzharysh. Girls' races on horseback. (Kyrgyzstan).

Kyz kuumai. Chasing the bride. A common village ritual in which the bride is provided with the fastest horse and must try to outrace the groom. If she outraces him, she can "choose" not to marry him. (Kyrgyzstan).

Kyzy. The Kyrgyz word for "daughter." In Kyrgyz, a girl is greeted by her father's first name, followed by *kyzy*, and then the girl's own given name. (Kyrgyzstan).

Kyzyl chai. "Red tea." A popular drink. (Kyrgyzstan).

La. A sound attached to words in Dzongkha or English to show respect. (Bhutan).

Laba diena. "Good day." A common Lithuanian greeting. (Lithuania).

Laban. A yogurt drink. (Oman).

Labas. "Hello." An informal Lithuanian greeting used among friends. (Lithuania).

Labas rytas. "Good morning." A common Lithuanian greeting. (Lithuania).

Labass. "No evil." A response to the Hassaniya greeting **Iyak labass**. (Mauritania).

Labas vakaras. "Good evening." A common Lithuanian greeting. (Lithuania).

Labess. A greeting that means "How are you?" and "Fine." (Morocco).

La cena. The Spanish word for "dinner." (Spain).

La comida. The Spanish word for "lunch." (Spain).

Laddie. A term people use to refer to males. (Scotland).

La dictadura. A period of time in which a military junta ruled for 12 years, beginning in 1968. (Peru).

Ladino. Descendants of the Spanish and Maya. They more closely identify with their Spanish heritage. (Guatemala).

La Fête Nationale. Bastille Day, celebrated 14 July. The holiday commemorates the storming of the Bastille prison in Paris during the French Revolution. (France).

Lafia ngai. "Much peace." A Sara greeting. (Chad).

Lagting. The upper chamber of the Norwegian Parliament. (Norway). *See also* **Storting.**

Lahaf. An embroidered headdress worn by women. (Oman).

Lahatra. Malagasy word for "fate." (Madagascar).

Lahiya lau. "In health." A Hausa response to the greetings **Ina kwana?** and **Ina ini?** (Niger).

Lahko noč. "Good night." A common Slovene greeting. (Slovenia).

La hora chapina. The Guatemalan hour. A term that refers to putting people before schedules in such a way that events rarely start on time. (Guatemala).

La hora Ecuatoriana. Ecuadorian time; referring to the Ecuadorian tendency to arrive late. (Ecuador).

La hora latina. "Latin time." The notion that individuals' needs are more important than schedules. Thus, being late is the norm. (Honduras).

Lahuta. A one-stringed instrument played with a bow. (Albania).

Lailat El-Dakhlah. An Arabic phrase meaning "wedding night." (Jordan).

La Isla de la Trinidad. Island of the Holy Trinity. (Trinidad and Tobago).

Lala salama. "Sleep peacefully." A common parting phrase used in the evening. (Kenya).

Lalé. A greeting used when joining a large group. Both palms are raised while greeting. (Chad).

Lali. Wooden drums. (Fiji).

La lucha. Professional wrestling. (Mexico).

Lamas. Buddhist monks who teach. They officiate at most events, from naming babies to village festivals to public ribbon cuttings. (Bhutan).

Lamba. Long white cotton wrap. Traditional attire for men and women in the highlands area. (Madagascar).

Lambamena. "Red cloth." A burial shroud. (Madagascar). *See also* **Famadihana.**

Lambaoany. A light, colorful wrap worn by men and women in coastal areas. (Madagascar).

Lambi. Conch. (Grenada).

Lam gi day? "What are you doing?" A common Vietnamese greeting. (Vietnam).

La multi ani. "Happy New Year." A Romanian greeting used at the beginning of the new year. (Moldova).

Lamvong. The Lao national folk dance, in which dancers form three rings and are encircled by the audience. (Laos).

Länder. German states that have their own legislatures and control over local issues. (Germany).

Landtag. The Liechtenstein Parliament. (Liechtenstein).

Lang Arm. Waltz music. Literally, "long arm." (Namibia).

Langouti. An ankle-length cotton garment tied at the waist. A traditional outfit worn by Hindu men. (Mauritius).

La novena. The nine days before Christmas that are marked by religious observances and parties. (Colombia).

Lao. "Old." A Mandarin Chinese term used with or instead of a title to show special respect to a friend. (China).

Lao Lum. "Lowland Lao." The largest ethnic group in Laos. The *Lao Lum* are culturally and linguistically related to the Isaan people of northeastern Thailand. (Laos).

Lao Sung. "Highland Lao." An ethnic group that includes the Hmong, Kor, and Yao peoples. Their origins are in southwestern China. (Laos).

Lao Theung. "Midland Lao." An ethnic group that includes the Khmu, Katang, Makong, and Xuay ethnic groups. (Laos).

Lap. Sautéed meat mixed with onions, lemongrass, and spices. Served with a rice-flour sauce. (Laos).

Laplap. A wraparound sarong worn by men and women. (Papua New Guinea).

Lappas. Two yards of ankle-length cloth worn by women; tied about the waist and topped with an African or Western blouse. Commonly made of brightly colored cotton. (Sierra Leone).

La punta. A popular style of music with a complex rhythm. It originated with traditional Garífuna music and dance. Played

Glossary of Cultural Terms

with instruments such as drums, conch shells, and maracas. (Honduras).

La revedere. "Good-bye." A Romanian parting phrase. (Moldova).

Lari. Georgia's national currency. (Georgia).

Larimar. A blue stone unique to the Dominican Republic. Used to make jewelry. (Dominican Republic).

Las Cortes Generales. Spain's bicameral legislature. (Spain).

Las murgas. Small groups of singers and actors who present parodies of the year's main events. (Uruguay).

Lassie. A term people use to refer to females. (Scotland).

Lat. Latvia's national currency. (Latvia).

Laulu. The Tuvaluan word for "spinach." (Tuvalu).

Lau Susuga. A general Samoan title suitable for chiefs and married or professional people. (American Samoa, Samoa).

Lavalava(s). Large rectangular pieces of cloth worn as clothing. (American Samoa, Micronesia, Samoa, Solomon Islands).

La Vanguardia. "The Vanguard." A literary movement that seeks to restore Nicaragua's cultural identity. (Nicaragua).

Lavash. Lightly browned flat bread, rolled out in large circles and baked in a **Tonir**. (Armenia).

Laver bread. A mixture of seaweed and oatmeal that is fried and served with bacon. (Wales). *Also called* **Bara lawr.**

La Vielle. French term meaning "elderly woman." If there is no male figurehead, families may be headed by the oldest woman in the family, who is called this name. (Ivory Coast).

La Violencia. Colombian civil war between conservatives and liberals from 1948 to 1957. (Colombia).

Lay. Condensed milk with sugar. (Gambia).

Leban. Diluted yogurt. (Kuwait).

Lebaran. A feast at the end of **Ramadan**. (Indonesia). *Also called* **Idul-Fitri.**

Leberknödelsuppe. A soup with liver dumplings. (Austria).

Lechon. A stuffed pig roasted over a charcoal fire. (Philippines).

Lechoza. Papaya. (Venezuela).

Lederhosen. Leather knee-length pants. Traditional clothing worn by men. (Austria, Germany).

Le Huit Mai. French Armistice Day. Celebrated on 8 May. (France).

Lek. Albania's national currency. (Albania).

Leka nosht. "Good night." A Bulgarian greeting. (Bulgaria).

Lempira. Honduras's national currency. (Honduras).

Lengua en salsa. "Tongue in sauce." A common Costa Rican dish. (Costa Rica).

Leone(s). Sierra Leone's national currency. (Sierra Leone).

Lesiba. A stringed reed. A popular traditional instrument often played by young men as a method of herding cattle. (Lesotho).

Leso. A printed shawl. (Comoros).

Le truck. A truck converted into a bus that is a popular form of local transportation. (French Polynesia).

Letterboxes. A colloquialism for mailboxes. (Wales).

Lettres. An education track that focuses on humanities and social sciences. (Tunisia).

Lëtzebuergesch. The Luxembourgish language. (Luxembourg).

Leu. Moldova and Romania's national currencies. (Moldova, Romania).

Lev. Bulgaria's national currency. (Bulgaria).

L'Exode. Young men that work for wages in neighboring countries and return to Niger during the rainy season. (Niger).

Liamuiga. The name, meaning "Fertile Island," given to Saint Kitts by the Caribs who lived on the island prior to its colonization by Europeans. (Saint Kitts and Nevis).

Licensiado. A professional title. (Peru).

Liceo. A government-subsidized secondary school. (Uruguay).

Lift. Elevator. (New Zealand).

Lihiya. A single length of printed cloth. The plural form is **Emahiya.** It forms the basis of traditional clothing for men and women. (Swaziland). *See also* **Knobkerrie, Lijobo.**

Lijobo. An animal skin worn at the waist. Part of male traditional dress. (Swaziland). *See also* **Knobkerrie, Lihiya.**

Likembe. A traditional instrument; a board with thin metal strips plucked with the thumbs. (Congo).

Lilangeni. Swaziland's national currency. (Swaziland).

Lim. A flute. (Bhutan).

Lime. A term that refers to the time people spend relaxing and socializing with each other. (Antigua and Barbuda, Trinidad and Tobago). *Also called* **Liming.**

Limey. A derogatory nickname for people from the United Kingdom. The source is believed to be the Montserratian lime juice used by the British navy to combat scurvy. (Montserrat).

Limin. A colloquialism for "hanging out with friends." (U.S. Virgin Islands). *Also called* **Out on a lime.**

Liming. A term that refers to the time people spend relaxing and socializing with each other. (Antigua and Barbuda, Barbados, Grenada). *See also* **Lime.**

Liming. Activities include listening to music, chatting, and relaxing. Dropping by a home unannounced is acceptable, but staying too long once doing so is rude. (Trinidad and Tobago).

Lingala. An upbeat Congolese dance music. (Congo, Kenya).

Liphalishi. A stiff porridge made from maize. (Swaziland).

Liputa. The Lingala word for **Pagne.** (Congo).

Liqoqo. A council of elders. (Swaziland).

Lira. The national currencies of various countries. (Italy, Malta, Turkey).

Litas. Lithuania's national currency. (Lithuania).

Llajua. A spicy salsa. (Bolivia).

Llamar. "To call." A Spanish verb. Typically pronounced "yah-MAHR." In parts of Argentina it is pronounced "shah-MAHR." (Argentina).

Llaneros. Venezuelan cowboys. (Venezuela).

Llano(s). (1) Spanish word for "plains." (Venezuela). (2) Wet, hot, forested lowlands found in the east and northeast of Bolivia. (Bolivia). *Also called* **El trópico.**

Llapingachos. Cheese and potato cakes. (Ecuador).

Loaka. A term that describes meat, fish, eggs, vegetables, or basic broth. (Madagascar).

Lobi. A Lingala word meaning both "yesterday" and "tomorrow." (Congo).

Lobola. The bride-price paid by the groom or his family to the bride's parents. Traditionally it included cattle, although cash is now accepted. (Malawi, Namibia, South Africa, Swaziland, Zambia, Zimbabwe).

Lobolo. The bride-price paid by the groom's family to the bride's parents in the form of cattle or cash. (Mozambique).

Lochs. Deep blue lakes. (Scotland).

Locro. Soup made with potatoes, meat, and vegetables. (Argentina, Ecuador). tea ceremony.

Loi. The Uzbek word for "mud." A term of special significance in the Uzbek (Uzbekistan).

Glossary of Cultural Terms

Lok Sabha. House of the People. The lower house in India's Parliament. (India). *See also* **Rajya Sabha.**

Lola. "Grandmother." A Tagalog word used as a term of address for elderly women. (Philippines).

Lolo. (1) Coconut milk. (Fiji, Tuvalu). (2) "Grandfather." A Tagalog word used as a term of address for elderly men. (Philippines).

Lonche. A light breakfast-type meal served around 6 p.m. (Peru).

Longyi. An ankle-length wraparound sarong worn by Burmese men and women. The male *longyi* is tied at the front, while the female *longyi* is tucked in at the side of the waist. Material patterns differ for men and women. Women wear the the *longyi* with a blouse. Men wear the *longyi* with an **Eingyi** and a **Taikpon.** (Myanmar).

Loonie. The Canadian dollar's nickname. Refers to the image of the loon minted on the gold-colored coin. (Canada).

Lorries. Small trucks. (Guyana).

Loshoto da ne chue. "Do not let evil hear." A Macedonian phrase said by older rural women to ward off bad luck. (Macedonia). *See also* **Skraja da e.**

Lotar. An instrument similar to a three-stringed banjo. (Morocco). *Also called* **Kanza.**

Loti. Lesotho's national currency. The plural form is *Maloti*. (Lesotho).

Lot song teow. Vehicles with two rows of seats; a form of public transportation. (Laos).

Louages. Group taxis that run on set routes between cities. (Tunisia).

Loubo. Yam flour, often used to make a stiff porridge. (Benin). *Also called* **Amala.**

Lovespoons. Intricately carved wooden spoons that people traditionally gave to their loved ones. (Wales).

Lovo. Ground oven. (Fiji).

Low. A type of island characterized by small sand-and-coral bars surrounding a lagoon, dotted with shrubs and coconut palms. (French Polynesia). *See also* **High.**

Loya Jirga. Grand Council. A body of locally elected and tribal officials that convenes to discuss special issues, such as constitutional amendments. (Afghanistan).

Loy Krathong. A Buddhist holiday that honors the water goddess for providing water throughout the year. People float small "boats" with candles, coins, or flowers on waterways. (Thailand).

Lucia. A festival coinciding with the longest night of the year (13 December). A girl assumes the role of St. Lucia and dresses in white with a crown of candles in her hair. She sings a special song and serves coffee and **Lussekatter**. This marks the beginning of the Christmas season. (Sweden). *See also* **Jul.**

Ludo. A board game. (Togo).

Luiet. A black or colorful cloth that Muslim women use to cover their dresses. The cloth can be loosely draped or sewn to be more tailored. (Eritrea).

Lukim iu. "See you later." A common Solomon Island Pijin parting phrase. (Solomon Islands).

Lumela. "Hello." A common Sesotho greeting. (Lesotho).

Lung. "Uncle." A term of address. (Laos, Thailand).

Lungi. (1) A circular piece of cloth, knotted at the waist, that extends to the ankles. Worn by rural men with a **Genji**. (Bangladesh). (2) The most common headwear for men. It is worn with a **Kolah**. (Afghanistan).

Lu pulu. Cooked taro leaves with coconut cream and corned beef. (Tonga).

Lusekwane. A traditional Swazi event and a type of tree used in the event. For the event, young men bring branches of the *lusekwane* tree to the royal residence to build a cattle byre. (Swaziland).

Lussekatter. "Lucia cats." A type of roll. (Sweden).

Luta livre. Traditional wrestling. (Guinea-Bissau).

Lutefisk. Cod or coalfish soaked in potash lye. (Norway).

Luumos. Weekly markets that sell livestock, household goods, fabric, and food. (Gambia).

Lycée(s). Secondary schools. (Comoros, France, Tunisia).

Lyceums. A three- or four-year course that prepares a student for higher education. (Greece).

Lyonpo. A Buddhist minister. (Bhutan).

Ma. (1) A term used to address older women, regardless of relationship. (Saint Lucia, Sierra Leone). (2) "Sister." A term used to address girls and young women, regardless of relationship. (Myanmar). (3) A Chinese word that has five different meanings, including "horse" and "mother." It can also function as a question marker, depending on the tone or voice inflection with which it is spoken. (Taiwan).

Ma'a el-salameh, deer balak. "Good-bye, take care." A common Arabic parting phrase. (West Bank and Gaza).

Ma'alesh. "Don't worry" or "Never mind." An Arabic term that is used to dismiss concerns or conflicts that are inevitable or not serious. Reflects the relaxed and patient Egyptian life. (Egypt).

Ma' al-salamah. An Arabic term meaning "go in safety." (Libya).

Maandazi. Small doughnuts. (Tanzania).

Ma'asina ruru. "Marching Rule." A nationalist movement of self-reliance opposed to British rule. *Ma'asina ruru* helped lay the groundwork for independence, even though it eventually failed in its own right. (Solomon Islands).

Ma'assalameh. "Good-bye." A common Arabic parting phrase. (Bahrain).

Ma'awiis. A Somali kilt. (Somalia).

Mabele. Sorghum. (Botswana).

Mabkhara. A special stand used to burn incense. (Bahrain). *See also* **Bakhour.**

Mabrouk. An Arabic phrase used to offer congratulations for weddings, graduations, new employment, etc. (Tunisia).

Macaroni pie. (1) A popular dish made with cheese or mincemeat. (Barbados). (2) Macaroni baked with cheese, butter, and milk. (Trinidad and Tobago).

Machbous. (1) A dish with rice, meat, tomatoes, and lentils. (Bahrain). (2) Rice flavored with saffron and served with a tomato sauce and lamb or chicken. (Kuwait).

Machetta. A headscarf worn by men on Fridays and religious holidays. Can also be used to protect one's face in sandstorms, mask foul odors, or be used as a towel. (Yemen).

Machismo. The male attitude of proving one's manliness or superiority. (Belize, Dominican Republic, Honduras, Mexico, Nicaragua, Panama, Philippines).

Macumbeiros. Witches. People believe that witches can free them from a problem or help them obtain wealth, usually at the expense of others. Deaths or accidents are often attributed to witchcraft. (Angola). *Also called* **Feiticeiros.**

Glossary of Cultural Terms

Mada'a. A water pipe filled with tobacco. (Yemen).

Madame. (1) "Mrs." A common title for married women. Used in French-speaking countries.. (2) A common title for female elders. (Namibia).

Madeeh. Islamic gospel music sung to commemorate the prophet Muhammad. It is also the foundation of **Haqibh**. (Sudan).

Mademoiselle. "Miss." A common title. Used in French-speaking countries..

Madrinha. Portuguese word for "godmother." (Portugal).

Mãe. "Mother." A term of address used as a sign of respect. (Angola, Cape Verde).

Maestro/a. A Spanish title used to address a teacher. Masculine *maestro,* feminine *maestra*. (Panama).

Mafola? "OK?" An informal Niuean greeting. (Niue).

Maftool. A dish of vegetables and meat served with **Couscous**. (West Bank and Gaza).

Magafaoa. Niuean word for "extended family." (Niue).

Magalimoto. Toy cars that are made out of scrap metal and bits of trash. (Malawi).

Mageu. A thick sorghum drink. (Botswana).

Maghlobah. Vegetables, meat, and rice served with salad and yogurt. (West Bank and Gaza).

Maghna-eh. A black traditional Iranian head covering worn by women. (Iran).

Magolli. An alcoholic drink most popular in rural areas. (South Korea).

Magrud. Semolina cookies stuffed with dates and dipped in syrup. (Libya).

Magtaal. Poetic songs of praise; the heart of much of Mongolian literature. (Mongolia).

Mahabharata. An epic Sanskrit poem that continues to influence national and regional literature. (India).

Ma Ha 'inyanim? "What's happening?" A Hebrew phrase that may follow the initial greeting **Shalom**. (Israel).

Maha la shegay? "What are people saying?" A Somali greeting used to ask "How are you?" (Somalia).

Mahangu. Millet. (Namibia).

Maharram. The Muslim New Year. (Indonesia).

Maha Shivaratree. A Hindu holiday in which it is popular to dress in white and pour sacred water on a representation of the god Shiva. The water is drawn from the Grand Bassin, a high-altitude lake that is located in a volcano crater. (Mauritius).

Mahjong. A Chinese table game played with tiles. A cross between dominoes and cards. (Hong Kong, Philippines).

Mahleb. A paste of crushed black seeds that women apply to their faces during a visit. (Oman).

Mahram. Arabic word for a male relative. (Qatar).

Mahshi. Stuffed vegetables. (Jordan).

Mahu. The Fon name of a supreme god of an indigenous belief system. (Benin).

Mai kana. "Come eat." A person is greeted with this phrase when passing a rural house. (Fiji).

Mai mota. "Person with the car." A name used to address taxi drivers. (Niger).

Main gasing. A traditional activity of spinning tops that weigh several pounds for long periods of time. (Malaysia).

Mai Pen Rai. "Never mind." A Thai expression that characterizes a general feeling that life is to be enjoyed for the moment; problems and setbacks should not be taken too seriously. (Thailand).

Maizītes. Small sandwiches. (Latvia).

Majbous. Rice cooked in a sauce until it is yellow and then served with chicken, fish, or meat. (United Arab Emirates).

Majelis Permusyawaratan Rakyat. The People's Consultative Assembly. (Indonesia).

Majiang. (China). *See* **Mahjong**.

Majilis. The Kazak Parliament. (Kazakstan).

Majlis. (1) Arabic word for "sitting room." Used to entertain guests. (Oman, Qatar, United Arab Emirates). (2) Parliament, the Islamic Consultative Assembly. (Iran). (3) A traditional Islamic administrative system that allows people to petition the **Emir** directly. (Bahrain). (4) The supreme legislative branch of government. (Turkmenistan).

Majlis al-Chaab. The People's Council, the legislative body. (Syria).

Majlis al-Dawla. Council of State. The upper body of the Omani Council. Consists of appointed senior dignitaries. (Oman).

Majlis al-Nuwaab. The Chamber of Deputies, the legislative body. (Tunisia).

Majlis al-Shura. Consultative Council in the national government. (Oman, Qatar, Saudi Arabia).

Majlis al-Shuyukh. The Mauritanian Senate. (Mauritania).

Majlis al-Umma. The National Assembly. (Kuwait).

Majlis al-Watani. The Mauritanian National Assembly. (Mauritania).

Majlisi Milliy. The upper chamber of the Tajik parliament, or **Majlisi Oli**. (Tajikistan).

Majlisi Namoyandogon. The lower chamber of the Tajik parliament, or **Majlisi Oli**. (Tajikistan).

Majlisi Oli. The Tajik parliament. (Tajikistan).

Makadii? "How are you?" A Shona phrase that follows an initial greeting such as **Mhoroi**. (Zimbabwe).

Makala. Fried dough. (Central African Republic).

Makaruna mbakbaka. Refers to any pasta simmered in tomato and lamb stock with a mixture of spices. (Libya).

Make. A social title added to an adult woman's name to show respect. Pronounced "MAH-gay." (Swaziland).

Makha Bucha. An important Buddhist holiday. Set according to the lunar calendar. (Thailand).

Making a turn. "I am leaving." A phrase used among friends and youth at parting. (Saint Vincent and the Grenadines).

Makkara. Sausage. (Finland).

Makossa. An indigenous style of Cameroonian music. (Cameroon, Equatorial Guinea).

Makrout. A semolina pastry with date filling. (Algeria).

Maktoub. "Fate." A concept used to explain difficult times. This attitude provides comfort and encourages perseverance. (Tunisia).

Makunji. Village chief. (Central African Republic).

Mak yong. A musical play. (Malaysia).

Malabar. A long-sleeved striped or plaid shirt reaching to the knees and worn over pants. Traditional attire for men in the highlands area. (Madagascar).

Malamba. Cane alcohol. (Equatorial Guinea).

Malekum Salaam. (Gambia). *See* **Waalaikum assalaam**.

Malica. Slovene word for a midmorning snack. (Slovenia).

Malo e lelei. "Hello." A common daytime greeting. (Tonga).

Malo e lelei ki he efiafi ni. "Good evening." A Tongan greeting. (Tonga).

Malo e lelei ki he pongipongi ni. "Good morning." A common Tongan greeting. (Tonga).

Glossary of Cultural Terms

Malo e tau mo eni. "Good morning." A common Tongan greeting. (Tonga).

Malo lava. "Hello." An informal Samoan greeting. (American Samoa, Samoa).

Malo soifua. A polite reference to good health and well-being. A common greeting. (American Samoa).

Maloti. (Lesotho). *See* **Loti**.

Malouf. A musical style played by small orchestras with instruments such as drums, lutes, sitars, and violins. (Tunisia).

Malu. A tatoo for women. It covers the top of the thigh to the knee. (American Samoa). *See also* **Pe'a**.

Mama. (1) "Mother." A term of address for older women. (Central African Republic, French Polynesia, Gabon, Papua New Guinea, Saint Kitts and Nevis, South Africa). (2) An expression of surprise or shock. One can also say **Aye**. (Central African Republic).

Mamá. "Mother." A term of address used as a sign of respect. (Angola, Cape Verde).

Mamaguy. (1) Grenadian patois for "flatter." (Grenada). (2) Trying to fool someone. (Trinidad and Tobago).

Mamaliga. Cornmeal mush. (Moldova, Romania).

Maman. French word for "mom." A term of address children use for adult women even if they are not related. (Ivory Coast, Togo).

Ma nabad baa? "Is there peace?" A Somali greeting used in the north. (Somalia).

Manao ahoana tompoko? "How are you, sir/madam?" A common Malagasy greeting. An informal greeting would omit the word *tompoko*. (Madagascar).

Manas. The longest and most significant Kyrgyz epic. *Manas* was an important folk hero who has come to represent the strength, independence, and unity of the Kyrgyz people. (Kyrgyzstan).

Manat. The national currency. (Azerbaijan, Turkmenistan).

Mandalas. A circular pattern fashioned out of different media, such as paint and sand. It is the creator's interpretation of religious concepts such as the universe or deity and is often used in meditation. (Bhutan).

Mandazi. A doughnutlike food. (Kenya).

Mandioca. Cassava. (Paraguay).

Mane. "To collect and/or bring together." (Kiribati). *See also* **Aba, Maneaba(s)**.

Maneaba ni Maungatabu. The Kiribati House of Assembly. (Kiribati).

Maneaba(s). A meeting house used for formal entertaining. It is the center of community life. Strict traditions govern construction, seating arrangements, member duties, etc. (Kiribati). *See also* **Aba, Mane**.

Maneapa(s). A community hall used for feasts. (Tuvalu). *Also called* **Ahiga**. *See also* **Fakaala**.

Mang. A Pilipino title used before a male elder's last name. (Guam).

Mangbele. Cassava dough wrapped and boiled in leaves. (Central African Republic).

Ma ngi fi rek. "I am all right; I am here." A Wolof response to the greeting **Na ka nga def?** (Gambia).

Mangwanani. "Good morning." A common Shona greeting. (Zimbabwe).

Manheru. "Good evening." A common Shona greeting. (Zimbabwe).

Manicou. A type of opossum. (Grenada).

Manioc. Cassava. (Gabon).

Ma Nishma? "What's up?" A Hebrew phrase that may follow the initial greeting **Shalom**. (Israel).

Manjar. A bread spread and baking ingredient that is made by boiling an unopened can of sweetened condensed milk for hours. (Chile).

Mannginge'. A traditional custom in which a Chamorro greets an elder by kissing his or her hand. (Guam).

Mansaf. A large tray of rice covered with chunks of stewed lamb (including the head) and **Jameed**. The Jordanian national dish. (Jordan).

Mansef. Rice, lamb, yogurt, bread, and nuts. (West Bank and Gaza).

Manta. A shawl worn by rural women. (Bolivia).

Mante. Dumplings with meat or vegetables. (Uzbekistan).

Manti. Large steamed dumplings filled with chopped beef, pumpkin, and onions. (Kazakstan).

Mantin-Majel. The Marshallese manner. Generally, it means a casual or carefree way of life. (Marshall Islands).

Man tou. Steamed bread. (China).

Mantu. Pasta dishes. (Afghanistan, Tajikistan).

Manty. Steamed meat and onions sealed in dough patties. (Kyrgyzstan).

Manueline. A unique baroque style. (Portugal).

Manyattas. Walled communities in which Karamojong live to protect their livestock and families from raids by rival groups. (Uganda).

Man, yoh overtake meh. "Friend, you surprised me." A local English Creole phrase. (U.S. Virgin Islands).

Maoloeud. (Chad). *See* **Mouloud**.

Maqhas. Coffee shops. (Kuwait).

Maquiladoras. Border industries where U.S. investments employ Mexican labor. (Mexico).

Maquis. Small outdoor restaurants that sell alcohol and basic dishes to travelers and local men. People may gather there to eat fried plantains, drink beer, and chat. (Ivory Coast).

Marabout(s). Muslim teachers and leaders. (Libya, Mauritania, Senegal).

Maracas. Rattles made of gourds. (Venezuela).

Marae. The sacred space in front of a Maori **Wharenui**. (New Zealand).

Marag laham. A lamb and vegetable stew. (Kuwait).

Marama. A handkerchief worn on the head by older rural women to keep hair away from the face. (Macedonia).

Maravi. "The sun's rays." The origin of the word *Malawi*. (Malawi).

Mardi. Celebrated on 10 November, a day for children to go to neighbors' houses, sing special national songs, dance, and ask to be let in out of the cold. They are given candy and fruit. (Estonia).

Marenda. A light midmorning meal of fish, cheese, and bread. (Croatia).

Marhaba. (1) "Hello." A casual Arabic greeting. (Iraq, Jordan, Lebanon, Saudi Arabia, Syria). (2) "Fine." An Arabic response to the greeting **Kefelhal?** (Eritrea).

Marhabah keif halak? "Hello, how are you doing?" A common Arabic greeting. (West Bank and Gaza).

Marhaban bikoum. "Hello to you." A common Arabic greeting. (Algeria).

Glossary of Cultural Terms

Mariachi. A type of band music that originated in Mexico. Bands vary in size but generally consist of a singer, violins, trumpets, and guitars. (Mexico).

Marimba. An instrument similar to a xylophone. (Guatemala, Honduras, Nicaragua).

Marisa. A sorghum beer. (Sudan).

Marka. Bosnia and Herzegovina's national currency. (Bosnia and Herzegovina).

Markka. The name of the former Finnish national currency. (Finland). *Also called* **Finmark.**

Maroon. A cooperative effort in which people come together to finish a work project and share a meal or have a party. (Grenada).

Marquetry. The art of affixing wood patterns on boxes, trays, and furniture. (Syria).

Marraine. "Godmother" in French. (Belgium).

Married quarters. A married couple's own apartment. (Hong Kong).

Martenitza. A celebration of spring. On 1 March people exchange *martenitza*, a red-and-white yarn design that symbolizes health. They wear the design until they see a stork or a blossoming tree. Then they either put the *martenitza* on a tree branch to bring spring or hide it under a rock to represent the wish that evil spirits in nature and humankind will go to sleep. (Bulgaria).

Mărțisor. A holiday on 1 March in which men give women and girls small brooches. (Romania).

Mas. (1) A title used to address an older man or a superior. (Montserrat). (2) Short for masquerade. Also known as Carnival. (Trinidad and Tobago).

Masa al-khair. (Bahrain). *See* **Mesah al-Khair.**

Masa' al-khayr. (Libya). *See* **Masa' el-khair.**

Masa al-nur. The Arabic reply to the greeting **Masa al-khair**. (Bahrain).

Masa' el-khair. "Good afternoon." A common Arabic greeting. (West Bank and Gaza).

Masakhane. "Let us build together." A Nguni phrase that was the motto of Nelson Mandela's campaign in 1994. (South Africa).

Maseche. A Malawian rattle. (Malawi).

Mash. Green lentils cooked with rice in a stew. (Turkmenistan).

Ma' Sha' Allah. (Libya). *See* **Insha'Allah.**

Ma Shlomcha? "How are you?" Addressed to men, a Hebrew phrase that may follow the initial greeting **Shalom**. (Israel).

Ma Shlomech? "How are you?" Addressed to women, a Hebrew phrase that may follow the initial greeting **Shalom**. (Israel).

Mashramani. An Amerindian word for the celebration at the end of a cooperative project. The name is also used for Republic Day, celebrated on 23 February, which marks the date Guyana became the Cooperative Republic of Guyana. (Guyana).

Masi. Cloth produced from bark and decorated with stencils to create elaborate patterns. (Fiji).

Masikati. "Good afternoon." A common Shona greeting. (Zimbabwe).

Maslahat. Meeting. (Turkmenistan).

Ma soeur. "My sister." A French term of address used among people of the same age. (Gabon).

Massar. A turban worn by men. (Oman).

Massegohoun. A traditional music rhythm. (Benin).

Más tarde. "Later." A common Spanish parting phrase. (Guatemala).

Mata-bicho. The term for "breakfast" that literally means "kill the beast" (the one growling in an empty stomach). (Angola, Mozambique).

Matai. A male or female chief that holds authority in the extended family or kinship group. He or she is selected based on loyal service to family members and the village community. Traditional qualifications include oratory skills and a body tattoo. (American Samoa, Samoa).

Mataqali. Fijian landholding units composed of families living communally. (Fiji).

Matatus. Small pickup truck taxis with cabs on the back that run on regular routes but without schedules. (Kenya).

Mate. (1) An herb tea that is served hot. Pronounced "MAH-tey." (Argentina, Brazil, Paraguay, Uruguay). (2) A term of address used between male friends. (Australia).

Mate dulce. An herb tea made with sugar. Women traditionally drink *mate dulce*. (Uruguay). *See also* **Mate.**

Mathapa. Manioc leaves. (Mozambique).

Matisa. "How are you?" A Nama/Damara greeting. (Namibia).

Matooke. Mashed bananas. (Uganda).

Matryoshka. Nested dolls. A Russian folk craft. (Russia).

Matua. A Niuean term for "parent" that refers not only to the biological parent but also to the guardian of a child. Sometimes it is used to address elderly family members. (Niue).

Matura. An exam that is required to continue on to higher education. (Liechtenstein, Slovenia).

Maulid. (Comoros). *See* **Mouloud.**

Maulid an-Nabi. (Nigeria). *See* **Mouloud.**

Mauloud-el-Nabi. (Gambia). *See* **Mouloud.**

Maung. "Younger brother." A term used to address boys, regardless of relationship. (Myanmar).

Maur. An English variation of the spelling of the term **Moor**. (Mauritania).

Maure. French term for **Moor**. (Mauritania).

Mauri. "Blessings." A common Kiribati greeting. (Kiribati).

Maw lam. Lao folk theater. (Laos).

Mawliid. (Somalia). *See* **Mouloud.**

Mawloud. (Guinea, Senegal). *See* **Mouloud.**

Maxi-taxis. Mini-buses. (Trinidad and Tobago).

Maybahay. A Pilipino title for a married hostess. (Philippines).

¿Mba'eichapa? "How are you?" A common Guaraní greeting. Pronounced "m-buy-ay-SHA-pah." (Paraguay).

Mbalatsara? "Doing well?" A common greeting in the north. (Madagascar).

Mbalax. A style of music that incorporates tribal drumming and Afro-Caribbean pop. (Senegal).

Mbaqanga. A popular style of dance music that originated in apartheid-era townships. (South Africa).

Mbaxal-u-Saloum. A sauce of ground peanuts, dried fish, meat, tomatoes, and spices. It is a traditional Wolof dish served with rice. (Senegal).

M'bda. "On you no evil." A Pulaar greeting. The response is **Jam tan**. (Mauritania).

Mbewa. Roasted mice on a stick. (Malawi).

Mbira. An instrument with small metal strips that are plucked by the thumbs. (Zimbabwe). *See also* **Jiti.**

Mbo. Fang word for cassava. (Equatorial Guinea).

Mbolo. "Hello." A common Fang greeting. (Equatorial Guinea, Gabon).

Glossary of Cultural Terms

Mbona. An elder's response to the child's greeting **Kwezi**. The elder clasps the child's hands and says *Mbona*. (Comoros).

Mbote. "Hello." A common Lingala greeting. (Congo).

Mdraha. A pebble-and-board game. (Comoros).

Me. A Montserratian word that indicates first person singular and past tense. (Montserrat). *See also* **Me no me know.**

Mealie meal. Cornmeal porridge. (Lesotho, Namibia, South Africa).

Me dear. An informal term of address. (Saint Kitts and Nevis).

Medex. An individual trained in primary health care. (Guyana).

Meet-and-greet. Conversations that are held on the street. (Jamaica).

Me'etu'upaki. "Paddle dance." A dance performed by male groups in which they gracefully twist paddles to the rhythm of a chorus and hollow log gongs. (Tonga).

Meeyonband. A bandana-type tie used as a belt. (Tajikistan). *Also called* **Chorsi.** *See also* **Joma.**

Mehana. A Bulgarian eating establishment that features traditional food, folk music, and dancing. (Bulgaria).

Mehikitanga. The father's eldest sister. She is the leader over that nuclear family in the extended-family system. (Tonga). *See also* **Fahu.**

Meke. Dances that describe legends and historical events. (Fiji).

Mekhmonlar. Uzbek word for "guests." (Uzbekistan).

Melkooptoviye Rynki. Wholesale markets. (Russia).

Melodeon. An instrument similar to an accordion. (Dominican Republic).

Meme. A term of address for older Owambo women. (Namibia). *See also* **Tate.**

Me na able. "I can't cope." An example of the Saint Vincent dialect of English. (Saint Vincent and the Grenadines).

Me no me know. "I did not know." A Montserratian phrase showing the different uses of the word **Me**. (Montserrat).

Menudo. Spicy tripe soup. (Mexico).

Merak. A relaxed pace of life. A Bosnian general attitude. (Bosnia and Herzegovina).

Merengue. A ballroom dance of Caribbean origin and the rapid music that accompanies the dance. (Colombia, Costa Rica, Dominican Republic, Panama, Saint Kitts and Nevis, Venezuela). *See also* **Meringue.**

Merhaba. "Hello." A Turkish greeting. (Turkey).

Meri. Brightly colored blouses worn by women over a **Laplap**. (Papua New Guinea).

Merienda. A snack between meals. (Colombia, Guam, Mexico, Philippines, Spain).

Meringue. A music style and dance that is a mixture of African rhythms and European music. Haiti's national dance. (Bahamas, Haiti). *See also* **Merengue.**

Mesadoras. The Dominican word for "rocking chairs." (Dominican Republic).

Mesah al-kair. (Yemen). *See* **Mesah al-Khair.**

Mesah al-Khair. [NOTE: Spelling varies because it is a transliteration of Arabic.] "Good evening." A common Arabic greeting. (Saudi Arabia).

Meshrano Jirga. House of Elders. Part of Afghanistan's bicameral National Assembly. (Afghanistan).

Meshwi. Shish kebab. (Jordan).

Meskel. A holiday in late September that celebrates the finding of Jesus Christ's "true cross" in the fourth century. (Eritrea, Ethiopia).

Mestiços. People of mixed Portuguese and African origin. (Angola).

Mestiza. A skirt, camisole, and mesh top with puffy butterfly sleeves, worn by women. (Guam).

Metemgee. A dish made with coconut milk, **Ground provisions**, meat or fish, and other ingredients. Similar to **Cook-up rice.** (Guyana).

Meter. "Godmother" in Dutch. (Belgium).

Metical. Mozambique's national currency. (Mozambique).

Meto. An elaborate system of navigation using wave and current patterns represented in stick charts. (Marshall Islands).

Métro. The name for subways throughout France. (France).

Métro Léger. The light-rail system in Tunis. (Tunisia).

Metta. Loving-kindness and the practice of goodwill. A pillar virtue in Buddhism. (Laos). *See also* **Brahma Vihara.**

Meu camba, fixe? "Friend, are you okay?" An informal Portuguese greeting used among young men. (Angola).

Me vex fu true. "I was really angry." A Montserratian phrase. (Montserrat). *See also* **Fu true.**

Me we see you. "I'll see you later." A common Jamaican English parting phrase. (Jamaica).

Meza. A traditional four- to five-hour meal for special occasions. (Lebanon).

Meze. (1) An antipasto of various hors d'oeuvres. (Albania, Bosnia and Herzegovina, Serbia and Montenegro, Turkey). (2) A mixture of ham, cheese, vegetables, and eggs. (Macedonia).

Mezza. A table full of appetizers, which include pastes made from chickpeas and eggplant, meat dishes with spices and wheat, pickles, olives, and breads. (Syria).

Mhoroi. "Hello." A common Shona greeting. (Zimbabwe).

Mida. A low, round, wooden table. (Tunisia).

Middag. The main meal of the day. (Sweden).

Mi de. "I'm fine." A Sranan Tongo response to a greeting such as **Fa waka?**, **Fa'y tan?**, or **Fa'y go?** (Suriname).

Midori No hi. Greenery Day. A day to celebrate nature's beauty; 29 April. (Japan).

Midsommar. Summer solstice celebrations in late June. Festivities include dancing around the maypole and having picnics. (Sweden).

Miklavžovanje. The holiday of St. Nicholas Eve. (Slovenia).

Milanesa. Fried, breaded steak. (Uruguay).

Milk bar. A corner shop where people buy items such as bread and milk. (Australia).

Milk tart. A custard-like pie. (South Africa).

Milli Majlis. Azerbaijan's Parliament. (Azerbaijan).

Milonga. A traditional Uruguayan dance. (Uruguay).

Mince. Ground meat. (Scotland).

Minestra. Vegetable soup. (Malta).

Min-gala-ba. A formal "Hello" in Burmese.

Mingas. Community improvement projects. (Ecuador).

Mi orait. Na yu? "I'm fine. And you?" A Melanesian Pidgin response to the greeting **Yu orait?** (Papua New Guinea).

Miorita. A well-known ballad. (Moldova).

Mir dita. Albanian for "Good day." (Macedonia).

Miremengjes. "Good morning." An Albanian greeting. (Albania).

Mire se erdhet. (1) "Welcome." An Albanian greeting to welcome guests. (Albania). *See also* **Mire se vini.** (2) A host and hostess's reply to the phrase **Mire se ju gjeta** before drinking. (Albania).

Glossary of Cultural Terms

Mire se ju gjeta. "I am glad I find you well." An Albanian phrase guests say before drinking. (Albania).

Mire se vini. "Welcome." An Albanin greeting to welcome guests. (Albania). *See also* **Mire se erdhet.**

Mirmenjezi. Albanian for "Good morning." (Macedonia).

Mir u pafshim. "Good-bye." An Albanian parting phrase. (Albania).

Mir wëlle bleiwe wat mer sin! "We want to remain what we are!" Luxembourg's national motto. This reflects Luxembourgers independence and unique identity in Europe. (Luxembourg).

Mishlah. A cloak men wear over a **Thobe**. (Qatar, Saudi Arabia).

Misniar. Informal wives. (Qatar).

Miso. Bean paste. (Japan).

Mititei. Grilled meat sausages. (Moldova, Romania).

Mittagspause. A traditional midday break. (Austria).

Mi wokabaot nomoa. "I'm just walking around." A Solomon Island Pijin response to the greetings **Iu go long wea?** and **Iu bin stap long wea?** (Solomon Islands).

Mixed. People who are primarily descendants of Afro- and Indo-Guyanese. (Guyana).

Miyess. A honey mead. (Eritrea).

Mlada Bosna. "Young Bosnia." A multiethnic group responsible for the assassination of the heir to the Austro-Hungarian throne, the spark that initiated World War I. (Bosnia and Herzegovina).

Mme. "Mother." A Sesotho term of address used for older women. (South Africa).

Mo-. A prefix used when referring to one person. (Botswana). *See also* **Ba-, Batswana, Motswana.**

Mobylettes. Mopeds. (Burkina Faso).

Modi ki bu sta? "How are you?" A standard Crioulo greeting. (Cape Verde).

Mogethin. "What did you come here for?" A greeting used between friends. (Micronesia).

Mohinga. A fish and noodle soup often enjoyed for breakfast. (Myanmar).

Moi. (1) "Hi." An informal Finnish greeting. (Finland). (2) The Uzbek word for "butter." A term of special significance in the Uzbek tea ceremony. (Uzbekistan).

Moien. "Morning." A common Luxembourgish greeting. (Luxembourg).

Mok kai. Poultry cooked in a banana leaf. (Laos).

Moko. Traditional facial tattooing, featuring elaborate designs. (New Zealand).

Mokorotlo. A traditional straw hat, conical in shape, that has an intricately designed knob on top. (Lesotho). *Also called* **Molianyeoe.**

Mok paa. Fish cooked in a banana leaf. (Laos).

Mola(s). Appliqué for clothing or textiles. (Costa Rica, Panama).

Mole. A spicy sauce served with meat. (Mexico).

Molianyeoe. A traditional straw hat that is conical in shape with an intricately designed knob on top. (Lesotho). *Also called* **Mokorotlo.**

Molo. Literally, "I see you." A Xhosa greeting meaning "Hello." (South Africa).

Momo. Tibetan ravioli. (Bhutan).

Mondongo. (1) Tripe and beef knuckles. (Honduras, Nicaragua). (2) Intestine soup. (Costa Rica).

Mon frère. "My brother." A French term of address used among people of the same age. (Gabon).

Mon frère, même mère, même père. "My brother, same mother, same father." An introduction that one takes special pride in due to large families where the man may have more then one wife. (Central African Republic).

Moni. "Hello." A greeting used by northern men and women after they clap their hands three times. (Mozambique).

Moni bambo! "Hello, sir!" A Chichewa greeting. (Malawi).

Moni mayi! "Hello, madam!" A Chichewa greeting. (Malawi).

Moning. "Good morning." An adapted English greeting. (Papua New Guinea, Togo).

Moning kaikai. "Morning food." The Melanesian Pidgin word for breakfast. (Papua New Guinea).

Monire adada! "Hello, sir!" A Chitumbuka greeting. (Malawi).

Monire amama! "Hello, madam!" A Chitumbuka greeting. (Malawi).

Monno. Millet porridge. (Gambia).

Monsha. The Kazak word for "sauna." (Kazakstan).

Monsieur. "Mr." A common title. Used in French-speaking countries..

Montuno. Baggy shorts and matching embroidered top. A traditional costume worn by men with **Cutarras** and palm-fiber hats. (Panama).

Monuina [e fenoga]! "Blessings [on the voyage]!" A Niuean parting phrase used if an individual is leaving for a long time. (Niue).

Mophane. Trees in the northeast that are used to harvest the **Phane** worm. (Botswana).

Mora-mora. A relaxed pace of life. (Madagascar).

Môre. "Good morning." An Afrikaans greeting. (Namibia).

Moreneng. The chief compound; a place for socializing. (Lesotho).

More times. "Until we meet again." An informal parting phrase. (Saint Vincent and the Grenadines).

Morin-khuur. A bowed lute with a carved horse head at the neck. A symbol of Mongolian culture. (Mongolia).

Morn. "Morning." A Norwegian greeting used regardless of the time of day. (Norway).

Morna. A style of music with a slow rhythm and melancholy lyrics. (Cape Verde).

Moro. "Good morning." An Otjiherero greeting. (Namibia).

Morogeh koman honah. "I'm glad to see you." A Machushi greeting. (Guyana).

Moroho. Cooked vegetables. (Lesotho).

Mosakhan. Vegetables, meat, and rice served with salad and yogurt. (West Bank and Gaza).

Mos Craciun. The Romanian name for Santa Claus. (Moldova).

Moshav. A small village where families live separately but cooperate in providing community needs and in marketing the village's products. (Israel). *See also* **Kibbutz.**

Moso'oi. A fragrant plant. (American Samoa). *See also* **Moso'oi festival.**

Moso'oi festival. A week-long festival held in October. (American Samoa).

Mosquito coils. Mosquito repellent. (Sierra Leone).

Mother. (1) A term of address used for older women. (Saint Kitts and Nevis). (2) A term of address also used for aunts. (Sierra Leone).

Motorela. A three-wheeled motorized carriage. (Philippines).

Glossary of Cultural Terms

Motovilec. A salad green called "corn salad" or "mâche." (Slovenia).

Motswana. A Tswana person. (Botswana). *See also* **Ba-, Batswana, Mo-.**

Motta. "Friend." A general Marshallese term of address that follows the greeting **Yokwe**. (Marshall Islands).

Motu. Niuean word for "islanders." (Niue).

Motum. Stone/earth ovens. (Solomon Islands).

Mouharem. The Islamic New Year holiday according to the lunar calendar. (Algeria).

Moulah. Sauce. (Chad).

Moulid. (Ethiopia). *See* **Mouloud.**

Moulid al-Nabi. (Iraq). *See also* **Mouloud.**

Moulid al-Nebi. (Jordan). *See* **Mouloud.**

Mouloud. [NOTE: Spelling varies because it is a transliteration of Arabic; the name may vary from country to country. Also, Muslim holidays are set according to the lunar calendar.] A Muslim holiday celebrating the birth of Muhammad. Celebrated in predominantly Muslim countries. (Burkina Faso, Morocco, Niger).

Mountain chicken. Frog, a popular dish. (Montserrat).

Mourides. A large Muslim brotherhood and spiritual order. (Senegal).

Moussaka. A casserole made with pork or lamb, potatoes, tomatoes, and yogurt. (Bulgaria).

Moussems. Muslim religious festivals that are held throughout the year. (Morocco).

Mo yeke. "Are you okay?" Part of a common Sango greeting, it usually follows the phrase **Bara ala** or **Bala mo** (Greetings to you!). (Central African Republic).

Mpanandro. "Day maker." People consult with the *mpanandro* person for help in choosing the best day to get married, start construction, and so on. (Madagascar).

Mpihira gasy. Traditional performers who sing, dance, and play music in an open-air concert. (Madagascar).

Msa'a al khair. (Jordan). *See* **Mesah al-Khair.**

Msa al Kheir. (Morocco). *See* **Mesah al-Khair.**

Mshvidobit. "Peace be with you." A Georgian parting phrase used for an extensive parting. (Georgia).

M'to kari. "I'm fine." A Sara response to the greeting **I baii?** (Chad).

Mtsvadi. Marinated, skewered, grilled meat. (Georgia).

Mua kia! "Good-bye!" A Niuean parting phrase used when addressing two people. (Niue).

Mua roi nuoc. Water puppetry. (Vietnam).

Muchas gracias. "Many thanks." After finishing a meal, each person, including the cook, uses this phrase to thank everyone at the table. (Guatemala).

¡Mucho gusto! "Pleased to meet you." A common Spanish greeting used for strangers. (Guatemala, Paraguay).

Mucho gusto de conocerle. "Glad to meet you." A Spanish greeting used when meeting another person for the first time. (Nicaragua).

Muciro. Beauty cream that is made from grated plant stems mixed with water. Used by women to clean and beautify their faces. (Mozambique).

Múcua. The fruit of the baobab tree. The white-and-pink edible interior is a favorite treat. It is also made into ice cream. (Angola).

Mudhita. Sympathetic or altruistic joy. One of Buddhism's four pillar virtues. (Laos). *See also* **Brahma Vihara.**

Mufradsh. A room with cushions and pillows on the floor. Used for visiting and chewing **Qat**. (Yemen).

Mugam. Folk music derived from classical poetry. Based on improvisation. (Azerbaijan).

Muhallebi. Milk pudding. (Turkey).

Mujahideen. Holy Muslim warriors. (Afghanistan).

Muktaaq. A term meaning whale meat, used by indigenous tribes in Canada. (Canada).

Mukulukhana. Witch doctors. (Mozambique). *Also called* **Nhangas.**

Mulafa. A large piece of colored cloth worn by Moorish women that is wrapped around the body and draped over the head. (Mauritania).

Muli bwanji? "How are you?" A common greeting. (Malawi, Zambia).

Muli shani? "How are you?" A Bemba phrase used to greet a friend. (Zambia).

Muli uli? "How are you?" A Chitumbuka phrase that follows the greetings **Monire adada!** and **Monire amama!** (Malawi).

Mullah(s). "Giver of knowledge." A Muslim religious leader. (Afghanistan, Iran).

Mullo. (Tajikistan). *See* **Mullah(s).**

Mulţumesc pentru masă. "Thank you for the meal." A Romanian phrase used to thank the cook. (Romania).

Mum. A synonym for "mom." (Scotland).

Mummy. A respectful term of address used to address older women, regardless of relationship. (Saint Lucia).

Mumu. A ground oven. (Papua New Guinea).

Muqmad. Dried beef in clarified butter. (Somalia).

Muraho. "Hello, it's been a while." A common Kinyarwanda greeting. (Rwanda).

Murawarawa. A strategy game played on a board with 18 to 32 holes. Each hole has two seeds in it. The object of the game is to collect the most seeds. (Mozambique).

Mürebbe. Preserves made of fruits or nuts. (Azerbaijan).

Musakhan. Chicken with onions, olive oil, pine seeds, and seasonings. (Jordan).

Musha'irahs. Poetry readings. (Pakistan).

Musibityendo ssebo/ngabo? "How are you, sir/madam?" A Luganda greeting. (Uganda).

Muslim. Literally, "one who has submitted." A follower of the religion **Islam**. (Mauritania).

Mutawassit. Intermediate school. (Saudi Arabia).

Muti. A curse. (Swaziland). *See also* **Batsakatsi.**

Mutolu kia! "Good-bye!" A Niuean parting phrase used when addressing three or more people. (Niue).

Muumuu. A long wraparound skirt worn by women. (Samoa).

Muwatiniin. Locals that are Arab descendants of great tribal confederations or long-time immigrants from Persia and Arabian Gulf countries. (United Arab Emirates).

Muyongo. Witchcraft. (Cameroon).

Mwabonwa. "Welcome." A common greeting used in the south. (Zambia).

Mwami. The Kinyarwanda word for "king." (Rwanda).

Mwana hangu. "My child/brother." A title used to address good friends. (Comoros).

Mwapoleni. "Welcome." A Bemba greeting used between friends. (Zambia).

Mwapolenipo mukwai. "Welcome, very respectfully." A Bemba greeting used to address elders. The *po-* suffix shows added respect. (Zambia).

Glossary of Cultural Terms

Mwaramutse. "Good morning." A common Kinyarwanda greeting. (Rwanda).

Mwiriwe. "Good afternoon" or "Good evening." A common Kinyarwanda greeting. (Rwanda).

Mzé. A title used to address an elder man. (Comoros).

Mzuri. "Good." A common Kiswahili response to the greetings **Habari?** and **Habari gani?** (Kenya).

Ña. A term of address for women, used with the first name. Commonly used in rural areas. (Paraguay).

Naa. "Aunt." A Lao term of address used when a person has no specific title. (Laos).

Naadam. Mongolian People's Revolution. A holiday celebrated on 11 to 13 July with horse races, wrestling, and other events. (Mongolia).

Naag Panchami. A summer festival in which snakes are venerated because of their association with Hindu gods. (India).

Nabad. "Peace." A common Somali greeting. (Somalia).

Nabad miya? "Is there peace?" A common Somali greeting used in the southern areas. (Somalia).

Nacatamales. (1) Pork tamales. (Honduras). (2) A dish of meat and vegetables, with spices. (Nicaragua).

Nadenitsa. Stuffed pork sausage. (Bulgaria).

Nadie es más que nadie. "No one is better than anyone else." A Spanish phrase that expresses a commonly held democratic viewpoint in Uruguay. (Uruguay).

Naengmyon. A cold noodle dish. (North Korea).

Na fo biah. "You must bear it." A common Krio response to the expressions **Na so God say** (It is God's will) and **Ow fo do?** (What can you do?). (Sierra Leone).

Na gosti. To go visiting. (Bulgaria, Macedonia).

Nagra. Flat shoes that curl upward in front. Part of a groom's wedding attire. (Bangladesh). *See also* **Pagri, Shirwani.**

Naguas. Colorful dresses worn by Ngöbe-Buglé women. (Panama).

Nahili sen? Gowy my? "How are you? Well?" (Turkmenistan).

Nai. Reed pipe or flute. (Lebanon, United Arab Emirates).

Nain dat. "That's all." A Krio parting phrase used to mean good-bye. (Sierra Leone).

Naira. Nigeria's national currency. (Nigeria).

Na ka nga def? "How are you?" A common Wolof greeting. (Gambia).

Nakfa. Eritrea's national currency. (Eritrea).

Nakhajash. The first meal of the day. It usually consists of coffee or tea and a pastry for adults and bread, butter, cheese, boiled eggs, honey or jam, and warm milk for children. (Armenia).

Nama. Meat. (Lesotho).

Nama ea khoho. Chicken. (Lesotho).

Nama ea khomo. Beef. (Lesotho).

Nama ea kolobe. Pork. (Lesotho).

Namaskar. A traditional greeting and parting gesture for superiors and elders. A person places the palms together with the fingers up in front of the chest or chin and says *Namaskar*. (Nepal). *See also* **Namaste.**

Namaskaram. A traditional southern Indian greeting in which one places the palms together with the fingers up below the chin and says *Namaskaram*. (India).

Namaste. A traditional greeting in which one places the palms together with the fingers up below the chin and says *Namaste*, sometimes bowing slightly. (Bhutan, Fiji, India, Mauritius, Nepal).

Nan. Unleavened bread. (Afghanistan, Uzbekistan).

Nana. A term Imazighen use to show respect to female elders, including siblings. (Algeria).

Ñandutí. Intricate and delicate lace. A craft introduced by the Spanish. (Paraguay).

Nane Nane. International Trade Day. Celebrated 8 August. (Tanzania).

Nang. "Ms." A Lao term of address used when a married woman has no specific title. (Laos).

N'anga. Witch doctors. (Zimbabwe).

Nanga def. "On you no evil." A common Wolof greeting. The response is **Jam rekk** (No evil). (Mauritania).

Nangi. "Younger sister." A term of address used among close friends and relatives. (Sri Lanka).

Nang sbek. Shadow plays in which the characters are black leather puppets. The plays often tell religious stories. (Cambodia).

Nao. "Man." A Kiribati word that is used to get someone's attention. (Kiribati).

Narcoterroristas. Drug traffickers. (Colombia).

Nareau. "The Creator." A supreme being the I-Kiribati worshiped before the introduction of Christianity. (Kiribati). *See also* **Te maaka.**

Narodna muzika. Folk music, which is especially favored in rural areas. (Serbia and Montenegro).

Narodni pesni. Folk songs that describe historical battles and life in Macedonia. (Macedonia).

Narodno Sobranyie. The Bulgarian National Assembly, which has 240 members. (Bulgaria).

Na schledanou. "Good-bye." A formal Czech parting phrase. (Czech Republic).

Nashif. Chopped beef with a spicy tomato sauce; traditionally eaten with **Kissar**. (Chad).

Nasi campur. Javanese vegetable dishes with white rice, noodles, and chicken. (Indonesia).

Nasi Lemak. Buttered rice with dried anchovies and peanuts. (Malaysia).

Nasisliniz? "How are you?" A common Turkish greeting. (Turkey).

Na so God say. "It is God's will." A common Krio expression. The response is **Na fo biah** (You must bear it). (Sierra Leone).

Nasvidenje. "Good-bye." A common Slovene phrase used when parting or exiting a room or an elevator, even if one does not know the others present. (Slovenia).

Nat. A spirit. Many of Myanmar's Buddhists practice *nat* worship; shrines to these spirits are common, especially in rural areas. (Myanmar).

Naten e mir. Albanian for "Good night." (Macedonia).

Nationalrat. National Council. The 183-seat lower house of the Austrian Parliament. (Austria). *See also* **Bundesversammlung.**

Natsionalnoye Sobranie. Belarus's National Assembly. (Belarus). *See also* **Palata Predstaviteley, Soviet Respubliki.**

Nau mai. "Welcome." A ceremonial Maori greeting. (New Zealand).

Nauriz. (Kazakstan). *See* **Naw Ruz.**

Navruz. (Uzbekistan). *See* **Naw Ruz.**

Navy biscuits. Crackers. (Solomon Islands).

Nawrooz. (Afghanistan). *See* **Naw Ruz.**

Glossary of Cultural Terms

Naw Ruz. The New Year. Celebrated in connection with the spring equinox. (Iran).

Nazdrave. Bulgarian word for "toasting." Done at the beginning and throughout a meal. (Bulgaria).

Na zdravie. "To your health." A Slovak phrase used to toast someone. (Slovakia).

Nbe sira dari. Dyula phrase that guests use to "ask for the road" from hosts after they accompany each other to the road at the end of a visit. (Ivory Coast).

Ndaga. A popular style of Senegalese music. (Gambia).

Ndaguta. "I am satisfied." A phrase used after a meal to show respect and indicate one has been well provided for. (Zimbabwe).

Ndalale. "I passed the night well, and you?" The response to the Umbundo greeting **Walale**. (Angola).

Ndi. "Good morning." A common Ewe greeting. (Togo).

Ndili bwino! "I am fine!" A Chichewa response to the greeting **Muli bwanji?** (How are you?). (Malawi).

Ndili makola! "I am fine!" A common Chitumbuka response to the greeting **Muli uli?** (How are you?). (Malawi).

Ndiwo. A sauce or condiment. Balled **Nsima** is often dipped in it. (Malawi).

Ndo. "Good afternoon." A common Ewe greeting. (Togo).

Ndombolo. An upbeat dance style performed in urban discos. (Congo).

Neeps. Boiled turnips. (Scotland).

Negrito. A Spanish word for "little dark one" or "little black one." In some places it is not considered rude to comment on such physical attributes. (Argentina).

Nei. "Miss" or "Mrs." A Kiribati title used in formal situations to show respect. (Kiribati).

Neih hau ma? (Hong Kong). *See* **Ni hao ma?**

Neih sihkjo faan meih a? "Have you eaten yet?" A common Cantonese greeting. (Singapore).

Neih sik msik a. "Have you eaten?" A typical Chinese greeting. (Hong Kong).

Neiko. "Woman." A Kiribati word that is used to get someone's attention. (Kiribati).

Nejasiniz? "How are you?" An Azeri phrase used after the initial greeting between acquaintances and friends. (Azerbaijan).

Ne-kaun-ba-deh. "I'm well." The response to the greeting **Ne-kaun-yeh-la?** (Myanmar).

Ne-kaun-yeh-la? "Are you well?" An informal Burmese greeting. The response is **Ne-kaun-ba-deh**. (Myanmar).

Nene. "Mother." An Albanian term used to address older women. (Albania).

New cedi. Ghana's national currency. (Ghana).

New Israeli shekel. Israel's national currency. (Israel, West Bank and Gaza).

New riel. Cambodia's national currency. (Cambodia).

Next time. A common parting phrase. (Jamaica).

Ne y yibeogo. "Good morning." A common Mooré greeting. (Burkina Faso).

Ne y zaabre. "Good afternoon." A common Mooré greeting. (Burkina Faso).

Ngalabi. A long drum played by the Baganda people. (Uganda).

Ngambe. Fortune-tellers. (Cameroon).

Ngapi. A fish or shrimp paste; added to a variety of dishes. (Myanmar).

Ngepi Nawa. "Good afternoon." An Oshiwambo greeting. (Namibia).

Ngola. The title of the king of the Ndongo; the word from which Angola derives its name. (Angola).

Ngoma. Popular traditional music. Dancers follow the rhythm of drums, accompanied by a chorus, xylophones, and whistles. (Tanzania).

Ngultrum. Bhutan's national currency. (Bhutan).

Ngunza. A thick sauce made from ground cassava leaves, tomato paste, and peanut butter. (Central African Republic).

Ngwenyama. The siSwati word for "lion." In 1921, King Sobhuza II was crowned *Ngwenyama* of the nation. His rule lasted until his death in 1982. (Swaziland).

Ngwetsa. A festival that celebrates the harvest. (Malawi).

Nhangana. Leaves of **Nhemba** beans. (Mozambique).

Nhangas. Traditional healers or witch doctors. (Mozambique).

Nhemba. A type of bean. (Mozambique).

Ni chi fan le ma? "Have you eaten yet?" A common Chinese greeting. The reply is "Yes," even if one has not eaten. (China).

Nien. The Vietnamese word for "years." (Vietnam).

Nieves. The Spanish word for "snows." (Saint Kitts and Nevis).

Nightcrawling. A method of dating in which a young man approaches a young woman's house at night and invites her to join him. (Marshall Islands, Micronesia).

Ni hao ma? "How are you?" A typical Chinese greeting. (China, Singapore).

Ni hau ma? (Malaysia, Taiwan). *See* **Ni hao ma?**

Nikoh. A blessing from a religious leader. The capstone of a three-day Tajik wedding. (Tajikistan).

Ni meza. "Fine." A typical response to the greetings **Amakuru?** (How's the news?) and **Bite se?** (How are things going?). (Rwanda).

Ni meza cyane. "Very fine." A typical response to the greetings **Amakuru?** (How's the news?) and **Bite se?** (How are things going?). (Rwanda).

Ni molo. Chilled coconut water. (Marshall Islands).

Niña. A less formal title used to address young women and girls. (El Salvador).

Ninde? "Who's there?" A response to a visitor's greeting announcing his or her presence. (Rwanda).

Ni Sa Bula! A formal Fijian greeting. (Fiji).

Nitijela. The national parliament. (Marshall Islands).

Njangis. Savings societies in which members pool their capital, provide loans to each other, and sponsor social activities. (Cameroon). *Also called* **Tontines**.

Njatjeta. "Hello." A common Albanian greeting. (Albania).

N Justa. "I've had enough." A Kriolu phrase used to decline a meal after having at least one bite. Pronounced "NG JUICE-ta." (Guinea-Bissau).

Nkhokwe. A structure for storing grain. (Malawi).

Nkhosi. The praise name for royalty. Can be used as a title when one is unsure of a person's title. (Swaziland).

Nliwalè. "Good morning." A common Kabyè greeting. (Togo).

N'na. Kabyè word for "mother." (Togo).

Nob. "Salute." A formal Lao greeting in which one places one's hands together in a prayer position at chest level but not touching the body. The higher the hands are held, the greater the sign of respect, although they should never be held above the level of the nose. Can also be used to express thanks or regret. (Laos).

Noche Buena. Christmas Eve. (Guatemala, Mexico).

Noël. The French word for "Christmas." (France, Gabon).

Glossary of Cultural Terms

Nofo a. Literally "You stay." A parting phrase said by the person leaving. The person staying responds with **'Alu a**. (Tonga).

No, gracias; estoy satisfecho. "No, thank you; I am satisfied." A host will continue to offer food until guests use this phrase. (El Salvador).

Noh. Highly stylized drama that blends together dance, music, and acting. (Japan).

Non. Unleavened bread. (Tajikistan).

Nong. "Little brother" or "little sister." A Thai title used to refer to younger or lower status people, regardless of relationship. (Thailand).

Nonishta. The Tajik word for "breakfast." (Tajikistan).

No no no. A phrase that expresses disagreement. Accompanies the gesture of raising the hand, palm out, and wagging an extended index finger from side to side. (Antigua and Barbuda).

Nonu. An apple-like fruit. (Samoa). *See also* **Vi**.

Nooruz. (Kyrgyzstan). *See* **Naw Ruz**.

No problem man. A good-natured answer to life's challenges even if there is no solution at hand; reflects Jamaicans flexible approach to life. (Jamaica).

Ñoquis. Gnocchi. (Uruguay).

Nori. Dried seaweed. (Japan). *See* **Norimaki**.

Norimaki. Sushi wrapped in dried seaweed. (Japan). *See* **Nori**.

Normal. "Fine." A Pidgin response to the greeting **Ha na?** (How are you?). (Cameroon).

Noroc. (1) "Cheers." A common Romanian greeting. (Moldova, Romania). (2) "Good luck." A Romanian phrase used after a close friend or family member sneezes. (Romania).

Norteamericanos. A Spanish term used to refer to people from the United States and North America. (Bolivia, Chile, Mexico, Paraguay).

Nosnja. A long white skirt and cotton blouse worn by Bosnian Serb women on special occasions. (Bosnia and Herzegovina).

Nošnja. Traditional attire that includes long skirts and cotton shirts for women and wide pants, vests over shirts, and **Opanke** for men. Worn by older people and varies depending on the region. (Serbia and Montenegro).

Nos vemos. A common Spanish parting phrase meaning "see you later." (Colombia, El Salvador, Guatemala, Venezuela).

Notables. A community's group of elders. (Comoros).

No tenga pena. "Don't worry." A phrase used to set others at ease in social interaction. (Guatemala).

No tro way you belly and tek trash tuff um. "Don't lose the substance for the shadow." A traditional saying. (Antigua and Barbuda).

Nouvelle cuisine. A style of cooking that emerged in the 1960s. The food is made of expensive ingredients, is light, has small portions, and is artistically presented. (France).

Novelas. (Angola). *See* **Telenovelas**.

Novenas. Nine days of prayer. The origin of the holiday Nine Mornings. (Saint Vincent and the Grenadines).

Noviy Gohd. The Russian term for the New Year celebration. (Kazakstan).

Novrus Bairami. The New Year celebration that occurs at the beginning of spring. Families make food for the celebration. Young people make fires and jump over them, dance, and play games. (Azerbaijan).

Now for now. A Grenadian English idiom for "urgent." (Grenada).

Nshima. (Zambia). *See* **Nsima**.

Nsima. A thick porridge made from cornmeal. (Malawi, Zambia).

Nsomba. Dried fish. (Malawi).

N'sta bom. "I am fine." A Crioulo response to the greeting **Modi ki bu sta?** (Cape Verde).

N sta bon. "I am fine." A Kriolu response to the greeting **Kuma?** (How are you?). (Guinea-Bissau).

Ntate. "Father." A SeSotho term used to address older men. (South Africa).

Ntchuva. A strategy game played on a board with 18 to 32 holes. Each hole has two seeds in it. The object of the game is to collect the most seeds. (Mozambique).

Ntlo. A traditional circular home built of stone and sticks held together with cow dung, which dries hard and can be painted. It has a thatched roof and windows. The diameter of the main house reflects socioeconomic status. (Lesotho). *Also called* **Rondavel(s)**.

Ntoma. A long colored cloth worn by men in the south that is wrapped around the body somewhat like a toga. (Ghana).

Nuestra Señora de la Alta Gracia. Our Lady of High Gratitude. A national holiday celebrated on 21 January. (Dominican Republic).

Nuestra Señora de las Mercedes. Our Lady of Mercies. A national holiday celebrated on 24 September. (Dominican Republic).

Nuevo sol. Peru's national currency. (Peru).

Nuoc mam. A fermented fish sauce that can be used as a dip or a seasoning. (Vietnam).

Nu'u. Village. (American Samoa).

Nvet. A traditional stringed rhythm instrument. (Equatorial Guinea).

Nyam. "To eat." A creole word with African origins. (Antigua and Barbuda, Saint Vincent and the Grenadines).

Nyama choma. Barbequed meat. (Tanzania).

Nya-na dhoo. "Good evening." A common Kabyè greeting. (Togo).

Nya-na wysy. "Good afternoon." A common Kabyè greeting. (Togo).

Nyatiti. An eight-string lyre played by the Luo to accompany lyrics about fables and legends. (Kenya).

Nyckelharpa. Key fiddle; a Swedish invention. (Sweden).

Nyepi. The Hindu New Year. (Indonesia).

O a mai oe? "How are you?" A common Samoan greeting. (Samoa).

O a mea sa fai? Roughly "What have you been up to?" (American Samoa).

Obi. A special sash worn with the traditional **Kimono(s)**. (Japan).

Obid. The main meal, which is eaten midafternoon. It consists of two main courses, the first being soup and the second containing meat or fish. (Ukraine).

Oblast(s). Political region(s). (Kazakstan, Kyrgyzstan, Russia).

Obrigada. (Mozambique). *See* **Obrigado**.

Obrigado. Portuguese word for "Thank you." Masculine *obrigado*, feminine *obrigada*. (Mozambique, Portugal).

Obyed. The Russian word for "lunch." (Kazakstan).

Ocal. (Bahrain). *See* **Ogal**.

Occasion. A "bush taxi" used to travel long distances. (Gabon).

Ochi. Greek word for "no." *Ochi* Day commemorates the day when Joannis Metaxas, then prime minister, said no to Hitler.

Glossary of Cultural Terms

Greece then entered World War II on the side of the Allies. (Greece).

Odelsting. The lower chamber of the Norwegian Parliament. (Norway). *See also* **Storting.**

Odika. A substance from wild mango pits used to make a gravy-like sauce called **Chocalat**. (Gabon).

Odini! A welcoming answer to visitors who call out the phrase **Odi! Odi!** (Malawi).

Odi! Odi! A phrase visitors use to announce their presence. (Malawi, Mozambique).

Odun Idi. A feast at the end of the Muslim holy month of **Ramadan**. The Arabic name is **Aid al Fitr**. (Benin).

Odun Lea. Muslim Feast of Sacrifice. The Arabic name is **Eid al-Adha**. (Benin).

Ogal. A weighted black cord worn by men to hold a headdress in place. (Kuwait).

Oghol. (Qatar). *See* **Ogal.**

Ohayou. "Good morning." An common casual greeting used among the youth. (Japan). *See also* **Genki?**

Ohayougozaimasu. "Good morning." A Japanese phrase used to greet a superior. (Japan).

Oi. "Hi." An informal Portuguese greeting. (Angola, Brazil, Mozambique).

Oilai kalon. Extended family. The center of Tajik society. (Tajikistan).

Oil down. A stew made of Callaloo, breadfruit, meat or salt fish, and coconut oil; the Grenadian national dish. (Grenada).

OK. "Hello, I'm OK, how are you?" A typical casual black Bahamian greeting. (Bahamas).

O kae? "How are you?" An informal Setswana greeting. (Botswana).

Okay, Okay. The response to the greeting **Alright**. (Antigua and Barbuda).

Okeme. The Luo word for the thumb piano. (Uganda).

Okoumé. A hardwood. (Gabon).

Olá. "Hello" or "Hi." A common Portuguese greeting. (Angola, Mozambique, Portugal).

Olá. Tudo bem? "Hello. Is everything fine?" A common Portuguese greeting. (Brazil).

Older father. A paternal uncle. Called *older father* or **Younger father** depending on the uncle's age in relation to the child's father. (Kenya).

Older mother. A maternal aunt. Called *older mother* or **Younger mother** depending on the aunt's age in relation to the child's mother. (Kenya).

Old Year's Night. New Year's Eve. Friends and relatives toast the coming year at each home they visit. (Saint Lucia).

Oling, oling. "Take, take." A phrase hosts use to encourage guests to eat more. (Uzbekistan).

Olla de carne. A beef stew with potatoes, onions, and vegetables. (Costa Rica).

Olodumare. The Yoruba name of the supreme God. (Benin). *Also called* **Olorun.**

Olorun. The Yoruba name of the supreme God. (Benin). *Also called* **Olodumare.**

O mais velho. A term meaning "the elder" used to refer to the eldest man (and head) of the extended family. (Angola).

Ombiasy. A person who heals or divines with charms and magic and can alter destiny. (Madagascar). *See also* **Vintana.**

Omeen. At the end of a meal, Muslims will say *Omeen* as they bring their hands together in a "prayer" position in front of the chest, raise them together to make an invisible circle, and return them to face level. (Kyrgyzstan).

Omurambas. Dry riverbeds that are a distinctive part of the Namibian landscape. (Namibia).

Omweso. A traditional strategy board game played with seeds or stones. (Uganda). *Also called* **Coro.**

Ona. "Grandmother." An Uzbek term used to address elderly women. (Uzbekistan).

Onces. Afternoon teatime when beverages, small sandwiches, and cookies or cakes are served. (Chile).

Ondol. Floor cushions for sitting that are heated from below. Used in traditional Korean homes. (South Korea).

One-pot. A common rural stew that may have different ingredients based on availability and is usually cooked on an outdoor coal pot. (Saint Lucia).

One time. A Grenadian idiom for "at the same time." (Grenada).

Oodarysh. The sport of wrestling on horseback. (Kyrgyzstan).

Oo la ndi? "Will you still sleep?" A Mungaka greeting used in the morning. The response is **Oo sat ni?** (Cameroon).

Oolesi. Papaya. (Tuvalu).

Oom. "Uncle." A term of respect used by Afrikaans-speaking people to address older males. (South Africa).

Oo sat ni? "Have you arisen?" The Mungaka response to the greeting **Oo la ndi?** (Cameroon).

Opa. "Big sister." An Uzbek term used to address female strangers. (Uzbekistan).

Opanke. Traditional shoes with upturned toes. (Bosnia and Herzegovina, Serbia and Montenegro).

Opintotuki. Finnish word for "stipend." (Finland).

Opko chaboo. A wedding custom in which a sheep is sacrificed for the meal. (Kyrgyzstan).

Oraet. "All right." A common Solomon Island Pijin parting phrase. (Solomon Islands).

Oraet, mi go nao. "All right, I'm leaving." A common Solomon Island Pijin parting phrase. (Solomon Islands).

Ordo. A game children play with sheep bones. (Kyrgyzstan).

Oreano. A unique Kiribati game in which two teams of 10 players throw a heavy, stone, soccer-sized ball wrapped in coconut husk fiber. A team scores if the opposing team drops the ball. The first team to earn 10 points wins. (Kiribati).

Oriort. A title of respect for single women; used with the last name. (Armenia).

Orisha. The Yoruba word for local divinities through which people worship the supreme God. (Benin). *See also* **Voodoos.**

Oro. A popular dance at wedding receptions and other celebrations. Consists of holding hands while dancing particular steps and constantly moving in a circle. (Macedonia).

Orozo Ait. [NOTE: Muslim holidays are set according to the lunar calendar.] A feast at the end of **Ramadan**. The Arabic name is **Aid al Fitr**. (Kyrgyzstan).

Or paa. A spicy fish soup. (Laos).

Orpack. A small piece of cloth worn by women. It is wrapped around the head and shoulders. (Azerbaijan).

Országgyulés. The Hungarian National Assembly; the 386-seat House of Parliament. (Hungary).

Orta oyunu. A type of comedy for the theater. (Turkey).

Os barbudos. A Portuguese term meaning "bearded ones." The origin of the name *Barbados* because of an abundance of bearded fig trees on the islands. (Barbados).

Oshana. (Namibia). *See* **Iishana.**

Glossary of Cultural Terms

Osnovna. The basic level of school, which is the first eight years. (Serbia and Montenegro).

Oso dresi. Home medicines typically linked to traditional religious rituals. (Suriname). *See also* **Busi dresi.**

Ota. "Grandfather." An Uzbek term used to address elderly men. (Uzbekistan).

Otai. A mixture of cut fruit. A refreshment often served to visitors. (Tonga).

Oud. A traditional type of lute. (Jordan, Kuwait, Lebanon, Libya, Sudan, Syria, Turkey, United Arab Emirates, Yemen).

Ouguiya. Mauritania's national currency. (Mauritania).

Oulaha. Advance notice. Given to hosts when someone visits from out of town, allowing the hosts time to prepare. (Comoros).

Out on a lime. A colloquialism for "hanging out with friends." (U.S. Virgin Islands). *Also called* **Limin.**

Outside children. Children born out of wedlock. No stigma is associated with the title. (Bahamas). *See also* **Sweethearting.**

-ovanje. A Slovene suffix that indicates the eve of a holiday. (Slovenia). *See also* **Miklavžovanje, Silvestrovanje.**

Over the road. A colloquialism for "across the street." (New Zealand).

-ovich. A Russian suffix meaning "son." Attached to the end of the father's first name to form a patronymic. (Kyrgyzstan, Uzbekistan).

-ovna. A Russian suffix meaning "daughter." Attached to the end of the father's first name to form a patronymic. (Kyrgyzstan, Uzbekistan).

Ow di bodi? "How are you?" A Krio greeting. A typical response is **A tel God tanki.** (Sierra Leone).

Ow fo do? "What can you do?" A common Krio expression. The response is **Na fo biah** (You must bear it). (Sierra Leone).

Oy gosh. A collection of household goods and clothes. (Turkmenistan).

Oz-komus. A mouth harp used to play traditional music. (Kyrgyzstan). *Also called* **Temir-komuz.**

Ozodii zanon. "Freedom for women." Because of this campaign, women are not required in Tajikistan to comply with certain traditional Islamic restrictions. (Tajikistan).

Pa. (1) A term used to address older men, regardless of relationship. (Sierra Leone). (2) "Aunt." An informal Thai title. (Thailand).

Paali. An ancient language from which Khmer is derived. *Paali* developed as a successor to Indian Sanskrit. (Cambodia).

Pa'anga. Tonga's national currency. (Tonga).

Pabellón criollo. A dish of black beans, rice, shredded meat, plantains, and **Arepa(s).** (Venezuela).

Paçe. A traditional breakfast served at a restaurant. It consists of a creamy soup made with a cow or calf head, tomato sauce, garlic, flour, butter, and seasonings. (Albania).

Pachamama. Goddess Mother Earth. Part of an indigenous tradition that Altiplano Bolivians mix with Catholic beliefs. (Bolivia). *See also* **Achachila, Ch'alla.**

Padarias. Neighborhood shops that sell bread and basic food items. (Brazil).

Padi. "Friend." A term used to address both friends and strangers. (Sierra Leone).

Padrinho. Portuguese word for "godfather." (Portugal).

Pad Thai. Pan-fried noodles. (Thailand).

Paella. Rice with fish, seafood, and/or meat. (Spain).

Pagne. A wraparound skirt. Worn by women in Central and West African countries..

Pagnes. Ivorian women wear these long, colorful bolts of cloth wrapped around the waist, along with a blouse. (Ivory Coast).

Pagri. A traditional cap. Part of a groom's wedding attire. (Bangladesh). *See also* **Nagra, Shirwani.**

Pahela Baishak. The New Year according to the Bangla calendar. (Bangladesh).

Pahu. An indigenous drum. The *pahu,* the guitar, and the **Toere** provide accompaniment to singing performances. (French Polynesia).

Pai. "Father." A term of address used as a sign of respect. (Cape Verde).

Paillotte. A thatched hut. (Comoros).

Pai Sai Maa. "Where are you coming from?" An informal Lao greeting. (Laos).

Päivää. A general Finnish greeting. (Finland).

Pajama. White religious clothing worn by men that is similar to a Western pajama bottom. Worn with **Panjabi.** (Bangladesh).

Pajomah. Long pants worn by women under a traditional dress (**Curta**). (Tajikistan). *Also called* **Aezor.**

Pakeha. New Zealanders of European descent. (New Zealand).

Pakinou. The Baoulé term for Easter. (Ivory Coast).

Palamene. The unicameral Parliament. (Tuvalu).

Palata Predstaviteley. Chamber of Representatives. Part of the Belarus National Assembly. (Belarus). *See also* **Natsionalnoye Sobranie.**

Palav. A dish of rice mixed with meat and carrots. (Tajikistan).

Paleche. White maize. It is replacing sorghum as the primary grain, though vulnerable to drought. (Botswana).

Palolo(s). Coral worms. A delicacy that Samoans gather during Swarm of the *Palolo,* which occurs in late October and early November, when the worms come out to propagate their species. (American Samoa, Samoa).

Paloo. A dish of rice with lamb, carrots, onions, and garlic. (Kyrgyzstan).

Palov. The Uzbek national dish, generally made with rice, meat, and carrots. (Uzbekistan).

Palow. Turkenistan's national dish, a mixture of sticky rice and meat, eaten frequently at celebrations. (Turkmenistan).

Palusami. Coconut cream baked in taro leaves. (American Samoa, Samoa).

Pamanhikan. An engagement tradition wherein the suitor's family visits the prospective bride's family to propose marriage. (Philippines).

Pamplemousse. Grapefruit. (Haiti).

Pán. "Sir." A formal title that precedes a professional title and/or the last name. (Czech Republic, Slovakia).

Pan. (1) "Mr." A title used with the last name. (Poland, Ukraine). (2) Steel drums used in many Grenadian music styles. (Grenada).

Pana. A staple root crop. (Solomon Islands).

Panadería. A bread shop. (Spain).

Panades. Fried corn shells with beans or fish. (Belize).

Pancasila. Five principles: belief in one God, humanism, unity of the state, consensus, and social justice. A national philosophy first embraced by the government in the 1970s. (Indonesia).

Panchai baja. Five-instrument musical ensembles that accompany special activities and festivals. (Nepal).

Pancit. A noodle dish. (Guam).

Glossary of Cultural Terms

Panele. "Miss." A Lithuanian title used with the last name during an introduction. (Lithuania).

Pangi. The Ndyuka term for a traditional wraparound dress. (Suriname). *Also called* **Kosu.**

Panglamaran. A formal ritual among Javanese families in which the parents of a prospective groom go to the parents of the prospective bride to ask permission for the marriage. (Suriname).

Pan-hsai-myo. Myanmar's ten traditional plastic arts, which include painting, sculpture, metalwork, and wood carving. (Myanmar).

Paní. "Madam." A formal title that precedes a professional title and the last name. (Czech Republic).

Pani. "Mrs." A title used with the last name. (Poland, Slovakia, Ukraine).

Panjabi. White religious clothing worn by men that is similar to a knee-length Western pajama top. Worn with **Pajama.** (Bangladesh).

Panna. "Miss." A title used with the last name. (Ukraine).

Panove. "Sirs" or "Gentlemen." A term of address used in official situations. (Ukraine).

Pan sobao. Puerto Rican flat bread that is made with flour, shortening, and water. (Puerto Rico).

P'ansori. Musical drama performed by a soloist. (South Korea).

Papá. "Father." A term of address used as a sign of respect. (Cape Verde).

Papa. (1) A term used to address older men. (French Polynesia, Gabon, Papua New Guinea). (2) A French word for "father." Used by children to address adults. (Ivory Coast, Togo). (3) A stiff cornmeal porridge that is eaten with every meal. (Lesotho). (4) A pandanus mat on which people sit. (Tuvalu).

Papa a la Huancaina. A baked potato topped with sliced eggs and a sauce. (Peru).

Papa graun. The system of tribally owned land, which allows everyone to own land by birthright. (Papua New Guinea).

Papah. A traditional high, round, lambskin hat worn by older men. (Azerbaijan).

Papai Noel. Father Noel. Brings gifts on Christmas Eve that are opened on Christmas Day. (Brazil).

Papá Noel. Father Christmas or Santa Claus. Brings gifts on Christmas Eve. (Argentina, Bolivia).

Papiamento. Dutch Creole. A language spoken on Saint Croix. (U.S. Virgin Islands).

Pâques. Easter. (Gabon).

Parang. Spanish Christmas carols. (Trinidad and Tobago).

Paranging. An activity in which groups of friends go from house to house singing Spanish Christmas carols as well as dancing, eating, and playing homemade instruments. (Trinidad and Tobago).

Parata. A sword dance. An important event at the Carnival celebration in Valletta. (Malta).

Pareu. Wraparound cloth. Traditional clothing worn by men and women. (French Polynesia, Niue).

Parish. A Grenadian region. Each is named after a Catholic saint. A festival is held in honor of the *parish* saint. (Grenada).

Pari-vente. A fund-raising party with free food but expensive beer; organized by women. (Chad).

Paron. A title of respect for older men or officials; used with the last name. (Armenia).

Paros cívicos. Strikes. Occasionally interfere with business hours. (Bolivia).

Parrain. "Godfather" in French. (Belgium).

Parrandas. A Christmas celebration in which groups of friends go door-to-door and sing Christmas songs. The singers expect food and drinks in return. (Puerto Rico).

Pasacalle. Folk music. (Ecuador).

Pasalubong. A small, inexpensive gift that a guest will bring for the host family after being away a long time. (Philippines).

Pasho. Maize paste. (Uganda).

Pasillo. Folk music that has slow, waltz-like rhythms. (Ecuador).

Påsk. Easter. Children celebrate by dressing up as old witches with brooms and going door-to-door (among friends and neighbors) to collect candy. Colored Easter eggs are also common. (Sweden).

Paskha. Special cakes. Family and friends gather to make *paskha* at Easter. (Belarus, Ukraine).

Pass a friend straight. Grenadian creole for passing by someone on the street; considered rude to do so without at least nodding or saying hello. (Grenada).

Passementerie. Decorative trim for clothing or furniture. (Colombia).

Pastel de choclo. A baked dish of beef, chicken, onions, corn, eggs, and spices. (Chile).

Pasterma. Dried salt mutton. (Albania).

Pasties. Meat pies in the shape of burgers. (Northern Ireland).

Pastizzi. Cheesecake. (Malta).

Pasulj. Beans. (Serbia and Montenegro).

Pâte. A doughy corn flour porridge eaten with a spicy stew. (Benin).

Pâte. The French word for a stiff porridge made of cornmeal and water and served with a spicy sauce of okra, spinach, and fish or meat. (Togo). *Also called* **Akoumé.**

Pates. A dish similar to a fish turnover. (U.S. Virgin Islands).

Pa thung. A wraparound skirt worn by women with a simple blouse. (Thailand). *Also called* **Sarong.**

Pâtisseries. A pastry shop that sells cakes. Some may sell crêpes. (France).

Patois. A French-based *creole* language. (Jamaica, Saint Lucia, Trinidad and Tobago, U.S. Virgin Islands).

Patuiki. Head chief. (Niue).

Pavement. A term for "sidewalk." (South Africa).

Pawa. A long shawl worn over the shoulders by Burmese women. (Myanmar).

Paw paw. A race in which students run carrying smaller students on their backs. (Sierra Leone).

Pawpaws. Papaya. (Congo, Grenada, Solomon Islands, Zimbabwe).

Pazar. Open-air markets. (Macedonia).

Pchiwang. Violin. Often accompanies folk music. (Bhutan).

Pe'a. A traditional body tattoo for men. (American Samoa, Samoa).

Peanut cake. A form of peanut brittle. (Bahamas).

Pears. Smooth-skinned avocados. (U.S. Virgin Islands).

Peas. A variety of legumes, including lentils, red beans, pigeon peas, chickpeas, etc. (Antigua and Barbuda, Barbados, Grenada, Jamaica, Saint Lucia).

Peas n' rice. Rice combined with **pigeon peas**, a certain type of bean. (Bahamas).

Pee. "Older brother" or "older sister." A Thai title used to refer to slightly older or higher-status people. (Thailand).

Glossary of Cultural Terms

Pe'epe'e. Coconut cream made by straining a mixture of warm water and mature coconut meat gratings and adding salt or lemon juice. Popularly used as a sauce. (Samoa).

Pelau. (1) A dish made with rice, beans, and chicken. (Montserrat, Saint Kitts and Nevis, Saint Vincent and the Grenadines). (2) A rice dish prepared with chickpeas. (Trinidad and Tobago).

Pelmeni. A pasta dish. (Russia).

Pelotear. In Cuba, a Spanish verb that means "to pass the buck." (Cuba).

Penlop(s). A regional governor. (Bhutan).

Pentecôte. The Christian holiday of Pentecost. (Gabon).

Pepernoten. Gingerbread. Thrown by the servants of **Sinterklaas** during parades. (Netherlands).

Pepper pot. A meat stew flavored with **Casareep**. (Guyana).

Pepperpot. A spicy vegetable stew. (Antigua and Barbuda, Barbados).

Perahan. A knee-length shirt worn with a **Tunban**. Typical clothing for Afghan men. (Afghanistan).

Perahan tunban. A knee-length shirt (**Perahan**) worn over baggy trousers (**Tunban**) that are pulled tight with a drawstring. Typical clothing for Afghan men. (Afghanistan).

Père Noël. The French name for Santa Claus. (France).

Perestroika. Restructuring. A policy of reform introduced by Mikhail Gorbachev in the late 1980s. (Latvia, Russia).

Pesach. [NOTE: Jewish holidays are set according to the lunar calendar.] Passover. Takes place six lunar months and two weeks after New Year's. (Israel). *See also* **Rosh Hashanah**.

Pesäpallo. Finnish baseball. (Finland).

Peso. The national currencies of various countries. (Argentina, Chile, Colombia, Cuba, Dominican Republic, Honduras, Mexico, Philippines, Uruguay).

Pétanque. French lawn bowling. (Burkina Faso, France, Singapore).

Peter. "Godfather" in Dutch. (Belgium).

Petits boubous. Muslim-style robes with a matching **Pagne**; worn by women. (Guinea).

Pet name. A nickname. Often a shortened or slightly altered version of a person's given name. (Jamaica). *Also called* **Yard name**.

Petrol. Gasoline. (New Zealand).

Peul. The French name for Mbororo. The Mbororo are descendants of the Fulbé and are migratory herders. (Central African Republic).

Phaakhamaa. A traditional sarong worn by men. (Laos).

Phaasin. A calf-length, sarong-style skirt worn by Lao women. Made of locally handwoven materials in multicolor designs. Worn with a Western-style blouse and a silver link belt. (Laos).

Phagwah. A celebration to welcome spring. (Guyana).

Phane. A worm that is considered a delicacy. It is gathered from **Mophane** trees, dried in hot ashes, and eaten. (Botswana).

Pi. Coconuts. (Tuvalu).

Pibimbap. Rice mixed with bits of meat and seasoned vegetables. (South Korea).

Picante. A Spanish term used to describe spicy food. (Mexico). *See also* **Caliente**.

Pierogi. Stuffed dumplings. (Poland).

Pierozhki. Meat- or potato-filled pastries. (Kazakstan).

Pigeon peas. A type of bean. (Bahamas). *See also* **Peas n' rice**.

Pigtails. A long, single plait at the back of the head; a hairstyle worn by men. (Saint Vincent and the Grenadines).

Pilau. Pilaf. (Afghanistan, Azerbaijan, Tanzania).

Pilav. Pilaf. (Turkey).

Pillau. Lightly fried rice with vegetables. (Pakistan).

Pi Mai. A three-day Lao New Year celebration in the spring. (Laos).

Piman zwazo. Small, hot pimentos that are often added to dishes. (Haiti).

Piment. Hot peppers. (Chad, Gabon).

Pinasse. Covered, motorized canoe. Commonly used on the Niger River year-round. (Mali).

Ping kai. Grilled poultry. (Laos).

Pinol. A natural beverage made of corn. (Nicaragua).

Pinyin. A romanized Chinese alphabet used for international communication and in schools to help teach Chinese. (China).

Pīrāgi. Meat-filled pastries. (Latvia).

Pirão. A paste of ground cassava, similar to thick porridge. A staple food at lunch and dinner. (Angola).

Pirogues. Traditional outrigger canoes. (French Polynesia).

Pirópos. Flattering personal comments made by Mexican men to women. The women generally do not respond. (Mexico).

Pirozhki. A stuffed pastry. (Moldova, Russia).

Pirukas. A pastry with meat and/or vegetables. (Estonia).

Pisco. Grape brandy. The Chilean national drink. (Chile).

Piti. A lamb broth with potatoes and peas cooked in clay pots in the oven. (Azerbaijan).

Pitso. A town meeting called by the local chief to share important news or discuss something. An impromptu party may follow good news. (Lesotho).

Pjazza. The village square; a popular location for socializing. (Malta).

Placinte. A flaky stuffed pastry. (Moldova).

Planting. Fancy embroidery in a contrasting color, placed around the shirt collar and pant cuffs. (Sierra Leone).

Plassas. "Sauce." Most commonly made from pounded cassava leaves, palm oil, and chili peppers. Eaten with rice. (Sierra Leone).

Plátanos. (1) Plantains. (Cuba, Dominican Republic, Nicaragua). (2) Bananas. (Guatemala).

Plaza Bolívar. A city park the size of a block that honors the Venezuelan hero Simon Bolívar; found in most cities near the city center. (Venezuela).

Plaza de armas. The town plaza. (Peru).

Plazas. Large parking areas that have supermarkets, banks, department stores, post offices, fast-food restaurants and other stores. (U.S. Virgin Islands).

Plena. A popular form of music for dancing and singing. A type of Puerto Rican folk music that deals with life's hardships. (Puerto Rico).

Plov. A popular Uzbek dish of rice, carrots, onions, and mutton. (Kazakstan).

-po. A suffix added to a greeting to indicate respect. (Zambia).

Pocket sulu. A tailored **Sulu** worn with a short-sleeved shirt and sometimes a tie. Worn by businessmen, clergy, and civil servants (Fiji). *Also called* **Sulu vakataga**.

Poda-podas. Small pickup trucks fitted with seats and a roof. They carry people, goods, and animals. (Sierra Leone).

Poe'. Fruit puddings made with coconut milk; a popular dessert. (French Polynesia).

Poftă bună. "Enjoy the meal." A Romanian phrase used at the beginning of the meal. (Romania).

Glossary of Cultural Terms

Poh piah. Spring rolls filled with shredded turnip, bamboo shoots, bean curd, prawns, and pork. (Singapore).

Poisson cru. Raw fish marinated in lime juice. Eaten with breadfruit cooked in coconut milk. (French Polynesia).

Pojadok. The Macedonian word for "breakfast." (Macedonia).

Poka. "Bye." An informal Russian parting phrase. (Belarus).

Polders. Western areas of land that have been reclaimed from the sea. (Netherlands).

Polhovka. A traditional fur hat made from dormouse skins. Worn in southern regions of Slovenia. (Slovenia).

Politburo. Vietnam's 19-member Government Council. (Vietnam).

Polla. Market. (Sri Lanka).

Pollera. (1) A full, colorful skirt. (Bolivia). (2) A full-length dress with embroidery. (Panama).

Pol sambol. Scraped and spiced coconut. (Sri Lanka).

Polska. Polka. A common type of music. (Sweden).

Polyclinics. Clinics that provide free medical and dental care to all Barbadians. (Barbados).

Pom. A Creole dish named for the ingredient **Pomtayer**. (Suriname).

Pomodoro. Tomato sauce. (Italy).

Pomtayer. A local root used in the dish **Pom**. (Suriname).

Ponas. "Mr." A Lithuanian title used with the last name upon introduction. (Lithuania).

Poncho. A blanket-like cloak with a slit in the middle for the head. (Colombia).

Ponerse las pilas. (1) "To insert batteries." A Spanish phrase. (Venezuela). (2) "To be aware" or "to watch out." A Venezuelan colloquialism. (Venezuela).

Ponia. "Mrs." A Lithuanian title used with the last name upon introduction. (Lithuania).

Pop downtown. "Go downtown." A New Zealand colloquialism. (New Zealand).

Popol Vuh. A literary work that describes the Maya creation story. Written in the mid-1500s. (Guatemala).

Por favor. "Please." A common Portuguese phrase. (Portugal).

Por la ventana. "Through the window." Refers to common-law marriage. (Dominican Republic).

Pôro. Male initiation rites that take place in Senoufo communities, once every seven years. (Ivory Coast).

Por puesto. A popular form of transportation in which taxi-like automobiles travel a regular route throughout the city, picking up and letting off passengers at any point. (Venezuela).

Porteño. The Buenos Aires Spanish accent that has been influenced by the Italian language. (Argentina).

Porteños. Argentine coastal inhabitants in the early 1800s who favored a centrist government that would be based in Buenos Aires. (Argentina).

Portuñol. A mixture of the Spanish and Portuguese languages. Spoken in northern border towns. (Uruguay). *Also called* **Brazilero.**

Posadas. Nightly parties that take place during Christmas celebrations. (Mexico).

Postre. Spanish word for "dessert." (Mexico).

Potica. A traditional nut roll served during Christmas and Easter. (Slovenia).

Potjiekos. "Pot food." Any meal cooked in a three-legged cast-iron pot over a fire. (Namibia, South Africa). *See also* **Braai(s).**

Pour-out. A bag of small change scattered by the best man onto the pavement or road after the bride and groom have driven away. (Scotland). *Also called* **Scramble.**

Pousse-pousse. Pedicab. A common form of transportation. (Madagascar).

Poutine. Fries covered with spicy gravy and cheese curds. A favorite fast food. (Canada).

Poya. A holiday held every full moon. (Sri Lanka).

Pozole. Pork-and-hominy soup. (Mexico).

Praça. The town plaza. A popular location to socialize. (Cape Verde).

Prang. "Fender bender." An Australian English colloquialism. (Australia).

Prasad. Blessings from the gods in the form of saffron powder, holy water from the Ganges River, and food. Offered to visitors in Hindu temples. (India).

Presepju. The nativity. A traditional part of Christmas. (Malta).

Pret. "Evil spirits." The Nepalese believe *pret* can cause disease, crop failures, or accidents. (Nepal). *See also* **Bhoot, Bokshi, Graha dasha.**

Priedka tat-Tifel. The traditional Boy's Sermon that is included in Midnight Mass. (Malta).

Prima. "Cousin." A feminine term of address used between good friends. (Guinea-Bissau). *See also* **Primo.**

Primatywny. Polish word for "primitive." A label for people who do not observe public courtesies. (Poland).

Primo. "Cousin." A masculine term of address used between good friends. (Guinea-Bissau). *See also* **Prima.**

Privet. [NOTE: Spelling varies because it is a transliteration of Russian.] "Hello." An informal Russian greeting. (Belarus, Moldova, Russia).

Privyet. (Kazakstan, Kyrgyzstan). *See* **Privet.**

Prodavnici. Small, family-owned stores. (Macedonia).

Profesor/a. (Peru). *See* **Profesor(a).**

Profesor(a). A professional title. Masculine *profesor*, feminine *profesora*. (Chile).

Proost. The Dutch equivalent of saying "Bless you." One can also say **Gezondheid**. (Netherlands).

Prosím. The word for "Please." It is polite to use this word before making any requests and for saying, "You're welcome." (Czech Republic, Slovakia). *See also* **D'akujem, Děkuji.**

Provincien. Provinces. (Belgium).

Pryvit. "Hi." An informal Ukrainian greeting. (Ukraine).

Pryvitanne! "Hi!" A Belarusian greeting used between young friends. (Belarus).

Puan. "Madam." A Malay title. (Malaysia).

Public house. Called a "pub," these establishments serve alcohol and food. People often gather here to socialize. (England, Ireland).

Public motor vehicle. PMV. A bus or truck used for public transportation. (Papua New Guinea).

Públicos. (1) Informal taxis that follow certain routes. (Dominican Republic). (2) Large cars that fit as many as six passengers and travel from specified terminals to fixed destinations with no stops in between. (Puerto Rico).

Public schools. A British idiom for "private schools." (England). *See also* **State schools.**

Pudding(s). A term used to refer to dessert. (Scotland, Wales). *See also* **Sweet.**

Pueblo. A Spanish word for "village." (Bolivia).

Glossary of Cultural Terms

Pugua. Betel nut mixed with powdered lime and wrapped in a pepper leaf. Chamorros often chew *pugua* after a meal. (Guam).

Pula. (1) "Rain." The name of the Batswana national currency. (Botswana). (2) "Good wishes." A Setswana phrase used as a greeting or at the end of speeches. (Botswana).

Pulaka. Swamp taro. (Tuvalu).

Puletasi. A fitted two-piece dress. (American Samoa, Samoa).

Pulkogi. Marinated beef. A Korean delicacy. (North Korea, South Korea).

Pulla. A sweetbread often flavored with cardamom. Comes in a variety of forms. (Finland).

Pulperias. Small shops that are run out of people's homes. *Pulperias* sell food, medicine, and cleaning and school supplies. (Honduras).

Pumari. Head dresses made of toucan and parrot feathers. Worn by Trio and Wayana Amerindians. (Suriname).

Punjabi. Colorful pants, tight from the calves down, with a matching knee-length tunic. Worn by unmarried girls and women in the Terai. (Nepal). *Also called* **Kurta surwal.**

Punjene paprike. Stuffed peppers. (Serbia and Montenegro).

Punt. Ireland's old currency, before the euro came into use. (Ireland).

Punta-rock. A favorite style of music and dance that has its roots in the Garífuna culture. (Belize).

Puntatrasera. A tender steak. (Venezuela).

Punto Guanacaste. A folk dance. The Costa Rican national dance. (Costa Rica).

Pupusas. Thick tortillas stuffed with meat, beans, or cheese. (El Salvador).

Pura vida. "Pure life." A common Costa Rican response to the greeting ¿Cómo estás? (Costa Rica).

Purdah. A state of living in which women are not seen by males, unless they are close family members. (Afghanistan).

Puri puri. Black magic. A belief that coexists with Christianity on both the community and individual level. (Papua New Guinea).

Purotu. "Missionary dresses." *Purotu* cover more of the body than traditional clothing. Worn by women performing slow hula dances. Literally, "Good in appearance." (French Polynesia).

Pushing. The action of a host accompanying a guest to the road. (Ivory Coast).

Pushtunwali. Code of the Pashtuns. A local behavioral code. (Afghanistan).

Pust. The Slovene equivalent of Mardi Gras. (Slovenia).

Puszi. A greeting in which Hungarians hug and kiss each other lightly on each cheek. (Hungary).

Putonghua. Mandarin Chinese. (China, Hong Kong, Singapore).

Putu. A hot pepper sauce Comorians use to season all types of food. (Comoros).

Pwe. A live show incorporating acting, singing, music, dancing, and sometimes clowns or puppets. (Myanmar).

Pyelmeni. Small boiled dumplings. A Russian dish. (Kazakstan).

Pyithu Hluttaw. People's Assembly. A 485-seat unicameral parliament elected in 1990 but never allowed to convene. (Myanmar).

Pysanka. Easter-egg painting. A Ukrainian art form. (Ukraine).

Pytt i Panna. A dish of potatoes, leftover meats, and onions, fried with an egg on top and served with pickled beets. (Sweden).

Qahwa. (Bahrain). *See* **Qahwah.**

Qahwah. [NOTE: Spelling varies because it is a transliteration of Arabic.] Coffee. (Qatar).

Qahwah Saadah. Bedouin coffee that is bitter and drunk quickly from small cups. (Jordan).

Qameez. A long tunic. (Pakistan). *See also* **Shalwar qameez.**

Qarakuli. A cap worn by men in the winter; made from the skin of a karakul sheep. (Afghanistan).

Qassatat. A pastry filled with either cheese or peas, and occasionally anchovies or spinach. (Malta).

Qat. An addictive stimulant leaf that grows on a bush. Chewed during afternoon visits, holidays, wedding celebrations, and so on. (Yemen).

Qawwali. An Islamic song of worship performed by Sufi mystics. Accompanied by instruments such as the **Dholak** and the **Rabab.** (Pakistan).

Qazi. A Muslim holy man who completes the marriage contract between the families of the bride and groom. (Pakistan).

Qedra. A spicy rice dish. (West Bank and Gaza).

Qeleshe. A traditional white cap worn by men. (Albania).

Qobqob. A gold headpiece worn by the bride during her wedding celebration. (Bahrain).

Qorma. A vegetable sauce. (Afghanistan).

Quadrille. A style of dance similar to square dancing, but with an island beat. (U.S. Virgin Islands).

Qubbajt. A pastry filled with nougat. (Malta).

¡Que aproveche! "Enjoy your meal." A Spanish phrase often used to politely refuse an invitation to join a meal. (Spain).

Québeckers. Canadians from Québec. (Canada). *Also called* **Québécois.**

Québécois. Canadians from Québec. (Canada). *Also called* **Québeckers.**

¿Qué hay de bueno? "What's good?" A common Spanish greeting. (Panama).

Que le vaya bien. "May it go well with you." A common Spanish parting phrase. (Guatemala, Honduras, Panama).

Quelle sont les nouvelles? French phrase meaning "What is the news?" After initial questions, Ivorians eventually ask each other this question, which opens the conversation to deeper discussion. (Ivory Coast).

Quena. An instrument similar to a recorder. Used to play traditional music. (Peru). *See also* **Antara, Charango.**

Quenelles. Small dumplings made with meat or fish and served with a sauce. (Luxembourg).

Quesadillas. Tortillas baked or fried with cheese. (Mexico).

Que sea lo que Dios quiera. "Whatever God wills." A Spanish expression Colombians use to express their faith. (Colombia).

¿Qué tal? "How are you?" or "What's up?" A common Spanish greeting. (Cuba, Guatemala, Panama, Puerto Rico).

Quetschentaart. Plum tart. (Luxembourg).

Quetzal. Guatemala's national currency. (Guatemala).

Quijongo. A traditional stringed instrument. (Costa Rica).

Quinceañera. A girl's 15th birthday party, which marks her entrance into the social world. (Ecuador, El Salvador).

Quinoa. A protein-rich grain often included in soup. (Bolivia).

Quisaca. Dried and ground cassava leaves cooked in water. (Angola).

Quoc-Hoi. The Vietnamese National Assembly. (Vietnam).

Glossary of Cultural Terms

Qur'an. The Koran; contains the word of **Allah** as revealed to the prophet Muhammad through the angel Gabriel. The scriptures of Islam. Used in Muslim-populated countries..

Qur'anic. (Cameroon, Chad, Comoros, Kuwait, Mauritania, Qatar, Senegal, Sudan, United Arab Emirates). *See* **Qur'an.**

Qurban khait. Day of Sacrifice. A Muslim holiday that honors Abraham's willingness to sacrifice his son. (Uzbekistan). *Also called* **Eid al-Adha.**

Rabab. A stringed instrument. Accompanies the **Qawwali**. (Pakistan).

Rababa. One- or two-stringed fiddle used to accompany singing. (United Arab Emirates).

Rabel. An instrument similar to a fiddle. (Chile).

Raclette. Melted cheese on a piece of potato. (Switzerland).

Radio trottoir. Pavement radio. A system of verbal relays that pass news and information with great speed. (Cameroon).

Radunitsa. A holiday to remember the dead. (Belarus).

Ragamuffin. A style of music that mixes rock and reggae. Also, the untucked fashion that these musicians wear. (Grenada).

Ragù. Sauce with meat. (Italy).

Raï. A style of music popular among young people. (Algeria, Morocco).

Rajya Sabha. Council of States. The upper house in India's Parliament. (India). *See also* **Lok Sabha.**

Rake n' scrape. A type of island music created with goatskin drums, saws, and maracas. (Bahamas). *See also* **Goombay.**

Rakhmat. "Thank you." A phrase used when departing after visiting friends or family. (Kyrgyzstan).

Raki. A strong alcoholic drink. (Albania).

Rakija. (1) An alcoholic drink. (Bosnia and Herzegovina, Serbia and Montenegro). (2) A brandy made of apples, grapes, or plums. (Macedonia).

Ramadan. [NOTE: Spelling varies because it is a transliteration of Arabic. Also, Muslim holidays are set according to the lunar calendar.] The month in which **Allah** revealed the **Qur'an** to the prophet Muhammad. During this month, Muslims fast from sunrise to sunset. Observed in Muslim-populated countries..

Ramadhan. (Oman). *See* **Ramadan.**

Ramakian. An important traditional literary work containing stories of the Hindu god Rama. Based on the epic Sanskrit poem the **Ramayana**. (Thailand).

Ramasan Bairam. A feast at the end of **Ramadan**. Celebrated by Muslims. (Albania, Bosnia and Herzegovina, Croatia).

Ramayana. An epic Sanskrit poem. Continues to influence national and regional literature. (Cambodia, India, Thailand).

Ramazan. (Uzbekistan). *See* **Ramadan.**

Ramazan Bairami. A feast at the end of **Ramadan**. Celebrated by Muslims. (Azerbaijan).

Ramazon. (Tajikistan). *See* **Ramadan.**

Ramen. A type of noodles. (Japan).

Ramzaan. (India). *See* **Ramadan.**

Ramzan. (Bangladesh). *See* **Ramadan.**

Ran annim. "Good morning." A greeting used by the Chuukese. (Micronesia).

Ranchera. A traditional form of music. (Mexico).

Rand. South Africa's national currency. (South Africa).

Ranovola. Golden water. A drink made from water boiled in the browned rice that remains stuck to the bottom of the pan after cooking. (Madagascar).

Rapa. A cloth women wear wrapped around the waist. (Cameroon). *Also called* **Pagne.**

Rappée. A pie made with grated potato and ground meat. (Canada).

Raqaq. A very thin bread served with a sauce. (United Arab Emirates).

Rara. (1) A more traditional version of **Carnaval**. Celebrated mainly in urban areas. (Haiti). (2) Local bands that perform in the streets from mid-January to Easter. (Haiti).

Ras El Am El Hejri. The Islamic New Year. (Tunisia).

Ras El Sans El Hejria. The Islamic New Year. (West Bank and Gaza).

Rashogolla. Dough boiled in syrup; a popular sweet. (Bangladesh).

Raspaitos. Shaved ice; a popular treat. (Venezuela).

Ratu. A title used with the first name when addressing a chief. (Fiji).

Rau luoc. Boiled vegetables. (Vietnam).

Ravane. A tambourine-like drum often ringed with bells. Accompanies the **Séga** dance. (Mauritius).

Ravitoto sy henakisoa. Ground manioc leaves with pork. A popular form of **Loaka**. (Madagascar).

Rayons. Districts within Azerbaijan. (Azerbaijan).

Razana. Ancestors. Intermediaries between the gods and the living. People report their activities and needs to the *razana*, who provide directives and taboos. (Madagascar). *See also* **Fadys.**

Razha. A dance involving sword throwing and an exchange of poetry. The Omani national dance. (Oman).

Real. Brazil's national currency. (Brazil).

Reamker. The Cambodian version of the Hindu **Ramayana**. An important literary work; stories from the epic are carved on the walls of the temple **Angkor Wat**. They are also acted out in shadow plays. (Cambodia). *See also* **Nang sbek.**

Rebab. A bowed instrument. Used in **Gamelan** ensembles. (Indonesia).

Rebaba. A one-stringed instrument. (Saudi Arabia).

Rebambaramba. "A free-for-all." A Spanish idiom unique to Cuban society. (Cuba).

Rebana. A single-headed drum. (Malaysia).

Rebetiko. A type of folk music with themes of poverty and suffering. (Greece).

Rebozo. A shawl used by women for a variety of purposes, including carrying a child or covering the head or arms. (Mexico).

Recuerdos. Tokens of affection or remembrance. (Ecuador).

Redda. A woman's wraparound skirt that is tucked in at the waist. Worn with a **Hatte**. (Sri Lanka).

Refresquerias. Fruit-and-drink stands that sell **Batidos de fruta.** (Venezuela).

Regalo. Spanish word for "gift." (Venezuela).

Regierungschef. The Liechtenstein prime minister; serves as head of government. (Liechtenstein).

Regressados. Refugees who have returned to their home regions. (Angola).

Regulos. Traditional chiefs, who have great influence over local matters. (Mozambique).

Rendang Padang. A spicy meat dish cooked in garlic, shallots, ginger, chilies, lemongrass, and coconut milk. (Indonesia).

Renminbi. China's national currency. (China). *See also* **Yuan.**

Glossary of Cultural Terms

Respect. "I respect you" or "It's nice to meet you." An informal greeting used among friends and youth. (Saint Vincent and the Grenadines).

Responsables populares de salud. Community health-care workers that are trained in basic skills by local nurses and doctors. They serve the rural population. (Bolivia).

Retablos. Wooden boxes that feature three-dimensional religious or everyday scenes; a form of folk art. (Peru).

Revista. A popular theater where politics and social issues are satirized. (Portugal).

Rezen. Breaded steak. (Slovakia).

Rhamadan. (Yemen). *See* **Ramadan.**

Rial. The name of the Iranian and Yemeni national currencies. (Iran, Yemen).

Rial Omani. The name of the Omani national currency. (Oman).

Ribab. A single-stringed instrument often used to accompany poetry. (Morocco). *Also called* **Amzhad.**

Rice pudding. Blood sausage. (Antigua and Barbuda). *Also called* **Black pudding.**

Riebel. Cornmeal stirred in a frying pan with milk, water, and salt. The Liechtenstein national dish. (Liechtenstein).

Riigikogu. The Estonian Parliament. (Estonia).

Rijerbal. Workers. A position in the traditional social system that is now incorporated into the formal government. (Marshall Islands). *See also* **Alaps, Irooj.**

Riksdag. The Swedish Parliament. (Sweden).

Ring. A colloquialism for "call on the telephone." (Australia).

Ringgit. Malaysia's national currency. (Malaysia).

Rinok. An open-air market where meat, cheese, fruits, vegetables, and spices are sold. (Kazakstan).

Risorgimento. The Italian unification movement that began in the 1800s. (Italy).

Riyal. The name of the Qatari and Saudi national currencies. (Qatar, Saudi Arabia).

Riyuq. Breakfast. (Iraq). *Also called* **Futur.**

Rogora khar? "How are you?" An informal way to begin a conversation. (Georgia).

Rogor brdzandebit? "How are you?" A more formal way to begin a conversation. (Georgia).

Romaji. A Japanese phonetic alphabet that uses Roman letters. (Japan). *See also* **Hiragana, Kanji, Katakana.**

Ro mazava. A stew made with **Zebus** and green leafy vegetables. (Madagascar).

Rondadors. Panpipes. (Ecuador).

Rondavel(s). (1) A traditional circular home built of stone and sticks held together with cow dung, which dries hard and can be painted. It has a thatched roof and a few windows. The diameter of the main house reflects socioeconomic status. (Lesotho). *Also called* **Ntlo.** (2) Round, thatched dwellings that are located within a family compound. (Botswana).

Roora. The bride-price paid by the groom's family to the bride's parents. Traditionally it included cattle, although cash is accepted. (Zimbabwe). *Also called* **Lobola.**

Rosh Hashanah. The Jewish New Year. (Bosnia and Herzegovina, Croatia, Israel).

Rosolje. A pink potato salad made with beets and herring. A Russian dish. (Estonia).

Roštilj. Grilled meats. (Serbia and Montenegro).

Rösti(s). Grated and fried potatoes. (Liechtenstein, Switzerland).

Roti. (1) Flat bread. (Fiji, India, Mauritius, Nepal, Pakistan, Trinidad and Tobago). (2) Flat bread wrapped around meat and vegetables. (Grenada, Guyana, Suriname).

Roti chanai. Bite-sized balls of cooked wheat dipped in lentil curry. (Malaysia).

Roti prata. An Indian dough-bread; a popular breakfast item. (Singapore).

Rottab. Fresh dates. (Bahrain). *See also* **Tamr.**

Route taxis. A form of transportation that follows set routes and has set fares. (Jamaica).

Roze-Maulud. A Muslim holiday celebrating the birth of the prophet Muhammad. (Afghanistan).

Rtveli. A rural harvest holiday in midautumn that celebrates variety and abundance. (Georgia).

Ruanas. Woven wool shawls. (Colombia).

Rubab. A traditional two-string guitar. (Uzbekistan).

Ruble. (1) Russia's national currency. (Russia). (2) Tajikistan's former national currency. (Tajikistan). *See also* **Somoni.**

Ručak. The main meal of the day. Eaten after work around 4 p.m. Includes soup and a meat dish. (Serbia and Montenegro).

Rucek. The Macedonian word for "lunch." (Macedonia).

Rüfen. Debris slides. Previously a natural threat, they are now enclosed and rendered harmless. (Liechtenstein).

Rugbrød. Pumpernickel bread or rye bread traditionally used for sandwiches. (Denmark).

Ruhname. President Saparmyrat Niyazov's thoughts on philosophy and Turkmen identity. (Turkmenistan).

Rui. Millet porridge. (Gambia).

Rumbero. A Spanish adjective that describes the Colombian ability to both work and play hard. (Colombia).

Rum shop(s). Small bars where men socialize, drink, and play dominoes and cards. (Grenada, Montserrat).

Rupee. The national currency of various countries. (India, Mauritius, Nepal, Pakistan, Sri Lanka).

Rupiah. Indonesia's national currency. (Indonesia).

Rupmaize. Rye bread. (Latvia).

Saaang, I gridi! "You are greedy!" A phrase people call out when a child does not share, or when someone finishes a plate of food without offering some to others. (Suriname).

Saan ka galing? "Where have you been?" A common, informal Pilipino greeting. (Philippines).

Saan ka pupunta? "Where are you going?" A common, informal Pilipino greeting. (Philippines).

Saba al-khair. (Bahrain). *See* **Sabah al-Khair.**

Saba al-nur. The proper reply to the Arabic greeting **Saba al-khair.** (Bahrain).

Sabah al-kair. (Yemen). *See* **Sabah al-Khair.**

Sabah al khair. (Jordan). *See* **Sabah al-Khair.**

Sabah al-Khair. "Good morning." A common Arabic greeting. (Saudi Arabia).

Sabah al-khayr. (Libya). *See* **Sabah al-Khair.**

Sabah el-khair. (West Bank and Gaza). *See* **Sabah al-Khair.**

Sabah El-Kheer. (Tunisia). *See* **Sabah al-Khair.**

Sabaidii. "May you have happy health." The most common Lao greeting. (Laos).

Sabar. A set of five to seven tuned drums. Played by the Wolof people to accompany dancing. (Senegal).

Saba Saba. Farmer's Day. Observed on 7 July. (Tanzania).

Sabji bazaar. A weekend open-air market. (Bhutan).

Sabkha. Salt flats. (United Arab Emirates).

Sabor. Croatia's parliament. (Croatia).

Glossary of Cultural Terms

Sachak. Cloth. (Turkmenistan).

Sachertorte. A rich chocolate cake with apricot jam and chocolate icing. (Austria).

Sadiq. "Friend." An Arabic term of address used for strangers. (Qatar).

Sadjèn. Food sacrifices made to the world of spirits. A central feature of **Agama Djawa**. (Suriname). *See also* **Slametan**.

Sadu. The traditional Bedouin handicraft of weaving rugs and tents using sheep, goat, or camel wool. (Kuwait).

Sadza. A stiff porridge made from white cornmeal. *Sadza* is rolled into a ball and dipped in a sauce. (Zimbabwe).

Saeima. The Latvian Parliament. (Latvia).

Safsari. A rectangular piece of cloth worn by older women that completely covers the clothing. Worn for protection from rain and dust. (Tunisia).

Sagas. Medieval Icelandic stories from A.D. 1200 to 1400. The *sagas* cover centuries of Scandinavian and British history. (Iceland).

Sagh ol. "Be well." An Azeri parting phrase. (Azerbaijan).

Sah. "Hello." A greeting used between rural Fang women. (Equatorial Guinea).

Saħħa. "Health to you." A Maltese parting phrase. (Malta).

Sai hankuri. "Have patience." A Hausa phrase. (Niger).

Saing-waing.

Sain uu. "Hello." A casual Mongol greeting. (Mongolia).

Sai pe, Malo. "Fine, thank you." A polite response to the Tongan greeting **Fefe hake?** (How do you do?). (Tonga).

Sa ka fet? "What's happening?" A common patois greeting. (Saint Lucia).

Sakau. An alcoholic beverage. (Micronesia).

Sakay. A side dish of jalapeños, ginger, and garlic. (Madagascar).

Saksak. A starchy extract from the sago palm. A staple food on the coast and in the lowlands. (Papua New Guinea).

Salaam. (1) "Peace." A common greeting. (Eritrea, Mauritius, Uzbekistan). (2) A gesture with the right hand used as an informal greeting. (Nepal, Singapore).

Salaam Alaikum. (Guinea). *See* **Assalaam alaikum**.

Salaam alaykum. (Mauritania). *See* **Assalaam alaikum**.

Salaam' alaykum. (Sudan). *See* **Assalaam alaikum**.

Salaam Aleikum. (Kyrgyzstan, Niger). *See* **Assalaam alaikum**.

Salaam alek(i). (Chad). *See* **Assalaam alaikum**.

Salaam ale kum. (Burkina Faso). *See* **Assalaam alaikum**.

Salaam Malekum. (Gambia). *See* **Assalaam alaikum**.

Sala gashi. "Go well in peace." A Sesotho parting phrase. (South Africa).

Sala hantle. "Stay well." A Sesotho parting phrase used by the person leaving. The person staying says **Tsamaea hantle**. (Lesotho).

Salam. (Azerbaijan, Iran, Sudan, Turkmenistan). *See* **Salaam**.

Salama. "Peace" (a common greeting) or "Peaceful" (a common response to a greeting). (Kenya, Madagascar, Tanzania).

Salamalek. (Turkmenistan). *See* **Assalaam alaikum**.

Salamaleykum. (Turkmenistan). *See* **Assalaam alaikum**.

Salamatsyzby. "Hello." The standard Kyrgyz greeting. (Kyrgyzstan).

Sala sentle. "Stay well." A parting phrase said to a person who is staying. (Botswana).

Salat. Praying five times daily facing Makkah, Saudi Arabia. One of the Five Pillars of Islam. (Iran, Malaysia). *See also* **Hajj, Saum, Shahada, Zakat**.

Salawar kameez. A traditional Punjabi pajama-like outfit. (Singapore).

Saldais ēdiens. Dessert; the third course of the main meal. (Latvia).

Salegy. Popular dance music that combines East African guitar rhythms with local beats. (Madagascar).

Salem. "Hi." A common Kazak greeting. (Kazakstan).

Salemetsis-ba? "How do you do?" A common Kazak greeting. (Kazakstan).

Salom. "Peace." A Tajik greeting used between friends. (Tajikistan).

Salomka. Straw plaiting used to create dolls, animals, baskets, and other decorative items. (Belarus).

Salon. (1) The living quarters, which consist of the living room and the bedrooms. (Gabon). (2) The sitting room. (Madagascar).

Saloneh. Mixed vegetables. (Bahrain).

Salteñas. Meat or chicken pies with potatoes, olives, and raisins. (Bolivia).

Saltfish. (1) Usually means cod that has been dried and salted. (Antigua and Barbuda, Jamaica, Montserrat). (2) Fish cured in salt. (Trinidad and Tobago).

¡Salud! "Health." A saying used if someone sneezes. (Mexico).

¡Saludos! "Hi." An informal Spanish greeting. (Dominican Republic).

Salut. (1) "Hello." A French greeting common among friends and youth. (Belgium, Canada, Central African Republic, France, French Polynesia, Lebanon, Romania, Switzerland). (2) A common parting phrase used among young people. (Luxembourg).

Salut, comment ça va? "Hi, how are you?" An informal French greeting. (Burkina Faso).

Salvator Mundi. The name of the sculpture of Christ in San Salvador's cathedral. One of the few major works of art in El Salvador left after natural disasters ruined older works. (El Salvador).

Salwaar kameez. A type of pantsuit with a long shirt. (Fiji).

Salwaar-kameez. (Mauritius). *See* **Salwaar kameez**.

Salwar. A long blouse worn over long pants with a matching shawl. (Suriname).

Salwar khamis. (Malaysia). *See* **Salwaar kameez**.

Sambal. Any foods fried with chilies. (Indonesia).

Samlor. A three-wheeled motorized taxi. (Thailand).

Samoon. An oval-shaped bread loaf. (Iraq).

Sampot. Worn by women, a large rectangular piece of colored cloth that is wrapped around the hips like a skirt down to the ankles. (Cambodia).

Samri. A dance performed at weddings and other social gatherings by women. (Kuwait).

-san. A suffix used with the family name. (Japan).

Sanatate. "Good health." A Romanian phrase used after a close friend or family member sneezes. (Romania).

Sancocho. (1) Vegetable-and-meat stew. (Colombia, Dominican Republic). (2) Chicken soup. (Panama).

Sandae. Masked theater. Performed at festivals and for entertainment. (South Korea).

Glossary of Cultural Terms

Sandinistas. A Marxist-oriented revolutionary group that gained control of the Nicaraguan government in July 1979 after a prolonged civil war. (Nicaragua).

Sanga ye? "How are you?" A common Pashto greeting. (Afghanistan).

Sangoma. A person consulted for divination. A traditional practice. (Swaziland). *See also* **Batsakatsi, Tinyanga.**

Sango nini? "What's new?" A Lingala phrase that follows the greeting **Mbote** (Hello). (Congo).

Sangría. A popular drink made with wine, fruit, and soft drinks. (Spain).

Sanibonani. "I see you." A siSwati greeting used to address two or more people. (Swaziland). *See also* **Sawubona.**

Santa Cruz. Words that mean "holy cross" in Spanish. Christopher Columbus gave this name to the island that is now St. Croix. (U.S. Virgin Islands).

Santería. Religious beliefs that combine Catholicism and ideas of African origin. (Cuba).

Santos. Carved religious figurines found in almost every home. A common folk art. (Puerto Rico).

Santur. A traditional stringed instrument. (Iran).

Sanusis. An Islamic religious and political group that fought Ottoman and Italian invasions into Libya and North Africa. (Libya).

Sanza. A thumb piano; a traditional instrument. (Central African Republic).

Sa-pi-bi-la? "Have you eaten?" A common Burmese greeting. (Myanmar).

Sarangi. A traditional four-stringed instrument used to accompany singing and dancing. (Nepal).

Sarape. A wool poncho that a man may wear over his shirt and pants when it is cold. (Mexico).

Saree(s). (Bangladesh, India, Mauritius, Sri Lanka). *See* **Sari.**

Sari. A long piece of cloth that is wrapped around the body in a special way. Worn by women. (Fiji, Nepal, Singapore, South Africa, Suriname).

Sari-saris. Small convenience stores run out of homes. (Philippines).

Sarma. Cabbage leaves stuffed with minced meat and rice. (Macedonia, Serbia and Montenegro).

Sarmale. Minced meat with rice, rolled in pickled cabbage or grapevine leaves. (Romania).

Sarmi. A pepper or cabbage stuffed with pork and rice. (Bulgaria).

Sarod. A traditional northern Indian instrument. (India).

Saron demung. A traditional Indonesian instrument similar to a xylophone. (Indonesia).

Sarong. A long cloth wrapped around the waist. Worn by both men and women, depending on the country. (Cambodia, Indonesia, Senegal, Sri Lanka, Suriname, Thailand).

Sarong soet. A large rectangular piece of colored cloth worn by men that is wrapped around the hips like a kilt down to the ankles. (Cambodia).

Sarung. A long piece of cloth worn about the waist by Muslim men when they attend mosque on Fridays. (Malaysia).

Sărut mâna. "Kiss your hand." A Romanian phrase men use to greet women as a sign of respect. (Romania).

Sarut mâna. "I kiss your hand." A Romanian phrase men use to greet women. (Moldova).

Sărut mâna pentru masă. "Kiss your hand for the meal." A Romanian phrase used to thank the person who cooked and served the meal. (Romania).

Sasa. A group dance involving slapping, clapping, and stylized hand, arm, and leg movements. (American Samoa).

Sashimi. Raw fish; a popular dish. (Japan, Micronesia).

Sat. "Chastity." The most important virtue a woman can bring to marriage. (Nepal).

Sata. A wraparound cloth worn by women. The term is used in the north. (Togo). *Also called* **Bsawao.** *See also* **Avo tata.**

Satay. Barbecued pork or chicken on a stick with peanut sauce. (Malaysia, Thailand).

Satsivi. Fried chicken or turkey soaked in walnut sauce and spices. (Georgia).

Satversme. The Latvian constitution. (Latvia).

Saucisse. French term for "grilled sausage." (Switzerland).

Saum. Fasting during **Ramadan.** One of the Five Pillars of Islam. (Iran, Malaysia). *See also* **Hajj, Salat, Shahada, Zakat.**

Sausage roll. A sausage wrapped in pastry. (New Zealand).

Sawasdee ka. "Hello" or "Good-bye." A greeting used by women in conjunction with the **Wai.** (Thailand).

Sawasdee kraab. "Hello" or "Good-bye." A greeting used by men in conjunction with the **Wai.** (Thailand).

Sawubona. "I see you." A common greeting. (South Africa, Swaziland).

Saya. A traditional Bolivian dance. (Bolivia).

Sayazhai. Kazak word for a "summer cottage." (Kazakstan).

Sayedaty. "Mrs." An Arabic title used with the last name. (Syria).

Sayedy. "Mr." An Arabic title used with the last name. (Syria).

Sayyed. "Mr." An Arabic title used with the last name. (West Bank and Gaza).

Sayyedeh. "Mrs." An Arabic title used with the last name. (West Bank and Gaza).

Saz. A type of long-necked lute. A common folk instrument. (Turkey).

Sbah al Kheir. (Morocco). *See* **Sabah al-Khair.**

S Bohom. "God be with you." A traditional Slovak greeting. (Slovakia).

School-leaving. Graduation. (Montserrat).

Schrebergarten. Small garden plots located in or near the city. Urban dwellers own or rent them. (Germany).

Schweizerdeutsch. Swiss German; it is the dialect used for everyday conversation in Switzerland. It can be hard for other German speakers to understand. (Switzerland).

Schwiizertütsch. The Swiss German dialect that is similar to the Alemannic dialect spoken in Liechtenstein. (Liechtenstein).

Schwinger. Traditional wrestling that is similar to Graeco-Roman wrestling but does not have weight classifications. (Switzerland).

Sciences. An education track that focuses on math and sciences. (Tunisia).

Scramble. A bag of small change that is scattered by the best man onto the pavement or road after the bride and groom have driven away. (Scotland). *Also called* **Pour-out.**

Sea bathe. Playing in shallow water. (Antigua and Barbuda).

Seanad. The Irish Senate. (Ireland).

Secretos en reunión es mala educación. "It is bad manners to tell secrets in gatherings." A common Spanish expression used if not everyone is included in mealtime conversation. (Peru).

Glossary of Cultural Terms

Séga. A Mauritian dance that integrates Creole texts and modern percussion instruments with the rhythm of African, Caribbean, and Latin American pop music. Traditional accompanying instruments are the triangle, the **Coco**, and the **Ravane**. (Mauritius).

Seghanapet. Toastmaster. Proposes toasts when guests are present. (Armenia). *Also called* **Tamada.**

Seimas. The Lithuanian Parliament. (Lithuania).

Sejm. The lower house of the Polish parliament. (Poland). *Also called* **Diet.**

Seke. "Hello." A common Temne greeting. (Sierra Leone).

Seker Bayramı. "Sugar holiday." A three-day holiday in which people eat sweets to celebrate the end of **Ramazan**. (Turkey).

Seke-seke. A percussion instrument used in Amerindian music. Consists of a closed piece of metal pipe with seeds or gravel, shaken to the rhythm. (Suriname).

Sekona singabusalina. "I am fine." A typical Ndebele response to **Siyabonga linjani?** (Hello, how are you?). (Zimbabwe).

Sœl. (Iceland). *See* **Sœll.**

Selam. "Salute." A Turkish greeting used by youth. (Turkey).

Selamat malam. "Good evening." A Malay greeting. (Singapore).

Selamat pagi. "Good morning." A typical Malay greeting. (Malaysia, Singapore).

Selamat petang. "Good afternoon." A Malay greeting. (Singapore).

Selamat sejahtera ke atas anda. "I wish you peace and tranquility." A formal Malay greeting. (Singapore).

Seljanka. A meat soup with pickles, onions, and olives. (Estonia).

Sœll. "Happy" or "glad." An Icelandic greeting. Masculine *Sœll*, feminine *Sœl*. (Iceland).

Selsko meso. A meat and mushroom dish. (Macedonia).

Selteh. Spicy stew made with fenugreek. (Yemen).

Semana de Turismo. Tourism Week. The week preceding Easter when people travel throughout the country and participate in a variety of local festivals. (Uruguay).

Semana Santa. Holy Week. Celebrated the week before Easter, an important time for family gatherings. (Costa Rica, Dominican Republic, El Salvador, Honduras, Mexico, Paraguay, Venezuela).

Semba. A popular musical style. (Angola).

Senat. The upper house of the Polish legislature. (Poland).

Sendero Luminoso. "Shining Path." A violent Maoist group that used guerrilla warfare to try to overthrow the government during the 1980s and 1990s. As many as 70,000 Peruvians have died in the battles between the government and the rebels. (Peru).

Senedd. The 60-member Welsh Assembly. (Wales).

Senhor. "Mr." A Portuguese title used with the surname. (Angola, Brazil, Cape Verde, Mozambique).

Senhora. "Mrs." A Portuguese title used with the surname. (Angola, Brazil, Cape Verde, Mozambique).

Señor. "Mr." A title used with the last name. Used in Spanish-speaking countries..

Señora. "Mrs." A title used with the last name. Used in Spanish-speaking countries..

Señorita. "Miss" or "young woman." A title used with the last name. Used in Spanish-speaking countries..

Sepaktakraw. A traditional competitive team sport played with a rattan ball. (Malaysia).

Sepo. The wedding custom of a dowry for the bride. (Kyrgyzstan).

Seqer. A women's party before a wedding. The bride's body hair is "waxed" off with a sugar, water, and lemon paste prior to applying designs of henna dye. (Tunisia).

Serranos. People from highland areas, said to be more formal, conservative, and reserved. (Ecuador). *See also* **Costeños.**

Servus. (1) "Hello." A casual greeting. (Austria, Romania, Slovakia). (2) "I am here to serve you." Latin word that is the root of the Hungarian terms **Szervusz** and **Szia**. (Hungary).

Sette Giugno. A public holiday commemorating an uprising against the British. Observed 7 June. (Malta).

Seu. A Portuguese title for men used with the first name in less formal situations. (Brazil).

Sevdalinka. Love songs. (Bosnia and Herzegovina).

Sevdidzan. Soft cake. A Bosniac dessert. (Bosnia and Herzegovina).

Seytesootiun. "See you later." A common Armenian parting phrase between friends. (Armenia).

Shaabi. A working-class, socially-minded form of urban Egyptian pop music with roots in folk music and dance. (Egypt). *See also* **Al-jil.**

Shabbat. Hebrew word for "Sabbath." (Israel).

Shabeen. An informal neighborhood bar. (Namibia).

Shab-i-Barat. A Muslim holiday. A special night to ask for blessings. (Bangladesh).

Shahada. The act of professing that there is no god but **Allah**. One of the Five Pillars of Islam. (Iran, Malaysia, Saudi Arabia). *See also* **Hajj, Salat, Saum, Zakat.**

Shah Namah. "Book of the Kings." The first great literary work in Dari; completed in A.D. 1010 by Firdausi. (Afghanistan).

Shaikh. An Arabic title used to greet men that are clergy or members of the royal family. (Bahrain, United Arab Emirates).

Shaikha. [NOTE: Spelling varies because it is a transliteration of Arabic.] A title used to greet women who are members of the royal family. (Bahrain).

Shaikhah. (United Arab Emirates). *See* **Shaikha.**

Shailah. A rectangular scarf that covers the head. Worn by women. (Qatar, United Arab Emirates).

Shak Barak? "How are you?" A common Arabic greeting. (Qatar).

Shalom. "Peace." A common Hebrew greeting and parting phrase. (Israel).

Shalwar. A pair of loose-fitting pants. (Pakistan). *See also* **Shalwar qameez.**

Shalwar qameez. An outfit, typically made of cotton, that consists of the **Shalwar** (a pair of loose-fitting pants) and the **Qameez** (a long tunic). Styles differ for men and women. (Pakistan).

Shamagh. A scarf worn by men. (Oman).

Sham el-Nasseem. A holiday celebrated at the beginning of spring. (Egypt).

Shamija. A scarf-like head covering. (Macedonia).

Shapka. A Russian fur hat worn in winter. (Kyrgyzstan, Russia). *See also* **Tumak, Ushanka.**

Sharba libiya. Meaning "Libyan soup," it is a dish made of lamb and tomato stock, orzo pasta, chickpeas, cilantro, lemon, mint, and curry. (Libya).

Shared accommodations. Nursing homes. (Northern Ireland).

Glossary of Cultural Terms

Shari'a. Islamic law. (Afghanistan, Bahrain, Kuwait, Nigeria, Pakistan, Qatar, Saudi Arabia, Somalia, Sudan, Syria, United Arab Emirates, Yemen).

Sharshaf. A black cloak worn by women over their clothes to hide their body and hair. (Yemen).

Shashlik. Skewered meat. (Tajikistan).

Shavu'ot. Pentecost. A Jewish holiday. (Israel).

Shawarma. Pita bread filled with spit-roasted meat and salad. (Israel).

Shawarma(s). A sandwich made with marinated chicken or beef with dressing and salad and wrapped in a thin dough wafer. The sandwich is wrapped in paper and peeled like a banana. (Kuwait, Qatar).

Shea butter. A fruit extract used in beauty products and foods. (Togo).

Shebka. Wedding jewels presented by the groom to the bride. They usually include gold and diamond earrings, a bracelet, and necklace. (Kuwait).

Sheik. [NOTE: Spelling varies because it is a transliteration of Arabic.] A tribal leader. (Yemen).

Sheikh. (Oman). *See* **Sheik.**

Shendet! "Stay healthy!" A common Albanian parting phrase. (Albania).

Sherut. Taxis that operate on fixed routes. (Israel).

Shetha tongni. Sharing jokes, stories, and local gossip. (Bhutan).

Sh'hili. South wind. (Tunisia). *Also called* **Sirocco.**

Shi. Soup with sour cabbage. (Russia).

Shi'a. (Pakistan, Syria). *See* **Shi'i.**

Shih. Municipalities. (Taiwan).

Shi'i. Shi'ite Muslims. Shi'ism reveres Muhammad's daughter, Fatima, her husband, Ali, their sons, Hassan and Hussein, and their descendants, called **Imams**. (Afghanistan, Azerbaijan, Bahrain, Iran, Iraq, Kuwait, Lebanon, Oman, Qatar, United Arab Emirates).

Shikamoo. "Is anyone there?" A typical Kiswahili greeting when approaching someone's home. The response is **Karibu**. (Tanzania).

Shinkansen. Bullet trains that provide rapid transportation between major Japanese cities. (Japan).

Shinty. A Celtic sport similar to hockey. (Scotland).

Shi-par-say-taw. "Let it be." A saying that characterizes people's laid-back approach to problems. (Myanmar).

Shir. An open deliberation forum of extended families or clan groups. Decisions are made by consensus. A *shir* can declare war or peace, settle family disputes, and so on. (Somalia).

Shirdeg. Richly ornamented felt carpets. (Mongolia).

Shiromani. Traditional cloth worn by Anjouan women over clothes and pulled up over their heads. (Comoros).

Shirt-jacket. (Antigua and Barbuda, Montserrat). *See* **Shirt-jac(s).**

Shirt-jac(s). A square-cut cotton shirt. (Barbados, Grenada, Guyana, Saint Kitts and Nevis, Saint Lucia).

Shirwani. A knee-length coat. Part of a groom's wedding attire. (Bangladesh). *See also* **Nagra, Pagri.**

Shishcheta. A pork shish kebab. (Bulgaria).

Shiva. The destroyer. One of three supreme gods of Hinduism. (Nepal). *See also* **Brahma, Vishnu.**

Shkubbah. A traditional card game. (Tunisia).

Shlonach. "How are you?" An Arabic greeting used to address women. (Qatar).

Shlonak. "How are you?" An Arabic greeting used to address men. (Qatar).

Shodo. Calligraphy. (Japan).

Shoguns. Japanese feudal lords who held political control from the 12th century until the late 19th century. (Japan).

Shok. "Comrade." A title used before 1990 with the last name in introductions. (Albania).

Shopska salata. A salad made with cucumbers, tomatoes, and **Cirene**. (Bulgaria).

Showa. "Enlightened peace." The name of Emperor Hirohito's reign, which was from 1926 to 1989. (Japan).

Show days. Festivals featuring athletics and handicraft displays. (Niue).

Shqip. The Albanian language, which is an Indo-European language directly descended from Illyrian. (Albania).

Shreemati. A title used with the last name for married women to show respect. (India).

Shudra(s). The lowest class in the Brahmin classification philosophy (not to be confused with the caste system). Composed of workers. Also used to refer to the people of the class. (India, Nepal). *See also* **Brahmin(s), Chaturvarna Vyavasta, Kshatriya, Vaishya.**

Shu'ra. A sauce made from chopped onions and spices marinated in warm cooking oil. (Bangladesh).

Shura. A governing council. (Afghanistan, Bahrain, Egypt).

Shuro. A typical meal of garbanzo bean flour and spices. (Eritrea).

Siapo. Traditional fabric made from bark that has been repeatedly pounded with a mallet. The fabric is printed with geometric patterns in dye made from clay and plants. (American Samoa, Samoa).

Sibhaca. A dance performed by young men in which they stamp their feet to the rhythm of music and chants. (Swaziland).

Si Dios quiere. "God willing." A Spanish phrase that expresses one's faith. (Colombia, Dominican Republic, Honduras, Nicaragua).

Siesta(s). Afternoon rest. Some businesses close for 1 to 3 hours; workers often go home to eat their lunch and relax. (Chile, Honduras, Mexico, Nicaragua, Paraguay, Peru, Spain, Uruguay).

Sièste. An afternoon break. Government offices and private stores close to escape from the afternoon heat. (Niger).

Sigheh. A temporary marriage that can last between a few days and 99 years. A woman marrying in this arrangement and any children born in the marriage do not have the same rights and privileges as conventional wives and children, although they are legitimate. (Iran).

Sijambo. "I'm fine." A common Swahili response to the greeting **Hujambo**. (Tanzania).

Si jeni? "How are you?" A common Albanian greeting. (Albania).

Sijo. An ancient poetic form. Themes include Confucian principles, love, nature, and politics. (South Korea).

Si keni kaluar? "How are you doing?" A common Albanian greeting. (Albania).

Silat. A style of martial arts. (Malaysia).

Silor. Mini-cab. A form of local transportation. (Thailand).

Silvestrovanje. New Year's Eve. (Slovenia).

S'il vous plaît. "Please." A valued French phrase. (France).

Sim. The Dzongkha word for "younger sister." (Bhutan).

Glossary of Cultural Terms

Sina. The informal pronoun "you." It is used with friends and relatives. (Estonia). *See also* **Teie.**

Sinappi. Mustard. (Finland).

Sing'anga. Traditional healers. (Malawi).

Singlish. A colloquial dialect that combines a modified English with elements of Chinese, Malay, and Tamil. (Singapore).

Sing-Sing. An intervillage ceremony of the highlands that involves thousands of costumed dancers. (Papua New Guinea).

Sinterklaas. St. Nicholas. He dresses like a Catholic bishop, rides a white horse, and leaves gifts in children's shoes. (Netherlands).

Sira beyi. Dyula phrase that hosts use to "give the road" to guests after they accompany each other to the road at the end of a visit. (Ivory Coast).

Sirenje. Feta cheese. (Macedonia).

Sirnica. Cheese pie. (Bosnia and Herzegovina).

Sirocco. A hot, sandy, south wind. (Algeria). *Also called* **Sh'hili.**

Sisi. A social title added to a girl's name to show respect. (Swaziland).

Sister. A term used to address females of the same age, regardless of relationship. (Ghana, Sierra Leone).

Sitar. A traditional stringed instrument. (India, Sri Lanka, Suriname, Tunisia).

Siva. A modern dance in which young women dance and sing as young men play the guitar and sing. (Tuvalu).

Siyabonga linjani? "Hello, how are you?" A Ndebele greeting. (Zimbabwe).

Sjenički sir. A soft and fatty cheese often crumbled on **Sopska.** (Serbia and Montenegro).

Sjómannadagurinn. Fisherman's Day. A holiday observed on the first Sunday in June. (Iceland).

Skål. A toast. (Sweden).

Skalmeje. The folk clarinet; a native instrument. (Denmark).

Skara. Grilled meat. (Bulgaria).

Skir ai. Rolling and blinking the eyes. A gesture that expresses disapproval. (Suriname).

Skraja da e. "Do not let evil hear." A Turkish phrase said by older rural women to ward off bad luck. (Macedonia). *See also* **Loshoto da ne chue.**

Skratsji. A percussion instrument consisting of a low wooden bench played with sticks. (Suriname).

Skupstina. The Parliamentary Assembly. (Bosnia and Herzegovina).

Skyr. A popular dish similar to yogurt. (Iceland).

Slametan. A ritual feast, typically held for births, circumcisions, marriages, and funerals. A component of **Agama Djawa**, the feast strengthens or repairs harmony between the spirits and the living. (Suriname). *See also* **Sadjèn.**

Slan. Literally, "safe." An Irish term used for "good-bye." (Ireland).

Slan agus Beannacht. A formal Irish parting phrase meaning "safe and blessed." (Ireland).

Slanina. Home-smoked bacon. (Slovakia).

Slendang. A shoulder drape worn with a **Sarong** and **Klambi koeroeng.** (Suriname).

Slivovica. Plum liquor. (Slovakia).

Smalahode. Sheep's head; a Norwegian specialty. (Norway).

Smock. A long tunic worn by men in northern Ghana. Made of wide strips of rough cotton cloth that are sewn together. (Ghana).

Smörgåsar. Open-faced sandwiches. (Sweden).

Smörgåsbord. A lavish buffet eaten on holidays or for special occasions. (Finland, Sweden).

Smørrebrød. Traditional open-faced sandwiches. (Denmark).

Snackette(s). A stand that sells finger food and drinks. (Guyana).

Snags. Sausages. (Australia).

Snedanne. Belarusian word for "breakfast." (Belarus).

Snidanok. The Ukrainian word for "breakfast." (Ukraine).

Snooker. A billiards game. (England).

Soba. (1) A type of noodles. (Japan). (2) A village chief. (Angola).

Sobranie. A term that may refer to Macedonia's national parliament or a municipality parliament. (Macedonia).

Soca. A mixture of soul music from the United States and calypso music. (Antigua and Barbuda, Bahamas, Barbados, Belize, Costa Rica, Grenada, Jamaica, Montserrat, Saint Kitts and Nevis, Saint Lucia, Saint Vincent and the Grenadines, U.S. Virgin Islands).

Sofra. A low table. Traditionally, people sit around the table on the floor. (Albania).

Sogetrag. An intercity bus service. (Guinea).

Sogi. A gesture used for greeting in which relatives press their faces to the other's cheek and sniff deeply. (Tuvalu).

Soju. A common alcoholic drink served with meals. (South Korea).

Sok sebai. A common Khmer greeting. (Cambodia).

Solevu. A great feast that accompanies wedding ceremonies. (Fiji).

Solitaire. A game and a decoration that consist of a polished round wooden support laden with semiprecious stones in carved holes. (Madagascar).

Soljanka. Russian soup. (Latvia).

Som. Kyrgyzstan and Uzbekistan's national currencies. (Kyrgyzstan, Uzbekistan).

Somogo do? "How is your family?" A common Dioula greeting. (Burkina Faso).

Somoni. Tajikistan's national currency. (Tajikistan).

Somsa. Fried dough pockets stuffed with meat and onions. (Turkmenistan).

Son. A genre of music that combines the sound of maracas, guitars, bongos, trumpets, and the **Tres.** (Cuba).

Songkhran. The Thai New Year. People throw buckets of water on each other and hold other festivities to celebrate. (Thailand).

Songkok. A black velvet cap worn by Muslim men on Fridays. (Malaysia).

Songlines. Aboriginal musical stories that focus on creation legends of the **Dream time.** (Australia).

Songo. A traditional strategy game played on a wooden board with pebbles or seeds. (Gabon).

Sonin yu baina? "What's new?" A casual Mongol greeting. (Mongolia).

Soon come. A common phrase that expresses a casual approach to life and a relaxed view of time. (Antigua and Barbuda, Jamaica).

Sopa de Maní. Peanut soup. (Bolivia).

Glossary of Cultural Terms

Sopaipillas. Deep-fried pumpkin dough sprinkled with sugar. (Chile).

Sopa Paraguaya. Cornbread baked with cheese, onions, and sometimes meat. (Paraguay).

Sop bening. Vegetable soup. (Indonesia).

Sopilka. A flute. (Ukraine).

Soppa ta' l-armla. "Widow's broth"; a common soup. (Malta).

Sopropo. Bitter melon. A popular tropical vegetable. (Suriname).

Sopska. A Greek-like salad. (Serbia and Montenegro).

Sorabe. A Malagasy script with Arabic origins used prior to introduction of the Latin alphabet. (Madagascar).

Sore. The time period just before evening when temperatures cool and work is finished. People bathe and dress in traditional attire to relax or visit. (Indonesia).

Sorpa. A broth used to make **Besbarmak**. (Kazakstan).

Sorpresas. Small egg-shaped cases that display miniature scenes and figures of everyday life. Literally, "surprises." (El Salvador).

Sorrel. A tart, acidic drink made from the petals of the sorrel plant. (Grenada, Saint Kitts and Nevis).

Sorullos. A locally prepared variety of **Frituras** made of corn flour. (Puerto Rico).

Soukous. A style of music that combines African and Caribbean influences. Played with a high-pitched guitar. (Congo, Equatorial Guinea, Togo).

Souk(s). An open-air market. (Egypt, Kuwait, Morocco, Oman, Saudi Arabia, Tunisia).

Souq. (Chad). *See* **Souk(s).**

Souse. Pickled pigs' feet. (Antigua and Barbuda, Montserrat, Saint Kitts and Nevis).

Souses. Boiled meat in a seasoned broth. (Grenada).

Souvlaki. A shish kebab with meat (pork or lamb), mushrooms, and vegetables. (Greece).

Soviet Respubliki. Council of the Republic. Part of the Belarus National Assembly. (Belarus). *See also* **Natsionalnoye Sobranie.**

Spadar. "Mr." A formal Belarusian title used with the last name. (Belarus).

Spadarynya. "Mrs." A formal Belarusian title used with the last name. (Belarus).

Spanglish. An informal dialect in which English words are mixed with spoken Spanish. (Puerto Rico).

Spanish rice. A rice dish cooked with vegetables. (Trinidad and Tobago).

Sparks. Intelligent and knowledgeable; may be a nickname for a highly educated man. (Saint Lucia).

Spaza. Small retail businesses run from suburban homes. *Spaza* shops sell a variety of items to neighborhood residents. (South Africa).

Spaziergang. Taking a walk; a popular Austrian pastime. (Austria).

Speaking Bajan. An English-based creole. (Barbados). *Also called* **Broken English.**

Speaking dialect. (Montserrat). *See* **Speaking Montserratian.**

Speaking Montserratian. A form of English mixed with elements of Irish brogue and various African tongues. (Montserrat).

Spektakel. Dutch creole word meaning "noise" or "din." (U.S. Virgin Islands). *See also* **What a pistarkel.**

Spetakel. Danish word meaning "noise" or "din." (U.S. Virgin Islands). *See also* **What a pistarkel.**

Spicy curry. A favorite dinner. (Guyana).

Spot on. "Right on." (Australia).

Sranan bubbling. A variant of reggae music. (Suriname).

Srange. A wedding custom in which the bride is detained by young men in her village until the groom ransoms her. (Slovenia).

Srednja škola. Optional middle school that includes grades 9 to 12. (Serbia and Montenegro).

Sredno uciliste. Vocational high school. (Macedonia).

Ssali kaleve. Warm, freshly cut toddy; often served with breakfast. (Tuvalu).

Ssrom. A unique form of wrestling in which contestants hold on to pieces of cloth tied around their opponent's legs during their match. (South Korea).

Sta ima? "What's up?" An informal Serbo-Croatian phrase that follows the greeting **Zdravo** (Hello). (Bosnia and Herzegovina).

Stalls. Booths. Vendors sell items from outdoor *stalls* during market days. (Wales).

Stamping drum(s). A bamboo tube covered on one end with cloth. It produces a tone when beat rhythmically on the ground. (Solomon Islands).

Standard(s). School levels or grades. (Lesotho).

Stara Nova Godina. Literally means "Old New Year's." Celebrated on 14 January, marked according to the Julian calendar still used by the Macedonian Orthodox Church. (Macedonia).

State schools. A British idiom for "public schools." (England). *See also* **Public schools.**

Steel drums. Lids of oil drums that have been hammered into the shape of an inverted turtle shell. (Trinidad and Tobago).

Stekt falukorv med senap och potatis. Fried slices of thick German sausage with mustard and boiled or fried potatoes. (Sweden).

Steupsing. A tooth-sucking noise used to display disgust, frustration, or disapproval. (Trinidad and Tobago).

Stewed chicken. Chicken simmered in carmelized sugar and oil. (Trinidad and Tobago).

Stewps. To suck air through the teeth. Expresses exasperation. (Saint Vincent and the Grenadines).

Stick fighting. A traditional Sudanese sport. (Sudan).

Stolovii. Workplace canteens. (Turkmenistan).

Stori. To talk. (Papua New Guinea, Solomon Islands).

Storting. The Norwegian Parliament. (Norway). *See also* **Lagting, Odelsting.**

Stovies. A dish of roast beef, onions, and potatoes. (Scotland).

Street blockoramas. Open-air parties. (Montserrat).

Street food. Snacks such as bread and margarine, fried potatoes, fried plantains, fruit, etc. (Sierra Leone).

Strina. An aunt who is the father's brother's wife. (Croatia). *See also* **Tetka, Ujna.**

Strippenkaart. A universal ticket for public transportation. (Netherlands).

Stroop. A sweet drink available in many flavors. (Suriname).

Stroopwafels. Syrup waffles; a favorite snack. (Netherlands).

Strukli. A salt or sweet-cheese dumpling. (Croatia).

Stupa. A Buddhist shrine. (Nepal).

Sua/Dona. A Portuguese title for women. Used with the first name in less formal situations. (Brazil).

Glossary of Cultural Terms

Sua phrara-chathan. A high-necked jacket worn by a groom. (Thailand).

Succot. [NOTE: The Jewish calendar is based on the lunar standard.] "Tabernacles." A weeklong festival that begins on the 15th of the month **Tishrei**. (Israel).

Sucking the teeth. A gesture in which individuals purse their lips and make a sound by sucking air through their teeth. Expresses disgust or anger. (Saint Kitts and Nevis).

Suck teeth. (Bahamas). *See* **Sucking the teeth.**

Sucre. Ecuador's former national currency. (Ecuador).

Su Diev. "Go with God." A common Lithuanian greeting. (Lithuania).

Sudzuka. A sausage. (Bosnia and Herzegovina).

Sujukh. Minced beef with greens and spices. (Armenia).

Sukuma wiki. Collard greens. (Kenya).

Sukupira. The main open-air market; located in Praia. (Cape Verde).

Sula. Juice. (Latvia).

Sült. Head cheese. (Estonia).

Sulu. An article of clothing consisting of colorful, medium-to-long wraparound cloth. (Fiji, Tuvalu).

Sulu vakataga. A tailored **Sulu** worn with a short-sleeved shirt and sometimes a tie. Worn by businessmen, clergy, and civil servants. (Fiji). *Also called* **Pocket sulu.**

Sulu vaka toga. (Fiji). *See* **Sulu.**

Summo lay? "How are your people?" A common Mandinka greeting. (Gambia).

Supakanja. Okra soup. (Gambia).

Supermercado. The Spanish word for "supermarket." (El Salvador).

Supper. A snack before bedtime. (Australia).

Suq. (Yemen). *See* **Souk(s).**

Surnai. A traditional Afghan instrument similar to a clarinet. (Afghanistan).

Suru. A raised platform with a table in the center and mats for sitting. (Uzbekistan).

Suruhana(s). Old women who provide folk medicine. *Suruhanas* mix local leaves, roots, and bark to prepare medicines. (Guam).

Surular. Platforms located in the courtyard of family compounds that are used to sleep and eat on during the summer. (Uzbekistan).

Survachka. A small decorated stick. On New Year's Day, children go door-to-door carrying the *survachka*, with which they tap people on the back in exchange for candy and money. (Bulgaria).

Susu mai. "Welcome" or "Come in." A respectful Samoan greeting. (American Samoa, Samoa).

Suwa. A beer. (Eritrea).

Svadva. A wedding reception. Involves food, music, and dancing. (Macedonia).

Sveika. "How are you?" A friendly Lithuanian greeting used when addressing a woman. (Lithuania).

Sveikas. "How are you?" A friendly Lithuanian greeting used when addressing a man. (Lithuania).

Sveiki. "How are you?" A friendly Lithuanian greeting used when addressing a group or in a formal situation. (Lithuania).

Sweet. A term used to refer to dessert. (Wales). *Also called* **Pudding(s).**

Sweethearting. A practice in which a man fathers children with multiple women. (Bahamas). *See also* **Outside children.**

Sylvester. Marks the beginning of the New Year's celebrations on 31 December with midnight fireworks and parties, followed by a public holiday on 1 January. (Germany).

Szervusz. "Hello." An informal Hungarian greeting. (Hungary). *See also* **Servus.**

Szia. "Hello." An informal Hungarian greeting. Also, a parting phrase. (Hungary). *See also* **Servus.**

Ta'ahine. "Miss." A Tongan title. (Tonga).

Taalofa! "Greetings!" A Tuvaluan greeting. (Tuvalu).

Ta'amu. A large, coarse root. (Samoa).

Taaniko. The Maori folk art of weaving flax to produce clothing with colorful geometric patterns. (New Zealand).

Taara. The name of a god Estonians worshiped prior to Christianity. (Estonia).

Tabang. Teahouses. (South Korea).

Tabaski. Feast of the Sacrifice. A Muslim holiday honoring Abraham's willingness to sacrifice his son. Celebrated in predominantly Muslim countries.. *Also called* **Eid al-Adha.**

Tabasky. (Mauritania). *See* **Tabaski.**

Tabbal. Drummer. (Iraq).

Tabboule. A popular salad made with parsley, minced onions, diced tomatoes, and other vegetables. (Lebanon).

Tabla. (1) Small different-sized hand drums. (India, Sudan). (2) Both a strategic board game and a card game. (Macedonia).

Tablados. Stages; used to perform Carnival theater productions. (Uruguay).

Tablah. A traditional drum. (Lebanon).

Tabots. Arks of the covenant. Many are found in Ethiopia's churches. (Ethiopia).

Tabouleh. (Syria). *See* **Tabboule.**

Tabuna. A round bread. *Tabuna* is also the name of the cylindrical clay oven in which the bread is baked. (Tunisia).

Tacos. Folded tortillas with meat or other filling. (Mexico).

Taekwondo. A martial art. (South Korea).

Tafadal. "Please come in." An expression of goodwill and welcome. (West Bank and Gaza).

Tafadhali. Swahili word for "please." (Congo, Tanzania).

Tafiti. A term describing traders who settled on Niue a century ago. (Niue).

Tagalog. A Pilipino dialect from Luzon. (Philippines).

Tahina. A sesame-seed paste. (Egypt).

Tahngdyr nahn. Flat bread. (Kyrgyzstan).

Tahteh. "Older sister." A Kazak term added to the end of a name to show respect to an older woman. (Kazakstan).

Tahyar. Embroidered skullcap. (Turkmenistan).

Tai chi. A martial art used for relaxation. (Vietnam).

Taijiquan. A traditional form of shadowboxing that provides exercise and therapy. (China, Singapore).

Taikpon. A round-necked jacket worn by Burmese men. Accompanies an **Eingyi** and a **Longyi**. (Myanmar).

Tai'mamahlao. "Having no shame." An ill-mannered person will be referred to as *tai'mamahlao*. This is a severe criticism. (Guam).

Taitah. Sour bread made of **Teff**, millet, or corn flour fermented in water. (Eritrea). *Also called* **Ingera.**

Taituuj. Fried banana pancakes. (Marshall Islands).

Tajine. A meat-and-vegetable stew. (Algeria, Morocco, Tunisia).

Tajub. A dance party at which Javanese families celebrate a marriage. (Suriname).

Tak. Danish word for "Thank you." (Denmark).

Glossary of Cultural Terms

Taka. Bangladesh's national currency. (Bangladesh).

Tak bhat. "To scoop rice." Because Buddhist monks cannot own anything, they receive their food from villagers who line up daily to *tak bhat*. (Thailand).

Take-away. Take-out. (Australia, England, Jamaica, Namibia, Scotland, Swaziland).

Tak for mad! "Thanks for the meal!" A Danish expression used to thank the hostess. (Denmark).

Takihi. Slices of taro and papaya wrapped in leaves and baked. (Niue).

Takk for maten. "Thank you for the food." A Norwegian phrase said before leaving the table at mealtime. (Norway).

Takk for sist! "Thanks for the last time!" A Norwegian greeting used when people have not seen each other for a while. (Norway).

Takro. A traditional sport in which players try to keep a wicker ball in the air without using their hands. (Thailand).

Tala. Samoa's national currency. (Samoa).

Talib. Arabic word for "student." (Afghanistan).

Taliban. "Seekers of knowledge." A group that gained control of Afghanistan in 1996 but were ousted during the U.S. war in Afghanistan (2001–2). (Afghanistan).

Talitali fiefia. "Welcome." A Tongan phrase used to greet visitors. (Tonga).

T'all. "Not at all." A phrase used in the Antiguan English dialect. (Antigua and Barbuda).

Tallarines. A pasta similar to spaghetti. (Uruguay).

Talofa lava. "Hello." A formal Samoan greeting. (American Samoa, Samoa).

Tamaaraa. A traditional feast common at holidays and other special occasions. (French Polynesia).

Tamada. Toastmaster. Proposes toasts when guests are present. (Armenia, Georgia).

Tamales. A cornmeal dough stuffed with a filling, wrapped in banana or plantain leaves, and then steamed. (Belize, Costa Rica, Mexico).

Tamalitos. Cornmeal dough wrapped in corn husks and steamed. (Guatemala).

Tambal. A stringed folk instrument played with small mallets. (Romania).

Tambora. A small drum. (Dominican Republic).

Tambores. Drums. (Uruguay).

Tamborito. Panama's national dance. (Panama).

Tamboura. An instrument similar to a harp, used to accompany singing. (United Arab Emirates).

Tambura. A stringed instrument. Used in the traditional music that accompanies folk dances. (Macedonia).

Tamburitza. A traditional instrument used to accompany the **Kolo**. (Croatia).

Tamil Eelam. An independent Tamil state. (Sri Lanka).

Ta'miyya. A traditional food prepared from fava beans. (Egypt).

Tamkharit. [NOTE: Muslim holidays are set according to the lunar calendar.] The Islamic New Year. Also, the day on which **Allah** determines people's destinies. (Senegal).

Tamr. Half-dried dates. (Bahrain). *See also* **Rottab**.

Tam-tam. Traditional dancing in which drummers play so that young women can dance in the moonlight. (Niger).

Tamure. A traditional style of dance that incorporates rapid hip and leg movements. (French Polynesia).

Tanboura. A dance performed at weddings and other social gatherings by women. (Kuwait).

Tandor. A clay oven. Used to prepare **non**. (Tajikistan).

Tanga. A small covered horse-drawn cart. (India).

Tangata'eiki. "Mr." A Tongan title. (Tonga).

Tangyertengi as. The Kazak word for "breakfast." (Kazakstan).

Tan kul. A sauce that is mixed with fish, meat, or beans for special occasions. (Chad).

Tannia. A type of root crop. (Montserrat).

Tannie. "Auntie." A term of respect used by Afrikaans-speaking people to address older females. (South Africa).

Tanoa. A special wooden bowl used to prepare **Yaqona**. (Fiji). *See also* **Bilo**.

Tante. "Aunt." A familial title used with strangers as well as family. (Guinea, Ivory Coast).

Tantie. A term children use to address adult women even if they are not related. Derived from the German word for "aunt." (Togo).

Taotaomo'na. Ghosts of Guam's ancient people. Chamorros believe they are revered protectors of the land and will cause near or actual harm to those who do not respect the land. (Guam).

Ta'ovala. A piece of fine material made from the leaves of the pandanus tree. Wrapped around the waist and tied with a coconut-fiber rope. Worn by men. (Tonga). *See also* **Kiekie, Tupenus**.

Tapa. Bark cloth. (Papua New Guinea, Tonga).

Tapado. A stew of beef, vegetables, and coconut milk. (Honduras).

Tapan. A type of drum. Used in the traditional music that accompanies folk dances. (Macedonia).

Tapas. An informal meal where guests take small bites from shared dishes. (Spain).

Tapochki. Slippers. (Kyrgyzstan).

Tap-tap(s). Brightly painted pickup trucks fitted with benches and covered tops. Travel fixed routes but not on a fixed schedule. (Haiti).

Tapu. Niuean word for "taboo." (Niue).

Taqya. Small, decoratively embroidered caps worn by older Kazak men and young boys. (Kazakstan).

Tar. A traditional stringed instrument. An ancestor to the guitar. (Azerbaijan, Iran).

Taraab. Music with Arab influence. (Kenya, Tanzania).

Tarator. A cold soup made of cucumbers, yogurt, garlic, dill, walnuts, and oil. (Bulgaria).

Tarawih. An evening prayer. (Algeria).

Tarha. A veil worn by women. (Sudan).

Tarranga. Hosting international guests. (Gambia).

Ta sain baina uu? "How do you do?" A standard Mongol greeting. (Mongolia).

Tasbe. Worry beads. (Afghanistan).

Tassa drums. Cone-shaped drums made of clay and goat skins. (Trinidad and Tobago).

Tass'bah Ala Kheer. "Good night." A standard Arabic greeting. (Tunisia).

Tata. "Father." A Xhosa term of address used for older men. (South Africa).

Tatami. Straw-mat floors. (Japan).

Tate. A term of address for older Owambo men. (Namibia). *See also* **Meme**.

Tatties. Potatoes. (Scotland).

Taualuga. A traditional dance performed by women. (American Samoa, Samoa).

Glossary of Cultural Terms

Taupou. The daughter of the village high chief. (Samoa).

Tautua. Loyal service. (American Samoa, Samoa). *See also* **Matai**.

Tavale. "Cousin." A term of address that may be used between male cousins. (Fiji).

Tave kosi. Meat or liver baked in yogurt. (Albania).

Tawiz. An amulet worn to protect against evil. (Afghanistan).

Tawjihi. An exam students must pass to attend a university. (Jordan, West Bank and Gaza).

Taxi brousse. A bush-taxi. (Central African Republic, Chad, Madagascar).

Taxi moto. A motorcycle taxi. (Rwanda).

Taxis de brousse. Bush-taxis. (Niger). *See also* **Autogare**.

Taxi velo. A bicycle taxi. (Rwanda).

Tchaa. A Kabyè term children use to address their fathers. (Togo).

Tcháu. "Good-bye." A common Portuguese parting word. (Angola, Brazil).

Tchisangua. A breakfast drink made of water, ground cornmeal, and sugar. (Angola).

Tchouk. Millet beer. (Togo).

Tea. (1) The evening meal. (Belize, Niue, Northern Ireland, Wales). (2) A term that refers to both the evening meal and afternoon refreshments. (Australia, England, New Zealand). (3) Any breakfast drink, such as tea, Milo, or Ovaltine. (Barbados). (4) Any hot drink. (Jamaica).

Tea kitchens. A type of restaurant that serves hot drinks, homemade cakes, and pastries in the afternoon. (Ireland).

Te ano. A traditional game similar to volleyball but with a heavier ball. (Tuvalu).

Teatime. Dinnertime. (Ireland).

Te bee. (Kiribati). *See* **Lavalava(s)**.

Tebetei. A fur hat decorated with a foxtail. (Kyrgyzstan).

Teff. A native grain. (Eritrea, Ethiopia). *See also* **Ingera, Injera**.

Teie. The formal pronoun "you." It is used when meeting someone for the first time, with older people, and with those in authority. (Estonia). *See also* **Sina**.

Te ka. "The car." An English word that has been adapted to the Kiribati alphabet and pronunciation. (Kiribati).

Tekemets. Woven rugs made of felt or wool. (Kazakhstan).

Télécarte. Phone cards. Used to operate pay phones. (France).

Telenovelas. Television soap operas. (Brazil, Mexico, Venezuela).

Televiisor. Estonian word for "television." (Estonia).

Telly. A television. (Australia).

Telpek. Hat made of sheep fur. (Turkmenistan).

Te maaka. Power or magic. A prevalent traditional belief prior to the introduction of Christianity. (Kiribati). *See also* **Nareau**.

Temir-komuz. A mouth harp. (Kyrgyzstan). *Also called* **Oz-komus**.

Tempos. Motorized three-wheel vehicles. (Nepal).

Ten. "Mr." A Kiribati title used in formal situations to show respect. (Kiribati).

Tena koe. A polite Maori way to say "Hello" to one person. (New Zealand).

Tena korua. A polite Maori way to say "Hello" to two people. (New Zealand).

Tena koutou. A polite Maori way to say "Hello" to many people. (New Zealand).

Tena Yistilin. "God give you health." A formal Amharic greeting. (Ethiopia).

Tenge. Kazakstan's national currency. (Kazakstan).

Tenor banjo. A ukulele. (Grenada).

Tenue de fonctionnaire. A civil servant suit, with shirt and pants made of the same cloth. (Burkina Faso).

Tere. "Hello." A common Estonian greeting. (Estonia).

Tere hommikust. "Good morning." A common Estonian greeting. (Estonia).

Tere Õhtust. "Good evening." A common Estonian greeting. (Estonia).

Tere päevast. "Good day." A common Estonian greeting. (Estonia).

Tereré. A mildly stimulating tea served cold. In Argentina it is often mixed with lemonade. (Argentina, Paraguay). *See also* **Mate**.

Terno. Worn by women, a full-length dress with a scoop neckline and butterfly sleeves. (Philippines).

Terra. Portuguese word for "homeland." (Portugal).

Tertulias. Social clubs that meet regularly in cafés to discuss ideas, events, and politics. (Spain).

Teshkoto Oro. A folk dance in which a series of steps depicts the fate of Macedonian fighters struggling against the Ottoman Turks. Females participate in some parts of this dance by portraying those who assisted the rebels in their battle. Dancers wear colorful embroidered costumes reflective of the clothing of past generations. (Macedonia).

Teši ma. "Pleased to meet you." A formal Slovak greeting. (Slovakia).

Těší mne. "Pleased to meet you." A Czech greeting. (Czech Republic).

Test match. An international cricket competition. (Montserrat).

Tet. The Vietnamese word for "holiday." (Vietnam).

Tetka. (1) An aunt that is a mother's or father's sister. (Croatia). *See also* **Strina, Ujna**. (2) "Auntie." An informal term of address used for older people who are not family. (Serbia and Montenegro).

Tet nguyen dan. [NOTE: Vietnamese holidays are set according to the lunar calendar.] The Lunar New Year. Celebrated in late January or early February. (Vietnam).

Teto. An Albanian word for "aunt," specifically the father's sister. (Albania). *Also called* **Halle**.

Tet thuong nguyen. [NOTE: Vietnamese holidays are set according to the lunar calendar.] A holiday celebrated on the first full moon of the new year. (Vietnam). *See also* **Tet trung nguyen**.

Tet trung nguyen. [NOTE: Vietnamese holidays are set according to the lunar calendar.] A day to pardon the sins of the dead by reading the **Vu lan**. Celebrated on the full moon of the seventh month. (Vietnam). *See also* **Tet thuong nguyen**.

Teuila Week. Tourism Week. Celebrated in September with a parade; sports competitions; music, dance, and cultural demonstrations; and other activities. Named after the national flower. (Samoa).

Teyze. "Aunt." A Turkish term of address for an older woman. (Turkey).

Teze. An Albanian word for "aunt," specifically the mother's sister. (Albania).

Thaan. A title added to the name of a person of high status. (Laos).

Glossary of Cultural Terms

Thadingyut. A light festival in September or October (determined according to the lunar calendar) at which people offer a candle or electric light to Buddha. (Myanmar).

Thai-Pongal. A Tamil holiday that marks the "return" of the sun after a month of evil days; the sun brings a new period of goodwill. (Sri Lanka).

Thanawi. Secondary school. (Saudi Arabia).

Thangka. Iconographic pictures painted on scrolls to depict Buddha, other great religious masters, and **Mandalas**. (Bhutan).

Thanh. The Vietnamese word for "fresh." (Vietnam).

Thanh nien. The Vietnamese word for "youth." A combination of the words **Thanh** "fresh" and **Nien** "years." (Vietnam).

The Festas Juninas. The June Festivals, which coincide with the feasts of St. John and St. Peter and are celebrated with local fair-type activities. (Brazil).

The food. A phrase that refers to lunch. (Saint Lucia).

The mainland. A phrase that refers to the island of Saint Vincent. (Saint Vincent and the Grenadines).

Thiebou dien. A meal of fish and rice. Popular at lunch. (Senegal).

Thingyan. A water festival marking the Buddhist New Year in April or May (determined according to the lunar calendar); Myanmar throw water on each other to clean away the dirt and sins of the previous year. (Myanmar).

Thit kho. Pork cooked in fish broth. (Vietnam).

Thobe. A long, light robe that reaches the ankles. Worn by men. (Bahrain, Qatar, Saudi Arabia).

Thu. A piece of cloth wrapped around the waist. Worn by men. (Micronesia).

Thukpa. Noodle soup. (Bhutan).

Ti. "You." An informal pronoun. (Bosnia and Herzegovina, Serbia and Montenegro, Slovenia).

Tia. "Aunt." A Portuguese term used to address older people. (Angola, Cape Verde, Guinea-Bissau, Mozambique).

Tiar. A title of respect for older men or officials; used with the last name. (Armenia).

Tiares. Leis made of white flowers. Worn by the bride and groom on their wedding day. (French Polynesia).

Ti boy. "Little boy." A creole phrase used by adults to address male children. (Saint Lucia).

Tibuta. A loose-fitting blouse gathered at the neck. Worn by women. (Kiribati).

Ticas. (Costa Rica). See **Ticos**.

-tico. A suffix used in Costa Rica to form a diminutive. (Costa Rica).

Ticos. A term used throughout Central America to refer to Costa Ricans. Comes from the habit of ending words and phrases with the suffix **-tico**. Masculine *ticos*, feminine *ticas*. The mixed company reference is *ticos*. (Costa Rica).

Tidak. The Indonesian word for "no." (Indonesia).

Tidnit. A four-stringed lute. (Mauritania).

Tienda. A small store. (El Salvador).

Tifaifai. A two-layer patchwork quilt. (French Polynesia).

Ti fi. "Little girl." A creole phrase used by adults to address female children. (Saint Lucia).

Tiga diga na. Peanut butter and tomato sauce. (Mali).

Tihar. [NOTE: Hindu holidays are based on the phases of the moon.] A holiday to worship the Goddess of Wealth. Celebrated for three days in October and/or November. Rows of light are displayed on every building. Married women go home to their parents, receive special treatment, ritually purify themselves, and pray for sons. (Nepal).

Tika. (1) A red dot made from vermilion powder. Worn by women on their foreheads to signify their husbands are alive. (Mauritius, Nepal). (2) Coconut oil often used on the hair and body. (Micronesia).

Tikin. A title of respect for married women; used with the last name. (Armenia).

Tikling. Herons. (Philippines). See also **Tinikling**.

Ti ma mai. "My little one." A creole phrase used by adults to address children. (Saint Lucia).

Timket. A holiday celebrating the baptism of Jesus. Celebrated in January. (Eritrea).

Timpana. Baked macaroni pastry. (Malta).

Tingatinga. A style of painting in which artists paint animals and natural scenes using tiny brightly colored dots. (Tanzania).

Tinikling. The Filipino national dance in which performers mimic the actions of the **Tikling** while dancing between bamboo poles. (Philippines).

Tinku. A traditional Bolivian dance. (Bolivia).

Tinyanga. A person who heals by faith or with traditional medicines. (Swaziland). See also **Batsakatsi, Sangoma**.

Tio. "Uncle." A Portuguese term used to address older people. (Angola, Cape Verde, Guinea-Bissau, Mozambique).

Tío/a. "Uncle" or "aunt." A Spanish term often used as a term of address. Masculine *tío*, feminine *tía*. (Panama).

Típico. Traditional Panamanian music. Played by a band composed of a singer and players with an accordion, a guitar, and percussion. Lyrics usually pertain to love and life. (Panama).

Tirgi. Open-air markets. (Latvia).

Tiripo kana makadiiwo. "We are fine if you are fine." A Shona response to the question **Makadii?** (How are you?). (Zimbabwe).

Tishrei. [NOTE: The Jewish year is based on a lunar calendar.] A Jewish month that corresponds to September/October. Begins with **Rosh Hashanah**. (Israel).

Tita. "Auntie." A Tagalog term used by young adults to address older adult female strangers. (Philippines).

-tito. A Spanish suffix used to form a diminutive. (Costa Rica). See also **-tico**.

Tito. "Uncle." A Tagalog term used by young adults to address older adult male strangers. (Philippines).

Tiurai. "July." *Tiurai* festivities begin with a cultural parade on 29 June. (French Polynesia).

Tjuri. A gesture that expresses dissatisfaction or annoyance; one points the lips and sucks in air between the teeth and lips while looking away. (Suriname).

Tô. A hard porridge made from sorghum, millet, or corn. (Burkina Faso, Ivory Coast, Mali).

To. Ewe word for "waters." Combined with **Godo**, meaning "other side," it forms the name of the lakeside village of Togodo, for which Togo is named. (Togo).

Tobaski. Feast of the Sacrifice. A Muslim holiday. (Gambia). See also **Eid-el-kabir**.

To didana! "See you later!" A Tajik parting phrase. (Tajikistan).

Todu maolek. "Everything is good." A Chamorro response to the greeting **Hafa tatatmanu hao?** (How are you?). (Guam).

Toere. An indigenous wooden drum often played together with the guitar and the **Pahu**. (French Polynesia).

Tofa soifua. "Good-bye." A Samoan parting phrase. (American Samoa, Samoa).

Glossary of Cultural Terms

Toi. The Kyrgyz word for "party." (Kyrgyzstan).
Tojiki. The Tajik language. (Tajikistan).
Tok Pisin. Melanesian Pidgin. (Papua New Guinea).
Tok Ples. "Talk place." A term that refers to local languages. (Papua New Guinea).
Tol. A child's first birthday. (South Korea).
Tolar. Slovenia's national currency. (Slovenia).
Tomorrow then. A common parting phrase. (Jamaica).
Tom yam. Lemon-flavored soup. Usually includes shrimp. (Thailand).
Tonadas. Chilean folk music that has been influential in political and social reform. (Chile).
Tonga na nyen? "How's it going?" Part of a common Sango greeting, it usually follows the phrase **Bara ala** or **Bala mo** (Greetings to you!). (Central African Republic).
Tonghak. An indigenous Korean religion. An eclectic combination of Buddhist, Confucian, and Christian beliefs. (North Korea). *Also called* **Ch'ondogyo.**
Tonir. A special oven dug in the ground. (Armenia).
Tontines. Savings societies in which members pool their capital, provide loans to each other, and sponsor social activities. (Cameroon). *Also called* **Njangis.**
Tonton. French term meaning "uncle." Ivorians may call each other by familial names to show respect and affection even if they are not related. (Ivory Coast).
Tontons macoutes. The secret police. Used by former Haitian president François Duvalier to kill his opponents and maintain rule from 1957 to 1971. (Haiti).
Too. A porridge made from cassava or rice powder. Eaten by the Malinké. Pronounced "TOE." (Guinea).
Toonai. Samoan word for "Sunday meal." (American Samoa, Samoa).
Tope. Palm wine. (Equatorial Guinea).
Topogios. Frozen fruit juice in plastic bags. (Honduras). *Also called* **Charamuscas.**
Toqi. A four-cornered or round hat. Worn by men. (Tajikistan). *Also called* **Tupi.**
Torge shygynyz. "Have the seat of honor." A Kazak phrase used to welcome guests in the home. (Kazakstan).
Torrejas. A type of food similar to French toast; served at Christmas. (Honduras).
Torta. Slovak word for "cake." (Slovakia).
Tortas. Hollow rolls stuffed with meat, cheese, or beans. (Mexico).
Tortilla. An omelette. (Cuba).
Tortilla española. An omelette with potatoes and onions. (Spain).
Tot siens. "Till we see each other again." An Afrikaans parting phrase. (South Africa).
Tour de France. An annual bicycle race. (France).
Toussaint. All Saints' Day. A holiday observed on 1 November. (French Polynesia, Gabon).
Tout va bien. French term meaning "All is well." It is a proper response to questions about one's general wellbeing. (Ivory Coast).
Tovarishch. "Friend" or "comrade." A Soviet-era title still used by some today. (Russia).
Town. An urban, commercial area. (Barbados).
Toy. A large wedding celebration with dancing and food. (Turkmenistan).

Tracht. A traditional costume. A woman's *tracht* includes a dress with a full skirt, an apron, and a headdress. Men's attire includes knee breeches, a straight loden jacket, and a flat black hat. The plural form is **Trachten**. (Liechtenstein).
Trachten. Traditional costumes. (Austria, Liechtenstein).
Trachtenanzug. A traditional suit worn by men. (Austria).
Trachtenjacken. A traditional woolen jacket worn by men. (Austria).
Trachtenkostüm. A traditional suit worn by women. (Austria).
Trade fair. A fair that sells a variety of goods and foods. Prices are lower than in stores and bargaining is acceptable. (Georgia).
Train à grande vitesse. The TGV. One of the world's fastest passenger trains. (France).
Träipen. Black pudding commonly eaten on Christmas Eve. (Luxembourg).
Tram. A streetcar. (Australia).
Tramping. Hiking. (New Zealand).
Tranquilidad. "Tranquility," an ultimate desire of Paraguayans. (Paraguay).
Transport. Private minivans that run regular routes. They leave from a central location when full and pick up or drop off passengers along the way. (Saint Lucia).
Tres. A small three-paired stringed instrument. (Cuba).
Trini. A language that uses English with French, Spanish, Hindi, and African influences and is often difficult for visitors to understand. (Trinidad and Tobago).
Trinkgeld. An extra tip. (Germany, Liechtenstein).
Tro-tro. A minibus used for short-distance travel. (Ghana).
Tsagaan Sar. "White Month" or "White Moon." The name of the Lunar New Year. Celebrated with family gatherings. (Mongolia).
Tsamaea hantle. "Go well." A parting phrase used by the person staying. The person leaving will say **Sala hantle**. (Lesotho).
Tsamaya sentle. "Go well." A phrase said to a person who is departing. (Botswana). *See also* **Sala sentle.**
Tsechhu. A three-day festival at which local monks perform legends from Buddhist scripture. (Bhutan).
Tsenatsil. A type of musical rattle. (Ethiopia).
Tshogdu. The Bhutanese National Assembly. (Bhutan).
Tshulnt. Traditional bean stew. (Israel).
Tsoho. "Old man." A term of address used for elderly men. (Niger).
Tsohoa. "Old woman." A term of address used for elderly women. (Niger).
Tsymbaly. A dulcimer. A traditional instrument. (Belarus).
Tsy misy. "Nothing." A Malagasy response to the question **Inona no vaovao?** (What is new?). (Madagascar).
Tú. "You." The informal singular Spanish pronoun. (Argentina, Chile, Dominican Republic, Paraguay).
Tuba. A type of fermented coconut juice. (Guam).
Tube. The London subway. (England).
Tudo bem? "How's it going?" A common Portuguese greeting used between urban youth. (Mozambique).
Tufahija. Boiled apple stuffed with nuts and sweet cream. (Bosnia and Herzegovina).
Tughrik. Mongolia's national currency. (Mongolia).
Tuisi. "Twist." *Tuisi* dances are popular fund-raising events enjoyed by young people. (Tuvalu).

Glossary of Cultural Terms

Tulafale. An orator. Speaks for a village chief during formal ceremonies and serves as the spokesperson for the entire village during inter-village disputes. (American Samoa).

Tulou. "Excuse me." A phrase used after a variety of offenses such as touching someone's head, walking between people having a conversation, reaching for something above someone's head, and so on. (Fiji, Tuvalu).

Tumak. A Russian fur hat worn in winter. (Kyrgyzstan). *See also* **Shapka**.

Tumba. Flies that lay eggs on wet clothing; if the eggs hatch, the flies can burrow into the skin. (Zimbabwe).

Tunban. Baggy trousers that are pulled tight with a drawstring. Worn with a **Perahan**. Typical clothing for Afghan men. (Afghanistan).

Tung. Albanian for "Hello" and "Good-bye." (Macedonia).

Tungjat jeta. "Have a long life." An Albanian greeting used by males from northern villages. (Albania).

Tuo zaafi. A thick porridge made of corn or millet. (Ghana).

Tupenus. Calf-length pieces of material wrapped around the waist. (Tonga). *See also* **Kiekie, Ta'ovala**.

Tupi. A four-cornered or round hat. Worn by men. (Tajikistan). *Also called* **Toqi**.

Tupuna. Respect for ancestors and their culture. (French Polynesia).

Turbofolk. Dance music popular among young people and prevalent in larger cities; a combination of folk tunes and rock instruments. (Serbia and Montenegro).

Turn the crack. A Scottish English idiom meaning "change the subject." (Scotland).

Turn their pots down. "To cook less." Typically during mango season, people cook less and eat large amounts of mangoes. (Antigua and Barbuda).

Turshi. Vegetables preserved in salt water. (Albania).

Turshija. Pickled vegetables. (Macedonia).

Tushuk. A velvet floor mat; used for sitting during meals. (Kyrgyzstan).

Tutaonana. "We will see each other." A common parting phrase. (Kenya).

Tuwo. The Hausa term for a thick, gelatinous millet paste. Usually eaten with a tomato or okra sauce. (Niger).

Twisting. Recreational dancing. (Kiribati).

Twoonie. A nickname for the Canadian two-dollar coin. (Canada).

Tyin Enmei. Falconry on horseback; a traditional equestrian sport. (Kyrgyzstan).

Tyski as. The Kazak word for the "midday meal." (Kazakstan).

Tze pau le ma. "Have you eaten?" A Chinese greeting. (Malaysia).

Tzuica. Plum brandy. (Romania).

U. "Uncle." A term used to address older men, regardless of relationship. (Myanmar).

Ubugali. A thick, doughy paste made from corn, sorghum, or cassava flour. (Rwanda).

Udon. A type of noodles. (Japan).

Ufi. Yams. (Samoa).

Uga. Coconut crab. (Niue).

Ugali. A stiff dough made from cassava, corn, millet, or sorghum. (Kenya, Tanzania).

Uha. Fish soup. (Belarus).

Uhn-uhn. Said while one nods to indicate "yes." (Madagascar). *See also* **Ahn-ahn-ahn**.

Ujamaa. "Familyhood." A principle emphasized in Tanzanian society. (Tanzania).

Uji. Porridge made from cornmeal, millet, or sorghum. (Kenya).

Ujna. An aunt that is a person's mother's brother's wife. (Croatia).

Ulak. A type of polo played with a goat carcass. (Kyrgyzstan).

Uli. Ornamental body paint that decorates ritual participants in religious ceremonies. (Nigeria).

Ulpan. Government-sponsored classes to learn Hebrew. (Israel). *See also* **Ulpanim**.

Ulpanim. An educational system that offers immigrants a chance to learn Hebrew. (Israel). *See also* **Ulpan**.

Ulster. A region comprised of the six counties in Northern Ireland and three counties in Ireland. (Northern Ireland).

Ulu. Breadfruit. (Samoa).

Ulumoega. Mats the bride's family offers to the groom's family after the wedding. (American Samoa, Samoa). *See also* **Falaninii, Ietoga**.

Um. (1) "Mother." An Arabic term of address used by children. (Qatar). (2) "Mother of." An Arabic title combined with a child's name to show respect. (Iraq, Jordan, United Arab Emirates).

Um ghayib. "Awaiting mother." A respectful term used to address a woman without children. (Iraq). *See also* **Abu ghayib**.

Umhlanga. The Reed Dance. A traditional Swazi event that honors the Queen Mother. Traditionally has served as a display of marriageable girls. Takes place in late August or early September. (Swaziland).

Umm. (Afghanistan). *See* **Um**.

Umu. (1) A traditional ground oven. (American Samoa, French Polynesia, New Zealand, Niue, Samoa, Tonga). (2) Cooking house; a separate structure that contains an open fire. (Tuvalu).

Umukechuru. "Old woman." An affectionate name for an elderly woman. (Rwanda).

Umusaza. "Old man." An affectionate name for an elderly man. (Rwanda).

Un cafecito. A thick black coffee served in a small cup; a symbol of hospitality and a way of extending friendship to visitors. (Venezuela).

Un chin. "A little bit." A Spanish phrase used in the Caribbean. (Dominican Republic). *See also* **Un poquito**.

Uncle. A term a younger person uses to address an older man, even if they are not related. (Barbados, Gambia, Ghana, Guam, Guyana, Saint Kitts and Nevis, Saint Lucia, Sierra Leone, Uganda). *See also* **Aunt(ie)**.

Un cousin. "A cousin" or a very distant relative. (Central African Republic).

Underground. The London subway. (England). *Also called* **Tube**.

Un frère. A half brother or another family relation. (Central African Republic).

Uni. An Australian colloquialism for "university." (Australia).

Unimane. "Old men" that comprise the **Maneaba(s)** council. (Kiribati).

Un poquito. "A little bit." A Spanish phrase. (Dominican Republic). *See also* **Un chin**.

U phela joang? "How are you?" A Sesotho phrase that follows the initial greetings **Khotso** or **Lumela**. (Lesotho).

Uphumaphi? "Where have you come from?" A common siSwati question. (Swaziland).

Glossary of Cultural Terms

Uppekkha. Equanimity. A Buddhist pillar virtue. (Laos). *See also* **Brahma Vihara.**

Upsa. A paste made from sun-dried cereals, usually cornmeal. (Mozambique). *Also called* **Xima.**

Ushanka. A Russian fur hat worn in winter. (Russia). *Also called* **Shapka.**

Ustashe. Fascist Croats. Collaborated with the Nazis during World War II and caused the deaths of thousands of civilian Jews, Serbs, and Gypsies. (Bosnia and Herzegovina, Croatia).

Usted. "You." A formal Spanish term of address. (Argentina, Chile, Dominican Republic, Honduras, Uruguay).

Uszka. A type of ravioli. (Poland).

U tsamaea kae? "Where are you going?" A common Sesotho question that follows the initial greeting. (Lesotho).

U tsoa kae? "Where have you been?" A Sesotho question that commonly follows the initial greeting. (Lesotho).

Uulu. "Son." A term used after a person's father's first name in a greeting. (Kyrgyzstan).

U-weekíi. Literally, "You have awaken." A Ndyuka greeting meaning "Good morning." (Suriname).

Uyaphi? "Where are you going?" A common siSwati question. (Swaziland).

Užgavinės. A pre-Lent holiday in which people dress in costumes and children go door-to-door asking for treats. (Lithuania).

Uzhyen. Russian word for a light evening meal. (Kazakstan).

Vaalaikum assalaam. (Uzbekistan). *See* **Waalaikum assalaam.**

Vaishya. The third class in the Brahmin classification philosophy, composed of merchants and farmers. (India). *See also* **Brahmin(s), Chaturvarna Vyavasta, Kshatriya, Shudra(s).**

Vaisyas. (Nepal). *See* **Vaishya.**

Vajrayana. Tibetan Buddhism. Shares the common Buddhist goals of reincarnation and individual release from suffering. (Mongolia).

Vaka. An outrigger canoe; commonly used for fishing. (Niue).

Vaka Atua. Powerful priests, prior to the introduction of Christianity, who acted as intermediaries between the people and the gods; they presided over special ceremonies. (Tuvalu).

Valiha. A cylindrical harp-like instrument. (Madagascar).

Valle. A folk dance. (Albania).

Vallenato. A tropical Colombian style of music. (Colombia).

Valli-e-faghih. The supreme leader of Iran. (Iran).

Vals. Swedish word for "waltz." (Sweden).

Valtioneuvosto. The Finnish cabinet. (Finland).

Vanakkam. "Hello." A Tamil greeting. (Singapore).

Vannakkam. (Sri Lanka). *See* **Vanakkam.**

Vanneyen. Chopped fish meatballs in a fish broth. (Mauritius).

Vánočka. A fruit bread; eaten during the days leading to Christmas and during Lent. (Czech Republic).

Vappu. May Day. Celebrated 1 May in honor of springtime and laborers. (Finland).

Varaynya. Preserves. (Kyrgyzstan).

Varenyky. Dumplings. (Ukraine).

Vary mitsangana. An outdoor vendor who sells hot food to be eaten while standing. (Madagascar).

Vasilopitta. A special cake with a coin in it. At midnight on New Year's Eve, the cake is cut into various pieces; whoever gets the coin is supposed to have good luck during the new year. (Greece).

Vastlapäev. A holiday on 15 February during which people go sledding and eat special foods. A long sled ride indicates good luck with the fall harvest. (Estonia).

Vau o kai! "Stop and eat with us!" A greeting to passersby who are friends or family members. A person will usually stop and chat briefly but does not normally stay to eat. (Tuvalu).

Vecera. The Macedonian word for "dinner." (Macedonia).

Večerja. Light supper. (Slovenia).

Vecheria. Dinner; eaten around 6 or 7 p.m. (Ukraine).

Vedarai. Cooked potatoes and sausage stuffed into pig intestines. (Lithuania).

Vedejparis. "Matchmaking couple." Traditionally, the *vedejparis* introduced the bride and groom. Today, it is an honorary position for admired friends. The *vedejparis* helps with wedding arrangements and serves as the ceremony's witnesses. (Latvia).

Vegemite. Yeast extract; used as a bread spread. (New Zealand).

Vegeta. A mixture of seasoning salt and dried vegetables. (Macedonia).

Veicaqe moli. "Kick the orange." A traditional Fijian game played by village women during January to celebrate the New Year. The winning team presents the losers with clothes; the losing team will mix and serve **Yaqona** to the winners that night. (Fiji).

Vejigantes. "Monsters." During various festivities, the *vejigantes* wear bells and elaborate papier-mâché masks with multiple horns. They roam the streets, threatening to "hit" people on the head with a dried pig's bladder. Children try to gather bells from *vejigantes'* costumes. (Puerto Rico).

Vencavka vo crkva. The religious ceremony that takes place on a couple's wedding day. The ceremony takes place in a church in the presence of family and friends. It is here the bride and groom exchange rings and vows. (Macedonia).

Venchaniye. An elaborate and traditional wedding ceremony. Literally, "coronation." (Russia).

Verabredung. German word for "appointment." (Germany).

Vereine. German word for "associations." (Liechtenstein).

Verivörst. Blood sausage. (Estonia).

Verkhovna Rada. The Ukrainian Parliament. (Ukraine).

Vær så god. A Danish phrase used when passing and receiving food. It means "Please, eat well." (Denmark).

Vesak. A holiday that celebrates the birth, enlightenment, and nirvana of Buddha. Held during the fifth lunar month. (Singapore).

Veselica. A summer picnic. (Slovenia).

Vi. (1) "You." A formal pronoun. (Serbia and Montenegro, Slovenia). (2) An apple-like fruit. (Samoa). *See also* **Nonu.**

Viadu. A sweet raison-almond bread. (Suriname).

Vidalita. A traditional Uruguayan dance. (Uruguay).

Vidimo se. "See you." An informal Serbo-Croatian greeting. (Bosnia and Herzegovina).

Vidovdan. A holiday on 28 June that commemorates the Battle of Kosovo. (Serbia and Montenegro).

Vigorón. A dish of vegetables and pork skins. (Nicaragua).

Vinaka. The phrase "Thank you" in Fijian. (Fiji).

Vintana. "Destiny," which brings good or bad luck based on the time and date of a person's birth. A Malagasy belief. (Madagascar). *See also* **Ombiasy.**

Viola. A kind of guitar. (Cape Verde).

Glossary of Cultural Terms

Virgen de la Caridad del Cobre. A holiday on 8 September that honors the patron saint of Cuba and African goddess Ochún. (Cuba).

Visakha Bucha. An important Buddhist holiday. Set according to the lunar calendar. (Thailand).

Viša škola. "Higher school." A two-year technical college. (Serbia and Montenegro).

Vishnu. The preserver. One of three supreme gods of Hinduism. (Nepal). *See also* **Brahma, Shiva.**

Viso. "Bye." An informal Lithuanian parting phrase. (Lithuania).

Viso gero. "Good-bye." A Lithuanian parting phrase. (Lithuania).

Viszlát. A Hungarian parting phrase. (Hungary).

Viszontlátásra. "See you again." A Hungarian parting phrase. (Hungary).

Vitumbua. (Tanzania). *See* **Kitumbua.**

Vivaha. The Hindu marriage ceremony. (Mauritius).

Vlaggetjesdag. Little Flag Day. Celebrated in May in coastal areas. Marks the beginning of the herring season. Ships leave the harbor, decorated with little flags. (Netherlands).

Voan-dalana. "Gifts from the journey." People returning from a trip or visiting from out of town will give *voan-dalana* to their extended family. (Madagascar).

Vodiondry. The bride-price. Literally, "lamb's rump." (Madagascar).

Volynka. A hornpipe. (Ukraine).

Vonts es? "How are you?" An Armenian question that usually follows an initial greeting. (Armenia).

Voodoos. The Fon word for local divinities through which people worship the supreme God. (Benin). *See also* **Orisha.**

Vos. "You." An informal singular Spanish pronoun. (Argentina, Paraguay).

Vouli. The informal name of the Greek Chamber of Deputies. (Greece). *See also* **Vouli ton Ellinon.**

Vouli ton Ellinon. The Greek Chamber of Deputies. (Greece).

Voy a pasear. "I am going visiting." A Spanish phrase. Visiting is a common weekend pastime. (Equatorial Guinea).

Vsichko hubavo. "All the best." A common Bulgarian parting phrase used between friends. (Bulgaria).

Vu lan. The Buddhist prayer book. (Vietnam).

Vyachera. Belarusian word for "supper." (Belarus).

Vyshyvanka. A traditional shirt or blouse embroidered in a regional pattern. The patterns have not changed for centuries. (Ukraine).

Waalaikum assalaam. [NOTE: Spelling varies because it is a transliteration of Arabic.] "And peace be upon you." A response to the greeting **Assalaam alaikum.** Used in countries with large or predominantly Muslim populations..

Wa'alaikum salaam. (Indonesia). *See* **Waalaikum assalaam.**

Wa alaykum Asalaam. (Syria). *See* **Waalaikum assalaam.**

Wa alaykum As-salaam. (Kuwait, Qatar). *See* **Waalaikum assalaam.**

Wa'alaykum assalaamu. (Yemen). *See* **Waalaikum assalaam.**

Wa alaykum salaam. (Mauritania). *See* **Waalaikum assalaam.**

Wa alek asalaam. (Chad). *See* **Waalaikum assalaam.**

Wa alikum assalaam. (United Arab Emirates). *See* **Waalaikum assalaam.**

Wa Alikum Assalam. Arabic phrase meaning "I offer you peace, too"; it is the proper response to the greeting **Assalamu alikum.** (Libya).

Wa di gwan? "What's happening?" A Creole greeting. (Belize).

Wadis. Dry riverbeds. (Libya, Oman).

Wafidiin. A person who has left his or her own country to live in another. (United Arab Emirates).

Wafuku. A long traditional robe with long sleeves, tied closed with a special sash. (Japan). *See also* **Kimono(s), Obi.**

Wah eye no see heart no grieve. "What you don't know won't hurt you." A traditional saying. (Antigua and Barbuda).

Wai. A Thai greeting in which one places the palms of the hands together at chest level with fingers extended. Men bow slightly; women curtsy. (Thailand).

Waisak. A Buddhist holiday. (Indonesia).

Walalapo Nawa. "Good morning." An Oshiwambo greeting. (Namibia).

Walale. A common Umbundo greeting meaning "Good morning," but literally "How did you pass the night?". The reply is **Ndalale.** (Angola).

Wali. Arabic word for "governor." (Oman).

Walk with. "Carry." A phrase used in the Antiguan English dialect. (Antigua and Barbuda).

Wa-lo hla-lo. "You are looking more plump and more beautiful." A common Burmese greeting. Plumpness (to a certain extent) is regarded as a sign of beauty and health. (Myanmar).

Wa muka? "Are you well?" A greeting from an elder to a child. (Botswana).

Wan. "Afternoon." A common Mandarin Chinese greeting. (China).

Wanan. "Evening." An informal Chinese greeting. (China).

Wantok. "One talk." A system in which individuals help and share possessions with relatives or others in their language group or village. Reciprocation is expected. Participants in the system are called *wantoks*. (Papua New Guinea, Solomon Islands).

Warambas. Flowing robes worn by men. (Gambia).

Waraq dawalee. Stuffed grape leaves. (West Bank and Gaza).

Ward(s). A neighborhood. A village is divided into *wards*, each of which is led by a **Headman.** (Botswana).

Warri. A strategy game in which one tries to capture the opponent's 24 seeds. (Antigua and Barbuda).

Wasabi. A hot, green Japanese paste containing horseradish. (Micronesia).

Waso. A full moon holiday in June or July. Begins the three-month period of the Buddhist Rains Retreat. (Myanmar).

Water closet. A toilet. (Slovakia).

Wat(s). (1) A Buddhist temple. (Laos, Thailand). (2) A stew made from chicken, beef, or vegetables. (Ethiopia).

Wayang. Chinese mobile street theaters. A popular event during holiday festivities. (Singapore).

Wayang kulit. Shadow puppet theater. (Indonesia, Malaysia).

Wayang topeng. Masked dances in which performers act out legends and stories. (Indonesia).

We go see. "See you later." A casual Grenadian creole farewell. (Grenada).

Wéi geet et? "How are you?" A common greeting. (Luxembourg).

Wei qi. A strategy game played in more educated circles. (China).

Glossary of Cultural Terms

Wela. The Umbundo term for a strategy game played with beads or seeds placed in holes on a wooden board or in the ground. (Angola). *Also called* **Kwela.**

Welsh cakes. Similar to small pancakes, these can be served hot or cold. (Wales).

Wesak Day. A holiday in May that commemorates the birth of Buddha. (Malaysia).

Wesak Poya. A day in May that celebrates Buddha's birth, enlightenment, and death. (Sri Lanka).

Whaaa? A phrase that indicates surprise or disbelief. (U.S. Virgin Islands).

Whaapun? "What's happening?" A common patois greeting. (Jamaica).

Wha' it saying? A Creolese greeting. (Guyana).

W'happen dey? "What's happening?" A casual Grenadian creole greeting. (Grenada).

Wharenui. A Maori "great house," or meeting place. (New Zealand).

What a pistarkel. "What a spectacle." A Creole phrase. (U.S. Virgin Islands). *See also* **Spektakel, Spetakel.**

Whei. "Hello." A Mandarin Chinese greeting. (Singapore).

Whitmonday A religious holiday around the time of Pentecost. (Montserrat).

Whuh wunna doin' tonight? "What are you all doing tonight?" A Bajan phrase. (Barbados).

Wie geht es Ihnen? "How are you?" A German phrase. (Austria).

Wiener schnitzel. Breaded veal cutlets. (Austria).

Wifey. A term used to refer to females. (Scotland).

Wilayaat. A district or region. (Algeria).

Wilayat. (Oman). *See* **Wilayaat.**

Wilayet. Region. (Turkmenistan).

Wind and grind. Dancing. (Grenada).

Wo. Corn flour. Used to make a stiff porridge. (Benin). *Also called* **Amiwo.**

Województwa. Polish word for "provinces." (Poland).

Wolesi Jirga. House of People. Part of Afghanistan's bicameral National Assembly. (Afghanistan).

Wôn. South Korea's national currency. (South Korea).

Wooshay! Wooshay! "Hello! Hello!" A common greeting used by the Kanouris. (Niger).

Workbook. A document received after completing eighth grade and passing a matriculation exam; necessary to get a job. (Bosnia and Herzegovina).

Wôro-wôro. Taxis that rent seats on fixed routes; they are available in Abidjan. (Ivory Coast).

Wuh you sayin'? "How are things?" An informal Bajan greeting used between young people. (Barbados).

Wuh yuh sayin'? How are you? (Trinidad and Tobago).

Wukking up. A uniquely Bajan dance style, usually performed to calypso music, that features rhythmic waist-winding movements. (Barbados).

Wurst. Sausage. (Germany).

Xhamadan. A wool vest worn by men. (Albania).

Xhaxha. An Albanian term used for an uncle on the father's side. (Albania).

Xiao. "Young." A Mandarin Chinese term used with or instead of a title to show special respect to a friend. (China).

Xima. A paste made from sun-dried cereals, usually cornmeal. (Mozambique). *Also called* **Upsa.**

Xin chao. A formal Vietnamese greeting used between strangers. (Vietnam).

Yaa "Hi." A casual greeting generally used among men. (Japan).

Yaka. Long, loose-fitting dresses with hand-embroidered collars. (Turkmenistan).

Yakhshi me seez? (Tajikistan). *See* **Yakshimisiz?**

Yakshimisiz? "Are you well?" A common greeting. (Uzbekistan).

Yang di-Pertuan Agong. The Supreme Head of State. Refers to the Malaysian king. (Malaysia).

Yaqona. A mildly stimulating drink made from the root and lower stem of a shrub in the pepper family; Fiji's national drink. Pronounced "YANGGONA." (Fiji). *Also called* **Kava.**

Yard name. A nickname. Often a shortened or slightly altered version of a person's given name. (Jamaica). *Also called* **Pet name.**

Yarmulke. An embroidered cap worn by men. (Israel). *Also called* **Kippah.**

Yashmagh. A checkered headscarf worn by men. (Iraq). *See also* **Kaffiyah.**

Yassa. Rice and chicken covered with a sauce made of sliced onions and spices. (Senegal).

Yaum an Nibi. A Muslim holiday commemorating the prophet Muhammad's birthday. (Guyana).

Yavusa. A chiefly system that ordered society for centuries. Established by early settlers. (Fiji).

Yayechnya. Scrambled or fried eggs. (Belarus).

Yeah, Gidday. A common greeting. (New Zealand). *See also* **Gidday.**

Yebo. "Yes." A Zulu and Swazi response to the greetings **Sawubona** (I see you) and **Kunjani?** (How are you?). (South Africa).

Yela. A musical style reserved for women. (Senegal).

Yen. Japan's national currency. (Japan).

Yerba. The Spanish word for "herb." (Paraguay).

Yerba mate. An herbal tea. (Bolivia).

Ye yapvo? "What's up?" A Shingazidja question that follows the initial greeting **Edje** (Hello). Used between social equals. (Comoros).

Yo. The Spanish word for "I." Usually pronounced "YOH," in Uruguayan Spanish it is pronounced "SHOW." (Uruguay).

Yoghurtvla. Yogurt pudding. (Netherlands).

Yokwe. A Marshallese greeting appropriate in almost any situation. It can mean "Hello," "Good-bye," "love," and more. Meaning is based on inflection. Pronounced "YAH-quay." (Marshall Islands).

Yom Kippur. Day of Atonement. A Jewish holiday. (Bosnia and Herzegovina, Croatia, Israel).

Yondo. A secret ritual of initiation into adulthood. (Chad).

Yorkshire pudding. A baked batter usually served in muffin form. (England).

You alright? "How are you?" A casual Montserratian greeting. (Montserrat).

You lie. A phrase that can mean "You are kidding." (Antigua and Barbuda).

Younger father. A paternal uncle. Called *younger father* or **Older father** depending on the uncle's age in relation to the child's father. (Kenya).

Younger mother. A maternal aunt. Called *younger mother* or **Older mother** depending on the aunt's age in relation to the child's mother. (Kenya).

Glossary of Cultural Terms

Yuan. The standard unit of China's national currency. (China). *See also* **Renminbi.**
Yuca. Cassava. (Cuba, Dominican Republic, Equatorial Guinea).
Yue. The Cantonese language. (China, Hong Kong).
Yuh stickin'. You are moving too slowly. (Trinidad and Tobago).
Yumbo. Ecuadorian folk music. (Ecuador).
Yu orait? "How are you?" A common Melanesian Pidgin greeting. (Papua New Guinea).
Yurta. A tent used by nomads. (Kazakstan).
Zadušnice. A day for Orthodox Serbs to honor the dead; occurs four times a year. (Serbia and Montenegro).
Zain, al-Humdulillah "Good, thanks be to **Allah**." A response to the Arabic greetings **Eshloanak** and **Eshloanich**. (Bahrain, Kuwait).
Zajal. A form of poetry in which improvised dialogue is sung between several poets. (Lebanon).
Zajjaleen. Singers who lead celebrations. (West Bank and Gaza).
Zajtrk. Slovene word meaning "breakfast." (Slovenia).
Zakat. Giving alms to the poor. One of the Five Pillars of Islam. (Iran, Kuwait, Malaysia, Saudi Arabia, Sudan). *See also* **Hajj, Salat, Saum, Shahada.**
Zakuski. Russian word meaning "appetizers." (Russia).
Zampoña. Panpipes. (Bolivia).
Zam-rock. A form of rock music with lyrics in local languages. (Zambia).
Zanahary. A supreme being of Malagasy indigenous beliefs. (Madagascar). *Also called* **Andriamanitra.**
Zang zho. Bowl of warm water used to wash one's hands before eating. (Bhutan).
Zanna. A long white dress worn by Muslim men on Fridays and religious holidays. Worn with a **Machetta**. (Yemen).
Zao. "Morning." An informal Chinese greeting. (China).
Zaouia. Small mausoleums built in memory of especially holy men. (Tunisia).
Zatar. Thyme. (West Bank and Gaza).
Zavtrak. The Russian word meaning "breakfast." (Kazakstan).
Zbogom. "Farewell" or "With God." A common parting phrase. (Bosnia and Herzegovina, Croatia).
Zdrasti. "Hello." An informal Bulgarian greeting. (Bulgaria).
Zdrave. "Hello." An informal Bulgarian greeting. (Bulgaria).
Zdraveite. "Hello." A formal Bulgarian greeting. (Bulgaria).
Zdravo. "Hello." A casual greeting. (Bosnia and Herzegovina, Croatia, Macedonia, Serbia and Montenegro, Slovenia).
Zdravstvuite. (Moldova). *See* **Zdravstvuyte.**
Zdravstvuite. Kak pozhivaete? "Hello. How are you?" A Russian greeting. (Belarus).
Zdravstvuy. "Hello." An informal Russian greeting. (Russia).
Zdravstvuyte. "Hello." A formal Russian greeting. (Kazakstan, Kyrgyzstan, Russia).
Zebus. Oxen-like cattle. (Madagascar).
Zed. The Canadian pronunciation of the letter *z*. (Canada).
Zeljanica. Spinach-and-cheese pie. (Bosnia and Herzegovina).
Zemidjan(s). Motorcycle taxis. (Benin, Togo).
Zenmoyang? "How's it going?" An informal Chinese greeting. (China).
Zeze. A one-string violin. (Malawi).
Zhanga Zhyl. The Kazak term for the New Year celebration. (Kazakstan).
Zhug. A relish in which bread is dipped. (Yemen).
Zikak. A type of fruit. (Haiti).
Zito. A mush made of wheat, sugar, and nuts. (Serbia and Montenegro).
Živijo. "Long live." A Slovene greeting or toast. (Slovenia).
Zloty. Poland's national currency. (Poland).
Zmittag. The main meal of the day. (Liechtenstein).
Zmorga. Breakfast. (Liechtenstein).
Znacht. Dinner. (Liechtenstein).
Zogbedji. An Ewe word meaning "inhospitable land." A burial site for people who died violently (accident, suicide, murder) or badly (illness, childbirth). (Togo).
Zokela. A style of music that blends traditional and Western music. (Central African Republic).
Zokra. A North African instrument similar to the bagpipes. (Libya).
Zolgah. A gesture used when meeting for the first time after the New Year. The younger person holds the elbows of the older person, whose forearms rest on the younger person's forearms; the older person lightly touches his or her lips to the younger person's forehead. (Mongolia).
Zongo. Separate sections of town in which nonindigenous people live. (Ghana).
Zonja. "Mrs." An Albanian title used with the first or last name. (Albania).
Zonjushe. "Miss." An Albanian title used with the first or last name. (Albania).
Zorries. Rubber or plastic flip-flops; the common footwear. (Micronesia).
Zoteri. "Mr." An Albanian title used with the first or last name. (Albania).
Zouglou. A style of music that originated in Ivory Coast; it features a fast beat and humorous lyrics. (Ivory Coast).
Zouk. A Caribbean style of music. (Burkina Faso, Suriname).
Zow. A puffed rice snack. (Bhutan).
Zrig. A whipped drink made of milk, water, and sugar. (Mauritania).
Zud. A type of weather in which blizzards send enough snow to cover the grass; livestock cannot graze and therefore die. (Mongolia).
Zui jin mang ma. "Have you been busy lately?" A Chinese greeting used between people who have not seen each other in a long time. (China).
Zuls. Traditional flutes. (Nicaragua).
Zummar. Flute player. (Iraq).
Zungueiras. Women who sell fruit and other goods on street corners or by walking through the city carrying their products on their heads. (Angola). *Also called* **Kitandeiras.**
Zupa. The Latvian word for "soup." (Latvia).
Zwarte Piet. "Black Peter." According to tradition in the Netherlands, he is the servant of St. Nicholas. (Netherlands).